Ethics of
Psychiatry

INSANITY, RATIONAL AUTONOMY, AND MENTAL HEALTH CARE

Ethics of Psychiatry

INSANITY, RATIONAL AUTONOMY, AND MENTAL HEALTH CARE

Includes essays by:

Thomas S. Szasz
Jerome Wakefield
Robert M. Veatch
Paula J. Caplan
Kerry Brace
Paul S. Appelbaum
Glen O. Gabbard
Peter R. Breggin
Donald H. J. Hermann
Lawrie Reznek
Bruce J. Winick

edited by
Rem B. Edwards

Prometheus Books
59 John Glenn Drive
Amherst, New York 14228-2197

Published 1997 by Prometheus Books

Ethics of Psychiatry: Insanity, Rational Autonomy, and Mental Health Care. Copyright © 1997 Rem B. Edwards. All rights reserved. No part of this publication may be reproduced, stored in a retrieval system, or transmitted in any form or by any means, electronic, mechanical, photocopying, recording, or otherwise, without prior written permission of the publisher, except in the case of brief quotations embodied in critical articles and reviews. Inquiries should be addressed to Prometheus Books, 59 John Glenn Drive, Amherst, New York 14228–2197, 716–691–0133. FAX: 716–691–0137.

01 00 99 98 97   5 4 3 2 1

Library of Congress Cataloging-in-Publication Data

Ethics of psychiatry : insanity, rational autonomy, and mental health care / edited
    by Rem B. Edwards.
        p.   cm.
    Includes bibliographical references.
    ISBN 1–57392–113–0 (pbk. : alk. paper)
    1. Psychiatric ethics.   I. Edwards, Rem, Blanchard.
RC455.2.E8P8   1996
174'.2—DC20   96–36439
                                                            CIP

Printed in the United States of America on acid-free paper

For the patients and the staff
of Lakeshore Mental Health Institute

Contents

4. Controversial Behavior Control Therapies

5. Ethical and Conceptual Issues in Civil Commitment

Preface

A great strength of the doctoral program in philosophy with a concentration in medical ethics at the University of Tennessee, Knoxville, is its ability to give students considerable clinical exposure in a variety of medical settings, including the vitally important clinical practicum at nearby Lakeshore Mental Health Institute. This book is dedicated to Lakeshore's patients and staff. At Lakeshore, our students rotate through each unit of the hospital spending a number of hours each week as participants and observers in clinical situations where value-laden decisions are made by, with, and about mental hospital patients. Regular seminars are held on hospital grounds, attended by hospital staff as well as our students, who report on and analyze the value dimensions of what they are observing. I developed this practicum during the summer of 1977 with the aid of a grant from the Institute for Human Values in Medicine, and it is now regularly offered by our medical ethics faculty.

In developing the Lakeshore practicum, an obvious need was recognized for curriculum materials for a prepracticum course that would provide students with an adequate conceptual background for understanding and appreciating their clinical experience. My book entitled *Psychiatry and Ethics* (1982) resulted from efforts to meet this need. Material of this sort eventually becomes dated. During the past fifteen years, there has been an incredible burst of creative thinking and publishing in the area of ethical issues in mental health care; the quality of the essays in this volume are a quantum leap ahead of those in the earlier book. This new and updated volume should be of great interest to present and future professionals in the areas of law, psychiatry, psychology, advocacy, social services, chaplaincy, and medical ethics who must comprehend and apply values and ethical principles to mental health care.

At Lakeshore Mental Health Institute, most medical professionals strive to fulfill the fundamental ethical obligation to restore, develop, and honor the rational autonomy of their patients. The same ethical principle is expressed in many journals, books, and articles dealing with values in psychotherapy. This book aims to organize a variety of attempts to understand and apply an ethics of respecting rational autonomy to the difficult circumstances in which mental patients find themselves.

An ethics centered on restoring and respecting rational autonomy can be adopted by persons of very diverse philosophical persuasions, though for reasons peculiar to their own standpoints. Kantians may adopt the ideal of promoting and honoring rational autonomy because it appropriately expresses the *categorical imperative,* according to which we should always treat persons as ends in themselves and never merely as means. Rule utilitarians can adopt the ethical rule "We ought to restore, develop, and respect rational autonomy" because they think that if everyone always followed this rule, the best overall consequences would result. Obtaining informed voluntary consent is a practical expression of respect for rational autonomy, and now there is massive evidence that this has great therapeutic significance. In both physical and psychical medicine, therapies that are freely and knowingly embraced are usually much more effective than coerced treatments because they are augmented by the choice, energy, effort, and commitment of patients. Act utilitarians can adopt the ideal of informed voluntary consent as a very basic rule of thumb for identifying kinds of acts that will likely have the best (or least harmful) consequences for those affected. Qualitatively hedonistic utilitarians like John Stuart Mill could adopt this ethical ideal (as Mill did in *On Liberty* and *Utilitarianism*) as the most effective way to maximize long-range happiness that is high in both quality and quantity of pleasure for the greatest number of sentient beings. Those who aspire to adopt values under ideal conditions of rational choice—freedom, enlightenment, and open-mindedness—can affirm that this both presupposes and results in an ethics of rational autonomy. Even ethical relativists can accept respect for rational autonomy as an essential side-constraint for negotiating and resolving value conflicts. Thus, there are many good reasons for adopting such an ethics, and we need not agree on the ultimate reasons in order to agree on the ethical practice.

In the section introductions to follow, references are made both to articles reprinted in that section and to other articles that appear only in the "Suggestions for Further Reading" at the end of each section. The former are not referenced; for the latter the author and/or the date of publication are given in parentheses. In selections to follow, transitional and interpretive words and phrases supplied by the editor are enclosed in brackets [ ]. Users of this book should take care to read the informative endnotes as well as the main texts of the articles, especially those by legal authors like Donald Hermann and Bruce Winick.

I want to express my sincere appreciation to each of the journals and publishers who gave permission to reprint the essays contained in this volume. No attempt was made to standardize the systems of reference used in the original articles. Retaining original notation styles will not create difficulties for intelligent readers. I would also like to express my deep appreciation to Dr. Laura Shanner of the University of Toronto for her recommendations for revisions, and to my editor, Steven L. Mitchell of Prometheus Books, for his encouragement and able assistance in the production of this book.

1.

VALUE DIMENSIONS OF "MENTAL ILLNESS" AND "MENTAL HEALTH"

INTRODUCTION

"Mental Illness" and "Mental Health" as Value-Laden Concepts

Most philosophically minded thinkers who have looked critically at the concepts of "mental health" and "mental illness" have found them to be inherently value-laden. This means that evaluative components as well as descriptive elements are inescapably a part of their meaning. We pack our value preferences and aversions into these notions. "Mental illness" includes things regarded as highly undesirable; and "mental health" includes things judged to be highly desirable. Our second section shows that this is just as true for particular psychiatric diagnostic categories as for general notions of mental illness and health. Concepts of physical health and illness are also infected by human values; but these evaluative components can be deceptively hidden, disguised, or unrecognized.

Applied to the fourth edition of the American Psychiatric Association's *Diagnostic and Statistical Manual of Mental Disorders*, 1994, this means that both the general definition of "mental disorder" and all particular diagnostic categories include evaluative as well as descriptive elements, whether or not these are consciously acknowledged. "Experts" in mental orders and disorders disagree vehemently about how to define the core concepts in the field, including which disvalues belong in "mental illness" and which positive goods are incorporated into "mental health." Try to identify the disvalues present within the following defini-

17

tions of mental illness and in others presented, defended, and critiqued in articles to follow.

1. **Thomas Szasz:** "The expression 'mental illness' is a metaphor that we have come to mistake for a fact. We call people physically ill when their body-functioning violates certain anatomical and physiological norms; similarly, we call people mentally ill when their personal conduct violates certain ethical, political, and social norms" (Szasz, 1991, p. 23).

"Mental illness is a myth. Psychiatrists are not concerned with mental illnesses and their treatments. In actual practice they deal with personal, social, and ethical problems in living" (Szasz, 1974, p. 262).

2. **DSM-IV:** "The concept of mental disorder . . . lacks a consistent operational definition that covers all situations. . . . Mental disorders have . . . been defined by a variety of concepts (e.g., distress, dyscontrol, disadvantage, disability, inflexibility, irrationality, syndromal pattern, etiology, and statistical deviation). . . . In *DSM-IV*, each of the mental disorders is conceptualized as a clinically significant behavioral or psychological syndrome or pattern that occurs in an individual and that is associated with present distress (e.g., a painful symptom) or disability (i.e., impairment in one or more important areas of functioning) or with a significantly increased risk of suffering death, pain, disability, or an important loss of freedom. In addition, this syndrome or pattern must not be merely an expectable and culturally sanctioned response to a particular event, for example, the death of a loved one. Whatever its original cause, it must currently be considered a manifestation of a behavioral, psychological, or biological dysfunction in the individual. Neither deviant behavior (e.g., political, religious, or sexual) nor conflicts that are primarily between the individual and society are mental disorders unless the deviance or conflict is a symptom of a dysfunction in the individual, as described above" (American Psychiatric Association, *DSM-IV*, 1994, pp. xxi–xxii).

3. **Michael S. Moore:** "Mental illness is not a myth. It is not some palpable falsehood propagated amongst the populace by power-mad psychiatrists, but a cruel and bitter reality that has been with the human race since antiquity" (Moore, 1984, p. 156).

"Insanity and mental illness mean, and historically have meant, irrationality; to be insane or mentally ill is to fail to act rationally often enough to have the same assumption of rationality made about one as it made of most of humanity . . . part of our fundamental notion of personhood [is] not applicable to the mentally ill. This includes notions about their lack of responsibility and inability to choose and act upon their own conception of the good" (Moore, 1984, p. 178).

4. **Rem B. Edwards**: "Definition: 'Mental illness' means only those undesirable mental/behavioral deviations which involve primarily an ex-

treme and prolonged inability to know and deal in a rational and autonomous way with oneself and one's social and physical environment. In other words, madness is extreme and prolonged practical irrationality and irresponsibility" (Edwards, 1981, p. 312).

For Thomas Szasz, the disvalues incorporated into society's notion of "mental illness" are those of *behavioral deviance* from psychosocial, ethical, and legal norms; for *DSM-IV*, the disvalues are *distress* (pain) and *dysfunction* (disability); for Moore and Edwards, they are the specific dysfunctions of *irrationality* and *irresponsibility*. Look for the disvalues incorporated into "mental illness" by other authors in this volume. For many years, the legal definition in the state of Tennessee was: "Mentally ill individual—An individual who, in the opinion of a licensed physician, suffers from a psychiatric disorder, alcoholism, or drug dependence" (Tennessee Laws Annotated). The troublesome phrase "in the opinion of a licensed physician" has now been dropped; but, when included, the relevant disvalues were *any mental/behavioral conditions disfavored as disorders* by any licensed physician, even if he or she never had a course in psychology.

Noted authorities in psychology also include their most favored positive values in their definitions of "mental health." Many prominent psychologists make "mental health" synonymous with the *summum bonum*, the ideally desirable human life, as amply illustrated in essays to follow. See especially several definitions of "mental health" quoted in the articles by Edwards and Wakefield, and explore the references on "Mental Health" given in the "Suggestions for Further Reading."

Good and Bad

Evaluative concepts like "mental illness" and "mental health" resemble paradigm value concepts like "good" and "bad." In the twentieth century, metaethicists have closely scrutinized the meanings of value notions, and a number of elements in our common notion of "good" have been recognized. "X is good" is widely acknowledged to mean: (a) that *someone* (not necessarily the speaker) approves of X, or takes a positive attitude or valuational stance toward it; (b) that X is being measured by some norm or standard; (c) that X exhibits certain empirical features or "good-making characteristics" that occasion someone's approval and fulfill the relevant norm or standard; and (d) that X is being commended to others for their approval and/or choice. Similarly, "X is bad" involves negative attitudes that are occasioned by the absence of desirable or the presence of undesirable properties, together with commendation or discommendation to others. Degrees of goodness or badness vary with degrees of norm fulfillment or nonfulfillment.

In particular cases, one or more of these meaning/measurement/ use elements may be more prominent than others. Without having positive feelings about them, apple graders or used car dealers can distinguish good from bad apples or cars by matching their perceived good-making or bad-making properties with some socially derived norm or standard. Yet, *someone* must approve red, juicy, well-shaped, worm-free apples if social criteria for separating good from bad apples are ever to be established. Positive or negative attitudes are indispensable when initially identifying and selecting the descriptive properties that function socially thereafter as norms or standards for differentiating between good from bad apples, cars, or what have you.

The Four Ds

If, as most of the following authors believe, concepts of both physical and mental health and disease are value-laden, then they consist of standards or norms by which the actual mental, behavioral, and physical traits of individuals are measured, and through which positive and negative attitudes are expressed. Disease concepts are constructed out of descriptive properties of which we strongly disapprove, either directly or as the cause or the effect of symptomatic traits directly disvalued. Disease concepts include one or more of four disvalued properties: (1) *distress*— pain or suffering; (2) *dysfunction*—disability or incapacity; (3) *deformity*—objectionable deviation from standard and desirable human form; or (4) *deadliness*—the propensity to kill prematurely. Both mental and physical disorders manifest distresses and dysfunctions. Deformities like being born with too many breasts (supernumery breasts), too many fingers or toes (polydactylism), or with a tail (only one of which is one too many for human beings), are much more relevant to physical than to mental disorders. Still, some forms of mental retardation like cretinism and Down's syndrome involve fairly obvious departures from typical and usually desired human form. Also, some organic mental disorders like Huntington's chorea and Alzheimer's are slow killers.

Like apple graders who need not emote negatively about the bad apples they discard, medical professionals, who concentrate on causes and cures, need not be aware of the evaluative dimensions of their work. Yet, if not themselves, *someone* must disvalue the distressing, dysfunctional, deforming, and deadly dimensions of diseases. Since things other than diseases, like war, weariness, and starvation, can cause the four Ds, additional descriptive criteria are required to differentiate between disease instances and nondisease instances of these four disvalues. Consider such differentiating criteria as: (1) being inside an individual; (2) enduring or recurring over time; (3) not being a "necessary evil" that accompanies natural and desirable human functions or maturation processes like teething, menopause, or childbirth; (4) having a mental cause; (5) having a physical cause; (6) being manifest at an intolerable level of intensity; (7) not being under long-term control; (8) not being susceptible to immediate voluntary control; (9) being manageable or treatable (at least in principle) by physicians, and so on. Many of these are offered in following essays as defining characteristics of diseases.

Evaluative versus Descriptive

Logically, medical concepts like "disease," "illness," "health," "normality," "treatment," and so on could be (1) purely evaluative, containing no empirical elements; (2) purely descriptive, containing no evaluative elements; or (3) value-laden, composed of both evaluative and descriptive elements. Selections to follow illustrate all of these positions on "mental health" and "mental illness." Thomas Szasz advocates position (1) for mental diseases and position (2) for physical diseases. He holds that the mental health establishment's notion of "mental illness" is evaluative, but he insists (mistakenly) that the "anatomical or physiological norms" of real physical diseases are purely statistical and descriptive, not normative. Critiques of Szasz's position will follow in selections by Michael Moore and Jerome Wakefield. J. T. Scadding, R. E. Kendell, and Christopher Boorse, all discussed by Wakefield, are rare recent theorists who subscribes to position (2) for both mental and physical diseases. Position (3), clearly the dominant view, is affirmed in this section by Michael Moore, Rem B. Edwards, and Jerome C. Wakefield, and in the next section by Robert M. Veatch. The relatively new discipline of evolutionary psychology, represented by Wakefield, promises to shed much new light on human nature and its aberrations. Descriptivists like Scadding and Boorse contend that natural values (survival and reproduction) created by evolutionary pressures are not values, but Wakefield knows that they are.

The Myth of Mental Illness

Thomas S. Szasz

My aim in this essay is to raise the question "Is there such a thing as mental illness?" and to argue that there is not. Since the notion of mental illness is extremely widely used nowadays, inquiry into the ways in which this term is employed would seem to be especially indicated. Mental illness, of course, is not literally a "thing"—or physical object— and hence it can "exist" only in the same sort of way in which other theoretical concepts exist. Yet, familiar theories are in the habit of posing, sooner or later—at least to those who come to believe in them—as "objective truths" (or "facts"). During certain historical periods, explanatory conceptions such as deities, witches, and microorganisms appeared not only as theories but as self-evident *causes* of a vast number of events. I submit that today mental illness is widely regarded in a somewhat similar fashion, that is, as the cause of innumerable diverse happenings. As an antidote to the complacent use of the notion of mental illness— whether as a self-evident phenomenon, theory, or cause—let us ask this question: What is meant when it is asserted that someone is mentally ill?

In what follows I shall describe briefly the main uses to which the concept of mental illness has been put. I shall argue that this notion has outlived whatever usefulness it might have had and that it now functions merely as a convenient myth.

From the *American Psychologist* 15 (1960):113–18. Article is now in the public domain.

Mental Illness as a Sign of Brain Disease

The notion of mental illness derives its main support from such phenomena as syphilis of the brain or delirious conditions—intoxications, for instance—in which persons are known to manifest various peculiarities or disorders of thinking and behavior. Correctly speaking, however, these are diseases of the brain, not of the mind. According to one school of thought, *all* so-called mental illness is of this type. The assumption is made that some neurological defect, perhaps a very subtle one, will ultimately be found for all the disorders of thinking and behavior. Many contemporary psychiatrists, physicians, and other scientists hold this view. This position implies that people *cannot* have troubles—expressed in what are *now called* "mental illnesses"—because of differences in personal needs, opinions, social aspirations, values, and so on. *All problems in living* are attributed to physicochemical processes which in due time will be discovered by medical research.

"Mental illnesses" are thus regarded as basically no different than all other diseases (that is, of the body). The only difference, in this view, between mental and bodily diseases is that the former, affecting the brain, manifest themselves by means of mental symptoms; whereas the latter, affecting other organ systems (for example, the skin, liver, etc.), manifest themselves by means of symptoms referable to those parts of the body. This view rests on and expresses what are, in my opinion, two fundamental errors.

In the first place, what central nervous system symptoms would correspond to a skin eruption or a fracture? It would *not* be some emotion or complex bit of behavior. Rather, it would be blindness or a paralysis of some part of the body. The crux of the matter is that a disease of the brain, analogous to a disease of the skin or bone, is a neurological defect, and not a problem in living. For example, a *defect* in a person's visual field may be satisfactorily explained by correlating it with certain definite lesions in the nervous system. On the other hand, a person's *belief*—whether this be a belief in Christianity, in Communism, or in the idea that his internal organs are "rotting" and that his body is, in fact, already "dead"—cannot be explained by a defect or disease of the nervous system. Explanations of this sort of occurrence—assuming that one is interested in the belief itself and does not regard it simply as a "symptom" or expression of something else that is *more interesting*—must be sought along different lines.

The second error in regarding complex psychosocial behavior, consisting of communications about ourselves and the world about us, as mere symptoms of neurological functioning is *epistemological*. In other words, it is an error pertaining not to any mistakes in observation or reasoning, as such, but rather to the way in which we organize and express our knowledge. In the present case, the error lies in making a symmetrical dualism between mental and physical (or bodily) symptoms, a dualism which is merely a habit of speech and to which no known observations can be found to correspond. Let us see if this is so. In medical practice, when we speak of physical disturbances, we mean either signs (for example, a fever) or symptoms (for example, pain). We speak of mental symptoms, on the other hand, when we refer to a patient's *communications about himself, others, and the world about him.* He might state that he is Napoleon or that he is being persecuted by the Communists. These would be considered mental symptoms *only* if the observer believed that the patient was *not* Napoleon or that he was *not* being persecuted by the Communists. This makes it apparent that the statement that "*X* is a mental symptom" involves rendering a judgment. The judgment entails, moreover, a covert comparison or matching of the patient's ideas, concepts, or beliefs with those of the observer and the society in which they live. The notion of mental symptom is therefore inextricably tied to the *social* (including *ethical*) *context* in which it is made in much the same way as the notion of bodily symptom is tied to an *anatomical* and *genetic context* (Szasz, 1957a, 1957b).

To sum up what has been said thus far: I have tried to show that for those who regard mental symptoms as signs of brain disease, the concept of mental illness is unnecessary and misleading. For what they mean is that people so labeled suffer from diseases of the brain; and, if that is what they mean, it would seem better for the sake of clarity to say that and not something else.

Mental Illness as a Name for Problems in Living

The term "mental illness" is widely used to describe something which is very different than a disease of the brain. Many people today take it for granted that living is an arduous process. Its hardship for modern man, moreover, derives not so much from a struggle for biological survival as from the stresses and strains inherent in the social intercourse of complex human personalities. In this context, the notion of mental illness is used to identify or describe some feature of an individual's so-called personality. Mental illness—as a deformity of the personality, so to speak—is then regarded as the *cause* of the human disharmony. It is implicit in this view that social intercourse between people is regarded as something *inherently harmonious,* its disturbance being due solely to the presence of "mental illness" in many people. This is obviously fallacious reasoning, for it makes the abstraction "mental illness" into a *cause,* even though this abstraction was created in the first place to serve only as a shorthand expression for certain types of human behavior. It now becomes necessary to ask: "What kinds of behavior are regarded as indicative of mental illness, and by whom?"

The concept of illness, whether bodily or mental, implies *deviation from some clearly defined norm*. In the case of physical illness, the norm is the structural and functional integrity of the human body. Thus, although the desirability of physical health, as such, is an ethical value, what health *is* can be stated in anatomical and physiological terms. What is the norm deviation from which is regarded as mental illness? This question cannot be easily answered. But whatever this norm might be, we can be certain of only one thing: namely, that it is a norm that must be stated in terms of *psychosocial, ethical,* and *legal* concepts. For example, notions such as "excessive repression" or "acting out an unconscious impulse" illustrate the use of psychological concepts for judging (so-called) mental health and illness. The idea that chronic hostility, vengefulness, or divorce are indicative of mental illness would be illustrations of the use of ethical norms (that is, the desirability of love, kindness, and a stable marriage relationship). Finally, the widespread psychiatric opinion that only a mentally ill person would commit homicide illustrates the use of a legal concept as a norm of mental health. The norm from which deviation is measured whenever one speaks of a mental illness is a *psychosocial and ethical one*. Yet, the remedy is sought in terms of *medical* measures which—it is hoped and assumed—are free from wide differences of ethical value. The definition of the disorder and the terms in which its remedy are sought are therefore at serious odds with one another. The practical significance of this covert conflict between the alleged nature of the defect and the remedy can hardly be exaggerated.

Having identified the norms used to measure deviations in cases of mental illness, we will now turn to the question: "Who defines the norms and hence the deviation?" Two basic answers may be offered: (*a*) It may be the person himself (that is, the patient) who decides that he deviates from a norm. For example, an artist may believe that he suffers from a work inhibition; and he may implement this conclusion by seeking help *for* himself from a psychotherapist. (*b*) It may be someone other than the patient who decides that the latter is deviant (for example, relatives, physicians, legal authorities, society generally, etc.). In such a case a psychiatrist may be hired by others to do something *to* the patient in order to correct the deviation.

These considerations underscore the importance of asking the question "Whose agent is the psychiatrist?" and of giving a candid answer to it (Szasz, 1956, 1958). The psychiatrist (psychologist or nonmedical psychotherapist), it now develops, may be the agent of the patient, of the relatives, of the school, of the military services, of a business organization, of a court of law, and so forth. In speaking of the psychiatrist as the agent of these persons or organizations, it is not implied that his values concerning norms, or his ideas and aims concerning the proper nature of remedial action, need to coincide exactly with those of his employer. For example, a patient in individual psychotherapy may believe that his salvation lies in a new marriage; his psychotherapist need not share this hypothesis. As the patient's agent, however, he must abstain from bringing social or legal force to bear on the patient which would prevent him from putting his beliefs into action. If his *contract* is with the patient, the psychiatrist (psychotherapist) may disagree with him or stop his treatment; but he cannot engage others to obstruct the patient's aspirations. Similarly, if a psychiatrist is engaged by a court to determine the sanity of a criminal, he need not fully share the legal authorities' values and intentions in regard to the criminal and the means available for dealing with him. But the psychiatrist is expressly barred from stating, for example, that it is not the criminal who is "insane" but the men who wrote the law on the basis of which the very actions that are being judged are regarded as "criminal." Such an opinion could be voiced, of course, but not in a courtroom, and not by a psychiatrist who makes it his practice to assist the court in performing its daily work.

To recapitulate: In actual contemporary social usage, the finding of a mental illness is made by establishing a deviance in behavior from certain psychosocial, ethical, or legal norms. The judgment may be made, as in medicine, by the patient, the physician (psychiatrist), or others. Remedial action, finally, tends to be sought in a therapeutic—or covertly medical—framework, thus creating a situation in which *psychosocial, ethical,* and/or *legal deviations* are claimed to be correctable by (so-called) *medical action.* Since medical action is designed to correct only medical deviations, it seems logically absurd to expect that it will help solve problems whose very existence had been defined and established on nonmedical grounds. I think that these considerations may be fruitfully applied to the present use of tranquilizers and, more generally, to what might be expected of drugs of whatever type in regard to the amelioration or solution of problems in human living.

The Role of Ethics in Psychiatry

Anything that people *do*—in contrast to things that *happen* to them (Peters, 1958)—takes place in a context of value. In this broad sense, no human activity is devoid of ethical implications. When the values underlying certain activities are widely shared, those who participate in their pursuit may lose sight of them altogether. The discipline of medicine, both as a pure science (for example, research) and as a technology (for example, therapy), contains many ethical considerations and judgments. Unfortunately, these are often denied, minimized, or merely kept out of focus; for the ideal of the medical profession as well as of the people whom it serves seems to be having a system of medicine (allegedly) free of ethical value. This sentimental notion is expressed by such things as the doctor's willingness to treat and help patients irrespective of their religious or political beliefs, whether they are rich or poor, etc. While there may be some grounds for this belief—albeit it is a view that is not impressively true even in these regards—the fact remains that ethical considerations encompass a vast range of human affairs. By making the practice of medicine neutral in regard to some special issues of value need not, and cannot, mean that it can be kept free from all such values. The practice of medicine is intimately tied to ethics; and the first thing that we must do, it seems to me, is to try to make this clear and explicit. I shall let this matter rest here, for it does not concern us specifically in this essay. Lest there be any vagueness, however, about how or where ethics and medicine meet, let me remind the reader of such issues as birth control, abortion, suicide, and euthanasia as only a few of the major areas of current ethicomedical controversy.

Psychiatry, I submit, is very much more intimately tied to problems of ethics than is medicine. I use the word "psychiatry" here to refer to that contemporary discipline which is concerned with *problems in living* (and not with diseases of the brain, which are problems for neurology). Problems in human relations can be analyzed, interpreted, and given meaning only within given social and ethical contexts. Accordingly, it *does* make a difference—arguments to the contrary notwithstanding— what the psychiatrist's socioethical orientations happen to be; for these will influence his ideas on what is wrong with the patient, what deserves comment or interpretation, in what possible directions change might be desirable, and so forth. Even in medicine proper, these factors play a role, as for instance, in the divergent orientations which physicians, depending on their religious affiliations, have toward such things as birth control and therapeutic abortion. Can anyone really believe that a psychotherapist's ideas concerning religious belief, slavery, or other similar issues play no role in his practical work? If they do make a difference, what are we to infer from it? Does it not seem reasonable that we ought to have different psychiatric therapies—each expressly recognized for the ethical positions which they embody—for, say, Catholics and Jews, religious persons and agnostics, democrats and communists, white supremacists and Negroes, and so on? Indeed, if we look at how psychiatry is actually practiced today (especially in the United States) we find that people do seek psychiatric help in accordance with their social status and ethical beliefs (Hollingshead & Redlich, 1958). This should really not surprise us more than being told that practicing Catholics rarely frequent birth control clinics.

The foregoing position which holds that contemporary psychotherapists deal with problems in living, rather than with mental illnesses and their cures, stands in opposition to a currently prevalent claim, according to which mental illness is just as "real" and "objective" as bodily illness. This is a confusing claim since it is never known exactly what is meant by such words as "real" and "objective." I suspect, however, that what is intended by the proponents of this view is to create the idea in the popular mind that mental illness is some sort of disease entity, like an infection or a malignancy. If this were true, one could *catch* or *get* a "mental illness," one might *have* or *harbor* it, one might *transmit* it to others, and finally one could get *rid* of it. In my opinion, there is not a shred of evidence to support this idea. To the contrary, all the evidence is the other way and supports the view that what people now call mental illnesses are for the most part *communications* expressing unacceptable ideas, often framed, moreover, in an unusual idiom. The scope of this essay allows me to do no more than mention this alternative theoretical approach to this problem (Szasz, 1957c).

This is not the place to consider in detail the similarities and differences between bodily and mental illnesses. It shall suffice for us here to emphasize only one important difference between them: namely, that whereas bodily disease refers to public, physicochemical occurrences, the notion of mental illness is used to codify relatively more private, sociopsychological happenings of which the observer (diagnostician) forms a part. In other words, the psychiatrist does not stand *apart* from what he observes, but is, in Harry Stack Sullivan's apt words, a "participant observer." This means that he is *committed* to some picture of what he considers reality—and to what he thinks society considers reality—and he observes and judges the patient's behavior in the light of these considerations. This touches on our earlier observation that the notion of mental symptom itself implies a comparison between observer and observed, psychiatrist and patient. This is so obvious that I may be charged with belaboring trivialities. Let me therefore say once more that my aim in presenting this argument was expressly to criticize and counter a prevailing contemporary tendency to deny the moral aspects of psychiatry (and psychotherapy) and to substitute for them allegedly value-free medical considerations. Psychotherapy, for example, is being widely practiced as though it entailed nothing other than restoring the patient from a state of mental sickness to one of mental health. While it is generally accepted that mental illness has something to do with man's social (or interpersonal) relations, it is paradoxically maintained that problems of values (that is, of ethics) do not arise in this process.[1] Yet, in one sense, much of psychotherapy may revolve around nothing other than the elucidation and weighing of goals and values—many of which may be mutually contradictory—and the means whereby they might best be harmonized, realized, or relinquished.

The diversity of human values and the methods by means of which they may be realized is so vast, and many of them remain so unacknowledged, that they cannot fail but lead to conflicts in human relations. Indeed, to say that human relations at all levels—from mother to child, through husband and wife, to nation and nation—are fraught with stress, strain, and disharmony is, once again, making the obvious explicit. Yet, what may be obvious may be also poorly understood. This I think is the case here. For it seems to me that—at least in our scientific theories of behavior—we have failed to *accept* the simple fact that human relations are inherently fraught with difficulties and that to make them even relatively harmonious requires much patience and hard work. I submit that the idea of mental illness is now being put to work to obscure certain difficulties which at present may be inherent—not that they need be unmodifiable—in the social intercourse of persons. If this is true, the concept functions as a disguise; for instead of calling attention to conflicting human needs, aspirations, and values, the notion of mental illness provides an amoral and impersonal "thing" (an "illness") as an explanation for *problems in living* (Szasz, 1959). We may recall in this connection that not so long ago it was devils and witches who were held responsible for men's problems in social living. The belief in mental illness, as something other than man's trouble in getting along with his fellow man, is the proper heir to the belief in demonology and witchcraft. Mental illness exists or is "real" in exactly the same sense in which witches existed or were "real."

Choice, Responsibility, and Psychiatry

While I have argued that mental illnesses do not exist, I obviously did not imply that the social and psychological occurrences to which this label is currently being attached also do not exist. Like the personal and social troubles which people had in the Middle Ages, they are real enough. It is the labels we give them that concerns us and, having labeled them, what we do about them. While I cannot go into the ramified implications of this problem here, it is worth noting that a demonologic conception of problems in living gave rise to therapy along theological lines. Today, a belief in mental illness implies—nay, requires—therapy along medical or psychotherapeutic lines.

What is implied in the line of thought set forth here is something quite different. I do not intend to offer a new conception of "psychiatric illness" nor a new form of "therapy." My aim is more modest and yet also more ambitious. It is to suggest that the phenomena now called mental illnesses be looked at afresh and more simply, that they be removed from the category of illnesses, and that they be regarded as the expressions of man's struggle with the problem of *how* he should live. The last mentioned problem is obviously a vast one, its enormity reflecting not only man's inability to cope with his environment, but even more his increasing self-reflectiveness.

By problems in living, then, I refer to that truly explosive chain reaction which began with man's fall from divine grace by partaking of the fruit of the tree of knowledge. Man's awareness of himself and of the world about him seems to be a steadily expanding one, bringing in its wake an ever larger *burden of understanding* (an expression borrowed from Susanne Langer, 1953). *This burden, then, is to be expected and must not be misinterpreted.* Our only *rational* means for lightening it is *more understanding,* and appropriate *action* based on such understanding. The main alternative lies in acting as though the burden were not what in fact we perceive it to be and taking refuge in an outmoded theological view of man. In the latter view, man does not fashion his life and much of his world about him, but merely lives out his fate in a world created by superior beings. This may logically lead to pleading nonresponsibility in the face of seemingly unfathomable problems and difficulties. Yet, if man fails to take increasing responsibility for his actions, individually as well as collectively, it seems unlikely that some higher power or being would assume this task and carry this burden for him. Moreover, this seems hardly the proper time in human history for obscuring the issue of man's responsibility for his actions by hiding it behind the skirt of an all-explaining conception of mental illness.

Conclusions

I have tried to show that the notion of mental illness has outlived whatever usefulness it might have had and that it now functions merely as a convenient myth. As such, it is a true heir to religious myths in general, and to the belief in witchcraft in particular; the role of all these belief-systems was to act as *social tranquilizers,* thus encouraging the hope that mastery of certain specific problems may be achieved by means of substitutive (symbolic-magical) operations. The notion of mental illness thus serves mainly to obscure the everyday fact that life for most people is a continuous struggle, not for biological survival, but for a "place in the sun," "peace of mind," or some other human value. For man aware of himself and of the world about him, once the needs for preserving the body (and perhaps the race) are more or less satisfied, the problem arises as to what he should do with himself. Sustained adherence to the myth of mental illness allows people to avoid facing this problem, believing that mental health, conceived as the absence of mental illness, automatically ensures the making of right and safe choices in one's conduct of life. But the facts are all the other way. It is the making of good choices in life that others regard, retrospectively, as good mental health!

The myth of mental illness encourages us, moreover, to believe in its logical corollary: that social intercourse would be harmonious, satisfying, and the secure basis of a "good life" were it not for the disrupting influences of mental illness or "psychopathology." The potentiality for universal human happiness, in this form at least, seems to me but another example of the I-wish-it-were-true type of fantasy. I do not believe that human happiness or well-being on a hitherto unimaginably large scale, and not just for a select few, is possible. This goal could be achieved, however, only at the cost of many men, and not just a few being willing and able to tackle their personal, social, and ethical conflicts. This means having the courage and integrity to forego waging battles on false fronts, finding solutions for substitute problems—for instance, fighting the battle of stomach acid and chronic fatigue instead of facing up to a marital conflict.

Our adversaries are not demons, witches, fate, or mental illness. We have no enemy whom we can fight, exorcise, or dispel by "cure." What we do have are *problems in living*—whether these be biologic, economic, political, or sociopsychological. In this essay I was concerned only with problems belonging in the last mentioned category, and within this group mainly with those pertaining to moral values. The field to which modern psychiatry addresses itself is vast, and I made no effort to encompass it all. My argument was limited to the proposition that mental illness is a myth, whose function it is to disguise and thus render more palatable the bitter pill of moral conflicts in human relations.

Note

1. Freud went so far as to say that: "I consider ethics to be taken for granted. Actually I have never done a mean thing" (Jones, 1957, p. 247). This surely is a strange thing to say for someone who has studied man as a social being as closely as did Freud. I mention it here to show how the notion of "illness" (in the case of psychoanalysis, "psychopathology," or "mental illness") was used by Freud—and by most of his followers—as a means for classifying certain forms of human behavior as falling within the scope of medicine, and hence (by *fiat*) outside that of ethics!

References

Hollingshead, A. B., & Redlich, F. C. *Social class and mental illness.* New York: Wiley, 1958.

Jones, E. *The life and work of Sigmund Freud.* Vol. III. New York: Basic Books, 1957.

Langer, S. K. *Philosophy in a new key.* New York: Mentor Books, 1953.

Peters, R. S. *The concept of motivation.* London: Routledge & Kegan Paul, 1958.

Szasz, T. S. Malingering: "Diagnosis" or social condemnation? *AMA Arch. Neurol. Psychiat.,* 1956, 76, 432–43.

Szasz, T. S. *Pain and pleasure: A study of bodily feelings.* New York: Basic Books, 1957. (a)

Szasz, T. S. The problem of psychiatric nosology: A contribution to a situational analysis of psychiatric operations. *Amer. J. Psychiat.,* 1957, 114, 405–13. (b)

Szasz, T. S. On the theory of psychoanalytic treatment. *Int. J. Psycho-Anal.,* 38, 166–82. (c)

Szasz, T. S. Psychiatry, ethics and the criminal law. *Columbia Law Rev.,* 1958, 58, 183–98.

Szasz, T. S. Moral conflict and psychiatry, *Yale Rev.,* 1960, 49, 555–66.

Some Myths About "Mental Illness"

Michael S. Moore

T he concept of mental illness has had a long and interesting history in man's thoughts about himself, his nature, and his responsibility. It stands at one junction of law, morals, and medicine, with the result that lawyers, psychiatrists, and philosophers have long shared a concern for the nature of the concept. This shared concern has not given rise to any consensus, however, and the debates, particularly between lawyers and psychiatrists, have often been acrimonious and unfruitful. Since the advent of "radical psychiatry," the theoretical justification of which is to be found notably in the works of Thomas Szasz, the battle lines have been redrawn somewhat along other than professional lines, but the result has not been added clarity about the nature of the concept of mental disease or its moral and legal relevance.

Indeed, quite the reverse has occurred, so that essentially ethical and political questions about psychiatric practices or legal doctrines with regard to the mentally ill are increasingly answered by the trundling out of the contemporary shibboleth that mental illness is a myth rather than in terms of the ethical and political arguments necessary to answer such questions. There is a disturbing tendency to regard complicated legal issues, notably the proper place of mental illness in various legal tests (of insanity in criminal trials, of incompetency to perform various legal acts or to stand trial, the tests for civil commitment), as solved by the new truth that mental illness is but a myth anyway. Equally disturbing is the apparent belief that problems of social policy and social justice, such as

From *Archives of General Psychiatry* 32 (December 1975): 1483–97. Copyright © 1975 by American Medical Association. Reprinted by permission.

what in fact society should do with dangerous persons who have not committed any criminal acts, are satisfactorily resolved if legislatures would but recognize mental illness for the sham that it is.

If mental illness were a myth, acceptance of such a truth would provide straightforward answers to such legal, ethical, and political questions. One would not have to muddle along in the grubby details of comparing awful prisons with almost as awful hospitals for the criminally insane. One would not have to grapple with difficult policy issues, such as the rationale for punishment generally and its relation to those found to be not guilty by reason of insanity, for it would be instantly clear that those we call mentally ill should be punished just like anyone else if they commit a criminal act; that they should have all the rights of an accused criminal if society should seek to deprive them of their liberty no matter how the proceeding or the place of confinement might be named; that legal tests should abolish the phrase; and, easiest of all, that psychiatrists should mind their own business and leave the law to the lawyers.

The problem is that mental illness is not a myth. It is not some palpable falsehood propagated among the populace by power-mad psychiatrists, but a cruel and bitter reality that has been with the human race since antiquity. This is such an obvious truism that to have stated it 20 years ago would have been an embarrassment. Since the advent of radical psychiatry and its legal entourage, however, such truths need restatement. Even more, they need restatement in a form specifically addressed to the various senses in which mental illness has been thought to be a myth. Since on my reading of the radical psychiatrists there seem to be five distinguishable points [only two of which appear below] they have in mind in thinking of mental illness as a myth, the discussion will proceed by considering them seriatim.

The Mythology of Radical Psychiatry

. . . In ordinary English, in order to make out a motivational explanation we need to know what the agent wanted and what he believed about the situation and his abilities to achieve through action what he wanted. In addition, we need to know that he is a rational creature in the fundamental sense of "rational" defined . . . [as] one who, other things being equal, will act so as to further his desires in light of his beliefs; and we need to know that other things are in fact equal, namely, that the agent does not have desires and beliefs that conflict with the desires and beliefs on which he is about to act.

The actions of the mentally ill may be nonrational or irrational in any of five following corresponding senses: (1) R may be an unintelligible thing to want, such as soaking one's elbow in the mud for its own sake;

(2) the belief that A will lead to R may be an irrational belief (e.g., a belief that saying "storks" instead of "stocks" will make one a mother); (3) the belief that one is in situation S may also be irrational (e.g., a belief that one is being persecuted by spirits); (4) there may be no set of beliefs and desires, no matter how bizarre, by virtue of which one can make out the action as the rational thing to do; or (5) the beliefs and desires of the particular practical syllogism may be inconsistent with other standing beliefs and desires.

The rationality of an *agent* is a function of the rationality of his actions over time. The more irrational behavior we observe of an individual in any of these five senses, the less rational we will judge him as an agent to be.

By and large, the empirical version of the myth argument is only intended to show that the behavior of the mentally ill is rational in the fundamental sense defined by the fourth premise above, i.e., there is *some* set of beliefs and desires (no matter how bizarre) furthered by the act in question. The crunch for even this limited attempt at making out the behavior of the mentally ill as rational, comes in making more precise the nature of the beliefs and desires of mental patients in terms of which their actions are to be so adjudged. More specifically, the fudge occurs with the use of *unconscious* beliefs and desires to fill in where we all know that mental patients did not consciously guide their actions to achieve such goals in light of such beliefs. Braginsky and colleagues are explicit about this: "It is obvious that rational goal-directed behavior does not guarantee that the individual appreciates what he is up to."[1] (p. 171) Szasz is particularly transparent in his glossing over of this distinction:

> In describing this contrast between lying and erring, I have deliberately avoided the concept of consciousness. It seems to me that when the adjectives "consciously" and "unconsciously" are used as explanations, they complicate and obscure the problem. The traditional psychoanalytic idea that so-called conscious imitation of illness is "malingering" and hence "not illness," whereas its allegedly unconscious simulation is itself "illness" ("hysteria"), creates more problems than it solves. It would seem more useful to *distinguish between goal-directed and rule-following behavior on the one hand, and indifferent mistakes on the other. . . .* In brief, *it is more accurate to regard hysteria as a lie than as a mistake.* People caught in a lie usually maintain that they were merely mistaken. The difference between mistakes and lies, when discovered, is chiefly pragmatic. From a purely cognitive point of view, both are simply falsehoods.[2] (pp. 142, 143)

The fudge occurs in the shift from our judgments of rationality being based on the agent's conscious beliefs and objectives to a notion of rationality by virtue of which we adjudge an action at least minimally rational if we can posit any set of beliefs or objectives with which we can explain the action. The problem is that it is notoriously easy to posit beliefs and desires to explain any finite sequence of the behavior of anything. Simply pick a consequence of the behavior and label it the objective, pick a set of beliefs by virtue of which it would appear likely that such a consequence would indeed ensue as a result of the behavior, and one is then in a position to adjudge the behavior as rational, relative to that objective and that set of beliefs. The shedding of leaves by a tree, the falling of stones, the pumping of blood by the heart, and the most chaotic word-salad of a schizophrenic are all "rational" activities judged by such a standard. The "action" of a tree in shedding its leaves is rational if we suppose that it desires to survive the coming winter, and believes that the only way to do this is to lower its sap level, thereby killing off its leaves. The same analysis can be applied to stones, hearts, and schizophrenics.

The reason such explanations are so easy to manufacture is because without the requirement that an agent be conscious of the beliefs and the desires by which we (and he) judge his action as rational, there is no means of fixing the nature of such beliefs or wants independently of the behavior to be explained and adjudged. Behavior is by itself inherently ambiguous as a criterion for such matters. If we know by some independent means that an agent believes that action A will lead to result R, and he does A, we have good grounds for attributing to him a desire for R; if we know that he desires R, and does A, we have equally good grounds for supposing that he believes that A will lead to R. However, if we know neither his beliefs nor his desires, but only that he does A and that A does result in R being the case, we have no means of singling out R as his motive, for any other consequence of A would do as well. "There is nothing in a pure behaviorist theory to prevent us from regarding each piece of behavior as a desire for whatever happens next."[3] (p. 108)

Szasz can thus ignore the conscious/unconscious distinction only at the price of significance. What he fails to realize is that any behavior can be seen as rational (or as in accordance with rules of a game, or as furthering certain goals—Szasz's substitute criteria for consciousness), if one allows oneself the freedom to *invent* the beliefs and desires in terms of which the behavior is to be so viewed.

It may be objected that good sense at least seems to be made in the use of unconscious beliefs and unconscious desires in explaining human action, even in orthodox psychoanalysis, and thus that the foregoing must be an inadequate account of motivated action and hence, of rational action. As Stuart Hampshire[4] and Dilman[5] have pointed out, unconscious beliefs and unconscious desires can make good sense, so long as they are used in a way that ties them to consciousness. One may have the same independent grounds for ascribing beliefs and desires to an agent if his first person statements of his *memory* of them are accorded the same authority as are his normal, first person, present tense reports of them. When in successful psychoanalytic therapy the patient comes to know his motives or beliefs, he comes to know them in the same noninferential, nonobservational way as we all normally know our own motives, and in such cases it makes sense to grant the usual authority to his sincere avowals of what they are. As long as the nature of such beliefs or desires is dependent on authoritative statements of the agent who himself remembers them (as opposed to inferring them from observing his own behavior or acceding to the authority of his analyst), significant explanations of his behavior can be formed using such unconscious motives.

So restricted, how much of the behavior of the mentally ill can even be said to be unconsciously motivated? Are there sets of beliefs and desires, conscious *or* unconscious, that explain the peculiar string of words and sounds sometimes uttered as a kind of word-salad by the mentally ill? Can one give such an explanation of the actions-by-omission of the vegetating catatonic, or of the violent actions against self-interest such as beating one's head against the wall? Note that the question is not whether one can or cannot come up with legitimate *causal* hypotheses about why the patient is in the state he is in. Nor is the question whether or not one can *invent* some set of beliefs and desires which, *if* the patient had them, would render his action rational. Rather, the question is whether such patients are performing an action for reasons which they either recognize, or if sufficient effort were made, could come to recognize as an action *they* were doing for reasons *they* found sufficient. Put this way, much of the behavior by which the more extreme forms of mental illness are diagnosed remains unmotivated and hence nonrational.

In any case, such behavior of the mentally ill as can be legitimately explained by reference to unconscious beliefs or unconscious desires is not fully rational. By hypothesis, such behavior is minimally rational because motivated. It is typically *irrational,* however, in each of the several other senses of "rationality" mentioned earlier—the desires may be unintelligible, the beliefs about means irrational (or at least the means/end calculation grossly inefficient), the beliefs about the situation in which the actor finds himself irrational, or the beliefs and desires inconsistent with standing beliefs and desires. Since these aspects of the irrationality of unconscious motive explanations have been explored by others,[6-9] they need not be pursued further here.

On occasion, the empirical version of the myth claim is put forward without any extensive reliance on some supposed unconscious beliefs or desires of the mentally ill. Laing in particular explicitly disavows[10] (p. 26) use of unconscious beliefs or desires in reaching his well-known conclusions that "*without exception* the experience and behavior that gets labeled schizophrenic is *a special strategy that a person invents in order to live in an unlivable situation.*"[11] (pp. 114, 115) Nonetheless, such studies do not show schizophrenics to be as rational as everyone else, for the conscious beliefs such patients admittedly do have are themselves irrational beliefs; and actions that are predicated on irrational beliefs, and actors who hold them, are, in common understanding, irrational.

This is quite clear with regard to many of Laing's reported patients. The woman who avoids crowds may be rational in so doing, *given* her belief that "when she was in a crowd she felt the ground would open up under her feet."[12] (p. 131) Similarly many of the peculiar actions of one who believes that "she had an atom bomb inside her"[13] (p. 75) may be rational, *given* such a belief. But the beliefs themselves are irrational, with the result that neither the agent nor the action they explain can be said to be rational. To be sure, Laing's studies of the "social intelligibility" of schizophrenic symptoms do not end with the discovery of such obvious beliefs; Laing often attempts to go further and explain how such beliefs could be formed by an individual in the patient's situation. The explanation Laing typically gives—the patient "adopts" the symptom as the only response to an intolerable situation—involves reference to further beliefs that are also irrational.

A convenient example is the case of "Joan," a catatonic woman who was not one of Laing's patients but whose case Laing believed to afford "striking confirmation" of his views regarding schizophrenia. Joan's own subsequent avowals were used by Laing in attributing to her catatonic withdrawal a rational basis. She recalled that when she was catatonic, she "tried to be dead and grey and motionless." She thought that her mother "would like that," for "she could carry me around like a doll." She also felt that she "had to die to keep from dying. I know that sounds crazy but one time a boy hurt my feelings very much and I wanted to jump in front of a subway. Instead I went a little catatonic so I wouldn't feel anything."

Laing finds in such statements the two typical motives for catatonic withdrawal. First, "there is the primary guilt of having no right to life . . . and hence of being entitled at most only to a dead life." Since Joan's parents had wanted a boy, and since "she could not be anything other than what her parents wanted her to be," she sought to be "nothing," i.e., a passive catatonic. Secondly, Joan's withdrawal was viewed by Laing as a defensive mechanism to avoid the loss of identity (Joan's metaphorical "dying") with which she was threatened by any normal relationship with others:

One no longer fears being crushed, engulfed, overwhelmed by realness and aliveness . . . since one is already dead [by the catatonic withdrawal]. Being dead, one cannot die, and one cannot kill. The anxieties attendant on the schizophrenic's phantastic omnipotence are undercut by living in a condition of phantastic impotence.[14] (p. 176)

None of this would convince us that Joan or others like her were rational in effective catatonic withdrawal (even if we were convinced that at least in her case the withdrawal was an *action* she performed for reasons at all, a conclusion contrary to that reached by the original reporters of her case[15]). Her action is based on a series of beliefs that are irrational, including her belief in a disembodied self, a belief in her parents' complete determination of her worth, and a belief in her own omnipotence and impotence.

It is sometimes believed that the rationality of beliefs is not a matter that can be objectively judged and that calling them irrational is simply a pejorative way of saying that they are false. The conclusion in the present context would be that people like Joan are thus as rational as the rest of us, only mistaken about certain facts. While the topic of rational belief is a difficult one, prima facie the most obvious way to differentiate beliefs that are irrational from those that are merely false is by looking at the influence relevant evidence would have on the holder of the belief. It is characteristic of irrational beliefs that their holder maintains them despite countervailing evidence or despite inconsistencies with other beliefs he has. There is a fixed or frozen nature about such beliefs, in the sense that they are not correctable by relevant evidence. Irrational beliefs are held with a strength (relative to other beliefs the actor has) disproportionate to the evidence known to the actor. Thus the man "who believes very strongly that his brother is trying to poison him (in spite of appearances) and who believes, rather weakly by comparison, that Boston is north of New York is likely to be flying in the face of evidence and the claims that the evidence renders likely"[16] (p. 33)—he is likely, in other words, to be irrational in his belief of his imminent poisoning.

The empirical version of the myth argument fails because it is empirically false. By our shared concept of what it is to be rational, the mentally ill are not as rational as the rest of the population. Only by muddling the concept of rationality have the radical psychiatrists appeared to call into question this obvious truth. Only by attributing unconscious beliefs and desires to the mentally ill for which there is no evidence, or only by referring to beliefs that are themselves irrational can motives be found for the peculiar behavior symptomatic of mental illness. Neither of these moves satisfies what we usually mean by "rational" as applied to actions and agents. One may, of course, like Humpty Dumpty, choose to make a word like "rationality" mean what he pleases, but surely it is unhelpful when one does so to then present the manufactured match between the facts and the new criteria for the word, as a discovery of new facts, previously overlooked because of the willful blindness of self-interested psychiatrists or whatever. To do so is to create one's own myths. . . .

The Myth as an Evaluation Masquerading as an Explanation: The Abuse of the Normative Connotations of "Mental Illness" by Orthodox Psychiatry

Sensitivity to the normative connotations of the concepts of "mental health" and "mental illness' is, I suspect, rather widespread. When one of the psychiatrists at the annual meeting of the American Psychiatric Association (APA) some years ago loudly diagnosed a women's-libber who was disrupting the meeting, as a "stupid, paranoid bitch," something other than a value-neutral explanation of her behavior was intended. The same suspicions are engendered when psychiatrists label homosexuals as mentally ill, or when "mental health" is used as a synonym for whatever way of life is adjudged good. The radical psychiatrists build on these kinds of examples to argue that "mental illness" and the predicate "mentally ill" are used *only* to make evaluations of others' behavior, and that these terms are particularly effective as evaluations because they are paraded as value-neutral, scientific explanations: "while allegedly *describing* conduct, psychiatrists often *prescribe* it."[17] (p. 18)

> The masquerading of promotive assertions in the guise of indicative sentences is of great practical significance in psychiatry. Statements concerning "psychosis" or "insanity" . . . almost always revolve around unclarified equations of these two linguistic forms. For example, the statement "John Doe is psychotic" is ostensibly indicative and informative. Usually, however, it is promotive rather than informative. . . .[18] (p. 131)

It may seem curious to claim that "mental illness" is used like "bad" or "wrong" or "ugh"—that is, used to pass moral evaluations—when by our shared notions of moral responsibility we use the same phrase to *excuse* those who are mentally ill. To attribute a harmful action to the actor's mental illness, then, cannot always be exactly the same as attributing it, say, to his "murderous personality." What Szasz sometimes has in mind in saying that "mental illness" is used prescriptively or promotively is not that moral judgments are made with such use; rather, psychiatric usage of the phrase is often promotive, etc., in the quite different sense that the capability of being morally responsible is denied. "Mental illness" for Szasz and others is evaluative often only in the sense that it denies the "personhood" of those to whom it is applied:

> What better way is there . . . for degrading the culprit than to declare him incapable of knowing what he is doing. . . . This is the general formula for the dehumanization and degradation of all those persons whose conduct psychiatrists now deem to be "caused" by mental illness.[19] (pp. 122, 123)

Although needlessly stated in inflammatory terms (as if orthodox psychiatry were universally motivated by a desire to degrade the mentally ill), Szasz here suggests a very important feature of mental illness. "Insanity" and "mental illness" mean, and have historically meant, "irrational"; to be insane, or to be mentally ill, is not to act rationally often enough to have the same assumption of rationality made about one as is made of most of humanity; and absent such an assumption of rationality, one cannot be fully regarded as a person, for our concept of what it is to be a person is centered on assuming rationality in the senses introduced earlier. Unless we can perceive another being as acting for intelligible ends in light of rational beliefs, we cannot understand that being in the same fundamental way that we understand each other's actions in daily life. Such beings lack an essential attribute of our humanity. It is thus easy to appreciate that historically the insane have been likened to young children, the intoxicated, and wild beasts; for absent the assumption of rationality, the mentally ill are, as Bleuler said of his schizophrenic patients, stranger to us than the birds in our gardens.

Such statements are of course offensive to the ears of those concerned about the moral claims and legal rights of mental patients. However, unless radical psychiatry and its lawyerly following can show, as I have argued earlier in this article it has not, that those we label mentally ill are just as rational as everyone else, part of our fundamental explanatory scheme and part of our fundamental notion of personhood are not applicable to the mentally ill. This includes notions about their lack of responsibility and their lack of an ability to choose and act upon their own conception of their good. If one believes (contra Szasz and followers) that there are in fact people who do not act rationally often enough for us to make the same assumption of rationality for them as we do for most of our fellows, then this "evaluative" feature of the phrase "mental illness" is accurate enough in its reflection of how the mentally ill fit into our fundamental conceptual scheme.

Szasz, at other times, seems to have in mind a second kind of normative use we do on occasion make of "mentally ill" in everyday expressions such as, "That was an insane thing to do," or "That's crazy!" In such usages we do seem to be expressing disapproval of the agent's ends and his actions, recommending that one ought not to do such things or seek such ends, etc. Thus Szasz is also accurate in noting that at times, "mentally ill" or "insane" can be used as terms of general disapproval: "The difference between saying 'He is wrong' and 'He is mentally ill' is not factual but psychological."[20] (p. 205) Other examples with which we began this section were the women's libber's diagnosis and the use of "mental health" as if it were synonymous with "good" by some psychoanalysts, e.g., Erich Fromm.

To the extent that orthodox psychiatry uses these words in this way it is plainly abusing them. The phrase "mental illness" and its companions are so abused, not by being applied to those who are in fact irrational, but by being applied to persons whose actions are often rational but of whose ends prevailing psychiatric opinion does not approve. An action that is fully rational in each of the senses examined earlier cannot, without ignoring the meaning of the words, be said to be insane or due to mental illness, no matter how deviant may be the end pursued. The fact that homosexuals have a preference for a sexual relationship not shared by most of the populace is hardly a ground (as the APA with strong dissent implicitly recognized recently in its deletion of homosexuality as an illness) for labeling that preference irrational (ill). Homosexuals may (sometimes, often, or always) be mentally ill, if their capacity for rational action is significantly diminished below our expectations; such irrationality is hardly shown, however, by their unpopular sexual desires alone if those ends are pursued on the basis of rational and consistent beliefs, without conflict with other strong desires, and by relatively efficient means.

The mistake of radical psychiatry is to assume that mental illness is a myth just because the phrase can be so abused. The mistake is to assume that because words such as "murder," "greediness," "mental illness," or even "good" can be used to express attitudes, kindle emotions, pass evaluations, and the like, they cannot also be used at the same time as a legitimate form of explanation and/or description, or at different times only as a description/explanation. Those moral philosophers who have raised another logical gulf between evaluative and descriptive statements insufficiently stress the fact that words used in evaluations can also be used to express descriptions. Merely because a woman may call the doctor who through surgical error kills her husband a murderer, despite the fact that one of the main criteria for that term's proper use is not met (viz., *intentional* killing), is not sufficient to show that the term "murderer" cannot have legitimate descriptive and explanatory uses.

To the extent that one views mental illness as a myth solely because of its evaluative connotations, one makes the same mistake. I do not believe one can accuse Szasz himself of this error because he conjoins this point with one of the preceding four points; mental illness is a myth because it has no descriptive meaning (take your pick of any of the first four myth arguments) *and* because it can be and is sometimes used to pass moral judgment on those so labeled. If, however, one rejects the first part of this thesis, the second is an insufficient basis on which to label mental illness a myth. "Mental illness" is perhaps a dangerous term because its normative connotations make possible the kind of abuse mentioned earlier; but then the same can be said of many of the terms with which we describe and explain human action, such as "greedy," "stupid," "murder," "manipulative," etc.

Some Legal Implications

The disease that radical psychiatry has contracted (and which appears to be contagious, at least for those lawyers who always knew that psychiatry was pseudoscience anyway) is the temptation to regard complex legal, social, ethical, and conceptual problems as solved once it administers a sufficient amount of antimyth antidote. In Szasz's case in particular, it is an attempt to use the therapeutic tools of modern philosophy to dissolve the problems, not to solve them.

If indeed one believes that there is no such thing as mental illness, that those we call mentally ill are fully as rational as anyone else only with different aims, that the only reason anyone ever thought differently was because of unsophisticated category mistakes or because of their adherence to the epistemology of a sick society, and that the phrase accordingly is only a mask used to disguise moral judgments in pseudoscientific respectability—one who in other words accepts the myth theses—will necessarily also believe that he wields an Alexandrian sword with which to cut through the knotty legal problems surrounding the treatment of the mentally ill. For once one subscribes to these versions of the myth argument, a number of radical consequences for the present treatment of the mentally ill are self-evident truths to all but the uninitiated: either the insanity defense should be abolished and those we call mentally ill punished like anyone else, or at the least the phrase should play no part as a separate defense; the incompetency plea should be either abolished or highly limited; those we call mentally ill should be sued for breach of contract like anyone else, not excused from their contractual obligations because of supposed incapacity to contract; no one should be civilly committed for mental illness, for the mentally ill know their own good and have the capacity to act in accordance with such conception no less than anyone else, the state thus having no parental role to play here; anyone inside or outside of a mental hospital should have the full civil rights of any citizen because he is just like any citizen. In short, one who subscribes to the myth argument will believe "that we abolish the problem of mental illness by abolishing the concept of mental illness."[21]

Unfortunately, the mentally ill and their attendant problems will not go away this easily. Unlike some of the conceptual problems against which the analytic philosophy on which Szasz relies has been directed in this century, there are no logical or methodological shortcuts by which one can dissolve the ethical, legal, and medical problems presented by the mentally ill. Belief that there are such shortcuts only impedes the search to solve these problems in a manner consistent with the accepted values of our society.

It is beyond the scope of this article to document in any complete way the impact that the myth argument has had on the legal issues mentioned above. I shall content myself with one example, the proposal to abolish the insanity defense. For there the conclusions of the myth argument are both clear and disturbing. The myth argument seems to have led in two related directions here.

1. The conclusions that some lawyers have drawn from one or more variants of the myth argument has been more limited than a complete abolition of the insanity plea. Rather, the conclusion drawn has been that the defense could be retained but any use of such allegedly meaningless phrases as "mental defect," "mental illness," "mental disease," or the like, be omitted. . . .

. . . As [former] Chief Justice [Burger] of the United States once said,

> No rule of law can possibly be sound or workable which is dependent upon the terms of another discipline whose members are in profound disagreement about what those terms mean.[22] (p. 860)

Citing and quoting Szasz among others, [former] Chief Justice Burger also adopted the view that "[mental] 'disease' . . . has no fixed, agreed or accepted definition in the discipline which is called upon to supply expert testimony, . . ." and that accordingly it was "a tenuous and indeed dangerously vague term to be a critical part of a rule of law on criminal responsibility."[23] (pp. 861, 862)

If "mental illness" were indeed in a sorry state depicted by the radical movement in law and psychiatry, its use should be discontinued. Yet it is not, for the reasons set forth in the body of this article, and the proposals to eliminate the phrase from legal tests of insanity, are as erroneous as the premises on which they are based.

2. The more radical conclusion to be drawn from the myth arguments is that the insanity defense should be abolished and that those

presently excused by the defense should be dealt with like any other offenders, viz., punished. This is the conclusion Szasz himself correctly perceives to be entailed by his myth arguments, and he unflinchingly endorses it: "mental illness should never be accepted as a release from criminal responsibility. . . ."[24] (p. 228)

Such a result does real violence to our notions of fairness. No one merits society's condemnation or punishment unless they are morally blameworthy, and no one is blameworthy if he acts as he does because of his mental disease. Szasz's conclusion is reminiscent of the Erewhonian practice of punishing the ill, and evokes in most of us the same distaste.

Szasz is not unaware of this fundamental objection. Rather than softening the argument, however, as many of his lawyerly admirers are inclined to do, he proclaims that indeed the mentally ill *deserve* to be blamed and punished like any criminals. This follows axiomatically from an unswerving adherence to that version of the myth argument that claims as a matter of fact that the mentally ill are really as purposive, as rational, as the rest of us. Thus,

> Insofar as men are human beings, not machines, they always have some choice in how they act—hence, they are *always* responsible for their conduct. There is method in madness, no less than in sanity.[25] (p. 135)

Just as those who act in ignorance of the law are not excused but expected to learn it, so those ignorant of themselves (the mentally ill), being fully purposive beings, are expected to educate themselves.

> Just as the recognition of ignorance and its correction are the responsibility of the adult citizen, so also are the recognition of mental illness and its correction.[26] (p. 133)

Ultimately, we should abolish the insanity defense—"this crime against humanity"[27] (p. 112)—because "by treating offenders as responsible human beings, we offer them the only chance . . . to remain human."[28] (p. 137) (Szasz is referring to the denial of the status of a person which is involved in using "insanity").

The problem with this response is the problem with the basic argument on which it rests, examined earlier—despite the mental gymnastics Szasz would lead us through, the purposive idioms are not as often applicable to explain the doings of the mentally ill as they are to explain the actions of most people; the mentally ill are not as rational as most people. Hence, to say that the mentally ill engage in criminal conduct for purposes sufficient to themselves, like any other criminals, or worse, that they should correct their condition just as the normal citizen is expected to correct any ignorance he may have about the law, is an erroneous, (and in this instance, cruel) distortion of the facts.

For lawyers, perhaps the most persuasive of the Szaszian arguments for either of the two conclusions regarding the insanity defense—that either the concept of mental disease or the entire defense should be abolished—has been the third version of the category mistake argument—"mental illness" is not the name of a mechanical cause, and, as set forth earlier, it is not. "Mental illness" and its subspecies, "schizophrenia," and other terms are not the names of physiological events that cause criminal actions. Thus, when Szasz attacks[29] (pp. 133–35)[30] (p. 191) the Durham decision[31] as "unadulterated nonsense" because in its explicitly causal language (the criminal act must be the *product* of mental disease) there has been committed a category mistake, he seems to have pointed to a serious defect.

The conclusion that is supposed to follow from this insight in the present context is that mental illness should not excuse; mental illness is only a pseudo-cause of the criminal behavior of the mentally ill. Once one sees through this myth, then he can see that that behavior is as uncaused as that of the rest of us; and with such contra-causal freedom comes responsibility. The softer version of this argument is that other conditions usually present in those we call mentally ill—compulsion, ignorance, or lack of mens rea—do excuse such persons without reference to the supposed causal agency of some entity called mental illness.[32-33] (pp. 985, 986) The heroic line is Szasz's—such persons should not be excused at all.

The mistake common to both positions is to be found in the assumption that it is only because "mental illness" was believed to name a mechanical cause that anyone ever thought it itself could be an excusing condition. This is indeed a popular misconception about the role of mental illness vis-à-vis our shared conceptions of responsibility. Yet that it is a misconception can be seen from the fact that, even if "mental illness" were the name of known, mechanical causes, it would not excuse because of such reference.

To believe that mental illness can excuse because it is or could be correlated with as yet unknown mechanical causes would be both to allow one's judgments of responsibility to depend entirely on speculative hypotheses about causes and to accept whole-hog the thesis that any mechanistic explanation of human action ipso facto excuses the actor from responsibility for that action. These two assumptions, however, would be sufficient to eliminate responsibility altogether as a viable concept. For if one is a determinist (which is likely if one believes in the existence of the requisite sorts of correlations between mental diseases and physiology), and if one allows the possibility of any kind of mechanical cause, known or unknown, to vitiate responsibility, then little seems to be left for particular excuses, such as mental illness, to do. One need only see the general implications of these same assumptions to see that everyone is already "excused" by an assumed, but yet unknown, mechanistic science of human behavior. The assumption that underneath the behavioral manifestations of disease there is a physiological explanation is not the source of our excusing the mentally ill from responsibility, no matter how popular the notion that that is the basis for our moral sentiments here.

As I[34] and others[35-38] have argued elsewhere in more detail, the reason it has been a century's-old and fundamental feature of our collective conscience that the mentally ill, who cause injurious results, are nonetheless not morally blameworthy is because, as set forth earlier, one who is mentally ill is not as rational as the rest of us in the senses of "rational" introduced earlier. If we cannot assume the rationality of another being, we cannot think of him as being morally responsible; for this assumption "is a precondition of any moral stance, and if it is jeopardized . . . the notion of moral responsibility is jeopardized in turn."[39] (p. 169) The presupposition of rationality is a necessary condition of taking any moral attitude toward another because it is a necessary condition for understanding that other in human terms, that is, in the idioms of practical reasoning, beliefs, motives, intentions, desires, and the like. Absent from such explanations we cannot understand another in the same fundamental way in which we understand our fellows in daily life, as set forth earlier. It is only beings that we understand in this way that we regard as moral agents.

Since mental illness negates our assumption of rationality, we do not hold the mentally ill responsible. It is not so much that we excuse them from a prima facie case of responsibility; rather, by being unable to regard them as fully rational beings, we cannot affirm the essential condition to viewing them as moral agents to begin with. In this the mentally ill join (to a decreasing degree) infants, wild beasts, plants, and stones—none of which is responsible because of the absence of any assumption of rationality. True, primitive people sometimes do hold such beings responsible, but then such peoples also invariably regard these things as purposive beings, i.e., rational. A widespread attribution of responsibility to infants, animals, and natural objects goes hand in hand with primitive animism or some other anthropomorphic view of the world.

Our intuitive feeling that the mentally ill should not be blamed (and, not being the subject of moral blame, excused from criminal liability), thus survives any insights about category mistakes lawyers or others might make in thinking of mental disease as a mechanical cause. Mental illness is not a mechanical cause of behavior, but then the assumption that it is or could be is not why we feel that the mentally ill should be excused to begin with.

Conclusion

. . . It has been the central purpose of this article to demonstrate that a critical reading of Szasz in terms of the philosophers on which he relies leaves "the myth of mental illness" as itself a myth, useful perhaps as a battle cry but hardly as the starting point for serious consideration of the legal status or medical treatment of the mentally ill.

The hoped for result of such a critique would be to channel the contemporary discussion of the insanity defense, civil commitment, the civil rights of the mentally ill, etc., away from the notion that mental illness is a myth and away from the methodological and philosophical grounds that allegedly support the myth conclusion. There may be strong arguments, e.g., that we in effect punish the insane anyway by involuntary detention in hospitals hardly worthy of the name, or that it is unjust for society to deprive anyone of his liberty absent either a violation of the law or a demonstrated dangerousness to others. These kinds of arguments do not depend on mental illness being nothing but a myth, and are the kinds of arguments genuinely relevant to the issues. Such arguments assume their proper role, however, only if one thinks more in terms of, say, Mill on liberty, than in terms of Szasz on myths.

Notes

1. Braginsky BM, Braginsky OD, Ring K: *Methods of Madness: The Mental Hospital as a Last Resort.* New York, Holt, Rinehart & Winston Inc., 1969.

2. Szasz TS: *The Myth of Mental Illness.* New York, Harper & Row Publishers Inc., 1961.

3. Kenny A: *Action, Emotion and Will.* London, Routledge & Kegan Paul Ltd., 1963.

4. Hampshire S: Disposition and memory. *Int. Psychoanal.* 43:59–68, 1962.

5. Dilman I: Is the unconscious a theoretical construct? *Monist* 56:313–42, 1972.

6. Alexander P: Rational behaviour and psychoanalytic explanation. *Mind* 71:326–41, 1962.

7. Mischel T: Concerning rational behaviour and psychoanalytic explanation. *Mind* 74:71–78, 1965.

8. Mullane H: Psychoanalytic explanation and rationality. *J. Philos.* 68:413–26, 1971.

9. Audi R: Psychoanalytic explanation and the concept of a rational action. *Monist* 56:444–64, 1972.

10. Laing RD, Esterson A: *Sanity, Madness, and the Family*. Baltimore, Penguin Books Inc., 1970.

11. Laing RD: *The Politics of Experience*. New York, Ballantine Books Inc., 1967.

12. Laing RD, Esterson A: *Sanity, Madness, and the Family*.

13. Ibid.

14. Laing RD: *The Divided Self*. Baltimore, Penguin Books Inc., 1965.

15. Hayward ML, Taylor JE: A schizophrenic patient describes the action of intensive psychotherapy. *Psychiatr. Q.* 30:211–48, 1956.

16. Ackermann RJ: *Belief and Knowledge*. New York, Doubleday & Co. Inc., 1972.

17. Szasz TS: *Law, Liberty, and Psychiatry*. New York, Collier Books, 1968.

18. Szasz TS: *The Myth of Mental Illness*.

19. Szasz TS: *The Manufacture of Madness*. New York, Harper & Row Publishers Inc., 1970.

20. Szasz TS: *Law, Liberty, and Psychiatry*.

21. Gerbode FA: Book review. *Santa Clara Lawyer* 13:616–22, 1973.

22. *Blocker* v. *United States*, 288 F 2d 853, 1961.

23. Ibid.

24. Szasz TS: *Law, Liberty, and Psychiatry*.

25. Ibid.

26. Ibid.

27. Szasz TS: *Ideology and Insanity*. New York, Doubleday & Co. Inc., 1970.

28. Szasz TS: *Law, Liberty, and Psychiatry*

29. Ibid.

30. Szasz TS: Psychiatry, ethics, and the criminal law. *Columbia Law Rev.* 58:183–98, 1958.

31. *Durham* v. *United States*, 214 F 2d 862, 1954.

32. Goldstein J, Katz J: Abolish the insanity defense—why not? *Yale Law J.* 72:853–80, 1963.

33. *United States* v. *Brawner*, 471 F 2d 969, 1972.

34. Moore MS: Mental illness and responsibility. *Bull. Menninger Clin.* 39:308–28, 1975.

35. Feinberg J: What is so special about mental illness? in *Doing and Deserving*. Princeton, NJ, Princeton University Press, 1970, pp. 272–92.

36. Fingarette H: *The Meaning of Criminal Insanity*. Berkeley, Calif., University of California Press, 1972.

37. Fingarette H: Insanity and responsibility. *Inquiry* 15:6–29, 1972.

38. Dennett DC: Mechanism and responsibility, in Honderich T (ed.): *Essays on Freedom of Action*. London, Routledge & Kegan Paul Ltd., 1973, pp. 159–84.

39. Ibid.

Mental Health as Rational Autonomy

Rem B. Edwards

It has often been noted that psychiatric labeling has grave moral consequences, i.e., consequences which seriously affect the moral standing, rights, and quality of life of other people. In the name of supposedly scientific and objective medicine, it legitimatizes the enormous power which psychiatrists and mental institutions have over other people, especially the weaker and more vulnerable members of society. Psychiatric labeling is a form of moral as well as medical behavior which has clear disadvantages as well as clear advantages. On the debit side, it serves to isolate socially those persons to whom labels of lunacy are applied; and it often generates enormous mistrust and alienation between them and their family and friends. It permanently stigmatizes those so characterized and negatively affects for years to come their opportunities for such basic amenities as self respect, employment, promotion, housing, education, marriage, and general social trust and acceptance. It dehumanizes and degrades those to whom it is applied, allowing us to regard and treat the mentally ill as slightly less than human. Nevertheless, it may still be a rationally acceptable and justifiable mode of interpersonal interaction, despite its obvious moral liabilities. Recognizing that psychiatric labeling of individual persons may have grave consequences, we should also acknowledge that the very act of defining and providing a range of application for such concepts as "mental health" and "mental illness" is itself a moral act which greatly affects the lives of others.

There is both an evaluative and a descriptive dimension to our con-

From *The Journal of Medicine and Philosophy* 6 (1981): 309–22. Reprinted by permission of Kluwer Academic Publishers.

cepts of "mental health" and "mental illness." The latter term applies to describable mental and/or behavioral deviations of which we strongly disapprove. In addition to statistical abnormality, the disapproval element is a necessary condition for applying the term; for there are many "healthy" minority deviations of which we strongly approve, such as the rare but precious intellectual genius, creativity and sensitivity of our most outstanding artists, writers, scientists, philosophers, and moral and religious leaders. It is a great but often-made mistake, however, to allow statistical deviation and the disapproval element to be sufficient conditions for applying the notion of "mental illness," for then we must allow every peculiar mental/behavioral process of which we disapprove to count as a mental illness. To avoid the excesses into which so much of psychiatry has lapsed in recent years, we must allow the notion to be applied only to a small sub-class of disapproved psychic processes, distresses, and behaviors. The issue is: do we wish to medicalize the whole of life, or do we wish instead to recognize and preserve other evaluative realms of discourse such as that of intrinsic value and disvalue, as well as distinctive moral, political, and religious norms?

Our present problem is not merely of academic interest, for there is a powerful tendency to work in modern secular, scientific society to allow older religious and moral values simply to fade away and to medicalize the whole sphere of moral, political, and religious deviation. When confronted by conditions and behaviors of which we disapprove, so many of us no longer use such ethico-religious terms as "ungodly," "sinful," and "immoral," or even such political terms as "unjust" or "undemocratic." Instead we apply such highly evaluative pseudo-scientific terms as "sick," "unhealthy," "immature," "a sad case," etc. We often do not realize that this whole way of talking tends to put ministers, political activists, and even serious-minded moralists as such out of business. Physicians and psychiatrists become the secular priests and final arbiters of what we should value and disvalue—in the name of "empirical" medicine. Many recent authors such as René Dubos, Ivan Illich, Nicholas Kittrie and Thomas Szasz have condemned such creeping medical imperialism and totalitarianism for a variety of reasons. Some protesters do so simply because they wish to make a place for moral, political, and religious norms and deviations which should not be confused with or collapsed into an all-embracing domain of "mental health" and "mental illness." This may involve recognizing and respecting other intrinsic, moral, social, political, and religious values and disvalues in their own right. E. Fuller Torrey was doing this when he criticized as follows the 1977 report of President Carter's Commission on Mental Health, which equated mental illness with the unhappiness which results from social injustice, discrimination, and poverty:

Certainly poverty and discrimination are terrible injustices that cause widespread anguish and unhappiness. But anguish and unhappiness are not mental illness, and herein lies the confusion. Poverty and discrimination are no more "mental health" problems than famine and war. They are human problems and should be attacked as such, with all the governmental and private resources at our disposal: jobs must be created; opportunities equalized; housing built; food supplies fairly distributed. Labeling them mental-health problems not only obscures their true importance but also creates the illusion that they can be "cured" if we will only put enough mental-health professionals into positions of power (Torrey, 1977, p. 10).

Resisting medical imperialism in psychiatric labeling may also involve an awareness of the grave moral consequences of psychiatric name-calling, or an appreciation of the horrendous physical and psychic consequences of much that passes for "therapy," or a sense of the desirability of protecting the integrity of language itself. Economic considerations also are very much involved in any decision to expand or restrict our notion of "illness," even of "mental illness." If a condition gets classified as an illness, insurance companies and government agencies such as Medicare and Medicaid will be expected to pay the bills in many cases; and if the condition is not so classified, these agencies will not pay. There are many good reasons for wanting to limit the scope of application for the notion of "mental illness," rather than allow it to swallow up *all* those states of mind, distresses, and deviant behaviors of which we disapprove. Surely things have gotten way out of hand when a psychoanalyst such as Fine (1967, p. 95) tells us, "neurosis is defined in the analytic sense as distance from the ideal; then it can be said to affect 99 percent of the population. Thus, the essential thesis of this paper emerges: The ultimate goal of psychoanalysis is the reform of society."

I shall now make a conservative proposal for the proper limitation of the very notion of "mental illness" which until recently has been a presupposition of our entire legal system, which is very close to what I have found many mental health professionals actually using in their work in mental hospitals, and which is also very close to what the term traditionally meant before the advent of the sort of medical imperialism which Kittrie (1971, pp. 340–410) has called "the therapeutic state," or which Illich (1976, pp. 31–60) has called "the medicalization of life." There is nothing final about this proposal. It is merely an attempt to generate a discussion of the proper limits of "mental illness," *recognizing that the lives of many people will be greatly affected by where we draw the line.*

Definition: "Mental illness" means only those undesirable mental/behavioral deviations which involve primarily an extreme and prolonged inability to know and deal in a rational and autonomous way with oneself and one's social and physical environment. In other words, madness is extreme and prolonged practical irrationality and irresponsibility. Correspondingly, "mental health" includes only those desirable mental/behavioral normalities and occasional abnormalities which enable us to know and deal in a rational and autonomous way with ourselves and our social and physical environment. In other words, mental health is practical rationality and responsibility. A number of other theorists such as Breggin (1974, 1975), Engelhardt, Jr. (1973), Fingarette (1972), and Moore (1975), have arrived at similar views.

There is much here that needs explaining. By "mental/behavioral" I mean thinking, willing and feeling which may manifest itself in publicly observable bodily alterations and activities. By "autonomy" I mean having and freely actualizing a capacity for making one's own choices, managing one's own practical affairs and assuming responsibility for one's own life, its station and its duties. Before defining "rationality," and specifying its relevant realm of application, let us first recognize that there is a large domain of human belief which falls quite legitimately into the category of contested beliefs and unanswered questions, and which should be regarded as only peripherally relevant to the identification of madness. Most of our political, philosophical, and religious beliefs, many scientific and factual beliefs, and many questions of value and practice belong to the class of contested beliefs and unanswered questions. There is no clear answer to what it is and what it is not rational to believe in these areas. I keep telling my colleagues in philosophy that in such matters, there is very little difference between being around a mental hospital and being around a department of philosophy! Political, philosophical, and religious beliefs especially should never provide us with *primary* grounds for diagnosing mental illness. If that restriction had been observed, attempts would not have been made to have Mary Baker Eddy declared insane and institutionalized involuntarily for being a Christian Scientist. Nor would Ezra Pound have been institutionalized for political dissent. Irrationality and irresponsibility with respect to knowing and dealing with oneself and one's social and physical environment should be the primary focus for defining and diagnosing mental illness. We cannot declare a Christian Scientist mentally ill for believing that a broken bone has been miraculously healed if indeed no fractures show up any longer on X-rays. However, if anyone for any reason insists that healing has occurred when the fractures are still showing up, or if a woman insists that she has a million children and spends all her time looking for them, or if someone insists that they no longer need to eat since they died yesterday and are now in Heaven, then questions of sanity may be very legitimately raised and would be so raised even by Christian Scientists. True, there will be some tough marginal cases such as that of the sociopath; but some cases will be clear enough. Situations will also arise in which philosophical and religious beliefs impinge upon personal, empirical, and social realities, but mental illness should not be diagnosed unless it manifests itself in these practical areas.

Are we all just a little bit crazy, as some psychotherapists and much of our popular wisdom and humor insinuate? This depends in part on whether we are willing to call *any* momentary lapse into irrationality and irresponsibility a form of "mental illness," or whether we wish to reserve the term only for extreme and persistent forms of such. Because of the grave consequences of psychiatric labeling, it seems morally desirable to limit it to the latter, and I am offering a moral argument for a very limited and conservative conception of "mental illness." As for the factors of duration and degree, there is no *precise* answer to the question of "how long?" or "how extreme?" But it seems both socially undesirable and linguistically unconventional (at least prior to our recent medicalization of the whole of life) to count momentary and relatively superficial confusions, lapses of memory, emotional traumas and perceptual errors, etc., as indications of mental illness. A moment of confusion does not count as a mental illness any more than a single sneeze counts as a respiratory disease. The concept of duration belongs in our definitions of all diseases. On my analysis, mental illness will be a matter of degree of both time and severity of impairment and as such will be on a continuum with the whole of life; and there will be a grey area of controversial borderline cases. But some instances of it will be unmistakable in their duration and degree. If we take the duration factor seriously, there will be no such thing as temporary insanity, but this has never been anything more than a legal fiction invented for excusing certain persons when no other legal rationale for doing so could be found. It is important that we understand that only relatively extreme forms of such mental/behavioral malfunctions count as mental disorders. Though the question is worth exploring, we should be wary of altering this to mean that any such malfunction which is *capable* of taking an extreme form is a mental illness, for then we would be right back to the medicalization of the whole of life. It should also be noted that the factual claim that extreme mental/behavioral malfunctions are grounded in some "underlying pathology," located in the brain, the unconscious, the enduring structure of the mind itself, or what have you, has not been built into our definition of mental illness. This is a hotly contested issue, especially between behaviorally oriented psychologists and their adversaries; and such a consideration can be introduced only when it has been confronted head-on and found to be justified. All the data are not in on this one yet.

Now, what is meant by "rational"? Whatever it is, mental disorders are shortcomings or departures from it, and only those disorders which involve the absence of it are to count as mental disorders. Other undesirable mental/behavioral deviations should be classified in other ways, such as intrinsically bad, immoral, criminal, irreligious, etc. There are a number of defining elements in our common notion of "rationality." This is an important word in our living languages, not a technical word invented by philosophers. But philosophers may contribute to its clarification, and there is widespread agreement among both philosophers and non-philosophers that rationality involves (1) being able to distinguish means from ends and being able to identify processes and manifest behaviors which likely will result in the realization of consciously envisioned goals; (2) thinking logically and avoiding logically contradictory beliefs; (3) having factual beliefs which are adequately supported by empirical evidence, or at least avoiding factual beliefs which are plainly falsified by experience; (4) having and being able to give reasons for one's behavior and beliefs; (5) thinking clearly and intelligibly, and avoiding confusion and nonsense; (6) having and exhibiting a capacity for impartiality or fair-mindedness in judging and adopting beliefs; (7) having values which have been (or would be) adopted under conditions of freedom, enlightenment, and impartiality. Rationality is a function of how we know, not of what we know. Ignorance is not insanity, but irrationality is. Stupidity, the deliberate choice of self-defeating ends, is also not insanity.

I am fully aware that many books could be and have in fact been written explicating all the complications of and full conceptual significance of these seven defining features of "rationality," but I do not have space here to rewrite such books. I do think that the last element is so difficult to apply that it should never be used in diagnosing insanity, though it has very legitimate philosophical uses. For purposes of defining "mental illness," I hope that enough has been said to indicate the sort of direction in which the notions of "rationality" and "irrationality" as deviations from such, have been traditionally understood. Of course, there are all sorts of degrees in the development of our human capacity for rationality, and it is only fairly extreme and persistent departures from some of our seven defining features of rationality which count as mental illness. Only a few of these factors need be involved in any particular case. Most people are not *very* rational, but most people are nevertheless sane. *Extreme* departures from sanity are not as difficult to identify in practice as some skeptical critics, especially lawyers and philosophers who have never spent any time around mentally disturbed persons, would have us to believe. Cases on the borderline of such extremities are the ones which understandably give headaches to mental health professionals, but such professionals can also cite many clear-cut cases involving extreme and prolonged incompetence and self-defeating performances in selecting effective means to avowed ends, of radically inconsistent practical belief systems, items of which are plainly controverted by empirical facts, of inability to cite reasons for belief and behavior, of persisting and pervasive conceptual confusions, and of entrenched inabilities to adopt fair-minded perspectives on either factual or valuational beliefs.

Since being rational involves having and acting upon factual beliefs supported by common experience and avoiding beliefs clearly at odds with common experience, it is easy to understand how persisting hallucinations and perceptual distortions contribute to irrationality. They involve loss of contact with our common world and generate beliefs about and behaviors directed toward things that are just not there. To the extent that unconscious conflicts, powers, and processes interfere with the functioning of conscious rational autonomy, they too are relevant for diagnosing mental illness.

No account of underlying pathology in the brain or in a Freudian psyche has been built into the definition here proposed of mental illness as loss of practical rational autonomy. Neither has the attempt to correlate mental illness with such pathology been excluded by such an analysis. Indeed, I wish to encourage an exploration of possible connections between mental illness so conceived and current concepts of and research on organic brain pathology, the standard functional psychoses and neuroses, and mental retardation. My suspicion is that standard (and desirable) brain structure, function, and chemistry can be correlated with all manifestations of rational autonomy, even if the precise relation between them always remains shrouded in metaphysical mystery. Though we do not know precisely how conscious thought and decision processes are related to brain function, we might still find that predictable correlations can be made between consciousness and brain. We might discover, and to some extent have actually found, that physical therapies such as psychotropic drugs, electroshock, and even carefully controlled psychosurgery have predictable connections with restoration to rational autonomy and mental health. True, drugs *may* be used as "chemical strait jackets." They may also be used to correct an imbalance in the dopamine circuit of the brain of the schizophrenic. A renewal of rational autonomy may thus be correlated experimentally with a return to more normal brain chemistry. The medical model is not included in our concept of mental illness/health, but its relevance is not excluded either. In this area much work remains to be done.

The problem of placing proper limits on the notion of mental disorder becomes especially acute when it is allowed to range over the whole spectrum of disapproved mental/behavioral phenomena, including those which have little or nothing to do with breakdowns of rational autonomy, but which still might be disapproved on moral, legal, or reli-

gious grounds. It is not very difficult to see that schizophrenics, paranoids, and manic depressives, etc., are irrational and have lost control;
but many people certainly have great difficulty seeing that irrationality
has much to do with many other conditions which are often classified as
mental disturbances. An example of such a highly controversial classification would be homosexuality uncomplicated by distress, which was
listed in 1968 as a mental disorder in the American Psychiatric Association's *Diagnostic and Statistical Manual of Mental Disorders, II,* but
which was not listed in *DSM-III* in 1980. Has Anita Bryant persuaded
us that this is really an ethico-religious problem after all, or have we been
convinced that it is really no problem at all? In the 19th century, masturbation was regarded as a manifestation of madness and treated with
the harshest of imaginable "therapies," but few persons even disapprove
of it these days, much less classify it as madness. *DSM-III* included caf-
feinism and excessive smoking as mental disorders. Will these have the
same ultimate fate as masturbation? Anyone who has read Szasz (1972)
knows that alcoholism and drug addictions are very debatable categories
of mental illness. As he puts it, "Bad habits are not disease: a refutation
of the claim that alcoholism is a disease." Is alcoholism a mental or a
moral problem? My own view is that alcohol abuse begins as a moral
problem and ends as a mental disease as it gradually becomes physically
addictive, deprives the individual of much rational autonomy, and in
some cases (Korsakov's psychosis) turns the brain to mush. I shall not
attempt to work through *DSM-II* or *DSM-III* in detail to see which
diagnostic categories might involve a confusion of irrationality with
immorality or irreligion. Let the A.P.A. do that! I wish only to assert that
not every disapproved mental/behavioral phenomenon should count as
mental illness, that we should make a concerted effort to disentangle
legitimate psychiatric valuations from moral and religious ones, and that
we should attempt to put a screeching halt to the rampant proliferation
of psychiatric diagnostic categories because of the grossly detrimental
effects of the very act of psychiatric labeling if for no other reason. I am
convinced that psychiatric labeling does have legitimate uses, but it also
has illegitimate ones, and it will be the mark of the wise psychiatrist, psychologist, and philosopher to be able to distinguish the two.

No doubt, many psychologists and psychiatrists will want to reject
the definitions of "mental illness" and "mental health" here proposed.
This is not a great embarrassment, however, for there is *no* definition of
these terms anywhere in the literature that many psychologists and psychiatrists would not want to reject. One of the truly embarrassing aspects
of this field of medicine is that there is so little agreement on theoretical
fundamentals. This always adds fuel to the fire of those who insist that
the "medical model" has no legitimate application to mental/behavioral

disorders. Why should anyone want to reject the conservative definition of "mental illness" in terms of impairment of rational autonomy here being proposed? I am confident that most objections will be based upon the tendency inherent in all medical imperialism to engulf all disapproved mental/behavioral conditions and processes under the label of "sick," and to recognize no separate domains of intrinsic, social, moral, political, legal, and religious values and disvalues.

The same imperialistic tendency is at work when we come to positive conceptions of "mental health." The tendency in so many cases is to equate this with *everything* desirable, not simply with the desirability of rational autonomy. *Every* desirable mode of experience, activity, self-realization, happiness and social organization are packed into imperialistic conceptions of "mental health." Consider and analyze for yourself the intrinsic, social, moral, religious, legal, etc., values which are packed into the following definitions.

1. "Health is a state of complete physical, mental and social well-being and not merely the absence of disease or infirmity" (The World Health Organization, 1978, p. 89).

2. "The crucial consideration in determining human normality is whether the individual is an asset or a burden to society and whether he is or is not contributing to the progressive development of man" (Alfred Adler as summarized by O. H. Mower in Boorse, 1976, p. 69).

3. "Let us define mental health as the adjustment of human beings to the world and to each other with a maximum of effectiveness and happiness. Not just efficiency, or just contentment—or the grace of obeying the rules of the game cheerfully. It is all of these together. It is the ability to maintain an even temper, an alert intelligence, socially considerate behavior, and a happy disposition. This, I think, is a healthy mind" (Karl Menninger in Boorse, 1976, p. 69–70).

4. "Mental health in the humanistic sense, is characterized by the ability to love and to create, by the emergence from the incestuous ties to family and nature, by a sense of identity based on one's experience of self as the subject and agent of one's powers, by the grasp of reality inside and outside of ourselves, that is by the development of objectivity and reason. . . . The mentally healthy person is the person who lives by love, reason and faith, who respects life, his own and that of his fellow man" (Fromm, 1955).

5. ". . . here we have to deal with those persons who fall ill as soon as they pass beyond the irresponsible age of childhood, and thus never attain a phase of health—that of unrestricted capacity in general for production and enjoyment" (Freud equating mental health with his "genital phase" of personality development, in Rickman, 1957, p. 66).

6. "True Sanity entails in one way or another the dissolution of the normal ego, that false self competently adjusted to our alienated

social reality; the emergence of the 'inner' archetypal mediators of divine power, and through this death a new kind of ego-functioning, the ego now being the servant of the divine, no longer its betrayer" (Laing, 1967).

Many wonderful things other than rational autonomy are mentioned in the foregoing imperialistic definitions of mental health, and we should realize that the judgment that they do not belong in such a definition is not by any means the same as the judgment that they are not wonderful! Nor is it the same as the judgment that we never need help and counseling in achieving these wonderful things. It simply recognizes that those who do such counseling should more honestly be termed applied axiologists, moral educators, spiritual mentors, political activists, etc. Szasz (1974, p. 262) has a point in condemning "mental illness" as a myth *where values other than those of rationality and autonomy are involved* in the therapist-patient relationship. *Beyond that point,* psychotherapists *are* dealing with what he terms "personal, social, and ethical problems in living." *Up to that point,* however, they are dealing with real insanity, which Szasz fails to see. The rationally autonomous person may *choose for himself* just how much value he will attach to social conformity and adjustment, productivity, pleasure, heterosexuality, socially considerate behavior, love, faith, creativity, introspection, mysticism, and all such good things. The rationally autonomous person may still need value education in such matters, and it may be a perfectly legitimate function of psychotherapists and mental hospitals to provide such, though not in the name of treating mental illness or under the guise of *medical* expertise.

We should acknowledge that two great and interrelated goods have been built into our very conception of sanity—rationality and autonomy. It is quite possible, however, to agree that these are great goods without agreeing upon precisely what kind of goods they are, and for most practical purposes it is not even necessary to agree upon the latter. Philosophers distinguish intrinsic goods, things worth having, experiencing, doing, preserving for their own sake from instrumental goods, things required for the actualization of other values beyond themselves. Are rationality and autonomy intrinsic ends in themselves? Are they merely indispensable means to other intrinsic goods such as enjoyment or long-range happiness defined in terms of enjoyment? Is their actualization inherently enjoyable in itself, so that they become an integral part of our happiness, as John Stuart Mill suggested? We need not agree upon such abstruse philosophical questions in order to agree that rationality and autonomy are great and indispensable human goods, and that life is so greatly impoverished that it merits the labels "insanity" or "mental illness" where these functions are significantly diminished.

Rationality and autonomy are controversial goods, not universally prized, however. Blind faith and obedience to external authority are greatly preferred by many (but not all) religious thinkers and by totalitarian political regimes everywhere. A well-functioning democracy must be heavily populated by citizens exemplifying a significant degree of rational autonomy, and in that sense there is a political dimension to our definitions of mental health and mental illness. And though *we* may conceive of rational autonomy as the very essence of moral agency, we should not forget that many religious and nondemocratic political perspectives regard rational autonomy with dismay and insist that *their* ideal moral agents renounce it, or better yet never develop it, for blind, unthinking, inherited or emotionally induced devotion to unquestioned authority. In the former Soviet Union, it was the rationally autonomous person who was involuntarily institutionalized in mental hospitals! Thus, it may not be possible to separate *completely* the values of mental health as rational autonomy from *all* political, moral, and religious values. We can separate them from *most* such values, i.e., all the others, however; and it is necessary in a democratic society to do so.

Finally, we should realize that the value dimensions of how we conceive of "mental illness" and "mental health" are relevant to the practice of medicine in a mental hospital. If a mental hospital declares (as one with which I am acquainted has done) that "The goal of the institute is to restore its patients to an optimum level of social, intellectual, emotional, and vocational functioning in the community," we need to ask whether this is a realistic goal and just what it implies practically for patients. My own view is that "optimum" is much too strong a word to use here, just as "complete" was much too strong in the World Health Organization definition of "health." As a general affirmation of charity toward all and malice toward none, such formulations have a legitimate place. But as an avowal of realistic goals, such a statement is surely too strong. *All* the institutional and social arrangements and efforts of society and all the energies of the individual are required for the *summum bonum*, whatever that might be conceived to be; and no medical institution should claim or aspire to have the power and the resources required for its achievement. Reaching the *summum bonum* should certainly not be a prerequisite for discharge from such a hospital, for no one would ever be discharged! In that sense such a goal is not a realistic one, especially for involuntarily committed patients. It would be much more sensible for mental hospitals to aim at a restoration to minimal sanity in the present conservative sense of the term, i.e., a degree of rational autonomy which is minimally sufficient for "making it" in society, recognizing that even this is relative to what any given society or functional segment thereof expects of its members and provides by way of support.

Although care for and cure of mental illness should be the primary functions of a mental hospital, they certainly need not be its sole legitimate functions, any more than the physical care for and cure of disease need be the sole legitimate function of general hospitals and other medical practitioners. Medical professionals both within and without mental hospitals may also willingly and legitimately accept the additional tasks of relieving and preventing pain even where there is no hope of a cure, of assisting in social adaptation, giving moral counsel, and even being religious mentors (chaplains have a place) if they find that their patients are willing to ask and pay voluntarily for such services, or that society is willing to provide such services for those who want them but cannot pay. My only concern is that they recognize and admit what they are doing and not confuse treating mental illness with every form of aiding in the pursuit of justice and happiness.

Note

Writing of this paper was supported by an N.E.H. Development Grant in Medical Ethics, ED-32672-78-652.

References

Breggin, P. R.: 1974, Psychotherapy as applied ethics, *Psychiatry* 34, 59–74.

Breggin, P. R.: 1975, Psychiatry and psychotherapy as political processes, *American Journal of Psychotherapy* 29, 369–82.

Boorse, C.: 1976, What a theory of mental health should be, *Journal for the Theory of Social Behavior* 6, 61–84.

Engelhardt, Jr. H. T.: 1973, Psychotherapy as meta-ethics, *Psychiatry* 36, 440–45.

Fine, R.: 1967, The goals of psychoanalysis, in Alvin R. Mahrer (ed.), *The Goals of Psychotherapy*, Appleton-Century-Crofts, New York, pp. 73–98.

Fingarette, H.: 1972, Insanity and responsibility, *Inquiry* 15, 6–29.

Fromm, E.: 1955, *The Sane Society*, Fawcett Publications, Greenwich, Conn., pp. 180–81.

Illich, I.: 1976, *Medical Nemesis: The Expropriation of Health*, Bantam Books, New York, pp. 31–60.

Kittrie, N.: 1971, *The Right to be Different: Deviance and Enforced Therapy*, The Johns Hopkins Press, Baltimore, pp. 340–410.

Laing, R. D.: 1967, *The Politics of Experience*, Ballantine Books, New York.

Moore, M. S.: 1975, Some myths about "Mental Illness", *Archives of General Psychiatry* 32, pp. 1483–97.

Rickman, J. (ed.): 1957, *A General Selection from the Works of Sigmund Freud*, Doubleday & Co., Garden City, New York, p. 66.

Szasz, T. S.: 1972, Bad habits are not diseases: A refutation of the claim that alcoholism is a disease, *The Lancet* 2, 83–84.

Szasz, T. S.: 1974, *The Myth of Mental Illness,* Harper & Row, New York.
Torrey, Fuller E.: 1977, Carter's little pills, *Psychology Today* 11, 10–11.
World Health Organization: 1978, A definition of health, in R. Beauchamp, and
    Le Roy Walters (eds.), *Contemporary Issues in Bioethics,* Dickenson Publish-
    ing Co., Encino, California, p. 89.

The Concept of Mental Disorder: On the Boundary Between Biological Facts and Social Values

Jerome C. Wakefield

This article presents an analysis of the concept of mental disorder. The focus is on *disorder* rather than *mental* because questions about the concept of disorder cause the most heated disputes in the mental health field. I argue that disorder lies on the boundary between the given natural world and the constructed social world; a disorder exists when the failure of a person's internal mechanisms to perform their functions as designed by nature impinges harmfully on the person's well-being as defined by social values and meanings. The order that is disturbed when one has a disorder is thus simultaneously biological and social; neither alone is sufficient to justify the label *disorder*.

There are many reasons why mental health professionals should care about the correct analysis of the concept of disorder. Concerns about the distinction between disorder and nondisorder are omnipresent in the mental health field and range from the sublime (how can one tell the difference between noble self-sacrifice and pathological masochism?) to the ridiculous (is snoring a disorder the treatment of which therefore warrants medical insurance reimbursement?) and on to the tragic (if a person diagnosed with acquired immunodeficiency syndrome expresses suicidal thoughts, is he or she suffering from an adjustment disorder or reacting normally to a life-threatening illness?). In terms of clinical practice, every diagnosis involves the ability to distinguish disorder from normal reactions to stressful environments and from other nonpathological problems, such as the marital, parent-child, and occupational conflicts

From the *American Psychologist* 47, no. 3 (1992): 373–88. Copyright © 1992 by the American Psychological Association. Reprinted by permission.

summarized in the V Code categories of the revised third edition of the *Diagnostic and Statistical Manual of Mental Disorders* (*DSM-III-R*; American Psychiatric Association, 1987). At an institutional level, "mental disorder" demarcates the special responsibilities of mental health professionals from those of other professionals such as criminal justice lawyers, teachers, and social welfare workers. Thus jurisdictional disputes are often disputes about the application of the term *mental disorder.*

Public concerns about misapplication of the term *disorder* underlie accusations of sexual, racial, and sexual orientational biases in diagnosis (Bayer, 1981; Bayer & Spitzer, 1982; Kaplan, 1983; Spitzer, 1981; Szasz, 1971; Wakefield, 1987, 1988, 1989b; Williams & Spitzer, 1983; Willie, Kramer, & Brown, 1973), as well as more general accusations that psychodiagnosis is often used to control or stigmatize socially undesirable behavior that is not really disordered (Eysenck, J. A. Wakefield, & Friedman, 1983; Foucault, 1964/1965; Goffman, 1963; Gove, 1980; Horwitz, 1982; Laing, 1967; Szasz, 1974). Awareness of past psychodiagnostic errors and abuses, such as diagnoses of "drapetomania" (the "disorder" that afflicted slaves who ran away from their masters; Cartwright, 1851/1981; Szasz, 1971), "childhood masturbation disorder" (Englehardt, 1974; Foucault, 1978), and "lack of vaginal orgasm" (Kaplan, 1983), sets the stage for today's controversies over diagnoses such as "self-defeating personality disorder" (American Psychiatric Association, 1987; P. J. Caplan, 1984), "premenstrual syndrome" (American Psychiatric Association, 1987; Ussher, 1989), "alcoholism" (Fingarette, 1988, 1990; Gorman, 1989a, 1989b; Vaillant, 1990), "hyperactivity" (Coles, 1987; Cowart, 1988; Kohn, 1989; Pond, 1960; Rutter, Graham, & Yule, 1970), "homosexuality" (Bayer, 1981; Bayer & Spitzer, 1982; Spitzer, 1981), and many others, all of which controversies would benefit from a clearer understanding of the concept of disorder. Finally, a correct understanding of the concept is essential for constructing "conceptually valid" (Wakefield, in press) diagnostic criteria that are good discriminators between disorder and nondisorder.

The concept of disorder is not the same as a theory of disorder. Physiological, behavioral, psychoanalytic, and other theories attempt to explain the causes and specify the underlying mechanisms of mental disorder, whereas the concept of disorder is the criterion used to identify the domain that all these theories are trying to explain. The concept is largely shared by professionals and the lay public (Campbell, Scadding, & Roberts, 1979) and is the basis for the attempt in *DSM-III-R* to construct universally acceptable atheoretical diagnostic criteria (Spitzer & Williams, 1983, 1988; Wakefield, in press). The concept is certainly more complex than the simple "suffering" and "problems in living" criteria that are sometimes suggested: Grieving a lost spouse involves considerable suffering and being in a bad marriage is a problem in living but neither is a disorder. Despite a vast literature spanning philosophy, psychology, psychiatry, and medicine devoted to the concept of mental disorder, there currently exists no widely accepted analysis that adequately explains even generally agreed upon, uncontroversial judgments about which conditions are disorders. I shall attempt to construct an account that explains such uncontroversial judgments; until such an analysis is available, using a definition of *disorder* as an arbiter of controversies is premature.

Among analyses of the concept of mental disorder, the most basic division is between value and scientific approaches. As Kendell (1986) put it,

> The most fundamental issue, and also the most contentious one, is whether disease and illness are normative concepts based on value judgments, or whether they are value-free scientific terms; in other words, whether they are biomedical terms or sociopolitical ones. (p. 25)

To construct a more adequate analysis and resolve the fact/value debate, I propose a hybrid account of disorder as harmful dysfunction, wherein *dysfunction* is a scientific and factual term based in evolutionary biology that refers to the failure of an internal mechanism to perform a natural function for which it was designed, and *harmful* is a value term referring to the consequences that occur to the person because of the dysfunction and are deemed negative by sociocultural standards.

Because the general concept of disorder, which applies to both mental and physical conditions, is the subject of the present analysis, examples from both the mental and physical realms are equally relevant and are used. I use *internal mechanism* as a general term to refer to both physical structures and organs and mental structures and dispositions, such as motivational, cognitive, affective, and perceptual mechanisms. Also, some writers draw distinctions among *disorder, disease,* and *illness. Disorder* is perhaps the broader term because it covers traumatic injuries as well as disease/illness. I ignore these differences and use the discussions of related terms as if they refer to *disorder* whenever they contribute useful insights.

First, I review the problems with six standard analyses of the concept of disorder and informally suggest how a harmful dysfunction approach might avoid these problems, if such a view could be precisely and clearly developed. I then analyze the critical concept of natural function so as to have a clear basis for attributing dysfunction (i.e., the loss of a natural function) and thus, in cases in which dysfunction is harmful, disorder.

Problems with Standard Analyses of Mental Disorder

THE MYTH OF THE MYTH OF MENTAL DISORDER

The first question in analyzing the concept of mental disorder is whether the concept exists. Several skeptical writers (e.g., Foucault, 1964/1965, 1978; Sarbin, 1969; Scheff, 1966, 1975; Szasz, 1974) have attempted to cast doubt on the concept's coherence. The skeptics typically claim that "mental disorder" is merely an evaluatory label that justifies the use of medical power (in the broad sense, in which all the professions concerned with pathology, including psychiatry, clinical psychology, and clinical social work, are considered medical) to intervene in socially disapproved behavior. The strength of the skeptical perspective is that it explains the frequency with which the label "mental disorder" has been misapplied, as in "drapetomania" and "childhood masturbation disorder." However, this strength is bought at a considerable price. According to the skeptical view, all applications of "mental disorder" are illegitimate, so the ability to distinguish correct from incorrect uses, target criticisms, and improve criteria is lost.

Two arguments are proposed by the skeptics. First, the skeptics present many practical, ethical, and epistemological concerns about psychodiagnosis. They note, for example, that people who are labeled as mentally disordered are often stigmatized, psychodiagnosis is often used for purposes of social control, and it is often difficult to tell whether someone is mentally disordered. Such concerns, legitimate and important though they are, must be separated from questions about the coherence and logic of the concept of disorder (Gorenstein, 1984; Horwitz, 1982). The need for such separation of issues can be illustrated with a physical example: People who are labeled as human immunodeficiency virus (HIV) positive are often socially stigmatized; such labeling is often used for purposes of social control; and, because of imperfections in available tests, it is sometimes hard to establish whether someone is HIV positive. Despite all these problems, the concept of HIV positivity is perfectly coherent and HIV-positive status does truly exist. Thus practical, ethical, and epistemological problems simply do not demonstrate that there is something wrong with the concept of mental disorder. Similar comments apply to attempts to discredit mental disorder through analysis of the historical processes that led up to the adoption of this concept (Foucault, 1964/1965) or of the sociological processes that influence diagnosis (Scheff, 1966, 1975).

The skeptics' second argument is more to the point because it directly addresses the nature of disorder. This argument has been put forward most explicitly by Szasz (1974), but it is implicit in most other skeptical positions as well. Szasz began with the assumption that physical disorder is a legitimate concept based on a clear foundation, namely, that a disorder consists of a physical lesion, with *lesion* referring to a recognizable deviation in anatomical structure. Szsaz continued with the observation that mental disorder is an extension of the concept of physical disorder to the mental realm. Therefore, mental disorders exist only if the very same concept of disorder that applies to physical conditions also applies to the mental conditions labeled as disorders. Otherwise, the application of *disorder* to mental conditions is merely an analogy or metaphor. Szsaz next maintained that *mental disorder* is used to label behavior that deviates from social norms and that the psychological functioning that is said to be a mental disorder is typically not accompanied by any identifiable lesion of the brain or of any other part of the body. (Szasz implicitly assumed that no lesions would be found in the future to explain such conditions.) Thus, the lesion concept of disorder that is applicable to physical conditions is not applicable to mental conditions, and mental disorders are not literally disorders. Szsaz concluded that "there is no such thing as 'mental illness' " (1974, p. 1). Sarbin (1969) similarly asserted that "contemporary users of the mental illness concept are guilty of illicitly shifting from metaphor to myth" (p. 15).

The weakness in Szasz's (1974) argument lies in the inadequacy of the lesion account of physical disorder. The account consists of two theses: (a) that a lesion (or abnormal bodily structure) is simply a statistical deviation from a typical anatomical structure and (b) that a physical disorder is simply a lesion. First, the idea that a lesion can be directly recognized by its deviant anatomical structure is incorrect. Bodily structures normally vary from person to person, and many normal variations are as unusual as any lesion. Moreover, some lesions are statistically nondeviant in a culture, such as atherosclerosis, minor lung irritation, and gum recession in American culture and hookworm and malaria in some others. Therefore recognition of a lesion is not simply a matter of observing anatomical deviance. Second, and more important, it is not the existence of a lesion that defines disorder. There are physical disorders, such as trigeminal neuralgia and senile pruritis (Kendell, 1975), for which there are no known anatomical lesions. Moreover, a lesion can be a harmless abnormality that is not a disorder, such as when the heart is positioned on the right side of the body but retains functional integrity. Kendell compared lesions that are disorders with similar lesions that are not disorders in order to show that the existence of lesions is not what distinguishes disorder from nondisorder in the physical realm:

> A child with spina bifida and an oligophrenic imbecile both suffer from congenital diseases—the first by virtue of an anatomical defect acquired

early in embryonic development, the second because of the absence of the enzyme needed to convert phenylalanine to tyrosine. But children with fused second and third toes have a similar congenital defect to those with spina bifida, and those with albinism also lack an enzyme involved in tyrosine metabolism, yet despite the presence of these lesions we do not normally wish to regard them as ill. (p. 308)

Thus the lesion account of physical disorder fails, and with it goes the skeptics' case that the concept of disorder cannot literally apply to mental conditions.

How, then, *do* we recognize deviations that are lesions and lesions that are disorders? Roughly, we recognize a variation in anatomical structure as a lesion rather than as a normal variation if the variation impairs the ability of the particular structure to accomplish the functions that it was designed to perform. Such an impairment of a specific mechanism might be referred to as a "part dysfunction" (Lewis, 1967; see also Klein, 1978). We recognize a part dysfunction/lesion as a disorder only if the deviation in the functioning of the part affects the well-being of the overall organism in a harmful way. For example, the reason that fused toes, albinism, and reversal of heart position are not considered disorders even though they are abnormal anatomical variations is that they do not significantly harm a person. Thus, a harmful dysfunction approach to the concept of disorder would seem to explain what the skeptics' lesion account cannot explain, namely, which anatomical deviations are lesions and which lesions are disorders.

If lesion is essentially a functional concept, then mental conditions and physical conditions can literally be disorders for the very same reason, that is, their functional implications. Considering that mental processes play important species-typical roles in human survival and reproduction, there is no reason to doubt that mental processes were naturally selected and have natural functions, as Darwin himself often emphasized (Boorse, 1976a). Because of our evolutionary heritage, we possess physical mechanisms such as livers and hearts; that same heritage gave us mental mechanisms such as various cognitive, motivational, affective, personological, hedonic, linguistic, and behavioral dispositions and structures. Some mental conditions interfere with the ability of these mental mechanisms to perform the functions that they were designed to perform. In such cases, there is a part dysfunction of the particular mental mechanism. The concept of disorder, whether applied to liver disorders, heart disorders, or mental disorders, refers to part dysfunctions that harm the person. Contrary to Szasz's (1974) and Sarbin's (1967, 1969) claims, the notion of a mental disorder is not a myth based on a bad metaphor but a literal application to the mental realm of the same harmful dysfunction concept of disorder that applies in the physical realm.

DISORDER AS A PURE VALUE CONCEPT

The typical response to the skeptics is to argue that mental disorder is an objective scientific concept, like physical disorder (examples of this scientific approach are provided later). However, other thinkers who try to show that mental disorders are genuine disorders accept the skeptics' contention that mental disorder is a value concept and argue that physical disorder is also a value concept.

> Quite correctly, the anti-psychiatrists have pointed out that psychopathological categories refer to value-judgments and that mental illness is deviancy. On the other hand, the anti-psychiatric critics themselves are wrong when they imagine physical medicine to be essentially different in its logic from psychiatry. A diagnosis of diabetes, or paresis, includes the recognition of norms or values. (Sedgwick, 1982, p. 38)

The pure value account of disorder asserts that disorder is nothing (or almost nothing) but a value concept, so that social judgments of disorder are nothing but judgments of desirability according to social norms and ideals. The pure value approach is to be distinguished from a mixed or hybrid approach (Boorse, 1975; Klein, 1978), of the kind to be defended later, in which values play some role but in which there are important factual components to the concept of disorder as well.

The value account reflects an important truth: Because disorders are negative conditions that justify social concern, social values are involved. On the other hand, the pure value view has the disadvantage that it makes disorder (both mental and physical) a completely value- and culture-relative notion with no scientific content whatsoever, thereby leaving the concept open to unconstrained use for purposes of social control. Nonetheless, a considerable number of writers have taken the pure value position or strongly emphasized the evaluative element in their analyses. Ausubel (1971) defined disease as "any marked deviation, physical, mental, or behavioral, from normally desirable standards of structural or functional integrity" (p. 60). Marmor (1973) stated, "To call homosexuality the result of disturbed development really says nothing other than that you disapprove of the outcome of that development" (p. 1208). Pichot (1986) asserted, "The definition of disease in every language is 'something bad' " (p. 56). King (1954/1981) wrote, "Disease is the aggregate of those conditions which, judged by the prevailing culture, are deemed painful, or disabling, and which, at the same time, deviate from either the statistical norm or from some idealized status" (p. 112). Engelhardt (1974) stated that "choosing to call a set of phenomena a disease involves . . . judgments closely bound to value judgments" (p.

241). The World Health Organization (1946/1981) defined health as "a state of complete physical, mental and social well-being" (p. 83). This appears to assume that disorder is any deviation from a completely desirable and ideal state. Sedgwick (1982) was perhaps the most articulate spokesman for the pure value position: "*All sickness is essentially deviancy* [from] some alternative state of affairs which is considered more desirable. . . . The attribution of illness always proceeds from the computation of a gap between presented behavior (or feeling) and some social norm" (pp. 32–34).

The fact that all disorders are undesirable and harmful according to social values shows only that values are part of the concept of disorder, not that disorder is composed only of values. Sedgwick (1982) suggested through vivid examples that there is nothing objective or scientific that distinguishes the conditions said to be disorders from other processes in nature, leaving the value element as the only identifying characteristic:

> There are no illnesses or diseases in nature. . . . The fracture of a septuagenarian's femur has, within the world of nature, no more significance than the snapping of an autumn leaf from its twig; and the invasion of a human organism by cholera-germs carries with it no more the stamp of "illness" than does the souring of milk by other forms of bacteria. . . . Out of his anthropocentric self-interest, man has chosen to consider as "illnesses" or "diseases" those natural circumstances which precipitate . . . death (or the failure to function according to certain values). (p. 30)

However, completely aside from values, there is a relevant difference between the cracking of a femur and the snapping off of an autumn leaf: The leaf is designed to fall off at a certain stage and the tree is not designed to require the leaf for its continued functioning, whereas the possession of an intact femur is part of the way a person, even an old person, is designed to function. Similarly, once it is extracted from the cow, milk certainly has no natural function, so the bacteria that invade and sour it are not causing a dysfunction, whereas the person who is infected with bacteria is in danger of losing functional integrity. Thus, if natural function is a scientific concept that cannot be reduced to values (as is argued later), then there is a scientifically definable difference between Sedgwick's (1982) examples of natural processes that are disorders and those that are not; that is, the ones that are disorders disrupt a natural function.

The most basic objection to the pure value position is that there are obviously a great many undesirable conditions that are not classifiable as disorders. Recognizing that not all undesirable states are considered dis-

orders, Sedgwick (1982) added to the value account one factual requirement—that the cause of the undesirable condition could not lie entirely
in external circumstances but must be inside the individual's body or
mind. This would explain why externally caused undesirable conditions
such as poverty, bad luck, or being sexually rejected are not disorders.
However, it would not explain why other undesirable conditions that are
internal, such as ignorance and the pain of teething, are also not considered disorders. A dysfunction account explains why these latter conditions are not disorders: Although they are internal, they do not involve
a breakdown in the functioning of an internal mechanism.

Another problem with the pure value position is that it does not
explain how people can be mistaken about disorder and how people who
share social norms and values can disagree about which conditions are disorders. For example, slaves who ran away from their masters were not in
fact suffering from a disorder of "drapetomania," even though the dominant social order saw the condition as undesirable, and many incarcerated
Soviet dissidents were not in fact mentally disordered despite the fact that
they violated social norms. If one embraces the pure value position, one
has no grounds for asserting that these diagnoses were incorrect in their
context. Moreover, our culture clearly disvalues such conditions as premenstrual syndrome, hyperactivity, and alcoholism, and yet there are
ongoing disputes about whether each of these is a disorder. The complex
factual arguments presented by both sides in these debates clearly indicate
that judgments about disorder depend on much more than values.

To say that a condition is undesirable or socially disvalued does not
imply anything about the cause of the condition. Thus, the pure value
view fails to account for the fact that attributions of disorder are attempts
to partially explain behavior and/or symptoms. For example, the question "Why is that man talking to himself?" can be coherently answered
by explanations in terms of rational action (e.g., "Because he is trying to
memorize a list by repeating it aloud") or the manifestation of a disorder (e.g., "Because he is suffering from schizophrenia"). Admittedly, an
explanation in terms of disorder says very little if nothing more is known
about the attributed disorder, but it eliminates enough alternative explanations to be useful. The explanatory content of disorder attributions
shows that they involve more than sheer value judgments. We shall see
later that the explanatory content of disorder attributions is nicely
explained by the functional approach.

DISORDER AS WHATEVER PROFESSIONALS TREAT

Frustration with failed attempts to analyze the concept of mental disorder often leads to the practical-sounding suggestion that a disorder is

simply any condition that health professionals treat. For example, Taylor (1976) asserted that a disorder consists in part of the "attribute of therapeutic concern for a person felt by the person himself and/or his social environment" (p. 591), and Kendell (1986) suggested that we stop trying to diagnostically distinguish disorders from "the problems that psychiatrists are currently consulted about" (pp. 41–42).

However, many concerns that are handled by health professionals clearly are not disorders, but are assigned to health professionals because of their special skills. For example, professionals are regularly called on to provide "treatment" in cases of childbirth, unwanted pregnancy, circumcision, cosmetic surgery, and distresses due to the normal vicissitudes of life. *DSM-III-R* has a special section of V Code diagnostic categories just for conditions that are not disorders but are often treated by mental health professionals, such as marital conflicts, adolescent-parent conflict, and occupational problems. These are conditions in which there is some harm, but not a genuine dysfunction or disorder.

Furthermore, both the patient and the therapist can be wrong about whether a condition is a disorder. For example, Victorian medical books indicate that many people came to physicians seeking treatment of the "masturbatory disease" from which, under the influence of the writings of the very same physicians, they thought they were suffering, and women sought out treatment—sometimes surgical—for the "perverse" clitoral orgasms that afflicted them (e.g., Acton, 1871; Barker-Benfield, 1983; Schrenck-Notzing, 1895/1956; Showalter, 1987; Ussher, 1989). Despite what the doctors and patients thought, the patients' masturbatory activities and clitoral orgasms were not in fact disorders, contrary to the whatever-professionals-treat approach. The possibility of error is explained by a functional approach: the diagnostician can simply have an incorrect belief about what a mechanism was naturally designed to do.

Finally, this approach would paradoxically imply that lack of social concern can eliminate disorder. Kendell (1975) himself, in an article in which he criticized the view he later adopted, noted that "equating illness with 'therapeutic concern' implies that no one can be ill until he has been recognized as such, and also gives doctors, and society, free rein to label all deviants as ill" (p. 307).

DISORDER AS STATISTICAL DEVIANCE

The skeptics claim that physical disorders are lesions and mental disorders are socially deviant behavior and thus the two are not instances of the same concept of disorder. However, if one accepts the skeptics' notion that a lesion is a statistical deviation in anatomical structure, then one might claim that lesions and deviant behavior do have something in common, namely, statistical deviance. If statistical deviance makes either a physical or a mental condition a disorder, then the same concept of disorder can be applied to both domains, and the criterion is purely objective and scientific.

The classical statement of the statistical approach to disorder is Sir Henry Cohen's (1981) definition of disease as "quantitative deviations from the normal" (p. 218), in which by *normal* he meant the statistical norm. Statistical abnormality is a requirement of many other definitions, including those of Taylor (1971), Scadding (1967), Kendall (1975), King (1954/1981), and even *DSM-III-R* (discussed later). As Claridge (1985) noted, Eysenck's (1986) dimensional system of diagnosis also presupposes a statistical approach to disorder.

One basic problem with this view is that excellence in strength, intelligence, energy, talent, or any other area is just as statistically deviant as its opposite. Moreover, an individual's fingerprint, the precise shape of his or her heart, and endless other neutral features can be deviant and even unique but still normal. An obvious suggestion to avoid this problem is to add the requirement that the deviance must be in a negative direction. (We shall see later that this is essentially the strategy of *DSM-III-R*.) However, there are many behaviors that are statistically deviant and undesirable but are not disorders; for example, such behavior can be criminal, discourteous, ignorant, morally repugnant, or disadvantageous. For a man, being five feet tall is statistically deviant and presumably undesirable but not a disorder; the same goes for men or women being clumsy, having a slow reaction time, and so on.

Another problem with the statistical deviance view of disorder is that many conditions that are statistically normal in their context are still disorders. For example, as noted earlier, minor lung irritation from pollution, atherosclerosis, periodontal disease, and dental caries all seem to be statistically normal in American society, and such disorders as hookworm and malaria are so endemic in other societies as to be statistically normal, but all these conditions are still considered disorders. In fact, there is nothing incoherent about a virtually universal disorder, as might occur as a result of an uncontrolled epidemic or radiation poisoning after a nuclear war. Thus statistical deviance cannot be part of what we mean by disorder.

Although statistical deviance is not the same as disorder, disorder often is statistically deviant. From a functional perspective, this is understandable. In general, mechanisms function as they were naturally designed to function; failures of function are usually deviant. As the preceding examples show, however, functional abnormality and statistical abnormality do not necessarily go together. Dysfunction is judged on the basis of standards set by the design of internal mechanisms rather than by statistical norms.

DISORDER AS BIOLOGICAL DISADVANTAGE

In order to conceptualize disorder in purely scientific terms, more than sheer statistical deviation is needed. If the definition must equally fit both physical and mental disorders, then a reasonable place to look for an account of disorder is within the biological sciences. The biological sciences are the scientific basis for physical medicine, and the mind is, after all, a part of the organism and has evolved like other parts of the organism. Mental mechanisms like those involved in perception, motivation, emotion, linguistic ability, and cognition play distinctive but coordinated roles in overall mental functioning, much as different organs play distinctive but coordinated roles in physical functioning. Thus, a biological account based on evolutionary theory has seemed to many to be potentially capable of handling the concepts of both mental and physical disorder in a scientific and value-free manner.

Note that although the use of an evolutionary perspective makes an account of the mind biological, it does not necessarily make it physiological or anatomical. The evolutionary approach accepts descriptions of mental and behavioral mechanisms as legitimate biological descriptions of the advantageous mechanisms that were naturally selected (Buss, 1991).

Three different accounts of disorder that involve evolutionary theory are considered in the remainder of this article; confusion might be avoided if they are distinguished here. The first, considered in this section, is the view of Scadding, Kendall, and Boorse, who used the evolution-derived general criterion of lowered survival or lowered reproductive fitness, as a purely scientific means for identifying disorders. The second evolutionary account, suggested in passing in the Disorder as Harmful Dysfunction section, considers an organism disordered when some mental mechanism (e.g., perception or the fear response) does not perform the specific function (e.g., convey information about the environment or help the organism to avoid certain dangers) that it was designed by evolution to perform. This too is a purely scientific criterion. The third evolutionary approach, which is argued in the aforementioned section to be the correct one, combines the second approach (using the specific natural functions of mechanisms) with a value component, so that a person is disordered only when some mechanism fails to perform the specific function it was designed to perform *and* the failure of the mechanism causes the person real harm.

Scadding (1967, 1990) proposed a purely scientific biological definition of disorder by in effect translating the earlier harmful statistical deviation account into a biologically disadvantageous deviation account:

> The name of a disease refers to the sum of the abnormal phenomena displayed by a group of living organisms in association with a specific

common characteristic, or set of characteristics, by which they differ from the norm for their species in such a way as to place them at a biological disadvantage. (Scadding, 1990, p. 243)

Kendell (1975) elaborated and extended Scadding's biological disadvantage analysis, and Boorse (1975, 1976a) offered a very similar approach.

Scadding (1967, 1990) never explained what he meant by biological disadvantage, and on the surface it would seem that *disadvantage,* contrary to intent, is a value term. Kendell (1975) and Boorse (1975, 1976a) tried to get around the value implication by using biological theory itself as an objective criterion for what constitutes the relevant type of disadvantage. According to the theory of evolution, the prime advantages to accrue from any internal mechanism or structure are survival and reproductive fitness. (Actually, from an evolutionary perspective, survival also serves the one ultimate goal of reproductive fitness, but so many of the organism's mechanisms are aimed directly at survival in a way that is relatively remote from reproductive activity that it is convenient to use both criteria.) Thus, both Kendell and Boorse claimed that a disorder is a condition that reduces longevity or fertility. This made the definition value-free by in effect equating lowered fertility and longevity with harm (Kendell, 1975).

The equation is faulty, however. A condition can reduce fertility without causing real harm; marginally lowered fertility is serious over the evolutionary time scale, but it may not affect an individual's well-being if the capacity for bearing some children remains intact. And some serious harms, such as chronic pain or loss of pleasure, might not reduce fertility or longevity at all; Kendell (1975) admitted there are many harmful physical conditions, such as postherpetic neuralgia and psoriasis, that are clear cases of disorder but have no effect on mortality or fertility. This is likely to be even more true of mental disorders. It would seem that the harm requirement must be added to, rather than derived from, the evolutionary requirement.

Another problem with Scadding's (1967, 1990) account is that his statistical deviance requirement runs afoul of the counterexamples to the statistical approach presented earlier. As Kendell (1975) noted of both Scadding's and his own position, "the majority are debarred from being regarded as ill" (p. 309). But this, as we have seen, is not part of our concept of disorder and leads to numerous actual and potential counterexamples. The reason that Scadding and Kendall cannot just scrap the statistical deviation requirement and take biological disadvantage as the whole definition of disorder is that disadvantage is relative. Without the statistical deviation requirement, any disadvantage relative to anyone superior in function could be labeled a disorder, leading to an impossibly demanding criterion. Klein (1978), in an analysis otherwise extremely similar to the one I propose, made this mistake of relativizing disorder to "optimal" part function: "Disease is here defined as covert, objective, suboptimal part dysfunction, recognizing that functions are evolved and hierarchically organized" (p. 70). This implies that the existence of even a few people with unusually high functioning would mean that everyone else has a dysfunction. For example, everyone with an IQ lower than 180 has a brain that is functioning less than optimally and so is diseased, according to Klein's proposal. But it is how we are designed to be, not how we might ideally be, that is relevant to judgments of disorder. The same problem, of disorder's including any deviation from optimal functioning, would arise for Scadding if he defined disorder simply as biological disadvantage without specifying that the disadvantage is relative to the statistically normal. If Scadding were to jettison the problematic statistical deviation clause, the validity of the definition in one respect would be increased at the cost of severely decreasing the validity in another respect.

Taken at face value, Scadding's (1967, 1990) account is subject to two additional objections. First, differential fertility rates may exist between populations defined by racial, ethnic, economic, sex, personality, and many other variables. Are all these variables to be considered candidates for pathology? For example, is it a disorder to be a young Black urban male in 1990s America because that "set of characteristics" corresponds to increased mortality? The problem is that the definition does not distinguish between disadvantage due to dysfunction of internal mechanisms and disadvantage due to harmful environments. Second, the definition implies that a disorder can be "cured" simply by taking steps to increase the life span and fertility of the people who have the disorder, even if no change is made in their mental condition.

Kendell (1975) recognized these problems and tried to solve them by requiring that the effects of the condition on mortality and fertility be "innate" or "intrinsic" rather than due to social factors such as rejection by others: "The criterion must be, would this individual still be at a disadvantage if his fellows did not recognize his distinguishing features but treated him as they treat one another?" (p. 314). But because humans are social animals, it is impossible to separate the functioning of the organism from all consideration of how others respond. For example, aphasia is certainly a disorder, but language functions as a communication device between individuals, so if the reactions of others to one's attempts to speak are entirely discounted from consideration, then there are no grounds for classifying aphasia as a disorder. Even in the case of schizophrenia, which Kendell argued is a pathology in part on the grounds that schizophrenic individuals have reduced fertility, it seems likely that the lower fertility is at least in part due to the reactions of potential partners to the schizophrenic person's mental condition, thus putting in question whether schizophrenia is indeed a disorder according to Kendell's account. (Similar questions can be raised about the source of schizophrenic individuals' higher mortality.) Moreover, many conditions, such as being male versus being female, seem to be intrinsically tied to higher mortality and yet are not disorders.

Scadding (1967, 1990), Kendall (1975), and Boorse (1975, 1976a) were right that there must be an evolutionary foundation to our judgments of disorder. The notion that something has gone wrong with the organism's internal functioning, which is critical for distinguishing between disorders and other negative conditions, can be captured only by comparing present functioning with what the organism's mechanisms were designed to do, and this requires a reference to the evolutionary explanation of the mechanism. However, the biological disadvantage approach mistakenly uses decreased longevity and fertility in the present environment as the criterion for mechanism dysfunction. The fact that the organism's mechanisms were originally selected because they increased longevity and fertility in a past environment does not imply that some mechanism is malfunctioning when longevity and fertility decrease in the present environment. Thus, despite its evolutionary roots, the biological disadvantage definition actually fails to require a dysfunction and thus is subject to counterexamples.

By directly relying on reproductive fitness in the present environment as their criterion for health, Scadding (1967, 1990) and Kendell (1975) committed a form of the "sociobiological fallacy" (Buss, 1991; see also Wakefield, 1989a). This fallacy consists of misinterpreting evolution as conferring on the organism a general tendency to maximize fitness. In fact, evolution confers a multiplicity of specific mechanisms that do not directly aim at fitness but do have fitness as an effect in the environments in which they were selected. For example, sexual attraction is not a mechanism that directly confers maximal reproduction; it confers desire for sexual contact, and that leads to reproduction under the circumstances in which the mechanism evolved. Today, with contraceptive technology available, the sexual attraction mechanism may not ensure reproduction in the same way, but that does not mean that there is something wrong with the mechanism. It is the failure of specific mechanisms to perform their assigned tasks, rather than lowered fitness in itself, that shows that something has gone wrong with the organism. I shall use this insight later to construct a better evolution-based account of the concept of disorder.

DISORDER AS UNEXPECTABLE DISTRESS OR DISABILITY

The most influential recent definition of mental disorder is the one developed by Robert Spitzer and his colleagues for *DSM-III-R*. I have presented a detailed analysis and critique of *DSM-III-R*'s definition elsewhere (Wakefield, in press), so the present discussion is limited to a few crucial points. Further support for the claims made here can be found in the aforementioned article.

The definition in *DSM-III-R* is inspired by an overall view of disorder very much like the harmful dysfunction approach I propose. For example, in their discussion of the approach to disorder in the third edition of the *Diagnostic and Statistical Manual of Mental Disorders (DSM-III*; American Psychiatric Association, 1980), which is essentially the same as *DSM-III-R*'s, Spitzer and Endicott (1978) listed "dysfunction" and "negative consequences" (which can be taken to be equivalent to "harm") as two of the necessary conditions for disorder. Moreover, *DSM-III-R* explicitly states that a disorder must be "a manifestation of a behavioral, psychological, or biological dysfunction in the person" (American Psychiatric Association, 1987, p. xxii). It is also required that a disorder must be associated with "present distress (a painful symptom) or disability (impairment in one or more important areas of functioning) or with a significantly increased risk of suffering death, pain, disability, or an important loss of freedom" (p. xxii), and this list might be considered to be an operationalized approximation to the requirement that there must be harm. So, at least in initial conception, *DSM-III-R*'s approach to disorder has much affinity to the harmful dysfunction view.

For two reasons, however, *DSM-III-R* does not actually define disorder as harmful dysfunction. First, as Spitzer and Endicott (1978) noted, one cannot simply define disorder in terms of dysfunction because dysfunction itself is a concept that requires analysis: "These criteria [for disorder] avoid such terms as 'dysfunction,' 'maladaptive,' or 'abnormal,' terms which themselves beg definition" (p. 17). So, although *DSM-III-R* as well as Spitzer and Endicott indicate in the statement of the definition that a disorder must be a dysfunction, the definition of disorder actually consists of a formula that analyzes dysfunction in clearer terms and in effect replaces dysfunction in the definition. The definition is thus adequate only to the extent that the analysis of dysfunction contained in the definition is adequate.

Second, a central goal of *DSM-III-R* is to present reliable operationalized diagnostic criteria for specific disorders. The definition of disorder is aimed at providing a general framework for constructing such criteria (Spitzer & Endicott, 1978). But dysfunction is not an operational concept, and for *DSM-III-R*'s purposes dysfunction must be translated into a more operational and reliable formula that captures the essential idea of dysfunction. The same point applies to harm, which must also be operationalized. Thus, the definition of disorder that actually guides the formulation of specific *DSM-III-R* diagnostic criteria is the operational definition that results after the notions of harm and dysfunction are translated into operational terms. As we shall see, it is in the process of operationalization that the problems with *DSM-III-R*'s definition occur, because the operationalization diverges substantially from the dysfunction requirement that it is meant to capture.

To stand in for the dysfunction requirement (and thus to discriminate those harms that are disorders from all the other harms to which people are subject), *DSM-III-R* specifies that a disorder "must not be merely an expectable response to a particular event" (American Psychiatric Association, 1987, p. xxii). The basic idea is that normal responses are expectable (e.g., fear is an expectable response to danger, and grief is an expectable response to loss of a loved one), whereas disordered responses are not expectable. *DSM-III-R* translates harm into a list of observable harms such as distress and disability; I shall take the latter two harms as an adequate approximation to *DSM-III-R*'s longer list. Thus *DSM-III-R* operationally defines disorder roughly as unexpectable distress or disability. It is this definition that manifests itself in *DSM-III-R* criteria for specific disorders; the terms *dysfunction* and *harm* never appear in those criteria, but statistical unlikelihood and distress/disability do.

However, the unexpectable distress or disability definition fails to capture the notion of a dysfunction, and this results not only in the invalidity of the definition itself, but also in the invalidity of many *DSM-III-R* diagnostic criteria that are patterned on the definition. First, many nondisordered negative reactions (e.g., stress responses and grief) are normally statistically distributed in intensity, so that many of such reactions will be sufficiently above the mean to be "unexpected" in the sheer statistical sense. The *DSM-III-R* definition allows the incorrect classification of such greater than average normal responses as disorders. For example, *DSM-III-R* classifies a condition as an adjustment disorder if symptoms following a psychosocial stressor "are in excess of a normal and expectable reaction to the stressors" (American Psychiatric Association, 1987, p. 330). This implies that any reaction to a stressor that is much above the mean in intensity is classifiable as a disorder. Similarly, a child is diagnosed with oppositional defiant disorder when, during a six-month period, he or she displays certain kinds of defiant behavior, such as loss of temper, arguing with adults, refusing to do chores, and swearing, at a rate that is "considerably more frequent than that of most people of the same age" (p. 57). These criteria confuse normal variation with disorder.

Second, there are many unexpectable conditions, from extreme ignorance to plain misfortune, that can cause distress or disability but are not disorders. Some telling examples are contained in *DSM-III-R*'s own V Codes. Although *DSM-III-R* states correctly that these conditions are not disorders, many types and intensities of marital, parent-child, and occupational problems that fall under the V Codes are unexpectable distresses and disabilities that are classifiable as disorders according to the *DSM-III-R* definition. As another example, consider an adolescent who runs away from home for a second time, breaks into a car, and steals something; these are potentially harmful and unexpectable behaviors. Such an adolescent is disordered according to the criteria for the *DSM-III-R* diagnosis of conduct disorder. Yet this adolescent may just be rebellious, foolish, or desperate rather than disordered.

Third, *DSM-III-R*'s diagnostic criteria incorrectly allow normal responses to abusive treatment to be classified as disordered. For example, chronic depressed feelings can be due to a dysfunctional cognitive or affective system, or they can be a normal response to chronically depressing external circumstances such as abuse, neglect, or illness. *DSM-III-R*'s criteria for dysthymia do not adequately discriminate these possible sources of depressive symptoms; they merely classify unexpectably high levels of negative affect as a disorder.

The unexpectability requirement leads to other problems as well. For example, a "merely expectable response" to an extreme trauma is posttraumatic stress disorder, and an expectable response to lack of contact with a caregiver in infancy is anaclitic depression, but these conditions are disorders nonetheless.

All these problems result from the fact that *DSM-III-R*'s operational definition of disorder fails to match the dysfunction requirement that inspired it. For example, a dysfunction requirement would imply that an adjustment disorder would have to involve a breakdown in the way the coping mechanisms were designed to function and not merely a greater than average response to stress. The acts of a desperate teenager may be foolish, but they need not involve a dysfunction. Posttraumatic stress disorder is classifiable as a disorder despite its expectability after trauma if, as appears plausible from the nature of the condition, it involves a breakdown in the functioning of coping mechanisms. What is needed to resolve these problems is a better analysis of dysfunction.

A last point concerns the translation of harm into distress or disability. The list of harms in *DSM-III-R* and various secondary publications is longer than and different from the specific list of harms in *DSM-III*. One suspects that any kind of harm that is due to a dysfunction of some internal mechanism could be called a disorder and therefore the list of possible harms is potentially endless. Although a typology of harms such as that provided by *DSM-III-R* is useful, it should not be forgotten that, as Spitzer and Williams (1982) stated, the underlying reason these effects are relevant to disorder is that they are negative and this evaluative element is fundamental to our judgments about disorder. This value component should be reflected in, rather than obscured by, the definition of disorder.

Disorder as Harmful Dysfunction

FUNCTIONS AS EFFECTS THAT EXPLAIN THEIR CAUSES

The preceding critique provides several important lessons. The concept of disorder must include a factual component so that disorders can be distinguished from a myriad of other disvalued conditions. On the other hand, facts alone are not enough; disorder requires harm, which involves values. Thus both values and facts are involved in the concept of disorder. With respect to the factual component of the concept, I suggested earlier that the problems with the lesion, statistical deviation, whatever professionals treat, biological disadvantage, and *DSM-III-R* analyses of disorder could all be avoided, and the facts cited in support of those approaches explained, by a suitable dysfunction analysis. The notions of function and dysfunction are central to the factual-scientific component of disorder.

However, all the preceding points were made informally, without a clear and precise analysis of dysfunction to support them. In a similarly informal way, the view that the concept of disorder somehow involves the concepts of function and dysfunction emerges with remarkable consistency in the remarks of many authors who otherwise differ in their views (e.g., Ausubel, 1971; Boorse, 1975, 1976a; A. L. Caplan, 1981; Flew, 1981; Kendell, 1975, 1986; Klein, 1978; Macklin, 1981; Moore, 1978; Ruse, 1973; Scadding, 1967, 1990; Spitzer & Endicott, 1978). Spitzer and Endicott (1978) noted the seeming necessity and virtual universality of using dysfunction to make sense of disorder: "Our approach makes explicit an underlying assumption that is present in all discussions of disease or disorder, i.e., the concept of organismic dysfunction" (p. 37).

Despite the virtually universal tendency to fall back on dysfunction to explain disorder and the potential explanatory power of the dysfunction approach, *dysfunction* rarely appears in actual definitions of disorder. Because there is no standard account of what dysfunction is, citing dysfunction provides no conclusive insight into disorder. Even the connection I assumed earlier among dysfunction, natural functions, and evolutionary theory is not obvious and needs to be justified. Still, if dysfunction can be analyzed in clearer and more basic terms, then an adequate and generally acceptable criterion for disorder might be constructed using the results.

What, then, is a dysfunction? An obvious place to begin is the supposition that a dysfunction implies an unfulfilled function, that is, a failure of some mechanism in the organism to perform its function. However, not all kinds of functions are relevant. For example, one's nose functions to hold up one's glasses, and the sound of the heart performs a useful function in medical diagnosis. But a person whose nose is shaped in such a way that it does not properly support glasses does not thereby have a nasal disorder, and a person whose heart does not make the usual sounds is not thereby suffering from a cardiac disorder. A disorder is different from a failure to function in a socially preferred manner precisely because a dysfunction exists only when an organ cannot perform as it is naturally (i.e., independently of human intentions) supposed to perform. Presumably, the functions that are relevant are natural functions, about which concept there is a large literature that I draw on shortly (Boorse, 1976b; A. L. Caplan, 1981; Cummins, 1975; Elster, 1983; Hempel, 1965; Klein, 1978; Moore, 1978; Nagel, 1979; Woodfield, 1976; Wright, 1973, 1976). For example, one of the heart's natural functions is to pump the blood, and that is why a cessation of pumping is a dysfunction. A natural function of the perceptual apparatus is to convey roughly accurate information about the immediate environment, and that is why gross hallucinations indicate dysfunctions. Some cognitive mechanisms have the function of providing a person with the capacity for a degree of rationality as expressed in deductive, inductive, and means-end reasoning (I am referring not to ideal rationality as represented by theoretical models, but to simply the degree of rationality that people manifest in everyday inferences), and that is why it is a dysfunction when the capacity for such reasoning breaks down, as in severe psychotic states.

To understand dysfunction, then, we need an analysis of natural function. Hempel (1965) usefully posed the problem of natural function as follows: Each organ has many effects, most of which are not its natural functions. For example, the heart has the effects of pumping the blood and making a sound in the chest, but only pumping the blood is a natural function. An analysis of natural function must specify what distinguishes an organ's natural functions from its other effects.

The concept of function also applies to artifacts, such as automobiles, chairs, and pens. It seems likely that the concept of function was analogically extended from artifacts to organs (Wright, 1973, 1976). Therefore, the use of the term *function* in the case of naturally occurring mechanisms must be a way to refer to properties that such mechanisms share with artifacts. Now, the function of an artifact is just the purpose for which the artifact was designed; for example, the functions of automobiles, chairs, and pens are, respectively, to enable us to transport ourselves, to sit, and to write, because those are the benefits the artifacts are designed to provide. But organisms and their organs occur naturally and were not really designed by anyone with a purpose consciously in mind, so design and purpose cannot be the shared property. Of course, evolutionary biologists commonly talk in terms of purpose and design when they talk about natural functions, but that just brings the puzzle back a step: What justifies such talk in the case of naturally occurring mechanisms? The extension of function from artifacts to natural mechanisms must be justified by some other shared property that lies beneath talk of design and purpose and gives that talk its importance.

The function of an artifact is important largely because, via its connection to design and purpose, it has tremendous explanatory value. The function explains why the artifact was made, why it is structured the way it is, why the parts interact as they do, and why one can accomplish certain things with the artifact. For example, we can partially explain why automobiles exist, why automobile engines are structured as they are, and why with suitable learning one can get from place to place with the help of an automobile, all just by referring to the automobile's function of providing transportation.

Functional explanations of artifacts have the odd feature that an effect (e.g., transportation) is claimed to somehow explain the very artifact (e.g., automobiles) that provides the effect. Consequently, it has sometimes been claimed that functional explanations violate the basic principle that a cause must come before its effect. However, a description of the function can legitimately enter into the explanation of the artifact if there is some additional theory that shows that the cited effect plays some role in the events that preceded the artifact's creation. For artifacts, that theory is very simple and well known. The benefit precedes the artifact in the sense that it is represented beforehand in the mind of the person who designs the artifact. Thus, a functional explanation (e.g., "The function of an automobile is to provide transportation" or, equivalently, "Automobiles exist in order to provide transportation") is a sketch of a fuller causal explanation: The artifact (e.g., an automobile) exists because someone desired a certain effect (e.g., transportation) and believed that creating that artifact was a way to obtain the effect, and the belief and desire, which preceded the artifact, caused the person to create the artifact.

I have argued that the function of an artifact is important because of its explanatory power and that function explanations of artifacts have a distinctive form—the existence and structure of the artifact are explained by reference to the artifact's effects. It is this form of explanatory implication that statements about artifact functions and natural functions have in common and that justifies extending talk of functions from artifacts to natural mechanisms. Natural mechanisms, like artifacts, can be partially explained by referring to their effects, and natural functions, like artifact functions, are those effects that enter into such explanations. For example, the heart's effect of pumping the blood is also part of the heart's explanation, in that one can legitimately answer a question such as "Why do we have hearts?" or "Why do hearts exist?" with "Because hearts pump the blood." The effect of pumping the blood also enters into explanations of the detailed structure and activity of the heart. Thus, pumping the blood is a natural function of the heart. Anatomical and physiological research is largely devoted to establishing the natural functions of organs and explaining the features of an organ in terms of their contributions to the organ's natural functions. Talk of design and purpose in the case of naturally occurring mechanisms is just a metaphorical way to refer to this unique explanatory property that the effects of a mechanism explain the mechanism. In sum, the concept of natural function can be analyzed as follows: A natural function of an organ or other mechanism is an effect of the organ or mechanism that enters into an explanation of the existence, structure, or activity of the organ or mechanism.

An important feature of functional explanations is that they can be plausible and very useful even when little is known about the actual nature of a mechanism. With natural mechanisms, as with artifacts, the benefits that they provide are so remarkable and depend on such intricate and harmonious interactions that it is often reasonable to infer that the benefit is not accidental. In such cases, if no alternative explanations exist, it is reasonable to infer that the artifact exists because it has these effects. For example, it cannot be merely a happy accident that the eyes enable us to see, the legs enable us to walk, and the heart pumps the blood any more than it is a happy accident that the automobile provides transportation. The eyes therefore must exist in part because they enable us to see; that is, the fact that the eyes provide sight must somehow enter into the explanation of why we have eyes. This makes seeing a function of the eyes. Obviously, one can go wrong in such explanatory attempts; what seems nonaccidental may turn out to be accidental. But often one is right, and functional explanatory hypotheses communicate complex knowledge that may not be so easily and efficiently communicated in any other way.

The preceding analysis applies equally well to the natural functions of mental mechanisms and thus forms a common basis for the attribution of physical and mental disorder. Like artifacts and organs, mental mechanisms, such as cognitive, linguistic, perceptual, affective, and motivational mechanisms, have such strikingly beneficial effects and depend on such complex and harmonious interactions that the effects cannot be entirely accidental. Thus, functional explanations of mental mechanisms are sometimes justified by what we know about how people manage to survive and reproduce. For example, one function of linguistic mechanisms is to provide a capacity for communication, one function of the fear response is to help a person to avoid danger, and one function of tiredness is to bring about rest and sleep. These functional explanations yield ascriptions of dysfunctions when respective mechanisms fail to perform their functions, as in aphasia, phobia, and insomnia, respectively.

DYSFUNCTION AND EVOLUTIONARY THEORY

We now have an account of natural functions as effects that explain the existence and structure of naturally occurring physical and mental mechanisms. Correspondingly, dysfunction is the failure of a mechanism to perform its natural function. The next step is to provide this abstract analysis with some theoretical substance by linking it to the theory of evolution.

As in the case of artifacts, natural function explanations appear on the surface to violate the principle that a cause comes before its effects. For example, "Sexual desire exists because it causes people to copulate and reproduce" seems to explain sexual desire in terms of something that normally comes after it. To understand exactly how and in what sense such effects can play a role in causing the respective mechanisms requires an additional theory.

In the case of artifacts, it is a prior mental representation of the effect that explains the existence of the artifact. Coming up with a similar demystifying causal explanation in the case of natural functions has posed an age-old mystery: Why, indeed, should our internal mechanisms be so beneficially designed? Until recently, the mystery could be dealt with only by assuming that there exists a God who purposely created our internal mechanisms with benevolent intentions. According to this theory, our internal mechanisms are artifacts created by a divine entity, so natural functions are reduced to a special case of artifact functions.

Today evolutionary theory provides a better explanation of how a mechanism's effects can explain the mechanism's presence and structure. In brief, those mechanisms that happened to have effects on past organisms that contributed to the organisms' reproductive success over enough generations increased in frequency and hence were "naturally selected" and exist in today's organisms. Thus, an explanation of a mechanism in terms of its natural function may be considered a roundabout way of referring to a causal explanation in terms of natural selection. Because natural selection is the only known means by which an effect can explain a naturally occurring mechanism that provides it, evolutionary explanations presumably underlie all correct ascriptions of natural functions. Consequently, an evolutionary approach to personality and mental functioning (Buss, 1984, 1991; Wakefield, 1989a) is central to an understanding of psychopathology.

Dysfunction is thus a purely factual scientific concept. However, discovering what in fact is natural or dysfunctional (and thus what is disordered) may be extraordinarily difficult and may be subject to scientific controversy, especially with respect to mental mechanisms, about which we are still in a state of great ignorance. This ignorance is part of the reason for the high degree of confusion and controversy concerning which conditions are really mental disorders. Paradoxically, this ignorance about the detailed nature and causal histories of mental mechanisms also makes it all the more necessary to rely on functional explanations based on inferences about what mental mechanisms are probably designed to do. In this respect, we are now at a stage of understanding that is comparable in some ways to the position of ancient physicians who had to rely on similar inferences in judging physical disorder. For example, although knowing nothing about the mechanisms involved in sight or the natural history of the eye, such physicians still understood on the basis of functional inferences that blindness and other physical conditions are dysfunctions. As we learn more about the naturally selected functions of mental mechanisms, our judgments about dysfunction will become correspondingly more confident.

THE HARM REQUIREMENT: WHY DYSFUNCTION IS NOT ENOUGH

Given that all disorders must involve failures of naturally selected mechanisms, it is tempting to simply identify disorder with dysfunction as delineated by evolutionary theory. This would realize the long-sought goal of making disorder a purely objective scientific concept. However, as I showed earlier with many examples, a dysfunction is not enough to justify attribution of disorder. To be considered a disorder, the dysfunction must also cause significant harm to the person under present environmental circumstances and according to present cultural standards. For example, a dysfunction in one kidney often has no effect on the overall well-being of a person and so is not considered to be a disorder; physicians will remove a kidney from a live donor for transplant purposes with no sense that they are causing a disorder, even though people are certainly naturally designed to have two kidneys. To take a more speculative example, even if we suppose that people are designed to age and die at roughly a certain rate, someone whose aging mechanism suffered a dysfunction that slowed the aging process and lengthened life would be considered not disordered but lucky, assuming that no harmful side effects occurred as a result. The requirement that there be harm also accounts for why albinism, reversal of heart position, and fused toes are not considered disorders even though each results from a breakdown in the way some mechanism is designed to function. Although every disorder must involve a failure of a naturally selected property, not every such failure is a disorder. The element of harm must also be involved.

There are two reasons for the divergence between harm (in the practical sense that is relevant to diagnostic concerns) and failure of naturally selected effects. First, the natural functions of internal mechanisms were determined by the selective pressures that operated in environments that existed when the human species evolved. In some cases, those selective pressures have changed so that a breakdown in a mechanism now does not have the negative consequences that it would have had then. For example, high levels of male aggression might have been useful under primitive conditions, but in present-day circumstances such aggressive responses might be harmful. Consequently, even if a disposition to highly aggressive responses is the natural function of some mechanism, the loss of that function might not now be considered a disorder.

Second, natural selection of a mechanism occurs when organisms that possess the mechanism have greater reproductive fitness than organisms that do not possess the mechanism. Small decreases in reproductive fitness can be important over the evolutionary time scale, but in the absence of any other negative effects they are not necessarily harmful in the practical sense relevant to disorder. Relative reproductive fitness must be distinguished from possession of some reproductive capacity; the ability to have children is commonly considered a benefit and its deprivation is commonly considered a disorder, although even this has been disputed because of its implications for the classification of homosexuality. The mental health theoretician is interested in the functions that people care about and need within the current social environment, not those that are interesting merely on evolutionary theoretical grounds.

Thus disorder cannot be simply identified with the scientific concept of the inability of an internal mechanism to perform a naturally selected function. Only dysfunctions that are socially disvalued are disorders. Note that in this article I have explored the value element in disorder less thoroughly than the factual element. This is in part because the factual component poses more of a problem for inferences about disorder and in part because the nature of values is such a complex topic in its own right that it requires separate consideration.

The following general concept of disorder results from the preceding analysis: A condition is a disorder if and only if (a) the condition causes some harm or deprivation of benefit to the person as judged by the standards of the person's culture (the value criterion), and (b) the condition results from the inability of some internal mechanism to perform its natural function, wherein a natural function is an effect that is part of the evolutionary explanation of the existence and structure of the mechanism (the explanatory criterion).

This concept of disorder as harmful dysfunction leads directly to a definition of mental disorder as a special case. But first one question must be resolved: Does the "mental" in "mental disorder" refer to the nature of the harmful effects (symptoms) or to the nature of the dysfunctional cause of the harm? For example, as already mentioned, *DSM-III-R* asserts that the harm must be "a manifestation of a behavioral, psychological, or biological dysfunction in the person" (American Psychiatric Association, 1987, p. xxii). The inclusion of biological dysfunctions (by which *DSM-III-R* means physiological as opposed to psychological or behavioral) as causes of mental disorders suggests that what makes a disorder mental is not the kind of dysfunction but the kind of symptom. This interpretation is consistent with Spitzer and Endicott's (1978) statement that "a mental disorder is a medical disorder whose manifestations are primarily signs or symptoms of a psychological (behavioral) nature, or if physical, can be understood only using psychological concepts" (p. 18). The last clause was added to deal with what would otherwise be the obvious counterexample of psychosomatic illness, in which the symptoms are physical but the disorder is mental. The need for an ad hoc clause to cover psychosomatic disorders already suggests that the definition is incorrect. In fact, it is clearly not the case that mental disorders are disorders with mental symptoms. For example, trigeminal neuralgia has pain as its main symptom, and pain is a mental phenomenon, but trigeminal neuralgia is not a psychological disorder. As the example of psychosomatic illness suggests, it is the nature of the cause of the symptoms, and not the nature of the symptoms themselves, that determines whether a disorder is mental. This is why pain due to a physical dysfunction does not constitute a mental disorder; even extreme pain need not indicate a dysfunction of any mental mechanism. A physiological dysfunction can be the source of mental disorder only if it causes a breakdown in the functioning of some mental mechanism that in turn causes symptoms. So for a disorder to be mental, there must be a mental dysfunction, although the mental dysfunction might be secondary to a physiological dysfunction. This yields the conclusion that a mental disorder is a harmful dysfunction in a mental mechanism or, equivalently, a harmful mental dysfunction. More formally, in parallel to the general concept of disorder, we have the following concept of mental disorder: A condition is a mental disorder if and only if (a) the condition causes some harm or deprivation of benefit to the person as judged by the standards of the person's culture (the value criterion), and (b) the condition results from the inability of some mental mechanism to perform its natural function, wherein a natural function is an effect that is part of the evolutionary explanation of the existence and structure of the mental mechanism (the explanatory criterion). The further question of how to distinguish mental from physical mechanisms in a principled way that goes beyond the sort of list presented earlier (e.g., cognitive, perceptual, emotional, linguistic, and motivational mechanisms) is beyond the scope of this article.

No doubt there is much to be done to clarify, extend, and improve this analysis. But if this analysis does indeed come closer than other analyses to expressing the concept that underlies judgments about mental disorder, then it is this conception that we must scrutinize if we are to understand the strengths and limits of the concept of mental disorder or attempt to improve the conceptual validity of our diagnostic criteria. However, it is worth noting that even the clearest concepts possess areas of ambiguity, indeterminacy, and vagueness, so even a correct analysis of the concept of mental disorder is unlikely to resolve all controversies, although it may illuminate why certain intractable cases are controversial.

THE CONCEPT OF DISORDER AND THEORIES OF DISORDER

I observed earlier that the concept of disorder has explanatory content; for example, to assert that a person is talking to him- or herself because he or she is suffering from a disorder suggests something about the explanation of the behavior. According to the view developed in the previous section, the explanatory content is as follows: To say that a harm is due to a disorder is to say that the harm is due to the fact that some internal mechanism is not functioning the way it was designed by nature to function. This attribution is inferential and goes beyond either the sheer existence of the manifest symptoms or the value judgment that the symptoms are harmful. However, in itself, a disorder attribution says nothing about the specific nature of the mechanisms that have gone awry. Consequently, judgments of disorder can be based on circumstantial evidence when knowledge of mechanisms is lacking, as when we infer that blindness and hallucinations are disorders without understanding anything about how perception works. Nevertheless, understanding the nature of mental mechanisms is ultimately critical to advancing the mental health field. Specifying the nature and functions of mental mechanisms and why they fail is the task of theories of mental disorder.

Theories of mental disorder are essentially theories of dysfunction. The harm component of the concept of disorder is judged by value standards that transcend the technicalities of any theory. A theory may alert us to hidden processes that have negative implications that we did not know about, but the reason that the processes are negative has to do with pretheoretical values.

The concept of disorder thus places two constraints on any theory of mental disorder. The value criterion implies that any successful theory of disorder must link up in the right way with the commonsense concept of harm. The explanatory criterion implies that any successful theory must offer an account specifically of dysfunctions.

Accounts of disorder in terms of genetic etiology obviously fit well with the approach to disorder I propose. There is a presumption that genetic mechanisms are naturally selected and have natural functions, implying that when something goes wrong there is a dysfunction. Thus, genetic etiology might easily satisfy the explanatory criterion. Moreover, genetic dysfunctions often cause harm, fulfilling the value criterion. However, even dysfunctional genetic mechanisms do not indicate disorder unless there is harm to the organism, as was illustrated in the examples of albinism, fused toes, and reversal of chest organ position.

The harmful dysfunction approach equally fits more psychological theories of disorder. A good example is Freud's repression account of neurotic disorder. It is sometimes mistakenly claimed that repression in itself is neurotic. This position would be bewildering as a theory of mental disorder because it contains no account of the function of repression, of how it comes to be dysfunctional, or of why repression itself is harmful. However, Freud's (1915/1957a, 1915/1957b) theory is much more sophisticated and is quite consistent with the framework imposed by the concept of disorder. Freud maintained that the mechanism of repression is designed to provide the benefit of keeping extremely painful ideas and affects from reaching consciousness and impairing the functioning of the organism. However, according to Freud, repression sometimes fails to perform its function in a satisfactory way, especially under the conditions imposed by modern civilization where so many desires and thoughts must be repressed. Consequently, indirect expressions of the repressed material sometimes reach consciousness in the form of neurotic symptoms. Thus, it is not the repression per se that constitutes the disorder; that would make no sense because neither harm nor dysfunction is necessary in successful repression. Instead the disorder is the failure of repression to do what it was designed to do (which implies a dysfunction) and the fact that harmful symptoms, such as painful anxiety, result from that failure. Note that the link via symptoms to the commonsense concept of harm is essential to the claim that the failure of repression is a disorder.

Similar considerations apply to the opposite end of the therapeutic theory spectrum, behavioral theory. It is sometimes claimed that a behavioral approach to the mind is not compatible with the traditional concept of mental disorder, because behaviorists consider all behavior to be the outcome of the same basic processes of reinforcement and learning, which are normal mechanisms. However, there is no inherent incompatibility between a behavioral approach and the harmful dysfunction concept of disorder. Behavioral theory can link up in a variety of ways with the critical concept of dysfunction (the harm requirement is easily met by many behaviors). One possibility is that learning mechanisms themselves may not operate in the way they were designed to operate. For example, simplifying greatly, Eysenck (1982, 1986) might be interpreted as arguing that certain personological characteristics can cause a person's learning mechanisms to respond to aversive stimuli more sensitively than they are designed to respond, yielding a variety of phobias and other maladaptive behaviors. A second possibility, which is hinted at in Salzinger's (1986) discussion of ethological approaches to behavior, is that there are submechanisms that facilitate the learning of specific classes of behaviors that are essential to survival and reproduction (e.g., ingestive, eliminative, sexual, parental, and agonistic mechanisms) and behavioral disorder results when these innate dispositions are not triggered by learning, as they are designed to be. Third, just as an emotionally normal infant can, in the absence of adequate or "expectable" caretaking stimuli, develop life-threatening anaclitic depression (Spitz, 1945), and a genetically normal fetus can develop pathological anatomical structures if "unexpected" chemicals come through the placenta, so a person with normal learning mechanisms can develop pathological behavioral dispositions that are outside the range that the learning mechanism was designed to produce, if the history of reinforcement includes stimuli outside the range that the mechanism was designed to "expect." For example, simplifying a bit, suppose that one function of learning mechanisms (i.e., one result of learning that selectively shaped the nature of learning mechanisms) is to associate the response of fear with danger, in such a way that the intensity of fear is roughly proportional to the degree of actual danger. Sometimes a severe trauma or other unusual sequence of stimuli causes the formation of an enduringly exaggerated sense of danger that causes substantial harm to the person. Such a disposition constitutes a disorder, because not only is there a dysfunction (learning is not leading to the kind of adaptive association between fear and danger that partially explains why learning mechanisms exist in the first place), but there is also harm (the exaggerated fear is painful and disabling).

CONCLUDING COMMENTS ON THE MISAPPLICATION OF THE CONCEPT OF "DISORDER"

The requirement that a disorder must involve a dysfunction places severe constraints on which negative conditions can be considered disorders and thus protects against arbitrary labeling of socially disvalued conditions as disorders. Unlike the skeptical view, the harmful dysfunction analysis distinguishes between sound and unsound applications of the term *mental disorder.* Diagnoses such as "drapetomania" (the "disorder" of runaway slaves), "childhood masturbation disorder," and "lack of vaginal orgasm" can be seen as unsound applications of a perfectly coherent concept that can be correctly applied to other conditions. Unlike the value view, the harmful dysfunction view allows us to reject these diagnoses on scientific grounds, namely, that the beliefs about natural functioning that underlie them—for example, that slaves are naturally designed to serve, that children are naturally designed to be nonsexual, and that women are naturally designed to have orgasms from vaginal stimulation in intercourse alone—are false.

Because of the complexity of the inferences involved in judgments of dysfunction and our relative ignorance about the evolution of mental functioning, it is easy to arrive at differing judgments about mental dysfunction even on the basis of the same data. For example, according to the eminent Victorian physician and sexologist William Acton (1871), the female sexual organs do not naturally function to produce orgasm during intercourse, and the occurrence of orgasm in a woman is a form of pathology due to an excess of stimulation beyond what her body was designed to tolerate. According to Masters and Johnson (1966, 1970, 1974), orgasm during intercourse is a natural function of the female sexual organs, and lack of orgasm in a woman is a disorder due to inadequate stimulation of the sort to which her body was designed to respond. Acton and Masters and Johnson knew that there are many women who do have orgasms in intercourse and many women who do not. Acton interpreted these facts to mean that there are a lot of women who are disordered because they suffer from overstimulation, whereas Masters and Johnson interpreted these facts to mean that there are a lot of women who are disordered because they suffer from understimulation. The nonstatistical nature of function and disorder, combined with ignorance of the evolutionary history of female sexual capacities, enabled these opposite beliefs to be consistent with the same set of data and with the same concept of disorder. Only further facts about the nature of the mechanisms involved in female sexual response, and the evolution of those mechanisms, can resolve such debates.

In principle, Acton and Masters and Johnson might have been able to reach agreement on what constitutes female orgasmic dysfunction if they had full knowledge of the evolutionary history of female sexual capacities. However, according to the view presented here, it is possible that agreement on the facts about function and dysfunction might not lead to agreement about which conditions are disorders because of differences in values (e.g., is orgasm in intercourse a desirable goal?). Such value differences, rather than any dispute over facts, may be what makes some diagnostic controversies, such as that over the pathological status of homosexuality, so intractable (Spitzer, 1981). The harmful dysfunction analysis thus provides a framework for identifying both the possibilities and the limits of agreement in such controversies.

References

Acton, W. (1871). *The functions and disorders of the reproductive organs in childhood, youth, adult age, and advanced life, considered in their physiological, social, and moral relations* (5th ed.). London: Churchill.

American Psychiatric Association. (1980). *Diagnostic and statistical manual of mental disorders* (3rd ed.). Washington, D.C.: Author.

———. (1987). *Diagnostic and statistical manual of mental disorders* (3rd ed., rev.). Washington, D.C.: Author.

Ausubel, D. P. (1971). Personality disorder is disease. *American Psychologist* 16, 59–74.

Barker-Benfield, G. J. (1983). The spermatic economy: A nineteenth-century view of sexuality. In T. L. Altherr (Ed.), *Procreation or pleasure? Sexual attitudes in American history* (pp. 47–70). Malabar, FL: Robert E. Krieger.

Bayer, R. (1981). *Homosexuality and American psychiatry: The politics of diagnosis.* New York: Basic Books.

Bayer, R. & Spitzer, R. L. (1982). Edited correspondence on the status of homosexuality in DSM-III. *Journal of the History of the Behavioral Sciences* 18, 32–52.

Boorse, C. (1975). On the distinction between disease and illness. *Philosophy and Public Affairs* 5, 49–68.

———. (1976a). What a theory of mental health should be. *Journal for the Theory of Social Behavior* 6, 61–84.

Boorse, C. (1976b). Wright on functions. *Philosophical Review* 85, 70–86.

Buss, D. M. (1984). Evolutionary biology and personality psychology: Toward a conception of human nature and individual differences. *American Psychologist* 39, 1135–1147.

———. (1991). Evolutionary personality psychology. *Annual Review of Psychology* 42, 459–491.

Campbell, E. J. M., Scadding, J. G., & Roberts, R. S. (1979). The concept of disease. *British Medical Journal* 2, 757–762.

Caplan, A. L. (1981). The "unnaturalness" of aging—a sickness unto death? In A. L. Caplan, H. T. Engelhardt, Jr., & J. J. McCartney (Eds.), *Concepts of health and disease: Interdisciplinary perspectives* (pp. 725–738). Reading, MA: Addison-Wesley.

Caplan, P. J. (1984). The myth of women's masochism. *American Psychologist* 39, 130–139.

Cartwright. S. A. (1981). Report on the diseases and physical peculiarities of the Negro race. In A. L. Caplan, H. T. Engelhardt, Jr., & J. J. McCartney

(Eds.), *Concepts of health and disease: Interdisciplinary perspectives* (pp. 305–326). Reading, MA: Addison-Wesley. (Original work published 1851)

Claridge, G. (1985). *Origins of mental illness.* Oxford, England: Blackwell.

Cohen, H. (1981). The evolution of the concept of disease. In A. L. Caplan, H. T. Engelhardt, Jr., & J. J. McCartney (Eds.), *Concepts of health and disease: Interdisciplinary perspectives* (pp. 209–220). Reading, MA: Addison-Wesley.

Coles, G. (1987). *Learning mystique.* New York: Pantheon.

Cowart, V. (1988). The ritalin controversy: What's made this drug's opponents hyperactive? *Journal of the American Medical Association* 259, 2521–2523.

Cummins, R. (1975). Functional analysis. *Journal of Philosophy* 72, 741–765.

Elster, J. (1983). *Explaining technical change.* Cambridge, England: Cambridge University Press.

Engelhardt, H. T., Jr. (1974). The disease of masturbation: Values and the concept of disease. *Bulletin of the History of Medicine* 48, 234–248.

Eysenck, H. J. (1982). Neobehavioristic (S-R) theory of neurosis. In G. T. Wilson & C. M. Franks (Eds.), *Contemporary behavior therapy* (pp. 205–276). New York: Guilford Press.

———. (1986). A critique of contemporary classification and diagnosis. In T. Millon & G. L. Klerman (Eds.), *Contemporary directions in psychopathology: Toward the DSM-IV* (pp. 73–98). New York: Guilford Press.

Eysenck, H. J., Wakefield, J. C., & Friedman, A. F. (1983). Diagnosis and clinical assessment: The DSM-III. *Annual Review of Psychology* 34,167–193.

Fingarette, H. (1988). *Heavy drinking: The myth of alcoholism as a disease.* Berkeley: University of California Press.

———. (1990). We should reject the disease concept of alcoholism. *Harvard Medical School Mental Health Letter* 6(8), 4–6.

Flew, A. (1981). Disease and mental illness. In A. L. Caplan, H. T. Engelhardt, Jr., & J. J. McCartney (Eds.), *Concepts of health and disease: Interdisciplinary perspectives* (pp. 433–442). Reading, MA: Addison-Wesley.

Foucault, M. (1965). *Madness and civilization: A history of insanity in the Age of Reason* (R. Howard, Trans.). New York: Pantheon. (Original work published 1964)

———. (1978). *History of sexuality: Vol. 1. An introduction.* New York: Pantheon.

Freud, S. (1957a). Repression. In J. Strachey (Ed. and Trans.), *The standard edition of the complete psychological works of Sigmund Freud* (Vol. 14, pp. 146–158). London: Hogarth Press. (Original work published 1915)

———. (1957b). The unconscious. In J. Strachey (Ed. and Trans.), *The standard edition of the complete psychological works of Sigmund Freud* (Vol. 14, pp. 166–215). London: Hogarth Press. (Original work published 1915)

Goffman, E. (1963). *Stigma: Notes on the management of spoiled identity.* Englewood Cliffs, NJ: Prentice-Hall.

Gorenstein, E. E. (1984). Debating mental illness: Implications for science, medicine, and social policy. *American Psychologist* 39, 50–56.

Gorman, D. M. (1989a). Is 'disease model' an appropriate term to describe the alcohol dependence syndrome? *Alcohol and Alcoholism* 24, 509–512.

Gorman, D. M. (1989b). Is the 'new' problem drinking concept of Heather & Robertson more useful in advancing our scientific knowledge than the 'old' disease concept? *British Journal of Addiction* 84, 843–845.

Gove, W. R. (1980). Labeling and mental illness: A critique. In W. R. Gove (Ed.), *The labeling of deviance: Evaluating a perspective* (2nd ed., pp. 53–99). Beverly Hills, CA: Sage.

Hempel, C. G. (1965). The logic of functional analysis. In C. G. Hempel (Ed.), *Aspects of scientific explanation and other essays in the philosophy of science* (pp. 297–330). New York: Free Press.

Horwitz, A. V. (1982). *The social control of mental illness.* San Diego, CA: Academic Press.

Kaplan, M. (1983). A woman's view of DSM-III. *American Psychologist* 38, 786–792.

Kendell, R. E. (1975). The concept of disease and its implications for psychiatry. *British Journal of Psychiatry* 127, 305–315.

———. (1986). What are mental disorders? In A. M. Freedman, R. Brotman, I. Silverman, & D. Hutson (Eds.), *Issues in psychiatric classification: Science, practice and social policy* (pp. 23–45). New York: Human Sciences Press.

King, L. (1981). What is disease? In A. L. Caplan, H. T. Engelhardt, Jr., & J. J. McCartney (Eds.), *Concepts of health and disease: Interdisciplinary perspectives* (pp. 107–118). Reading, MA: Addison-Wesley. (Original work published 1954)

Klein, D. F. (1978). A proposed definition of mental illness. In R. L. Spitzer & D. F. Klein (Eds.), *Critical issues in psychiatric diagnosis* (pp. 41–71). New York: Raven Press.

Kohn, A. (1989, November). Suffer the restless children. *Atlantic Monthly,* pp. 90–100.

Laing, R. D. (1967). *The politics of experience.* London: Penguin Books.

Lewis, A. (1967). Health as a social concept. In A. Lewis (Ed.), *The state of psychiatry* (pp. 113–127). New York: Science House.

Macklin, R. (1981). Mental health and mental illness: Some problems of definition and concept formation. In A. L. Caplan, H. T. Engelhardt, Jr., & J. J. McCartney (Eds.), *Concepts of health and disease: Interdisciplinary perspectives* (pp. 391–418). Reading, MA: Addison-Wesley.

Marmor, J. (1973). [Comments]. In A symposium: Should homosexuality be in the APA nomenclature? *American Journal of Psychiatry* 130, 1270–1316.

Masters, W. H., & Johnson, V. E. (1966). *Human sexual response.* Boston: Little, Brown.

———. (1970). *Human sexual inadequacy.* Boston: Little, Brown.

———. (1974). *The pleasure bond: A new look at sexuality and commitment.* Boston: Little, Brown.

Moore, M. S. (1978). Discussion of the Spitzer-Endicott and Klein proposed definitions of mental disorder (illness). In R. L. Spitzer & D. F. Klein (Eds.), *Critical issues in psychiatric diagnosis* (pp. 85–104). New York: Raven Press.

Nagel, E. (1979). *Teleology revisited and other essays in the philosophy and history of science.* New York: Columbia University Press.

Pichot, P. (1986). [Comment in Discussion section]. In A. M. Freedman, R. Brotman. I. Silverman, & D. Hutson (Eds.), *Issues in psychiatric classification: Science, practice and social policy* (p. 56). New York: Human Sciences Press.

Pond, D. (1960). Is there a syndrome of "brain damage" in children? *Cerebral Palsy Bulletin* 2, 296.

Ruse, M. (1973). *The philosophy of biology.* London: London University Press.

Rutter, M., Graham, P., & Yule, W. (1970). *A neuropsychiatric study in childhood.* Philadelphia: Lippincott.

Salzinger, K. (1986). Diagnosis: Distinguishing among behaviors. In T. Millon & G. L. Klerman (Eds.), *Contemporary directions in psychopathology: Toward the DSM-IV* (pp. 115–134). New York: Guilford Press.

Sarbin, T. (1967). On the futility of the proposition that some people be labeled "mentally ill." *Journal of Consulting Psychology* 31, 447–453.

———. (1969). The scientific status of the mental illness metaphor. In S. C. Pong & R. B. Edgerton (Eds.), *Changing perspectives in mental illness* (pp. 1–16). New York: Holt, Rinehart & Winston.

Scadding, J. G. (1967). Diagnosis: The clinician and the computer. *Lancet* 2, 877–882.

———. (1990). The semantic problem of psychiatry. *Psychological Medicine* 20, 243–248.

Scheff, T J. (1966). *Being mentally ill: A sociological theory.* Chicago: Aldine.

———. (Ed.). (1975). *Labeling madness.* Englewood Cliffs, NJ: Prentice-Hall.

Schrenck-Notzing, A. (1956). *The use of hypnosis in psychopathia sexualis* (C. D. Chaddock, Trans.). New York: Julian Press. (Original work published 1895).

Sedgwick, P. (1982). *Psycho politics.* New York: Harper & Row.

Showalter, E. (1987). *The female malady: Women, madness, and English culture, 1830–1980.* London: Virago Press.

Spitz, R. (1945). Hospitalism, *The Psychoanalytic Study of the Child* 1, 53–74.

Spitzer, R. L. (1981). The diagnostic status of homosexuality in DSM-III: A reformulation of the issues. *American Journal of Psychiatry* 138, 210–215.

Spitzer, R. L., & Endicott, J. (1978). Medical and mental disorder: Proposed definition and criteria. In R. L. Spitzer & D. F. Klein (Eds.), *Critical issues in psychiatric diagnosis* (pp. 15–39). New York: Raven Press.

Spitzer, R. L., & Williams, J. B. W. (1982). The definition and diagnosis of mental disorder. In W. R. Gove (Ed.), *Deviance and mental illness* (pp. 15–31). Beverly Hills, CA: Sage.

———. (1983). International perspectives: Summary and commentary. In R. L. Spitzer, J. B. W. Williams, & A. E. Skodol (Eds.), *International perspectives on DSM-III* (pp. 339–353). Washington, DC: American Psychiatric Press.

———. (1988). Basic principles in the development of DSM-III. In J. E. Mezzich & M. V. Cranach (Eds.), *International classification in psychiatry: Unity and diversity* (pp. 81–86). Cambridge, England: Cambridge University Press.

Szasz, T. S. (1971). The sane slave. *American Journal of Psychotherapy* 25, 228–239.

Szasz, T. S. (1974). *The myth of mental illness: Foundations of a theory of personal conduct* (Rev. ed.). New York: Harper & Row.

Taylor, F. K. (1971). A logical analysis of the medico-psychological concept of disease. *Psychological Medicine* 1, 356–364.

———. (1976). The medical model of the disease concept. *British Journal of Psychiatry* 128, 588–594.

Ussher, J. M. (1989). *The psychology of the human body*. New York: Routledge.

Vaillant, G. E. (1990). We should retain the disease concept of alcoholism. *Harvard Medical School Mental Health Letter* 6(9), 4–6.

Wakefield, J. C. (1987). Sex bias in the diagnosis of primary orgasmic dysfunction. *American Psychologist* 42, 464–471.

———. (1988). Female primary orgasmic dysfunction: Masters and Johnson versus DSM-III-R on diagnosis and incidence. *Journal of Sex Research* 24, 363–377.

———. (1989a). Levels of explanation in personality theory. In D. M. Buss & N. Cantor (Eds.), *Emerging issues in personality psychology* (pp. 333–346). New York: Springer-Verlag.

———. (1989b). Manufacturing female dysfunction: A reply to Morokoff. *American Psychologist* 44, 75–77.

———. (in press). Disorder as harmful dysfunction: A conceptual critique of DSM-III-R's definition of mental disorder. *Psychological Review* 99 (2).

Williams, J. B. W., & Spitzer, R. L. (1983). The issue of sex bias in DSM-III: A critique of "A woman's view of DSM-III" by Marcie Kaplan. *American Psychologist* 38, 793–798.

Willie, C. V., Kramer, B. M., & Brown, B. S. (Eds.). (1973). *Racism and mental health*. Pittsburgh, PA: University of Pittsburgh Press.

Woodfield, A. (1976). *Teleology*. Cambridge, England: Cambridge University Press.

World Health Organization. (1981). Constitution of the World Health Organization. In A. L. Caplan, H. T. Engelhardt, Jr., & J. J. McCartney (Eds.), *Concepts of health and disease: Interdisciplinary perspectives* (pp. 83–84). Reading, MA: Addison-Wesley. (Original work published 1946)

Wright, L. (1973). Functions. *Philosophical Review* 82, 139–168.

———. (1976). *Teleological explanations*. Berkeley: University of California Press.

Suggestions for Further Reading

Antipsychiatric Psychiatrists and Their Critics

Edwards, Rem B., "Mental Health as Rational Autonomy." *The Journal of Medicine and Philosophy* 6 (1981):309–22.

Fisher, Seymore, and Roger P. Greenberg, "Prescriptions for Happiness." *Psychology Today* 28, no. 5 (1995): 32–37.

Isaac, Rael Jean, and Virginia C. Armat, *Madness in the Streets: How Psychiatry and the Law Abandoned the Mentally Ill.* New York: The Free Press, 1990.

Laing, R. D., *The Politics of Experience.* New York: Ballantine Books, 1967.

Masson, Jeffrey M., *Against Therapy: Emotional Tyranny and the Myth of Psychological Healing.* New York: Atheneum Books, 1988.

Reznek, Lawrie, *The Philosophical Defence of Psychiatry.* London: Routledge, 1991.

Roth, Martin, and Jerome Kroll, *The Reality of Mental Illness.* Cambridge: Cambridge University Press, l986.

Sedgwick, Peter, *Psycho Politics.* New York: Harper & Row, 1982.

Szasz, Thomas, *Ideology and Insanity: Essays on the Psychiatric Dehumanization of Man.* Syracuse, N.Y.: Syracuse University Press, 1991.

———, *Law, Liberty, and Psychiatry.* New York: Macmillan, 1963.

———, *The Manufacture of Madness.* New York: Harper & Row, 1970.

———, *The Myth of Mental Illness*, revised edition. New York: Harper & Row, 1974.

———, *The Myth of Psychotherapy.* Garden City, N.Y.: Anchor Books, 1979.

Vatz, Richard E., and Lee S. Weinberg, *Thomas Szasz: Primary Values and Major Contentions.* Amherst, N.Y.: Prometheus Books, 1983.

Insanity as Irrationality and Irresponsibility

Breggin, Peter R., *The Psychology of Freedom*. Amherst, N.Y.: Prometheus Books, 1980.

Moore, Michael S., *Law and Psychiatry: Rethinking the Relationship*. New York: Cambridge University Press, 1984.

Radden, Jennifer, *Madness and Reason*. London: George Allen & Unwin, 1985.

Stauch, Marc, "Rationality and the Refusal of Medical Treatment: A Critique of the Recent Approach of the English Courts." *Journal of Medical Ethics* 21 (1995): 162–65.

Winick, Bruce J., "On Autonomy: Legal and Psychological Perspectives." 37 *Villanova Law Review* 1705 (1992): 1755–68.

Mental Health

Boorse, Christopher, "Concepts of Health." In Donald VanDeVer and Tom Regan, eds., *Health Care Ethics: An Introduction*. Philadelphia: Temple University Press, 1987.

———, "What a Theory of Mental Health Should Be." *Journal of Social Behavior* 6, no. 1 (April 1976).

Jahoda, Marie, *Current Concepts of Positive Mental Health*. New York: Basic Books, 1959.

Offer, Daniel, and Melvin Sabashin, eds., *Normality: Theoretical and Clinical Concepts of Mental Health*. New York: Basic Books, 1974.

———, *The Diversity of Normal Behavior: Further Contributions to Normatology*. New York: Basic Books, 1991.

———, *Normality and the Life Cycle: A Critical Introduction*. New York: Basic Books, 1994.

Sider, Roger C., "Mental Health Norms and Ethical Practice." *Psychiatric Annals* 13 (1983):302–309.

Weiner, Neal O., *The Harmony of the Soul: Mental Health and Moral Virtue Reconsidered*. Albany: State University of New York Press, 1993.

2.

THE MEDICAL MODEL
AND DISVALUES IN
PSYCHIATRIC CLASSIFICATION

INTRODUCTION

General acceptance of the modern Western view of mental illness as a *medical* problem is a relatively recent historical development. Prior to the eighteenth-century Enlightenment, the insane were not usually thought of as sick. Instead they were regarded as sinners, criminals, witches, or possessed by demons; society responded to them with condemnation, execution, imprisonment, ostracism, torture, and exorcism. Institutions for their social isolation, confinement, degradation, and torture were created in a number of countries as early as the sixteenth century. Bedlam in England was established in the thirteenth century. The eighteenth-century Enlightenment endorsed the convictions that madmen are sick, morally innocent, entitled to the benefits and privileges of the "sick role," can and should be treated for relief by medical science, and are entitled to humane living conditions in mental institutions. The rationalistic Enlightenment transformed mental dungeons into medical hospitals and applied an ethicomedical model to the mentally deranged. The Western world was painfully slow to adopt and implement these enlightened ideas; to this day, say critics of mental asylums, they have never been properly implemented in most places. In the first selection, Robert M. Veatch explains and emphasizes the blameless sick role, along with many other evaluative and empirical features of the medical model.

The Ethicomedical Model

The so-called medical model included a profound but easily overlooked ethical dimension from its inception. It would be more accurate to call it the "ethicomedical model." Philippe Pinel, the great French Enlightenment medical reformer of mental institutions, wrote, "The mentally ill, far from being guilty persons who merit punishment, are sick people whose miserable state deserves all the consideration due to suffering humanity." Enlightenment thinkers accented ethical dimensions of medical care for mental patients like humane treatment and blamelessness for being sick. Our own society continues to refine its awareness of the ethical dimensions of doctor-patient relationships in all of medicine.

Despite the good intentions of the reformers who first applied an ethicomedical model to mental disturbances, critics of today's mental institutions insist that medicalizing mental/behavioral deviancy was a total mistake from the outset. Applying the medical model to mental illness involves both egregious conceptual confusion and unacceptable moral consequences, proclaims a whole chorus of critics led by Thomas Szasz and other antipsychiatric psychiatrists such as Peter Breggin, Fuller Torrey (for a time), and R. D. Laing; by sociologists and social psychologists such as Erving Goffman, Benjamin and Dorothea Braginsky, Robert Perrucci, T. J. Scheff, Theodore R. Sarbin; and by judges, lawyers, and civil libertarians like Bruce Ennis, Richard Emery, and former Chief Justice Warren Burger.

Thomas Szasz and other antipsychiatric psychiatrists do not wish to eliminate the profession and practice of psychotherapy. They only want to reclassify psychic treatment as instruction rather than therapy, to place it within an educational rather than a medical model, and to eliminate all involuntary instances of it. They do not deny that many people need help with their "problems in living," and that many professionals are well trained to give that help. Not all forms of helping are medical in nature, however. Psychotherapists do not treat diseases, and they should be reclassified and paid as educators, not as more expensive medical practitioners. Skilled psychoeducators merely teach people how to behave themselves, how to know, change, and accept themselves, and how to resolve their problems in living; but there is nothing medical about that!

Medicalizing Moral Vices

Antipsychiatrists contend that establishment psychotherapists do not treat real diseases; they merely employ the language and powers of medicine to enforce controversial political, social, religious, and moral values. This is illustrated, perhaps, by the diagnostic categories of the bible of the mental health establishment—the American Psychiatric Association's *Diagnostic and Statistical Manual of Mental Disorders, Fourth Edition* (*DSM-IV*), 1994. This new bible seems to medicalize the immoralities of the traditional "Seven Cardinal Sins"—pride, covetousness, lust, anger, gluttony, envy, and sloth. Most of these—at least in their most extreme forms—are now diseases. Today *pride* is merely a component of "narcissistic personality disorder" (pp. 658–61). *Covetousness* presently belongs to "conduct disorder" (pp. 85–91), "manic episode" (pp. 328–30), "kleptomania" (pp. 612–13), and "antisocial personality disorder" (pp. 645–50). *Lust* is no longer a character defect, at least in its heterosexual form; but lack of lust is! See "hyposexuality" (pp. 496–98), "sexual aversion disorder" (pp. 499–502), "male erectile disorder" (pp. 502–504), etc. Excluding homosexuality, deviant forms of lusting after the wrong objects are now disvalued, not as vices, but as illnesses. Consider "fetishism" (p. 526), "pedophilia" (pp. 527–28), and "zoophilia" (p. 532). *Anger* has become "intermittent explosive disorder" (pp. 609–12) or a prominent feature of "paranoid personality disorder" (pp. 634–38) and "borderline personality disorder" (pp. 650–54). *Gluttony* is now "binge eating disorder" (pp. 729–31). *Envy* is a conspicuous feature of "histrionic personality disorder" (pp. 655–58), "narcissistic personality disorder" (pp. 658–61), and "passive-aggressive personality disorder" (pp. 733–35). *Sloth* is assimilated into "dependent personality disorder" (pp. 665–69). Other moral vices, like cowardice ("avoidant personality disorder" [pp. 662–65] and "dependent personality disorder" [pp. 665–69]), intemperance, lying, bullying, gambling, drunkenness, and so on, have been medicalized in *DSM-IV.* But do they really belong within the ethicomedical model? Also, are some traditional virtues now so discredited that they are regarded as mental disorders? Have conscientiousness and responsibility become instances of "obsessive-compulsive disorder"? And is chastity now a variant of "sexual aversion disorder"?

To decide whether the medical model applies legitimately to "mental disorders" in general, or to particular psychopathological diagnoses, we must first analyze the medical model. The experts generally agree, but they disagree about some details. For example, Thomas Szasz would repudiate Robert Veatch's claim that all disease concepts (including the physical) are value-laden, while agreeing with his insistence on organicity; but their shared conviction that all real illnesses have purely physical "original entry" causes is surely mistaken. Many diseases have no magic moment of causal origination, and social and psychological stresses contribute significantly to the development of physical diseases like hypertension, coronary disease, ulcers, spastic colons, and some cancers.

Identifying Real Diseases

Can the medical model be used successfully to determine whether mental illness in general, and specific psychiatric diagnoses in particular, are real diseases, as Veatch and others propose? Try playing this game yourself. Use the following medical model outline (roughly as understood by Veatch) as a checklist for determining whether controversial diagnostic deviancies like alcoholism, homosexuality, and others, discussed in upcoming articles, are really medical in nature, or whether they belong more properly to other models of deviancy.

Antipsychiatrists contend that the medical model does not apply properly to the "mythical" concept of "mental illness" or to any particular diagnostic category of behavioral deviancy. Do all the features of the medical model outlined above survive careful critical scrutiny? A better understanding of physical and mental illnesses may indicate that the ethicomedical model applies legitimately to each. A viable ethicomedical model should provide criteria for differentiating between medical norms and moral, political, legal, social, religious, and other norms; and it should explain how to avoid confusing medical with nonmedical values. Try to make this work while reflecting on articles in this section that deal with problematic diagnostic categories like alcoholism, homosexuality, "self-defeating personality disorder," "premenstrual dysphoric disorder," and "delusional dominating personality disorder."

Most essays to follow are self-explanatory and self-contained, but a few words about some may be illuminating. Today's college-age students are often surprised to learn that alcoholism has not always been recognized as a disease, and that the medicalization of this moral problem in living is still rejected by serious critics like Herbert Fingarette, Stanton Peele, and many others. There were earlier anticipations; but the diseasing of inebriation, now heavily promoted by the medical establishment, began in earnest in the 1930s. In 1933, with the approval of both the American Medical Association and the American Psychiatric Association, the National Conference on Nomenclature of Disease issued *The Standard Classified Nomenclature of Disease*, which listed "alcoholic addiction" as a disease. Alcoholics Anonymous, founded in 1935, helped to popularize the view at a time when most Americans regarded drunkenness as a moral, not a medical, problem. During the 1950s, major medical organizations found it expedient to reaffirm the disease concept of alcoholism because so few people had accepted it. In 1951, the World Health Organization listed alcoholism as a disease; in 1952, the American Psychiatric Association included it in the first edition of its diagnostic manual; and in 1956, the disease concept of alcoholism was reaffirmed by the American Medical Association (Miller and Chappel, 1991).

	Alcoholism	Homosexuality	Self-Defeating Personality Disorder	Premenstrual Dysphoric Disorder	Delusional Dominating Personality Disorder	Other
The Medical Model affirms that:						
1. Disease is deviancy, i.e., aberrant or undesirable attributes that fall below a socially defined minimum of acceptability						

2. For which the "Sick Role" is assigned, consisting of:
A. Exemption from normal everyday responsibilities (duties)
B. Exemption from responsibility (blameworthiness) for one's condition, either:
  1. For *becoming or causing oneself to be* sick, or
  2. For *being* sick, which means that one cannot get well by an act of will, choice, or self-control; being sick is nonvoluntary
C. Having duties to:
  1. Want or try to get well, and
  2. Seek technically competent help						

3. Being sick is *organic or physical* in that:
A. The *symptoms* (fever, nausea, vomiting, diarrhea, elevated heart rate and blood pressure, etc.) are organic or physical
B. The *medical responses* (medicines, operations, devices) are physical (as opposed to psychological, social, etc.)
C. The *causes* are physical, both:
  1. The *proximal* (*immediate*) cause, and
  2. The *ultimate* (or *original entry*) cause						

4. The proper professional experts to manage these problems are *physicians*						

As Robert Wright will indicate in an upcoming article, we seem to have many misconceptions about alcoholism. Many of us believe that some people are genetically determined to become alcoholics; but, as critics of the disease model of alcoholism like Fingarette (1988) and Peele (1989) indicate, only 18 percent of male offspring with an alcoholic parent become alcoholics themselves (and 82 percent do not). Female offspring are even less vulnerable. A genetic predisposition is there, but it is very weak.

It is now widely believed that treatment programs like that offered by Alcoholics Anonymous and medical practitioners are very successful in helping alcoholics to quit drinking; but innumerable studies show that over the long run these programs have no more success than no treatment at all! True, some treated alcoholics quit; but the same percentage of untreated alcoholics also quit! Are the billions of dollars spent each year on treating alcoholics wasted if treatment is no more successful than spontaneous recovery? Most treatment programs provide strong and helpful social support and encouragement for the decision to quit, but in the end success consists in the heavy drinker's deciding not to drink again. The disease model of alcoholism involves the paradox that alcoholics are entitled to the sick role because they have lost control over their drinking; yet, cure, or at least alleviation, consists in their controlling it.

Alcoholism is not accepted as a disease by the Supreme Court of the United States. In 1988, after Wright's article was written, the Court issued its ruling in the *Traynor v. Turnage* case. Here, two drunken veterans who wanted to go back to school sobered up for it only after the ten-year limitation on their G.I. Bill educational benefits had expired. Existing regulations made allowances for delays by illnesses. The Court had to decide if the plaintiffs' prolonged inebriation was caused by the disease of "alcoholism," or if it resulted from "willful misconduct." The Court decided that it was willful misconduct.

Homosexuality was once a mental disorder, but is not now. In the first and second editions of the *DSM*, all forms of homosexuality were listed as disorders. The homosexual community protested vehemently that the American Psychiatric Association merely promoted a dubious moral stance, confused morality with medicine, and used the power and prestige of medicine to stigmatize homosexuals. In 1973, the APA agreed to eliminate homosexuality as a mental disorder; but when *DSM-III* was published in 1980 the task of demedicalizing was only partly accomplished. Ego-dystonic homosexuals, those miserable with themselves and their lifestyle, remained in *DSM-III*; but that also was eliminated when the revised edition, *DSM-III-R*, appeared in 1987. Yet, a slot for ego-dystonic homosexuals remains in *DSM-IV*, 1994, under diagnostic category "302.9 Sexual Disorder Not Otherwise Specified," which includes "Persistent and marked distress about sexual orientation" (p. 538). Does distress always indicate mental illness? Might not distressed homosexuals be simply responding to social rejection?

Another article in this section deals with feminist concerns about diagnostic discrimination against women.

The Medical Model: Its Nature and Problems

Robert M. Veatch

With few exceptions addiction to morphine and heroin should be regarded as a manifestation of a morbid state.

British Rolleston Committee, 1926

Addiction should be regarded as an expression of mental disorder, rather than a form of criminal behavior.

Brain Committee, 1961

. . . the addict should be regarded as a sick person . . . and not as a criminal, provided he does not resort to criminal acts.

Brain Committee, 1965

. . . according to the prevalent understanding of the words, crime is not a disease. Neither is it an illness, although I think it should be!

Karl Menninger, 1968

Ultimate policy control of the programs as well as day-by-day supervision must be securely lodged in *medical* rather than political, probation, parole, or police hands.

Consumer Union Report on Licit and Illicit Drugs, 1972

In sociological parlance, a model is a complex, integrated system of meaning used to view, interpret, and understand a part of reality; and one of the most deeply rooted such systems in our rationalistic and scientifically oriented Western society is the medical model. A pervasive and complex instrument for interpreting a wide range of behavior, the med-

---

From *Hastings Center Studies* 1 (1973): 59–76. Copyright © 1973 by the Hastings Center. Reprinted by permission.

ical model has served well as a means of organizing our attitudes and actions toward a variety of human abnormalities. In fact, it has served so well that attempts are continually being made to expand its boundaries to include forms of abnormal behavior which had previously been interpreted within other models.

Today an entire series of behaviors are doubtful candidates for the category of illness, that is, for interpretation in the medical model: narcotic addiction, mental deviancy, unwanted pregnancy, alcoholism, homosexuality, unwanted folds in the facial skin, and virtually all criminal behavior. At least some members of our society view all or some of these conditions as most meaningfully understood in the medical model, as part of the health-illness complex in some sense or another. Some generations ago, other forms of abnormality were in a similar position as dubious illnesses: tuberculosis, leprosy, epilepsy, psychosis from lead poisoning. The fact that we have a history of expanding the medical model to include an ever-widening circle of forms of human variant behavior previously interpreted as resulting from moral, religious, or political aberration is sometimes used as an argument from precedent, i.e., with further enlightenment (i.e., scientific understanding) we shall see how the presently ambiguous variant behaviors also fit into the medical model.

What, then, is the nature of the medical model, its basic elements, and its implications for society? Before outlining what I see as the basic characteristics of the medical model, however, we must first examine the nature of illness as one among many forms of socially constructed deviancy. Having done this, we can then consider what I see as four essential characteristics of the medical model. Finally, we shall conclude by exploring the implication of the medical and other models for marginal forms of deviancy.

Illness as a Socially Constructed Deviancy

THE SOCIAL CONSTRUCTION OF DEVIANCY

In the past two decades the sociology of medicine and the sociology of knowledge have together made great progress in gaining insight into the human interpretation of human behavior. Individuals who are ill, according to our ordinary understanding, are in possession of biological attributes seen as abnormal in some sense. While we are all familiar with concepts of psychogenic and psychosomatic illness, the man on the street normally conceives of illness as a biological aberration. Beginning, however, with Parsons' work in the 1950s, it became apparent that the process of being labeled as ill was much more complex. Illness is a socially assigned category given meaning from society to society by social interpretation and evaluation of the biologically abnormal characteristics. Thus Freidson argues that two kinds of imputed deviance figure in the notion of illness: biological and social.[1]

It is clear that biological aberration alone is not enough to make a person ill. The seven-foot-tall basketball player is hardly ill. He is admittedly grossly abnormal—and rewarded for it. Thus some kinds of biological aberration are deviant (both socially and biologically), yet positively evaluated. Still other kinds of biological deviance are not positively evaluated, but are not negatively valued either—sporadic dense pigmentation of the skin called "freckles," for instance. In the sociology of deviance, normally the term deviance is limited to negatively evaluated deviance. However, it is possible to possess a *negatively* evaluated attribute which is clearly biological in nature and still not have the condition interpreted in the medical model. In a racist society, for instance, which evaluates generally distributed black pigmentation negatively, possessors of that biological characteristic will encounter discrimination but are not considered sick.

All forms of deviancy have in common the fact that they are necessarily social constructions. Freidson argues, "Human, and therefore social, *evaluation of what is normal, proper, or desirable is as inherent in the notion of illness as it is in notions of morality*."[2] We should not lose sight of the fact that all understandings of reality are sociocultural constructions. Working with perceptual raw data, which are nothing more than an endless series of impressions, human beings, as members of social groups, construct categories and systems of meaning and value which make sense out of an otherwise meaningless stream of existence.[3] This is true even for such fundamental systems of meaning as the Western scientific world view. But it is more obviously true for the socially constructed patterns by which types of deviancy are evaluated and for the establishment of roles which organize the life of the deviant.

To claim that all understandings of reality are sociocultural is emphatically not the same as saying that all meanings and values are culturally relative. It is simply to say that *understandings* and *systems* of meaning which are used by human beings to interpret experience are necessarily products of a culture. Certainly language is a critical element in interpretation and understanding of experience, and language is a cultural construction. Likewise world views, underlying systems of meaning and value, are the products of a culture. But in making this claim we are purposely leaving open the question of whether there may be "in reality" values and meanings upon which our socioculturally constructed systems of understanding are based, and which could give rise to meaningful debate about whether or not such social constructions are "constructed properly."[4]

To have one's body invaded by bacterial organisms which produce fever, nausea, and vomiting is not the same as being sick. Animals quite ordinarily may have the former characteristics, but it is not until social interpretation is given to those characteristics that the affected one is "sick." To be sick is to have aberrant characteristics of a certain sort which society as a whole evaluates as being bad and for which that society assigns the sick role.[5] According to the Parsonian formulation, the sick role includes two exemptions from normal responsibilities and two obligations or new responsibilities.[6] First, the person in the sick role is exempt from normal social responsibilities. Second, the person in the sick role is exempt from responsibility for his condition and cannot be expected to get well by an act of decision or will; he cannot be expected to "pull himself together." The third characteristic of the sick role is that it is itself undesirable. There is an obligation to want to get well.[7] Finally, one in the sick role has an obligation to "seek technically competent help."

No matter how unusual, "unnatural," or even death-inducing a set of characteristics may afflict him, the individual is not "sick," and thus exhibiting behavior interpreted in the medical model, until a social judgment is made. Among other things, that social judgment must include a negative evaluation. That is true for any class of deviant behavior no matter what its origin.[8]

This critical point should not be lost throughout the remainder of this discussion. Even organic sickness in the most narrow and traditional sense as interpreted in the medical model necessarily contains a socially bestowed negative evaluation. Sedgwick and others are thus on the right track in attacking Szasz, Leifer, Goffman, and other critics of treating mental illness in the medical model, when they base their argument on the assumption that mental illness differs from organic illness. These critics claim that while organic illness refers to biological conditions which are objective and exist independent of any human value judgments, mental illness is a social, value-laden category.[9] I shall later disagree with Sedgwick's conclusion that because organic and mental illness share in common a socially constructed negative evaluation which is in either case a value judgment, mental deviation should, therefore, be classified as an illness. That shall be argued later, but at this level Sedgwick is certainly correct and reflects sound thinking in the sociology of knowledge and the sociology of medicine. If one refuses to place mental deviation in the same "illness" category as organic illness, it must be done on grounds other than that the former involves social value judgments and the latter supposedly does not.

THE DIFFERENTIATION OF SOCIAL DEVIANCES

Having identified all illness as a type within the broader category of social deviance, it is now important to differentiate it from other types and to trace the history of that differentiation and the study of it. Nowadays it is a commonplace to recognize that in an earlier age deviances were not well differentiated. The ill person, the criminal, the possessed, the religiously inspired were not well separated into different roles. Likewise the functionaries with special roles were not differentiated. In many societies, the medical practitioner, law enforcer, psychologist, and priest were combined in one role, that of the medicine man-priest. One of the primary characteristics of "higher" civilization, however, according to this school of functional analysis, is the differentiation of different functionary roles.

Talcott Parsons again has provided the definitive analysis of the differentiation of the medical model from other major forms of deviancy which he saw as important conceptual models in societies.[10] Parsons differentiated deviancies on two major axes.[11] First, he separated those deviancies which involve disturbances in commitments to norms and values (giving rise to the deviancies of crime and sin respectively) from those deviancies attributed to "the exigencies of the situation in which the person must act" (deviancies of disloyalty and illness). The second axis of differentiation separates those deviancies of the person as a whole from those which involve only a problem of accepting particular obligations. Disturbances of particular obligations (disloyalty and crime) are differentiated from disturbances of the total person (immorality and illness). When these two variables are crossed as the major axes of differentiation, illness is thus separated from immorality in being situational rather than normative in focus; from disloyalty by being a disturbance of the total person rather than of particular obligations; and from crime or illegality on both of the axes.

In less sophisticated analyses, the polarity is erroneously reduced to the extremes of crime and illness. For example, the title of an important study, formulating policy for two major relevant professional groups on the subject of drug addiction, poses the question—"Drug Addiction: Crime or Disease?"[12] It is little wonder that the authors had difficulty reaching a conclusion. Once again the origins of the study suggest that the *Sitz im Leben* may be important for the understanding of the theoretical categories for classifying negatively evaluated deviancies and the unique interests and perspectives of the professional groups in the debate. The study was conducted by the professional associations representing the cadres of experts in the two models posed as alternatives for interpretation of drug addiction: the American Bar Association and the American Medical Association. One wonders what the alternative models would have been if the study had been sponsored by associations of priests, behavioral psychologists, or sociologists.

For understanding the medical model and the disputes currently arising about doubtful illnesses such as narcotic addiction, it is crucial to realize the nature of the primary axes of major differentiations of types of deviancy. At the level of the Parsonian differentiation, if a deviance is to be seen as situational (rather than normative) and total (rather than particular), the only category available is "illness." Since one of the primary motives (functions) for classifying a doubtful illness as illness is to gain these characteristics, it may be that we are in need of more than one category with such characteristics, and that only failure to carry the analysis far enough has left but one appropriate category, that of illness. Much of the difficulty about classifying doubtful illnesses may rest here.

The task of model differentiation has been carried somewhat further by the work of Siegler and Osmond. Working with a series of questionable forms of negatively evaluated deviancies (schizophrenia, alcoholism, drug addiction) they have constructed a series of models of interpretation now numbering eight: the medical, moral, psychoanalytic, social, family interactional, impaired, psychedelic, and conspiratorial models.[13]

The classification of marijuana use may well rest at this level of debate. If it is the case that marijuana is relatively harmless to the physical health of the self and to others, it is still possible to argue that it is wrong to use it on the grounds that it would lead to a life style which is incompatible with the value system of those doing the disapproving. On the other hand, proponents of marijuana's legitimacy would simply reply by arguing that its use is consistent with a better set of values. Independent of whether a deviancy is included in the medical model, one must still deal with the social value judgment that the deviancy is evaluated negatively rather than positively. Thus it would be possible to have a deviancy which clearly fits the characteristics of the medical model and to still reject that this medical deviancy is negatively evaluated. For the use of drugs or any other deviant behavior to be a medical problem, the behavior must first of all be considered bad.

The Characteristics of the Medical Model

Having argued that the medical model is a systematic mode of interpretation of a type of social deviance and that it, therefore, incorporates negative evaluations of the deviancy, we must now move on to specify the characteristics of the medical model—those elements which differentiate this model from other models of interpretation of deviancy. It is our thesis that a negatively evaluated deviancy will be perceived as fitting the medical model to the extent it conforms to these characteristics.

We have identified four characteristics which seem to be essential. A deviancy will be placed within the medical model if it is seen as (a) nonvoluntary and (b) organic, if (c) the class of relevant, technically competent experts is physicians, and if (d) it falls below some socially defined minimal standard of acceptability. A negatively evaluated deviancy will be perceived as fitting the medical model to the extent that it conforms to these characteristics. Every example of negatively evaluated deviancy which is a doubtful illness and therefore only ambiguously included in the medical model can be shown, we believe, to be questioned on at least one of these grounds.

NONVOLUNTARINESS

Probably the most central characteristic of the medical model is incorporated in the second exemption from the sick role. As Parsons defined it, the person in the sick role is exempt from responsibility for his condition. A sinner or criminal or morally irresponsible person would be seen as deficient in character to the extent that he has brought on his condition; the person in the sick role is not. More significantly, one in the sick role is not expected to use willpower or self-control to overcome his condition. This is a crucial dimension of the medical model and one of the reasons for its attractiveness. The other major candidates for models of interpretation—especially the criminal, moral, and sinner models—normally suggest deficiency of the will of the deviant person. In the Parsonian major axes of differentiation, all of the other forms of deviancy are probably voluntary forms of deviancy. The one exception would be some interpretations of the sinner role, especially in a Calvinistic form of double predestination where, logically at least, the sinner is predestined to his sinner role by the decree of God and, therefore, is not responsible for his condition. Needless to say, the doctrine of double predestination is not very viable in contemporary society, and if an individual is to be considered nonculpable for his actions, another model of interpretation must be found.[14]

It seems clear that one of the primary functions of the medical model is to remove culpability. The attempt to place narcotic addiction, violence associated with rage, and larceny and assault by children into the medical model is in large part a move to remove blame by removing attribution of voluntary control of the action. We think there is sound empirical and moral reason for efforts to remove culpability from many forms of deviance. Nevertheless, there are serious problems in using the medical model to do this.

First, we believe it is reductionistic to force all forms of blameless deviance into the medical model. We have already seen that there are forms of nonculpable religious deviance for which the individual is in no way to be blamed. There are, at least at the theoretical level, many other types of nonvoluntary deviancy which should not be forced into the medical model. This will be discussed more fully in the next section.

Second, increasing scientific study of biology and medicine has jeopardized the notion of blamelessness for even some of the human conditions most traditionally classified in the medical model. Certainly a heart attack is partially preventable, and an individual who fails to watch diet, exercise, and standards for physical examination may be seen as blameworthy if he has a coronary. Exposure to bacteria may be willful, through failure to observe sanitary and inoculation precautions known or thought to be effective. A parent may be blamed and feel guilty if his child suffers an attack of a preventable disease. The elaborate precautions taken by parents of the previous generation to avoid contact with children with polio suggests the extremes to which traditional illnesses can be culpable. Even cancer is now subject to the norms of the "seven danger signals." Genetic counseling and screening is moving rapidly to make even genetic disease a culpable event albeit culpable at the parental level. This suggests that the notion of nonresponsibility in the sick role is in jeopardy although the assumption that one cannot get well by an act of the will alone certainly remains central to all of these illnesses. The medical model may be less functional for the removal of culpability in the future than it has been in the past.

Third, the *utility* of attributing nonculpability is most recently being challenged. Over the past century there has been increasing enlightenment about the implausibility and injustice in assigning blame to individuals who are quite possibly acting in a nonvoluntary manner. The medical model served this purpose well. Very recently, however, the virtue of culpability is being rediscovered, especially by radical groups of mental patients, minors, political radicals, and advocates of alternative life styles. They recognize that to place an individual in the medical model is to remove blame, but to remove blame is to remove responsibility, and to remove responsibility is to challenge the dignity of the individual and the validity of the values he claims to be acting upon. Removing culpability by means of the assumption that the act is nonvoluntary is thus not without its price. Those who place great significance on the values of diversity, autonomy, and individual freedom and dignity will accordingly be very cautious in assigning a deviant behavior to the medical model.[15]

This, of course, is a discussion of the functional status of the medical model in removing culpability. In the end, assigning a deviancy to the medical model or to models which imply voluntarism (and, therefore, praiseworthiness and blameworthiness for actions) depends at least in part on the ontological status of the concept of individual free will. The question of whether there really is such a thing as free will is one of the classic debates in philosophy and probably will not be resolved definitively in the near future. Those who opt (or are determined) for the deterministic interpretation of man's nature will be more inclined to the medical model, while those who are determined (or opt) for a position more supportive of the free will position will be more cautious.

It is important to realize, however, that Western society in general and the United States in particular is heavily committed to the voluntarist tradition. The victories of the political voluntarists combine with the victories of the Arminian and anti-predestinarian theological forces to make American society probably the most heavily committed to voluntarism of any society in history. This reality is manifested even in the Skinnerian claim that we must choose to use the correct conditioning techniques for the correct ends if our society is to survive in an age beyond freedom and dignity. Such an extreme commitment to voluntarism probably predisposes us to abandon the medical model in its classical form as scientific and technological breakthroughs rationalize and routinize illness. We may well be coming to the day when all illness will be divided into two classes: those blameworthy at the individual level when some individual preventive actions could have been taken and were not, and those blameworthy at the national level where the National Institutes of Health will be blamed for failure to develop scientific explanation and cure. This possible trend toward the decline of the medical model as an interpretation of deviance stands directly in opposition to Parsons' suggestion that American value predispositions to "activism," "instrumentalism," and "worldliness" lead us to place selectively high emphasis on the health-illness complex.[16]

I have argued that many questionable forms of deviancy may be brought into the medical model in order to remove culpability and imputation of blame by removing the attribution of voluntary choice. There are good functional and philosophical reasons, I believe, for continuing to hold that many of these forms of deviancy (narcotic addiction, alcoholism, other erratic behavior) really are based on an element of voluntary choice. Probably the man in the street is really not convinced that the alcoholic, the addict, the "criminal," are really acting from some drive or determining force independent of voluntary control. So long as that belief remains, it will be impossible to incorporate these deviancies into the medical model in any complete way. Let us now turn, however, to those deviancies which are assumed, according to the belief system of the society, to be nonvoluntary.

ORGANICITY

. . . While clear-cut traditional diseases are conceived of as somatic, all of the doubtful illnesses also are related in some way to a somatic component. I shall propose four different stages for subsystem analysis: the deviant behavior itself, the response (treatment), the proximal cause, and the ultimate cause.

(1) *Behavioral Stage.* Taking narcotic addiction as our model, we shall see that the confusion about organicity (and, therefore, about the appropriateness of the medical model) begins at the level of the deviant behavior itself. What is the behavior (symptom) which arouses our interest in narcotic addiction? On the one hand, there are clearly organic symptoms experienced by the addict in withdrawal—nausea, vomiting, dilated pupils, diarrhea, elevated heart rate and blood pressure—which are negatively evaluated. In this dimension narcotic addiction is not very different from invasion of an influenza virus. Yet narcotic addiction also produces psychological symptoms—euphoria, craving, feelings of dependency. Perhaps the social and cultural impact arouses the most interest, however. The narcotic addict's symptoms, albeit derivatively, include social impact which is economic and political and a life style (e.g., that of the stereotype opium den) which probably are the major worries of the public. Thus even at the behavioral level there is confusion about the subsystem classification. It appears, however, that some addicts, maintained on maintenance heroin, survive and behave quite normally. William Halsted, one of the four founders of Johns Hopkins School of Medicine and a practicing physician, continued to function effectively for roughly half a century as an addict.

(2) *Response Stage.* At another stage, that of response to the deviant behavior, narcotic addiction may also be classified as organic.[17] The addict may be maintained on maintenance doses or brought down on gradually declining doses of narcotics. He may have his behavior blocked by blocking agents such as N-allylnormorphine, or he may be conditioned away from his addiction using succinylcholine. The same may be said for alcoholism and nicotinism. But other forms of response are possible to these doubtful illnesses, including jail, social and psychological manipulation, preaching, moral exhortation, and peer group pressure. On the other hand, clearly nonsomatic forms of social deviancy can be controlled by the use of organic agents as a response, especially if one includes conditioning agents. I believe that organicity of the response, like organicity of the deviant behavior itself, should not be sufficient to classify the behavior within the medical model. A problem is created here because if the response is organic (a drug, a surgical procedure, or a physiologically acting device) it may require an "organicity expert" (a

physician) to administer the response. This necessarily brings the deviancy closer to the medical model, but physicians will be among the first to reject their functioning as societal control agents for types of deviant actors whom physicians classify as other than ill. The most dramatic example of the situation requiring an "organicity expert" for response, although the situation cannot be adequately interpreted in organic categories alone, is probably the abortion chosen because of, say, high parity and low socioeconomic status. The condition which is to be controlled (the pregnancy) and the method of response (dilation and curettage, saline injection, or hysterectomy) are clearly organic in every conceivable way. Yet it is only with the greatest effort (and then probably for pragmatic political purposes and not very effectively) that abortion for socioeconomic reasons is forced into the medical model.

(3) *Proximal Cause Stage.* The contrast between an abortion for socioeconomic reasons and one for "medical" reasons such as a cancerous uterus indicates the third stage of subsystem analysis. In the abortion for the cancerous uterus the cause of the "problem" is also organic. In narcotic addiction the cause of the deviant behavior may also be seen as organic. There certainly are organic changes in the body when one is addicted.

On the other hand, other theories of addiction deal with immediate causes of the behavior which are more psychological. The notion of "needle addiction" probably suggests a psychological causation model. We need to distinguish between the immediate causes of addiction, which are at least partially organic in character, from earlier causes. Let us use the terms proximal and ultimate causes.[18]

(4) *Ultimate Cause Stage.* Even if the proximal or immediate cause of addictive behavior is organic, which it may well be, it is still an open question whether the earlier or "ultimate" cause is organic. There are at least three addiction theories proposed today.[19] The psychological theories are based on the belief that there are "addiction-prone personalities." Through childhood or other personality structuring, the individual acquires a behavioral pattern which is served by addiction; the appropriate response would require restructuring of the psychological make-up of the addict. Sociological theories place causation in the surrounding environment of the addict. Racial, economic, and political conditions, according to this view, predispose the individual to addiction. A third theory of causation is biochemical. While holders of all theories are willing to concede that the proximal cause of addiction has a biochemical component, holders of the biochemical causation theory place organic chemical factors in a much more central place. One version of the theory holds that the morphine molecule causes physical changes which are permanently coded in the nervous system of the individual,

perhaps changes in the receptor site. This, however, from our perspective would still not be an ultimate biochemical causation theory. If, however, one were to argue that there are anatomical or biochemical predisposing factors which lead certain individuals to addiction—say by the presence of aberrant enzymes or biochemical ratios—then organic causation would be ultimate in the sense in which we are using the term. There are analogous causation theories for homosexuality and schizophrenia. Narcotic addiction is organic at the level of ultimate cause only according to the biochemical causation theory.

The confusion over the placing of narcotic addiction into the medical model on the dimension of organicity is thus seen. It is only ambiguously organic at each of the four stages of analysis: behavior, response, proximal, and ultimate cause. No wonder there is doubt about the appropriateness of the medical model.

Other "illnesses" also raise confusion about the dimension of organicity. A heart attack, for instance, is clearly organic or somatic at the level of the behavioral symptom which is the origin of concern. Likewise, the treatment may be primarily organic, as is the proximal cause. But at the stage of the ultimate cause, there is more doubt. Certainly social factors predispose to heart attack. The sedentary life or poor social patterns may increase risk, but then more narrowly organic factors might do so also.

Cystic fibrosis may be the prototypical organic disease. Its symptoms are somatic, as is the intervention with vasodilators and respiratory aids. The genetic origin, which is not clearly understood and not diagnosable prenatally, leads us to believe that the causation is somatic and little can be done to modify the disease process. At all four stages, it is plausible to believe that the somatic component dominates.

In contrast, alcoholism seems to be heavily somatic in its symptomatology, but the response may be organic (as in succinylcholine "therapy") or social (as with Alcoholics Anonymous). The immediate cause of the behavior of the alcoholic is clearly organic, and we know precisely what the chemical is; but an organic theory of an ultimate cause must share a place with psychological, social, and cultural level causal theories. Alcoholism's organic proximal cause, behavior, and possible treatment do not make alcoholism as clearly an organic disease as is the case of cystic fibrosis.

Homosexuality lends itself to organic interpretation primarily at the causal level with research on androsterone/estrogen ratios suggesting abnormal balances in homosexuals. Treatment, however, has tended to be psychological. It appears that the more clearly the deviance is associated with organicity at the four stages we have identified, the more neatly it fits the medical model.

The relationship between organicity and nonvoluntariness is important. There is quite clearly an association between a belief in organicity and nonvoluntariness. If behavior is "in the chemistry," we are convinced it is not in the control of the will. For the most part this association tends to be borne out, but there are enough instances where behavior which is clearly nonorganic at all four stages is nonculpable and, on the other hand, instances of behavior which is organic yet culpable, that the correlation is not perfect. When these inconsistencies arise, the appropriateness of the medical model is questioned.

The World Health Organization's definition of health as "complete physical, mental, and social well-being, and not merely the absence of disease or infirmity" is an innovative definition in which an attempt is made to stretch the concept of health and illness beyond the organic metaphorically to the nonorganic. Whether or not this reforming definition will lead to a change in the meaning of the term is not to be decided here. The reason for this move, however, is apparent. Proponents of this definition are attempting to gain the virtue of nonculpability for nonorganic forms of negatively evaluated deviancy as well as to mobilize the imperatives which have been associated with health and illness, i.e., the right to health and the obligation to give its attainment high priority. I believe there are great dangers in this expansionistic conception of health. Rather it seems preferable to make clear the missing categories—namely, nonculpable deviancy caused psychologically, socially, and culturally, for example, by the lack of various forms of psychological, social, and cultural welfare. The case can then be made that such psychological, social, or cultural support, too, is fundamental to man's existence, at least as fundamental as health in the somatic sense.

If it is the case that deviancies can be meaningfully differentiated as organic and nonorganic as well as voluntary and nonvoluntary, then we must disagree with Sedgwick in the conclusion he draws in his argument against Szasz, Laing, Goffman, and others. Earlier I indicated that Sedgwick was correct in his claim that both organic and mental deviancies require social evaluations. Merely establishing, however, that the two phenomena are not to be differentiated on *this* dimension does not establish the positive argument that therefore "mental illness *is* illness." Against Sedgwick, I would argue that even though they are the same in both being negatively evaluated social deviancies, they differ in that one is organic while the other is in the psychological realm. This, we shall argue, has important practical as well as theoretical implications.

Thus far, I have focussed on the primarily analytical argument, claiming that the medical model, at least in its original and pure form, applies to nonvoluntary and organic deviations from the norms established by a society. Let us now turn to the practical implications. By far the most important practical consequence of the limitation of the medical model refers to the professional cadre who will become involved depending upon the model employed. Before taking up that point in the next section of the paper, however, I wish to consider a question growing out of the alternative role models implied in the different subsystems.

In a theoretical discussion of types of roles, Lemert distinguishes between primary and secondary deviant roles.[20] This distinction, also reflected in Parsons' axis of differentiation between total and partial deviance, is between roles which totally reorganize one's life and roles which permit one to continue in other roles with minimal impact. Freidson applies this distinction to the medical model and argues that there are really different types of deviant roles in the health-illness complex.[21] Minor medical difficulties, of which the cold is the type case, produce only a primary role. The individual with a cold does not normally fully adopt the sick role with its new exemptions and responsibilities. On the other hand, the person with a major disease such as polio clearly adopts all of the characteristics of the role. The sick role, or at least the patient role, is thus a secondary role, while minor forms of deviancy in the medical model (a cold, a cut finger, a headache) generate only a new primary role actor.

Now the question arises if there is a precisely parallel pattern in deviancies which, according to our philosophy of causation, are best understood as nonorganic. There is no theoretical reason why that would be the case. There may well be something uniquely associated with organicity which would lead to the development of a secondary deviant role. The notions of contagion, the need for rest for bodily repair, the effectiveness of special technical instruments and procedures for "healing" the sick person may generate pressures to remove the (organically) sick individual from his normal roles in favor of the sick role which are far greater than for the nonorganically caused deviancy. People interpreted as being psychologically deviant may be more likely to continue in their normal primary roles. Those with deviancies thought to be socially caused are quickly put in the criminal role, but the role implies voluntary deviance in the social realm. The concept of nonvoluntary socially determined deviancy is a newer concept and one for which virtually no one is assigned a secondary role. To collapse the different subsystems may well have a serious impact on the development of primary and secondary deviant roles.

THE PHYSICIAN AS THE TECHNICALLY COMPETENT EXPERT

The third characteristic of the medical model is that the technically competent expert is the physician (often supported by a cadre of associates and assistants). The sick role includes an obligation to seek technically competent help appropriate to the need of the sickness. Parsons goes on specifically to state that the technically competent expert is "in the most usual case" the physician. This seems to be one of the most clearly established characteristics of the medical model. One of the important ideological implications of the sick role as Parsons states it is that in addition to removing the sick one from the realm of responsible actors it places him under the control of the medical professional.

The physician has authority; he gives "doctor's orders." More than this, the medical professional has first claim to jurisdiction in labeling of illness.[22] When a case is unambiguously within the medical model, it may well be appropriate for the medical professional to have the primary responsibility for labeling of a specific illness. Thus, when one has a small growth on the skin and wants to know whether it is cancer, a boil, or a normal bump, it is appropriate to turn to a physician. That, it seems to us, is where the authority must stop. It is not appropriate, for instance, for the medical professional to carry out the social evaluation of the badness or the goodness of the cancer (granted that the naming and diagnosing function of the physician must include telling the "seriousness" of the medical condition, the prognosis under various alternatives).

All too often, however, doubtful or ambiguous illnesses are placed into the medical model for the purpose of determining whether or not they are indeed illnesses rather than other forms of deviancy. This is fundamentally different from approaching a physician to determine whether or not a lump is a cancer. Let us grant that the experts in any form of deviancy, if they exist at all, have authority to diagnose the presence of deviancies which are clearly within their realm. But that does not mean that they have authority to arbitrate a dispute about whether an identified but marginal deviancy is within their model.

The British have been particularly guilty of this in the handling of narcotic addiction. In 1924 the British wanted to know whether narcotic addiction should be dealt with in the medical model or some alternative (the criminal being the most viable alternative). To resolve this they turned to the Rolleston Committee, a committee of distinguished physicians. It never seems to have been realized that precisely at that point was the decision made—by the public—to place narcotic addiction into the medical model. The conclusion of the group of physicians—that narcotic addiction was an illness—was anticlimactic and theoretically unsound.

If the question is to determine whether a deviancy is in one model or another, the methodology must involve, as a minimum, not only the acceptance of the deviancy by the experts of one model, but also the rejection of the deviancy by the experts of all the other relevant models. Thus, one might use the Siegler-Osmond list of models and insist that the opinion of functionaries in each model be obtained. Since the moral model has the entire public as the expert class, in effect it is the public which must make the decision to classify a deviancy within or without a model. Turning to the experts within the medical model for this function is a theoretically confused move.

The behavior under consideration is nonorganic, nonculpable, but negatively evaluated deviancies. The question is whether such types of behavior should be within the medical model. Recognizing that the medical model not only specifies the obligation to seek technically competent help, but also specifies that those experts are medical professionals, i.e., physicians, the implication is clear. Medically trained professionals are to be placed in control of such behavior and its correction if it is placed in the medical model. This seems to me both dangerous and unjustified in the light of the training and skills of such professionals. It is shocking to realize that, using the basic subsystems as differentiation points, the psychiatrist is the only professional in Western society who receives his primary training in one of the subsystems yet practices primarily in another.

The World Health Organization definition of health as encompassing total well-being means that, in effect, the medical professional is the one to turn to for technically competent help in such failures in well-being as marriage problems, poverty, and unanswered prayers. This will require either radical retraining and redefinition of the medical professional or, more practically, the development of clearer categories of deviant roles.

In the medical model the early generation of a secondary deviant role places the deviant (ill) one under the control of the medical professional and removes control from the layman. We should, therefore, be careful not to extend this removal of individual freedom and dignity into nonorganic forms of behavior too hastily. If the ratio of primary and secondary roles may be different in organic and nonorganic deviancy, it may well be that the creation of technically competent experts in these nonorganic realms may not follow the same patterns either. Perhaps we will be unable to produce such technically competent experts at all, or we may not be able to differentiate subspecialties in the same way. The expansion of the medical model to cover such categories could only be dangerous.

RESTORATION OF A MINIMAL STANDARD OF HEALTH

There is a fourth characteristic of the medical model, one which is probably the most difficult to grasp. I argued, in the first section of this paper, that even illness in the most traditional (i.e., nonculpable and organic) sense requires a social evaluation which is negative. The sick role is a socially disapproved, though legitimate, role. This is true by definition. One would not be sick but simply either unusual or super-healthy if he were abnormal in a manner which was not socially disapproved. We have purposely bracketed until now the question of the nature of the norm from which the deviant deviates in the medical model. Whatever it is, it is clear that the name for the norm is "health." Based on the previous discussion we would define health in a preliminary way as an organic condition of the body judged by the social system of meaning and value to be good.

Health, however, is an abstract norm, and abstractions in the human cultural symbol system function on at least two levels. On the one hand, in the abstract form, health exists as an ideal, a norm in the sense of being the highest or ideal type. Health in this meaning would be the organic condition of the body judged by the social system to be the best possible organic condition for a body. Abstract nouns also function in language to refer to some minimal standard, often, but not always, associated with a statistical mean or mode. In this sense, healthiness may be only a condition of the body judged by the social system of meaning and value to be better than a minimal standard. Thus, it is quite meaningful to say of two individuals that they are both healthy, but one is healthier. That statement would be impossible unless we could use the term in both senses simultaneously. "Healthy" refers simply to the minimal societal standard, but the "health" to which the word "healthier" refers is an ideal such that one individual approaches that ideal more closely. This dual function of abstract nouns in language is not unique to the concept health, but applies to all such abstract concepts.

In the medical model the most narrow reference seems to be to the minimal standard of healthiness. A deviancy fits most clearly in the medical model when it is perceived as falling below a minimal standard of healthiness. However, in the broader and more ambiguous sense, the problem of improving someone's health beyond the minimal standard to approach the ideal is only with difficulty assimilated to the medical model.

Our conceptualizations are frequently determined by the formulation of polarizations. Thus, the public health movement has posed the poles of restoring and preserving health. Both functions are clearly within the medical model in the more restricted sense. But this formulation often makes one lose sight completely of the possibility of an option to improve health beyond the normal. A number of somatic improvements are conceivable and perhaps technically feasible. They might include reduction of normal amounts of sleep needed, equipping the body to manufacture amino acids which now need to be obtained from animal protein, elimination of the menstrual cycle, and elimination of baldness. Would such activities be classed within the medical model? I think only with difficulty. They fit the medical model imperfectly and are analogous to other conditions which fit some, but not all, of the characteristics of the medical model.

While there is no necessary reason why medical practitioners should be limited to restoring and preserving minimal, socially defined standards of health, at least in Western medicine, the priority of these tasks seems well established. Even the normative principles of medical ethics reflect this orientation. At least according to one major strand of professional medical ethics, the primary moral principle is "first of all do no harm." This maxim differs in a significant way from classical utilitarianism even if it were applied solely with reference to the patient. The "don't harm rather than maximize the good" maxim is built on the same notion of a theoretical, socially defined minimal standard or baseline. It gives rise to a philosophical problem which we might call the "baseline problem." The idea of normalcy from which one can measure health and illness, benefit and harm, commission and omission of an act, ordinary and extraordinary means, or positive and negative incentives, is not well explored in the philosophical literature—and should be. In any case, it seems to have been incorporated into the medical as well as the legal and normative ethical tradition. An action is less ambiguously included in the medical model when it is an effort to restore or preserve that baseline of minimally accepted health rather than to improve health beyond that baseline to an ideal.

The Medical Model and Marginal Deviancies

In the last section of this paper, I traced what I see as four essential defining characteristics of the medical model. For a type of deviant behavior to be interpreted as falling clearly within the medical model, it must first of all be negatively evaluated. Then it must be seen as (1) nonvoluntary, (2) organic, (3) within the province of the medical professional, and (4) falling below some societally defined minimal standard of health. To the extent that the deviancy fits all of those characteristics, it will clearly be within the medical model. It is, however, when the behavior fails to meet one or more of these characteristics, or is called into question on one or more of them, that the medical model begins to seem less appropriate. The difficulty with such doubtful illnesses as narcotic addiction is thus apparent. For many, addiction remains a voluntary choice which sufficient willpower could overcome. The testimonies of former addicts about how difficult the habit was to overcome only support this view. For many, addiction is nonorganic at the stages of behavior, response (treatment), proximal or ultimate cause. In part because of these factors, these doubters may (but not necessarily will) reject the physician as the appropriate technical professional to respond to addiction. While addiction is clearly statistically aberrant, it may not always be considered below a minimal standard of health and may, especially in the case of marijuana, not be negatively evaluated as an alternative life style at all. With doubts at all of these levels, it is hardly surprising that narcotic addiction and similar deviancies are disputed in classification.

I believe that the bulk of the problem comes from reductionistic tendencies to polarize deviancy between the extremes of crime and illness and the use of the single category of illness to cover all nonvoluntary deviancy. If all of the variables mentioned in this paper were cross tabulated, 48 models would result (voluntary/nonvoluntary × organic/psychological/social/cultural × technical expert/no technical expertise × restoring health/preserving health/improving health). If differentiation within categories such as the social and cultural subsystems were included, the figure would be that much higher. I feel that the expansion of the medical model to cover the other models is dangerous when unique characteristics exist for the other models and treating such deviancies as unique entities would be more realistic.

Particularly interesting and troublesome will be the models which combine the assumed need for technically competent biomedical experts with the characteristics of the other three dimensions which tend away from the medical model. We have seen that in relation to each of the characteristics of the medical model, there may be conditions requiring medical expertise for the resolution of perceived problems which are not considered to be unambiguously within the medical model. The clearest example may arise on the subsystem dimension. There are (or at least theoretically may be) deviancies which are considered nonorganic in ultimate and proximal cause as well as in behavior, yet susceptible to chemical, surgical, or other medical "treatment" (response). We know, with a degree of certainty, that amygdalotomy will control violent behavior while we may not be certain that the "cause" of the behavior is somatic. We know chemical agents can condition avoidance of alcohol even if we are not sure the cause of alcoholism is biochemical. Likewise, we know that voluntarily induced somatic complaints are amenable to treatment by a physician. Recent discussion of hair implants has raised the question whether such procedures are sufficiently medical to justify tax deduction. This and other procedures may be medical in all senses except that they improve the bodily condition beyond societal standards of minimal acceptability. These cases will raise serious conflict for the medical professional as well as for the tax collector.

These ambiguous categories (voluntarily induced somatic complaint;

nonvoluntary, nonorganic complaint; and somatic complaint requiring extension beyond societal standards of minimal acceptability) are frequently labeled "elective" in contrast to "therapeutic" procedures. The term applies equally well to abortions for serious social reasons or "cosmetic" surgery which is considered beyond the minimal standards of physical health. These terms are terribly imprecise and probably misleading. In fact, in a country where free choice is valued, all medical procedures are elective for the patient (except in the case of incompetents where guardians elect medical treatments or, if necessary, courts will appoint a new guardian for the purposes of election). On the other hand, if "therapeutic" means simply "corrective" it might apply equally to nonsomatic as well as somatic complaints provided the fourth criterion of intervention necessary to produce a minimal standard established by society is met. It might be better to abandon these terms, recognizing instead that, increasingly, medically trained experts will be called upon to provide response to conditions which are not clearly in the medical model or are clearly not in the medical model. . . .

Notes

1. Eliot Freidson, *Profession of Medicine* (New York: Dodd, Mead, 1971), p. 211.

2. Ibid., p. 208. Italics in the original.

3. See Peter L. Berger and Thomas Luckmann, *The Social Construction of Reality* (Garden City, N.Y.: Doubleday, 1966).

4. In fact, it is our position that there are "absolute and objective" values and meanings upon which one may properly or improperly construct a sociocultural understanding, but to argue this point, just as to argue the point of whether or not there are in fact real physical objects in reality to which our natural scientific sense impressions should correspond, is to lead into the realm of metaphysics and theology. I have made such arguments elsewhere (*Hastings Center Studies* 1 [Number 1, 1973], pp. 50–65), but would claim that the present discussion is independent of these debates about the nature of the transcendent. For a similar position see Peter L. Berger, "Appendix II. Sociological and Theological Perspectives," in *The Sacred Canopy* (Garden City, N.Y.: Doubleday, 1967), pp. 179–88.

5. Of course, it may be, at least for a holder of the view that real values and meanings exist in the transcendent world of objectivity, that some individuals have characteristics which ought to be seen and treated by a society and yet are not—or, on the other hand, are seen and treated by society as sick but ought not to be. The fact is however that one really is sick in the sense of living the sick role if and only if the social judgment is made by society or some portion of it.

6. Talcott Parsons, *The Social System* (New York: The Free Press, 1951), pp. 428–79. This chapter is probably the most significant in (and the origin of) contemporary sociology of medicine. It grows out of an earlier field study of

medical practice conducted by Parsons. It is important to realize that not only sociology of medicine, but some important categories in theoretical sociology, especially the sociology of the professions and the sociology of deviance, grow out of this medical context. We would suspect that the use of the medical model as the paradigm for study of these more general issues has generated the expansionist tendencies for the medical model, the sick role and related theoretical constructs, the use of the model to cover all legitimated, nonculpable forms of deviancy, and the transfer of the obligation to seek technically competent help to the obligation to use medical personnel. Other sociological interpretations of illness as a form of legitimated deviancy can be found in David Mechanic, *Medical Sociology* (New York: The Free Press, 1968); Robert N. Wilson, *The Sociology of Health* (New York: Random House, 1970); Stanley H. King, "Social Psychological Factors in Illness," in Howard E. Freeman, Sol Levine, and Leo G. Reeder (eds.), *Handbook of Medical Sociology* (Englewood Cliffs, N.J.: Prentice-Hall, 1963), pp. 99–121, especially p. 112; and Robert N. Wilson, "Patient-Practitioner Relationships," in ibid., pp. 273–95, especially pp. 276–77.

In addition there are now several examples in the literature of authors who begin with the notion of illness as socially constructed deviancy and build this into a critical commentary on the incorporation of major forms of deviancy into the medical model. These include Erving Goffman, *Asylums* (Garden City, N.Y.: Doubleday, 1961); Thomas Szasz, *The Myth of Mental Illness* (New York: Harper & Row, 1961), and *The Manufacture of Madness* (New York: Harper & Row, 1970).

7. There is some disagreement about whether the person in the sick role has an obligation to "want" to get well or only to "try" to get well. Normally desires or wants are not obligated. Robert N. Wilson in *The Sociology of Health* (New York: Random House, 1970), p. 17, claims simply that there is "an obligation to 'get well' and to cooperate with others to this end." If, however, the sick role is by social definition undesirable, probably Parsons' formulation of the obligation to "want to get well" is appropriate. Parsons in "Definitions of Health and Illness in the Light of American Values and Social Structure," in E. G. Jaco (ed.), *Patients, Physicians and Illness* (New York: The Free Press, 1958), p. 176, says the sick person has an "obligation to try to 'get well.'"

8. Classifying illness as one among many types of socially defined deviant behavior which are disapproved does not mean that blame is imputed. The literature distinguishes between "legitimated" and "nonlegitimated" forms of social deviancy.

9. See the article by Peter Sedgwick in *Hasting Center Studies* 1 (1973): 3, reprinted in *Psychiatry and Ethics,* edited by Rem B. Edwards (Amherst, N.Y.: Prometheus Books, 1982), pp. 49–60.

10. Talcott Parsons, "Definitions of Health and Illness in the Light of American Values and Social Structure," pp. 165-87.

11. Ibid., p. 173.

12. *Drug Addiction: Crime or Disease?* Interim and Final Reports of the Joint Committee of the American Bar Association and the American Medical Association on Narcotic Drugs (Bloomington: Indiana University Press, 1961).

Antony Flew, *Crime or Disease?* (New York: Macmillan, 1973), creates the same polarization for the opposite motive in a discussion of the nature of mental disorder. He finds the removal of responsibility implied in the "disease" model a threat to individual dignity and is thus critical of its application to criminal behavior.

13. Miriam Siegler and Humphry Osmond, "Models of Madness," *British Journal of Psychiatry* 112 (1966), 1193–1203; "Models of Drug Addiction," *International Journal of Addictions* 3, no. 1 (1968): 3–24; and "The Impaired Model of Schizophrenia," *Schizophrenia* 1, no. 3 (1969): 192–202; and Miriam Siegler, Humphry Osmond, and S. Newell, "Models of Alcoholism," *Quarterly Journal of the Study of Alcoholism* 29, no. 3 (1968): 571–91. Unfortunately, the authors in this series do not devote much attention to the theoretical distinctions responsible for the differentiation of their interesting list of models.

14. We shall sometimes use the term nonculpable in place of nonvoluntaristic. Technically, however, an important difference should be noted. A deviancy such as marijuana smoking may be viewed as voluntary and yet nonculpable if one simply challenges the negative evaluation. Culpability thus implies simultaneously willful control and negative evaluation.

15. See Goffman, *Asylums,* pp. 153–54.

16. Parsons, "Health and Illness," pp. 178ff.

17. *Treatment* is a term which probably could be applied to this level, but in some contexts implies a medical model metaphor. This is possibly not always true—crops are treated with insecticide—but we prefer to use the more neutral term "response."

18. Ultimate is clearly a relative word. The Western notion of causation often implies an infinite regress. I, however, shall consider a cause ultimate at the level of the individual to be organic if the first entry into the human organism in the causation chain is organic.

The British Rolleston Committee documented its use of the distinction between organic and nonorganic causation models when it defined drug addiction as the use of a drug for purposes other than the relief of symptoms of an organic disease.

19. Edward M. Brecher and the Editors of Consumer Reports, *Licit and Illicit Drugs* (Boston: Little, Brown and Company, 1972), pp. 67–68, offers a brief summary.

20. Edwin Lemert, *Social Pathology* (New York: McGraw-Hill, 1964).

21. Freidson, *Profession of Medicine,* pp. 231–34.

22. See ibid., p. 251.

Alcohol and Free Will

Robert Wright

"He's a sick person," says Jane Wyman of Ray Milland. "It's as though there were something wrong with his heart or his lungs." The movie is *The Lost Weekend,* and Milland is Don Birnam, an aspiring writer whose potential is stifled only by his perennial willingness to pawn anything, including his typewriter, for enough money to drink himself unconscious. Wyman, Birnam's aspiring fiancée, is explaining why he deserves forgiveness and patience. It's not as though his disintegration were his fault, she's saying; the man has a disease.

The movie, released in 1945, could hardly have been better timed. For the previous ten years, Alcoholics Anonymous had been pushing the idea that alcoholism is a disease, and in 1946, about the time *The Lost Weekend* was winning a fistful of Academy Awards, the idea received the imprimatur of science with the publication of E. M. Jellinek's "Phases in the Drinking History of Alcoholics." Jellinek (who, perhaps not coincidentally, based his study on questionnaires designed and distributed by AA) found that alcoholism follows a roughly predictable pattern, from social drinking through various stages of excess, culminating in secret drinking, blackouts, and other symptoms. For the true alcoholic, Jellinek found, this grim cycle is virtually inexorable, and once he is in its grip, a single drink can destroy all self-control. Salvation lies in accepting that he has a disease—that he will never be able to drink like other people, and complete abstinence is his only alternative to a squalid, perhaps short, life.

With the help of AA (not to mention Jane Wyman), Jellinek's model

From *The New Republic,* Issue 3 (December 14, 1987): 804. Reprinted by permission of *The New Republic.* Copyright © 1987, The New Republic, Inc.

took root. Today a huge majority of Americans—and of the psychologists, physicians, and other therapists who treat alcoholics—consider alcoholism a disease.

Still, when this idea's implications are made explicit, the average citizen's enthusiasm for it may cool. Should the insurance premiums of teetotalers and moderate drinkers go to pay for other people's excesses, as they must in the numerous states whose legislatures have dictated that group health insurance cover alcoholism? Should Veterans Administration hospitals and Medicare, amid present fiscal pressures, spend tax dollars on people who can't stay off the bottle? And what is the import of the Federal Rehabilitation Act, which defines alcoholism as a handicap and prohibits federal agencies and federally subsidized institutions from discriminating against the handicapped?

On December 7 the Supreme Court is hearing the case of two reformed alcoholics who contend that the VA owes them an education because their drinking kept them from exhausting educational benefits within the ten years of military discharge normally allotted. They note that the VA grants extensions for mental or physical problems "not the result of . . . willful misconduct" and maintain that their drinking wasn't willful; they were victims of a disease. To withhold these benefits, they say, would be to discriminate against the handicapped. This may seem like a trivial matter, but there is a slippery slope here. In a federal appeals court in Philadelphia, a former Marine is suing to collect a VA disability pension on grounds that alcoholism renders him unemployable.

Assuming the Supreme Court doesn't duck the disease issue with a narrow ruling (an option left wide open by a tricky jurisdictional issue), the upshot of its decision will probably be either: (1) that alcoholism is indeed a disease, powerful enough to extinguish volition; or (2) that drinking, even for an alcoholic, is ultimately a choice freely made, the consequences of which the drinker must bear. Neither of these findings is in the interest of enlightenment. If the Court really wants to clear things up, it should dispense with the concepts of "disease" and of "willful" behavior altogether. The debate over alcoholism's essential nature is a prime example of how vestiges of the scientific and philosophical past can impair judicial reasoning and the making of public policy.

The rationale for considering alcoholism a disease has evolved since Jellinek's landmark paper. In the . . . book *Heavy Drinking,* a formidable critique of alcoholism as a disease, Herbert Fingarette, a philosopher at the University of California, Santa Barbara, shows that research in recent decades has painted a more complex picture than the common phrase "alcohol dependence syndrome" implies. Studies suggest that alcoholics do not, in fact, all follow the same route to dissolution, and that some can even learn to drink moderately; alcoholism, Fingarette argues, is not a single, binary condition whose course is predictable, but a grab bag of different kinds of problems.

In response, defenders of the disease concept say that there may be several kinds of disease under the rubric of alcoholism, just as there are various strains of flu. And, they add, some problem drinkers whose patterns diverge from the norm aren't "real" alcoholics anyway. Still, even as they dismiss Fingarette's criticisms, these people are also doing some strategic repositioning. They are staking their case less to the supposed clinical coherence of alcoholic behavior and more to fresh evidence of that behavior's biological underpinnings.

For instance, some people appear to be genetically predisposed to problem drinking. Alcoholics' children who are adopted by nonalcoholics are several times more likely to become alcoholic than the adopted children of nonalcoholic parents. And studies of identical twins reared apart also point to a genetic factor. Further, there are physiological abnormalities—in biochemistry, and in brain-wave patterns under certain laboratory conditions—that occur disproportionately in alcoholics. In fact, some occur disproportionately in the children of alcoholics, even children who have never had a drink. All of this, the argument goes, underscores the soundness of the disease label and the fallacy of blaming alcoholics for their problems. Since the biological deck is stacked against them, it is wrong, as one researcher at the National Council of Alcoholism put it, to label them "moral weaklings."

It is hard to attack this line of argument, because it is hard to discern it clearly in the first place. Some alcoholism-as-disease advocates talk as if the physiological correlates of alcoholism might be causes of the disease, whereas others seem to view them more as biological labels, identifying alcoholics as fundamentally different from the rest of us. To the extent that a unifying theme exists, it is the belief that the more "biological" a given behavior is, the less control the behaver has over it.

This belief does not exactly belong along the frontiers of modern thought. To talk as if some behaviors (the free-will kind) have a purely psychological basis while others (the disease kind) have a partly physiological basis is like distinguishing between election victories due to a candidate's popular support and victories due to the number of votes received. It is a basic, if usually unspoken, tenet of modern behavioral science that physiological and psychological processes are not alternative explanations of behavior but parallel explanations. We presume that all aspects of subjective experience—ideas, emotions, epiphanies, cravings— have physiological counterparts; that every behavior, while explicable in terms of thoughts and feelings, could also be explained as the result of a particular flow of neuronal, hormonal, and other biochemical information; that all behavior is in the deepest sense physically compelled. This is just an assumption, of course, but it is an assumption central to science, and research in neurology, psychology, and genetics has tended to substantiate it.

Indeed, so has the very fact that many alcoholics have a characteristic brain-wave pattern; they have characteristic patterns of behavior and sensation, so any good scientific materialist would suspect the existence of characteristic physiological patterns. Granted, if the physiological patterns were neater and cleaner than the behavioral patterns, then the alcoholism-as-disease crowd could take heart; if there were a physiological abnormality that all alcoholics and no nonalcoholics possessed, then the claim that alcoholism is a single, coherent syndrome would be in some measure strengthened. But so far the physiological evidence is fragmented, just like the behavioral evidence: some alcoholics have this unusual trait, others have that one, and others have none. And all of these physiological traits can be found, with less frequency, in the non-alcoholic population.

Alcoholism-as-disease proponents may think this sermon about the philosophy of behavioral science pedantic and beside the point. The point, they will say, is that the physiological correlates of alcoholism, like the alcoholic behaviors themselves, appear to be, in some cases, hereditary. Alcoholics, in other words, are born, not made. Strictly speaking, of course, this isn't true. To say that alcoholism has a heritable component is not to say that alcoholism is ever preordained by the genes. It is to say that some people who inherit alcoholics' genes have a genetic predisposition toward heavy drinking, that the range of circumstances that will lead to alcoholism is broader for them than for most people.

Now, it may be that this fact should deepen our compassion for alcoholics. But if it qualifies them as disease victims, and leaves them blameless for their behavior, then for the sake of consistency we are going to have to begin cutting down on the use of blame generally—and of credit. For there is now evidence that genes can similarly predispose people toward violent behavior, stellar intellectual achievement, and various other things. So should we consider violence a "disease" and exonerate murderers? Should we withhold praise from great mathematicians because their genes gave them a head start?

And these questions are just the beginning of the trouble. Science appears to be on the verge of perceiving a host of obscure connections between genes and behavior. Fingernail biting, reading pulp novels, altruism, entrepreneurship—thousands of such behaviors, some trivial and some consequential, may well turn out to vary according to genes. And even those behaviors not linked in this way will turn out to be under short-term physiological control, as the complex network of biochemical influences comes into focus. So if we are going to follow the alcoholism-as-disease logic, and equate genetic inclinations and physiological influences with the surrendering of volition, then we are going to have to give up on the concept of volition altogether. It is redundantly true that the more we understand about the mechanics of behavior, the more deterministic behavior will seem. (And it is worth noting that, notwithstanding the aversion of free-will aficionados to genetic explanations of behavior, it won't really matter whether the determinism appears to be mostly genetic or mostly environmental. When it comes to the question of free will, determinism is determinism is determinism.)

The alcoholism-as-disease advocates sometimes show encouraging signs of understanding all this, but they never seem to grasp its generality. In its friend-of-the-court brief in the Supreme Court case, the National Council of Alcoholism argues, "Whether any particular individual who drinks will become an alcoholic is largely the result of forces beyond his or her control. Extensive research has demonstrated that the disease of alcoholism is produced by a confluence of genetic/biochemical, environmental, and sociocultural factors." Can anyone think of a behavior that doesn't fit that description?

My point is not that we should abandon the concepts of blame and credit. Whatever science seems to say about the deterministic nature of human behavior, the inescapable fact is that no society can function well without holding people responsible for their actions. This is one of life's four or five great ironies: we are all victims of (or beneficiaries of) an extremely complex conspiracy between our genes and our environment, yet all of us must be held accountable for the results; otherwise, things fall apart. So, as the march of science yields more and more evidence that people are basically machines, we are going to have to get used to the idea of blaming robots for their malfunctions. It feels strange at first, but you get used to it after a while.

There are those who concede that the disease conception of alcoholism doesn't withstand scientific or philosophical scrutiny yet insist on preserving it as a "useful fiction." They say that (*a*) by absolving alcoholics of blame, this fiction keeps them from being saddled with "irrational guilt feelings," and (*b*) the word "disease" underscores the importance of abstinence. The obvious responses are: (*a*) What's so irrational about feeling guilty when you're flushing your life down the toilet and bringing your family along for the ride? For every alcoholic who is immobilized by guilt, there are probably several who use the "disease" idea to insulate themselves from the guilt that might otherwise incite a recovery; (*b*) People have been known to abstain completely from things—coffee, for example—without first concluding that they had a disease. AA could drop the word "disease" without appreciably altering its prescription for recovery.

Perhaps the most common "useful fiction" argument is that the disease conception of alcoholism keeps the treatment funds (now totaling an estimated $1 billion a year) flowing—from the government, from health insurance companies, from paternalistic corporations. Of course, the people most vociferously advancing this argument pay their rent with these funds, thus casting some doubt on their objectivity. Moreover, in *Heavy Drinking,* Fingarette shows that the efficacy of treatment programs remains unclear; because many treatment centers deal with precisely those patients who are most likely to recover on their own—the affluent, employed, and well-educated—seemingly impressive recovery statistics often mean less than meets the eye.

None of this is to say that corporations and insurance companies should stop pouring money into alcoholism treatment, or that alcoholic veterans shouldn't receive free therapy. Perhaps objective analysis—that is, analysis performed by someone other than the treatment industry's hired guns—would show that, given the costs and the benefits, it's often cheaper in the long run to subsidize certain kinds of treatment. (And certainly a socially inexpensive effort like AA is worth the trouble.) But this analysis shouldn't be short-circuited by the groundless presupposition that alcoholism is a disease in the sense that cancer is or a handicap in the sense that blindness is.

The treatment-industry spokesmen who are always waving around those suspiciously large estimates of the societal costs of untreated alcoholism like to maintain that they're not trying to tug at anyone's heartstrings. "We're talking dollars and cents," the director of the National Association of Addiction Treatment Providers told me. "We want to get beyond the compassion issue." Well, fine; let's get beyond it. The first step is to quit using the word "disease"—which, all told, is just a crutch.

Homosexuality

Richard C. Friedman
and Jennifer I. Downey

The deletion of homosexuality from the *Diagnostic and Statistical Manual* of the American Psychiatric Association in 1980 marked a dramatic reversal of the judgment that homosexuality is a behavioral disorder. In the practice of medicine, especially psychiatry, it is important to distinguish between that which is abnormal and that which is not.[1] Reviewing the present state of knowledge about homosexuality is of interest not only for medical and historical reasons, but also because of the central role of this sexual orientation in the adaptive psychological functioning of countless people.

The studies reviewed here are largely studies of white, middle-class people. Space does not allow for a discussion of cultural and ethnic diversity with regard to sexual orientation.[2]

Definitions

The term *homosexual* entered common usage in 1869.[3] The word *gay*, used to signify "homosexual," took on that meaning over the past 25 years in the context of the gay-rights movement. In common parlance, *gay* refers to males and sometimes to females, whereas *lesbian* is reserved exclusively for females. *Sexual fantasy*, in contrast to *sexual activity*, refers to private psychological imagery associated with feelings that are explicitly erotic or lustful and with physiologic responses of sexual arousal. The term *sexual orientation* refers to a person's potential to

From *The New England Journal of Medicine* 331 (1994): 923–30. Reprinted by permission of *The New England Journal of Medicine*. Copyright © 1994, Massachusetts Medical Society.

respond with sexual excitement to persons of the same sex, the opposite sex, or both. *Ego identity* refers to the sense of connection between a person and a particular social group whose values that person shares. Identity is formed during adolescence and early adulthood from experiences earlier in development.[4] The sense of being gay or lesbian is a facet of ego identity.[5] It may be entirely private, or it may be communicated to others, in which case it becomes part of one's social role.

Sexual Behavior

About half a century ago, Kinsey et al. collected sexual histories from thousands of Americans who, though diverse, were not a representative sample of the general population.[6, 7] Kinsey reported that 8 percent of men and 4 percent of women were exclusively homosexual for a period of at least three years during adulthood. Four percent of men and 2 percent of women were exclusively homosexual after adolescence. Thirty-seven percent of men and 20 percent of women reported at least one homosexual experience that resulted in orgasm.[6, 7]

Subsequent studies of subjects more representative of the general population have yielded lower estimates of homosexual behavior.[8, 9] Fay et al. compared data obtained from national surveys of male sexual behavior carried out in 1970 and 1988 with the data originally collected by Kinsey. In 1970, according to Fay et al., 20 percent of men had had at least one homosexual experience resulting in orgasm but only 7 percent had had such experiences after the age of 19.[10] Only 3 percent of the adult male population studied had homosexual contacts either occasionally or more often. In both the 1970 and in 1988 studies, the proportion of men with homosexual contact during the preceding year was approximately 2 percent.[10] In a recent review of studies conducted in the United States on sexual behavior, Seidman and Rieder estimated that 2 percent of men are currently exclusively homosexual and that an additional 3 percent are bisexual.[11]

Data on the current prevalence of homosexual behavior among women are scant. In a review of the literature on male and female homosexuality and bisexuality throughout the world, however, Diamond concluded that approximately 6 percent of men and 3 percent of women have engaged in same-sex behavior since adolescence.[12]

Homosexuality may be underreported because of social prejudice. Also, many homosexually arousable women may be included in the population reported as heterosexual, since women may engage in sexual intercourse without sexual arousal. Studies that assess the frequency of intercourse but not sexual fantasy may therefore be misleading in this regard.

By the age of 18 or 19 years, three quarters of American youth, regardless of their sexual orientation, have had sexual relations with another person.[11] Gay males are more likely than heterosexual males to become sexually active at a younger age (12.7 vs. 15.7 years) and to have had multiple sexual partners. The ages at the time of the first sexual experience with another person are closer for lesbians and heterosexual females (15.4 vs. 16.2 years).[13]

Of heterosexually active adults in the general population, about 20 percent of men have had 1 sexual partner during their lives, 55 percent have had up to 20 partners, and about 25 percent have had 20 or more partners.[11] Some older studies conducted before the epidemic of the acquired immunodeficiency syndrome (AIDS) indicated that homosexual men were more likely than heterosexual men to have had a very large number of sexual partners.[14] More recent population-based studies have found this to be relatively uncommon. For instance, Fay et al.[10] found that of men who had homosexual contact after the age of 20, almost all had 20 or fewer homosexual partners in their lifetimes. Of 1450 men in the sample, only 2 were reported to have had 100 or more same-sex partners.[10] The inconsistency in the data on the number of sexual partners of homosexual men probably reflects flaws in the sampling techniques of the earlier studies (e.g., recruiting subjects in gay bars) and their completion before the human immunodeficiency virus (HIV) epidemic. The overlap between gay and heterosexual men with respect to the number of partners is considerable, although a small subgroup of gay men have had sex with a great many more partners than almost any heterosexual men. Women have been studied less than men, but the existing data show that lesbians resemble heterosexual women more than gay men in their sexual behavior.[15] For instance, women of any sexual orientation are more likely to view sexual desire as a function of emotional intimacy and to value romantic love and monogamy. Almost all married women are sexually active only with their husbands, and unmarried women are very unlikely to have more than one partner in a given three-month period.[11] Blumstein and Schwartz reported that women in lesbian couples had fewer outside partners than women in heterosexual couples. Lesbian couples generally have less sexual activity than their heterosexual counterparts but report higher levels of intimacy and as much or more satisfaction with the sexual relationship.[16]

A substantial minority of adults in the United States abstain from sex, regardless of sexual orientation. In one study, 13 percent of homosexual and bisexual men reported having no sexual partner in the previous year, and in another, 43 percent of lesbians had been abstinent for a year or more.[17,18] Among unmarried heterosexual adults, women are also more likely to be abstinent than men.[11]

Diverse sexual practices occur in different groups regardless of sexual orientation, although with variable frequency. Thus, recent studies suggest that the majority (over 75 percent) of heterosexual and homosexual adults in the United States engage in oral-genital sex.[9, 16] Homosexual couples may do so more frequently, however. Kanouse et al. reported that about 55 percent of homosexual men and 26 percent of heterosexual men and women had engaged in oral sex in the month before the survey.[17, 19]

Although anal sex is practiced by 10 percent of heterosexual couples at least occasionally,[11] male homosexual couples engage in it more frequently. A recent study in Los Angeles reported episodes of anal sex in the four weeks before the survey to be six times more frequent among homosexual men than among heterosexual men studied at the same time.[16, 17, 19]

The high risk of contracting infection with HIV among homosexual men is usually attributed to contact with semen during unprotected receptive anal intercourse or other practices associated with the exchange of body fluids. Efforts to educate gay men in safe-sex practices to prevent HIV infection have been only partially effective in changing behavior.[20] Those who continue to engage in unprotective anal intercourse with multiple partners tend to be younger, to belong to minority groups, or engage in sexual acts more frequently, to use drugs or alcohol in connection with sex, to have psychiatric disorders, and if previously tested for HIV, to be seronegative.[21, 22] Such men have adequate cognitive information about HIV transmission but may entertain a false notion that they personally are "safe" when they engage in high-risk sexual behavior. Lapses in safe-sex precautions by men who ordinarily do practice safe sex are also common—in 45 percent over the previous six months in one study.[23]

A small number of lesbians have been reported to be HIV-positive, almost always as a result of exposure to risk factors other than contact with a partner of the same sex.[24] However, since vaginal secretions and menstrual blood are known to be implicated in female-to-male transmission of the virus, lesbians in relationships with seropositive women or who have multiple partners, including men or women of unknown HIV status, are routinely advised to use safe-sex practices. Nonetheless, no medically tested strategy for women to avoid contact with body fluids of same-sex partners has been developed that adequately addresses the particular issues presented by female anatomy and physiology.

Homosexual males have an increased risk of a variety of sexually transmitted diseases other than HIV infection. These include gonorrhea, syphilis, and human papillomavirus infection, as well as hepatitis B.[25, 26] Perianal carcinomas also occur more frequently in this group.[27] Lesbians do not have a higher risk of any sexually transmitted diseases than heterosexual women.[28]

Homophobia

The term *homophobia* was coined in 1967 to signify an irrationally negative attitude toward homosexual people.[29] In the United States, two particularly prominent influences fostering antihomosexual attitudes have been religious fundamentalism and heterosexualism, the belief in the moral superiority of institutions and practices associated with heterosexuality.[30]

A widespread tendency to view homosexuality as a stigma and to depict homosexual people in terms of negative stereotypes has only very recently begun to lessen. A majority of respondents to a national poll in 1987 indicated that they would prefer not to work around homosexual people.[31] Studies of homophobic people indicate that they are likely to be authoritarian, conservative, and religious; to have resided in areas where negative attitudes toward homosexuals are viewed as normal; and not to have had personal contact with gay or lesbian people.[32] Most gay and lesbian people have been harassed or threatened because of their sexual orientation, and a sizable minority have been assaulted.[33] Many negative beliefs about homosexual people are similar to those associated with other prejudices, such as racism.[31, 34]

In some respects, however, irrationally negative attitudes toward homosexual people are different from other forms of prejudice. For example, a young gay or lesbian person may grow up passing as heterosexual in an environment in which his or her family and friends are all heterosexual and homophobic. A recent national survey of gay men and lesbians revealed that the average time between a person's recognition of his or her own sexual orientation and its disclosure to someone else was more than four years.[35] Many gay and lesbian people never reveal their sexual orientation, even to family members.[35, 37]

Antihomosexual attitudes are prominent in many sectors of the American medical community, and numerous physicians find it necessary to hide their sexual orientation from colleagues and patients. There are no accurate data on the frequency of such "closeting," but it is undoubtedly common.[38] Homophobic attitudes have been reported among physicians, medical students, nurses, social workers, and mental health practitioners.[39-45]

It is likely that many students enter professional schools with antihomosexual values that go unchallenged during their education. A recent survey of American medical schools, for example, found that on average only three and a half hours were devoted to the topic of homosexuality during the four-year curriculum.[46] This is notable, since there is evidence that experience with gay and lesbian faculty members and participation in educational activities such as small-group discussions may influence students to develop more favorable attitudes toward homosexual people.[47]

AIDS

By December 1993, the number of cases of AIDS diagnosed in adolescents and adults in the United States totaled 355,936. Among the 311,578 men with AIDS, 62 percent had as their primary risk factor sex with other men, whereas only 2 percent contracted AIDS from heterosexual activity. Women accounted for a much smaller number of AIDS cases (44,357). When AIDS in women was related to sexual activity, it was most often associated with heterosexual contact with an HIV-positive man (35 percent of cases).[48]

Like the deadliest epidemics and wars, the AIDS crisis affects all members of society, not just those immediately at risk. Although it is not confined to homosexual men, the epidemic has increased their degree of stigmatization. Lesbians are at no increased risk of AIDS, but they are also stigmatized, because the public often wrongly assumes that all homosexual people are at high risk. Gay patients with AIDS are exposed to antihomosexual bias from employers, social services agencies, insurance carriers, and health care providers. Because of bias and fear of contagion, some persons and organizations may be reluctant to provide entitlements or carry out indicated medical procedures.

Undergoing a serologic test for HIV is often deeply frightening. Despite this, rates of psychiatric symptoms and syndromes have not been shown to be generally increased among HIV-positive patients as compared with those who are HIV-negative. Vulnerable subgroups, however, may have psychiatric symptoms and disorders, triggered by HIV testing or other vicissitudes of HIV infection. HIV itself and the opportunistic infections and cancers associated with it may directly cause a variety of neurologic syndromes (e.g., AIDS encephalopathy) that affect cognition, motivation, social judgment, and mood.[49-51]

Homophobia and the tendency to stigmatize the chronically ill may lead to deleterious social isolation by influencing those in the patient's support system to shun him or her. When internalized, these attitudes may motivate the HIV-positive to avoid others. That person must decide whom to tell and may again experience conflicts about coming out as a gay person. The nuclear family sometimes first learns that a person was HIV-positive or even that the person was gay when they are notified of his or her death.

Seropositive gay patients are likely to live in a community of the bereaved.[52] In the AIDS epidemic, many people endure serial losses. Those who have lost lovers often try to establish intimate sexual relationships with others while they are still grieving. The new partners may also be seropositive. HIV-positive partners who become involved with each other when both are asymptomatic experience mutual apprehension about when one or both will become ill. An HIV-positive person who has an HIV-negative partner often fears that he or she will infect the partner, and this fear may be reciprocated. The vitality of a sexual relationship can be compromised by the constant vigilance needed to engage in sexual practices that are reasonably safe.

People who die of AIDS are often cared for by their lovers, and the strain placed on intimate and sexual relationships is substantial. Losing the sexual dimension of a partnership may be associated with shame at the loss of bodily functions, attractiveness, and sexual interest. The partner who remains well must sometimes cope with choices regarding celibacy or infidelity in situations in which the sexual activity of the couple is curtailed. There is no specific social niche for lovers, as there is for husbands and wives. For example, there is no English word comparable to "widower" for one who has survived the loss of a same-sex lover.

Many of these issues also pertain to bisexual men, particularly those who present themselves as heterosexual while they are secretly involved with other men. A wife's first awareness that her husband has been homosexually active may come when she learns that he is HIV-positive or has AIDS.

One study showed an increased frequency of completed suicide among homosexual men with AIDS.[53] Studies of suicidality in patients with AIDS and those tested for HIV have not found an increased incidence, however.[49, 50] The population at risk for suicide seems to be composed of those whose history and psychiatric status had already increased their risk of suicide before the development of AIDS. The complex topic of rational suicide is beyond the scope of this article.

Helpful medical and psychological interventions for seropositive people and their affected family members and friends include self-help groups, counseling and psychotherapy, and pharmacotherapy. For many, coping with being HIV-positive includes maintaining involvement in life's activities, connectedness to others, and hope.[49-51]

Psychopathologic Issues

Independent studies with diverse designs have failed to find any increased frequency of various forms of psychopathology among homosexual people as compared with heterosexual people.[54] If identifying data on projective tests are deleted, it is impossible to distinguish homosexual from heterosexual people.[55] This finding is compatible with clinical reports that emphasize similarities in psychodynamic motivations despite differences in sexual orientation.[56, 57] Studies testing the hypothesis that homosexual people have phobic anxiety about heterosexuality have had negative results.[58] Research on specific disorders, such as sexual abuse of children, has not revealed an increased frequency of homosexual perpetrators.[59] These data, in conjunction with research on the family, have invalidated the once popular idea that castrating mothers and detached or hostile fathers are necessary and sufficient causes of male homosexuality.[60] The origins of sexual orientation appear to be multifactorial and diverse.[57]

INTERNALIZED HOMOPHOBIA

Developmental issues pertaining to sexual orientation are somewhat different in the two sexes. Usually boys follow an orderly sequence in which sexual feelings occur during childhood, followed by masturbation with sexual fantasies during early adolescence, sexual activity with others in mid to late adolescence, and a sense of identity as heterosexual, homosexual, or (in rare cases) bisexual during late adolescence or early adulthood.[60] Those who are on a developmental path toward predominant or exclusive homosexuality often feel homosexual attraction during childhood even though they may never have met a homosexual person and do not actually know what homosexuality is. The developmental pathways leading to a homosexual orientation are more varied in girls and women, although in one subgroup the pathway is similar to that described for boys and men.[61]

Gay adults often describe themselves as having felt "different" from other children.[56] The factors leading to a sense of difference are diverse and include both homosexual feelings and cross-gender interests and traits. In boys these tend to be aesthetic and intellectual; in girls, they are athletic. Beginning in childhood, many gay and lesbian people have feelings of shame at being considered deviant, as well as feelings of self-hatred because they identify with those who devalue them.[36, 62] Such feelings arise from identification with the aggressor, a mental mechanism experienced by many victims of abuse.

Many gay and lesbian people have had painful childhoods. Perhaps for this reason, lifetime rates of major depression and abuse of or dependence on alcohol and other drugs have been reported to be increased among homosexual men, although their current rates of psychiatric disorders are not.[63, 64] The disparity between the current and the past incidence of psychopathology awaits explanation. One hypothesis is that homosexual men ultimately develop effective ways of coping with stressors.

SUICIDE AND GAY YOUTH

Three psychological postmortem studies conducted in different areas of the United States have not demonstrated an increased frequency of people identified as homosexual among those who committed suicide. On the other hand, some studies of youths who have attempted suicide have revealed a disproportionately high number of homosexual persons.[65-69] In a study of 137 homosexual youths Remafedi et al. found that 41 had attempted suicide.[70] More than half the attempts were of moderate-to-severe lethality and involved inaccessibility to rescue—variables associated with completed suicide. The literature suggests that conflicts about the disclosure of sexual orientation (coming out) may influence young people to attempt suicide if they are otherwise predisposed. Many of those who attempt suicide have not yet disclosed their sexual orientation to anyone. Some people who have committed suicide and have not been identified as homosexual may have taken their lives because of conflict about a homosexual orientation that had been hidden from others.

Suicide attempts in all young people, regardless of sexual orientation, are associated with a common set of predisposing influences. Among vulnerable gay and lesbian young people, the physician should be particularly sensitive to self-hatred arising in response to homosexual feelings, conflicts about coming out, and homophobia among those in the patient's social support system.[35, 36] A dysfunctional family often scapegoats a young person who is identified as unacceptable and attempts to recruit medical authorities to make that person conform to the family's norms.

ALCOHOLISM AND SUBSTANCE ABUSE

An increased frequency of alcoholism among lesbians as compared with heterosexual women has been reported in some studies.[63, 71] Some researchers have reported a trend toward an increase in alcoholism or problem drinking among homosexual men.[63, 72, 73] The use of illicit drugs, at least occasionally, has also been reported to be more frequent among homosexual women than among heterosexual women, and a similar trend has been observed among men.[63] Because such data are sparse and studies have been confounded by the inclusion of subjects recruited in gay bars, it is impossible at this time to reach definitive conclusions about the frequencies of alcoholism and substance abuse in relation to sexual orientation.

Normal Development in Homosexuals

By the time of adolescence, some people's erotic feelings and attractions are predominantly or exclusively homosexual. The American Academy of Pediatrics has developed guidelines for physicians treating such patients.[37, 74] Ideally, complex developmental processes culminate in positive gay or lesbian identity and self-acceptance.[5] Although gay and lesbian groups are diverse and no single developmental line can summarize developmental issues, pathways leading to durable, loving sexual partnerships are common among lesbians and gay men.[16, 75, 76]

Confusion about sexual orientation is common during adolescence, however, and most adolescents who participate in homosexual activity or have homosexual feelings do not become gay or lesbian adults. Careful history taking often makes it possible to identify patients with predominant or exclusive homosexual responsivity and to support those who need assistance in establishing a gay identity. These patients must be distinguished from the many others who are confused by concurrent homosexual and heterosexual feelings. Here, the physician can often assist the patient in avoiding the premature foreclosure of homosexual or heterosexual identity until further development has occurred.

A sizable minority of lesbians and gay men are married, or once were,[77, 78] and many are parents. Conservative estimates exceed 1 million each for lesbian mothers[79, 80] and gay fathers.[80, 81] At least 6 million children have gay or lesbian parents.[80, 82] The literature on children of lesbian mothers indicates no adverse effects of a homosexual orientation, as evidenced by psychiatric symptoms, peer relationships, and overall functioning of the offspring.[79, 83-85] The frequency of a homosexual orientation has not been greater in such children than in children of heterosexual mothers. The data on children of gay fathers are more scant. No evidence has emerged, however, to indicate an adverse effect of sexual orientation on the quality of fathering.[80, 86] Enough information has accumulated to warrant the recommendation that sexual orientation should not in itself be the basis for psychiatric and legal decisions about parenting or planned parenting.

Ever-increasing numbers of homosexual persons and couples are requesting medical assistance in achieving parenthood through new reproductive techniques, including the donation of gametes (both egg and sperm) and the use of gestational surrogates. The data reviewed above support the judgment that medical decisions about the use of such techniques should not be based on sexual orientation alone.

Change in Sexual Orientation

Most people who seek to alter their sexual orientation consider themselves homosexual and wish to become heterosexual. Studies of changes in sexual orientation have varied in quality, and there are no adequate long-term outcome data. Many men who view themselves as homosexual have actually been attracted to women at some time during their lives. In this group, the homosexual-heterosexual mental balance may sometimes shift during therapy. The meaning attributed to sexual fantasies in determining the sense of identify may also change, so that the person may come to believe that his or her sexual orientation has changed. Homosexual fantasies often persist, however, or recur. Among homosexual men who have never experienced sexual attraction to women, there is little evidence that permanent replacement of homosexual fantasies by heterosexual ones is possible.[87-93]

The data on women, though extremely sparse, suggest that there is more variation with respect to the plasticity of sexual fantasies than with men.[61, 94] Many women seem to be able to experience bisexual fantasies or to participate in bisexual activity without necessarily constructing an identity or a social role as bisexual or lesbian. A subgroup has been described, however, whose pattern of psychosexual development is similar to that of many men. In these women, exclusively homosexual fantasies have been present since childhood, and their total replacement by heterosexual fantasies is unlikely.[61]

Patients who seek a change in their sexual orientation are diverse with respect to sexual attitudes, values, and psychopathological features. Some are motivated by homophobia, and the wish to change subsides as this is addressed. Others reject their homosexual orientation for other reasons, often religious. Sometimes the incompatibility between sexual desires and personal values cannot be resolved by therapeutic interventions. Those who deliver health care have a continuing role in helping such people preserve self-esteem and avoid anxiety and depression as much as possible.

Psychobiologic Aspects

GENETICS

In a recent study using DNA linkage analysis, Hamer et al. concluded that a gene that influences homosexual orientation in males is contained on the X chromosome.[95] Thirty-three of 40 homosexual pairs of siblings were found to be concordant for five markers in the distal region of the X chromosome, and the remaining 7 were discordant at one or more of these loci. Since certain types of families in which homosexuality was aggregated were selectively studied, no inference about the frequency of X-linked male homosexuality in the general population was possible.[95]

Bailey et al. reported increased concordance for homosexuality among male and female monozygotic twins, as compared with dizygotic twins.[96-98] Their data were consistent with results from a number of other studies of sexual orientation in twins[99, 100] and of familial aggregation of homosexuality.[95, 101, 102] One recent study found no difference in rates of concordance for homosexuality between monozygotic and dizygotic male and female twins, but the zygosity and sexual orientation of the co-twin were determined from the index subject's self-report.[103] A genetic influence on homosexual orientation is also suggested by a few cases of identical twins concordant for homosexuality who were separated early in life and reared apart.[99, 104]

SEX HORMONES AND PSYCHOSEXUAL DEVELOPMENT

Neither plasma hormone values nor other endocrine tests reliably distinguish groups with regard to sexual orientation.[105-107] Studies of mammalian sexual behavior led to the hypothesis that a prenatal androgen deficit results in male homosexuality and that a prenatal androgen excess results in female homosexuality.[108]

Another reason for hypothesizing that prenatal sex-steroid hormones may influence sexual orientation derives from behavioral antecedents of homosexuality. During the childhood of gay men, aversion to play that involves fighting and rough-and-tumble team sports is common.[60, 63, 109] The opposite pattern—vigorous tomboyishness—is common among girls who later became lesbians. In humans and many other mammals, prenatal sex-steroid hormones influence prepubertal nonsexual behavior, including rough-and-tumble play.[107] This raises the question whether a childhood predilection for or aversion to rough-and-tumble activities could be related to differences in prenatal androgen secretion.

Homosexual men and women report more "cross-gender" behavior (often considered to be nonconformity with sex roles) during childhood than heterosexual men and women.[63, 109-112] Most boys with psychiatric disorders of gender identity who have been followed become homosexual as adolescents or adults, although most homosexual adults have not had this syndrome as children.[113-115] No follow-up studies of females have been carried out. However, childhood gender-identity disorder has not been demonstrated to be influenced directly by biological factors.[116]

FURTHER IMPLICATIONS OF INTERSEX STUDIES

Important general principles of psychosexual development have been derived from studies of patients with unusual sexual disorders.[117-119] Although each syndrome is of interest, studies of females with congenital adrenal hyperplasia treated early in life illustrate a point of general relevance. Whereas the evidence for an effect of prenatal androgens on childhood sex-role behavior is robust in these patients and in others exposed to masculinizing hormones during gestation, the evidence for an effect on later-occurring sexual orientation is modest.[107] Although homosexual responsivity develops in more of these patients than in controls, most report exclusively heterosexual behavior as adults.

BRAIN DIFFERENCES ASSOCIATED WITH SEXUAL ORIENTATION

Unreplicated reports have been published of the increased size of the superchiasmatic nucleus of the hypothalamus, decreased size of the third anterior interstitial nucleus, and increased size of the anterior commissure in homosexual men.[120-122] Studies of left- and right-sided dominance[123-26] and of cognitive functioning[127, 128] have not been conclusive. Finally, a number of studies indicate that homosexual men tend to be born later in groups of siblings than do heterosexual men. Neither the reason for this nor its importance is yet apparent.[129]

Preliminary evidence suggests that to some extent sexual orientation is influenced by biologic factors, although the intermediate mechanisms remain to be described. Since sex differences in behavior appear to be influenced by prenatal sex hormones, the hypothesis that complex changes in prenatal androgen secretion influence sexual orientation remains viable, although unproved.[106, 107, 121, 122, 130]

Some prenatal hormonal events may be under genetic influence, whereas others may occur as a result of environmental factors. An example is prenatal stress, which inhibits the secretion of testosterone, influences the sexual behavior of rats, and may influence sexual orientation in humans (although it has not been proved to do so).[131-34] In some people neither genetic nor prenatal hormonal influences may determine sexual orientation. Diverse lines of psychosexual development could lead to the same behavioral end point with regard to sexual orientation.

Conclusions

Although there has been rapid growth recently in our knowledge about human sexual orientation, fundamental questions remain.[105, 135] Enough data have accumulated to warrant the dismissal of incorrect ideas once widely accepted about homosexual people. Many areas of law and public policy are still influenced by views discarded by behavioral scientists.[30, 83, 136] Thus, homosexual acts are still considered criminal in many states. Decisions about custody, visitation, and adoption are frequently made on the basis of sexual orientation. Homosexual partners are not afforded the same protection as marital partners. In addition, homosexual people receive unequal treatment in the military. There are no data from scientific studies to justify the unequal treatment of homosexual people or their exclusion from any group.

Notes

1. Bayer R. *Homosexuality and American psychiatry: the politics of diagnosis.* New York: Basic Books, 1981.

2. Herdt G. Cross-cultural issues in the development of bisexuality and homosexuality. In: Perry ME, ed. *Handbook of sexology*. Vol. 7. *Childhood and adolescent sexology*. Amsterdam: Elsevier, 1990.

3. Money J. *Gay, straight, and in-between: the sexology of erotic orientation*. New York: Oxford University Press, 1988.

4. The problem of ego identity. In: Erikson EH. *Identity and the life cycle: psychological issues*. Vol. 1. New York: International Universities Press, 1959: 101–64.

5. Troiden RR. Becoming homosexual: a model of gay identity acquisition. *Psychiatry* 1979; 42: 362–73.

6. Kinsey AC, Pomeroy WB, Martin CE. *Sexual behavior in the human male*. Philadelphia: W. B. Saunders, 1948.

7. Kinsey AC. Pomeroy WB, Martin CE, Gebhard PH. *Sexual behavior in the human female*. Philadelphia: W. B. Saunders, 1953.

8. Gebbard PH. *Incidence of overt homosexuality in the United States and Western Europe: NIMH Task Force on Homosexuality: final report and background papers*. Rockville, Md.: National Institute of Mental Health, 1972: 22–29.

9. Billy JO, Tanfer K, Grady WR, Klepinger DH. The sexual behavior of men in the United States. *Farm Plann Perspect* 1993; 25: 52–60.

10. Fay RE, Turner CF, Klassen AD, Gagnon JH. Prevalence and patterns of same-gender sexual contact among men. *Science* 1989; 243: 338–48.

11. Seidman SN, Rieder RO. A review of sexual behavior in the United States. *Am J Psychiatry* 1994; 151: 330–41.

12. Diamond M. Homosexuality and bisexuality in different populations. *Arch Sex Behav* 1993; 22: 291–310.

13. Rotheram-Borus MJ, Gwadz M. Sexuality among youths at high risk 1993. *Child Adolesc Psychiatr Clin North Am* 1993; 2: 415–31.

14. Bell AP, Weinberg MS. *Homosexualities: a study of diversity among men and women*. New York: Simon & Schuster, 1978.

15. Nichols M. Lesbian relationships: implications for the study of sexuality and gender. In: McWhirter DP, Sanders SA, Reinisch JM, eds. *Homosexuality/heterosexuality: concepts of sexual orientation*. New York: Oxford University Press, 1990: 350–64.

16. Blumstein P, Schwartz P. *American couples: money, work, sex*. New York: William Morrow, 1983.

17. Kanouse DE, Berry SH, Gorman EM, et al. *Response to the AIDS epidemic: a survey of homosexual and bisexual men in Los Angeles County*. Santa Monica, Calif.: RAND, 1991.

18. Loulon J. R1566 lesbians and the clinical application. *Women Ther* 1988; 7(2–3): 221–34.

19. Kanouse DE, Berry SH, Gorman EM, et al. *AIDS-related knowledge, attitudes, beliefs and behaviors in Los Angeles County*. Santa Monica, Calif.: RAND, 1991.

20. Kelly JA, Murphy DA, Roffman RA, et al. Acquired immunodeficiency syndrome/human immunodeficiency virus risk behavior among gay men

in small cities: findings of a 16–city national sample. *Arch Intern Med* 1992; 152: 2293–97.

21. Rotheram-Borus MJ, Rosario M, Meyer-Bahlburg HFL, Koopman C, Dopkins SC, Davies M. Sexual and substance use acts of gay and bisexual male adolescents in New York City. *J Sex Res* 1994; 31: 47–57.

22. Linn LS, Spiegel JS, Matthews WC, Leake B, Lien R, Brooks S. Recent sexual behaviors among homosexual men seeking primary medical care. *Arch Intern Med* 1989; 149: 2685–90.

23. Kelly JA, Kalichman SC, Kauth MR, et al. Situational factors associated with AIDS risk behavior lapses and coping strategies used by gay men who successfully avoid lapses. *Am J Public Health* 1991; 81: 1335–38.

24. Chu SY, Buehler JW, Fleming PL, Berkelman RL. Epidemiology of reported cases of AIDS in lesbians, United States 1980–89. *Am J Public Health* 1990; 80: 1380–81.

25. Handsfield HH, Schwebke J. Trends in sexually transmitted diseases in homosexually active men in King County, Washington, 1980–1990. *Sex Transm Dis* 1990; 17: 211–15.

26. Hart G. Factors associated with hepatitis B infection. *Int J STD AIDS* 1993; 4: 102–106.

27. Holly EA, Whittemore AS, Aston DA, Ahn DK, Nickoloff BJ, Kristiansen JJ. Anal cancer incidence: genital warts, anal fissure or fistula, hemorrhoids, and smoking. *J. Natl Cancer Inst* 1989; 81: 1726–31.

28. Edwards A, Thun RN. Sexually transmitted diseases in lesbians. *Int J STD AIDS* 1990; 1: 178–81.

29. Weinberg GH. *Society and the healthy homosexual*. New York: St. Martin's Press, 1972.

30. Greenberg DF. *The construction of homosexuality*. Chicago: University of Chicago Press, 1988.

31. Herek GM. Stigma, prejudice, and violence against lesbians and gay men. In: Gonsiorek JC, Weinrich JD, eds. *Homosexuality: research implications for public policy*. Newbury Park, Calif.: Sage, 1991: 60–80.

32. *Idem*. Beyond "homophobia": a social psychological perspective on attitudes toward lesbians and gay men. *J Homosex* 1984; 10: 1–21.

33. Herek GM, Berrill K, eds. Violence against lesbians and gay men: issues for research, practice and policy. *J. Interpersonal Violence* 1990: 5(3).

34. Allport GW. *The nature of prejudice*. Cambridge, Mass.: Addison-Wesley, 1954.

35. Herdt G, ed. *Gay and lesbian youth*. New York: Harrington Park Press, 1989.

36. Stein TS. Overview of new developments in understanding homosexuality. *Rev Psychiatry* 1993; 12: 9–40.

37. American Academy of Pediatrics Committee on Adolescence: homosexuality and adolescence. *Pediatrics* 1993; 92: 631–34.

38. Scheier R. For gays in medicine's closet, a haven. *American Medical News*. January 13, 1989: 29–30.

39. Gartrell N, Kraemer H, Brodie HK. Psychiatrists' attitudes toward female homosexuality. *J Nerv Ment Dis* 1974; 159: 141–44.

40. Douglas CJ, Kalman CM, Kalman TP. Homophobia among physicians and nurses: an empirical study. *Hosp Community Psychiatry* 1985; 36: 1309–11.

41. Kelly JA, St. Lawrence JS, Smith S Jr, Hood HV, Cook DJ. Medical students' attitudes toward AIDS and homosexual patients. *J Med Educ* 1987; 62: 549–56.

42. Royse D, Birge B. Homophobia and attitudes towards AIDS patients among medical, nursing, and paramedical students. *Psychol Rep* 1987; 61: 867–70.

43. Wisniewski JJ, Toomey BG. Are social workers homophobic? *Social Work* 1987; 32: 454–55.

44. Randall CE. Lesbian phobia among BSN educators: a survey. *J Nurs Educ* 1989; 28: 302–306.

45. Garnets L, Hancock KA, Cochran SD, Goodchilds J, Peplau LA. Issues in psychotherapy with lesbians and gay men: a survey of psychologists. *Am Psychol* 1991; 46: 964–72.

46. Wallick MM, Cambre KM, Townsend MH. How the topic of homosexuality is taught in U.S. medical schools. *Acad Med* 1992; 67: 601–603.

47. Stevenson MR. Promoting tolerance for homosexuality: an evaluation of intervention strategies. *Sex Res* 1988; 25: 500–11.

48. Centers for Disease Control and Prevention. *HIV/AIDS Surveillance Report*. December 1993.

49. AIDS and mental health—part I. *The Harvard Mental Health Letter*. 1994; 10(7): 1–4.

50. AIDS and mental health—part II. *The Harvard Mental Health Letter*. 1994; 10(8): 1–4.

51. King MB. *AIDS, HIV, and mental health*. Cambridge, England: Cambridge University Press, 1993.

52. Martin JL. Psychological consequences of AIDS-related bereavement among gay men. *J Consult Clin Psychol* 1988; 56: 856–62.

53. Marzuk PM, Tierney H., Tardiff K, et al. Increased risk of suicide in persons with AIDS. *JAMA* 1988; 259: 1333–37.

54. Gonsiorek JC. The emphirical basis for the demise of the illness model of homosexuality. In: Gonsiorek JC, Weinrich JD, eds. *Homosexuality: research implications for public policy*. Newbury Park, Calif.: Sage, 1991: 115–37.

55. Hooker E. The adjustment of the male overt homosexual. *J Proj Tech* 1957; 21: 18–31.

56. Isay RA. *Being homosexual: gay men and their development*. New York: Farrar, Straus, Giroux, 1989.

57. Friedman RC, Downey J. Psychoanalysis, psychobiology, and homosexuality. *J Am Psychoanal Assoc* 1993; 41: 1159–98.

58. Freund K, Langevin R, Chamberlayne R, Deoscran A, Zajac Y. The phobic theory of male homosexuality. *Arch Gen Psychiatry* 1974; 31: 495–99.

59. Groth AN, Birnbaum HJ. Adult sexual orientation and attraction to underage persons. *Arch Sex Behav* 1978; 7: 175–81.

60. Friedman RC. *Male homosexuality: a contemporary psychoanalytic perspective*. New Haven, Conn.: Yale University Press, 1988.

61. Golden C. Diversity and variability in women's sexual identities. In: Boston Lesbian Psychologies Collective eds. *Lesbian psychologies: explorations and challenges.* Urbana: University of Illinois Press, 1987: 19–34.

62. Malyon A. Psychotherapeutic implications of internalized homophobia in gay men. *J Homosexuality* 1982; 17: 59–69.

63. Saghir MT, Robins E. *Male and female homosexuality: a comprehensive investigation.* Baltimore: Williams & Wilkins, 1973.

64. Williams JBW, Rabkin JG, Remien RH, Gorman JM, Ehrhardt AA. Multidisciplinary baseline assessment of homosexual men with and without human immunodeficiency virus infection. II Standardized clinical assessment of current and lifetime psychopathology. *Arch Gen Psychiatry* 1991; 48: 124–30.

65. Robins E. *The final months: a study of the lives of 134 persons who committed suicide.* New York: Oxford University Press, 1981.

66. Rich CL, Fowler RC, Young D, Blenkush M. San Diego suicide study; comparison of gay to straight males. *Suicide Life Threat Behav* 1986; 16: 448–57.

67. Hendin H. Suicide among homosexual youth. *Am J Psychiatry* 1992; 149: 1416–17.

68. Prenzlauer S, Drescher J, Winchel R. Suicide among homosexual youth. *Am J Psychiatry* 1992; 149: 1416.

69. Shaffer D. Political science. *The New Yorker.* May 3, 1993, 116.

70. Remafedi G, Farrow JA, Deischer RW. Risk factors for attempted suicide in gay and bisexual youth. *Pediatrics* 1991; 87: 869–75.

71. Lewis CE, Saghir MT, Robins E. Drinking patterns in homosexual and heterosexual women. *J Chr. Psychiatry* 1982; 43: 277–79.

72. Lohrenz LJ, Connelly JC, Coyne, L, Spare KE. Alcohol problems in several midwestern homosexual communities. *J Stud Alcohol* 1978; 39: 1959–63.

73. Pillard RC. Sexual orientation and mental disorder. *Psychiatr Ann* 1988; 18: 52–56.

74. Slater BR. Essential issues in working with lesbian and gay male youths. *Prof Psychol Res Pract* 1988; 19: 226–35.

75. McWhirter DP, Mattison AM. *The male couple: how relationships develop.* Englewood Cliffs, N.J.: Prentice-Hall, 1984.

76. Hanley-Hackenbruck P. Working with lesbians in psychotherapy. *Rev Psychiatry* 1993; 12: 59–83.

77. Ross MW. *The married homosexual man: a psychological study.* London: Routledge & Kegan Paul, 1983.

78. Green GD, Bozett FW. Lesbian mothers and gay fathers. In: Gonsjorek JC, Weinrich JD, eds. *Homosexuality: research implications for public policy.* Newbury Park, Calif.: Sage, 1991: 197–214.

79. Gottman JS. Children of gay and lesbian parents. In: Bozett FW, Sussman MB, eds. *Homosexuality and family relations.* New York: Harrington Park Press, 1990: 177–96.

80. Patterson CJ. Children of lesbian and gay parents. *Child Dev* 1992; 63: 1025–42.

81. Bozett FW. Children of gay fathers. In: Bozett FW, ed. *Gay and lesbian parents.* New York: Praeger, 1987: 39–57.

82. Harvard Law Review, eds. *Sexual orientation and the law.* Cambridge, Mass.: Harvard University Press, 1990.

83. Kirpatrick M, Smith C, Roy R. Lesbian mothers and their children: a comparative survey. *Am J Orthopsychiatry* 1981; 51: 545–51.

84. Golombok S, Spencer A, Retter M. Children in lesbian and single-parent households: psychosexual and psychiatric appraisal. *J Child Psychol Psychiatry* 1983; 24: 551–72.

85. Green R, Mandel JB, Hetvedt ME, Gray J, Smith L. Lesbian mothers and their children: a comparison with solo parent heterosexual mothers and their children. *Arch Sex Behav* 1986; 15: 167–84.

86. Miller B. Gay fathers and their children. *Fam Coord* 1979; 28: 544–52.

87. Socarides CW. *Homosexuality.* New York: J. Aronson, 1978.

88. Bieber I, Dain HJ, Dince PR, et al. *Homosexuality: a psychoanalytic study.* New York: Basic Books. 1962.

89. Liss JL, Welner A. Change in homosexual orientation. *Am J Psychother* 1973; 27: 102–104.

90. Acosta FX. Etiology and treatment of homosexuality: a review. *Arch Sex Behav* 1975; 4: 9–29.

91. Pattison EM, Pattison ML. "Ex-gays": religiously mediated change in homosexuals. *Am J Psychiatry* 1980; 137: 1553–62.

92. Haldeman DC. Sexual orientation conversion therapy for gay men and lesbians: a scientific examination. In: Gonsiorek JC, Weinrich JD, eds. *Homosexuality: research implications for public policy.* Newbury Park, Calif.: Sage, 1991: 149–61.

93. Nicolosi J. *Reparative therapy of male homosexuality.* Northvale N.J.: J. Aronson, 1991.

94. Boston Lesbian Psychologies Collective, eds. *Lesbian psychologies: explorations and challenges.* Urbana: University of Illinois Press, 1987.

95. Hamer DH, Hu S, Magnuson VL, Hu N, Pattatucci AM. A linkage between DNA markers on the X chromosome and male sexual orientation. *Science* 1993; 261: 321–27.

96. Bailey JM, Pillard RC. A genetic study of male sexual orientation. *Arch Gen Psychiatry* 1991; 48: 1089–96.

97. Bailey JM, Pillard RC, Neale MC, Agyei Y. Heritable factors influence sexual orientation in women. *Arch Gen Psychiatry* 1993; 50: 217–23.

98. Buhrich N, Bailey JM, Martin NG. Sexual orientation, sexual identity, and sex-dimorphic behaviors in male twins. *Behav Genet* 1991; 21: 75–96.

99. Whitam FL, Diamond M, Martin J. Homosexual orientation in twins: a report on 61 pairs and three triplet sets. *Arch Sex Behav* 1993; 22: 187–206.

100. Kallmann FJ. *Heredity in health and mental disorder: principles of psychiatric genetics in the light of comparative twin studies.* New York: Norton, 1953.

101. Pillard RC, Poumadere J, Carretta RA. A family study of sexual orientation. *Arch Sex Behav* 1982; 11: 511–20.

102. Pillard RC, Weinrich JD. Evidence of familial nature of male homosexuality. *Arch Gen Psychiatry* 1986; 43: 808–12.

103. King M, McDonald E. Homosexuals who are twins: a study of 46 probands. *Br J Psychiatry* 1992; 160: 407–409.

104. Eckert ED, Bouchard TJ, Bobken J, Heston LL. Homosexuality in monozygotic twins reared apart. *Br J Psychiatry* 1986; 148: 421–25.

105. Gooren L, Fliers E, Courtney K. Biological determinants of sexual orientation. *Annu Rev Sex Res* 1990; 1: 175–96.

106. Meyer-Bahlberg HFL. Psychobiologic research on homosexuality. *Child Adolesc Psychiatr Clin North Am* 1993; 2: 489–500.

107. Friedman RC, Downey J. Neurobiology and sexual orientation, current relationships. *J Neuropsychiatry Clin Neurosis* 1993; 5: 131–53.

108. Phoenix CH, Goy RW, Gerall AA, Young WC. Organizing action of prenatally administered testosterone propionate on the tissues modifying mating behavior in the female guinea pig. *Endocrinology* 1959: 65: 369–82.

109. Bell AP, Weinberg MS, Hammersmith SK. *Sexual preference, its development in men and women*. Bloomington: Indiana University Press. 1981.

110. Zucker KJ, Green R. Psychological and familial aspects of gender identity disorder 1993. *Child Adolesc Psychiatr Clin North Am* 1993; 2: 513–43.

111. Whitam FL, Zent M. A cross-cultural assessment of early cross-gender behavior and familial factors in male homosexuality. *Arch Sex Behav* 1984; 13: 427–39.

112. Whitam FL, Mathy RM. Childhood cross-gender behavior of homosexual females in Brazil, Peru, the Philippines, and the United States. *Arch Sex Behav* 1991; 20: 151–70.

113. Green R. Gender Identity in childhood and later sexual orientation: follow-up of 78 males. *Am J Psychiatry* 1985; 142: 339–41.

114. *Idem. The "sissy boy syndrome" and the development of homosexuality.* New Haven, Conn.: Yale University Press, 1987.

115. Bailey JM, Zucker KJ. Childhood sex-typed behavior and sexual orientation: a conceptual analysis and quantitative review. *Dev Psychol* (in press).

116. Coates S. Gender identity disorder in boys: an integrative model. In: Barron JW, Eagle MN, Wolitzky DL, eds. *Interface of psychoanalysis and psychology*. Washington, D.C.: American Psychological Association, 1992: 245–65.

117. Money J, Schwartz M, Lewis VG. Adult erotosexual status and fetal hormonal masculinization and demasculinization: 46, XX congenial virilizing adrenal hyperplasia and 46, XY androgen-insensitivity syndrome compared. *Psychoneuroendocrinology* 1984; 9: 405–14.

118. Money J, Ehrhardt AA. *Man and woman, boy and girl.* Baltimore: Johns Hopkins University Press, 1972.

119. Meyer-Bahlburg HFL. Gender identity development in intersex patients. In: *Sexual and gender identity disorders. Child Adolesc Psychiatr Clin North Am* 1993; 2: 501–12.

120. Swaab DF, Hofman MA. An enlarged suprachiasmatic nucleus in homosexual men. *Brian Res* 1990; 537: 141–48.

121. LeVay S. A difference in hypothalamic structure between heterosexual and homosexual men. *Science* 1991; 253: 1034–37.

122. Allen LS, Gorski RA. Sexual orientation and the size of the anterior commissure in the human brain. *Proc Natl Acad Sci USA* 1992; 89: 7199–202.

123. Geschwind N, Galaburda AM. Cerebral lateralization: biological mechanisms, associations and pathology. I. A hypothesis and a program for research. *Arch Neurol* 1985; 42: 428–59.

124. *Idem.* Cerebral lateralization: biological mechanisms, associations, and pathology. II. A hypothesis and a program for research. *Arch Neurol* 1985; 42: 521–52.

125. McCormick CM, Witelson SF, Kingstone E. Left-handedness in homosexual men and women: neuroendocrine implications. *Psychoneuroendocrinology* 1990; 15: 69–76.

126. Rosenstein LD, Bigler ED. No relationship between handedness and sexual preference. *Psychol Rep* 1987; 60: 704–706.

127. Sanders G, Ross-Field L. Neuropsychological development of cognitive abilities: a new research strategy and some preliminary evidence for a sexual orientation model. *Int J Neurosci* 1987; 36: 1–16.

128. McCormick CM, Witelson SF. A cognitive profile of homosexual men compared to heterosexual men and women. *Psychoneuroendocrinology* 1991; 16: 459–73.

129. Blanchard R, Zucker KJ. Reanalysis of Bell, Weinberg, and Hammersmith's data on birth order, sibling sex ratio, and parental age in homosexual men. *Am J Psychiatry* 1994; 151: 1375–76.

130. Gorski RA. Sexual differentiation of the endocrine brain and its control. In: Motta M, ed. *Brain endocrinology.* 2nd. ed. New York: Raven Press, 1991: 71–104.

131. Ward IL, Reed J. Prenatal stress and prepubertal social rearing conditions interact to determine sexual behavior in male rats. *Behav Neurosci* 1985; 99: 301–309.

132. Ward IL. Prenatal stress feminizes and demasculinizes the behavior of males. *Science* 1972; 175: 82–84.

133. Ellis L, Peckham W, Ashley Ames M, Burke D. Sexual orientation of human offspring may be altered by severe maternal stress during pregnancy. *J Sex Res* 1988; 25: 152–57.

134. Bailey JM, Willerman L, Parks C. A test of the maternal stress theory of human male homosexuality. *Arch Sex Behav* 1991; 20: 277–93.

135. Byne W, Parsons B. Human sexual orientation: the biologic theories reappraised. *Arch Gen Psychiatry* 1993; 50: 228–39.

136. Gonsiorek JC, Weinrich JD. eds. *Homosexuality: research implications for public policy.* Newbury Park, Calif.: Sage, 1991.

Gender Issues in the Diagnosis of Mental Disorder

Paula J. Caplan

Historically, it has been considered acceptable—indeed, womanly—for two or more women or girls to band together to help the poor, the sick, the helpless, the oppressed, children, or men. The only time it has not been considered acceptable for women to do this has been when the help was for themselves or for other women. Women who have done the latter have been branded as selfish, unwomanly, belligerent, strident, and so on; they have been accused of complaining too much or of ignoring the needs of other people. They have been threatened with ostracism by the host culture.

In spite of such threats, some women have continued to insist that women's concerns be given high priority. . . .

I shall present a very brief sampling of some of the ways in which sexism among mental health professionals has resulted in serious oversights, inadequate treatment, and even mistreatment and harm—primarily to females but also sometimes to males. It is important to keep in mind that sexism is not the only bias that profoundly skews and twists the process of diagnosis. Racism, ageism, classism, and homophobia are some of the other deep-seated prejudices that are reflected in the creation and assignment of diagnostic labels by mental health professionals.

Although there is space here to mention only a few examples, I have chosen these carefully to provide a sense of the enormous range of diagnostic problems and harm that result from sexism.

From *Women and Therapy* 12, no. 4(1992): 71–82. Reprinted by permission of The Haworth Press, Inc. Copyright © 1992, The Haworth Press, Binghamton, New York.

Learning Disabilities

In my earliest years as a clinical psychologist, I specialized in children's learning problems (Kinsbourne & Caplan, 1979). One of the most widely accepted bits of "wisdom" in that field was, and still is, that far more boys than girls have learning disabilities. Recent research (Shaywitz, Shaywitz, Fletcher, & Escobar, 1990) suggests that, in fact, learning disabilities are equally common in both sexes. Nevertheless, in virtually all clinical settings, more boys than girls are brought in with complaints about learning problems; and I wondered whether that pattern of *noticing* and referral for learning disabilities reflected the pattern of *real* learning disabilities. My own research (Caplan, 1973, 1977; Caplan & Kinsbourne, 1974) a number of years ago suggested that girls' learning disabilities and other academic problems are more likely than boys' to be overlooked and underdiagnosed, and there seemed to be several reasons for this:

First, since it is considered less important for girls than for boys to be academically successful, low academic performance by girls appears less likely to be labeled a problem than low academic performance in boys; therefore, girls' learning difficulties are unnoticed or, when noticed, not considered to warrant referral, remediation, or any other kind of treatment (this is the "As long as she's pretty and nice, she'll get a husband. She doesn't need to be smart" attitude).

Second, girls are socialized to deal with frustration and failure in less disruptive, antisocial ways than are boys. As a consequence, a learning disabled girl is more likely than an equally learning disabled boy to deal with that frustration in ways that lead her teachers or parents to take her to professionals in the hope that they can "do something" to keep her under control.

This pattern is harmful to girls and to boys in different ways. Many girls' learning problems are simply never noticed, and boys who already have one problem (e.g., learning disability) develop a second problem (disruptive behavior) as part of their attempt to cope in a sex-appropriate, traditionally masculine way. Canadian psychologist Meredith Kimball (1981) has identified the deep-seated sexism in North American educational systems' allocation of funds for remediation of learning disabled children. Kimball points out that it is commonly believed (although by no means based on solid evidence) that boys have more reading disabilities than girls and that girls have more trouble (although, interestingly, these are not usually dignified with the term "learning disability") with so-called visual-spatial tasks, which are assumed to be important for doing math and sciences.

Where do public monies for remediation go? Overwhelmingly, they are poured into remedial *reading* programs, and little or no remediation is provided for children with visual-spatial problems. A similar disproportion characterizes the research that is done on learning disabilities: Overwhelmingly, it is focused on reading problems, the problems thought to plague boys far more than girls. Although some might argue that reading is the most important school-related skill and therefore deserves more attention and funding, even North America's post-Sputnik stress on the importance of education in mathematics and sciences did not result in any substantial increase in a focus on visual-spatial problems.

Psychiatric Diagnoses

When the American Psychiatric Association last revised its massive handbook, *Diagnostic and Statistical Manual of Mental Disorders* (DSM)—which is probably the most widely used listing of psychiatric labels—they included two new, dangerously misogynist diagnostic categories. A great deal has been written elsewhere (see Caplan, 1987, for details and additional references) about the numerous problems and dangers involved in these categories, which are "self-defeating personality disorder" (SDPD) and "late luteal phase dysphoric disorder" (LLPDD), but I shall briefly mention some of the major ones here.

Self-defeating personality disorder was initially to be called "masochistic personality disorder," and even though the title was changed, the criteria and the implications are the same. The criteria applied to these people include putting other people's needs ahead of their own, not feeling appreciated even though they really are, and settling for less when they could have more.

This diagnostic label is dangerous because:

1. It applies to what I call the "good wife syndrome": Women in North America are traditionally raised to put other people's needs ahead of their own and to settle for less when they could have more (it's called being unselfish, not being a demanding shrew, and/or having poor self-esteem so that one doesn't *realize* that one could do better), and it has been well-documented that women's traditional work (housework and childcare) in fact is *not* appreciated. Thus, after a woman has conscientiously learned the role her culture prescribes for her, the psychiatric establishment calls her mentally disordered. It does *not* do anything similar for men. It does not classify as a psychiatric disorder the inability to identify and express a wide range of emotions, a "disorder" which has been proven to characterize enormous numbers of North American males.

2. It is a description of the typical battered or severely emotionally abused woman. Such women characteristically experience a dangerous plummeting in their self-esteem because of the abuse, and, trying to be good women and good wives, they may become even more self-denying, giving, and undemanding than other women in an attempt to persuade the abuser to stop the abuse. Applying the label of "self-defeating personality disorder" to these women is a pernicious form of victim-blaming. Although users of the DSM are cautioned not to apply this label when abuse was the major cause of the woman's apparently "self-defeating" behavior, it has been well-documented (see Firsten, 1991, for a review) that therapists almost never ask their clients about abuse, and when they do, the clients are reluctant (ashamed, scared) to talk about it. As Poston and Lison (1989) report, "Many would sooner ask a client if she is hearing voices than ask her if she has sexual abuse in her background, even though figures would indicate that the chances of an abusive background far outweigh the occurrence of hearing voices" (p. 21).

3. The label is dangerous because it leads both therapists and the women so diagnosed to believe that the problems come from within, that the women have a sick need to be hurt, humiliated, unappreciated, etc. Since my book, *The Myth of Women's Masochism,* was published (1987), hundreds of women have told me that in years of traditional psychotherapy, their therapists told them regularly that they brought all their problems on themselves. When the women say, for instance, "But Fred was wonderful to me when we were dating. It wasn't until our wedding night that he started to beat me," the therapist all too often replies, "Ah, yes! So *consciously* you didn't choose an abusive man. But your self-defeating motives are *unconscious!*" Such "treatment" is, I believe, a major cause of depression in women: They are unjustifiably given the message that there is no point in their trying to get out of an abusive or otherwise distressing relationship or situation, because their sick, unconscious motives will inevitably lead them straight into more trouble.

4. Prime movers of the DSM revisions have themselves pointed out that people diagnosed in this way typically have what is called a "negative therapeutic reaction," that psychotherapy makes them worse (Kass, MacKinnon, & Spitzer, 1986). No surprise, I say, because if I have a broken leg, and the doctor puts a cast on my arm instead, my leg will certainly get worse. If a woman is being abused or severely emotionally neglected and unappreciated by her intimate partner, then a therapist who takes the approach that

she enjoys her misery and has an unconscious need to suffer not only does not help but actively makes her worse.

[Editorial note: as a result of criticism and adverse publicity brought by Dr. Caplan and others, SDPD was dropped from *DSM-IV,* 1994. LLPDD discussed below was retained and changed to Premenstrual Dysphoric Disorder (PDD)].

The other misogynist diagnosis, LLPDD [or PDD], is a fancy term for premenstrual syndrome as a psychiatric disorder. What's wrong with that? Several things.

1. While we all know women who have genuine physical or mood problems that seem to be regularly associated with their menstrual cycle, the danger is in calling these troubles psychiatric problems. Robert Spitzer, chief author of the most recent DSM revisions, told a press conference that psychiatrists don't know any psychiatric treatment that will help women with PMS but that PMS as a psychiatric diagnosis is essential to enable psychiatrists to figure out what they can do for these women. Although Spitzer may have good intentions, since psychiatric labeling tends to have negative and even dangerous consequences, until there is reason to believe that PMS is a psychologically caused problem *and/or* is helped by psychiatric treatment, there is no justification for using this label. Women who have PMS have enough trouble without having to worry that they are crazy. Furthermore, our society typically seizes on any suggestion of women's emotional weakness to justify keeping women out of well-paying, responsible jobs. (By contrast, although it is known that men's job performance varies according to predictable cycles, since there is no easy-to-pinpoint marker like monthly bleeding with which to associate those changes, men are regularly allowed to work at such dangerous jobs as piloting airplanes without being checked for where they are in their cycles.)
2. Nutritional, vitamin, and exercise treatments of various kinds have been shown to be helpful to many women who have PMS. These forms of treatment are not widely recommended (perhaps not even known) by the psychiatric and medical community, and calling PMS a psychiatric problem makes it even less likely that women will be told about such useful courses of action.

Perhaps the most striking feature of SDPD and LLPDD [PDD] is that the DSM includes no equivalent diagnostic categories for males, that is, there is no male SDPD parallel in the sense of having a category that describes an extreme form of males' socialization, such as "Macho Personality Disorder," [or the "John Wayne Syndrome" as Caplan calls it elsewhere] and there is no male equivalent of LLPDD [PDD] such as "Testosterone-Based Aggressive Disorder."[1]

Why Isn't the Health Insurance Industry Scared?

The health insurance industry ought to be up in arms about both of these diagnoses. Why? Because most nice women and virtually all battered women could be erroneously given the label of "self-defeating personality disorder," and once they are in psychiatric treatment, since they are not psychiatrically disordered they will be unlikely to "get well"; thus, the therapy is likely to be interminable. Women who enter psychiatric treatment for their PMS will, of course, experience little or no improvement for this physiologically-based disorder, and since they don't "get well," they may regularly lie on a psychiatrist's couch—until they reach menopause, at which time they will no doubt be considered in need of psychotherapy for their menopausal disorder. I have repeatedly contacted the health insurance lobby in the United States and the Canadian department of Health and Welfare, but they have chosen not to express any opposition to these categories, even though one would think that they would be worried that their coffers will be rapidly drained.

The Abuse of Mothers of Sexually Abused Children

After a few, brief years during which many brave adults revealed that they had been sexually abused as children and were believed, there has been a dangerous, unbelieving backlash. The media are filled with allegations that children claim they are sexually abused by their fathers only because the children's nasty, scheming mothers force them to say it, in an effort to hurt their ex-husbands. Some mental health professionals, egged on by an enthusiastic legal profession, have legitimized this backlash through the use of the psychiatric label, "Munchausen's syndrome by proxy." The label "Munchausen's syndrome" is a psychiatric diagnosis applied to people (usually women) who are described as going from one physician to another in the mistaken belief that they have something physically wrong with them, that they have a pathological need to believe they are physically ill. Typically, I have heard psychiatrists describe such a person as "never being satisfied until she gets someone to operate on her." Now, "Munchausen's by proxy" is being applied to a woman whose child reports being sexually abused. The diagnosis is supposed to indicate that the woman has a need to believe that something terrible is happening not to her but rather to her child.

This is a particularly terrifying, nauseating development. For so long, mothers have been damned by therapists for *not* reporting sexual abuse in their children—mother's explanations that they *did not know* it was happening are ignored, and therapists say they *must have known unconsciously*—and now, they are being damned and pathologized if they *do* make the report. When their children are being seriously harmed, the harm to the children is too often ignored and disbelieved, while the spotlight is turned on the allegedly sick mother. This is one of the more vicious and irresponsible forms of mother-blaming, a phenomenon whose pervasiveness among mental health professionals has been well-documented.

Conclusion

The sheer variety of gender biases in diagnoses represented in this brief paper reflects the power and the pervasiveness of sexism in the realm of diagnosis. This means that both conclusions drawn from research mired in these biases and the clinical and human applications of biased categories need rapid and radical transformation.

Note

1. After this paper was presented at the 1988 Gender, Science, and Medicine Conference, Margrit Eichler and I proposed, for educational and consciousness-raising purposes, the diagnostic category described in the Appendix as a way to redress the sexist imbalance in the DSM. Curious to see what would happen, we submitted the category to the DSM–IV Revisions Task Force, and excerpts from the disturbing, sometimes hilarious, but always revealing correspondence from some of the Task Force members about this category have now been published in a paper called "How *Do* They Decide Who Is Normal? The Bizarre, But True, Tale of the *DSM* Process" (Caplan, 1991). A comprehensive review of the research relevant to the category has also been published (Pantony & Caplan, 1991). We note that, in our hurry to get the proposal circulated, we inadvertently omitted a great many possible criteria that we feel ought to have been included, such as some related to homophobia, racism, classism, materialism, ableism, weightism, and so on.

References

Caplan, Paula J. (1973). The role of classroom conduct in the promotion and retention of elementary school children. *Journal of Experimental Education*, Spring. 41(3).

———. (1977). Sex, age, behavior, and subject as determinants of report of learning problems, *Journal of Learning Disabilities*, 10, 314–316.

———. (1987). *The myth of women's masochism*. NY: Signet.

Caplan, Paula J. (1991). How *do* they decide what is normal? The bizarre, but true, tale of the DSM process. *Canadian Psychology* 32(2), 162–170.

———. (1995). *They say you're crazy: How the world's most powerful psychiatrists decide who's normal.* Reading, Mass.: Addison-Wesley.

Caplan, Paula J., & Kinsbourne, Marcel. (1974). Sex differences in response to school failure. *Journal of Learning Disabilities,* 7, 232–235.

Firsten, Temi. (1991). Violence in the lives of women on psych wards. *Canadian Woman's Studies,* 11(4), 45–48.

Kass, Frederic, MacKinnon, Roger A., & Spitzer, Robert L. (1986). Masochistic personality: An empirical study. *American Journal of Psychiatry,* 143, 216–218.

Kimball, Meredith. (1981). Women and science: A critique of biological theories. *International Journal of Women's Studies,* 4, 318–335.

Kinsbourne, Marcel, & Caplan, Paula J. (1979). *Children's learning and attention problems.* Boston: Little, Brown.

Pantony, Kaye Lee, & Caplan, Paula J. (1991). Delusional dominating personality disorder: A modest proposal for identifying some consequences of rigid masculine socialization. *Canadian Psychology,* 32(2), 120–133.

Poston, Carol, & Lison, Karen. (1989). *Reclaiming our lives: Hope for adult survivors of incest.* Boston: Little, Brown.

Shaywitz, Sally E., Shaywitz, Bennett A., Fletcher, Jack M., & Escobar, Michael. (1990). Prevalence of reading disability in boys and girls: Results of the Connecticut longitudinal study. *Journal of American Medical Association,* 264(8), 998–1002.

Appendix

DELUSIONAL DOMINATING PERSONALITY DISORDER (DDPD)*

Individuals having this disorder are characterized by at least 6 (?) of following 14 criteria (note that such individuals nearly always suffer from at least one of the delusions listed):

1. Inability to establish and maintain meaningful interpersonal relationships
2. Inability to identify and express a range of feelings in oneself (typically accompanied by an inability to identify accurately the feelings of other people)
3. Inability to respond appropriately and empathically to the feelings and needs of close associates and intimates (often leading to the misinterpretation of signals from others)
4. Tendency to use power, silence, withdrawal, and/or avoidance

---

*The criteria for Delusional Dominating Personality Disorder was first printed by *Canadian Psychology* 32(2), pp. 120–133.

rather than negotiation in the face of interpersonal conflict or difficulty

5. Adoption of a gender-specific locus of control (belief that women are responsible for the bad things that happen to oneself, and the good things are due to one's own abilities, achievements, or efforts)

6. An excessive need to inflate the importance and achievements of oneself, males in general, or both. This is often associated with a need to deflate the importance of one's intimate female partner, females in general, or both

7. The presence of any one of the following delusions:
   A. the delusion of personal entitlement to the service of
      1. any woman with whom one is personally associated
      2. females in general for males in general
      3. both of the above
   B. the delusion that women like to suffer and to be ordered around
   C. the delusion that physical force is the best method of solving interpersonal problems
   D. the delusion that sexual and aggressive impulses are uncontrollable in
      1. oneself
      2. males in general
      3. both of the above
   E. the delusion that pornography and erotica are identical
   F. the delusion that women control most the world's wealth and/or power but do little of the world's work
   G. the delusion that existing inequalities in the distribution of power and wealth are a product of the survival of the fittest and that, therefore, allocation of greater social and economic rewards to the already privileged are merited
      (Note: The simultaneous presence of several of these delusions in one individual is very common and frequently constitutes a profoundly distorted belief system)

8. A pronounced tendency to categorize spheres of functioning and sets of behavior rigidly according to sex, e.g., belief that housework is women's work

9. A pronounced tendency to use a gender-based double standard in interpreting or evaluating situations or behavior (e.g., a man who makes breakfast sometimes is considered to be extraordinarily good, but a woman who sometimes neglects to make breakfast is considered deficient)

10. A pathological need to affirm one's social importance by dis-

playing oneself in the company of females who meet any three of the following criteria:
   A. are conventionally physically attractive
   B. are younger than oneself
   C. are shorter in stature than oneself
   D. weigh less than oneself
   E. appear to be lower on socioeconomic criteria than oneself
   F. are more submissive than oneself
11. A distorted approach to sexuality, displaying itself in one or both of these ways:
   A. an excessive need for flattery about one's sexual performance and/or the size of one's genitals
   B. an infantile tendency to equate large breasts on women with their sexual attractiveness
12. A tendency to feel inordinately threatened by women who fail to disguise their intelligence
13. An inability to derive pleasure from doing things for others
14. Emotionally uncontrolled resistance to reform efforts that are oriented toward gender equity; note that the tendency to consider oneself a "New Man" neither proves nor disproves that the patient fits within this diagnostic category and patients who fit this description should *not* be diagnosed as having obsessive-compulsive disorders, since obsessive compulsive disorder affects only a limited part of the personality and functioning, whereas this disorder is pervasive and profound, a maladaptive organization of the entire personality.

Note: In keeping with the stated aims of the DSM, the proposed category is atheoretical, but there is little or no evidence that it is biologically based. In fact, there is a great deal of evidence that it is an extremely common disorder that involves a great deal of psychological upset both to the patient and to those with whom the patient deals. There is also evidence that the disorder is socially-induced and . . . that the younger the patient when . . . treatment is begun, the better the prognosis.

Suggestions for Further Reading

Psychiatric Classification

American Psychiatric Association, *Diagnostic and Statistical Manual of Mental Disorders, Fourth Edition*. Washington, D.C.: American Psychiatric Association, 1994.

Michels, Robert, and John M. Oldham, "Value Judgments in Psychoanalytic Theory and Practice." *Psychoanalytic Inquiry* 3, no. 4 (1983): 599–608.

Millon, Theodore, "Classification in Psychopathology: Rationale, Alternatives, and Standards." *Journal of Abnormal Psychology* 100 (1991): 245–61.

Reich, Walter, "Psychiatric Diagnosis as an Ethical Problem." In Bloch, Sidney, and Paul Chodoff, eds., *Psychiatric Ethics*, 2d ed. New York: Oxford University Press, 1991, ch. 7.

Rosenhan, David, "On Being Sane in Insane Places." *Science* 179, no. 7 (1973): 250–58.

Sadler, John Z., Osborne P. Wiggins, and Michael A. Schwartz, *Philosophical Perspectives on Psychiatric Diagnostic Classification*. Baltimore: Johns Hopkins University Press, 1994.

The Medical Model

Alper, Joseph, "Biology and Mental Illness." *The Atlantic Monthly* (Dec. 1983): 70–76.

Andreasen, Nancy C., and Donald W. Black, *Introductory Textbook of Psychology*, 2d ed. Washington, D.C.: American Psychiatric Press, 1995, especially ch. 5 on "The Neurobiology of Mental Illness."

Dinan, T. G., ed., *Principles and Practice of Biological Psychiatry*. London: Clinical Neuroscience Publishers, 1990, 2 vols.

Eisenberg, Leon, "The Social Construction of the Human Brain." *American Journal of Psychiatry* 152, no. 11 (Nov. 1995): 1563–75.

Greenberg, Aaron S., and J. Michael Bailey, "The Irrelevance of the Medical Model of Mental Illness to Law and Ethics." *International Journal of Law and Psychiatry* 17, no. 2 (1994): 153–73.

Reznek, Lawrie, *The Philosophical Defence of Psychiatry.* London: Routledge, 1991.

Roth, Martin, and Jerome Kroll, *The Reality of Mental Illness.* Cambridge: Cambridge University Press, 1986, ch. 5.

Siegler, Miriam, and Humphrey Osmond, *Models of Madness, Models of Medicine.* New York: Harper & Row, 1974.

U.S. Congress, Office of Technology Assessment, *The Biology of Mental Disorders.* Washington, D.C.: U.S. Government Printing Office, 1992.

Alcoholism

American Psychiatric Association, "Practice Guidelines for the Treatment of Patients with Substance Use Disorders: Alcohol, Cocaine, Ophoids." *The American Journal of Psychiatry* 152, no. 11 (Nov. 1995 Supplement): 1–59.

Andreasen, Nancy C., and Donald W. Black, *Introductory Textbook of Psychology,* 2d ed. Washington, D.C.: American Psychiatric Press, 1995, ch. 14.

Fingarette, Herbert, *Heavy Drinking: The Myth of Alcoholism as a Disease.* Berkeley: University of California Press, 1988.

Goff, J. Larry, "Alcoholism: Disease or Wilful Misconduct." *The Journal of Psychiatry and Law* 18 (Spring 1990): 59–107.

Jellinek, E. M., *The Disease Concept of Alcoholism.* New Haven, Conn.: Hillhouse Press, 1960.

Kolata, Gina, "Alcoholic Genes or Misbehavior?" *Psychology Today* (May 1988): 34–37.

Maltzman, Irving, "Is Alcoholism a Disease?" *Integrative Physiological and Behavioral Science* 26, no. 3 (1991): 200–10.

Miller, Norman S. and John N. Chappel, "History of the Disease Concept of Alcoholism" *Psychiatric Annals* 21 (April 1991): 196–205.

Peele, Stanton, *The Diseasing of America: Addiction Treatment out of Control.* Lexington, Mass.: Lexington Books, 1990.

Rose, R. M., and J. Barrett, eds., *Alcoholism: Origins and Outcome.* New York: Raven Press, 1988.

Searles, John, "The Role of Genetics in the Pathogenesis of Alcoholism." *Journal of Abnormal Behavior* 97 (1988): 153–67.

Sykes, Charles J., *A Nation of Victims: The Decay of the American Character.* New York: St. Martin's Press, 1992, chs. 11 and 12.

Vaillant, George E., *The Natural History of Alcoholism Revisited.* Cambridge, Mass: Harvard University Press, 1995.

Homosexuality

Bayer, Ronald, *Homosexuality and American Psychiatry, The Politics of Diagnosis.* New York: Basic Books, 1981.

Bayer, Ronald, and Robert L. Spitzer, "Edited Correspondence on the Statue of Homosexuality in DSM-III." *Journal of the History of the Behavioral Sciences* 18 (1982): 32–52.

Friedman, R. C., and Jennifer I. Downey, "Homosexuality." *New England Journal of Medicine* 331, no. 14 (October 1994): 923–30.

Gonsiorek, J., "The Empirical Basis for the Demise of the Illness Model of Homosexuality." In Gonsiorek, J., and Weinrich, J., eds., *Homosexuality: Research Implications for Public Policy.* Newbury Park, Calif.: Sage, 1991. Other essays in this volume are very relevant.

Green, Richard, "Homosexuality as a Mental Illness." In: Caplan, Arthur L., et al., eds., *Concepts of Health and Disease,* Reading, Mass.: Addison-Wesley, 1981, pp. 333–51.

Haldeman, D.C., "The Practice and Ethics of Sexual Orientation Conversion Therapy." *Journal of Consulting and Clinical Psychology* 62, no. 2 (1994): 221–27.

Kirk, Stuart A., and Herb Kutchins, *The Selling of DSM: The Rhetoric of Science in Psychiatry.* New York: Aldine De Gruyter, 1992, pp. 81–90.

Margolis, Joseph, "Homosexuality." In: Tom Regan and Donald VanDeVeer, eds., *And Justice for All: New Introductory Essays in Ethics and Public Policy.* Totowa, N. J.: Rowman and Littlefield, 1982, pp. 42–63.

Murphy, Timothy, "The Ethics of Conversion Therapy." *Bioethics* 5, no. 2 (1991): 123–38.

———, "Redirecting Sexual Orientation: Techniques and Justifications." *The Journal of Sex Research,* 29, no. 4 (1992): 501–23.

Nagel, Thomas, *Mortal Questions.* London: Cambridge University Press, 1979, pp. 39–52.

Nicolosi, Joseph, *Reparative Therapy of Male Homosexuality.* Northvale, N.J.: Jason Aronson, 1993.

Ruse, Michael, *Homosexuality: A Philosophical Inquiry.* New York: Blackwell, 1988.

Stoller, et al., "A Symposium: Should Homosexuality be in the APA Nomenclature?" *American Journal of Psychiatry* 130 (1967): 1270–1316.

Feminist Concerns

Ballou, M., and N. W. Gabalac, *A Feminist Position on Mental Health.* Springfield, Ill.: Charles C. Thomas, 1985.

Boverman, Ingek, et al., "Sex-Role Stereotypes and Clinical Judgments of Mental Health." *Journal of Consulting and Clinical Psychology* 34 (1970): 1–7.

Brown, L. S., "Ethical Issues in Feminist Therapy." *Psychology of Women Quarterly,* 15 (1991): 322–36.

Caplan, Paula J., "How *Do* They Decide Who is Normal? The Bizarre, but True, Tale of the *DSM* Process." *Canadian Psychology/Psychologie canadienne* 32, no. 2 (1991): 162–70.

———, *The Myth of Women's Masochism.* Toronto: University of Toronto Press, 1985.

———, *They Say You're Crazy.* Reading, Mass.: Addison-Wesley, 1995.

Chelser, Phyllis, *Women and Madness.* New York: Harcourt Brace Jovanovich 1989.

Enns, C. Z., "Twenty Years of Feminist Counseling and Therapy: From Naming Biases to Implementing Multifaceted Practice." *Counseling Psychology* 21 (1993): 3–87.

Greene, B., "Teaching Ethics in Psychotherapy." *Women and Therapy* 15 (1994): 17–28.

Hill, M., "On Creating a Theory of Feminist Therapy." *Women and Therapy* 15 (1994): 53–66.

Hohmann, Ann H., "Gender Bias in Psychotropic Drug Prescribing in Primary Care." *Medical Care* 27, no. 5 (1989): 479–90.

Lerman, H., "The Practice of Ethics within Feminist Therapy." *Women and Therapy* 15 (1994): 85–92.

Oakley, Ann, *Essays on Women, Medicine, and Health.* Edinburgh: Edinburgh University Press, 1993.

Rodin, Mari, "The Social Construction of Premenstrual Syndrome." *Social Science and Medicine* 35 (1992): 49–56.

Velasquez, M. J., "Bringing Ethics Alive: Training Practitioners about Gender, Ethnicity, and Sexual Orientation Issues." *Women and Therapy* 15 (1994): 1–16.

Religion, Craziness, and Mental Well-Being

American Psychiatric Association, "APA Guidelines Regarding Possible Conflicts Between Psychiatrists' Religious Commitments and Psychiatric Practice." *American Journal of Psychiatry* 147 (1990): 542.

Braun, Joseph, "Ethical Issues in the Treatment of Religious Persons." In Rosenbaum, Max, ed., *Ethics and Values in Psychotherapy: A Guidebook.* New York: The Free Press, 1982, ch. 6.

Elkins, David N., "Psychotherapy and Spirituality: Toward a Theory of the Soul." *Journal of Humanistic Psychology* 35, no. 2 (1995): 78–98.

Ellis, A., "Is Religiosity Pathological?" *Free Inquiry* 8 (1988): 27–32.

Greenberg, David, and Eliezer Witztem, "Problems in the Treatment of Religious Patients." *American Journal of Psychology* 45, no. 4 (1991): 554–65.

Hall, Todd W., Theresa C. Tisdale, and Beth F. Brokaw, "Assessments of Religious Dimensions of Christian Clients: A Review of Selected Instruments for Research and Clinical use." *Journal of Psychology and Theology* 22, no. 4 (1994): 395–421.

Hawkins, Ioma L., and Sylvia L. Bullock, "Informed Consent and Religious Values: A Neglected Area of Diversity." *Psychotherapy* 32, no. 2 (1995): 293–399.

Hoshmand, Lisa T., "Psychology's Ethics of Belief." *American Psychologist* 50 (1995): 540–41.

Jones, Stanton L., "A Constructive Relationship for Religion with the Science and Profession of Psychology: Perhaps the Boldest Model Yet." *American Psychologist* 49 (1994): 184–99.

Larson, David B., E. M. Pattison, D. G. Blazer, A. R. Omran, and B. H. Kaplan, "Systematic Analysis of Research on Religious Variables in Four Major Psychiatric Journals." *American Journal of Psychiatry* 143, no. 3 (1986): 329–34.

Lukoff, David, Francis Lu, and Robert Turner, "Toward a More Culturally Sensitive DSM-IV: Psychoreligious and Psychospiritual Problems." *The Journal of Nervous and Mental Disease* 180, no. 11 (November 1992): 673–82.

Post, Stephen, "*DSM-III-R* and Religion." *Social Science and Medicine* 35 (1992): 81–90.

Richardson, James T., "Religiosity as Deviance: Negative Religious Bias in and Misuse of the *DSM-III.*" *Deviant Behavior* 14 (1993): 1–21.

Turner, Robert P., David Lukoff, Ruth T. Barnhouse, and Francis G. Lu, "Religious or Spiritual Problem: A Culturally Sensitive Diagnostic Category in the DSM-IV." *The Journal of Nervous and Mental Disease* 183, no. 7 (1995): 435–44.

Soviet Psychiatry

Babayan, Edward, *The Structure of Psychiatry in the Soviet Union.* New York: International Press, 1985.

Block, Sidney, *Psychiatric Terror.* New York: Basic Books, 1977.

———, "The Political Misuse of Psychiatry in the Soviet Union." In Bloch, Sidney, and Paul Chodoff, eds., *Psychiatric Ethics,* 2d ed. New York: Oxford University Press, 1991, ch. 24.

———, *Soviet Psychiatraic Abuse: The Shadow over World Psychiatry.* London: Gollancz, 1984.

Fireside, Harvey, *Soviet Psychoprisons.* New York: W. W. Norton, 1979.

Stone, Alan A., *Law, Psychiatry, and Morality.* Washington, D.C.: American Psychiatric Press, 1984, ch. I.

Yeo, Clayton, "Psychiatry, the Law and Dissent in the Soviet Union." *International Commission of Jurists* (June 1975): 34–41.

3.

RIGHTS AND DUTIES IN PSYCHOTHERAPIST/PATIENT RELATIONS

INTRODUCTION

Rights and Duties

After several decades of struggle, the rights of mentally handicapped persons are now widely recognized, but not always honored in practice. What is a right? The general concept of a right was nicely expressed in chapter 5 of John Stuart Mill's *Utilitarianism*:

> When we call anything a person's right, we mean that he has a valid claim on society to protect him in the possession of it, either by the force of law or by that of education and opinion. If he has what we consider a sufficient claim, on whatever account, to have something guaranteed to him by society we say that he has a right to it. . . . To have a right, then, is . . . to have something which society ought to defend me [or anyone] in the possession of.

A right is a justified moral claim or entitlement against others, but a claim to what? To anything that anyone wants? No! Rights assure only the most basic things that any reasonable being would want and judge to be essential for living a worthwhile life—things like life itself, liberty of action, security in one's person and property, equality of opportunity, basic education, basic health care, and the like.

One person's right usually correlates with another person's obligation or duty. There may be duties without corresponding rights (e.g., charity or gratitude); but there are no rights, except empty ones, without corresponding duties. Thus, "X has a right to y" usually means that others have a duty to refrain from obstructing X's pursuit or possession of y, if X so chooses (negative rights), and/or to provide X with y, if she or he so chooses (positive rights). *Moral* rights correspond to the most basic societal, professional, or personal obligations that are ratified by free, open-minded, and enlightened conscience. They ideally ought to be recognized even where they are not. *Legal* rights correlate with duties codified into positive law and legally assured. A right is *absolute* when it is binding in *all* relevant circumstances and should never be overridden. A *defeasible* right is binding under normal circumstances but may be trumped by more important rights and their corresponding *prima facie* obligations. There is honest disagreement about whether there are any absolute rights and about what considerations justly override defeasible rights, but progress toward reflective consensus is made through continuing dialogue and debate.

Professional codes of ethics, judicial decisions, governmental regulations, state laws, accrediting agencies, medical ethicists, and personal reflections provide guidance to medical practitioners concerning the moral and legal rights of mentally handicapped persons. Beginning in the 1960s, landmark legal cases like *Rouse v. Cameron* (1966), *Wyatt* v. *Stickney* (1971), *McCray* v. *Maryland* (1971), and *O'Connor* v. *Donaldson* (1975) helped transform moral rights into legal rights. Elemental legal rights for mentally handicapped persons are now formally assured, though not always honored in practice. These include rights to adequate treatment by a capable and sufficient staff, to informed voluntary consent to or refusal of treatment, to an individualized treatment plan, to privacy and dignity, to freedom from harm and abuse, to a humane physical and psychological environment, to the least restrictive environment for treatment, to be presumed competent until and unless proved incompetent, to confidentiality with respect to sensitive personal information, to be free from sexual exploitation, to register and vote, to marry, to make a will, to engage in lawful business activities, to dispose of property, to sue or be sued, to obtain jobs, education, housing, and the like without discrimination, to be free from unnecessary or excessive medication, to be free from physical restraints and isolation (except when medically necessary or necessary to protect others), not to be subjected to experimental treatment or research without informed voluntary consent, to use and wear personal possessions and clothes, to use and control one's personal money and assets, to be paid adequately for work done for the institution, to have visitors, to access telephones at reasonable hours, to uncensored correspondence, to receive mail, to regular exercise, to freedom of religion, to adequate legal representation and due process of law, to be informed about one's rights, to have access to a patient advocate, and so on.

The exercise of the rights of mentally handicapped persons is complicated by considerations of competency. Others should protect and defend the basic rights of mentally handicapped persons, especially where they are not capable of standing up for themselves.

Informed Voluntary Consent

The most basic patient right in contemporary medical and legal ethics is that of informed voluntary consent. This right identifies the most morally appropriate way to structure power relationships within the medical setting. It is touched upon or presupposed by most if not all the articles in this section and in this book. The right to informed voluntary consent asserts (1) that competent adult patients are entitled to make final decisions about submitting to any medical procedure, and (2) that they are entitled to refuse any medical procedure to which they do not freely give their knowing consent. Correspondingly, medical personnel should not perform diagnostic, therapeutic, and experimental medical procedures on competent adult patients unless they knowingly and freely consent. This right correlates with staff obligations to (1) educate and inform patients about relevant medical concerns and procedures, and (2) avoid obtaining consent using deception, coercion (threat, force, or harm) or enticement (undue incentives)—these call the voluntariness of consent into question. To be adequately informed, patients must be instructed about (1) the nature of the medical procedures being contemplated, (2) their benefits, (3) their risks (kinds, degrees, and probabilities) of harm, and the risks of harm from no treatment at all, (4) alternative procedures and therapies, (5) the physician's willingness to answer questions, and (6) the patient's right to refuse treatment without penalty. Truthfulness with patients is a logical presupposition of informed voluntary consent.

The principle of informed voluntary consent promotes and protects fundamental positive values like patient rationality and autonomy or self-determination, and/or the enjoyment thereof. It prevents the dehumanization and distress that result when rational autonomy is not respected in practice. Rational autonomy is violated by deception, withholding information, coercion, enticement, or manipulation. Such violations destroy patients' self-respect and sense of being in control, and they alienate patients and cause them to mistrust their caregivers.

If not for moral, then for self-interested reasons medical personnel should adopt the ethics of obtaining informed voluntary consent from competent patients. The law, with its penalties for noncompliance, is squarely on the side of patients in such matters, and medical personnel must obtain voluntary informed consent to avoid civil prosecution for negligence, or criminal prosecution for assault and/or battery.

Both the law and the enlightened conscience recognize legitimate exceptions to the right to informed voluntary consent. Such consent cannot and need not be obtained (1) in emergency situations where patients are unconscious, or in such deep shock that they cannot communicate, or in such overwhelming physical and/or emotional pain that they are incapacitated for decision-making, (2) when mentally incompetent due to immaturity (minors), serious mental illness, or extreme mental retardation, (3) when the right is voluntarily waived, or (4) when physicians legally have "therapeutic privilege" to exercise their judgement that a patient would be gravely harmed by medical information.

Competency and Incompetency

Informed voluntary consent is intimately related to competency. The duty to obtain it presupposes that the patient is competent; but the concept of informed consent can provide criteria for determining competency to accept or refuse treatment. If patients can understand the nature of proposed medical procedures, their risks and benefits, alternative therapies, and so on, and can make decisions based on this information, then they are competent to consent to therapy; if not, they are not. Applying the principle of informed voluntary consent to psychiatric patients is complicated by the fact that the knowing and willing parts of their souls may be the diseased parts.

Should medical personnel presume from the outset that mental patients are not competent to consent to or refuse treatment? No, a presumption of complete incompetency for everything would be too much like the illegal presumption that defendants are guilty until proved innocent. The ideal presumption, now required by law, is that patients are competent until and unless this presumption is defeated by their own behavior. Psychiatric illness is highly episodic, and patients should be approached afresh each new day with the presumption of competence. Day to day, even hour by hour, judgments of patients' abilities to understand and manage their practical affairs, including treatment, must be made by the medical personnel who deal constantly and directly with them. Most mental patients have periods of lucidity between psychotic episodes, are able to understand and cope in some areas of life even if they have blocks in others, and can best achieve responsible rational autonomy only if it is thrust upon them at appropriate times.

Legally, a formal judicial competency hearing may be required when specific types of competency, like that to stand trial, or to dispose of property, or to refuse treatment, are at issue. As a general rule, determinations of competency to choose and refuse psychotropic drugs and other treatments are made in hospitals and clinics by attending physicians. Medical determinations may be challenged and taken to a treatment team, to an ethics review committee, or even to court; but usually this does not happen. Normally it is the doctors who decide who gets to decide.

In judicial competency hearings, judges decide who gets to decide, presumably only after patients receive due process of law; but how do judges know if patients are competent? Do they know more than everyone else about how to determine this? The law does not specify in detail what to consider in determining competency, or how high to set standards for understanding and choosing. Judges are in the same boat with everyone else. In fact, they often just accept the recommendations of physicians! Paternalism in determining who is qualified to choose or refuse therapy creeps in just as readily at the judicial level as at the psychotherapeutic level, but perhaps a bit of paternalism is appropriate where there is reasonable doubt that patients can understand and appreciate the significance of their decisions.

Formal judicial competency hearings supposedly provide procedural safeguards against exploitation and abuse, but in practice they may be only empty formalities. At such hearings, the mere presence of a patient in a mental hospital may count as sufficient evidence of incompetency. Yet, in the influential *Wyatt* v. *Stickney* case in 1972, Judge Frank Johnson proclaimed, "No person shall be deemed incompetent . . . solely by reason of his admission or commitment to the hospital." Family members may easily deprive mental hospital patients of property by having them declared incompetent to manage their business affairs and by obtaining guardianship or power of attorney over their finances. Incompetency is often decided at cursory hearings where patients are not present, have inadequate legal representation, and are not even informed that court action is taking place. Competency hearings degenerate easily into farces, and procedural safeguards afford real protection only when administered by persons of good will and keen moral and legal sensitivities, prodded perhaps by vigilant patient advocates. Lacking power, status, money, and advocates, mental patients may discover that even the right to appeal such legally sanctioned exploitation is just another meaningless procedural safeguard. A strong independent advocacy system in every psychiatric institution would contribute immensely to protecting patients' rights.

When mentally handicapped patients are incompetent to choose or refuse treatment, the fundamental ethical principle of informed voluntary consent is set aside and does not apply directly to them, for they have no rational autonomy to protect. Yet, the principle still applies to the proxy consenters who must decide on their behalf. Proxy consent may be given in the clinical setting, not by treating physicians, but by family, friends, or legal guardians. Essays to follow explore the appropriateness of permitting psychiatric patients to make their own treatment decisions, and when to substitute proxy consenters.

Competency for decision-making is an elusive notion, but most authorities agree that its elements are both rational/cognitive, and volitional/affective/decisional. Most discussions of competency, like that of James F. Drane to follow, concentrate primarily on the cognitive element, the ability to understand. Understanding comes in degrees, and Drane proposes a sliding scale of competency that ranges, for consent purposes, from minimal understanding and acquiescence when a diagnosis is sure and the available therapy is effective and safe, to much more complex understanding and reason-giving under conditions of great risk and uncertainty. For irreversible refusals of lifesaving therapy where the diagnosis is certain, treatment is effective and relatively risk-free, and refusals seem outrageously bad, a fairly high standard of reason-giving should be required.

Since both autonomy or decision-making capacity, as well as rationality or ability to understand, are essential for competency, incompetency may result from a deficiency in one or both. Drane recognizes this, but, like most authorities on competency, he gives very little consideration to affective/motivational/volitional inadequacy. Other authors (Bursztajn, et al., 1991, Becker and Kahana, 1993) have focused on these other features of competency. The following discussion supplements Drane's presentation.

If ignorance and incapacity to understand undermine the rationality component in competency, what would undermine the autonomy component? Persons assessing competency need to look at both. Some patients might be incompetent to choose or refuse therapy because their decision-making capacity is significantly impaired, even though they understand everything. The list is incomplete, but perhaps the motivational/choosing parts of the soul could be defective enough for incompetency if:

1. Decisions are determined by pathological conscious or unconscious processes. Presumably, psychotherapists know how to identify these states. Consider this case: A thirty-five-year-old woman with an M.A. degree in business administration is a rising executive star in a major corporation and is engaged to be married. One night she and her fiance are walking in a park, and a cat jumps on her from out of a tree and bites and scratches her head, face, and neck. The cat is apprehended and tests positively for rabies. Since childhood, this woman has detested having shots. When she was small, her brothers had to go with her and hold her down for the family physician to give her routine inoculations. Now, after considering and understanding everything, she refuses treatment for rabies because it involves a prolonged series of injections. She claims to prefer death from rabies over having the shots.

This patient might agree to being gassed unconscious for the shots, but assume for the sake of the argument that no one thinks of this alternative, or that she will not accept it. Would it be appropriate to declare this woman incompetent to refuse this treatment because she is victimized by a phobia? All members of her family support this alternative and agree that her refusal of lifesaving medical care is outrageously bad. Any of her brothers will volunteer to be a proxy decision-maker for her. They are confident that she will soon express "retrospective gratitude" if her refusal is overridden.

Might not many psychopathological conditions other than phobias and obsessions incapacitate a person for medical decision-making while leaving cognitive functions relatively intact?

2. Patients may want and choose incompatible things, even after extended discussions in which they seem to understand everything, as in this case: An elderly woman living alone is discovered in mid-winter to have frozen toes and a gangrenous foot. To save her life, doctors are convinced that her foot must be amputated. After explaining that she will lose her life unless her foot is removed, the physician asks her to consent to amputation. She replies that she does not want to lose her foot. "Then do you want to lose your life?" "No, I want to live." "Then you must give us permission to remove your foot." "No, I want to keep my foot." "Then do you want to die?" "No, I love life." "So you will give us permission to amputate the foot." "No, you must save my foot." And so the dialogue goes, almost endlessly.

Is this patient volitionally incompetent? Should her daughter, who will readily approve the amputation, be appointed as her surrogate decision-maker?

(3) Patients may obstinately refuse to consider the medical alternatives and/or the options for living a meaningful life after treatment. Consider the case of the star athlete who must have a leg amputated and thinks that he would then have absolutely nothing to live for, as described near the end of James Drane's article. The athlete is mentally intact, capable of understanding, but will not do so because of situationally based depression and anxiety.

Is Drane correct in judging that this athlete is incompetent to refuse lifesaving medical care? Might not many mental patients obtusely refuse to consider the alternatives?

(4) Patients are so emotionally or affectively blunted or distorted that they are unable to appreciate the significance of the acceptance/refusal decisions that they make. Persons with major affective disorders might be incompetent in this way to choose or refuse treatment.

The Rights to Receive and to Refuse Treatment

Once institutionalized involuntarily, must patients actually receive treatment, not just custodial care? And may they refuse treatment? Morton Birnbaum introduced the concept of a "right to treatment" for mental hospital patients in 1960, and this right was affirmed thereafter in a number of judicial decisions. Its range of application is much narrower than the phrase itself suggests, for it has a restricted legal focus. Its relation to the right to choose or refuse treatment needs clarification.

Voluntary patients have no legal right to treatment because *in theory* they are free to leave the hospital at any time. Only involuntary patients have this right. Its logic is disjunctive; it is a right *either* to be released in the absence of effective treatment *or* to be provided with adequate treatment in exchange for involuntary deprivation of liberty. The goal of such treatment is not absolute cure. Rather, it aims only the restoration of a minimal level of functioning sufficient for the earliest possible return to constitutionally guaranteed liberty. In response to this right, many states simply released most of their involuntary patients rather than provide them with costly treatment, even though only *minimal* treatment conditions were required. The legal right to treatment mandated only minimal humane living conditions in a therapeutic environment, but it became a powerful impetus for deinstitutionalization.

If misunderstood, the right to treatment could degenerate into another rationale for forcing treatment upon unwilling patients. To be compatible with a right to refuse treatment, the right to treatment must be understood as a right to *choose or refuse* treatment, which correlates with the duty of the institution to *make treatment available,* without forcing it upon unwilling patients. In refusing treatment, however, involuntary patients thereby elect indefinite confinement.

The right to refuse treatment is assured and exercised without serious challenge by all competent persons, given the moral and legal principles of democratic society. In the past, involuntary commitment to mental hospitalization completely suspended this right. Today, involuntary commitment for treatment leaves the question of involuntary therapy at least partly unresolved. Hospital employees are no longer authorized to do anything they please to mental patients in the name of therapy. Involuntary commitment is not equivalent to involuntary treatment.

Paternalistic, coercive treatments for clearly incompetent patients seem perfectly justifiable. Where patients are truly incapacitated for making treatment decisions, the moral duty to respect their rational autonomy is set aside; and moral duties of benevolence and/or harm-prevention prevail. Psychotherapists may disregard the choices and preferences of incompetent patients, especially where their decisions would likely result in serious and perhaps irreversible harm to themselves.

Specific Patient Rights and Corresponding Duties

Many specific moral and/or legal rights of mental patients and the corresponding duties of medical personnel are explored in the following selections, beginning with Kerry Brace's excellent analysis and defense of the moral ideal of preserving, restoring, and protecting rational autonomy as the primary goal of and ultimate presupposition of psychotherapy. Then follow discussions of (1) determining competency, (2) the right to treatment, (3) the right to refuse treatment, especially drug therapy, (4) the right to confidentiality, limited by therapists' duties to warn others of threatened harm, and to report abuses of children and medical perils like AIDS to the proper authorities, and (5) the right of present and former patients not to be sexually exploited by therapists.

An update on the duty to warn seems appropriate. This duty is much opposed by both psychotherapists and their patients for many good reasons, as Paul Appelbaum explains in his article to come. In the *Nasser v. Parker* case decided by the Virginia Supreme Court in 1995, the court ruled that a psychiatrist and hospital had no duty to protect prospective victims of a former patient because no "special relation" with this patient was ever established. In this case, a patient threatened to kill a woman who had rejected him. The man's psychiatrist arranged for him to be admitted to a mental hospital as a "voluntary" patient; but he left the hospital the next day; and several days later he shot and killed the woman and himself. The psychiatrist and hospital did not warn the woman that the patient had left the hospital, so her father sued them. Judges on the Virginia Supreme Court heard the appeal of the case. They ruled that having a "special relationship" meant "taking charge" of a patient, and that this was not done; thus, there was no duty to warn. Other courts, along with most medical ethicists, might judge that a "special relationship" is established with patients simply by providing them with treatment on a continuing basis, and that the Virginia court reached the right verdict for the wrong reason. In any event, as Appelbaum shows, there is massive noncompliance with the burdensome and ethically problematic duty to warn. Perhaps the courage of noncompliant psychotherapists will be bolstered by this legal counter to *Tarasoff*.

Finally, at times, psychotherapists may be highly attracted sexually to their patients, and vice versa. The psychotherapeutic establishment affirms decisively that vulnerable mentally handicapped patients have a strong right to be free of sexual exploitation by their therapists. The good reasons for taking this position are well explained in an upcoming essay by Françoise Baylis. The American Psychological Association affirmed in 1992 that sexual relations are allowed between therapists and former patients after an interval of two years; but this position faces serious objections like those raised in the coming essay by Glen O. Gabbard.

Nonrelativist Ethical Standards for Goal Setting in Psychotherapy

Kerry Brace

The goals that are developed in psychotherapy and the processes by which they are developed are considerably influenced by the values held not only by the client but also by the therapist (Bergin, 1985; Drane, 1982; Oliver & Rogers, 1986). Because of this there arises the danger that goals and goal setting in psychotherapy could be arbitrary in the sense that they reflect merely the value preferences of particular therapists or clients.

This issue is especially important for therapists with constructivist viewpoints. For them, psychotherapy involves not only discovery and alteration of a client's (family or individual) given characteristics, but the development of ways to construe the client's nature and situation that will be conducive to desirable changes. Because therapist and client create this construal out of their own internal and interpersonal processes, their value beliefs are likely to be major determinants of its form. In recognizing that they have a choice of various ways to describe and understand their clients and that clients' welfare may be at stake in the choice, constructivists have expressed an increased sense of being involved in ethical choices (Efran, Lukens, & Lukens, 1988; Epstein & Loos, 1989). As I see it, this is an overarching concern in psychotherapy, because ethical or moral decisions can be defined as choices as to what is good or bad or what is a right or wrong way to attain something good or to avoid something bad, and such choices are essential in the psychotherapeutic process.

From *Ethics & Behavior* 2, no. 1 (1992): 15–38. Copyright © 1992, Lawrence Erlbaum Associates, Inc. Reprinted by permission.

The purpose of this article is to propose a means by which therapists can determine whether their goal setting is justifiable from a standpoint that is not relative to their personal values but universal in the sense of being conformable to ethical standards. It represents one constructivist's attempt to find ethical grounding for therapeutic choices.

I argue that purely relativist standards for guiding moral choices are not adequate in psychotherapy or counseling because this particular context demands moral standards that apply regardless of personal views of what is good or right: respect for clients' welfare and respect for their self-determination. To benefit clients is the *raison d'être* for psychotherapy. (This discussion is limited to psychotherapy in which clients engage willingly. When psychotherapy is forced on a person by a third party, different considerations arise that are not addressed here.) At least in the case of voluntary psychotherapy there is no justification for its occurrence unless it benefits the client. Regardless of what the therapist and the client view as good or desirable, what goes on in psychotherapy needs to be directed toward the client's welfare. This principle accommodates relativism in the sense that it is recognized that people may differ in what they consider to be desirable; but it is universal in the sense that in psychotherapy what clients consider beneficial or harmful for themselves and what in fact is beneficial or harmful to them must always be taken into account.

As Kitchener (1984) pointed out, the fact that there are some exceptional cases in which a moral principle does not apply does not detract from its general validity. An exception arises, for example, if a client perceives his or her welfare as requiring unjustifiable harm to another or others. A batterer might believe his own well-being depends on keeping his wife frightened of him and under his control. The therapist could not seek to foster what the client perceives as his own welfare in this situation. However, the fact that such exceptions may arise does not remove the therapist's general responsibility to seek clients' best interest.

Respect for clients' self-determination can also be seen as universally necessary in voluntary psychotherapy. This is so because psychotherapy is carried out for the purpose of enabling clients to make changes in their lives that *they* want to make. The therapist will often have views that differ from the client's views regarding what thoughts and actions will be instrumental to the client's desired changes and may exert influence to get the client to adopt means to change that he or she would not have chosen independently. The therapist may also believe that what clients desire will not in fact be beneficial to them and may influence them toward changing their desires. However, what clients desire for themselves is what therapy is for—whether this be specific goals that they have brought to therapy or goals influenced by the therapist. In short, clients' self-determination is essential in psychotherapy because the purpose of therapy is to accomplish the client's goal.

The following discussion outlines possible philosophical bases for nonrelative ethical standards, then describes the principles of respect for clients' welfare and respect for clients' self-determination. An examination of what is involved in the practical application of these principles in psychotherapy and counseling follows. This leads to a set of rules that can be used by therapists and counselors who would like to have something beyond personal values to guide the process of goal setting.

The proposed rules can be related to Kitchener's (1984) model of levels of ethical justification in counseling. Her model is based on Drane's (1982) explication of levels of ethical discourse and Hare's (1981) discussion of the distinction between intuitive and critical-evaluative levels of ethical reasoning. The *intuitive level* refers to people's "immediate, prereflective response to most ethical situations based on the sum of their prior ethical knowledge and experience" (Kitchener, 1984, p. 44). The *critical-evaluative level* includes three sublevels that involve various types of reasoned judgment and evaluation used in making ethical decisions. The first of the sublevels is *ethical rules,* "directives which prescribe or proscribe certain acts" (Drane, 1982, p. 26). Kitchener focused mainly on the codified statements of professional ethical guidelines as exemplifying this sublevel. This discussion amplifies the content of this sublevel and proposes specific guidelines related to choice of instrumental and end goals in psychotherapy and counseling. Kitchener's next sublevel is that of *principles,* the higher level norms on which rules are based. Drane (1982) defined *principles* as "ethical values in verbal or propositional form which either have or presume to have universal applicability" (p. 31). Respect for clients' welfare and respect for their self-determination can be viewed as principles in this sense.

The third sublevel in Kitchener's model is *ethical theory*—that is, philosophical reasoning or religious belief that justifies, supports, explains, or qualifies the ethical principles (Drane, 1982). I address this level first, with a brief consideration of possible philosophical grounds for a nonrelativist moral viewpoint in psychotherapeutic goal setting.

Philosophical Bases for Nonrelativist Standards

The principles of respect for clients' welfare and self-determination can be viewed as applicable regardless of particular personal-cultural values held by the therapist and client. In this respect, they are unlike most of the consensus values of therapists discussed by Bergin (1985) and Jensen and Bergin (1988), which include, for example, "having a sense of identity and feelings of worth; being skilled in interpersonal communication, sensitivity, and nurturance; being genuine and honest; having self-control and personal responsibility; being committed in marriage, family, and other relationships . . ." (Jensen & Bergin, 1988, p. 295). These values generally can be seen as matters of personal or cultural preference.

Some ethical theorists have argued that there are no universal ethical standards, that moral rules are all merely preferences predominant in particular cultures (a view known as *ethical relativism*), or that they are merely expressions of individuals' preferences (a view known as *subjectivism*). However, there are important arguments against these views (Rachels, 1986).

As for the subjectivist thesis that moral standards are merely personal preferences, the basic argument to the contrary is that, in order to be acceptable, moral standards need to be backed up by reasons. As Rachels (1986) pointed out, the fact that truths in the area of moral standards are not on the same order as truths about physical nature does not imply that they are nothing but expressions of subjective feelings: "Moral truths are truths of reason; that is, a moral judgment is true if it is backed by better reasons than the alternatives" (p. 35).

> We cannot make something good or bad just by wishing it to be so, because we cannot merely will that the weight of reason be on its side or against it. And we can be wrong about what is good or bad, because we can be wrong about what reason commends. (pp. 35–36)

Just as other moral judgments require the support of reason, in order to be considered ethical, judgments as to what goals are conducive to clients' welfare and self-determination must be "backed by better reasons than the alternatives" (Rachels, 1986, p. 35). A subjectivist might ask, "Whose reasons?" because the reasons accepted could vary with the persons involved. A possible answer in the context of psychotherapy is, "The reasons agreed on by the client and therapist, when the therapist acts with respect for the client's best interest and self-determination." The fact that reasons may vary with the interpersonal context negates neither the need for acceptable reasons in each context nor the possibility that the principles of respect for the client's best interest and self-determination may apply generally in psychotherapy.

One basic argument against ethical relativism is that, although some rules by which people guide their actions are particular to their culture (e.g., the rule that certain topics are not fit for public discussion), other rules are essential to the survival of society (e.g., "Don't kill"). Rules of the latter type can be considered nonrelative. I propose an analogous distinction between two types of values operative in psychotherapeutic goal setting: relative personal-cultural values, such as Bergin's (1985) "consensus values"; and the nonrelative values of respect for clients' welfare and self-determination.

Gert (1988) provided a carefully reasoned discussion of moral rules as universal. An important part of his argument is that there are some things that no rational individual would want to have done to himself or herself, unless there is something that justifies having them done in a particular situation. The moral rules prohibit doing such things. Gert's (1988, p. 284) list of moral rules includes:

1. Don't kill.
2. Don't cause pain.
3. Don't disable.
4. Don't deprive of freedom.
5. Don't deprive of pleasure.
6. Don't deceive.
7. Keep your promise.

Gert may have considered the principle of working for another's best interest as a moral ideal rather than a moral rule, partly because he defined *moral rules* as rules that can be obeyed all the time. However, in the context of a helping relationship like psychotherapy, "keep your promise" does entail working for the client's welfare.

Engelhardt (1986) argued against the possibility of universal moral standards partly on the basis of different views of moral issues among different cultures and religions. He provided reasons to show that it is not possible to "establish by sound rational argument a particular concrete moral viewpoint as properly decisive" (p. 40). This leaves agreement among a group of people as the only means of establishing moral guidance for behavior.

However, Engelhardt distinguished between two dimensions of morality that correspond to Rachels's nonrelative and culture-relative types of rules: one that is "content-poor" (i.e., not much is specified) and that spans "numerous divergent moral communities" (p. 54) and one that has contents that are more extensive and specific to "particular moral communities" (p. 54). This suggests that there are a few things that can be widely agreed upon as morally acceptable, as well as many ideas regarding what is morally acceptable upon which people will differ.

It seems that Gert's moral rules designated as universal would certainly be widely agreed on across almost all cultures and belief systems. For our purposes, it is probably not necessary to distinguish between universal in the sense of being very widely agreed on (which would derive from Engelhardt's view) and universal in the sense of being rationally necessary (which would derive from Gert's view). In both cases, the ethical principles and criteria for following them discussed here can be taken as applicable to virtually all psychotherapy and counseling situations and can be used by therapists and counselors who would like to have some nonrelativist standards on which to base their goal setting.

Respect for Persons and the Client's Welfare

Based on a review of literature on values in social work, Horne (1987) focused on "respect for persons" as the one that is basic and central: "Basically all other values are derived from and are a part of the meaning of this moral principle" (p. 9). The American Psychological Association's (1990) "Ethical Principles of Psychologists" begins with the statement, "Psychologists respect the dignity and worth of the individual" (p. 390).

What does respect for persons entail? According to Horne, "The most common way of describing what is meant by this concept is that people should be treated as ends in themselves, not as means to ends" (pp. 11–12). This principle is the core concept in one important system of moral philosophy developed by Kant. According to Kant (1785/1959), to treat persons as ends implies treating them with respect, not because of their particular qualities or actions but because of their inherent worth as human beings.

Horne pointed out that the belief in the inherent worth of persons has been justified in various ways. According to Kant, the individual's absolute worth derives from the ability to think and act rationally; this rationality implies autonomy, that is, "our ability to act in the pursuit of our own self-chosen goals" (Horne, 1987, p. 13). Hence any diminishment of one person's self-determination by another would mean disregarding the principle of respect for persons.

However, as Watson (1980) pointed out, the context of social work makes it apparent that rationality and autonomy cannot be an adequate basis of respect for persons, because some clients (e.g., senile elders or young children) may not demonstrate rationality or capacity for autonomy. The same would hold, of course, in the context of counseling or psychotherapy. Watson (1980) included other human characteristics as grounds for respect of human beings, such as "the capacity to be emotionally secure, the desire to give and the desire to receive love and affection, as well as the distinctive endowments of a human being" (p. 61).

Another possibility is that respect for persons could be justified on the basis of another widely accepted ethical principle: "Do unto others as you would have them do unto you." Because most people would like to be respected as having unconditional worth as a human being, we should also accord this respect to others. This idea is supported by the reasoning of contemporary moral philosophers such as Rachels (1986) and Gert (1988). Their understanding is that, because moral standards need to be applied impartially, if one would advocate applying a principle to oneself, one must also advocate applying it to others.

Two of the principles discussed by Kitchener (1984)—beneficence and nonmaleficence—can be seen as components of respect for persons. The phrase "respect for the client's welfare" is used here to include both of these principles. *Beneficence* means "doing good to others" (Kitchener, 1984, p. 49) and, as a principle for therapy, mandates that the therapist must actively foster the client's welfare. In psychotherapy there is an explicit or implied promise that the therapist will do this. It is because of this promise that, in psychotherapy, respect for persons can be viewed as including a commitment to seek the client's best interest because not keeping a promise is an instance of not showing respect.

Nonmaleficence means not to cause harm or put one at risk of harm, and this is patently essential in observing respect for persons. In Gert's (1988) system of universally applicable moral rules, the most basic rules prohibit the causing of harm to others unjustifiably. From this viewpoint, nonmaleficence governs everyone, and the therapist's duty not to harm clients is equivalent to each human's duty to others. Of course psychotherapy may cause the client emotional pain at times. If this happens with the client's consent and if the pain results in or contributes to beneficial changes desired by the client which in the client's valuation would outweigh the pain, then this is a case in which causing pain can be ethically justified. For a discussion of how benefits and harms may be weighed in clinical settings, see Culver and Gert (1982).

Self-Determination

In this discussion, *self-determination* is defined as the experienced sense of doing according to one's own desire when that desire is not subject to manipulation by another person. (It does not address the philosophical issue of free will versus determinism.) There have been at least two different interpretations of the meaning of self-determination. The first of these is *negative freedom,* that is, freedom from interference with one's chosen actions. Self-determination as negative freedom is essential to respect for persons in the Kantian perspective of people as essentially rational and autonomous.

The other interpretation of self-determination is referred to as *positive freedom,* which has been defined by Butrym (1976) as "an extension of the range of choices available both within the personality and in the external environment" (p. 52). Although self-determination interpreted this way implies that the range of choices available to people should be maximized, it also allows for restriction of some choices: A helper, in this case, a therapist, should work to change a client's desires if they would lead to self-degradation or exploitation of others (Bernstein, 1975).

Plant (1970) pointed out that self-determination interpreted as positive freedom could sanction a denial of the right to freedom from interference. In the psychotherapeutic context, the therapist may influence the client in order to have the client reach a goal seen as good by the therapist, even through coercion or manipulation, if self-determination means only positive freedom.

When it is clear that what someone wants to do is unacceptably harmful to self or others, respect for persons requires denial of their self-determination. The problem is that, although sometimes it is relatively clear that a self-determined action will be harmful—for example, when there is a threat of bodily injury or death to self or another—at other times it may not be clear whether a self-determined action will lead to harm. Another complication is that the harm created by a self-determined action would need to be weighed against the harm inherent in denying self-determination. For example, even if a therapist was sure that a client would be harmed by staying in a current living situation, it might be considered more harmful to undermine the client's intention to stick it out because that would be a denial of self-determination.

Actions intended to be beneficial but done without the consent of the person to be benefitted (thus violating his or her self-determination) are referred to as *paternalistic*. Culver and Gert (1982) developed a procedure for determining whether such actions are justified. The conditions that justify paternalistic actions in psychotherapy are discussed by Brace and VandeCreek (1991).

Respect for the Client's Welfare in Goal Setting

GOAL EXAMINATION AND CONSISTENCY OF GOALS

Assume that acting in the client's best interest is a primary ethical standard in psychotherapy. The client may enter therapy with a particular goal stated explicitly which, however, is not in his or her best interest according to his or her own valuation. For example, a college student might request counseling stating that his or her goal is to improve motivation for academic performance. Assessment might reveal that this client really does not value the kind of work for which he or she is studying. Thus, stated goals need to be examined by both therapist and client to see whether they are actually in the client's best interest, rather than adopted without such examination.

The client's best interest will vary depending on what the client values and the relative importance of various values to the client. Each of the client's various values may or may not be conducive to the solution of the presenting problem or to the client's well-being. During the process of therapy, the therapist and client can work together to assess which values are most important to the client. They can also determine which values of lesser importance conflict with and which support the most important values. The therapist may be able to show the client how acting on one value results in blocking the realization of a more important value. A common example would be the husband who wants to maintain control over his wife's actions and in acting to fulfill this value alienates her so that he loses her affection and love. If clients see that something they value is blocking the achievement of a goal related to a more important value, they may want to alter the contrary value. Thus, when goals specified by the client are mutually incompatible, this needs to be pointed out and the client given a chance to formulate mutually consistent goals.

JUSTIFICATION OF CHOICE OF GOALS

Wylie (1989) described the psychotherapy relationship as being of an inherently problematic ethical nature. She pointed out that, although it is generally acknowledged that to act in the client's welfare is the paramount principle, in psychotherapy the meaning of welfare is often not clear or is subject to various interpretations. Given the same presenting situation, client welfare may mean different things to a psychoanalyst and a family therapist, and widely differing procedures would be used to work toward the client's welfare, the means chosen being determined to a large extent by the way the welfare of the client is defined. It is possible that in some or many cases various means or approaches to change could all be acceptable as being in the client's best interest. For example, in family therapy, the individual self-differentiation recommended by Bowen (1966) could lead to a family situation as satisfactory to all members as structural realignments (changes in relationship rules and patterns) recommended by Minuchin (1974). To fulfill the standard of seeking the client's best interest, it is necessary for the therapist to perform the widest feasible consideration of potential instrumental goals (means of treatment) and end goals for a particular client and to make a conscious choice of goals that the current knowledge base and informed reasoning would best support. Also, the therapist may find that a chosen treatment proves ineffective. In this case, seeking the client's best interest requires changing treatment means or making an informed referral (Keith-Spiegel & Koocher, 1985).

In many therapeutic situations, the effects of therapist values on choice of goals may not be obvious—especially if the therapist's habitual patterns of thought are taken for granted to be beneficial to clients. Hence, intentional deliberation would be required of the therapist in order to ensure that what he or she values as a goal is ethically defensible as being in the client's best interest. The basic point here is that ethical practice requires a conscious, intentional investigation of what the client's best interests actually are and examination of goals to determine whether they would promote these interests.

CLIENT-THERAPIST AGREEMENT ON GOALS

The principle of self-determination adds to this point the qualification that the client should be "in on" this investigation as fully as possible and that there should be agreement between therapist and client that the goals chosen are in the client's best interest. It seems that this may result in a more effective therapy because it should lead to results that are most satisfying for the client and, therefore, most likely to be maintained or to lead to further desired changes.

THOROUGH ASSESSMENT

Thorough assessment is a necessity in ensuring that the client's best interest is served by therapy. Along with knowing about intrapsychic and interpersonal factors, knowing about the client's family context or considering possible physical factors may be crucial. In a case described by Wylie (1989; discussed in more detail later), assessment of the family situation was important for prevention of the death of the client's father. In another case mentioned by Wylie, a woman died of a brain tumor because the therapist did not consider the possibility of an organic condition. Such occurrences prove the necessity of thorough assessment. Of course there are always practical limits on how much the therapist can find out about the client, and much information about the client may not be relevant to determining the best goals and treatment. However, the therapist does have an obligation to explore all areas of information that standard therapeutic practice would indicate to be of potential importance.

ERRORS IN CLINICAL JUDGMENT

Another important consideration in ensuring that therapeutic goals are really in the client's best interest has to do with potential errors in clinical judgment. A number of authors have reported that certain kinds of errors in judgment are likely to occur in psychotherapeutic treatment. Examples include: effects of preconceived notions or expectancies, lack of awareness of factors influencing one's judgment, overconfidence in the accuracy of one's judgment (Arkes, 1981), making probability judgments on the basis of representative characteristics without evaluating the actual probability (Dawes, 1986), selective evocation by the therapist of evidence from the client that confirms his or her existing hypotheses (Snyder & Thomsen, 1988), and various biases in attributions about causes of behavior (Jordan, Harvey, & Weary, 1988). The therapist needs to be aware of the danger of falling into such mistakes and must be circumspect about avoiding them or correcting them in order to be as sure as possible that end goals and instrumental goals are in the client's best interest.

FIDELITY AND HONESTY

Fidelity and honesty can also be seen as necessary factors in consideration of the client's best interest. Fidelity is one of the principles discussed by Kitchener (1984) as being relevant to counseling psychology. It means keeping the implied and explicit promises made when entering voluntarily into a relationship. Thus, a breach of confidentiality would be a violation of this principle because confidentiality is promised to the client. Because therapists promise to help clients, it is also a breach of fidelity for therapists not to refer clients elsewhere when they believe they cannot help.

Not to deceive is one of the universal moral rules discussed by Gert (1988) and, as a positive principle, may be referred to as honesty. Some schools of therapy advocate deception of the client in some cases (Henderson, 1987). If, as Gert suggested, no rational person would want to be deceived without some good reason for wanting this, respect for the client's best interest requires honesty—except when the breach of honesty is an instance of justified paternalism (discussed later). It is clear that therapeutic measures using deception of clients violate the principle of respect for self-determination because they entail doing something to or for them without giving them a chance to determine whether they want it done. As discussed in Brace and VandeCreek (1991), paternalistic actions of this type are rarely justifiable in psychotherapy.

CONTEXT AND JUSTICE

It is clear that changes made by clients as a result of therapy can affect people with whom the client is related, such as family, friends, or co-workers. The principle of respect for persons implies that the therapist has a responsibility to consider the client's environment in setting and working toward goals with the client.

Wylie (1989) described the case of a depressed and anxious young woman who was being treated by psychotherapist Mark Karpel. She had dropped out of college four times and was unable to find work. When Karpel saw her parents along with her, he found out that the father was also deeply depressed. As a young man, the father had failed in his career and attempted suicide several times. He was currently working in a low-status job. Observing the negative interactions in the family, Karpel thought that the daughter's doing worse than the father may have been an important factor in keeping the father from suicide. Because working only for the daughter's welfare could have meant disaster for the father—which in turn could have exacerbated the daughter's condition—Karpel saw a systemic approach as necessary in order to act ethically in this situation. A wider view of alternatives here allowed a more accurate view of the daughter's best interest, as well as consideration of her father's best interest. A poor outcome would be expected if the therapist in this case had happened to be one whose therapeutic values and consequent goal negotiation had an exclusive focus on the individual client.

The principle of justice is related to consideration of the client's environment. According to Kitchener (1984) *justice* means "that equal persons have the right to be treated equally and nonequal persons have a right to be treated differently if the inequality is relevant to the issue in question" (p. 49). This generally refers to fair distribution of services or opportunities, and this matter is beyond the scope of this study. In the context of group or family therapy, justice could mean aiming for equal benefit for all members. In individual therapy, given respect for persons in general, therapists should consider the effects of therapy on people other than clients and do what they can to ensure that the least amount of harm come to them. However, therapists can hardly be expected to seek to benefit significant others to the same extent that they do their clients.

Client Self-Determinination in Goal Setting

INFLUENCE OF THERAPISTS' VALUES

An essential prerequisite for respecting client self-determination in therapy is to consider the nature of the therapist's influence on the client. To the extent that the therapist-client relationship is perceived by both parties as a more expert helper–less expert person in need of help relationship, clients may be pressed into revising their views as to what change is desirable. Thomasma (1984) pointed out that there is an imbalance of knowledge and power between helping professionals and clients in need of help. Clients have lost some degree of autonomy—their choices are more limited than they would be if help were not needed. Thomasma saw this situation as obliging the professional to make decisions with particular attention to the values of the client.

Beitman (1987) cited evidence from Beutler (1983) and Strong (1978) which indicated that "Successful psychotherapy seems to be characterized by changes in patient values and beliefs toward those of the therapist, even though therapists vary widely in belief and value postures" (p. 222). Beitman saw therapists as "teaching their patients to be like them or to assume roles of which they approve" (p. 223). As Owen (1986) pointed out, the false presumption that the helper is scientifically objective and operates from a value-free stance is likely to lead to the client being molded in the helper's image. This presumption would reduce the possibility of clients questioning whether what the helper presents as valuable is really valuable for them.

Bergin (1980) cited empirical studies showing that therapists, even when intending to do so, do not remain value-free in what they actually say. Owen (1986) gave the example of independent studies of Carl Rogers's interview style by Murray (1956) and Truax (1966), both of whom found that Rogers rewarded what he liked and punished what he did not like in what clients said—so that his values rather than the clients' values regulated the structure, content, and outcomes of therapeutic sessions. Rogers himself acknowledged that therapy promotes a new idea of the human being (Owen, 1986), and he probably would not have claimed that being client centered necessarily means simply going along with the client's values. More likely he believed that the client would benefit by adopting Rogerian values. The same could be said for a dedicated practitioner of psychoanalysis, gestalt, cognitive-behavioral, or many other psychotherapeutic orientations.

Oliver and Rogers (1986) expressed apprehension that pervasive values of current psychotherapy, such as self-actualization, independence, and intimacy, may be treated as moral imperatives. (As discussed before, such values are personal or cultural preferences; it is helpful to distinguish them from nonrelative principles.) Wilkes (1981) expressed this danger in another way: When one person presumes to help others attain more of their potential, it is the helper who defines the potential. The helper is convinced that he or she can let clients know "what they really want or really are (as opposed to what they actually want or think they are)" (Horne, 1987, p. 28).

IMPORTANCE OF MAKING VALUES EXPLICIT IN THERAPY

It seems clear that the context of psychotherapy does pose a serious threat to client self-determination because of the potential for imposition of therapists' values. However, the fact that therapists operate while holding particular personal values does not necessarily lead to imposing these personal values on clients. Aside from it not being possible, it is probably not even desirable to try to exclude therapists' value beliefs from the goal-setting process. Rather, to protect client self-determination, unawareness of the effects of these beliefs needs to be excluded. According to Bergin (1985), "Because values are necessarily embedded in the treatment process, they should be made explicit and should be openly used to guide and evaluate therapy" (p. 99). Bergin further stated that

> being explicit actually protects clients. The more subtle our values, the more likely we are to be hidden persuaders. The more open we are about our views, the more choice clients will have in electing to be influenced or not to be influenced. (p. 107)

Clients are in therapy because they are seeking a direction beyond what is currently available to them, and therapists can provide this out of their own value systems. As long as this is done with the awareness of both parties, it would not constitute imposition of values; rather, it would be creating the option of alternative values for the client. It is not necessarily inconsistent to believe in self-determination and to encourage the client to try new things. It depends on how the therapist's values were presented and how they were perceived by the client. Do the therapist's values come across as implying goals that are "moral imperatives" for the client or options for the client to consider? As Aponte (1985) noted, it may be necessary for therapists sometimes to seek to alter clients' values intentionally. (Remember the case of the batterer who values his fearsomeness.) Even this could be done with respect for client self-determination, if the clients were made explicitly aware of their own and their therapists' relevant values and of the need for them to consider for themselves whether the proposed alteration in values would be to their own and others' best interest.

From a constructivist viewpoint, the client's best interest is not an objective reality to be discovered, but something defined by the verbal exchange between client and therapist (Epstein & Loos, 1989). Respect for self-determination would oblige therapists operating from this viewpoint not to take upon themselves the definition of the client's best interest, but to make the client aware of the dialectical process of definition of best interest and to ensure that the client's view predominates.

Interaction of Therapist and Client Values

A more detailed look at the interaction of the values held by therapists and clients may give a better understanding of how clients' self-determination can be maintained. When clients engage in therapy at their own volition, the process of goal setting involves therapist and client coming to a sufficient degree of agreement as to what kind of change will move the client from a less valued to a more valued condition. There are two general types of movement that could lead to or contribute to this agreement. The therapist could assess what kind of change clients want (perhaps helping them clarify what they do want if they are not already clearly aware of this), put aside his or her personal view of the value of the desired change, and endeavor to facilitate just what the clients order. Another possibility is that the therapist could assess the kind of change valued by clients in terms of his or her own values. Then agreeing on goals involves the therapist (intentionally or unintentionally) exerting persuasive influence on clients so that clients realize the kind of change that the therapist sees as valuable for them. The two alternative modes of goal setting—therapist accommodation to client values and client acceptance of therapist values—may be viewed as poles of a continuum, with the process of goal setting involving varying relative degrees of both modes.

The client, coming to a therapist and desiring to make some change, is requesting to be influenced, just as patients would expect to act on the basis of a physician's advice. To provide service, the therapist obviously must have some effect on what the client does. However, this can be done without denying clients' right to act on their own will if the therapist informs the client of various possible actions that could change their undesired situations and makes explicit that the choice of whether to implement such actions rests with the client and that other alternatives might be learned from other sources. This allows both the increased potential denoted by positive freedom and the avoidance of coercion denoted by negative freedom.

Clients often have a good idea of the end goal that would be right for them (e.g., feel less depressed or get daughter to eat enough), but cannot ask for what they need in order to reach it because they do not know what is needed. The therapist's role can be to provide ideas of alternative behaviors—instrumental goals differing from what clients could have come up with on their own—that clients can freely choose to put into action or not. For example, at the outset of therapy, parents may place exclusive value on control and believe that they only need to learn to control an adolescent's behavior more effectively; the therapist may value the development of independence and believe that parents need to find areas in which they can reduce their control over the adolescent. However, both parties are interested in achieving the same end goal, namely, a more satisfactory or less stressful relation between the parents and the adolescent. In such cases, client self-determination can be preserved if the therapist presents his or her belief about the means to the end goal as something for the clients' consideration or experimentation.

Oliver and Rogers (1986) considered client self-determination to be a myth on the basis of Strong's (1982) social influence model of psychotherapy. According to Strong's model, the therapist's influence is the primary factor in the client's behavior change, and the therapist manipulates clients in such a way as to make them (mistakenly) attribute the changes to themselves. Therapists who want to support client self-determination need to be aware of the influence they exert on clients and explicitly need to give them the option of accepting or declining that influence in such a way that not accepting it is a viable alternative. As Bergin (1985) put it, "The more open we are about our views, the more choice clients will have in electing to be influenced or not be influenced" (p. 107). The duplicity, or unintentional misleading of clients that is assumed in Strong's model (i.e., with therapists not letting clients know how they are being influenced), can be viewed as something to be avoided or overcome. Therapists could acknowledge their own contributions to clients' desired changes; they could also honestly communicate their views regarding clients' own contributions.

Evaluative Criteria

Based on this discussion, a set of criteria can be formulated with which therapists can assess their observance of the principles of the client's best interest and self-determination in practice. The criteria are expressed in the form of evaluative questions. The list is not complete or definitive. The criteria are intended to exclude assumption of values that can be considered relative to particular persons or cultures and to be rationally necessary if therapists are to respect clients' best interest and self-determination. Thus, with an awareness of these criteria, the goal-setting process can be judged from a perspective beyond personal values. Suggestions for practical implementation accompany each of the criteria.

To evaluate consideration of the client's welfare the following questions are relevant:

1. Has the stated goal been examined before being adopted and found to be in the client's best interest, not just adopted without such examination?

Fulfilling this criterion will generally involve helping clients to clarify their understanding of the interpersonal context of the stated goal and their motives or reasons for wanting the goal. Consider the case of the failing student going to a university counseling center with the stated goal of improving his motivation. Discussion of the interpersonal context might reveal that he had long admired an uncle's skilled craftsmanship, had found enjoyment in being taught by the uncle and in working at the craft, and had shown considerable talent. However, he had never considered the craft as a career because his parents were professionals and he had unthinkingly accepted their assumption that he too would study for a profession. Clarifying the fact that his reason for wanting to stay at the university was to accommodate to his parents' wishes could lead to recognition that his stated goal was not in his best interest.

Clients may present with a stated goal that represents a belief that a particular instrumental goal must be achieved in order to realize an end goal. For example, a man experiencing sexual dysfunction may believe that the dysfunction is due to his having been molested as a child, though he has no memory of such an occurrence. His stated goal may be to remove his dysfunction by recovering the memory. In such cases, it is possible that the client is right about the means of treatment to be used, but there could also be alternative approaches that would be preferable or necessary. While respecting the client's views, the therapist will have to evaluate other possible ways to achieve the end goal and present his or her views to the client for consideration.

2. Are the goals consistent with one another?

The question of mutual consistency of goals may not be evident in the stated presenting problem. The conflicting goals are likely to be things clients want but do not say that they want. The therapist discovers them by asking, "What (unstated) contradictory goals have been impeding the attainment of the stated goal, and is the client expecting me to help with them also?" An example is someone seeking help overtly for improved job performance and covertly to get professional support for the belief that his or her heavy drinking is under control.

Mutually inconsistent goals may also emerge upon examination of the interpersonal context, as in the example of the man who wants to maintain the affection of a wife who is becoming alienated from him. The therapist may have to talk to the wife to find out that the man is overcontrolling and that the wife has changed in her attitude toward being controlled. When there are mutually incompatible goals, the therapist provides feedback about the nature of the incompatibility and gives the client the opportunity to revise his or her goals in order to work toward something attainable.

3. Have adequate reasons been provided to justify the particular end goals that have been chosen rather than other alternative end goals?

The basic factor in answering this question might be referred to as *systematic doubt*. Once a goal has been formulated, the therapist engages in questioning whether the reasons for pursuing this particular goal are adequate and encourages the client to do the same. Again, this requires explication of the client's situation. For example, a woman may want to lose 15 lb. more than she ever has to reach a normal weight. However, one may find that to do this would require extreme austerity on her part, that none of her friends and family view her as unattractive the way she is, and that the weight loss is not needed to maintain her health. The client's only reason for her goal is to look better. Although giving the client the option of pursuing this goal for this reason, the therapist might also propose an alternative goal for the client's consideration—one that may be more in her best interest: to develop the ability to feel satisfied with her current body weight, A different set of conditions could represent immediately clear reasons for losing 15 lb., for example, if the woman is at risk of cardiac failure or wants to be in a situation where something she highly values depends on not being overweight.

4. Have adequate reasons been provided to justify the use of the particular instrumental goals that have been chosen rather than alternative instrumental goals? If the instrumental goals chosen are found ineffective, are they discarded and replaced with others?

A knowledge base derived from training, experience, and use of supervision is the primary factor in answering the first of these questions. Once the end goal is clear, the therapist needs to have information about what psychotherapeutic activity, if any, is most likely to facilitate achievement of the goal. Ideally this means knowledge of research demonstrating the effectiveness of certain treatments for certain kinds of clients with certain kinds of goals. When this is not available, therapists must turn to information from their own or others' experience regarding what works.

An important blind alley to avoid is the attitude that "This is what I do, so it is what is to be done for this client." If the therapist is an adherent of a particular psychotherapeutic theory, this step requires being able to assume an outsider's perspective. The therapist should consider whether a treatment approach more conducive to the client's best interest might be formulated more effectively in terms of a theory other than his or her own; if so, the therapist should be ready to refer this client. For example, most behavior therapists would want to refer a client who wants to figure out the meaning of some spectacular dreams.

To determine whether a treatment is working effectively or not, it is necessary to recognize when the proposed end goal is attained. O'Hanlon and Weiner-Davis (1989) put this requirement succinctly, getting clients to specify how they will know when they have achieved their goals. For example, clients might know that they feel better about themselves when they find they can engage in a conversation with attractive people without fumbling for words. When clients have an active part in specifying overt changes, they can report more effectively on whether the treatment is having the desired effect.

5. Has the full range of potential causal and contributing factors been assessed as far as possible in the formulation of instrumental goals? (For example, biological, intrapsychic, interpersonal, and family systems levels might need to be considered.)

The clinical knowledge base is important in fulfilling this criterion also, because the therapist confronted with a given presenting problem needs to know the various factors that could be causing or contributing to it. This is not to say that each factor that has led up to the current situation always must be discovered and addressed in therapy, because some approaches achieve the client's desired results effectively without delving into the life-history antecedents of the presenting problem (DeShazer, 1985). However, there are some cases when assessment and treatment of causal factors are essential for acting in the client's best interest. Therapists need to be able to recognize when causal factors could be important and to address them when they are. They need to know, for example, that certain psychological symptoms may result from brain tumors or injury. Or a client's family situation may be so abusive or the work situation so stressful that it would be futile to attempt to attain an end goal of anxiety reduction without addressing situational change.

6. Has the clinician considered possible errors in clinical judgment (e.g., having one's understanding of the client shaped by preconceived notions or expectations), which could affect the nature of the goals that are developed, and taken any necessary steps to prevent or correct such errors?

The key to preventing errors in clinical judgment from adversely affecting clients' welfare is to become aware of the kinds of errors in judgment that clinicians are prone to make. Then one can catch oneself making them before acting on the basis of faulty judgment. Unfortunately, there are many ways in which clinicians' judgments about clients can err, more than can be summarized here. The reader is therefore referred to the articles on this subject by Arkes (1981), Dawes (1986),

Jordan et al. (1988), and Snyder and Thomsen (1988). An element common to many of the errors is assuming one knows more than one actually does know. So a general prophylactic for clinical thinking is frequently to ask oneself, "With what degree of certainty, if any, do I know this?"

> 7. Has the therapist been careful to ensure that the treatment will not harm the client, or that if some harm is necessary for the treatment, it is outweighed by the potential benefit of the treatment, and occurs with the informed consent of the client?

The therapist can fulfill this criterion first by hypothesizing and asking clients about undesirable effects that could be anticipated from a proposed treatment or intervention. Then, rather than just making assumptions, the therapist can talk with the client about the likelihood of such effects and whether the possible benefits of treatment would make it worth enduring them. If a treatment is undertaken that does entail some form of suffering for the client, the therapist can keep asking the client at appropriate intervals whether he or she still wants to proceed with it. The clinician may be justified in encouraging the client to endure some emotional pain involved in the treatment if there is sound evidence that this will lead to a reduction in overall suffering for the client, as in the case of exposure to a feared stimulus as a treatment for simple phobia. However, to respect the client's self-determination, the therapist should make it explicit that he or she can refuse such treatment.

> 8. In setting goals, has the therapist kept any implicit and explicit promises made to the client?

The primary implicit promise made to clients is that the therapist will act in their best interest and help them achieve their desired changes. This promise will be kept in the course of fulfilling the other criteria discussed here. Keeping explicit promises, such as confidentiality and terms of a particular therapeutic contract, is generally a straightforward matter but requires careful self-monitoring on the therapist's part.

> 9. Has as much equal weight been given to the interest of each individual affected by the goals as possible?

This question is especially relevant in the context of family therapy in which the welfare of each family member has to be considered, and opposing interests of different members must be balanced or reconciled. An example can be found in the case mentioned earlier of parents who bring in a young adolescent child because they are having more difficulty than before in getting the child to comply with their wishes. The therapist has to consider the adolescent's developmental interest in decreasing dependence on the parents, as well as the parents' desire to be sure their child stays safe and to have a primarily harmonious relationship with the child. In this case, the opposing interests might be reconciled by suggesting areas in which the parents could safely allow the child more independence.

In individual therapy, the primary duty is for the client's welfare, but the therapist should investigate how clients' achievement of therapeutic goals is likely to affect others. It may be possible to help clients avoid causing negative effects on others in making their desire changes or to mitigate such effects. For example, the client may be a spouse or lover who wants to break off a relationship with someone who wants the relationship to continue. The words and manner the client uses in communicating with the person to be left could make a considerable difference in that person's subsequent emotional state, and the therapist could help the client find ways to minimize the other's pain.

In some cases (like the one treated by Mark Karpel which was already discussed), the client's goal may represent a serious danger to someone else; so the therapist needs to know enough about the client's interpersonal context to assess whether this might be so. If it is, the therapist can involve the other in therapy or, directly or through the client, take other measures to protect the endangered person.

To evaluate respect for client self-determination, the following questions are relevant:

10. Has the therapist made any of his or her values that may affect goal setting known or explicit to the client?

Making one's values explicit to the client requires two kinds of self-awareness on the therapist's part. The first is an awareness of the values by which one guides one's own life. This enables one to recognize more readily the value-laden statements one makes in therapy. There is undoubtedly a vast array of values held by practicing therapists: traditionalist, feminist, existential, utilitarian, religious, and so on. Therapists need to be aware that their own values are just one out of many possible morally justifiable sets of values. (To me this means that various value systems can incorporate or be compatible with the universal elements of morality previously discussed.) Therapists who have not considered that values unlike their own can be justifiably held by others are not likely to have an interest in protecting clients' self-determination by making their own values explicit.

The other type of self-awareness required in order for therapists to make their values explicit is moment-to-moment self-observation during therapy. If therapists will listen alertly to their own words, before or after speaking them, they can often catch expressions of personal values and explicitly mark these for their clients. For example, "I think that it is good to be able to experience painful emotions and not have to avoid them. This is something I value personally."

11. If initially stated goals of the therapist and clients differ and if clients modify their goals toward those of the therapist during the course of therapy, does this happen with the clients' conscious volition?

Fulfilling this criterion depends on fulfilling the previous one, but includes monitoring the client's words, as well as one's own, for expressions of values. When one finds that the client now espouses a value one had heard before only from oneself, this can be pointed out to clients with the suggestion that they reflect on whether the value is something they would willingly choose to adopt.

12. If paternalistic means are used by the therapist, are they justifiable?

This requires understanding what constitutes paternalism (i.e., action intended to benefit the client but done without the client's consent) and the conditions that justify such actions. These matters are discussed in detail by Brace and VandeCreek (1991). The basic requisites for justifying paternalistic action are that the harm prevented for the person treated clearly outweighs the harm caused and that the harm prevented by always taking the action in similar situations outweighs the harm caused. It is usually easy to avoid paternalism simply by getting the client's consent for the treatment or intervention in question. If one respects self-determination, paternalistic action is not something to be taken lightly. When consent is not forthcoming and one still thinks the action is necessary, one should make a careful analysis of whether it is justified, preferably in consultation with other professionals.

Questions relevant to both the client's welfare and to self-determination are:

13. Has the therapist avoided deceiving the client in developing instrumental and end goals?

As previously noted, deception of the client in therapy is a type of paternalism because it by-passes the obtaining of consent, and therapists who wish to respect clients' self-determination would want to avoid deception unless it is clearly justified in a particular situation. Deception generally refers to a deliberate act, rather than something done accidentally, so the desire to avoid it becomes the crucial factor in actually doing so. This may be problematic when one is tempted to use deception because it looks like the most efficient means to help a client achieve a goal. Therapists may want to weigh for themselves the arguments for the importance of self-determination in comparison to the importance of the possible efficiency of deception in therapy.

A therapist may also inadvertently misinform a client. A way to avoid this (as with the eighth criterion) is to maintain a critical view of one's relative degree of certainty about one's statements to clients and make this explicit to them. For example, to the man who believes he was abused as a child but cannot remember it, the therapist might say, "It is possible that your being abused as a child has led to this current problem, but there could also be other explanations. We really do not know at this point, and may or may not be able to find out."

14. Is there explicit agreement between client and therapist that the end goals are in the client's best interest and should be adopted?
15. Is there the same type of agreement regarding the instrumental goals?

These criteria simply add to the first four criteria the condition that clients freely and overtly agree that their therapeutic goals and the means to reach them are really in their best interest—as opposed to having this decided solely by the therapist. The collaborative approach to goal setting that has been assumed throughout this discussion ensures this kind of agreement on the part of clients. Through a process of reciprocal feedback, the therapist increases his or her understanding of the client's situation, and the client increases his or her self-understanding and contextual understanding. On this basis, both therapist and client modify or stabilize their views about what changes and what means are in the client's best interest. The therapist makes sure that both parties are explicitly aware of what happens in this process.

It is likely that fulfilling these criteria in itself will contribute to clients' achievement of their goals. The clarification of goals and the consideration of interpersonal context are almost sure to increase clients' understanding of their situations, and the thoroughgoing regard for clients' self-determination should foster their sense of being self-determining.

References

American Psychological Association. (1990). Ethical principles of psychologists (rev.). *American Psychologist* 45, 390–95.

Aponte, H. J. (1985). The negotiation of values in therapy. *Family Process* 24, 323–38.

Arkes, H. R. (1981). Impediments to accurate clinical judgment and possible ways to minimize their impact. *Journal of Consulting and Clinical Psychology* 49, 323–30.

Beitman, B. D. (1987). *The structure of individual psychotherapy.* New York: Guilford.

Bergin, A. E. (1980). Psychotherapy and religious values. *Journal of Consulting and Clinical Psychology* 48, 95–105.

———. (1985). Proposed values for guiding and evaluating counseling and psychotherapy. *Counseling and Values* 29, 99–116.

Bernstein, S. (1975). Self-determination: King or citizen in the realm of values. In F. E. McDermott (Ed.), *Self-determination in social work* (pp. 33-42). London: Routledge & Kegan Paul.

Beutler, L. F. (1983). *Eclectic psychotherapy.* New York: Pergamon.

Bowen, M. (1966). The use of family theory in clinical practice. *Comprehensive Psychiatry* 7, 345–74.

Brace, K., & VandeCreek, L. (1991). The justification of paternalistic actions in psychotherapy. *Ethics & Behavior* 1, 87–103.

Butrym, Z. (1976). *The nature of social work.* London: Macmillan.

Culver, C. M., & Gert, B. (1982). *Philosophy in medicine: Conceptual and ethical issues in medicine and psychiatry.* New York: Oxford University Press.

Dawes, R. M. (1986). Representative thinking in clinical judgment. *Clinical Psychology Review* 6, 425–41.

DeShazer, S. (1985). *Keys to solution in brief therapy.* New York: Norton.

Drane, J. F. (1982). Ethics and psychotherapy: A philosophical perspective. In M. Rosenbaum (Ed.), *Ethics and Values in psychotherapy: A guidebook* (pp. 15-50). New York: Free Press.

Efran, J. S., Lukens, R. J., & Lukens, M.D. (1988, September/October). Constructivism: What's in it for you? *Family Therapy Networker,* pp. 27-35.

Engelhardt, H. T. (1986). *The foundations of bioethics.* New York: Oxford University Press.

Epstein, E. S., & Loos, V. E. (1989). Some irreverent thoughts on the limits of family therapy: Toward a language-based explanation of human systems. *Journal of Family Therapy* 2, 405–29.

Gert, B. (1988). *Morality.* New York: Oxford University Press.

Hare, R. (1981). The philosophical basis of psychiatric ethics. In S. Block & P. Chodoff (Eds.), *Psychiatric ethics.* Oxford, England: Oxford University.

Henderson, M. C. (1987). Paradoxical process and ethical consciousness. *Family Therapy* 14, 187–93.

Horne, M, (1987). *Values in social work.* Aldershot, England: Wildwood House.

Jensen, J. P., & Bergin, A. E. (1988). Mental health values of professional therapists: A national interdisciplinary survey. *Professional Psychology: Research and Practice* 19, 290–97.

Jordan, J. S., Harvey, J. H., & Weary, G. (1988). Attributional biases in clinical decision making. In D. C. Turk & P. Salovey (Eds.), *Reasoning, inference, and judgment in clinical psychology* (pp. 90–106). New York: Free Press.

Kant, I. (1959). *Foundations of the metaphysics of morals* (L. W. Beck, Trans.). Indianapolis, Ind.: Bobbs-Merrill. (Original work published 1785)

Keith-Spiegel, P., & Koocher, G. P. (1985). *Ethics in psychology: Professional standards and cases.* New York: Random House.

Kitchener, K. S. (1984). Intuition, critical evaluation and ethical principles: The foundation for ethical decisions in counseling psychology. *The Counseling Psychologist* 12 (3): 43–55.

Minuchin, S. (1974). *Families and family therapy.* Cambridge, Mass.: Harvard University Press.

Murray, E. J. (1956). A content-analysis method for studying psychotherapy. *Psychological Monographs* 70 (13, Whole No. 420).

O'Hanlon, W. H., & Weiner-Davis, M. (1989). *In search of solutions.* New York: Norton.

Oliver, P., & Rogers, S. J. (1986). The virtue of explicit values in the social sciences. *Australian Psychologist* 21, 195–210,

Owen, G. (1986). Ethics of intervention for change. *Australian Psychologist* 21, 211–18.

Plant, R. (1970). *Social and moral theory in casework.* London: Routledge & Kegan Paul.

Rachels, J. (1986). *The elements of moral philosophy.* Philadelphia: Temple University Press.

Snyder, M., & Thomsen, C. J. (1988). Interactions between therapists and clients: Hypothesis testing and behavioral confirmation. In D. C. Turk & P. Salovey (Eds.), *Reasoning, inference, and judgment in clinical psychology* (pp. 124–52). New York: Free Press.

Strong, S. R. (1978). Social psychological approach to psychotherapy research. In S. L. Garfield & A. E. Bergin (Eds.), *Handbook of psychotherapy and behavior change* (pp. 101–35). New York: Wiley.

Strong, S. R. (1982). Emerging integrations of clinical and social psychology: A clinician's perspective. In G. Weary & H. L. Mirels (Eds.), *Integrations of clinical and social psychology* (pp. 181–213). New York: Oxford University Press.

Thomasma, D. (1984). Human values and ethics: Professional responsibility. In T. Vallance (Ed.), *Values and ethics in human development professions* (pp. 11–17). Dubuque, Iowa: Kendall/Hunt.

Truax, C. B. (1966). Reinforcement and non-reinforcement by Rogerian psychotherapy. *Journal of Abnormal Psychology* 71, 1–9.

Watson, D. (1980). *Caring for strangers.* London: Routledge & Kegan Paul.

Wilkes, R. (1981). *Social work with undervalued groups.* London: Tavistock.

Wylie, M. S. (1989). Looking for the fence posts. *Family Therapy Networker* 13, 23–33.

The Many Faces of Competency

James F. Drane

The doctrine of informed consent . . . creates many dilemmas because it tries to balance very different values—specifically, on one side beneficence (health or well-being); on the other, autonomy (or self-determination). Most of the ethical commentary on informed consent and a majority of the court cases deciding consent questions have focused on the physician's responsibilities to disclose information and to keep the medical setting free of coercion. But more and more frequently clinical questions arise about the capacity or competence of a specific patient to give an informed consent.

If the patient is not competent, then his or her consent does not constitute an authorization to treat, no matter how thorough the disclosure or how free from coercion the medical setting. Incompetence also calls into question a patient's refusal of treatment. Patient competence in effect is a condition for the validity of consent. Incompetence both creates a new obligation to identify a surrogate and provides a basis for the physician to set aside the informed consent requirement in favor of what he or she thinks is best for the patient.

Only recently have scholars begun to pay attention to this element in the informed consent doctrine. Loren Roth, Paul Appelbaum, Alan Meisel, and Charles Lidz found that different clinicians use very different tests to judge competence.[1] They reduced these to five categories: (1) making a choice; (2) reasonable outcome of choice or ability to produce a reasonable choice; (3) choice based on rational reasons; (4) abil-

From *The Hastings Center* (1985): 17–21. Copyright © 1985, The Hastings Center. Reprinted by permission.

ity to understand the decision-making process; and (5) actual understanding of the process. Later, Appelbaum and Roth suggested four possible standards for judging competency: (1) evidencing a choice; (2) factual understanding of issues; (3) rational manipulation of information; and (4) appreciation of the nature of the situation. They found any one of the four to be acceptable, as long as it was justified by a reasonable policy perspective.[2] Other authors have argued for a single standard: For Grace A. Olin and Harry S. Olin, competence means ability to retain information. For Howard Owens reality testing is the standard. Bernard Gert and Charles Culver in their book, *Philosophy in Medicine,* helped clarify the term by showing different ways competence is used in ordinary and professional language. Alan A. Stone has written extensively on informed consent and severely criticized court decisions that extended competency even of involuntary mental patients to refuse treatment. Mark Siegler made conceptual points about the meaning of competency, and more than any other writer connected the issue to the medical setting in which it emerges.[3]

Finally, the President's Commission for the Study of Ethical Problems in Medicine and Biomedical and Behavioral Research in a recently published report discussed competency, which the Commission prefers to call decision-making capacity.[4] The Commission spelled out the components of competency or decisional capacity: the possession of a set of values and goals, the ability to communicate and understand information, and the ability to reason and deliberate. Although they did not adopt any one of the standards listed by Roth and Appelbaum, the Commissioners were very critical of the first two tests: "evidencing a preference" and "reasonable outcome" of the patient's decision.

Despite all the work done to date, the competency question remains unsettled. What should the standard of competence be in order to ensure valid consent or refusal of consent to medical procedures? To be acceptable, any standard of competence must meet several important objectives. It must incorporate the general guidelines set out in legal decisions; it must be psychiatrically and philosophically sound; it must guarantee the realization of ethical values on which the consent requirement is based; and it must be applicable in a clinical setting.

In practice some tests seem too lenient and expose patients to serious harm. Others seem too stringent and turn almost all seriously ill patients into incompetents, thereby depriving them of rights and dignity. The solution proposed here is based on no one standard, but works out a sliding scale for competency. Accordingly as the medical decision itself (the task) changes, the standards of competency to perform the task also change.

The Competency Assessment

As long as a patient does or says nothing strange and acquiesces to treatment recommended by the medical professional, questions of competency do not arise. These questions arise usually when the patient refuses treatment or chooses a course of action which, in the opinion of the physician in charge, threatens his or her well-being. Either consenting to treatment or refusing consent may raise a suspicion of unreasonableness. More careful evaluation is then called for before a final determination of competency is made.

Competency assessment usually focuses on the patient's mental capacities: specifically the mental capacities to make a particular medical decision. Does this patient understand what is being disclosed? Can this patient come to a decision about treatment based on that information? How much understanding and rational decision-making capacity is sufficient for this patient to be considered competent? Or how deficient must this patient's decision-making capacity be before he or she is declared incompetent? A properly performed competency assessment should eliminate two types of error: preventing competent persons from deciding their own treatments; and failing to protect incompetent persons from the harmful effects of a bad decision.

The assessment process leads to a decision about a decision. A good clinical determination must balance the different and sometimes competing values of rationality, beneficence and autonomy. Rationality, or reasonableness, is an underlying assumption in competency determinations. In an emergency we presume that a rational person would want treatment and the informed consent requirement is set aside. But rationality cannot be set aside in nonemergency settings. A particular medical setting establishes certain expectations about what a reasonable person would do, and these expectations play an important role in competency determinations.

The patient's well-being (beneficence) also has to be considered in assessing competence. The same laws that establish the right to give or refuse informed consent express concern about protecting patients from the harm that could result from serious defects in decision-making capacity. Finally, a competency assessment must respect the value of autonomy. Patients must be permitted to determine their own fate, and a decision cannot be set aside simply because it differs from what other persons think is indicated.

A Sliding-Scale Model

How should the physician proceed when deciding on a patient's competence? The model proposed here posits three general categories of medical situations; in each category, as the consequences flowing from patient decisions become more serious, competency standards for valid consent or refusal of consent become more stringent. The psychiatric pathologies most likely to undermine the mental capacities required for each type of decision are listed in the tables given later.

A number of assumptions underlie the use of a sliding scale or variable standard rather than one ideal competency test. First, the objective content of the decision must be taken into consideration so that competency determinations remain linked to the decision at hand. Second, the value of reasonableness operates at every level. When people sit down to play chess, certain expectations are created even though no particular decisions are required. If, however, one player makes peculiar moves, the other will have to wonder whether his partner is competent or knows what he is doing. Something similar is assumed in the patient-physician partnership. Third, the reasonableness assumption justifies some paternalistic behavior. The physician or another surrogate is authorized by this model to decide what is best for the patient who is incompetent. In more cases than a patient-rights advocate would prefer, the patient's decision is set aside in favor of beneficence. The clinical values of health and patient well-being are balanced with the libertarian values of autonomy and self-determination.

Easy, Effective Treatments

Standard No. 1. The first and least stringent standard of competence to give a valid consent applies to medical decisions that are not dangerous and are objectively in the patient's best interest. Even though these patients are seriously ill, and therefore impaired in cognitive and volitional functioning, their consent to an effective, safe treatment is considered informed so long as the patient is aware of what is going on. *Awareness,* in the sense of being in contact with one's situation, satisfies the cognitive requirement of informed consent. *Assent* alone to the rational expectations of others satisfies the volitional component. When an adult goes along with what is considered appropriate and rational, then the presumption of competency holds. Higher standards for capacity to give a valid consent to this first type of medical intervention would be superfluous.

Consider the following two examples. Betty Campbell, a twenty-five-year-old secretary who lives alone, has an accident. She arrives at the hospital showing signs of mild shock and suffering from the associated mental deficiencies; but her consent to blood transfusion, bone-setting, or even to some minor surgery need not be questioned. Even though there is no emergency, if she is aware of her situation and assents to receiving an effective, low-risk treatment for a certain diagnosis, there is no reason to question her competence to consent.

Phil Randall's situation is quite different. A twenty-three-year-old veteran who has been addicted to drugs and alcohol, he is on probation and struggling to survive in college. When Phil stops talking and eating for almost a week, his roommate summons a trusted professor. By this time Phil is catatonic, but the professor manages to get him on his feet and accompanies him in a police car to the state hospital. The professor gets through to Phil sufficiently to explain the advantages of signing in as a voluntary patient. Phil signs his name to the admission form, authorizing commitment and initial treatment. His consent to this first phase of therapy is valid because Phil is sufficiently aware of his situation to understand what is happening, and he assents to the treatment. Later on, when his condition improves, another consent may be required, especially if a more dangerous treatment or a long-term hospitalization is required. The next decision will require a higher degree of competence because it is a different type of task.

Having a lenient standard of competence for safe and effective treatments eliminates the ambiguity and confusion associated with phrases like "virtually competent," "marginally competent," and "competent for practical purposes." Such phrases are used to excuse the common sense practice of holding certain decisions to be valid even though the patients are considered incompetent by some abstract standard, which ignores the specific task or type of medical decision at hand.

The same modest standard of competence should apply to a dying patient who refuses to consent to treatments that are ineffective and useless. This is the paradigm case in the refusal-of-ineffective-treatment category.

Most of the patients who would be considered incompetent to make treatment decisions under this first category are legally incompetent. Those who use psychotic defenses that impede the awareness of their situation and any decision-making ability are the only other patients who fall outside the wide first criterion. Even children who have reached the age of reason can be considered competent. According to law however, those below the ages of twenty-one or sometimes eighteen are presumed incompetent to make binding contracts, including health care decisions.

But exceptions are common. The Pennsylvania Mental Health Procedures Act (1976), for example, decided that fourteen-year-old adoles-

A Sliding-Scale Model for Competency

STANDARD NO. 1

Objective Medical Decisions

A. *Incompetent*		B. *Competent*
unconscious	effective treatment for acute	children (10 and above)
severe retardation	illness	retarded (educable)
small children	diagnostic certainty ineffective treatment	clouded sensorium
total disorientation	high benefit/low risk	mild senile dementia
severe senile dementia	limited alternatives	intoxicated
autism	severe disorder/major	conditions listed under
psychotic defenses	distress/immediately	#2 and #3 (A & B)
denial of self and situation	life-threatening	
delusional projection		

(consent) ... (refusal)

Competency Standards

Minimal Requirements:
1. *Awareness:* orientation to one's medical situation
2. *Assent:* explicit or implied

STANDARD NO. 2

Objective Medical Decisions

A. *Incompetent*		B. *Competent*
severe mood disorders	chronic condition/doubtful diagnosis	adolescent (16 and over)
phobia about treatment	uncertain outcome of therapy	mildly retarded
mutism	for acute illness	personality disorders;
short term memory loss	balanced risks and benefits:	narcissistic, borderline and obsessive
thought disorders	possibly effective, but burdensome	conditions listed under #3 (A & B)
ignorance	high risk, only hope	
incoherence		
delusion		
hallucination		
delirium		
conditions listed under		
#1 (A & B)		

(consent or refusal)

Competency Standards

Median Requirements:
1. *Understanding:* of medical situation and proposed treatment
2. *Choice:* based on medical outcomes

STANDARD NO. 3

Objective Medical Decisions

A. *Incompetent*		B. *Competent*
indecisive or ambivalent	effective treatment for acute	above legal age
over time	illness	reflective and self-critical
false beliefs about reality	diagnostic certainty	mature coping devices:
hysteria	high benefit/low risk	altruism
substance abuse ineffective treatment	limited alternatives	anticipation
neurotic defenses:	severe disorder/major	sublimation
intellectualization	distress/immediately	
repression	life-threatening	
dissociation		
acting out		
mild depression		
hypomania		
conditions listed under		
#1 and #2 (A & B)		

(consent) ... (refusal)

Competency Standards

Maximum Requirements:
1. *Appreciation:* critical and reflective understanding of illness and treatment
2. *Rational decision:* based on relevant implications including articulated beliefs and values

cents were competent to give informed consent to psychiatric hospitalization. Adolescents are also considered competent in many jurisdictions to make decisions about birth control and abortion. I am suggesting that, for this first type of decision, children as young as ten or eleven are competent.

Authors like Alexander M. Capron, Willard Gaylin, and Ruth Macklin support a lowering of the age of competency to make some medical decisions.[5] The President's Commission also endorses a lower age of competence. The physician, however, cannot ignore the law and must obtain the consent of the child's legal guardian. But if a minor is competent or partially competent, there is good reason to involve him or her in the decision-making process.

Less Certain Treatments

Standard No. 2. If the diagnosis is doubtful, or the condition chronic; if the diagnosis is certain but the treatment is more dangerous or not quite so effective; if there are alternative treatments, or no treatment at all is an alternative, then a different type of task is involved in making an informed treatment decision. Consequently, a different standard of competence is required. The patient now must be able to understand the risks and outcomes of the different options and then be able to make a decision based on this understanding. In this setting competence means ability to understand the treatment options, balance risks and benefits, and come to a deliberate decision. In other words, a higher standard of competence is required than the one discussed above. Let me give some examples of this type of decision, and the corresponding competency standards.

Antonio Marachal is a retired steel worker who has been hospitalized with a bad heart valve. Both the surgeon and his family doctor recommend an operation to replace the valve. Mr. Marachal understands what they tell him, but is afraid of undergoing the operation. He thinks he'll live just as long by taking good care of himself. His fear of surgery may not be entirely rational, but the option he prefers is real and there is no basis for considering his refusal to be invalid because of incompetence.

Or consider Geraldine Brown, a forty-year-old unmarried woman who is diagnosed as having leukemia. Chemotherapy offers a good chance for remission, but the side effects are repugnant and frightening to her. After hearing and understanding the diagnosis, alternatives, risks, and prognosis, she refuses, deciding instead to follow a program that centers on diet, exercise, meditation, and some natural stimulants to her immune system. Objectively, the standard medical treatment is preferable to what she decides, but informed consent joins objective medical data with subjective personal factors such as repugnance and burden. In this case the objective and subjective components balance out. A decision one way or the other is reasonable, and a person who can understand the options and decide in light of them is competent.

Although ability to understand is not the same as being capable of conceptual or verbal understanding, some commentators assume that the two are synonymous in every case. Many would require that patients remember the ideas and repeat what they have been told as a proof of competence. Real understanding, however, may be more a matter of emotions. Following an explanation, the patient may grasp what is best for her with strong feelings and convictions, and yet be hard-pressed to articulate or conceptualize her understanding or conviction.

Competence as capacity for an understanding choice can also be reconciled with a decision to let a trusted physician decide what is the best treatment. Such a choice (a waiver) may be made for good reasons and represent a decision in favor of one set of values (safety or anxiety reduction) over another (independence and personal initiative). As such, it can be considered an informed consent and create no suspicion about competence.

Ignorance or inability to understand, however, does incapacitate a person for making this type of decision. This is especially so when the ignorance extends to the options and persists even after patient and careful explanation. Patience and care may sometimes require that more than one person be involved in the disclosure process before a person is judged incompetent to understand. An explanation by someone from the same ethnic, religious, or economic background may also be necessary.

Dangerous Treatments

Standard No. 3. The most stringent and demanding criterion for competence is reserved for those treatment decisions that are very dangerous, and run counter to both professional and public rationality. Here the decision involves not a balancing of what are widely recognized as reasonable alternatives or a reasonable response to a doubtful diagnosis, but a choice that seems to violate reasonableness. The patient's decision now appears irrational, indeed life-threatening. And yet, according to this model, such decisions are valid and respectable as long as the person making them satisfies the most demanding standards of competence. The patient's decision is a different type of task than the others we have considered. As such, different and more stringent criteria of capacity are appropriate.

Competence in this context requires an ability on the part of the decision maker to appreciate what he or she is doing. Appreciation requires the highest degree of understanding, one that grasps more than just the medical details of the illness, options, risks, and treatment. To be competent to make apparently irrational and very dangerous choices, the patient must appreciate the implications of the medical information for his or her life. Competence here requires an understanding that is both technical and personal, intellectual and emotional.

Because such decisions contravene public standards of rationality, they must be subjectively critical and reflective. The competent patient must be able to give reasons for the decision, which show that he has thought through the medical issues and related this information to his personal values. The patient's personal reasons need not be scientific or publicly accepted, but neither can they be purely private or idiosyncratic. Their intelligibility may derive from a minority religious view, but they must be coherent and follow the logic of that belief system. This toughest standard of competence demands a more rational understanding: one that includes verbalization, consistency, and the like. Some examples will illustrate.

Bob Cassidy, an eighteen-year-old high school senior and an outstanding athlete, is involved in an automobile accident which has crushed his left foot. Attempts to save the limb are unsuccessful, and infection threatens the boy's life. Surgeons talk to his parents who immediately give permission for amputation of the leg below the knee. Since Bob is legally no longer a minor, however, his consent is required for the surgery, but he refuses. "If I cannot play sports, my life is meaningless," he says. First the doctors try to talk to him, then his parents, finally some of his friends. But he refuses to discuss the matter. When anyone comes to his room he simply closes his eyes and lies motionless. "If they cannot make my foot as good as before, I want to die," he tells them. "What good is it to live with only one leg? Without sports I can't see anything worth living for." Bob is using unhealthy coping behavior to handle his situation. He refuses to consider the implications of what he is doing and shows signs of being seriously depressed. No arguments or justifications are offered to counter the indications of immaturity and mild emotional illness. For these reasons he is incompetent for the task he presumes to undertake.

Charles Kandell is a Jehovah's Witness and refuses a blood transfusion after a bad accident at his job. He is not yet in shock, but will shortly be in danger of death. His wife and family support his refusal and pledge to help care for his children. The doctor asks Charles if he fears judgment from God if blood were given against his will. He is adamant, explaining to the medical group that he has lived his life by these beliefs, knows the possible consequences, and holds eternal life to be more important than life here on earth. This decision meets the high standards required for such a decision, and should be respected as a competent refusal.

A patient need not have a serious psychiatric pathology in order to be considered incompetent to make such serious decisions. On the other hand, not every mental or emotional disturbance would constitute incompetence. A certain amount of anxiety, for example, accompanies any serious decision. A patient may suffer some pain, which would not necessarily impair such a decision. Even a degree of reactive depression may not incapacitate a patient for this type of decision. But any mental or emotional disorder that compromises appreciation and rational decision making would make a person incompetent. Persons, for example, who are incapable of controlling their destructive behavior cannot be considered competent to decide about treatments that have destructive features. Consequently, a patient who is hospitalized for a self-inflicted injury would not be considered competent to refuse a life-saving treatment. And dangerous decisions that are inconsistent with life-long values are strongly suspect as being products of incompetence.

The paradigm case of consent to ineffective treatment is a decision to engage in a high-risk drug trial unrelated to one's own illness.

Objections to the Sliding Scale

Certain objections to this sliding scale notion are easy to anticipate. Libertarian thinkers will see it as justifying paternalistic behavior on the part of physicians and diminishing the patient's discretion to do whatever he or she prefers no matter what the consequence. True, by these standards some patient decisions would not be respected, but competency was originally required and continues to be needed in order to set aside certain dangerous and harmful decisions. This model provides guidelines for determining which patient decisions fall within the original purpose for a competency requirement. Besides, the sliding scale provides a justification even for decisions that are considered by some to be irrational. Instead of limiting freedom, it safeguards patient autonomy while balancing this value with well-being.

Admittedly, in the least stringent category the outcome, which is beneficial to the patient, plays a role in establishing the rationality of the decision and the competency of the decision maker. The President's Commission rejected a standard based on outcome for the following reason: if only the physician can determine outcome, and outcome constitutes the only test of a competent choice, then competence is a matter of doing what the doctor thinks best. But outcome is not *the* standard of competence in this model. Rather it is an important factor in only one class of medical decisions. In other decisions patients may competently go against medical assessments of outcome. In fact, a decision that leads to an outcome that professionals and nonprofessionals alike would consider the most unacceptable—unnecessary death—can be considered a valid and competent option according to this model.

Objections will also be raised against the most stringent standard for judging competence. If every patient must understand thoroughly and make a rational decision in order to be considered competent, then too many people will be considered incompetent. Consequently, the medical delivery system will be clogged with surrogate decision making, and many patients will be robbed of dignity and self-determination. The most stringent standard in this model requires just such capacities for competence, but only in cases where the patient has most to lose from his or her choice. If patients in category three suffer a decline in autonomy (and they do because some decisions will not be respected), this is balanced by a gain in beneficence.

Balancing Values

A balancing of values is the cornerstone of a good competency assessment. Rationality is given its place throughout this model. Not only does the sliding scale reflect a rational ordering of things, but reasonableness is an underlying assumption for each standard of competence. Maximum autonomy, however, is also guaranteed because patients can choose to do even what is not at all beneficial (participate in an experiment which has little chance of improving their condition) or refuse to do what is most beneficial. Finally, beneficence is respected because patients are protected against harmful choices, when these are more the product of pathology than of self-determination.

Notes

1. Loren H. Roth, Charles W. Lidz, and Alan Meisel, "Toward a Model of the Legal Doctrine of Informed Consent," *American Journal of Psychiatry* 134 (1977), 285–89; Loren H. Roth, Alan Meisel, and Charles W. Lidz, "Test of Competency to Consent to Treatment," *American Journal of Psychiatry* 134 (1977), 279–84; Paul S. Appelbaum and Loren H. Roth, "Clinical Issues in the Assessment of Competency," *American Journal of Psychiatry* 138 (1981), 1462–67; and Loren H. Roth and Paul S. Appelbaum, "The Dilemma of Denial in the Assessment of Competency to Refuse Treatment," *American Journal of Psychiatry* 139 (1982), 910–13.

2. Paul S. Appelbaum and Loren H. Roth, "Competency to Consent to Research," *Archives of General Psychiatry* 39 (1982), 951–58.

3. G.A. Olin and H.S. Olin, "'Informed Consent in Voluntary Mental Hospital Admission," *American Journal of Psychiatry* 132 (1975), 938–41; H. Owens, "When is a Voluntary Commitment Really Voluntary?" *American Journal of Orthopsychiatry* 47 (1977), 104–10; Charles Culver and Bernard Gert, *Philosophy in Medicine* (New York: Oxford University Press, 1982); Alan Stone, "The Right to Refuse Treatment," *Archives of General Psychiatry* 38 (1981),

358–62; Alan Stone, "Informed Consent: Special Problems for Psychiatry," *Hospital and Community Psychiatry* 30 (1979), 231–37; Mark Siegler, "Critical Illness: the Limits of Autonomy," *Hastings Center Report* 7 (October 1977), 12–15; and Mark Siegler and A.D. Goldblatt, "Clinical Intuition: A Procedure for Balancing the Rights of Patients and the Responsibilities of Physicians," in S.F Spicker. J.M. Healey, and H.T. Engelhardt, eds., *The Law-Medicine Relation: A Philosophical Exploration* (Dordrecht, Holland: D. Reidel Publishing Co., 1981).

4. The President's Commission for the Study of Ethical Problems in Medicine and Biomedical and Behavioral Research, *Making Health Care Decisions,* Vol. I (Washington: U.S. Government Printing Office, 1982).

5. Willard Gaylin and Ruth Macklin, eds., *Who Speaks for the Child?* (New York: Plenum Press, 1982).

The Right to Refuse Psychotropic Drugs

Heather Sones

The right to refuse medical treatment has been accepted by the courts, health care personnel and consumers throughout Canada and the United States. Yet for some situations, the right to refuse medical treatment remains a matter of serious public debate. One of the most complex of these circumstances occurs when an institutionalized person is to be treated with a psychotropic drug.

Psychotropic drugs, particularly the antipsychotics, revolutionized mental health care in the 1950s. They are the most commonly prescribed treatment in psychiatric facilities and are frequently administered on general hospital wards and in long-term care.[1]

Most of the literature on the right to refuse psychotropic drugs has focused on patients who have been committed to psychiatric facilities involuntarily. Considerably less has been written on the issue with respect to people in other care facilities. This is unfortunate, as many people in other facilities are confined involuntarily for all practical purposes, although no formal commitment proceedings have occurred. In one Canadian nursing home, for example, this author found it to be common practice for nurses to slip "as needed" psychotropic drugs into some residents' drinks. No consent was obtained, no formal procedures were provided for determining incompetency, and the decision to administer often depended entirely on the individual nurse. Given the large number of persons in long-term care facilities and the rate at which they are prescribed psychotropic drugs, the issue of the right to refuse is of major concern.

From *The Canadian Nurse/L'infirmière canadienne* 89, no. 5 (1993): 27–30. Reprinted by permission.

Recent legal developments in Canada and the United States have tended to support the right of patients, even involuntarily committed psychiatric patients, to refuse treatment.[2] In Canada, statutes have varied on the matter, with some providing for the right to refuse and others allowing forced treatment in any case of involuntary commitment.[3] However, provincial statutes are gradually moving into line with the Canadian Charter of Rights and Freedoms, which prohibits legal discrimination based on mental disability.[4]

Regardless of legal support, the right to refuse is poorly protected in practice. Determinations of competency to make treatment decisions are not being made at commitment proceedings. Once patients are under care, health care workers often make subjective findings of incompetence; indeed, involuntary commitment or the refusal of drugs may in themselves be used as proof of incompetence: "Patients tend to be considered competent to give consent, but incompetent to withhold it."[5]

Even when consent for a psychotropic drug is sought, information about side effects is often omitted,[6] and patients tend not to be informed of their right to refuse. Where legal safeguards do exist, the letter of the law has been virtually ignored.[7]

Arguments Against

The major ethical argument against the right to refuse psychotropic drugs is based on the moral principle of beneficence.[8] Proponents of this argument claim that the greatest ethical obligation of health care personnel is to do what is good for the client, even if it must be done against the client's will. They say that people who have been prescribed psychotropic drugs are not always in a position to know what is good for them, due to cognitive or affective dysfunction.

Another ethical argument used against the right to refuse is based on the principle of nonmaleficence. Because of staff fears, clients who are allowed to refuse psychotropics may experience inhumane treatment, such as extended seclusion, physical restraints and punishment.[9]

The ethical principle of autonomy is occasionally used to argue against the right to refuse as well. For example, one author says that forcible treatment is likely to increase clients' overall autonomy through an increased ability to become an active participant in treatment and by allowing for earlier release from psychiatric facilities.[10]

Legally, a number of principles contradict the right to refuse psychotropic drugs. One such principle is the "right of treatment" doctrine, which arose largely as a result of the inadequate treatment received by large numbers of involuntary mental patients in the United States before the 1970s.[11] A second legal principle in this category is the "least restrictive treatment" doctrine. This doctrine supports the treatment of involuntary clients, while at the same time promoting the opportunity to refuse medication if there is an "equally effective therapy available that is not as restrictive."[12]

In Canada, a constitutional clause may limit the extent to which provincial statutes can support the right to refuse: "The Canadian Charter of Rights and Freedoms guarantees the rights and freedoms set out in it, subject only to such reasonable limits as can be demonstrably justified in a free and democratic society."[13] Conceivably, Canadian courts could adopt limits similar to those that override the privacy right in the U.S. constitution. These limits include *parens patriae* (or the power of the state to intervene to prevent a patient's condition from deteriorating), police power (to protect other clients from harm) and a consideration of the state's financial burden in operating psychiatric facilities.

The strongest medical and therapeutic argument against the right to refuse psychotropic drugs relates to the effectiveness of treatment. The role played by these drugs in the deinstitutionalization of mental patients since the 1950s gives powerful testimony to their effectiveness in many cases.

Other medical and therapeutic arguments are primarily reactions to critics of the forced administration of psychotropic drugs. These include the argument that psychiatric diagnoses tend to be more specific and refined than many people believe. It has also been argued that the side effects of psychotropic drugs are overstated, partly because schizophrenic and geriatric populations have a high baseline incidence of dyskinetic movement.[14] Some health care professionals argue that the full disclosure of side effects required for informed consent would have an adverse effect on clients' mental states and cause them to lose trust. Finally, many physicians are concerned about the threat to their role in treatment decisions.[15]

Arguments For

Surprisingly, many of the same principles are used to support the right to refuse. For example, the major ethical argument supporting the right to refuse treatment is based on the moral principle of autonomy. This argument contends that a client's right to self-determination should prevail, even if it means withholding treatment intended for the client's good. The argument opposes not only forcible drug administration, but also other practices that reduce autonomy, such as the surreptitious administration of drugs and the withholding of drug information.

The principle of non-maleficence is also used in arguments supporting the right to refuse. Criticisms based on the side effects of psychotropic drugs, for example, as based on this principle. Furthermore, suggestions have been made that psychotropic drugs are sometimes used as punishment or for "staff convenience to control behavior, especially in overcrowded, understaffed facilities."[16] These last suggestions also call up the ethical principle of beneficence, as they hint that psychotropic drugs are sometimes used as a substitute for more beneficent measures.

A number of legal principles are promoting growing legal support for the right to refuse psychotropic drugs. One of these is the principle of the inviolability of the person, that is, the right to control over one's own body. The rights to freedom of thought, speech and religion may also support the right to refuse. In the U.S. case *Winter v. Miller*, for example, a ruling was made in favor of a Christian Scientist who had refused treatment on religious grounds.[17] As mentioned previously, the Canadian Charter of Rights and Freedoms also prohibits legal discrimination on the basis of mental disability.

A number of other legal arguments relate to competency. One argument is reflected in the growing trend toward determining competence with respect to the particular function requiring competence.[18] For example, legal competence (the ability to manage one's property and affairs) is being disassociated from factual competence (the ability to make decisions about treatment). Furthermore, mental illness is no longer seen as conclusive evidence of incompetence—competence is not considered to be the same as rationality, and persons tend to be presumed competent at certain times and not at others, as in the case of senile dementia. It has also been argued that low levels of understanding are acceptable when the risk of side effects is high.[19]

Medical support for the right to refuse also exists. Critics of psychotropic drugs argue that although they are often effective, "the results frequently appear paradoxical or idiosyncratic."[20] It is also argued that psychiatric diagnoses themselves are often suspect. Nursing home surveys have indicated that suboptimal choices of medication are common,[21] and reports that have emerged from major litigations and legislative inquiries indicate that medication administration is often "neglectful and abusive."[22]

The strongest medical arguments supporting the right to refuse psychotropic drugs relate to the side effects. With psychotropics, long-term therapy is necessary, as it may take four to six weeks for the drug to become effective. Yet the potential side effects of psychotropic drugs are not only numerous but may include serious symptoms such as irreversible tardive dyskinesia, which may occur as early as five weeks into therapy.[23] In some cases, the side effects "can be more disruptive than the illness itself."[24]

Finally, the process of obtaining informed consent can have positive therapeutic benefits in itself. Informing a client of potential side effects, for example, may prompt monitoring for side effects and encourage reporting to staff. Informed consent may also enhance clients' self-esteem, and it allows for more trusting and hence therapeutic relationships with health care personnel. One study of patients who were permitted to decline medication found that their treatment was not seriously impaired.[25] Furthermore, psychotropic drugs may have an anti-therapeutic effect when a patient perceives them to be destructive.

Recommendations

Involuntary institutionalization should not be equated with incompetency to make treatment decisions. This distinction should be clearly communicated in [state or] provincial statutes. The statutes should also outline a clear procedure for determining competency with respect to treatment decisions, a procedure that should generally involve a court or ethics committee review.

A procedure is also needed for determining whether or not to medicate when a court or ethics committee has deemed a client incompetent to decide. The procedure may involve a further court or ethics committee decision, or a decision by a court-appointed guardian. It has been argued that courts are more likely than guardians to use the "substitute judgment" approach, where an attempt is made to determine what a client would have decided if competent. Guardians, it has been argued, are more likely to use the "best interest" approach, in which the opinions of health professionals tend to outweigh client preference.[26]

Special provisions would still be necessary for clients who alternate frequently between periods of competency and incompetency, and for emergencies.

For clients who alternate between competency and incompetency, it would be impractical to hold a judicial review each time a determination of competency is required. Nonetheless, procedural safeguards are essential. There is a pressing need for a standardized test for competency to consent to or refuse a psychotropic drug. If, during a period of competency, a client gives written consent for future drug administration, then a refusal during an apparent period of incompetency could prompt the health care personnel to administer the competency test. The test would have to be witnessed by two staff members (if a guardian is not available), who would sign the recorded results. If incompetency is determined, the drug could be forcibly administered. The client would have to be retested daily, and if competency fails to return within a specified period, a court or ethics committee review would be necessary. On regaining competency, the client would again be offered the chance to consent or refuse.

Emergencies should be defined as situations in which clients are at serious risk of harming themselves or others. In administering a psychotropic drug in such a situation, the drug should be determined to be the least restrictive alternative and less harmful than the anticipated violence. Again, the standardized specific competency test could then be used until client competency is regained. A judicial or ethics committee review should be necessary after a specified time limit.

In each case, a client should be deemed competent to make treatment decisions whenever incompetence for this function cannot be shown. A client who is competent to make treatment decisions should be allowed to consent to or refuse psychotropic drug treatment, whether the client is involuntarily committed or not. Risks and benefits should be explained, alternatives should be presented, and the client should be clearly told of his or her right to refuse.

. . . Until the concept of the right to refuse treatment is clarified, nurses and other participants in client care must protect their patients' rights and interests.

Notes

1. Feather, R.B. The institutionalized mental health patient's right to refuse psychotropic medication, *Perspectives in Psychiatric Care*, 23(2), 1985, 45–68: Sherman, D.S. Psychoactive drug misuse in long term care: Some contributing factors. *Journal of Pharmacy Practice*, 1(3), 1988, 189–94.

2. Schafer, Arthur. The right of institutionalized psychiatric patients to refuse treatment. *Canada's Mental Health*, 33(3), 1985, 12–16.

3. Keyserlingk, Edward W. Consent to treatment—the principles, the provincial statutes, and the Charter of Rights and Freedoms, *Canada's Mental Health*, 33 (3), 1985, 7–11.

4. Canadian Charter of Rights and Freedoms. 1, Part I of *The Constitutional Act, 1982.*

5. Feather, 1985.

6. Taft, L.B., and Barkin, R.L. Drug abuse? Use and misuse of psychotropic drugs in Alzheimer's care, *Journal of Gerontological Nursing*, 16 (8), 1990, 4–10.

7. Feather, 1985.

8. Descriptions of the principles of nonbeneficence, nonmaleficence and autonomy are adapted from Shannon, T.A. (ed), chapt. 1, in *Bioethics*, 3rd edition, Mahwah, N.J., Paulist Press, 1987.

9. Feather, 1985.

10. Turnquist, A.C. The issue of informed consent and the use of neuroleptic medications, *International Journal of Nursing Studies*, 20(3), 1983, 181–86.

11. Feather, 1985.

12. Oriol, M.D., and Oriol, R.D. Involuntary commitment and the right to refuse medication, *Journal of Psychosocial Nursing and Mental Health Services*, 24(11), 1986, 15–20.

13. Canadian Charter, s.1.

14. Turnquist, 1983.

15. Winters v. Miller, 446 F. 2d 65 1971.

16. Feather, 1985.

17. Feather, 1985.

18. Keyserlingk, 1985.

19. Schafer, 1985.

20. Feather, 1985.

21. Vickerman, L. Involuntary medication: Your patient advocacy role is on the line, *The Canadian Nurse,* 80(5), 1984, 32–34.

22. Feather, 1985.

23. Turnquist, 1983.

24. Oriol and Oriol, 1986.

25. Appelbaum, P.S., and Gutheil, T.G. Drug refusal: A study of psychiatric inpatients, *American Journal of Psychiatry,* 137, 1980, 340–44.

26. Schafer, 1985.

The Right to Refuse Mental Health Treatment: A Therapeutic Jurisprudence Analysis

Bruce J. Winick

The controversy concerning the recognition and definition of a right to refuse mental health treatment has largely ignored the question of whether such recognition would be therapeutically beneficial or detrimental to the patient. Would such recognition lead to refusal of needed treatment so that patients will "rot with their rights on," as some have suggested?[1] Will allowing offenders the choice whether to participate in correctional rehabilitation programs increase recidivism? Will patients forced to accept mental health treatment over objection improve and come, in time, to thank their doctor, retrospectively approving beneficial treatment they never would have accepted voluntarily?[2] On the other hand, might recognition of a right to refuse treatment empower patients and offenders in ways that could have therapeutic value? Might it provide them with a context in which they could acquire decisionmaking skills, learn to engage in self-determining behavior, and attain functional capacities that will be useful in community adjustment? Will providing patients and offenders with treatment choice enhance the potential that such treatment will be efficacious? Will according patients (or offenders) a right to refuse treatment change the therapist-patient (or counselor-offender) relationship in ways that will enhance or diminish its therapeutic potential?

These are questions that have not been examined empirically, but which are critical to resolving the right to refuse treatment dilemma. Whether a right to refuse treatment should be recognized ultimately may

From *International Journal of Law and Psychiatry* 17, no. 1 (1994): 99–117. Copyright © 1994, Elsevier Science Ltd. Reprinted by permission.

be a constitutional question, but judicial and statutory definitions of its parameters and of the procedural requirements necessary to implement it can be critically affected by the answers to these empirical questions. Moreover, because constitutional adjudication itself usually involves the balancing of conflicting interests, the answers to these questions should provide data that is essential to a constitutional analysis of the right to refuse treatment. This article accordingly attempts a therapeutic jurisprudence analysis of the right to refuse treatment.[3] It examines principles of cognitive and social psychology and psychodynamic theory in order to speculate about the likely impact of recognizing that patients and offenders have a right to refuse treatment, and a corresponding opportunity to choose such treatment. It is hoped that this theoretical speculation will generate empirical investigation that, in turn, will aid in a more informed development of the law in this area.

The Psychological Value of Choice

An extensive body of psychological literature points to the positive value of allowing individuals to exercise choice concerning a wide variety of matters affecting them.[4] Patient choice in favor of treatment, for example, appears to be an important determinant of treatment success.[5] Treatment imposed over objection may not work as well. Patients, like people generally, often do not respond well when told what to do. This may be even more true of criminal offenders, who have demonstrated their unwillingness or inability to behave in accordance with society's rules. Unless people themselves see the merit in achieving a particular goal, they often will not pursue it or will do so only halfheartedly. Indeed, sometimes even when the costs of noncompliance with a goal are high, some people may resent the pressure imposed by others and refuse to comply. Sometimes they even may act perversely in ways calculated to frustrate achievement of the goal. By contrast, an individual voluntarily accepting treatment is exercising choice. The law strongly favors allowing individual choice rather than attempting to achieve public or private goals through compulsion.[6] Aside from the political values reflected in this preference, it is strongly supported by utilitarian considerations.

Cognitive and social psychology provide a theoretical explanation for why permitting individual choice may have the effect of enhancing the potential for success.[7] People directed to perform tasks do not feel personally committed to the goal or personally responsible for its fulfillment.[8] This feeling may apply even for tasks the individual is directed to perform in furtherance of his or her own best interests, such as medical treatment. When physicians do not allow patient participation in treatment decisions and do not explain treatment to them, patients often fail to comply with medical advice.[9] Choice, on the other hand, may bring a degree of commitment which mobilizes the self-evaluative and self-reinforcing mechanisms that facilitate goal achievement.[10] To the extent that a patient's agreement to accept a course of treatment recommended by a therapist constitutes an affirmative expression of choice by the patient in favor of treatment, such choice itself may be therapeutic. Compliance with a treatment plan is often indispensable to successful treatment.[11] Unless patients show up for scheduled appointments or take their prescribed medication, treatment cannot succeed. This would seem especially true for treatments like psychotherapy, correctional counseling, and other forms of verbal therapy,[12] and even for many forms of behavioral therapy.[13] These techniques all are largely dependent for their success on the conscious involvement and active cooperation of the patient. However, patient involvement and cooperation would seem essential for even organic forms of treatment.

The conscious, voluntary agreement to accept a course of treatment constitutes the setting of a goal. The setting of explicit goals is itself a significant factor in their accomplishment.[14] This "goal-setting effect" is "one of the most robust . . . findings in the psychological literature."[15] The conscious setting of a goal is virtually indispensable to its achievement.[16] A patient's voluntary agreement to a course of treatment recommended by a therapist constitutes the setting of a goal, the acceptance of a prediction by the therapist that the patient can achieve the goal and will do so, and at least an implicit undertaking by the patient that he or she will attempt the task. The therapist's prediction that the proposed therapy will succeed and the patient's acceptance of this prediction set up expectancies that help to bring about a favorable treatment outcome.[17]

A patient's expectancies concerning treatment success, as well as a number of other cognitive mechanisms, seem to be significantly related to treatment response. There is increasing recognition that the mind plays a crucial role in both the patient's susceptibility to a variety of medical conditions and his or her response to treatment.[18] In its treatment of illness, medicine traditionally has focused almost exclusively on treating the body, often neglecting the role of the mind. Even when fighting organic illnesses with organic treatment techniques, the role of the mind may be significant in producing positive outcomes.[19] Expectancy theory helps to explain the therapeutic power of such phenomena as the placebo effect, the Hawthorne effect, and the medicine man.[20] Although as yet imperfectly understood, these phenomena suggest the existence of a powerful relationship between a patient's expectations that he or she will improve and his or her perceived and even actual improvement. An increasing variety of medical and psychological conditions are treated with hypnosis and positive imaging techniques that ask the patient to visualize his or her body fighting illness and the ultimate restoration to health.[21] The positive attitudes and expectations thereby created are thought to allow the patient to mobilize his or her psychic resources in ways that may play a critical role in the therapeutic process.[22]

How do these positive attitudes and expectancies work to influence treatment success? Social cognitive theory posits that predictions and expectations concerning the achievement of goals, including treatment goals, stimulate feelings of self-efficacy in the individuals which in turn spark action and effort in furtherance of the goal.[23] The setting of treatment goals serves to enhance motivation and increase the patient's effort through self-monitoring, self-evaluation, and self-reactive processes.[24] Setting such goals helps to structure and guide the patient's behavior over the often long course of treatment.[25] It provides direction for the patient and focuses his or her interest, attention, and personal involvement in the treatment.[26] A patient's voluntary acceptance of a therapist's treatment recommendation may facilitate an internalization of the treatment goal that can produce the personal commitment and expenditure of energy needed to achieve it.[27]

Motivation to succeed is an ingredient in goal achievement. Ability to accomplish a goal, although necessary, will not produce success by itself; unless individuals are motivated to succeed, they will not commit the effort needed to bring about success. Psychologist Edward Deci's distinction between intrinsic and extrinsic motivation[28] helps to explain why choice works better than compulsion. Intrinsic motivation involves self-determining behavior and is associated with "an internal perceived locus of causality, feelings of self-determination, and a high degree of perceived competence or self-esteem."[29] With extrinsic motivation, on the other hand, the perceived locus of causality is external and feelings of competence and self-esteem are diminished.[30] When people are allowed to be self-determining, they function more effectively, with a higher degree of commitment and greater satisfaction.[31] These feelings increase motivation to succeed, stimulate positive expectations and attitudes, and spark effort.[32]

The exercise of treatment choice also may trigger what Leon Festinger described as "cognitive dissonance"—the tendency of individuals to reinterpret information or experience that conflicts with their internally accepted or publicly stated beliefs in order to avoid the unpleasant personal state that such inconsistencies produce.[33] Cognitive dissonance affects not only perception, but behavior as well, producing effort in furtherance of the individual's stated goal in order to avoid the dissonance that failure to achieve it would create.[34] In the treatment context, cognitive dissonance can cause the patient to mobilize his or her energies and resources in order to accomplish the treatment goal. These motivating effects of cognitive dissonance will be even stronger to the extent that the patient's commitment to achievement of the goal is made to a respected therapist or counselor or publicly communicated to others whose respect the patient values.[35]

Thus, according to several strands of psychological theory, voluntary choice of treatment, particularly if recommended by a trusted and respected therapist or counselor, engages a number of important intrinsic sources of motivation and creates the positive expectancies that help to bring about treatment success.[36] These intrinsic sources of motivation and positive expectancies are more likely to be activated when the individual makes a choice that he or she regards as voluntary. To the extent that a decision is externally imposed on the individual, or the individual perceives the choice to be coerced, motivation to succeed predictably will be reduced. The positive expectancies and attitudes that appear to be so significant to treatment response would seem likely to occur only to the extent that a real contractarian relationship exists between therapist and patient. The condition of voluntary choice is satisfied in most outpatient treatment contexts, but perhaps rarely in traditional public mental hospitals, where clinicians dictate treatment that is imposed whether or not the patient consents,[37] or in prisons in which treatment is given involuntarily[38] or is perceived to be a condition of release. Some jurisdictions, however, recognize a right to refuse treatment that is applicable in public mental health institutions and prisons,[39] and institutionalized individuals in these jurisdictions are able, at least theoretically, to exercise treatment choice. . . .

This theoretical explanation of the therapeutic value of choice finds support in empirical research in a variety of areas suggesting that allowing individuals to exercise choice increases the likelihood of success. For instance, research with children has demonstrated that involving them in treatment planning and decisionmaking leads to greater compliance and increases the efficacy of treatment.[40] Similarly, allowing students to make choices about educational programs causes them to work "harder, faster, and [react] more positively to the situation than when they [are] unable to make such choices."[41] Anecdotal reports and informed clinical speculation, supported by several empirical studies, suggest that medical and mental health treatment are more effective when provided on a voluntary rather than involuntary basis.[42] An extensive review of the literature on psychotherapy and psychotropic medication, the two most prevalent forms of treatment for those suffering from mental illness, found no persuasive evidence that coercive application of these techniques to involuntarily committed patients was effective.[43]

While more research is needed before definitive conclusions can be reached concerning the effectiveness of treatment applied coercively,[44] the available evidence supports the conclusion that patient choice increases the likelihood of treatment success and that coercion does not work as well. Choice seems to increase positive outcomes in a variety of treatment contexts, although the question of its impact on patients with psychosis has not been adequately studied. For example, a patient in a florid state of schizophrenia, who is disoriented and hallucinating, may not possess a sufficient degree of competence to make a meaningful choice in favor of treatment.[45] How much understanding and volition are necessary to engage the psychological mechanisms discussed earlier that can contribute to a positive treatment response? Will choice by such a patient have the effect of producing the positive expectancies and intrinsic motivation that seem to be related to favorable treatment outcome? Theoretical explanations for the relationship between patient choice and treatment success are based on studies with less impaired populations. Can these findings be generalized to more impaired patients suffering from at least severe cases of major mental illness? These questions remain largely unexamined empirically.

Even if such patients do not possess competence to enable their choices to trigger these positive psychological effects, however, allowing them as great a degree of choice as circumstances permit may still be therapeutic. The aim of treatment interventions for acutely psychotic patients is to ameliorate severe symptomatology and restore the patient to as great a degree of competence as is possible. After a brief period of medication, for example, most seriously disturbed patients will be sufficiently competent that their choices about future treatment presumably will have positive therapeutic value.

An additional therapeutic value of choice, especially for disabled and disadvantaged populations like mental patients and criminal offenders, is that having and making choices is developmentally beneficial. Except for young children, and sometimes even including them, the more choice we give individuals, the more they will act as mature, self-determining adults. Indeed, a sense of competency and self-determination provides strong intrinsic gratification and may be a prerequisite for psychological health.[46] Treating individuals as competent adults able to make choices rather than as incompetent subjects of our paternalism, pity, or even contempt, predictably will have a therapeutic effect. This may be especially true for mental patients, who too often are infantilized by the treatment they receive from institutional clinicians and staff.[47] But it also may be true for prisoners, particularly those incarcerated for lengthy periods, who develop a form of institutional dependency.[48]

The denial of choice—which occurs in a legal system that rejects a right to refuse treatment—can be antitherapeutic, producing what in therapeutic jurisprudence terminology is called "law related psychological disfunction."[49] Exercising self-determination is thought to be a basic human need.[50] A variety of studies show that allowing individuals to make choices is intrinsically motivating, while denying choice "undermines [their] motivation, learning, and general sense of organismic well-being."[51] Indeed, the stress of losing the opportunity to be self-determining may cause "severe somatic malfunctions" and even death.[52] When people feel they have no influence over matters that vitally affect them, they may also develop what Martin Seligman called "learned helplessness." Seligman's experimental work with animals and human subjects led him to posit that repetitive events outside an individual's control may produce a generalized feeling of ineffectiveness that debilitates performance and undermines motivation and perceptions of competence.[53] Institutionalized individuals coerced into accepting treatment might come to view themselves as incompetent in ways that could perpetuate and perhaps even worsen their mental health and social problems. This loss of control may produce depression[54] and decrease motivation.[55] Moreover, it may set up expectancies of failure in the individual that may undermine commitment and diminish subsequent performance.[56]

Denying people a sense of control over important areas of their lives thus can have strongly negative consequences. By contrast, when individuals exercise control and make choices, they experience increased opportunities to build skills necessary for successful living. As a result, they may gradually acquire feelings of self-efficacy, which in turn become important determinants of motivation and performance.[57] Hopefully, if given meaningful choices, these individuals will come to view themselves as in control of their lives, rather than as mere passive victims of forces they can neither understand nor control. . . .

Enhancing the Therapeutic Relationship

These psychological perspectives also suggest that according patients and offenders a right to refuse treatment might have the salutary effect of restructuring the therapist-patient (and counselor-offender) relationship in ways that will enhance its therapeutic potential. There is increasing recognition that in psychotherapy, the therapist-patient relationship itself plays an essential role in producing positive outcomes.[58] The effectiveness of psychotherapy is heavily dependent on the quality of the therapeutic relationship. The most effective therapeutic relationships are those in which mutual trust and acceptance are established and maintained and in which the patient perceives that the therapist cares about and is committed to pursuing his interests.[59] Patients improve as a result of therapeutic relationships that generate the perception that the therapist is interested in and dedicated to the patient's well-being.[60] To succeed, the therapist must establish his or her credibility and trustworthiness at an early time in the relationship. A relationship in which the therapist is permitted to treat the patient as an object of paternalism whose participation in the therapeutic decisionmaking process is unnecessary and undesirable will not inspire such trust and confidence, and therefore may be counterproductive. Indeed, a relationship in which the therapist ignores the patient's expressed wishes concerning treatment may produce the perception that the therapist is more concerned with the welfare of the institution than with that of the patient, and is not truly committed to the patient's best interests. A paternalistic approach that ignores the patient's wishes and concerns is likely to be perceived as offensive by the patient and an affront to his or her dignity and personhood.[61] Rather than producing trust and confidence, such an approach can inspire resentment and resistance.

Therapists, particularly those in public institutions, too often seem to misperceive the importance of the therapist-patient relationship. Not only do these therapists thereby forego therapeutic opportunities, but by their actions they may actually create a harmful division between therapist and patient. Too often there is no real connection or sense of community between therapist and patient. As a result, no real sense of trust and confidence develops on the part of the patient. Yet such trust and confidence may be a prerequisite for engaging those positive attitudes and expectancies that play an important role in producing a successful treatment response. There are therapists who could learn much from the teachings of theologian Martin Buber, whose writings explore the nature of relationships based on mutual dialogue.[62] Buber's notion of an "I-Thou" relationship characterized by mutual respect, openness, and affirmation of the other can be a useful model for restructuring the therapist-patient relationship. This model can transform the therapeutic relationship from one of paternalistic monologue to one of true dialogue, thereby increasing its therapeutic potential.

Recognition of a right to refuse treatment can reshape the therapist-patient relationship into a tool that is both more humane and more effective. It will increase the likelihood that therapists will respect the dignity and autonomy of their patients, and recognize their essential role in the therapeutic process. This reshaping of the therapist's role can increase the potential for a true therapeutic alliance in which therapists treat their patients as persons.[63] The result can be more patient trust, confidence, and participation in decisionmaking in ways that can cause patients to internalize treatment goals. A therapeutic relationship restructured in this fashion can enhance the patient's intrinsic motivation and the likelihood that the goal-setting effect, commitment, and the reinforcing effects of cognitive dissonance will occur.

A real therapist-patient (or counselor-offender) dialogue concerning treatment planning and decisionmaking can only bolster the patient's faith in the therapist and in his or her dedication to the patient's best interests. This faith and the expectations it generates may be essential to producing the Hawthorne effect or other interactive mechanisms that can increase the likelihood of therapeutic success.[64] Without trust, the therapeutic opportunities provided by the therapist-patient relationship are drastically reduced.

The need for trust, cooperation, and open communication is particularly important in the context or psychotherapy and other forms of verbal counseling, which are totally dependent on willing patient communication in the therapeutic relationship. What Freud characterized as the "fundamental rule" of psychotherapy requires the patient to communicate openly and candidly with the therapist.[65] Such basic techniques for probing the patient's unconscious as free association and interpretation of dreams necessitate a patient who is forthcoming with the therapist. Patient cooperation, necessary for these verbal techniques to have any chance of succeeding, assume a high degree of patient trust in the therapist and a relationship that is basically contractarian rather than coercive in nature.

The ability of the therapist successfully to manipulate the transference phenomenon is similarly dependent upon a high degree of patient trust in the therapist. Transference is the process by which the patient's feelings, thoughts, and wishes concerning certain important figures in his or her life (particularly in early life) are transferred or displaced to the therapist.[66] This process is an essential device by which the therapist helps the patient to understand his or her emotional problems and their origins. Transference is a key element in the therapist-patient alliance.[67] Indeed, it has been characterized as "unequivocally the heart of psychoanalysis."[68] Freud himself strongly stressed the role of transference as an ally of the analyst and the motivating force in treatment.[69] According to Freud, a positive transference provides the "strongest motive for the patient's taking a share in the joint work of analysis."[70] Transference thus is both a crucial therapeutic tool and a motivating force for committing the patient to the therapeutic alliance. It is the "unconscious affective bond that forms the basis for analytic work and underlies the patient's desire to remain in treatment. . . ."[71]

For transference to play this essential role in the therapeutic relationship, the therapist must gain the patient's trust and inspire confidence and respect. A basic sense of trust is a prerequisite to the optimal functioning of the working alliance. Patients "often require an awareness of the person and personality of the analyst as someone appropriately interested, caring, warm, and wishing to be helpful at the beginning of treatment in order to establish the self-object transferences that stabilize the treatment and make optimal therapeutic work possible."[72] Indeed, "[n]o analysis can proceed without the functioning of a rational, trusting therapeutic alliance."[73]

There is increasing recognition that the key to successful psychotherapy is the therapeutic alliance itself. The classical analytic concept of the psychotherapist-patient relationship envisioned the therapist as a neutral screen for the patient's transferential projections. But this concept has more recently been broadened to focus attention on the therapeutic value of the relationship itself. This broadening is often discussed as the "real relationship."[74] It represents more than a mere acknowledgement of the therapist's humanness, but also a recognition that what is transformative or curative in the therapeutic process is the actual, caring, human relationship between therapist and patient.[75] Thus, the therapeutic relationship itself is a therapeutic agent. To reach its therapeutic potential, the therapist must establish an environment of safety and trust.[76] A voluntary relationship in which the patient sees the therapist as his or her agent, assisting him or her to accomplish goals that the two of them define, rather than as a paternalistic director of the process, is more likely to create the atmosphere of trust and openness that is necessary for the therapeutic relationship to bring about healing and change.

A legal system in which the therapist needs the informed consent of the patient is thus more conducive to allowing the relationship itself to realize its potential as a therapeutic agent. An informed consent requirement, by encouraging a therapist-patient dialogue, can create a significant therapeutic opportunity. Discussion and negotiation about a patient's objections to treatment can provide an important context for probing conscious and unconscious resistance, for fostering a positive transference, and for earning the patient's trust and confidence.

A therapeutic relationship characterized by voluntariness rather than coercion is particularly important in the institutional contexts—hospital and prison—in which the right to refuse treatment question most often arises. It is in these contexts that distrust of the therapist and concern about his conflicting allegiance to his institutional employer is at its highest. For therapy to be successful, the therapist or counselor must distance himself from the institution's security and management staff and functions. The institutional resident, accustomed to being treated as an object—as a means to the accomplishment of institutional ends—will naturally be suspicious and distrustful of therapists who treat him on a coercive basis. Providing therapy or counseling on a truly voluntary basis will provide a sharp contrast to the way the individual is treated by other institutional staff and can establish a climate that may allow the patient or offender to view his therapist as an ally. It can break down distrust and inspire confidence in and commitment to the therapeutic relationship, which can emerge as an oasis in the desert of institutional life.

These considerations favoring a therapeutic relationship based on voluntariness obviously have special force in the context of verbal psychotherapy or counseling. They also seem applicable, however, in the context of behavior therapy, many of the techniques of which, in order to succeed, require patient cooperation and involvement as well as trust and confidence in the therapist.[77] Moreover, although to a considerably lesser extent, these considerations may apply as well even in the context of the organic treatment techniques. Choosing the appropriate medication, for example, and maximizing the potential that it will be used appropriately, will often require communication with the patient and a high degree of cooperation.[78]

In all types of medical decisionmaking, allowing the patient to exercise choice inevitably enriches and improves the quality of the decisionmaking process.[79] Successful treatment planning and implementation require a thorough analysis of the patient's problems, of the social context that often perpetuates them, and of the patient's strengths and weaknesses. Patient trust, cooperation, and full and open communication are essential if the therapist is to obtain this information from the patient, who frequently is the best, if not the only, source. Moreover, the aphorism "two heads are better than one" is especially apt in this context. Higher quality treatment decisionmaking is more likely when the therapist-patient dialogue, kept open by allowing the patient a legal right to participate in decisionmaking, produces the decision rather than the therapist making it unilaterally. Treatment decisionmaking often involves difficult value choices. How risks and benefits of alternative courses of treatment are weighed depends on the incentive preferences of the individual. The therapist will not always share the patient's values and preferences. Moreover, when the therapist is not the patient's long-term physician— as in mental institutions and prisons—he or she will be unaware of their absent dialogue. The doctor may "know best" about the clinical aspects of risks and benefits of alternative treatments.[80] However, the doctor cannot possess knowledge superior to that of the patient concerning the patient's preferences. Dialogue, although it may cost more in terms of therapist time, produces treatment decisionmaking that is more accurate and thus more likely to be efficacious. In addition, the patient is more likely to accept and comply with treatment when the decision is a product of a process in which he or she has participated.[81] . . .

Notes

1. *See, e.g.,* Appelbaum & Gutheil, *The Boston State Hospital Case: "Involuntary Mind Control," the Constitution, and the "Right to Rot,"* 137 AM J. PSYCHIATRY 720 (1980); Gutheil, *In Search of True Freedom: Drug Refusal, Invol-*

untary Medication, and "Rotting with Your Rights On," 137 AM. J. PSYCHIATRY 327 (1980) (editorial).

2. *See, e.g.,* A. STONE, MENTAL HEALTH LAW: A SYSTEM IN TRANSITION 69–70 (1975) (describing this reaction as the "thank-you" theory); D. WEXLER, MENTAL HEALTH LAW 45–48 (1981) (analyzing the "thank you" theory in context of narcotics abusers); Gove & Fain, *A Comparison of Voluntary and Committed Psychiatric Patients,* 34 ARCH. GEN. PSYCHIATRY 669, 675 (1977); Kane, Quitkin, Rifkin, Wegner, Rosenberg & Borenstein, *Attitudinal Changes of Involuntarily Committed Patients Following Treatment,* 40 ARCH. GEN. PSYCHIATRY 374, 376 (1983); Schwartz, Vingiano & Beziganian-Perez, *Autonomy and the Right to Refuse Treatment: Patient's Attitudes After Involuntary Medication,* 39 HOSP. & COMMUNITY PSYCHIATRY 1049 (1988) (empirical study showing that medication refusers treated over objection, if rehospitalized, would assent to drug treatment); *but see* Beck & Golowka, *A Study of Enforced Treatment in Relation to Stone's "Thank You" Theory,* 6 BEHAV. SCI. & L. 559, 565 (1988) (empirical study of involuntarily hospitalized patients showing no evidence to support "thank you" theory in 62% of cases).

3. Therapeutic jurisprudence suggests the need for an assessment of the therapeutic impact of legal rules. The law itself impacts upon therapeutic values—sometimes positively, but sometimes negatively. While other considerations may properly shape legal rules, a sensible policy analysis of law should take into account its consequences for the health and mental health of the individuals and institutions it affects. Therapeutic jurisprudence accordingly calls for theoretical speculation about and empirical investigation of the therapeutic or antitherapeutic effects of the law. *See generally* D. WEXLER & B. WINICK, ESSAYS IN THERAPEUTIC JURISPRUDENCE (1991); Wexler & Winick, *Therapeutic Jurisprudence as a New Approach to Mental Health Law Policy Analysis and Research,* 45 U. MIAMI L. REV. 979 (1991). In our prior writings, David Wexler and I have suggested the need for a therapeutic jurisprudence assessment of the right to refuse treatment. See WEXLER & WINICK, *supra* at 303, 310–11; Wexler & Winick, *supra* at 990–92. This article attempts such an analysis.

4. *See* Winick, *On Autonomy: Legal and Psychological Perspectives,* 37 VILL. L. REV. 1705, 1755–68 (1992) (summarizing literature on the psychology of choice).

5. Winick, *Competency to Consent to Treatment: The Distinction Between Assent and Objection,* 28 HOUS. L. REV. 15, 46–53 (1991).

6. Winick, *supra* note 4, at 1707–55.

7. *See* S. BREHM & J. BREHM, PSYCHOLOGICAL REACTANCE: A THEORY OF FREEDOM AND CONTROL 301 (1981); Carroll, *Consent to Mental Health Treatment: A Theoretical Analysis of Coercion, Freedom, and Control,* 9 BEHAV. SCI. & L. 129,137–38 (1991); Winick, *Harnessing the Power of the Bet: Wagering with the Government as a Means of Accomplishing Social and Individual Change,* 45 U. MIAMI L. REV. 737, 752–72 (1991) (hereinafter *Wagering with the Government;* Winick, *supra* note 5, at 46–53; Winick, *Competency to Consent to Voluntary Hospitalization: A Therapeutic Jurisprudence Analysis of Zinermon v. Burch,* 14 INT'L J. L. & PSYCHIATRY 169, 192–99 (1991) (hereinafter *Competency to Consent to Voluntary Hospitalization*).

8. A. BANDURA, SOCIAL FOUNDATIONS OF THOUGHT AND ACTION: A SOCIAL COGNITIVE THEORY 338, 363, 368, 468–69, 470–71, 475–76, 478–79 (1986).

9. P. APPELBAUM, C. LIDZ & A. MEISEL, INFORMED CONSENT: LEGAL THEORY AND CLINICAL PRACTICE 28 (1987); D. MEICHENBAUM & D. TURK, FACILITATING TREATMENT ADHERENCE: A PRACTITIONER'S GUIDE-BOOK 20, 76–79 (1987); B. MOYERS, HEALING AND THE MIND 50 (1993); see Appelbaum & Gutheil *Drug Refusal: A Study of Psychiatric Inpatients,* 137 AM. J. PSYCHIATRY 340, 341 (1980); Shultz, *From Informed Consent to Patient Choice: A New Protected Interest,* 95 YALE L. J. 219, 293 & n.323 (1985). Treatment adherence in general increases when the patient is given choice and participation in the selection of treatment alternatives and goals. See MEICHENBAUM & TURK, *supra* at 157, 159, 175; Kanfer & Gaelick, *Self-Management Methods, in* HELPING PEOPLE CHANGE 334–47 (F. Kanfer & A. Goldstein eds. 1986).

10. BANDURA, *supra* note 8, at 338, 363, 368, 468, 478–70; BREHM & BREHM, *supra* note 7, at 301; MEICHENBAUM & TURK, *supra* note 9, at 156–57; Carroll, *supra* note 7, at 129, 137–38.

11. *See generally* MEICHENBAUM & TURK, *supra* note 9.

12. *See* Council of the Am. Psychiatric Ass'n, *Position Statement on the Question of Adequacy of Treatment,* 123 AM. J. PSYCHIATRY 1458, 1459 (1967) ("[I]t may be said in general that the effectiveness of the psychotherapies is proportional to the degree of cooperation that is present . . . .") Katz, *The Right to Treatment—An Enchanting Legal Fiction,* 36 U. CHI. L, REV. 755, 777 (1969); Michels, *Ethical Issues of Psychological and Psychotherapeutic Means of Behavior Control: Is the Moral Contract Being Observed?,* 3 HASTINGS CENTER REP. 11, 11 (1973); Stromberg & Stone, *A Model State Law on Civil Commitment of the Mentally Ill,* 20 HARV. J. LEGIS. 276, 328 (1983); Winick, *The Right to Refuse Mental Health Treatment: A First Amendment Perspective,* 44 U. MIAMI L. REV. 1, 83–84 (1989).

13. *See* E. ERWIN, BEHAVIOR THERAPY: SCIENTIFIC, PHILOSOPHICAL AND MORAL FOUNDATIONS 180–81 (1978); MEICHENBAUM & TURK, *supra* note 7, at 150; Bandura, *Behavior Therapy and the Models of Man,* 29 AM. PSYCHOLOGIST 859, 862 (1974); Marks, *The Current Status of Behavioral Psychotherapy: Theory and Practice,* 133 AM. J. PSYCHIATRY 253, 255 (1976); Winick, *Legal Limitations on Correctional Therapy and Research,* 65 MINN. L. REV. 331, 360–61 (1981); Winick, *supra* note 12, at 80.

14. Campbell, *The Effects of Goal-Contingent Payment on the Performance of a Complex Task,* 37 PERSONNEL PSYCHOLOGY 23, 23 (1984); Huber, *Comparison of Monetary Reinforcers and Goal Setting as Learning Incentives,* 56 PSYCHOL. REP. 223 (1985); Kirschenbaum & Flanery, *Toward a Psychology of Behavioral Contracting,* 4 CLINICAL PSYCHOL. REV. 598, 603–609 (1984); Locke, Shaw, Saari & Latham, *Goal Setting and Task Performance* 1969–1980, 90 PSYCHOL. BULL. 125, 125–31 (1981); Terborg & Miller, *Motivation, Behavior, and Performance: A Closer Examination of Goal Setting and Monetary Incentives,* 63 J. APPLIED PSYCHOL. 29, 30–31 (1978).

15. Campbell, *supra* note 14, at 23; Locke, Shaw, Saari & Latham, *supra* note 14, at 145.

16. BANDURA, *supra* note 8, at 469 ("Those who set no goals achieve no change . . . .").

17. *See id.* at 412–13, 467; Deci & Ryan, *The Empirical Exploration of Intrinsic Motivational Processes,* 13 ADVANCES IN EXPER. SOC. PSYCHOLOGY 39, 59 (1980).

18. *See generally* N. COUSINS, HEALTH FIRST: THE BIOLOGY OF HOPE AND THE HEALING POWER OF THE HUMAN SPIRIT (1990); H. DIENSTFREY, WHERE THE MIND MEETS THE BODY: TYPE A, THE RELAXATION RESPONSE, PSYCHONEUROIMMUNOLOGY, HYPNOSIS, BIOFEEDBACK, NEUROPEPTIDES, AND THE SEARCH FOR IMAGERY, AND THE MIND'S EFFECT ON PHYSICAL HEALTH (1991); H. DUNBAR, EMOTIONS AND BODILY CHANGES (1954) (discussing psychosomatic medicine, a psychological approach to medicine treating the mind and body as one entity); MOYERS, *supra* note 9; Engel, *The Need for a New Medical Model. A Challenge for Biomedicine,* 196 SCIENCE 129 (1977) (proposing a psychosocial view of health, taking into account the interaction of biological, psychological, and social factors in the onset of physical disorders); Frank, *The Faith that Heals,* 137 JOHNS HOPKINGS MED. J. 127 (1975) (observing that diverse modes of medical treatment owe their success or failure to the patient's state of mind and expectations, and not solely to the treatment regimen itself).

19. *See* COUSINS, *supra* note 18, at 192 (commenting on the role of patient's outlook and attitudes on the onset and course of disease); *id.* ("[T]he wise physician makes a careful estimate of the patients' will to live and the ability to put to work all the resources of spirit that can be translated into beneficial biochemical changes."); *id.* ("[F]ew things are more important than the psychological management of the patient" in all medical contexts.); *id.* at 217–20 (discussing survey of oncologists showing their belief that positive patient attitude and participation in treatment were beneficial); MOYERS, *supra* note 9, at 130 (commenting on the role of lifestyle and attitudes on such conditions as cancer and heart disease).

20. *See, e.g.,* J. BOURKE, THE MEDICINE MEN OF THE APACHE 2 (1971) (observing that the ability to inspire belief in patients that he has "the gift" is a prerequisite to being "a diyi" or medicine man); H. BRODY, PLACEBOS AND THE PHILOSOPHY OF MEDICINE: CLINICAL, CONCEPTUAL, AND ETHICAL ISSUES 18–20 (1980) ("[T]he patient's expectations of symptom change is held to be causally connected to the change that occurs"); M. JOSPE, THE PLACEBO EFFECT IN HEALING 93–108, 130 (1978) (analyzing the Hawthorne effect in terms of expectancy theory); O. SIMONTON, S. MATTHEWS-SIMONTON & J. CREIGHTON, WELL AGAIN 22 (1978); Beecher, *The Powerful Placebo,* 159 J.A.M.A. 1602 (1955) (documenting the power of the placebo); Evans, *Expectancy, Therapeutic Instructions, and the Placebo Response,* in PLACEBO: THEORY, RESEARCH, AND MECHANISMS 215, 222–24 (1985) (concluding that the "placebo response is mediated by expectations generated within the context of the doctor-patient relationship"); Frank, *Biofeedback and the Placebo Effect,* 7 BIOFEEDBACK & SELF-REGULATION 449 (1982) (examining placebo effect in terms of expectancy theory); Horvath, *Placebos and Common Factors in two Decades of Psychotherapy Research,* 104 PSYCHOL. BULL. 214, 215 (1988) ("Expectancy factors have been shown to influence therapeutic outcome"); Wolf, *Effects of Placebo Administra-*

tion and Occurrence of Toxic Reactions, 155 J.A.M.A. 339 (1974) (documenting beneficial effects of placebos). For an alternative analysis of the placebo effect in terms of classical conditioning, see DIENSTFREY, *supra* note 18, at 86–87; Ader, *The Placebo Effect as Conditioned Response,* in EXPERIMENTAL FOUNDATIONS OF BEHAVIORAL MEDICINE: CONDITIONING APPROACHES 47 (R. Ader, H. Weiner & A. Baum eds. 1988).

21. *See, e.g.,* P. BROWN, THE HYPNOTIC BRAIN: HYPNOTHERAPY AND SOCIAL COMMUNICATION (1991); G. EPSTEIN, HEALING VISUALIZATIONS: CREATING HEALTH THROUGH IMAGERY (1989); M. ERICKSON, THE COLLECTED PAPERS OF MILTON H. ERICKSON ON HYPNOSIS (E. Ross ed. 1988); Barber, *Changing "Unchangeable" Bodily Processes by (Hypnotic) Suggestion: A New Look at Hypnosis, Cognition, Imagining, and the Mind-Body Problem,* in IMAGINATION AND HEALING (A. Sheikh ed. 1984); Orne & Dinges, *Hypnosis, in* 2 COMPREHENSIVE TEXT OF PSYCHIATRY 1501, 1511–12 (H. Kaplan & B. Sadock eds. 5th ed. 1989); Wilson & Barber, *The Fantasy-Prone Personality: Implications for Understanding Imagery, Hypnosis, and Parapsychological Phenomena,* in IMAGERY: CURRENT THEORY, RESEARCH AND APPLICATION 340 (A. Sheikh & J. Wiley eds. 1983).

22. *See* COUSINS, *supra* note 18, at 237–39 (discussing the psychic interplay and its effects on wound healing, the course of progressive illnesses such as AIDS, and the functioning of the immune system); DIENSTFREY, *supra* note 18; MOYERS, *supra* note 9, at 48; Dubos, *Introduction, in* N. COUSINS, ANATOMY OF AN ILLNESS AS PERCEIVED BY THE PATIENT: REFLECTIONS ON HEALING AND REGENERATION 11, 18, 22–23 (1979); Shultz, *supra* note 9, at 292–93.

23. *See* BANDURA, *supra* note 8, at 413. See also Rotter, *Generalized Expectancies for Internal Versus External Control of Reinforcement,* 80 PSYCHOL. MONOGRAPHS 1 (1966) (behavior varies as a function of the individual's generalized expectancies that outcomes are determined by his own actions or by external sources beyond his control); Horvath, *supra* note 20, at 218 ("The belief that the treatment works in the manner outlined in the rationale motivates the client to perform the tasks of the therapy.").

24. *See* BANDURA, *supra* note 8, at 469–72; MEICHENBAUM & TURK, *supra* note 9, at 158–61.

25. See BANDURA, *supra* note 8, at 469.

26. *See id.* at 472.

27. *Cf. id.* at 477–78 (observing that pledging goal commitments publicly, or to other people, enhances the amount of personal effort expended in their pursuit).

28. *See* E. DECI, INTRINSIC MOTIVATION (1975) (hereinafter INTRINSIC MOTIVATION) (reviewing studies in intrinsic motivation and discussing development of its interplay with extrinsic rewards and controls); E. DECI, THE PSYCHOLOGY OF SELF-DETERMINATION (1980) [hereinafter THE PSYCHOLOGY OF SELF-DETERMINATION]; Deci & Ryan, *supra* note 17, at 41–43, 60–63, 67.

29. DECI, THE PSYCHOLOGY OF SELF-DETERMINATION, *supra* note 28, at 41.

30. *Id.*

31. *Id.* at 208–10. *See also* C. KIESLER, THE PSYCHOLOGY OF COMMITMENT: EXPERIMENTS LINKING BEHAVIOR TO BELIEF 164–67 (1971) (finding

most effective method for behavior therapists to obtain desired results with patients was to give patients perception that they had freedom and control).

32. *See* BANDURA, *supra* note 8, at 390–449; DECI, THE PSYCHOLOGY OF SELF-DETERMINATION, *supra* note 28, at 208–10; M. FRIEDMAN & G. LACKEY, JR., THE PSYCHOLOGY OF HUMAN CONTROL: A GENERAL THEORY OF PURPOSEFUL BEHAVIOR 72–74 (1991) (noting that control leads to self-confidence, which in turn leads to positive behavior); Deci & Ryan, *supra* note 17, at 41–42, 60–61.

33. L. FESTINGER, A THEORY OF COGNITIVE DISSONANCE 2–3, 18–24, 73 (1957) [hereinafter COGNITIVE DISSONANCE]; L. Festinger, CONFLICT, DECISION, AND DISSONANCE 43 (1964). For a review of empirical studies on cognitive dissonance, *see* J. Brehm & A. Cohen, EXPLORATIONS IN COGNITIVE DISSONANCE 221–44 (1962).

34. FESTINGER, COGNITIVE DISSONANCE, *supra* note 33, at 19.

35. *See* BANDURA, *supra* note 8, at 477–78; MEICHENBAUM & TURK, *supra* note 9, at 170, 174; Winick, *Wagering with the Government, supra* note 7, at 763–64.

36. *See supra* notes 7–35 and accompanying text. *See generally* BANDURA, *supra* note 8, at 467, 471–72; DECI, INTRINSIC MOTIVATION, *supra* note 28; DECI, THE PSYCHOLOGY OF SELF-DETERMINATION, *supra* note 28; Carroll, *supra* note 7, at 129, 137–38; Deci & Ryan, *supra* note 17, at 41–42, 60–63, 67.

37. *See, e.g., Dautremont v. Broadlawn Hosp.*, 827 F.2d 291, 298 (8th Cir. 1987) (hospitalized civil patients may be involuntarily treated with psychotropic drugs against their will).

38. *See, e.g., Washington v. Harper*, 494 U.S. 210 (1990) (upholding involuntary administration of antipsychotic medication to prisoner).

39. *See, e.g.,* 2 M. PERLIN, MENTAL DISABILITY LAW: CIVIL AND CRIMINAL §§ 5.01–69 (1989); Winick, *supra* note 12; Winick, *The Right to Refuse Psychotropic Medication: Current State of the Law and Beyond, in* THE RIGHT TO REFUSE ANTIPSYCHOTIC MEDICATION 7 (D. Rapoport & J. Parry eds. 1986).

40. *See, e.g.,* Lewis, *Decision Making Related to Health: When Could/Should Children Act Responsibly?, in* CHILDREN'S COMPETENCE TO CONSENT 75, 76–77, 78–79 (G. Melton, P. Koocher & M. Saks eds. 1983); Melton, *Children's Competence to Consent, A Problem in Law and Social Science, in* CHILDREN'S COMPETENCE TO CONSENT, *supra* at 1, 11; Melton, *Decision Making by Children: Psychological Risks and Benefits, in* CHILDREN'S COMPETENCE TO CONSENT, *supra* note 21, 30–31, 37; Melton, *Children's Participation in Treatment Planning: Psychological and Legal Issues,* 12 PROF. PSYCHOL. 246, 250–51 (1981).

41. Bringham, *Some Effects of Choice on Academic Performance, in* CHOICE AND PERCEIVED CONTROL 131, 140 (L. Perlmutter & R. Monty eds. 1979). See also Amabile & Gitomer, *Children's Artistic Creativity: Effects of Choice in Task Materials,* 10 PERSONALITY & SOC. PSYCHOL. BULL. 209, 213 (1984) (restriction of choice negatively affected creativity); Deci, Nezlek & Sheinman, *Characteristics of the Rewarder and Intrinsic Motivation of the Rewardee,* 40 J. PERSONALITY & SOC. PSYCHOL. 1, 9 (1981) (students in autonomy-oriented classrooms shown to have higher intrinsic motivation and self-esteem than students in control-oriented classrooms).

42. *See* AM. PSYCHIATRIC ASS'N TASK FORCE REPORT NO. 34: CONSENT TO VOLUNTARY HOSPITALIZATION 1 (1993) (voluntary hospitalization may lead to more favorable outcomes compared to involuntary hospitalization), *id.* at 5 ("The American Psychiatric Association strongly believes that it is preferable whenever possible for patients to be able to initiate their own psychiatric treatment."); APPELBAUM, LIDZ & MEISEL, *supra* note 7, at 28; S. BRAKEL, J. PARRY & B. WEINER, THE MENTALLY DISABLED AND THE LAW 178, 181 n.34 (3d ed. 1985); BREHM & BREHM, *supra* note 7, at 301; MEICHENBAUM & TURK, *supra* note 9, at 175; Appelbaum, Mirkin & Bateman, *Empirical Assessment of Competency to Consent to Psychiatric Hospitalization*, 183 AM. J. PSYCHIATRY 1170, 1170 (1981); Carroll, *supra* note 7, at 129, 137–38; Culver & Gert, *The Morality of Involuntary Hospitalization*, in THE LAW-MEDICINE RELATION: A PHILOSOPHICAL EXPLORATION 159, 171 (S. Spicker, J. Healy & T. Engelhardt eds. 1981); Freedberg & Johnston, *Effects of various Sources of Coercion on Outcome of Treatment of Alcoholism*, 43 PSYCHOL. REP. 1271, 1271, 1277 (1978); Nicholson, *Correlates of Commitment Status in Psychiatric Patients*, 100 PSYCHOL. BULL, 241, 243–44 (1986); Perlin & Sadoff, *Ethical Issues in the Representation of Individuals in the Commitment Process*, 45 LAW & CONTEMP. PROBS. 161, 190–91 (1982); Rogers & Webster, *Assessing Treatability in Mentally Disordered Offenders*, 13 LAW & HUM. BEHAV. 19, 20–21 (1989); Stein & Test, *Alternatives to Mental Hospital Treatment*, 37 ARCH. GEN. PSYCHIATRY 392, 392–93 (1980); Stromberg & Stone, *supra* note 12, at 327, 328; Ward, *The Use of Legal Coercion in the Treatment of Alcoholism: A Methodological Review*, in ALCOHOLISM: INTRODUCTION TO THEORY AND TREATMENT 272 (D. Ward ed. 1980); Note, *Developments in the Law—Civil Commitment of the Mentally Ill*, 87 HARV. L. REV. 1190, 1399 (1974). *See also* Washington v. Harper, 494 U.S. 210, 249 n. 15 (1990) ("The efficacy of forced drugging is also marginal; involuntary patients have a poorer prognosis than cooperating patients.) (Stevens, J., dissenting); Rennic v. Klein. 462 F. Supp. 1131, 1144 (D. N.J. 1978) ("[T]he testimony . . . indicated that involuntary treatment is much less effective than the same treatment voluntarily received.").

43. Durham & La Fond, *A Search for the Missing Premise of Involuntary Therapeutic Commitment: Effective Treatment of the Mentally Ill*, 40 RUTGERS L. REV. 303, 351–56, 367–68 (1988) (hereinafter *Involuntary Therapeutic Commitment*). *See also* Durham & La Fond, *The Empirical Consequences and Policy Implications of Broadening the Statutory Criteria for Civil Commitments*, 3 YALE L. & POLICY REV. 395 (1985) (analyzing adverse effects of a statutory broadening of civil commitment standards).

44. *See* WEXLER & WINICK, *supra* note 3, at 248 n.101 (noting the scarcity and inadequacy of existing studies and suggesting the need for more empirical research on the issue).

45. *See* Zinermon v. Burch, 494 U.S. 113 (1990) (patient with schizophrenia who was delusional and hallucinating and who expressed the view that the mental hospital he was entering was "heaven" held incompetent to consent to voluntary hospitalization). This article does not analyze the concept of competency. For analysis of competency in various legal contexts, see Winick, *Competency to be Executed: A Therapeutic Jurisprudence Perspective*, 10 BEHAV. SCI.

& L. 317 (1992) (competency to be executed); Winick, *supra* note 5 (competency to consent to treatment); Winick, *Competency to Consent to Voluntary Hospitalization, supra* note 7 (competency to consent to hospitalization); Winick, *Incompetency to Stand Trial: An Assessment of Costs and Benefits, and a Proposal for Reform,* 39 RUTGERS L. REV. 243 (1987) (competency to stand trial). Nor does this article examine the conditions under which an incompetent patient's choice may be overridden pursuant to the state's *parens patriae* power. See Winick, *supra* note 4, at 1772–77. Recognition that patients have a constitutional right to refuse treatment does not, of course, mean that a patient's right is absolute. For analysis of when state interests may outweigh the patient's asserted right to refuse treatment, see Winick, *supra* note 13 (examining state interests in correctional rehabilitation); Winick, *supra* note 39 (examining state interests in the civil context).

46. Carroll, *supra* note 7, at 129, 137–38; Deci & Ryan, *supra* note 17, at 42, 61, 72–73.

47. *See generally* E. GOFFMAN, ASYLUMS: ESSAYS ON THE SOCIAL SITUATIONS OF MENTAL PATIENTS AND OTHER INMATES 3–74(1962) (discussing the phenomena of institutional dependence); Devillis, *Learned Helplessness in Institutions,* 15 MENTAL RETARDATION 10 (1977); Doherty, *Labeling Effects in Psychiatric Hospitalization: A Study of Diverging Patterns of Inpatient Self-labeling Process,* 32 ARCH. GEN. PSYCHIATRY 562 (1975). *See also* Johnson v. Solomon, 484 F. Supp. 278, 308 (D. Md. 1979) ("Inappropriate and excessive hospitalization fosters deterioration, institutionalization, and possible regression.") (footnotes omitted). In addition to breeding learned helplessness, see Devillis, *supra; infra* note 53 and accompanying text, such total institutions condition passivity and helplessness by reinforcing it and by discouraging assertiveness and autonomous behavior.

48. *See* GOFFMAN, *supra* note 47, 16–17, 25–31, 39, 53–55, 61, 68–70.

49. *See* WEXLER & WINICK, *supra* note 3, at 313; Wexler & Winick, *supra* note 3, at 979, 994.

50. DECI, THE PSYCHOLOGY OF SELF-DETERMINATION, *supra* note 28, at 208–09 (discussing "intrinsic motivation" as providing energy for various functions of will). See also H. HARTMANN, EGO PSYCHOLOGY AND THE PROBLEM OF ADAPTATION (1958) ("independent ego energy"); White, *Motivation Reconsidered: The Concept of Competence,* 66 PSYCHOL. REV. 297 (1959) ("effectance motivation").

51. DECI, THE PSYCHOLOGY OF SELF-DETERMINATION, *supra* note 28, at 209 (discussing studies).

52. *Id.*

53. M. SELIGMAN, HELPLESSNESS: ON DEPRESSION, DEVELOPMENT, AND DEATH (1975); HUMAN HELPLESSNESS: THEORY AND APPLICATIONS (J. Garber & M. Seligman eds. 1980); Maier & Seligman, *Learned Helplessness: Theory and Evidence,* 105 J. EXPERIMENTAL PSYCHOL. 33 (1976); Overmier & Seligman, *Effects of Inescapable Shock Upon Subsequent Escape and Avoidance Responding,* 63 J. COMP. & PHYSIOLOGICAL PSYCHOL. 28 (1976). Seligman, *Learned Helplessness,* 23 ANN. REV. MED. 407 (1972). *See also* BREHM & BREHM, *supra* note 7, at 378 (1981); LENORE WALKER, THE BATTERED WOMAN 42–54 (1979)

(applying learned helplessness to the battered woman syndrome); Peterson & Bossio, *Learned Helplessness, in* SELF-DEFEATING BEHAVIORS: EXPERIMENTAL RESEARCH, CLINICAL IMPRESSIONS, AND PRACTICAL IMPLICATIONS 235 (C. Peterson & Bossio eds. 1989); Thornton & Jacobs, *Learned Helplessness in Human Subjects,* 87 J. EXPERIMENTAL PSYCHOL. 367 (1971).

54. *See* FRIEDMAN & LACKEY, *supra* note 32, at 73; Peterson & L. Bossio, *supra* note 53, at 26.

55. *See* Deci, Nezlek & Sheinman, *supra* note 41; Deci & Ryan, *supra* note 17, at 59.

56. *See* FRIEDMAN & LACKEY, *supra* note 32, at 73.

57. *See* BANDURA, *supra* note 8, at 390–449; BREHM & BREHM, *supra* note 7, at 301, 376; Carroll, *supra* note 7, at 129, 137–38; Deci & Ryan, *supra* note 17, at 41–42, 60–61.

58. *E.g.,* BREHM & BREHM, *supra* note 7, at 151–55, 300–01; WEXLER & WINICK, *supra* note 3, at 173; Deci & Ryan, supra note 17, at 70; Lambert, Shapiro & Bergin, *The Effectiveness of Psychotherapy, in* HANDBOOK OF PSYCHOTHERAPY AND BEHAVIOR CHANGE 157–211 (S. Garfield & A. Bergin eds., 3d ed. 1986) (hereinafter HANDBOOK).

59. See authorities cited in *supra* note 58. The therapist-patient relationship, although especially significant in the context of psychotherapy, is also important in all areas of medical practice. *See, e.g.,* COUSINS, *supra* note 18, at 18 (discussing confidence by the patient in the doctor and in the patient's own healing resources); MOYERS, *supra* note 9, at 50 (discussing a "prevention partnership in which a patient is empowered to be a partner with . . . [the doctor] in the healing process."); Appelbaum & Gutheil, *supra* note 9, at 341 (noting correlation between adherence to drug treatment by psychiatric inpatients and the quality of the doctor-patient relationship).

60. BREHM & BREHM, *supra* note 7, at 151–52, 300–02; WEXLER & WINICK, *supra* note 3, at 173; Beutler, Crago & Arizmendi, *Therapist Variables in Psychotherapy Process and Outcome, in* HANDBOOK, *supra* note 58, at 280–81; Orlinsky & Howard, *Process and Outcome in Psychotherapy, in* HANDBOOK, *supra* note 58, at 311.

61. J. FEINBERG, HARM TO SELF 4–5, 23, 27 (1986); Goldstein, *For Harold Lasswell: Some Reflections on Human Dignity, Entrapment, Informed Consent, and the Plea Bargain,* 84 YALE L.J. 683, 691 (1975); Meisel & Roth, Toward an Informed Discussion of Informed Consent: A Review and Critique of the Empirical Studies, 25 ARIZ. L. REV. 265, 284 (1993); Winick, *supra* note 5. at 17.

62. *See* M. BUBER, I AND THOU (1937); M. BUBER, BETWEEN MAN AND MAN (1947). For a proposal calling for the restructuring of the attorney-client relationship in the poverty law context that builds upon Buber's work, see Alfieri, *The Antinomies of Poverty Law and a Theory of Dialogical Empowerment,* 16 N.Y.U. REV. L. & SOC. CHANGE 659 (1987–88).

63. *See* P. RAMSEY, THE PATIENT AS PERSON: EXPLORATIONS IN MEDICAL ETHICS (1970).

64. *See* Jospe, *supra* note 20, at 93–108, 130; text accompanying *supra* note 20.

65. S. Freud, AN OUTLINE OF PSYCHOANALYSIS, in 23 STANDARD EDITION OF THE COMPLETE PSYCHOLOGICAL WORKS OF SIGMUND FREUD 141 (1964).

66. *See, e.g.*, AM. PSYCHIATRIC ASSN, A PSYCHIATRIC GLOSSARY 106 (6th ed. 1988) (hereinafter A PSYCHIATRIC GLOSSARY); Adler, *Transference, Real Relationship and Alliance*, 61 INT'L J. PSYCHO-ANAL. 547, 547 (1980); Greenson, *The Working Alliance and the Transference Neurosis*, 34 PSYCHOANAL. Q. 155 (1965); Karasu, Psychoanalysis and Psychoanalytic Psychotherapy, in 2 COMPREHENSIVE TEXTBOOK OF PSYCHIATRY 1442, 1446–47 (H. Kaplan & B. Sadock eds., 5th ed. 1989).

67. See A PSYCHIATRIC GLOSSARY, *supra* note 66 at 106; Adler, *supra* note 66, at 548 ("[T]ransference and alliance seem inextricably intermeshed.").

68. Karasu, *supra* note 66, at 1446.

69. *See* Adler, *supra* note 66, at 548; Friedman, *The Therapeutic Alliance*, 50 INT'L J. PSYCHOANAL. 139 (1969).

70. S. FREUD, ANALYSIS TERMINABLE AND INTERMINABLE, *in* 23 THE COLLECTED WORKS OF SIGMUND FREUD 233 (1937), *cited in* Adler, *supra* note 66, at 548.

71. Karasu, *supra* note 66, at 1446.

72. Adler, *supra* note 66, at 553. *See* also Viederman, *The Real Person of the Analyst and his Role in the Process of Psychoanalytic Cure*, 39 J. AM. PSYCHOANALYTIC ASS'N 451, 457–58 (1991) (need for first phase of analysis to offer an environment of safety and trust in the therapist-patient relationship in order for the therapeutic potential of transference to be achieved). For a parallel perspective drawn from cognitive psychology, see BREHM & BREHM, *supra* note 7, at 151–53, 300–01; Deci & Ryan, *supra* note 17, at 70.

73. Karasu, *supra* note 66, at 1449.

74. *See, e.g.*, Adler, *supra* note 75.

75. Personal communication from Daniel C. Silverman, M.D., Associate Psychiatrist In Chief, Beth Israel Hospital, Boston, Massachusetts, and Assistant Professor of Psychiatry, Harvard Medical School, Cambridge, Massachusetts, June 3, 1991. *See, e.g.*, Aaron, *The Patient's Experience of the Analyst's Subjectivity*, 1 PSYCHOANALYTIC DIALOGUE 29, 33 (1991) ("The relational approach that I am advocating views the patient-analyst relationship as continually established and re-established through ongoing mutual influences in which both patient and analyst systematically affect, and are affected by, each other. A communication process is established between patient and analyst in which influence flows in both directions."); *id.* at 41 (analysis viewed as co-participation); *id.* at 43 (analysis viewed as "mutual," with "both patient and analyst functioning as subject and object, as co-participants"); Adler, *supra* note 66, at 552–54; Binstock, *The Therapeutic Relationship*, 21 J. Am. PSYCHOANALYTIC ASS'N 543 (1973); Hoffman, *Discussion: Toward a Social-Constructivist View of the Psychoanalytic Situation*, 1 PSYCHOANALYTIC DIALOGUE 74, 75 (1991) (a real personal relationship and a mutual exploration of each one's perception of the analytical relationship creates the opportunity "for a special kind of affective contact with the analyst that is thought to have therapeutic potential").

76. Karasu, *supra* note 66, at 1449; Viederman, *supra* note 72, at 548.

77. See supra note 13 and accompanying text.

78. Appelbaum & Gutheil, supra note 9, at 341. In addition, many of the organic treatment techniques, like psychotropic drugs, are not administered in isolation, but are part of an integrated treatment plan that involves verbal psychotherapy or counseling. In the case of schizophrenia or severe depression, for example, medication is needed to control symptoms that would prevent the patient from accepting other forms of therapy. Antipsychotic drugs that minimize the visual or auditory hallucinations or agitation that often characterize schizophrenia, and antidepressant drugs that control the severe withdrawal and feelings of worthlessness and profound sadness that often characterize major affective depression, are necessary to render the patient accessible to verbal, social, and occupational therapy approaches. Even if such medication would be effective in reducing severe symptomatology when administered coercively, the verbal therapy that should follow the reduction in symptoms would seem to be more effective to the extent that the individual chooses it voluntarily.

79. See J. KATZ, THE SILENT WORLD OF DOCTOR AND PATIENT 102–03 (1984) (analyzing the informed consent doctrine as furthering the doctor-patient relationship); COUSINS, supra note 22, at 55 ("[F]ull communication between the patient and physician is indispensable not just in arriving at an accurate diagnosis but in devising an effective strategy for treatment.); Altman, Health Official Urges Focus by Doctors on Caring as well as Curing: A More Active Role for Patients is Recommended, N.Y. Times, § 1, at 6, col. 3 (Aug. 15, 1993) ("Doctors need to consider their patients as knowledgeable allies, not as passive recipients of care, and involve them fully in the entire care process, including decision-making about treatment . . . .") (quoting Michael H. Merson, M.D., World Health Organization official).

80. But see KATZ, supra note 79, at 166–69 (discussing the uncertainty inherent in medical science).

81. See KATZ, supra note 79, at 103; MEICHENBAUM & TURK, supra note 9, at 63, 71–76, 84–85.

The Duty to Protect Potential Victims of Patients' Violence

Paul S. Appelbaum

The Genesis of a Broader "Duty to Protect"

In 1969, an Indian graduate student at the University of California, Berkeley, Prosenjit Poddar, entered psychotherapy with a psychologist at the university health service. Poddar had done poorly after his romantic attentions had been rebuffed by an American girl, Tatiana Tarasoff, whom he had dated for several months the previous year. He had become depressed and withdrawn, neglecting his appearance, his studies, and his health. Obsessed with the woman who had spurned him, Poddar met with her several times in the months before entering therapy and tape-recorded their conversations, trying to ascertain why she did not love him.[1]

Soon after the start of psychotherapy, the treating psychologist became concerned about Poddar's potential for harming Tatiana Tarasoff. Whether Poddar told the psychologist directly about his intent to kill her (as her parents later alleged)[2] or whether he merely manifested his obsession with her and the psychologist learned from a friend of Poddar that he had purchased a gun[3] is unclear. Whatever the basis for the psychologist's concern, he consulted with two supervising psychiatrists and then notified the campus police that he would be requesting commitment of the patient. He asked to detain Poddar while the necessary paperwork was completed.

The police picked up Poddar, but after talking with him, finding him "rational," and eliciting his promise that he would stay away from Tatiana Tarasoff, who was then out of the country on vacation, they let him go. No further action was taken by the therapists, apparently because they felt uncomfortable about having breached Poddar's confidentiality by informing the university police of their intention to commit him. Poddar never returned to therapy, but he did seek out Tatiana's brother, whose roommate he became and from whom he learned of her return to the country. Roughly two months after the attempt had been made to commit him, Poddar went to the Tarasoff house, armed with a pellet gun and a kitchen knife, and found Tatiana alone. She refused to speak with him and began screaming, at which point Poddar shot her, chased her as she attempted to flee, and stabbed her to death. He then returned to her house and called the police.

Faced with this horrifying crime, Tatiana's parents sought to hold the therapists and the campus police responsible for what had occurred. They filed suit alleging negligence on the therapists' part for failing effectively to detain Poddar and for failing to warn them (Tatiana being unreachable) of the threat to their daughter's life. Clearly, they were striking out across uncharted legal territory. Poddar never had been hospitalized, and thus the linchpin of all previous decisions in which psychiatrists had been found liable was missing in this case. If the courts agreed with the family that the therapists (setting aside any duties the police may have had) had a duty to protect Tatiana Tarasoff, they would have to base their decision on a new theory of psychiatric liability.

In the event, that is exactly what happened. The California Supreme Court, ruling that the suit could proceed to trial, held that a therapist who "determines, or pursuant to the standards of his profession should determine, that his patient presents a serious danger of violence to another" has a duty to take whatever steps are "reasonably necessary" to protect the intended victim.[4] The source of this duty was the "special relationship" that the court concluded existed between a therapist and a patient, and the additional obligations such a relationship imposed.

Invocation of "special relationships" has served as a mechanism by which courts can bypass the law's deeply rooted hesitancy about imposing affirmative duties on one person to protect or rescue another.[5] In Anglo-American law in general, no sanctions are applied to persons who fail to assist their fellows, even when assistance may be life-saving and may require only minimal effort. Thus, a person who knowingly walks past a toddler drowning in a wading pool—a situation in which a moment's intervention would have saved the child's life—bears no civil or criminal responsibility for the toddler's demise. Were the child's parents or babysitter to behave similarly, however, they would be held culpable, since they had a legally cognizable "special relationship" with the child.

There is no touchstone to determine when a special relationship exists. Indeed, the determination is often driven by the desired outcome: when courts believe, on whatever grounds, that a duty to rescue should be imposed, they proclaim a special relationship; when they feel otherwise, they solemnly declare its absence. Among the relationships deemed special have been common carrier-passenger, innkeeper-guest, employer-employee, shopkeeper-business visitor, host-social guest, and school-pupil.[6] Courts have justified each of these exceptions to the general rule by pointing to some characteristic of the relationship that warrants imposing a special, heightened duty.

In the case of the psychotherapist-patient relationship, the *Tarasoff* court's analysis of why a duty to rescue or protect should be imposed was skeletal. The court referred to several lines of cases that it apparently considered analogous. One was the release and escape decisions discussed earlier. The implication here seemed to be that, although Poddar's therapists did not exercise physical control over him, they had the opportunity to do so, given the commitment laws of the state of California. Thus, a duty arose comparable to the one that would have applied if he had been in their custody. A second line of cited cases dealt with physicians who had failed to warn patients' family members that the patients' conditions were infectious. The rationale here appeared to be that, just as physicians have specialized knowledge of the dangers of transmission of communicable diseases, so Poddar's therapists had knowledge of his dangerousness that was not available to the public at large. Along with this knowledge came an obligation to act.

Two additional facets of the *Tarasoff* decision are worthy of comment. First, the court restricted the ambit of obligation owed by therapists to identifiable victims of their patients. As explicitly affirmed in a later case,[7] this limitation excludes liability for patients whom therapists might only know to be dangerous to the public at large. Second, in contrast to this limiting of the persons to whom a duty was owed, the extent of therapists' duties to protect qualified individuals was quite broad. In this regard, it is important to note that there were actually two decisions by the California Supreme Court in this case; the second and definitive decision in 1976 displaced its predecessor of two years earlier.[8] The first decision had imposed only a duty to *warn* potential victims. When the case was reheard, in part at the request of a number of psychiatric and mental health organizations, the court apparently was persuaded that warnings alone often would be inadequate to protect victims. In place of a duty to warn, the court imposed a broader, less precise duty to protect—that is, to take "whatever other steps are reasonably necessary under the circumstances."[9]

Pushing aside the narrow requirements of the earlier release and escape cases. *Tarasoff* imposed a sweeping duty on all classes of therapists to protect identifiable potential victims of their patients. Since California was often a bellwether state, particularly where new developments in tort law were concerned, many observers assumed that the ruling would be adopted elsewhere. For the psychotherapeutic professions, this was a matter of urgent concern.

Clinicians' Reactions to *Tarasoff*

Most psychiatrists and other mental health professionals were upset by the *Tarasoff* court's imposition of a duty to protect third parties. Alan Stone, whose comments often typified the reaction of his colleagues, was vice-president of the American Psychiatric Association when the final opinion in *Tarasoff* appeared. He called the decision "extremely irrational"; and looking beyond the reasoning of the opinion itself to what he presumed was the court's underlying motivation, he declared it "one of the most extreme examples" of California's "effort to compensate everyone for everything."[10] Stone also found a connection between California's recent reform of its civil commitment statute—which was designed to make it more difficult to hospitalize patients—and the newly proclaimed duty to protect.[11] According to Stone, the California Supreme Court, compelled by the new statute to find other mechanisms than hospitalization to protect the public from the risk of harm at the hands of the mentally ill, shifted the burden of providing for public safety from the state hospital system to psychotherapists.

Stone's suspicions were shared by some lawyers, including William Curran, whose column on law and medicine appeared regularly in the *New England Journal of Medicine*. With the decision in *Tarasoff*, he wrote, the California Supreme Court had "made the physician a guarantor against harm to [a third party], here not even a patient, on the basis of its own concept of monetary justice."[12] Bernard Diamond, psychiatrist and professor of criminology and law at the University of California, Berkeley, described the state's psychiatrists as "going around bemoaning their fate and cursing under their breath this judicial intervention in what they regard as their private affairs with their patients."[13]

What caused this intense reaction by mental health professionals and their sympathizers? Unlike new restrictions on civil commitment, whose perceived effects were limited to clinicians' professional lives and only became apparent over time, the threat posed by *Tarasoff* and similar cases was immediate and much more direct. Psychiatrists and other mental health professionals suddenly found themselves at risk for costly, embarrassing, and painful court proceedings if their patients committed violent acts. And they suspected that the deck was stacked against them.

The *Tarasoff* court had required psychotherapists to anticipate their patients' violence "pursuant to the standards of [their] profession." Until roughly the time of the *Tarasoff* litigation, this was something that most psychiatrists thought themselves fully capable of doing. For decades forensic psychiatrists had assisted the courts in sentencing, release, and other decisions by offering their conclusions concerning defendants' and prisoners' propensities for violence. Indeed, some influential psychiatrists considered themselves so accomplished at this task that they argued for the abolition of prisons, with wrongdoers instead turned over to psychiatrists for treatment.[14] This proposal contained the implicit assumption that psychiatrists would also know when treatment had been effective—that is, when further violence was not likely to occur—at which point those confined would be freed to rejoin society. Transition to this form of therapeutic criminology was accomplished in part through the adoption of statutes in some states permitting indefinite sentences to forensic facilities for selected classes of defendants, often termed "defective delinquents" or "sexually dangerous persons."[15]

By the 1960s and early 1970s, however, faith in psychiatrists' predictive abilities had begun to crumble; indeed, several studies that appeared during this period suggested that psychiatrists performed relatively poorly at the task. Most of these studies involved follow-ups of defendants or prisoners who were predicted to be dangerous, but who were released from custody because of some legal imperfection in their detention or because a judge disagreed with the psychiatric prognostication.[16] All of the studies showed that only a small fraction of those released were later arrested for violent acts, inviting the conclusion that psychiatrists vastly overpredicted future violence.[17] Thus, by 1974, opinion among experts in dealing with violent patients had swung so far in the other direction that the American Psychiatric Association's Task Force on Clinical Aspects of the Violent Individual could reach the following conclusion: "Neither psychiatrists nor anyone else [has] reliably demonstrated an ability to predict future violence or 'dangerousness.' Neither has any special psychiatric 'expertise' in this area been established."[18]

Psychiatrists and other psychotherapists, still assimilating the data on their deficiencies as predictors of violence, were stunned to be thrust back into this role by the courts and to face the risk of liability for failure at what the experts said was an impossible task. The *amicus curiae* brief of the American Psychiatric Association and other mental health groups supporting the request for a rehearing of the original *Tarasoff* decision argued that "[t]his Court's newly formulated duty to warn directly conflicts with this growing body of scientific evidence."[19] To many commentators, it made no sense to charge psychotherapists with negligence for failing to do what even their most diligent peers could not accomplish.[20]

But it was more than concern over personal liability that led to the vociferous reaction to *Tarasoff.* Many therapists believed that the decision challenged the integrity of the psychotherapeutic process. Beginning with Freud, therapists had argued that the confidentiality of the information conveyed by patients had to be protected stringently if psychotherapy were to succeed.[21] How else could they persuade patients to confide their dreams, fears, and fantasies, all of which was essential if they were to obey the psychodynamic psychotherapist's dictum that whatever came to mind must be shared?[22] If families, friends, or the public at large were to learn what patients said in therapy, the treatment of these patients whose confidentiality had been abrogated would end, and other patients would be deterred from seeking treatment in the first place. Once one agreed that psychotherapy made important contributions to the functioning and well-being of thousands of patients—and most clinicians averred that it did—one had to conclude that mechanisms were needed to ensure that information provided by patients did not leave the confines of the consulting room.

Surveys of therapists and their patients, many undertaken in the wake of the *Tarasoff* decisions, confirmed that these views were widely held. In one study, 98 percent of a sample of mental health professionals said that they believed confidentiality was essential for therapy.[23] In a California study of psychiatrists and psychologists, 79 percent of respondents believed that patients would divulge less information if they knew there was a risk of disclosure.[24] Studies of patients seemed to confirm these beliefs. In a New Jersey study of patients in therapy, 22 percent said that they had hesitated to seek treatment because of fears concerning disclosure of confidential information; since the sample came entirely from people who had overcome their concerns and entered therapy, the percentage of potential patients with such fears was presumably even higher.[25] Similarly, 67 percent of psychiatric in-patients in a Pennsylvania survey said that they would be angry or upset if they discovered that hospital staff members had revealed their communications to other people without their consent.[26]

The premise underlying these views of both therapists and patients—that confidentiality is crucial to psychotherapy and deserves societal recognition—was accepted in the majority of states at the time of the Tarasoff decision, as reflected in statutes affording special protection to psychotherapeutic communications.[27] These laws created a testimonial "privilege" that enabled patients to prevent their therapists from revealing in court or other legal proceedings information communicated in therapy sessions, in contravention of the ordinary powers of the courts to subpoena all relevant information.[28] Although frequently riddled with exceptions,[29] these privilege statutes conveyed to psychotherapists and their patients a sense of the special confidential nature of things said in the therapist's office, and they acknowledged the special and presumably valuable character of the therapist-patient relationship.

Tarasoff seemed to threaten all that. The California Supreme Court explicitly considered whether California's privilege statute and another law on confidentiality of mental health records should be read as indicating a statutory preference for sheltering patients' confidences over protecting third parties. But in the end, the court ruled to the contrary: "The protective privilege ends where the public peril begins."[30] In one sense, the psychotherapeutic professions had come to the same conclusion on their own. The American Medical Association's Principles of Medical Ethics, which governed psychiatrists as well as other physicians, had already made it clear, as the *Tarasoff* court noted, that confidentiality could be breached when "it becomes necessary in order to protect the welfare of the individual or of the community."[31] But *allowing* psychotherapists to reveal confidential communications in the (presumably rare) circumstances when they thought that such action was required differed considerably from *demanding* that they do so under ill-defined circumstances of "serious danger" to other people.[32] Concern about the loss of professional discretion to the courts undoubtedly played a role here. Beyond that, however, commentators voiced the fear that potential liability, combined with the difficulties of predicting violent behavior and the already demonstrated tendency of mental health professionals to overpredict dangerousness, would lead to far more breaches of confidentiality than might otherwise take place.[33]

As skeptical as psychiatrists were learning to be about their abilities to predict patients' future violence, they had little hesitation in offering forecasts of the effects that the anticipated abrogation of the principle of confidentiality would have on psychotherapeutic practice. The chairman of the APA's Committee on Confidentiality declared that the *Tarasoff* decision "wipes out" the doctor-patient relationship.[34] Psychiatrists offered a litany of projected problems:

- Psychotherapists, caught between concerns over liability for failing to predict violence and liability for needlessly breaching patients' confidences, would be deterred from attempting to treat potentially violent patients.[35]
- Assuming that therapists were willing to continue to treat patients with suspected potential for violence, the patients themselves would be discouraged from seeking treatment by their knowledge of therapists' duty to protect. This tendency would be magnified by the warning about the duty that conscientious therapists would feel obliged to offer at the initiation of therapy. Among those dissuaded from crossing the thresholds of therapists' offices would be persons who unrealistically feared that they might be violent (a common fan-

tasy, even in high-functioning groups), as well as members of groups with the greatest propensity for violence—juvenile delinquents, prisoners, and parolees—in whose successful treatment society had a particular interest.[36]

- Patients who overcame such inhibitions and entered therapy would nonetheless be hesitant to share violent fantasies out of concern that these might provoke a warning. This would render therapy ineffective and result in a net increase in the amount of violence with which society had to contend.[37]

- Therapists themselves, concerned about the risks of malpractice suits, might distort the course of therapy, either to focus inappropriately on patients' passing thoughts of violence or to avoid listening to such fantasies—a "hear no evil, have no duty" approach. Alternatively, psychotherapists might be so unnerved by the obligation to detect violence potential that the whole process of therapy could go awry.[38]

- Once a warning was issued, therapy would essentially end. As in the case of Prosenjit Poddar, dangerous persons would be released to prey on their victims without the treatment that alone could alter the anticipated outcome. Not only would the breach of confidence itself ensure this end, but the patient's perception that the therapist was allied with the victim, rather than with the patient, would seal the therapy's doom.[39]

- Beyond the negative effects of warnings on therapy, their presumed benefits would not accrue. Since many potential victims are intimates of patients, they either are already prepared for the dangers they face or are helpless or unwilling to remove themselves from the situation.[40] Battered wives are a classic example.[41]

- Warnings would induce considerable anxiety in potential victims and might not aid them greatly, given the difficulties involved in protecting themselves from an assault without complete disruption of their lives.[42] Indeed, potential victims might sue therapists for the emotional distress caused by warnings that turned out to be unnecessary.[43]

- Third parties who received warnings and were not inclined toward strictly passive measures of defense might undertake preemptive strikes on patients. Warnings might therefore place patients in danger, even when the patient would probably never have harmed the prospective victim.[44]

- Therapists—psychiatrists, in particular—who have the power to initiate involuntary commitment in their jurisdictions, would solve their dilemma at a stroke by hospitalizing any patient about whom they had the slightest concerns regarding violence.[45] This would lead to overuse of scarce and expensive hospital beds and would needlessly deprive patients of their liberty. Indeed, one psychiatrist-lawyer actually urged mental health professionals to follow this course, leaving all release decisions to judges, since the latter—unlike psychiatrists—are immune from suit. This massive display of civil disobedience, she believed, would force the legal system to its senses, leading to a repudiation of the duty to protect.[46]

Psychiatrists' responses to the duty to protect varied, however, and particularly as time passed, voices endorsing the duty—although not always in the form crafted by the *Tarasoff* court—began to emerge. From the start, many psychiatrists acknowledged a moral duty to protect potential victims, even as they resisted its codification in law.[47] Others accepted versions of the legal duty that held therapists to clearer and less demanding standards for the difficult tasks of predicting and preventing violence.[48] The American Medical Association endorsed taking "reasonable precautions for the protection of intended victims, including notification of law enforcement authorities" when there is a "reasonable probability" that a patient may carry out a threat to "inflict serious bodily harm to another person."[49] Some clinicians claimed there was no conflict between a duty to protect and the duties incumbent in ordinary clinical care.[50] Indeed, it could only benefit patients themselves to avert acts of violence.[51] A therapeutically oriented law professor suggested that the duty to protect might even encourage more appropriate choices of treatment, especially if it led to incorporation of the potential victim—often an intimate—into joint therapy with the patient.[52]

Most of the more positive reactions came a decade or more after *Tarasoff* appeared. In the meantime, no other court decision had induced a similar wave of dread among psychotherapists. The dread, of course, was predicated on the assumption that *Tarasoff* would set the pattern for other courts around the country. For a few years, this seemed not to be happening. By the early 1980s, however, the floodgates opened.

Evolution of the Duty to Protect

Courts asked to consider questions of therapists' liability after *Tarasoff* invariably looked to the analysis in that case as their starting point. Some courts were content merely to apply the California doctrine to the facts before them, without substantial modification.[53] As with most new legal doctrines, however, a fair amount of experimentation by the courts took place, producing both expanded and restricted versions of the duty to protect.

As radical as Tarasoff seemed when it was decided, the duty created by the California Supreme Court was circumscribed in several ways. The first of these limitations to be rejected by another court was the requirement that the victim be "identifiable" before a duty to protect could be invoked. It is difficult to know just how carefully the *Tarasoff* court considered the implications of this identifiability rule in the first place. Since Tatiana Tarasoff was easily recognized as the target of Poddar's threats, it may be that the court's opinion was shaped to fit the peculiarities of the case, with the judges' being reluctant to define a duty that was not required by the facts at hand. Or perhaps the specification that the victim be known is an anachronism left over from the initial decision in the case, in which the duty enunciated consisted of an obligation to warn potential victims. One cannot easily warn someone whose identity is obscure.

Whatever the case, the identifiability requirement had a major flaw. Accepted at face value, it suggested that a psychotherapist had no duty to protect the victims of a patient who proclaimed his intention to shoot the first three people he saw on the street after leaving the therapist's office, whereas it would apply if the patient specified a single intended victim. Given this inconsistency, it was only a matter of time before the identifiability requirement was challenged.

The challenge came in a Nebraska case, *Lipari v. Sears, Roebuck and Co.*[54] Mrs. Lipari and her husband, who were unknown to the patient/assailant, were sitting in a nightclub when the patient entered and sprayed the room with bullets. Mrs. Lipari was wounded and her husband was killed. She claimed that the Veterans Administration, which had been treating the patient in an out-patient clinic, should have known that he was dangerous and should have taken steps to prevent the shooting. When the defendants objected that the Liparis were not identifiable victims, the federal district court hearing the case refused to limit the duty to protect in that way. As long as victims were part of a class of persons to whom "an unreasonable risk of harm" could be "reasonably foreseen," the therapists had a duty to protect them. Other cases since *Lipari* have held similarly.[55]

Another limitation of the ruling in *Tarasoff* was that it applied the duty to protect only to cases involving persons physically endangered by a patient. Nothing was said about a therapist's responsibility to prevent damage to property. The Vermont Supreme Court, however, faced with a case in which a patient burned down his parents' barn, held that the same rationale applied to protecting victims' possessions as well.[56] Moreover, that court also extended the duty to protect beyond the doctoral-level mental health professionals (psychiatrists and psychologists) who were the target of the suit in *Tarasoff*. A master's-level counselor, who was the patient's primary therapist in the Vermont case, was held liable for his purported negligence. The court's language suggested that all mental health professionals were now at risk if they failed to protect potential victims.

Other courts have extended the reach of possible liability for violating the *Tarasoff* duty to protect in a variety of ways. It has been applied to emergency settings, where there was no preexisting relationship between the psychiatrist and the patient, and to a situation in which the victim had been warned previously, appeared to be aware of the patient's potential for violence, and failed to protect herself.[57] Therapists have also been held liable for harm to the child of a victim, who witnessed the attack by a patient, on the theory that, if the victim herself were identifiable, it was foreseeable that her son might be in her presence and might be traumatized by the event.[58]

Perhaps most troubling to clinicians are the small number of cases in which the duty to protect has been invoked despite the fact that none of the prerequisites of the *Tarasoff* ruling seem to have been met. The prototypical case is *Davis* v. *Lhim,* in which a psychiatrist was held responsible for a patient's murder of his mother in Alabama several months after his discharge from a Michigan state hospital.[59] An expert witness for the plaintiff testified that the patient's act was foreseeable and that the victim was identifiable because a hospital emergency room record several years earlier had noted that the patient had threatened his mother with harm unless she gave him money. Despite this testimony, the trial record suggests that the in-patient psychiatrist had no reason to anticipate that the patient was dangerous or that the mother would be at any significant risk (she died as she was struggling with her son to take away a shotgun he was brandishing, perhaps for the purpose of harming himself); nor is it at all clear that meaningful steps could have been taken to protect her. The only plausible justification for the decision holding the psychiatrist liable is a desire on the part of the court to compensate the survivors without regard to fault on the part of the psychiatrist. Cases such as *Davis* struck fear into the hearts of psychotherapists around the country.[60]

In contrast to cases that have interpreted *Tarasoff* broadly, a number of courts have taken a narrow view of its scope. Several decisions have turned down opportunities to extend the duty to protect to cover non-identifiable (but perhaps foreseeable) victims, electing instead to cling tightly to the original California formulation of the duty.[61] Other courts have restricted the application of the duty to protect, in two major ways: by requiring that the patient must make a specific threat of violence before a duty is invoked; and by limiting the duty to circumstances in which actual control of the patient is possible. . . .

Consequences of Adopting a Duty to Protect

The projected consequences of the duty to protect were premised on two assumptions: that psychotherapists would behave differently in the wake of the decision in *Tarasoff,* specifically that they would much more often break confidentiality to protect potential victims; and that patients, learning of this new threat to the privacy of their communications, would react adversely, avoiding therapy entirely or using it in unproductive ways. Each of these premises, however, turned out to be flawed.

Perhaps most surprising were the results of two major surveys of psychotherapists, undertaken shortly after *Tarasoff* was decided, that examined changes in therapists' behavior when their patients endangered others. The first study surveyed psychiatrists and psychologists in California within one year of the final ruling in *Tarasoff.*[62] The study found that 50 percent of respondents said they had issued warnings about patients' potential violence *prior* to the final decision in *Tarasoff,* while 38 percent had done so in the year since the decision. Although the data do not permit conclusions to be drawn about the extent of changes in behavior— since responding therapists had been practicing for an average of 13 years prior to the decision, so the time periods contrasted were by no means comparable—they do indicate an unexpected prevalence of protective behavior by the study sample before the *Tarasoff* litigation ended.[63] This finding suggested that the impact of *Tarasoff* would be more limited than had been anticipated, since therapists already had been breaching confidentiality to protect potential victims. Thus, many of the purported harms, including discouraging patients from pursuing therapy, presumably had been accruing even before *Tarasoff* came along.

Why were therapists behaving in this way in the absence of legal compulsion? The answer to this question came from a second study that took a different approach to measuring the impact of *Tarasoff.* This national survey, conducted in 1980, looked at a stratified random sample of 2,875 psychiatrists, psychologists, and social workers.[64] Respondents were queried about the most recent case they had treated involving a dangerous patient. As expected, clinicians who were aware of *Tarasoff* and believed that the duty to protect was legally or ethically binding on them were more likely to have warned potential victims than were therapists who were unaware of or who rejected the duty.[65] The differences were even greater when an actual threat had been made.[66] On the other hand, there were no significant differences in the rates of warning victims, the police, or other authorities between therapists who accepted a duty to protect on an ethical basis and therapists who felt themselves legally bound to act on victims' behalf. Among respondents outside California, 60 to 71 percent believed that they had a professional ethical duty to protect, while 78 to 83 percent believed that they had a personal ethical duty to do so. The widespread acceptance of an ethical duty to protect made the additional impact of the *Tarasoff* ruling on therapists' conduct marginal.[67]

Notes

1. The facts of the *Tarasoff* case can be found in *Tarasoff* v. *Regents of the University of California*, 551 P.2d 334 (Cal. 1976) [subsequently cited as *Tarasoff II*]; in the appeal of the criminal case brought against Poddar, *People* v. *Poddar*, 518 P.2d 342 (Cal. 1974); and in A. A. Stone, *Law, Psychiatry and Morality* (Washington, D.C.: American Psychiatric Press, 1984), chapter 7. Each source provides a slightly different view of the facts, and none is comprehensive.

2. *Tarasoff II, supra* note 15.

3. Stone, *supra* note 15.

4. *Tarasoff II, supra* note 15, p. 340.

5. S. Levmore, "Waiting for Rescue: An Essay on the Evolution and Incentive Structure of the Law of Affirmative Obligations," *Virginia Law Review* 72: 879–941 (1986).

6. Ibid., pp. 899–900.

7. *Thompson* v. *County of Alameda*, 614 P.2d 728 (Cal. 1980).

8. *Tarasoff* v. *Regents of the University of California*, 529 P.2d 553 (Cal. 1974) [subsequently cited as *Tarasoff I*].

9. It is not clear to what extent the rehearing by the California Supreme Court was a response to the anguished cries of mental health professionals about the 1974 opinion. The earlier decision had found that the police, too, could be held liable for their actions. Police groups were outraged, claiming that they could not perform their complex functions if they always had to be concerned about the possibility of being sued for their decisions. The revised *Tarasoff II* opinion executed a 180-degree turn on this question, holding that, as a matter of public policy, the police should continue to be shielded—as they had been historically—from liability for their negligent acts. Second thoughts by the justices about the propriety of imposing liability on the police may well have been their primary motivation for rehearing the case.

10. M. McDonald. "Court Reaffirms 'Warning' Decision," *Psychiatric News* 11 (l): 1ff (August 6, 1976).

11. Stone, *supra* note 15.

12. W. J. Curran, "Confidentiality and the Prediction of Dangerousness in Psychiatry," *New England Journal of Medicine* 293: 285–86 (1975).

13. M. McDonald, "The Tarasoff Warning Decision," *Psychiatric News* 11 (24): 1ff (December 17, 1976).

14. K. Menninger, *The Crime of Punishment* (New York: Viking Press, 1968).

15. Group for the Advancement of Psychiatry, *Psychiatry and Sex Psychopath Legislation: The 30s to the 80s* (New York: GAP, 1977).

16. The studies are nicely summarized in J. Monahan, *Clinical Prediction of Violent Behavior* (Rockville, Md.: NIMH, 1981).

17. The studies, as a group, are problematic with regard to their methods and the scope of the conclusions that can be drawn from them. See the critique by T. R. Litwack and L. B. Schlesinger, "Assessing and Predicting Violence: Research, Law, and Applications," in I. Weiner and A. Hess, eds., *Handbook of*

Forensic Psychology (New York: Wiley, 1987), pp. 205–49. Among the difficulties with the studies are deficiencies in the ascertainment of violence during the follow-up period (most studies relied on arrest records, which are always inadequate as a reflection of actual behavior); biases in the selection of the study groups (many studies were "experiments of nature," in which persons released because of legal decisions were followed to ascertain subsequent violence; the most dangerous of these people were undoubtedly *not* released, lowering the rate of true positive predictions); and many of the "predictions" on which the designations of "dangerous" persons were based were probably made on a *pro forma* basis and do not reflect genuine efforts at prediction.

18. American Psychiatric Association, "Report of the Task Force on Clinical Aspects of the Violent Individual" (Washington, D.C.: APA, July 1974), p. 28.

19. Brief *amicus curiae* of American Psychiatric Association et al., *Tarasoff* v. *Regents of the University of California,* 551 P.2d 334 (Cal. 1976), p. 9. In one of those amusing peculiarities of life, the lawyer who signed the brief on behalf of the mental health coalition was named Freud.

20. A. A. Stone, "The *Tarasoff* Decisions: Suing Psychotherapists to Safeguard Society, " *Harvard Law Review* 90: 358–78 (1976).

21. For a classic statement of the importance of confidentiality in psychotherapy, see R. Slovenko, *Psychotherapy, Confidentiality, and Privileged Communication* (Springfield, Ill.: Charles C. Thomas, 1966), chapter 6; see also American Psychiatric Association, "Model Law on Confidentiality of Health and Social Service Records. *American Journal of Psychiatry* 136: 137–48 (1979).

22. Although the necessity of revealing potentially compromising information is most evident in traditional psychodynamic psychotherapy, it exists in other forms of psychotherapy as well, including structural, behavioral, interpersonal, cognitive, and gestalt approaches. The ethical codes of all the psychotherapeutic professions require adherence to the principle of confidentiality in the treatment setting, albeit with some exceptions. See the codes compiled in Gorlin, R. A. ed., *Codes of Professional Responsibility,* 2d ed. (Washington, D.C.: BNA Books, 1990).

23. R. D. Jagim, W. D. Wittman, and J. O. Noll, "Mental Health Professionals' Attitude Toward Confidentiality, Privilege, and Third-party Disclosure," *Professional Psychology* 9: 458–66 (1978).

24. T. P. Wise, "Where the Public Peril Begins: A Survey of Psychotherapists to Determine the Effects of *Tarasoff*," *Stanford Law Review* 135: 165–90 (1978).

25. J. J. Lindenthal and C. S. Thomas, "Psychiatrists, the Public and Confidentiality," *Journal of Nervous and Mental Disease* 170: 319–23 (1982).

26. D. Schmid, P. S. Appelbaum, L. H. Roth, and C. W. Lidz, "Confidentiality in Psychiatry: A Study of the Patient's View." *Hospital and Community Psychiatry* 34: 353–55 (1983).

27. Some of these statutes covered only communications with psychiatrists (by means of a physician-patient privilege), but many were extended to psychologists and other classes of psychotherapists. See D. Woodman, "Protection

of 'Privileged Communications' in Civil Cases," *National Law Journal,* August 20, 1979, pp. 22–23.

28. Privilege statutes relating to psychotherapy fall into several categories. Some states afford privilege to all communications of patients to their physicians, including psychiatrists. Separate statutes may cover other classes of psychotherapists. In other jurisdictions, a distinct psychotherapist-patient privilege statute exists, which excludes nonpsychiatric physicians. As new groups of psychotherapists (for example, social workers) have gained prominence and political clout, they have often been added to existing statutes or covered by laws that apply specifically to them.

29. R. Slovenko, "On Testimonial Privilege," *Contemporary Psychoanalysis* 11: 188–205 (1975).

30. *Tarasoff II, supra* note 15, p. 347.

31. American Medical Association, *Principles of Medical Ethics* (Chicago: AMA, 1957), Section 9. Two small-scale studies in the 1950s indicated that a majority of the psychiatrists and psychologists surveyed supported this principle. See R. B. Little and E. A. Strecker, "Moot Questions in Psychiatric Ethics," *American Journal of Psychiatry* 113: 455–60 (1956); M. Wiskoff, "Ethical Standards and Divided Loyalties," *American Psychologist* 15: 656–60 (1960).

32. This objection was mounted with particular force to the initial opinion in *Tarasoff,* which appeared to limit the therapist's options to warning the potential victim, even if other actions more protective of confidentiality could be taken. See A. A. Stone, "APA and 'Tarasoff,' " *Psychiatric News* 10(11): 2 (June 4, 1975).

33. Stone, *supra* note 34.

34. McDonald, *supra* note 24.

35. Stone, *supra* note 34.

36. Stone, *supra* note 34.

37. H. Gurevitz, "*Tarasoff:* Protective Privilege versus Public Peril," *American Journal of Psychiatry* 134: 289–92 (1977); Stone, *supra* note 34.

38. Wise, *supra* note 38.

39. Stone, *supra* note 34.

40. P. S. Appelbaum, "Rethinking the Duty to Protect," in J. C. Back, ed., *The Potentially Violent Patient and the* Tarasoff *Decision in Psychiatric Practice* (Washington, D.C.: American Psychiatric Press, 1985), pp. 110–30.

41. E. Walker, *The Battered Woman* (New York: Harper & Row, 1979).

42. S. L. Halleck, *Law in the Practice of Psychiatry* (New York: Plenum Medical Book Co., 1980); J. C. Beck, "Violent Patients and the *Tarasoff* Duty in Private Psychiatric Practice," *Journal of Psychiatry and Law* 13: 361–78 (1985).

43. E. J. Griffith and E. E. H. Griffith, "Duty to Third Parties, Dangerousness, and the Right to Refuse Treatment: Problematic Concepts for Psychiatrist and Lawyer," *California Western Law Review* 14: 241–74 (1978).

44. APA et al. *amicus* brief, *supra* note 33.

45. P. S. Appelbaum, "The New Preventive Detention: Psychiatry's Problematic Responsibility for the Control of Violence," *American Journal of Psychiatry* 145: 779–85 (1988).

46. L. T. Greenberg, "The Psychiatrist's Dilemma." *Journal of Psychiatry and Law* 17: 381–411 (1989).

47. Stone, *supra* note 34.

48. Appelbaum, *supra* note 54; M. J. Mills, "The So-called Duty to Warn: The Psychotherapeutic Duty to Protect Third Parties from Patients' Violent Acts," *Behavioral Sciences and the Law* 2: 237–57 (1985).

49. "Recent Opinions of the Judicial Council of the American Medical Association," *Journal of the American Medical Association* 251: 2078–79 (1984).

50. J. C. Beck, "The Potentially Violent Patient: Legal Duties, Clinical Practice, and Risk Management," *Psychiatric Annals* 17: 695–99 (1987).

51. S. Rachlin, "Psychiatric Liability for Patient Violence," in H. Van Praag, R. Plutchik, and A. Apter, eds., *Violence and Suicidality: Perspectives in Clinical and Psychobiological Research* (New York: Brunner-Mazel, 1990), pp. 19–33.

52. D. B. Wexler, "Patients, Therapists and Third Parties: The Victimological Virtues of *Tarasoff,*" *International Journal of Law and Psychiatry* 2: 1–28 (1979).

53. See, e.g., the first case outside of California to follow the *Tarasoff* doctrine: *McIntosh* v. *Milano*, 403 A.2d 500 (N.J. Super. Ct., 1979).

54. *Lipari* v.. *Sears, Roebuck and Co.*, 497 F, Supp. 185 (D. Neb. 1980).

55. See, e.g., *Peterson* v. *Washington*, 671 P.2d 230 (Wash. 1983); and *Schuster* v. *Altenberg*, 424 N.W.2d 159 (Wis. 1988). Both of these cases involved harm inflicted by a patient behind the wheel of an automobile, a fact situation in which it would seem unlikely that the victim could be identified in advance. See also *Hamman* v. *County of Muricopa*, 775 P.2d 1352 (Ariz. 1989).

56. *Peck* v. *Addison County Counseling Service*, 499 A.2d 422 (Vt. 1985). Arson, it should be noted, is the property crime that comes closest to constituting violence against persons, since the likelihood that people will be injured by the fire or as a result of attempting to control it is relatively great. The Vermont court suggested as much in its opinion. Whether the decision would have been the same if, for instance, the issue had been malicious destruction of a tractor is unclear. No other court, to my knowledge, has applied *Tarasoff* to a case exclusively involving damage to property.

57. Both of these circumstances were presented in the facts underlying the 9th Circuit Court of Appeals' decision in *Jablonski* v. *U.S.*, 712 F.2d 391 (9th Cir. 1993).

58. *Hedlund* v. *Superior Court of Orange County*, 669 P.2d 41 (Cal. 1983).

59. *Davis* v. *Lhim*, 335 N.W.2d 481 (Mich. Ct. App. 1983). The decision was later overruled on other grounds—namely, that the state was immune to suit for the discretionary behavior of its employees, which included decisions about whether to discharge patients. See *Canon* v. *Thumundo*, 422 N.W.2d 688 (Mich. 1988).

60. The facts in *Rotman* v. *Mirin*, a Massachusetts case that was settled out-of-court after a jury found for the plaintiff, are similarly incongruent with the *Tarasoff* doctrine. Dr. Mirin had for several years been treating a man who

was obsessed with a former girlfriend. The patient had been hospitalized at times, and the girlfriend and her family were well aware of the possible danger he posed. Outside the hospital, however, he had been stable, with no indication of any increase in risk over time. Dr. Mirin had instructed the patient's mother to call him at the first sign of the patient's decompensation. Nonetheless, when the patient began to decompensate over a weekend, shortly after he had been seen by Mirin, the mother did not call, and he murdered his former girlfriend before the next appointment was to take place. It is difficult to see in what way Dr. Mirin's behavior fell below the professional standard of care. Indeed, one cannot readily identify what step (other than keeping the patient indefinitely hospitalized) Dr. Mirin could have taken, but did not take. Nonetheless, a jury was persuaded to impose a multimillion dollar judgment against Dr. Mirin, on the grounds that he had been negligent. See *Rotman* v. *Mirin*. No. 88–1562 (Mass. Super. Ct. 1988).

61. See, e.g., *Furr* v. *Spring Grove State Hospital*, 454 A.2d 414 (Md. Ct. Spec. App. 1983); *Leedy* v. *Hartnett*, 510 F. Supp. 1125 (M.D. Pa 1981); and *Leonard* v. *Iowa*, No. 247/91–270 (Iowa Sup. Ct., Sept. 23, 1992).

62. Wise, *supra* note 38. In a random sample of 530 licensed psychologists and all 3,155 psychiatrists belonging to the California Psychiatric Association, only 34 percent and 35 percent, respectively, returned the questionnaire. This is a low rate of return even for mail surveys of this type (in which it is always difficult to motivate subjects to participate). The absence of responses from almost two-thirds of the sample introduces biases of unknown type and dimensions into the results. For example, if therapists who had previously warned potential victims were more interested in the issue and more likely to respond, the resulting data concerning psychotherapists' behavior are likely to be seriously skewed. There is no way of knowing how representative the reported data are.

63. Further complicating any attempt to interpret the study is the author's framing of time periods of interest. By labeling only the behavior of therapists after the issuance of the final (1976) opinion as "post-*Tarasoff*," she neglects the potential impact on clinicians' behavior of the publicity surrounding the murder, the criminal trial and its appeal, the filing of the civil suit against Poddar's therapists, and the initial (1974) much-discussed decision in the case. At a minimum, it would have been interesting to know what percentage of the therapists who reported issuing warnings before 1976 had done so only after the 1974 opinion.

64. D. J. Givelber, W. J. Bowers, C. L. Blitch, "*Tarasoff*, Myth and Reality: An Empirical Study of Private Law in Action," *Wisconsin Law Review* 443–97 (1984). This study had a better response rate—60 percent—although only 48 percent of psychiatrists returned the questionnaire.

65. Only the difference for psychiatrists reached statistical significance.

66. The differences were significant for all three groups.

67. It is, of course, possible that *Tarasoff* and the ensuing discussion helped to shape these ethical norms.

Confidentiality

Robert M. Wettstein

Confidentiality is often considered the sine qua non of psychiatric treatment. Absent confidentiality, it is argued, the patient would refuse to enter psychiatric care, would fail to develop the trust in the therapist, and would fail to share the information needed to accomplish treatment. The importance of preserving confidentiality is evident through its proclamation in the Hippocratic oath 2,500 years ago (Beauchamp and Childress 1989).

With the increasing complexity of contemporary society, confidentiality has come into conflict with other interests, some belonging to the patient and others to society. The patient-centered Hippocratic tradition has become less useful to today's practitioner. Thus, confidentiality has perhaps become the most prevalent type of ethically troubling incident for mental health professionals (Pope and Vetter 1992). Confidentiality was found to be the most frequent ethical principle intentionally violated by psychologists (Pope and Bajt 1988). Formal charges of breach of confidentiality against American Psychiatric Association members and processed through the American Psychiatric Association have increased in frequency over recent decades, according to the most recently published data (Moore 1985). Increasing incursions into the privacy of the psychiatrist-patient relationship from largely nonclinical interests make confidentiality of enduring if not increasing importance, although some physicians in exasperation have abandoned the notion in practice as a mythical fiction (Siegler 1982). . . .

From *Review of Psychiatry* 13 (1994): 343–64. Reprinted by permission.

Definitions

At the outset, it is important to distinguish among privacy, confidentiality, and testimonial privilege. *Privacy* is a complex concept that is largely self-regarding, in other words, focused on itself as the subject (Winslade and Ross 1985). It expresses a zone or area of private life free from government intrusion and has been recently recognized constitutionally as well. Thus, the state and others have limited access to the person, whether the body or the mind. The latter, informational privacy, is the principal concern here.

Confidentiality, as distinct from privacy, is an ethical duty of nondisclosure. The recipient of confidential information must protect that information from access by others and resist disclosing it. In contrast to privacy, confidentiality necessarily involves another party with whom private information is shared on the basis of trust. Thus, privacy applies to individuals, whereas confidentiality is applicable to relationships (Dyer 1988). A patient can suffer a loss of privacy, but not necessarily sacrifice confidentiality; when confidentiality is breached, however, both occur (Beauchamp and Childress 1989).

Confidentiality is typically addressed as a concern of professional ethics rather than law, although there are many statutes and regulations that prescribe and proscribe the release of confidential information either orally or from medical records. Furthermore, ethical standards, which are established by professional organizations, are often incorporated into legal standards of practice by medical licensure boards, giving them additional influence. Legal obligations about releasing records as opposed to patient communications may differ, but the ethical considerations are identical.

The notion that psychiatrist-patient confidentiality always supersedes all other interests has been abandoned by the organized profession, most psychiatrists, and the public. The patient-centered view of confidentiality has given way to the recognition that the psychiatrist has ethical and moral responsibilities to others as well. Thus, there are both ethical and legal exceptions to confidentiality, the most important of which is patient waiver of confidentiality. These exceptions either permit or require (i.e., mandatory reporting statutes) otherwise confidential information to be released by the therapist.

The term *breach of confidentiality* is often used loosely and improperly. Some therapists have claimed that every loss of confidentiality, no matter what the reason or mechanism, constitutes a breach of confidentiality. However, in this chapter, *breach of confidentiality* is defined as the unconsented release of patient information in the absence of a legal compulsion or authorization to release it. A loss of confidentiality through the patient's voluntary waiver is not a breach of confidentiality or infringement on his or her moral claim to informational privacy. It does not violate the patient's autonomy, since that is his or hers to allocate. Similarly, a therapist who reports a child abuse victim to a child protective services agency under a mandatory reporting statute is not breaching the patient's confidentiality. And a therapist who warns an endangered third party, contrary to the patient's wishes, in a jurisdiction where the therapist has a legal responsibility to protect a third party is not breaching that patient's confidentiality.

By this definition, a breach of confidentiality always violates the profession's ethics with regard to confidentiality; a therapist is not ethically permitted to breach confidentiality, and there are no permitted breaches. Legal exceptions to confidentiality thereby become ethical exceptions as well. By contrast, those psychiatrists who retain the view that confidentiality may never be sacrificed for other interests are saying that even a patient-initiated release of information is a breach of that psychiatrist's personal ethics or morality (Suarez and Balcanoff 1966); by the present account, such a disclosure is not a violation of the profession's ethics.

The relationship between ethical and legal standards of professional conduct is complex. A breach of confidentiality from an ethical viewpoint often, but not always, corresponds to a breach of confidentiality from a legal viewpoint. Ethical and legal breaches of confidentiality are not always coincident. Ethical standards of professional conduct may be more stringent than legal standards. Ethically, the psychiatrist is charged with the responsibility to "safeguard patient confidences within the constraints of law" (American Psychiatric Association 1993, Section 4). In effect, the profession's ethics have accommodated the society's interests in obtaining otherwise private information.

Having subordinated the ethical code to the law, the profession and the psychiatrist may not properly claim that the psychiatrist is only obligated to the patient's interests. If the law requires a release of confidential information, then the psychiatrist is ethically required to do so, although there may be competing ethical obligations. Further, once the psychiatrist obeys the law, his or her conduct would not be unethical, at least from the standpoint that a profession's ethics determine standards of professional conduct. Nevertheless, the presence of a law, and the ethical obligation of the psychiatrist to obey it, does not resolve the ethical and moral conflicts, but it does complicate them (Beauchamp and Childress 1989). Psychiatrists may perceive their conduct to be unethical when it is contrary to the best interests of the patient or others. By definition, the code creates dilemmas for the therapist when the law requires or allows the therapist to act in a manner contrary to the best interests of the patient or others.

A violation of confidentiality law constitutes a legally actionable tort, which, standing alone, would be considered an ethical breach. Conversely, releasing private information, though legally permissible, may in some circumstances constitute an ethical breach. An example of such an ethical breach is when a psychiatrist knows that the executor of an estate will use the requested information about the deceased patient for purposes of defaming the patient; the executor may have legal access to the information, but it may be unethical for the psychiatrist to reveal it. Other examples include the psychiatrist's failing to inform the patient of the consequences of consenting to information disclosure or the psychiatrist's disclosing more information than is necessary for a given purpose. In some cases, the law about releasing confidential information may be ambiguous or nonexistent.

Privilege, on the other hand, is strictly a legal concept, although it too has its origins in principles of ethics. Privilege refers to a statutory rule of evidence that makes that information admissible or not in court during litigation (Weiner and Wettstein 1993). Privilege is a rule of nondisclosure in court. As such, testimonial privilege encompasses just a small portion of the confidentiality concerns faced by clinicians. Exceptions to the testimonial privilege often, but not always, correspond to the exceptions to confidentiality as defined by the profession's ethics.

The type and extent of information subject to confidentiality and privilege are not always clearly identified. Most respected are the patient's communications, along with the fact of treatment. Beyond that, the therapist's observations, interpretations, diagnosis, treatment recommendations, and test or laboratory data and information provided by family members are not necessarily as readily protected, although the claim can be made that they should be. The distinction made here is the privacy of the patient versus that of the therapist or family (Winslade and Ross 1985).

Basis of Confidentiality

Two fundamental ethical traditions form the basis for confidentiality of health care information: deontology and utilitarianism.

From the deontological perspective, confidentiality honors an individual's autonomy and respects his or her human dignity. Though not a moral principle itself, confidentiality respects the person's privacy interests. By corollary, some states have granted confidentiality legal constitutional status. Utilitarians, in contrast, emphasize the instrumental value of confidentiality. In this regard, confidentiality is seen as necessary to protect and preserve the psychiatrist-patient relationship. In short, confidentiality is necessary for health care, whether for this patient or any other. The consequentialist sees confidentiality as protecting an intimate or trusting relationship, whereas the deontologist keeps information confidential out of respect for the patient's privacy.

Under either ethical theory, the competent patient retains the right to control confidential information whether or not its release would be harmful. This right helps to promote the patient's autonomy and self-determination. Similarly, the incompetent patient may not autonomously release confidential information. The patient, rather than the therapist, is the source for this control and its waiver. Further, the expectation of control should rest with the patient, not the therapist (Winslade and Ross 1985), although that may conflict with the unequal power noted in many fiduciary relationships. Thus, when a therapist urges a position of absolute or strict confidentiality and refuses to release information (in court or otherwise) even though this release is requested by the patient, the autonomy interests of the patient are offended, as they are by paternalism generally. Therapist-centered informational control is not the predominant view of ethics codes, society, or most practitioners, and it is easy to neglect the patient's autonomy in this regard.

Empirical Aspects of Confidentiality

Research regarding confidentiality has focused on nonpatient community samples, patients (outpatients and inpatients), and health care professionals. Researchers have investigated a variety of aspects of confidentiality, including attitudes, preferences, expectations, behavior, past experiences, and knowledge of the relevant ethical principles and law. . . . Research has often been directed toward confirming or rejecting the utilitarian hypothesis of confidentiality: in other words, that confidentiality is essential to mental health treatment and that in the absence of confidentiality, individuals will avoid or delay seeking treatment, terminate it prematurely, or fail to disclose important information to the therapist, thus impairing treatment. . . .

Although there are conflicting data and many methodological problems, available research generally supports the utilitarian hypothesis of confidentiality, at least for some patients. However, not every patient is concerned about confidentiality and not to the degree that clinicians might imagine. Not every patient would be deterred from entering or fully participating in treatment if the limits to confidentiality were fully explained. Patients generally value confidentiality and expect and trust that their therapists will preserve it, although they may not be familiar with the specific rules of law or ethics regarding confidentiality. Patient trust appears to be more predicated on clinicians' professional ethics than on legal rules, given how ignorant most patients are about the latter.

From the available research data (which are largely self-report), there appear to be several, rather than one, empirically derived standards of practice with regard to informing patients about confidentiality and its limits. To various degrees and at various times, patients in fact are informed about these issues. Practice standards may change for psychologists, because the current American Psychological Association's *Ethical Principles of Psychologists and Code of Conduct* (1992) newly requires that discussions of confidentiality, including its limitations, occur "at the outset of the relationship and thereafter as new circumstances may warrant" (Section 5.01), unless contraindicated. This process has been called "forewarning" or "prewarning" (Faustman and Miller 1987), but it has often been rejected because of the likelihood that the patient will have forgotten the warnings by the time that the potential confidentiality breach arises in treatment or because patients may be deterred from fully participating in treatment.

In contrast, the American Psychiatric Association (1993, Section 4) does not require warnings of the limits of confidentiality at any time during treatment, but only specifies that confidentiality should be discussed when particular situations arise in which information is requested by, or should be released to, third parties. However, clinicians have been encouraged to review the specific limits of confidentiality before discussing human immunodeficiency virus infection with a patient (American Psychiatric Association 1988/1992).

Because patients vary so widely in the importance they place on confidentiality, it becomes more important for the clinician to discuss confidentiality and its limits with the patient sooner rather than later in treatment. Many clinicians need to improve their detailing of the limits of confidentiality. In many clinics and institutions, the limits of confidentiality are increasingly set forth in written contracts or information brochures, usually as part of the process of obtaining informed consent to treatment (Somberg et al. 1993).

Mandatory Child Abuse Reporting

Mandatory child abuse reporting statutes have been extant in the United States for the last quarter century. Child abuse reports are among the most common intrusion on the confidentiality of health care information. In 1989, more than 2.4 million reports of suspected child abuse were officially filed, a number that has increased over the years (Daro and Mitchel 1990). We do not know how many reports were filed without the knowledge or consent of the victim and perpetrator. Only half of the cases reported by professionals and 15% of the cases reported anonymously are ever substantiated (Zuravin et al. 1987).

Mandatory child abuse reporting is primarily designed to identify, protect, and treat the child victim, but it has also been used to treat and punish the perpetrator (Smith and Meyer 1984). Child abuse reporting statutes generally require that mental health professionals and others formally report suspected child abuse or neglect without regard for whether the individual or family is currently in treatment for the problem at hand. The child need not be at risk of life-threatening or imminent harm before reporting is mandated, which is the basis for the emergency exception to confidentiality. In fact, reporting is usually made on the basis of recent past abuse rather than future abuse. The clinician is not responsible for investigating the complaint, nor should that be done. By law, the mandated reporter also is not to consider the likely outcomes of reporting; in other words, reporting remains mandatory even if it does more harm than good to the treatment or to the people involved. Although the statutes provide immunity from civil suits for good-faith reporting, they also prescribe civil and possibly criminal penalties for failure to report (Watson and Levine 1989). The statutes, however, vary as to the definitions of abuse and neglect, reportable circumstances, and who is a mandated reporter; for example, some do not require reports when the perpetrator discloses the abuse (Smith and Meyer 1984).

EMPIRICAL FINDINGS

Studies of actual or hypothetical child abuse reporting by mental health professionals consistently reveal a significant amount of nonreporting. As many as 75% of clinicians reported that they did not in the past or would not, given a specific case vignette, report a case of suspected child abuse, with an average failure-to-report rate of 40% (Brosig and Kalichman 1992). Factors relevant to a failure to report include characteristics of the clinician (e.g., attitudes, training, experience) or of the case (e.g., type, severity, and evidence of abuse), legal considerations, and organizational influences. Clinicians appear to fall into patterns as to whether they are consistent reporters, inconsistent ("discretionary") reporters, or nonreporters (Zellman 1990). Compared with nonpsychiatric physicians and school principals, psychologists and psychiatrists were more likely to be discretionary rather than consistent reporters (Zellman 1990).

Nonreporters of child abuse provide a variety of rationales for their failure to report. These include the belief that there was insufficient evidence of abuse or neglect, unwillingness to breach confidentiality, anticipated disruption in treatment or the family unit itself, poor quality of child protective services, and the claim that the clinician could better help the child or family (Zellman 1990).

Treating a population of sex offenders, Berlin and colleagues (1991) provided some cogent data to support the utilitarian hypothesis with regard to child abuse reporting. After the Maryland reporting statute was broadened to mandate child abuse reporting when this abuse was disclosed by sex offenders in treatment (in addition to mandating this reporting when the abuse was disclosed by their victims), self-referrals for treatment and self-reported relapses by those already in treatment abruptly ended (Berlin et al. 1991). Anecdotal information has also revealed harmful results of reporting distant-past abuse, whether this abuse is reported by adults who were victimized as children or by offenders who later enter treatment (Weinstock and Weinstock 1988).

Although many clinicians assume (consonant with the utilitarian hypothesis) that reporting suspected child abuse will necessarily interfere with treatment, that has not been demonstrated. Watson and Levine (1989) examined clinical records after child abuse was in fact reported or was discussed with the patient but not reported. Negative outcomes, usually termination, occurred in 31% of the cases in which the perpetrator was in treatment and in 17% of the cases involving third-party perpetrators (e.g., mother's boyfriend, not in treatment). A positive outcome occurred in 7% of the former and 33% of the latter cases. Positive results of reporting were thought to occur by virtue of strengthening the therapeutic alliance via reporting to an outside agency (i.e., the therapist becomes a "protector" against the perpetrator). The authors concluded that reporting abuse is "not always detrimental . . . and may even be helpful" and that "trust, not absolute confidentiality . . . is essential for the psychotherapeutic relationship" (Watson and Levine 1989, p. 255). Even more positive effects of mandatory reporting were obtained by Harper and Irvin (1985), who studied cases on a child psychiatry inpatient unit. Mandatory reporting strengthened the therapeutic alliance with the parents through external limit setting and enhanced the child's well-being with almost no negative results.

ETHICAL ISSUES AND CONFLICTS

Mandatory child abuse reporting laws pose a sharp conflict between two pairs of responsibilities: 1) promoting the best interests of the patient and maintaining the confidentiality of an evaluation or course of treatment and 2) protecting the child (whether or not the child is the reporter's patient) and obeying the law (American Psychiatric Association 1993, Section 3; American Psychological Association 1992, Principle F). Whether they report or not, clinicians are also obligated to "do no harm." Clinicians are faced with choosing between complying with the law, a social (control) responsibility, and pursuing what they may believe to be the child's best interests. Reporting statutes present conflicts between law and professional ethics and between competing professional ethical duties. They often pit the interests of the child against those of the perpetrator and the self-interests of the therapists against the interests of their patients. Of course, it is often unclear what constitutes the best interests of the adult patient or the allegedly abused child. Further, the consequences of the clinician's intervention or lack thereof for the adult patient and abused child may also be uncertain.

The proponents of mandatory child abuse reporting statutes assert that social interests such as protecting children easily outweigh confidentiality because the risk of physical or emotional (i.e., developmental) injury to the child exceeds the risk of emotional harm to the patient from disclosure (Weisberg and Wald 1984). Its detractors contend that mandatory reporting, due to underreporting and overreporting, offers uncertain benefits to children and society, undermines confidentiality, "usurps" professional judgment, and is ultimately "counterproductive" (Agatstein 1989).

The ethical conflicts are especially troublesome when the child is not the patient, when the offender (whether incestuous or extrafamilial) is in treatment for the child abuse, when the offender is already incarcerated (in a sexual offender treatment program in prison), when past abuse rather than ongoing abuse is at issue, or when the perpetrator can be prosecuted because of and with the psychiatrist's mandated report. (In the last case, the psychiatrist in effect acts as an informant and is compelled to testify at the criminal trial against the patient, which is permitted by some evidentiary privilege laws.) In any one or a combination of these situations, there are increased risks that reporting will be antitherapeutic, will fail to protect the specified child victim or future potential victims at large, or will be punitive.

Some mental health clinicians defensively avoid the ethical conflict by colluding with the patient to surreptitiously deny or minimize this and all future abuse allegations ("I won't ask and you shouldn't tell"), by overscrupulously complying with the reporting law to avoid personal liability, by defying the law by never reporting, by refusing to work with sexual offenders or abused children, or by remaining ignorant of the technicalities of the reporting statute. Some "discretionary" reporters, though violating the law, search for a solution to the ethical conflict by improperly assuming responsibilities such as investigation of the abuse allegations.

When the clinician resolves the conflict in favor of reporting, the potential harmfulness of the report, and perhaps even the conflict itself, can be mitigated with several interventions. The clinician honors the beneficence duty by informing the family that suspected child abuse will be reported and exploring the reaction to that information (Racusin and

Felsman 1986). The mandatory reporting statutes do not require that the family be informed, but it may help maintain the therapeutic alliance, especially if the perpetrator is not in treatment and external limits are needed. It may even be possible to obtain the family's consent to filing the report. The clinician may also explain to the family that the report is required as a matter of law and is not designed to punish or deprive. Having (pre)warned the patient or family as to the limits of confidentiality is also ethically useful here.

Beyond the use of some clinical devices to mitigate the ethical conflict or the harm that ensues from reporting, psychiatrists are charged by the American Psychiatric Association (1993) with "contributing to an improved community" (Section 7). In this regard, reforms of the child abuse reporting statutes have been proposed. These reforms include making reporting elective rather than mandatory; excluding mandatory reporting when the perpetrator is already in treatment and compliant with it or when the reports would be based on the perpetrator-patient's disclosures to the therapist; excluding reports of distant-past child abuse that has ceased; prohibiting criminal prosecutions based on or using the patient's disclosures to the therapist, including the reporter's testimony "against" the patient; permitting clinicians to use professional discretion in deciding whether or not to file; eliminating criminal sanctions for failure to report; and sharpening the definition of abuse and neglect so it is less ambiguous (Agatstein 1989; Coleman 1986; R. D. Miller and Weinstock 1987; Smith and Meyer 1984; Weinstock and Weinstock 1988). Enactment of these proposals, at least for perpetrators in treatment, may help shift the balance of interests back toward respecting confidentiality, as opposed to the trend toward criminal prosecution of child abusers that has been evident in recent years (Wettstein 1992). The reemphasis on promoting therapeutic considerations in the long term would be welcome, given that so many who are abused become abusers themselves (Berlin et al. 1991).

Duty to Protect Third Parties

The therapist's duty to protect the public from a potentially violent patient was created two decades ago after the two California Supreme Court decisions in *Tarasoff* (1974, 1976). Even before this case arose, however, the American Psychiatric Association's first annotated principles indicated, as they still do today, that "psychiatrists at times may find it necessary, in order to protect the patient or the community from imminent danger, to reveal confidential information disclosed by the patient" (American Psychiatric Association 1973, Section 9). The danger in many duty-to-protect third-party situations, however, is not "imminent," so the duty can well exceed the reach of this ethical principle.

The contemporary legal duty to protect is based on both case law and, more recently, statutory law. These statutes, present in nearly half the states, immunize the therapist from third-party liability once the therapist complies with the law by taking some prescribed action such as warning the victim, notifying the police, or civilly committing the patient (Weiner and Wettstein 1993). The statutes have been designed to limit the therapist's liability unleashed through case law in that state or other states and to allow for a variable amount of professional discretion in the discharge of therapists' obligations (Appelbaum et al. 1989).

The duty to protect resembles child abuse reporting in several respects. Both are legally derived mandates imposed on health care professionals that create legal standards of care, and both are relatively recent phenomena. Both immunize the therapist from personal liability for releasing otherwise confidential information. Both involve the therapist as social control agent and triangulate the interests of the patient, the clinician, and the potential victim.

EMPIRICAL FINDINGS

Frequency of warning and reporting. The prevalence of breaching confidentiality to protect third parties has not been well studied. Wise (1978) found that 38% of psychotherapists had warned someone of a patient's violent threats in the prior year and 50% had done so in their practice lifetimes. Givelber and colleagues (1984) found that 14% of psychiatrists nationally warned third-party victims in the previous year. Of these, 45% thought that doing so was contrary to their best clinical judgment—a greater percentage than that reported when information was disclosed to third parties for other purposes. Since *Tarasoff,* therapists claimed they were increasingly inclined to warn potential third-party victims of their patients (Wise 1978).

On a related issue involving a study of therapists' opinions about mandatory reporting, group therapists favored mandatory reporting laws when patients threatened physical harm to identified others (89%), more so than to nonidentified others (29%) (Roback et al. 1992).

Outcomes of warning and reporting. Few studies provide any quantitative data about the outcomes when therapists notify potential victims or call the police about violent patients. In a small study of institutional psychiatrists, warnings that were not discussed with the patient ahead of time—or warnings that the investigator believed post hoc were not warranted—were associated with negative results such as subsequent violence, suicide, and feelings of betrayal and rage (Beck 1982). However, most warnings had no apparent impact on the patient or the treatment, and a few were said to have reduced the likelihood of violence. In another study, premature terminations of inpatient and outpatient treatment were reported after the psychiatrist notified the threatened victim (Beck 1985). In summary, the available research does not permit a conclusion as to the respective frequencies of possible outcomes of trying to protect third parties.

Therapists also appear to misunderstand the duty to protect as involving a duty to warn rather than to protect the intended victim (Beck 1985; Givelber et al. 1984). Some mistake it for a duty to prevent suicide (Wise 1978).

ETHICAL ISSUES AND CONFLICTS

As noted, the duty to protect third parties extends the available ethical and legal exceptions to confidentiality in emergency situations. Disclosing otherwise confidential information in psychiatric (i.e., life-and-death) emergencies has been ethically well justified, but many *Tarasoff*-like clinical situations cannot be so characterized. Although the interest in preventing physical harm to another person readily trumps the patient's privacy interests in principle, violating confidentiality in a given case is justifiable only when it in fact promotes the victim's safety.

Frequently, however, clinicians have erroneously believed that non-clinical warning of the victim rather than therapeutic intervention is required to discharge their responsibilities under the law. Some duty-to-protect statutes have contributed to this problem by emphasizing the need for notifying the police and victims, while minimizing the usefulness of clinical judgment and discretion in managing potentially violent patients. Further, the immunity provisions for reporting provide an incentive to automatically report any patient's violent threats, even when there is no violent intent or means to accomplish the act or when a clinical resolution such as hospitalization would have been satisfactory. The coercive influence of the law then substitutes for professional judgment. If asked, clinicians may then acknowledge that their warnings were counterproductive in reducing the risk of violence and were contrary to their clinical judgment and the therapeutic interests of the patient.

In effect, too often the duty to protect can function as a mandatory reporting statute. Perhaps without noticing, clinicians have grown to accept the clinical duty to protect with its attendant costs to clinical care. The risk is that clinicians may have resolved the conflict among the interests of the patient, victim, and themselves in their own favor, contrary to the responsibility of a professional. In contrast, a professional is obligated to honor the interests of the patient above his or her own.

Unlike child abuse reporting, no criminal sanctions apply for failing to protect an injured third party, but therapists nevertheless face a variety of ethical perils. Although the therapist who warns an intended victim based on an empty threat of violence might still enjoy statutory immunity, that disclosure might not be ethical if there is no reasonable basis for revealing confidential information. Ethical problems might also occur if the warning were predicated on the therapist's best interests, if the extent of the disclosure far exceeded that which was needed to protect the victim, if the patient were already in custody, or if the therapist knew that the warning would precipitate violence by the victim. There might be similar ethical reservations when a therapist warns a victim knowing that the patient deliberately confabulated the threat to harass the purported victim via the therapist. More uncertain still would be the therapist's warning, in a nonemergency situation, if the law in the jurisdiction in question did not provide for a duty to protect in the first place.

As is the case in child abuse reporting, several clinical-ethical techniques may be useful in maximizing the therapeutic potential for third-party warnings while minimizing their harm. Assuming that the therapist decides to warn the specified victim rather than clinically manage the potential violence, the therapist can involve the patient in the reporting, obtain the patient's consent to warn, have the patient make the telephone warning while he or she is still in the therapist's office, invite victims who are significant others into the treatment with the patient, and at least inform the patient as soon as possible about the need to warn (Roth and Meisel 1977; Wulsin et al. 1983). In this way, the patient's treatment interests need not be sacrificed for the protection of an unknown person, and the relationship with the patient may be less adversarial. At times, it may be desirable from an ethics perspective for the therapist to incur some personal risk of third-party liability when the likelihood of patient violence is small but the risk of violating confidentiality is substantial (Weinstock 1988).

Prosecution use of third-party warnings. Recent legal developments in California raise the ethical stakes of the duty to protect in a manner unforeseen by most. Case law involving homicides committed after third-party warnings has held that the warnings, in addition to the patient's statements that gave rise to them, are admissible in the subsequent criminal prosecutions of the patient, including death penalty determinations (*People* v. *Wharton* 1991). Thus, the therapist becomes a prosecution witness against the patient (usually by then he or she is a former patient). When the patient is familiar with this law of privilege, whether through the therapist's prior discussions or independently, the therapist could become a target for the patient's violence (Leong et al. 1992; *Menendez* v. *Superior Court* 1992). Of course, in these criminal prosecutions, as in many prosecutions involving mandatory child abuse reports, the risk of further harm to the victim has long ago ceased.

This turn of events increases concerns about still another potential misuse of psychiatry—one that increases the risks of violence against the therapist. Many will doubt whether violent patients will be as willing to seek care and whether therapists will be as available to care for them. Many will wonder more about the value of third-party warnings versus the increasing sacrifice of confidentiality through loss of a testimonial privilege in criminal trials. But some will claim that patient knowledge of the possibility of compelled psychiatric testimony about possible statements and behavior will deter patients from becoming violent (Klotz 1991). Whatever the outcomes, these developments will certainly complicate how therapists resolve their legal obligations to protect others, treat the patient, and secure their own personal and professional livelihoods.

Conclusion

With changes in society come changes in the practice of medicine. The role, identity, and function of psychiatrists have already changed and will continue to change in the future. Along with these changes come increasing incursions into the physician-patient relationship and confidentiality and the growth of legal exceptions to confidentiality. There have been many such incursions, and there will always be more. Confidentiality is a dynamic concept, and the ethics and law regarding confidentiality continue to evolve. As a profession, psychiatry has had to abandon its stance that the psychiatrist owes a duty just to the patient, although some may still cling to this notion. No longer do psychiatrists own complete control over information generated clinically, if they ever did. Confidentiality is no longer of overriding importance, overcoming all other interests. Treatment relationships are no longer simply, and forever, dyadic. Thus, confidentiality is better viewed as a spectrum concept than a categorical one; absolute confidentiality no longer exists, and degrees or levels of confidentiality fit the clinical realities. Yet psychiatry as a profession is ambivalent about this state of affairs (Gillon 1985). Although the psychiatric profession recognizes that psychiatric treatment and privacy no longer trump all other interests, we still tend to think and act as if they do.

Even without the claim that confidentiality supersedes all other interests, many therapists assert that treatment cannot proceed in the absence of absolute confidentiality. Review of the available data, however, provides some—but not universal—support for the consequentialist hypothesis. This hypothesis may be more or less correct for certain patients, categories of patients (e.g., sex offenders and repeatedly violent patients in treatment), or treatment situations (involuntary treatment). This issue awaits further study.

Although we may understand something about the value of confidentiality in psychiatry, the heart of the ethical dilemmas regarding violation of confidentiality lies elsewhere. Decisions about whether to violate confidentiality in a particular case are often predicated on the "best interests" of the patient or a third party. Regrettably, ascertaining what constitutes the best interests of the parties is complex, and the impact of any potential clinical intervention or lack thereof is fraught with uncertainty. Rarely can we say with confidence that warning an endangered third party or reporting suspected child abuse, in contrast to the available alternatives, will clearly promote that party's best interests. Equally problematic are attempts to total the benefits and burdens to the respective parties, along with any duty to respect persons.

Especially because confidentiality can no longer be guaranteed, we need to facilitate patient trust in the psychiatrist. There is much that psychiatry can do here. Psychiatry can work to ensure that confidentiality exceptions remain limited in scope, that information is released only to the extent and the persons necessary to accomplish that purpose, and that records are securely protected. Psychiatrists must educate patients about the boundaries of confidentiality and about who has access to their records and communications. Psychiatrists need to give patients more responsibility for this information, improve patient access to records, involve patients in decision making about release of information, and reaffirm that the patient, and no one else, retains the locus of control of information. Through this work, psychiatrists demonstrate their honesty and commitment to the treatment, reassure the patient, and increase the patient's trust and confidence in their work together.

References

Agatstein DJ: Child abuse reporting in New York State: the dilemma of the mental health professional. *New York Law School Law Review* 34: 117–68, 1989

American Psychiatric Association: The principles of medical ethics with annotations especially applicable to psychiatry. *Am J Psychiatry* 130: 1058–64, 1973

American Psychiatric Association: AIDS policy: confidentiality and disclosure (*Am J Psychiatry* 145: 541, 1988), superseded by Position Statement on Confidentiality, Disclosure, and Protection of Others, 1992

American Psychiatric Association: *The Principles of Medical Ethics With Annotations Especially Applicable to Psychiatry.* Washington, D.C., American Psychiatric Association, 1993

American Psychological Association: *Ethical Principles of Psychologists and Code of Conduct.* Washington, D.C., American Psychological Association, 1992

Appelbaum PS, Kapen G, Walters B, et al.: Confidentiality: an empirical test of the utilitarian perspective. *Bull Am Acad Psychiatry Law* 12:109–16, 1984

Appelbaum PS, Zonana H, Bonnie R, et al.: Statutory approaches to limiting psychiatrists' liability for their patients' violent acts. *Am J Psychiatry* 146: 821–28, 1989

Baird KA, Rupert PA: Clinical management of confidentiality: a survey of psychologists in seven states. *Professional Psychology: Research and Practice* 18: 347–52, 1987

Beauchamp TL, Childress JF: *Principles of Biomedical Ethics,* 3rd Edition. New York, Oxford University Press, 1989

Beck JC: When the patient threatens violence: an empirical study of clinical practice after *Tarasoff. Bull Am Acad Psychiatry Law* 10: 189–201, 1982

Beck JC: Violent patients and the *Tarasoff* duty in private psychiatric practice. *Journal of Psychiatry and Law* 13: 361–76, 1985

Berlin FS, Malin HM, Dean S: Effects of statutes requiring psychiatrists to report suspected sexual abuse of children. *Am J Psychiatry* 148: 449–53, 1991

Bernard JL, O'Laughlin DL: Confidentiality: Do training clinics take it seriously? *Law and Psychology Review* 14: 59–69, 1990

Brosig CL, Kalichman SC: Clinicians' reporting of suspected child abuse: a review of the empirical literature. *Clinical Psychology Review* 12: 155–68, 1992

Cheng TL, Savageau JA, Settler AL, et al.: Confidentiality in health care. *JAMA* 269: 1404–1407, 1993

Coleman P: Creating therapist-incest offender exception to mandatory child abuse reporting statutes—when psychiatrists know best. *University of Cincinnati Law Review* 54: 1113–52, 1986

Daro D, Mitchel L: *Current Trends in Child Abuse Reporting and Fatalities: The Results of the 1989 Annual Fifty State Survey.* Washington, D.C., National Committee for the Prevention of Child Abuse, 1990

Dyer AR: *Ethics and Psychiatry: Toward Professional Definition.* Washington, D.C., American Psychiatric Press, 1988

Faustman WO, Miller DJ: Considerations in prewarning clients of the limitations of confidentiality. *Psychol Rep* 60: 195–98, 1987

Gillon R: Confidentiality. *Br Med J* 291: 1634–36, 1985

Givelber DJ, Bowers WJ, Blitch CL: *Tarasoff,* myth and reality: an empirical study of private law in action. *Wisconsin Law Review* 1984: 443–97, 1984

Harper G, Irvin E: Alliance formation with parents: limit-setting and the effect of mandated reporting. *Am J Orthopsychiatry* 55: 550–60, 1985

Harris L: Most people think doctors do a good job of protecting the privacy of their records. *Hosp Community Psychiatry* 30: 860–61, 1979

Haut MW, Muehleman T: Informed consent: the effects of clarity and specificity on disclosure in a clinical interview. *Psychotherapy* 23: 93–101, 1986

Hillerbrand ET, Claiborn CD: Ethical knowledge exhibited by clients and nonclients. Professional Psychology: *Research and Practice* 19: 527–31, 1988

Kaplan MS, Abel GG, Cunningham-Rathner J, et al.: The impact of parolees' perception of confidentiality of their self-reported sex crimes. *Annals of Sex Research* 3: 293–303, 1990

Klotz JA: Limiting the psychotherapist-patient privilege: the therapeutic potential. *Criminal Law Bulletin* 27: 416–33, 1991

Leong CB, Eth S, Silva JA: The psychotherapist as witness for the prosecution: the criminalization of *Tarasoff. Am J Psychiatry* 149: 1011–15, 1992

Lindenthal JJ, Thomas CS: A comparative study of the handling of confidentiality. *J Nerv Ment Dis* 168: 361–69, 1980

Lindenthal JJ, Thomas CS: Psychiatrists, the public, and confidentiality. *J Nerv Ment Dis* 170: 319–23, 1982

Lindenthal JJ, Thomas CS: Attitudes toward confidentiality. *Administration in Mental Health* 11: 151–60, 1984

McGuire JM, Toal P, Blau B: The adult client's conception of confidentiality in the therapeutic relationship. *Professional Psychology: Research and Practice* 16: 375–84, 1985

Menendez v *Superior Court,* 834 P2d 786 (Cal Sup Ct 1992)

Merluzzi TV, Brischetto CS: Breach of confidentiality and perceived trustworthiness of counselors. *Journal of Counseling Psychology* 30: 245–51, 1983

Miller DJ, Thelen MH: Knowledge and beliefs about confidentiality in psychotherapy. *Professional Psychology: Research and Practice* 17: 15–19, 1986

Miller RD, Weinstock R: Conflict of interest between therapist-patient confidentiality and the duty to report sexual abuse of children. *Behavioral Sciences and the Law* 5: 161–74, 1987

Miller RD, Maier GJ, Kaye K: *Miranda* comes to the hospital: the right to remain silent in civil commitment. *Am J Psychiatry* 142: 1074–77, 1985

Moore RA: Ethics in the practice of psychiatry: update on the results of enforcement of the code. *Am J Psychiatry* 142: 1043–46, 1985

Muehleman T, Pickens BK, Robinson F: Informing clients about the limits to confidentiality, risks, and their rights: is self-disclosure inhibited? *Professional Psychology: Research and Practice* 16: 385–97, 1985

Otto RK, Ogloff JRP, Small MA: Confidentiality and informed consent in psychotherapy: clinicians' knowledge and practices in Florida and Nebraska. *Forensic Reports* 4:379–89, 1991

People v *Wharton,* 280 Cal Rptr 631 (Cal Sup Ct 1991)

Pope KS, Bajt TR: When laws and values conflict: a dilemma for psychologists. *Am Psychol* 43: 828–29, 1988

Pope KS, Vetter VA: Ethical dilemmas encountered by members of the American Psychological Association. *Am Psychol* 47: 397–411, 1992

Pope KS, Tabachnick BG, Keith-Spiegel P: Ethics of practice: the beliefs and behaviors of psychologists as therapists. *Am Psychol* 42: 993–1006, 1987

Racusin RJ, Felsman JK: Reporting child abuse: the ethical obligation to inform parents. *Journal of the American Academy of Child Psychiatry* 25: 485–89, 1986

Roback HB, Ochoa E, Block F, et al.: Guarding confidentiality ill clinical groups; the therapist's dilemma. *Int J Group Psychother* 42: 81–103, 1992

Roth LH, Meisel A: Dangerousness, confidentiality, and the duty to warn. *Am J Psychiatry* 134: 508–11, 1977

Rubanowitz DE: Public attitudes toward psychotherapist-client confidentiality. *Professional Psychology: Research and Practice* 18: 613–18, 1987

Schmid D, Appelbaum PS, Roth LH, et al.: Confidentiality in psychiatry: a study of the patient's view. *Hosp Community Psychiatry* 34: 353–55, 1983

Shuman DW, Weiner MS; The privilege study: an empirical examination of the psychotherapist-patient privilege. *North Carolina Law Review* 60: 893–942, 1982

Siegler M: Confidentiality in medicine—a decrepit concept. *N Engl J Med* 307: 1518–21, 1982

Simmons DD: Client attitudes toward release of confidential information without consent. *J Clin Psychol* 24: 364–65, 1968

Smith SR, Meyer RG: Child abuse reporting laws and psychotherapy: a time for reconsideration. *Int J Law Psychiatry* 7: 351–66, 1984

Somberg DR, Stone GL, Claiborn CD: Informed consent: therapists' beliefs and practices. *Professional Psychology: Research and Practice* 24: 153–59, 1993

Suarez JM, Balcanoff EJ: Massachusetts psychiatry and privileged communication. *Arch Gen Psychiatry* 15: 619–23, 1966

Szasz TS, Nemiroff RA: A questionnaire study of psychoanalytic practices and opinions. *J Nerv Ment Dis* 137: 209–21, 1963

Tarasoff v *Regents of the University of California,* 529 P2d 553 (Cal Sup Ct 1974), vacated; 551 P2d 334 (Cal Sup Ct 1976)

Taube DO, Elwork A: Researching the effects of confidentiality law on patients' self-disclosures. *Professional Psychology: Research and Practice* 21: 72–75, 1990

VandeCreek L, Miars RD, Herzog CE: Client anticipations and preferences for confidentiality of records. *Journal of Counseling Psychology* 34: 62–67, 1987

Watson H, Levine M: Psychotherapy and mandated reporting of child abuse. *Am J Orthopsychiatry* 59: 246–56, 1989

Weiner BA, Wettstein RM: *Legal Issues in Mental Health Care.* New York, Plenum, 1993

Weinstock R: Confidentiality and the new duty to protect: the therapist's dilemma. *Hosp Community Psychiatry* 39: 607–609, 1988

Weinstock R, Weinstock D: Child abuse reporting trends: an unprecedented threat to confidentiality. *J Forensic Sci* 33: 418–31, 1988

Weisberg R, Wald M: Confidentiality laws and state efforts to protect abused or neglected children: the need for statutory reform. *Family Law Quarterly* 18: 143–212, 1984

Weiss BD: Confidentiality expectations of patients, physicians, and medical students. *JAMA* 247: 2695–97, 1982

Weiss BD, Senf JH, Carter JZ, et al.: Confidentiality expectations of patients in teaching hospital clinics versus private practice offices. *Soc Sci Med* 23: 387–91, 1986

Wettstein RM: A psychiatric perspective on Washington's sexually violent predators statute. *University of Puget Sound Law Review* 15: 597–633, 1992

Winslade WJ, Ross JW: Privacy, confidentiality, and autonomy in psychotherapy. *Nebraska Law Review* 64: 578–636, 1985

Wise TP: When the public peril begins: a survey of psychotherapists to determine the effects of *Tarasoff. Stanford Law Review* 31: 165–90, 1978

Woods KM, McNamara JR: Confidentiality: its effect on interviewee behavior. *Professional Psychology* 11: 714–21, 1980

Wulsin LR, Bursztajn H, Gutheil TG: Unexpected clinical features of the *Tarasoff* decision: the therapeutic alliance and the "duty to warn." *Am J Psychiatry* 140: 601–603, 1983

Zellman GL: Child abuse reporting and failure to report among mandated reporters. *Journal of Interpersonal Violence* 5: 3–22, 1990

Zuravin SJ, Watson B, Ehrenschaft M: Anonymous reports of child physical abuse: are they as serious as reports from other sources? *Child Abuse Negl* 11: 521–29, 1987

The AIDS Patient on the Psychiatric Unit: Ethical and Legal Issues

Howard Zonana, Michael Norko, and David Stier

Should all psychiatric inpatients be screened for AIDS antibodies prior to admission? Can sexual relationships between patients be prevented? Should HIV status be made known to other patients or to residential facilities at the time of discharge? These are but a few of the questions confronting psychiatric inpatient units beginning to deal with the epidemic.

As of July 1988, 58,000 cases of acquired immunodeficiency syndrome (AIDS) had been reported to the Centers for Disease Control (CDC) from the United States. It is estimated that another 1 to 1.5 million persons in the United States are currently infected with the human immunodeficiency virus (HIV), and that 270,000 individuals will have developed AIDS by 1991.[1]

Several features of HIV disease portend a consistent increase in the number of HIV infected persons within the inpatient psychiatric population. First, intravenous drug abusers are well represented on psychiatric units, and the prevalence of HIV antibody among this group is already as high as 50% to 60% in some urban areas.[1] With time, many more of these individuals will develop full-blown AIDS. Second, the virus directly invades the central nervous system[2] resulting in a subacute encephalopathy known as "AIDS related dementia," which is characterized in its early stages by memory loss, apathy, psychomotor retardation, attentional deficits, behavioral changes, and often depression.[3] Finally, psychiatric symptoms are not uncommonly seen in persons following a diagnosis of AIDS, AIDS related complex (ARC), or HIV infection, and may include manifestations of anxiety, depression, and suicidality."[4,5]

From *Psychiatric Annals* 18 (10 October 1988): 587–93. Reprinted by permission.

Psychiatric inpatient facilities began to report their experiences with AIDS patients around 1985. In those early reports, staff reactions were dominated by the fear of infection. One staff member is reported as having insisted on being gowned, masked, and gloved before entering the room of a patient previously diagnosed with AIDS.[6] In a small 1985 survey of psychiatric nursing staff of a ward to which an AIDS patient had just been admitted, 64% expressed concern about contracting AIDS, 73% believed AIDS could be transmitted through the air or by casual interpersonal contact, and 36% reported "highest anxiety" in relation to this patient.[7] When the first patient with diagnosed AIDS arrived at a mid-Manhattan psychiatric ward, a staff nurse who worked with him panicked after developing some minor physical symptoms, thinking that she had AIDS. The head nurse was afraid to touch him and admitted that it bothered her "just to breathe the air" in his room.[8] Other staff reacted by distancing (by wearing gloves when not required), denying any emotional reactions, and feeling pressured to reassure other staff members.

With experience, education, and new scientific knowledge about transmission of the disease, the initial panic has waned, and ward staffs can cope more effectively with the challenge of caring for AIDS patients.[9,10] In 1987 the CDC recommended that *all* body substances of *all* individuals be treated as though biohazardous (i.e., "universal" blood and body fluid precautions).[11] These precautions are now being employed more routinely in medical settings especially in endemic locations. No precautions have been stipulated for casual interpersonal contact, except with food preparation by patients and in the case of patients unable to control their secretions. These protective regulations are simple, but they are limited in scope. Psychiatric ward staff today must confront much more complex issues in the care of their HIV infected patients.

As the nature and properties of the pathogen become better understood and the likelihood of effective treatments become a reality, many of these care related issues are in flux. Because of the political climate and widespread fears, AIDS has not [been] and cannot be treated as just another infection by psychiatric hospital staffs. A few of the controversial topics that this article will discuss include:

- AIDS antibody testing, routine screening and informed consent
- Confidentiality of test results with respect to other patients, hospital staff, and residential treatment facilities
- Sexual activity in hospitals
- Civil commitment
- Medical management
- Policy development

AIDS Testing

The routine method of testing for HIV infection involves a sequence of laboratory tests for the presence of antibody to HIV, the enzyme linked immunosorbent assay (ELISA) and the Western blot (WB). A repeatedly positive ELISA followed by a positive WB yields a "confirmed" positive result. However, the testing is complicated by the potential for incorrect results. Because neither test is perfectly sensitive or specific for anti-HIV, some false positive results are expected. The false positive rate is also dependent on the prevalence of infection in the populations tested: the less prevalent the infection, the higher the false positive rate.[12] If the true prevalence of HIV infection in psychiatric inpatients is 0.2% (approximately four times the CDC estimate of prevalence in the general population), then 25 false positives would result for each 10,000 patients tested. If the true prevalence is 2.0% (40 times higher than in the general population), then for each 10,000 patients tested just 3 false positives would be expected.[11] In addition, some false negatives are expected, because the latency period of weeks to months between the onset of HIV infection and the appearance of detectable antibodies implies that some potentially infectious individuals will not be detected by the ELISA-WB sequence.[13] A small minority of patients have recently been shown to contain the virus in macrophages and not develop antibodies over an extended period lasting months to years.

Currently, mandatory screening of individuals for the presence of HIV antibody takes place only in selected circumstances.[14-16] At the federal level, all military recruits and active military personnel are screened, as are all federal prisoners when beginning or concluding their sentences. In Illinois and Louisiana, couples wishing to marry must be tested (though they are not prohibited from marrying if test results are positive), and the Texas legislature has mandated premarital screening when and if HIV seroprevalence in the state reaches 0.83% of the population. By general agreement across the nation (and by statute in some states), blood, sperm, and organ banks screen donations. Finally, testing for HIV antibody is mandated in Florida for persons convicted of prostitution, in Nevada for the licensure of prostitutes, and in Illinois for convicted sex offenders. Mandatory screening, then, is still largely the exception; in most settings, including hospitals, individuals are tested for HIV on a voluntary basis. In California and Massachusetts, written informed consent to testing is required by law.[17,18]

Should psychiatric inpatients be routinely screened for HIV infection? It might be argued that mass screening of ward patients would provide reliable information about infection rates in this population and would identify those patients who are capable of transmitting disease, allowing them to be educated so that high risk behavior could be altered. On the other hand, screening would be costly, would not identify all infected patients (false negatives), would result in numbers of healthy patients being labeled ill (false positives), and would not necessarily achieve more effective protection than does the current use of universal body substance precautions. It would also provide an illusion of safety for staff if precautions were not followed for those other than the patients who test positive. The epidemiology of HIV infection in the psychiatric population could be ascertained through entirely anonymous sampling methods similar to those employed in the sentinel hospital programs.[1] Finally, mandatory testing could involve costly consequences to the patient such as job loss, loss of medical insurance, alienation from family, stigmatization, and increased suicidal behavior. This action, although justifiable in cases of medical necessity, is particularly, intrusive in a psychiatric setting where the person's ability to cope may already be severely compromised. Thus, at the present time, mandated screening is difficult to defend on ethical grounds in the absence of more compelling medical rationale. This situation would immediately alter if a treatment were available, the rate of the infection increased substantially, or antigen testing became accurate and readily available.

Under which circumstances should psychiatric inpatients be tested? Clinical evaluation will identify those patients who are statistically at high risk for infection (e.g., gay men, users of intravenous drugs, prostitutes, hemophiliac patients) as well as some statistically lower risk persons who are realistically or irrationally concerned about their possible exposure to HIV. Testing for HIV antibody may be offered to these patients, along with appropriate counseling about the reliability of test results, the probability that the infection will become symptomatic, and practices that decrease the risk of HIV transmission. From the patient's standpoint, the prognostic value of testing in the medical setting must be weighed against the patient's psychological readiness to deal with the information as well as the potential negative social consequences of receiving a positive test result, such as denial of housing, employment, or insurance. Some thought should be given to suggesting that the testing be performed at anonymous test sites provided by most state health departments, if the patient is concerned about the results or even the fact of testing appearing in the medical record.

Some unusual circumstances may tip the balance in favor of testing, from the point of view of both the patient and the community. In Connecticut, for example, the Psychiatric Security Review Board (PSRB), which is responsible for monitoring insanity acquittees, must assess such acquittees' dangerousness to the public when considering conditional release from psychiatric commitment. The PSRB determined that the presence or absence of HIV infection was an important element in their assessment and received an opinion from the state attorney general authorizing HIV testing of any persons under their jurisdiction whom the board considered possibly dangerous on that basis.

Psychiatrists who evaluate patients presenting with elements of dementia are more likely than ever to consider AIDS in the differential diagnosis, due to increased knowledge about the neuropsychiatric sequelae of HIV infection and to the growth of the HIV positive population. Thus, the HIV antibody test assumes a role of direct diagnostic as well as prognostic significance in psychiatry. Also, the psychiatrist may join other physicians in having a "duty to diagnose" AIDS related disease. This duty may be discharged if the patient refuses the test and understands the consequences of that refusal. There is also a body of case law in which physicians were held liable for failure to diagnose communicable diseases that resulted in spread and harm to family members of the patients.[19-23]

It is difficult to argue for mandatory screening of new admissions (without consent) to psychiatric units when such screening is not supported for surgical units where the risk of exposure is substantially higher. At present, when testing is not conclusive, observing universal precautions seems the most prudent course of action.

Confidentiality

Confidentiality is one of the most difficult areas in psychiatric practice and patient management. It is clear that two legitimate and competing needs are at issue: the need of HIV infected individuals to be free of discrimination and stigmatization resulting from disclosure of their immunologic status versus the medical needs of the patient and the need to prevent unnecessary spread of the infection. To protect the rights of HIV infected persons, California enacted a statute prohibiting the disclosure of results of the HIV antibody test without the written consent of the patient. Consent must be obtained for each instance of disclosure and must specify to whom the disclosure would be made.[18] Several other states, including Florida, Hawaii, Kentucky, Maine, Massachusetts, and Wisconsin, have more recently followed suit with similar provisions.[16] More recently, California and Texas have amended these statutes to allow for the disclosure of information to spouses of HIV positive patients (several other states are considering similar legislation).

Other regulations exist for the protection of the public. All 50 states and the District of Columbia require that known cases of AIDS be reported to the public health authorities,[24] whereas a far smaller number of jurisdictions (Colorado, Arizona, Idaho, Montana, South Carolina, and

Wisconsin) require that positive HIV antibody test results be reported.[16] However, even some of the states with confidentiality laws allow release of HIV related information to medical personnel in a medical emergency; others require notification of emergency personnel who are exposed to HIV while rendering emergency care.

Aside from disclosures to state health departments, inpatient facilities are faced with the more commonplace concerns of how to deal with the medical records and requests for discharge summaries. Initially, many hospitals kept the results of HIV testing separate from the patient's chart. Today, most facilities place the results in the record but may keep such data off of computers which have hospital-wide accessibility. In addition, when requests for summaries from outside agencies (e.g., insurance companies) arrive, decisions must be made as to what data are necessary for the purposes requested. There are a number of situations in which summaries, progress notes, or lab reports are disclosed for purposes which are not relevant to and do not require knowledge of the patient's HIV status. Patients may not fully appreciate that signing a release for a discharge summary from a psychiatric inpatient unit may also include data regarding HIV status.

The APA and the AMA have recently established guidelines about AIDS related issues, such as confidentiality and disclosure, and inpatient treatment.[25, 26] The guidelines attempt to balance the patient's rights, the health of exposed third parties, and health professionals' safety.

The APA policy recommends that physicians inform patients during the initial clinical evaluation of the general limits of confidentiality. If the physician has reason to suspect that the patient is HIV positive or is engaging in behaviors with a high risk of HIV transmission, or if the physician intends to inquire specifically about the patient's HIV status, the physician should notify the patient, in advance, of the limits of confidentiality. Occasionally, a clinician will learn of the patient's HIV status before a warning can be given. This occurs with child abuse situations as well. Such situations should be carefully reviewed by staff, and hospital policy discussed with the patient as soon as possible.

The limits of confidentiality are tested where the patient is documented to be HIV positive, is engaging in behaviors placing others at risk of HIV infection, and despite the physician's attempts at counseling and education (and appropriate clinical management), the patient refuses to stop such behavior or to notify the persons at risk. In these situations, APA policy holds that it is ethically permissible for the physician to notify identifiable persons at risk. In situations where unknown persons in the community are at risk, it is ethically permissible for the physician to notify the appropriate public health agency.

Although disclosure may be ethically permissible, state laws may prohibit or require disclosure. Because this is a rapidly evolving area, physicians are encouraged to remain informed about their state's relevant statute(s). The AMA policy is similar to that of the APA except that it recommends disclosure to a public health agency in lieu of or before notifying a third party.

Tarasoff duties to protect third parties from a patient's violence have been adopted by case law or statute in most states where cases have been brought by plaintiffs. These duties may also pressure the physician to disclose a patient's HIV status. There are a number of civil actions pending against physicians for failure to diagnose or warn, and the number of such actions will certainly rise. At the moment, it is most prudent to consider each case individually, as the responsible physician must ultimately make the decision when and if a disclosure is warranted. Such disclosures should be infrequent on inpatient units, as there should be time to counsel and work with patients prior to discharge.

Disclosure to treatment staff is another controversial issue. The APA policy calls for disclosures only to appropriate staff when required for treatment. Routine screening and disclosures for the protection of staff are not appropriate. All patients should be considered at potential risk of transmitting or receiving HIV infection.[26]

Hospitals have a duty to safeguard patients from themselves and other patients. When individual patients engage in risk behavior, all appropriate clinical steps should be taken to control the behavior and isolate or seclude the patient if necessary. Only when all measures fail to control risk behavior is it appropriate to inform other patients of an individual patient's known HIV status.[27]

Discharge of psychiatric patients with positive HIV status also raises difficult questions. HIV seropositivity in itself could be argued as evidence of dangerousness. However, this raises the unacceptable specter of psychiatric units used as quarantine facilities. Thus, APA policy states that discharge decisions should be based solely on the patient's mental condition.

Issues of disclosure to third parties or public health agencies may come into consideration at the time of discharge. Such disclosure may be made for the purpose of warning potential identifiable victims of infection, as discussed above. Another issue is raised with respect to aftercare facilities and providers. Halfway houses, day programs, and drug treatment programs often request discharge summaries or whole portions of the medical record and might specifically inquire about a patient's HIV status. Disclosures to other facilities, although not mentioned in existing APA policy, would reasonably be handled in the same manner as disclosures within a facility, i.e., routine disclosures and disclosures solely for the protection of staff should not be made. Legitimate treatment goals may be served by disclosure to appropriate aftercare treatment staff, if, for example, ongoing medical care is required. Before such disclosure is made, and at the time disposition is proposed to the patient, the need for disclosure should be discussed with the patient and made only with his or her consent. Some aftercare facilities have refused admission for HIV positive patients. Many states have antidiscrimination statutes, and such discrimination should be opposed and legal relief pursued with the aid of patient advocacy groups.

Special Duties to Other Patients

Inpatient psychiatric units have a responsibility to provide for the safety of all patients. Mentally ill patients are often quite vulnerable, are generally not free to come and go, and are exposed to other mentally ill patients who may be agitated or violent. Several special duties to protect patients arise in situations involving HIV positive inpatients.

As a general rule, inpatient units prohibit sexual contact between patients for a variety of reasons, including abuse of more vulnerable patients, risk of pregnancy, risk of venereal disease, and the possible harmful effect to the patient's condition that prompted hospitalization in the first place. Even with such prohibition, sexual contact occurs, especially in large, poorly staffed, chronic care facilities. With the increasing prevalence of HIV infection, however, sexual contact between patients can have lethal consequences. Many patients may be unaware of the risks of AIDS, unaware of the means of protecting themselves, and many may be incapable of weighing this information or using it rationally.

It is, therefore, incumbent upon psychiatric inpatient facilities to protect against spread of HIV infection via sexual contact between patients. One measure is patient education. It is both appropriate and useful for inpatient units to educate all patients about AIDS, not only to diminish risk of sexual contact on the unit but to diminish patients' overall vulnerability to HIV infection and to decrease their irrational fears of HIV infection.

Making condoms available to patients might solve several of the problems of sexual contact, but the extent to which condoms would prevent the spread of HIV infection would depend on their proper usage, which is problematic. Furthermore, condom usage would not solve the psychological issues that make sexual contact between patients inadvisable. As of this date, hospital policies vary regarding the free availability of condoms. Some facilities will allow physicians to prescribe condoms for patients. A few have made them generally available.

Prevention of sexual contact will ultimately depend on adequate patient observation, clinical intervention, and the use of isolation, seclusion, and possible restraint with incorrigible patients. Acute and chronic units pose different problems, as patients may have grounds privileges and are given increased responsibility. Within many of the larger facilities, it is not possible to monitor sexual behavior without introducing draconian procedures, which would probably be ineffective and would undermine the therapeutic milieu. Efforts can be made more realistically toward those patients known by virtue of past behavior or current threats to represent a danger.

In the past, when patients have engaged in sexual relations, institutional policies have called for incident reports, physical examinations, tests for syphilis and gonorrhea, and pregnancy tests. Contemporary policies may necessitate HIV testing, disclosure to the contactee of an HIV positive patient's status, and counseling regarding HIV infection, HIV testing, and AIDS.

Civil Commitment

Civil commitment may be an appropriate response to the mentally ill patient who poses a danger to others by engaging in behaviors with a high risk of HIV transmission. *Tarasoff* duties presume not only warnings but a duty to exercise reasonable care to protect other individuals. Thus, just as an acutely psychotic patient who expressed homicidal ideation and possessed a weapon would be involuntarily committed, so might a psychotic patient known to be HIV positive who expressed a desire to spread the disease to others via sexual contact or shared needles. The physician must clearly understand, however, that the basis for commitment is not the patient's HIV status or sexual behavior, but the patient's mental illness that creates danger to others. Probate courts have only started to review such cases and will often try to find other grounds to decide the case.[28]

Psychiatric hospitalization is not an effective public health measure. The number of patients hospitalized because of the danger they present to others via HIV infection will be small compared with the total HIV population. Involuntary hospitalization under these circumstances is a clinical response to an individual situation. The fact that public health measures regarding AIDS and HIV are virtually nonexistent should not tempt psychiatry to fill the void. The lack of public health policy has forced the legal system to resort to criminal prosecutions and civil litigation for knowingly causing transmission of the virus.

Staff Refusals to Treat and Medical Management

Medical professionals have historically demonstrated a willingness to devote themselves to patient care even in situations of personal risk. Society's expectation, and that of the professions, is that medical personnel will continue such care with respect to HIV positive patients. APA policy specifically states that HIV positive status, in and of itself, should not "impede the delivery of appropriate medical-psychiatric treatment." Although individual situations vary and warrant case-by-case scrutiny, health care personnel who refuse to care for HIV positive patients may be forced to resign from their positions. Certainly, the degree of exposure to HIV on inpatient psychiatric units is significantly less than in the operating room. However, as an increasing number of AIDS patients are hospitalized and dying on inpatient units, attention to CDC guidelines will play an increasingly important role in patient care, both to staff and patients.

HIV and AIDS will undoubtedly force psychiatric units to enhance their medical treatment and diagnostic capacities. More patients will develop intercurrent infections that will require active treatment. Tuberculosis, syphilis, and other contagious diseases may become more prevalent. More patients will be dying and facilities will have to provide more terminal care than they have had to in the recent past.

Hospital Guidelines Committee

The clinical, legal, and ethical issues involved in providing psychiatric care to HIV positive individuals are myriad and require close attention. Although APA guidelines provide some framework and state laws provide some restrictions and requirements, there are many unresolved issues and many complex and difficult individual situations. All psychiatric institutions should establish some committee capable of developing and reviewing institutional policy to clarify the interaction of institutional, local, and state requirements and needs. Clear policy is also helpful in avoiding pitfalls such as inappropriate disclosure to third parties, disclosure without adequate prior notice to the patient, and infection control.

The AIDS epidemic has had a growing effect on the large state psychiatric facilities in or near urban areas with high risk populations, as more patients develop full-blown AIDS or its complications. Private and public facilities with active drug treatment units have also had to confront these issues for the past seven years. It is likely that psychiatric facilities will play an increasing role in the care of these patients. Policies and guidelines must be developed so that this care can be provided effectively and humanely.

Notes

1. Centers for Disease Control: Human immunodeficiency virus infection in the United States: A review of current knowledge. *MMWR* 1987; 36 (S-6): 1–19.

2. Ho DD, Pomerantz RJ, Kaplan JC: Pathogenesis of HIV infection. *N Engl. J. Med* 1987; 317 (3): 278–86.

3. McArthur JC: Neurologic manifestations of AIDS. *Medicine* 1987; 66 (6): 407–37.

4. Faulstich ME: Psychiatric aspects of AIDS. *Am J Psychiatry* 1987; 144 (5): 551–56.

5. Burton SW: The psychiatry of HIV infection. *Br Med J* 1987; 295: 228–29.

6. Selzer JA, Prince R: Milieu complication of the psychiatric inpatient treatment of the AIDS patient. *Psychiatr Q* 1985; 57 (1): 77–80.

7. Rosse RB: Reactions of psychiatric staff to an AIDS patient, letter. *Am J Psychiatry* 1985; 142 (4): 523.

8. Polan HJ, Hellerstein D, Amchin J: Impact of AIDS-related cases on an inpatient therapeutic milieu. *Hosp Comm Psychiatry* 1985; 36 (2): 173–76.

9. Amchin J, Polin HJ: A longitudinal account of staff adaptation to AIDS patients on a psychiatric unit. *Hosp Comm Psychiatry* 1986; 37 (12): 1235–38.

10. Baer JW, Hall JM, Holm K, et al.: Challenges in developing an inpatient psychiatric program for patients with AIDS and ARC. *Hosp Comm Psychiatry* 1987; 38(12): 1299–1303.

11. Centers for Disease Control: Recommendations for prevention of HIV transmission in health-care settings. *MMWR* 1987; 36 (2S): 3S–18S.

12. Meyer KB, Pauker SG: Screening for HIV: Can we afford the false-positive rate? *N Engl J Med* 1987; 317 (4): 258–41.

13. Ranki A, Valle SL, Krohn M, et al.: Long latency precedes overt sero-conversion in sexually transmitted human immunodeficiency-virus infection. *Lancet* 1987; i: 589–93.

14. Proposals to screen for HIV antibodies, *BioLaw Update* 1987; June: U432–U439.

15. Illinois requires AIDS test for couples wishing to marry. *BioLaw Update* 1987; October.

16. Gostin L, Ziegler A: A review of AIDS-related legislative and regulatory policy in the United States. *Law, Medicine, & Health Care* 1987; 15 (1–2): 5–16.

17. State legislatures pass more than 50 laws in 1986 on AIDS. *BioLaw Update* 1987; June.

18. Binder RL: AIDS antibody tests on inpatient psychiatric units. *Am J Psychiatry* 1987; 144 (2): 176–81.

19. *Davis* v. *Rodman*, 222SW2d612 (1921).

20. *Hofmann* v. *Blackmon* 241S2d752 (1970).

21. *Wojcik* v. *Aluminum Co. of America*, 183NYS2d351 (1959).

22. *Gill* v. *Hartford Accident and Casualty Co.*, 337S2d421 (1976).

23. *Gammell* v. *U.S.*, 727F2d950 (1984).

24. Curran WJ, Clark ME, Gostin L: AIDS: Legal and policy implications of the application of traditional disease control measures. *Law, Medicine & Health Care* 1987; 15 (1–2): 27–35.

25. Mills M, Wofsky CB, Mills J: Acquired immunodeficiency syndrome—Infection control and public health. *N Engl J Med* 1986; 314 (14): 931–32.

26. AIDS policy: Confidentiality and disclosure. *Am J Psychiatry* 1988; 145 (4): 541–42.

27. Mathews GW, Neslund VS: The initial impact of AIDS on public health law in the United States. *JAMA* 1987; 257 (3): 344–52.

28. In the Matter of Commitment of B.S., 517A2d146 (1986).

Therapist-Patient Sexual Contact: A Nonconsensual, Inherently Harmful Activity

Françoise Baylis

Therapist-patient sexual contact includes all touching of body parts "intended to arouse or satisfy sexual desire in the patient, the therapist, or both" (1). Therapist-patient sexual contact is a nonconsensual activity, and since sexual contact without consent is sexual abuse, the terms "sexual contact" and "sexual abuse" are used interchangeably throughout this text. It may be that the patient initiates the contact and the therapist responds to the patient's advance; that the therapist initiates the contact and the patient seems agreeable; or that the therapist initiates the contact using threat, and the patient acquiesces out of fear. Regardless of who initiates the contact (or how), in all cases, therapist-patient sexual contact constitutes a profound betrayal of trust on the part of the therapist and a profound violation of the patients. As such, it is a most egregious act on the part of the therapist and one that is rightly prohibited by many professional codes of ethics.

The American Psychiatric Association's *Principles of Medical Ethics with Annotations Especially Applicable to Psychiatry* affirms that "Sexual activity with a patient is unethical" (2); and the American Psychological Association's *Ethical Principles of Psychologists and Code of Conduct* affirms that "Psychologists do not engage in sexual intimacies with current patients or clients" (3). The *Canadian Medical Association Code of Ethics Annotated for Psychiatrists* states, "the ethical psychiatrist will scrupulously avoid using the psychiatrist-patient relationship to gratify his own emotional, financial, and sexual needs" (4). The *Canadian Code of Ethics for Psychologists* states that the psychologist should "not exploit

From *Canadian Journal of Psychiatry* 38 (September 1993): 502–506. Reprinted by permission.

any relationship established as a psychologist to further personal, political or business interests including taking advantage of trust or dependency to engage in sexual activities" (5). The *Code of Ethics of the Canadian Association of Social Workers* states, "the social worker will act to ensure that the difference between professional and personal relationships with clients is explicitly understood and respected. . . . Sexual intimacy with a client is unethical" (6).

Despite these unequivocal admonishments, some therapists continue to have sexual contact with their patients. In June 1991, a prominent psychiatrist with a reputation as one of the best psychotherapists in Canada was found guilty on four counts of indecent assault and one count of sexual assault. His accusers were four female former patients, two of whom had previously complained about his abuse to another psychiatrist and one of whom had registered a formal complaint with the British Columbia College of Physicians and Surgeons. The four women testified that the therapist abused them, enslaved them, chained and whipped them (7).

In Canada, the prevalence of therapist-patient sexual abuse has not been well documented. In the United States, however, there are a number of studies documenting the incidence of such abuse. Given the strong correlation between Canada and the United States for other abuse statistics (8), U.S. statistics on therapist-patient sexual abuse can be cited "as supportive of similar Canadian experience" (9). Recent U.S. national surveys based on confidential self-reports by psychiatrists, psychotherapists and psychologists (hereafter referred to as therapists), show that between seven percent and 15% of respondents engage in sexual relations with their patients (10). To be sure, these numbers are conservative estimates, given the following: 1. the type of research methodology used (for example, self-reports); 2. the stigma attached to therapist-patient sexual contact; and 3. the risk of professional sanctions after any admission of therapist-patient sexual contact. Nonetheless, these statistics clearly indicate that therapist-patient sexual contact is not a rare or isolated occurrence. Rather, it appears that a significant minority of therapists abuse their patients sexually and probably have done so for some years. Moreover, the vast majority of abused patients are female and the vast majority of abusers are male (11). Only recently, however, has the medical profession and the public begun to acknowledge the health care profession's resistance to dealing with the issue of therapist-patient sexual contact (12) and to attempt to address this serious problem (9).

The most important reasons for prohibiting therapist-patient sexual contact are the absence of consent, and the likelihood of harmful consequences. This paper examines the reasons for prohibiting therapist-patient sexual contact and concludes that therapist-patient sexual relations are always nonconsensual and inherently harmful. This conclusion applies irrespective of who initiates the sexual contact.

The Absence of Consent

Intentionality, substantial understanding, substantial voluntariness and autonomous authorization are the key elements of morally valid consent (13). For consent to be morally valid, there must be an intentional autonomous authorization based on a substantial understanding of the relevant information given in a context that is substantially free of controlling influences (for example, deceit, constraint or coercion).

Sexual relations between a therapist and a patient raise concerns with respect to each of these key elements. These concerns undermine the claim that sexual relations between a therapist and a patient are consensual and should be shielded from state intervention. Each of these concerns will be considered in turn.

INTENTIONALITY

Can a patient make an intentional choice to enter into a sexual relationship with a therapist? When a patient enters therapy, and during the course of treatment, she is in an extremely vulnerable position or state of mind. (Therapist-patient sexual abuse is not a gender-free issue. Most of the abusers are male and most of the victims are female. So as not to mask this important aspect of the problem, female pronouns are used to designate the patient and male pronouns are used to designate the therapist.) She is therefore "likely to have significantly impaired ability to decide whether or not to have sexual contact with the therapist" (14). This impairment may be a function of the underlying disorder for which she originally sought treatment, or the result of transference which has resulted in the idealization and erotic valuation of her therapist. Whatever the cause of the impairment, the patient's decision-making ability is likely to be compromised. This calls into question the "intentionality" or "willingness" of any choice or action relevant to the sexualization of the therapeutic relationship.

SUBSTANTIAL UNDERSTANDING

Can a patient who responds to sexual advances made by a therapist or who attempts to sexualize the therapeutic relationship substantially understand the likely consequences of such actions?

Most therapist-patient sexual relations are short term and physical rather than long term and affective and are "the product of a hasty infatuation on the part of the patient and/or therapist" (14). Many patients do not appreciate this fact and anticipate instead a long-term meaningful attachment. In addition, many patients do not appreciate how the therapeutic relationship is likely to be compromised once it is sexualized. When a patient becomes her therapist's sexual partner, the therapist may lose the distance required to provide the patient with effective care, or the gratification of sexual desires may take precedence over the patient's legitimate treatment needs. The patient's failure to appreciate the likely nature and consequences of therapist-patient sexual contact calls into question the "understanding" of any choice or action relevant to the sexualization of the therapeutic relationship.

SUBSTANTIAL VOLUNTARINESS

Can a patient freely choose therapist-patient sexual contact? Or rather, since everyone is constrained to some degree by external circumstances and the influence of others, at what point does constraint or influence undermine a patient's ability to freely choose therapist-patient sexual contact? Any response to this question must take into account the unique potential for explicit and implicit coercion within the therapist-patient relationship. In this relationship, the patient is the dependent, emotionally vulnerable person providing the therapist with unique knowledge of her needs and weaknesses. This knowledge can be used to manipulate or to pressure her in one or more ways, including: the misrepresentation of sexual contact as therapy; the false promise of an unaffected therapeutic relationship; and the threat of the withdrawal of care. In addition to such overt attempts at coercion, other more subtle coercive efforts are based on power and gender differences within the therapist-patient relationship. These explicit and implicit forms of coercion will be considered, in turn, starting with the misrepresentation of sexual contact as therapy.

From the mid-1960s to the late 1970s, a number of therapists openly argued that sexual contact with patients was a legitimate practice (12). While such claims are now rarely defended publicly, some therapists still consider therapist-patient sexual contact to be a legitimate form of therapy. In 1989, Gartrell (1) reported that 19% of therapists who engaged in therapist-patient sexual contact claimed to do so "to enhance the patient's self-esteem and/or to provide a restitutive emotional experience for the patient." In the case mentioned earlier, the therapist denied the accusations of sexual assault, while testifying that he practiced a form of relaxation therapy "whereby undressing and stroking could occur to encourage patients to talk openly about their emotional states" (15).

From a professional perspective, however, sexual contact is not a legitimate form of therapy. The Canadian Psychiatric Association, in its position paper "Sexual Exploitation of Patients," speaks authoritatively on this point: "eroticizing the physician/patient relationship is unacceptable under any circumstances and cannot be rationalized as therapy" (16). Thus, for the therapist to represent sexual contact as part of, or consistent with, his patient's treatment is to deceive his patient and thereby preclude voluntariness.

Another form of deception that equally undermines voluntariness is the therapist's fraudulent representation of sexual contact as being inconsequential to his ability to provide the patient with effective care. If the patient falsely believes that the therapeutic relationship will not be affected by any sexual relationship, one might say that she demonstrates extreme naivete, or simply poor judgment. If the therapist encourages her to believe this, however, then there clearly is an attempt to deceive through false promise. The therapist, as the professional, knows (or should know) that dual relationships introduce other interests and thus threaten to interfere with, to dilute, or otherwise diminish the purity of the concern that the therapist has for a patient (17). For the therapist to convince the patient otherwise is for the therapist to deceive the patient.

In addition to deception, voluntariness may be undermined by an implicit or explicit threat to withdraw treatment if the patient refuses sexual involvement. During the course of treatment, a therapist may imply or state specifically that continued treatment is contingent upon the gratification of sexual desires. Out of fear of abandonment, the patient may acquiesce. However, the threat (whether implicit or explicit) removes the possibility of free choice.

Apart from such overt attempts to deceive or coerce the patient, voluntary consent to therapist-patient sexual contact is further precluded by the power imbalance that pervades the relationship.

The Council on Ethical and Judicial Affairs of the American Medical Association states: "several elements of the physician-patient relationship can be combined to give the physician disproportionate influence over the patient. In the physician-patient relationship, the physician possesses considerable knowledge, expertise and status. A person is often most vulnerable, both physically and emotionally, when seeking medical care" (18).

Similarly, the Canadian Psychiatric Association, with specific reference to psychiatrists, acknowledges that "the power and prestige of the physician, with the right to touch and explore physically and psychologically place him or her in an advantageous position. It cannot be accepted that physicians and patients are similar to any consenting adults" (16).

In response, one might object by stating that not all therapists are physicians. The fact remains, however, that therapists and patients are not similarly situated; they do not have equal power in the relationship. A patient needing psychotherapy is a person in distress, presumably seeking to alleviate a mental disorder, to resolve an emotional or attitudinal problem or to modify behavior that undermines emotional and social well-being. The patient places hope and trust in the therapist's ability to help relieve her distress and is therefore particularly vulnerable to his suggestions. This creates a situation ripe for coercion.

In addition to the professionally based power differential, in most instances there is also a gender-based power differential. While some female therapists do sexually abuse their male patients, and some therapists sexually abuse patients of the same sex, as noted previously, the vast majority of abused patients are female and the vast majority of the abusers are male (1, 19). A recent U.S. national survey reported that approximately 85% to 90% of all sexual abuse involved a male therapist and a female patient (11).

This frank predominance of sexual contact between male therapists and female patients takes place in a cultural context that tolerates, and in some instances promotes, discrimination toward and violence against women. In Canada, between 1974 and 1987, 39% of the homicides solved by the police were the result of domestic violence. Of these domestic homicides, 37% were committed by men who killed their wives or women they were living with (20). In 1984, the Badgley Report (21) concluded that approximately 54% of all Canadian females had been raped or sexually assaulted at least once in their life time. (Sexual assault, as defined by the Badgley Committee, includes threats of unwanted sexual acts as well as unconsented to sexual acts.) More recently, it has been stated that, every year, one in eight Canadian women are abused by their male partners (22). Only in January of 1983, however, was the *Criminal Code* amended to remove spousal immunity for sexual assault.

The point of these last remarks is to emphasize that abuse (and, in particular, sexual abuse) is not a gender-free issue, and one should not be comfortable with any attempt to mask this important aspect of the problem. With specific reference to physician-patient sexual abuse, Katherine Morgan (9) writes most forcefully:

> The gender opaque formulation of philosophical arguments leads the reader to see the moral participants involved as generic, non-differentiated individuals who are inter-changeable players in the sexual contact game. This encourages a view of the players as equally situated and, in principle, equally powerful in the decision-making process. This is pernicious in two ways. First it renders relatively invisible the enormous power differential built in between any physician and patient, and second, it supports a completely mythic notion of gender equality.

In summary, the power imbalance between the sexes, the power imbalance between the therapist and the patient and overt attempts to coerce the patient either by deception or threat preclude voluntariness.

AUTONOMOUS AUTHORIZATION

Can a patient autonomously authorize therapist-patient sexual contact? Autonomous authorization requires that the patient do "more than express agreement with, acquiesce in, yield to, or comply with an arrangement or a proposal" (13). On this view, a patient may submit or yield to therapist-patient sexual contact without thereby consenting to such contact. For there to be morally valid consent there must be an autonomous authorization—an act of "will" as contrasted with an act of submission.

By its very nature, however, the therapist-patient relationship precludes such an act of will. Typically, circumstances do not allow for free choice based on personal values and preferences such that one could legitimately describe an agreement to engage in therapist-patient sex as a voluntary act of authorization. At most there can be compliance, submission and acquiescence.

In summary, "there is no such thing as gaining consent for sexual involvement with a patient" (9). That is, patients cannot provide a morally valid consent to sexual relations with their therapists because the key elements—intentionality, substantial understanding, substantial voluntariness and autonomous authorization—cannot be met.

The Likelihood of Harmful Consequences

The potential harm to the patient caused by therapist-patient sexual contact is sometimes far reaching and subtle, and sometimes immediate, blatant, profound and lasting. There is potential harm to patients, patients' families and the profession. These will be considered in reverse order.

Therapist-patient sexual contact can potentially harm the profession because it undermines the public's confidence in its integrity and trustworthiness. Of particular concern to the public is the fact that the profession would allow among its members persons of questionable moral character and place professional loyalty above patients' well-being. Therapist-patient sexual abuse can also harm the family and friends of those who are abused. Specifically, it contributes to family breakdown, the inability to be an effective parent and the alienation of extended family members and friends (12). Finally, therapist-patient sexual contact clearly harms the patients. A 1983 study by Bouhoutsos et al. (23), based on data on 559 patients, reported that 90% of the victims of therapist-patient sexual abuse suffered harm; 11% of these patients were hospitalized and 1% committed suicide.

PHYSICAL AND PSYCHOLOGICAL HARM
CAUSED BY SEXUAL ABUSE

The harm caused by therapist-patient sexual abuse can be both physical and psychological. Physical harm, as a result of violence, is minimal. The use of force or weapons is generally unnecessary, given the unequal distribution of power inherent in the therapist-patient relationship. Psychological harm resulting from therapist-patient sexual abuse, however, may be considerable and may manifest itself as a physical harm. For example, a number of physical health problems (manifestations of underlying psychological distress) can be attributed to therapist-patient sexual contact. Patients who have been sexually abused report "abdominal pain, eating disorders, or drug and alcohol abuse" (9), symptoms which do not predate the onset of the sexual relationship.

It has also been suggested that:

> the sequelae of therapist-patient sexual involvement form a distinct clinical syndrome for the patient, with both acute and chronic phases. Aspects of the Therapist-Patient Sex Syndrome include: 1. ambivalence; 2. guilt; 3. feelings of isolation; 4. feelings of emptiness; 5. cognitive dysfunction (especially in the areas of attention and concentration frequently involving flashbacks, nightmares, intrusive thoughts and unbidden images); 6. identity and boundary disturbance; 7. inability to trust (often focused on conflicts about dependence, control and power); 8. sexual confusion; 9. lability of mood (frequently involving severe depression); 10. suppressed rage; and 11. increased suicidal risk (12).

Two of these aspects merit further comment. It is not unusual for a patient who is involved sexually with her therapist to become isolated from family and friends. A consequence of this isolation is that when the therapist-patient sexual relationship ends, as it invariably does, the patient lacks the support necessary to help her deal with feelings of hurt, anger, humiliation, loneliness, abandonment, embarrassment, guilt, anxiety, shame and hopelessness. In addition to the isolation, there is a sense of betrayal associated with the breach of trust. The perpetrator is not a stranger, but a trusted person with whom the patient had a fiduciary relationship—a relationship in which a person with particular knowledge and abilities accepts the trust and confidence of another to act in the person's best interests. Trust and confidence are placed in the therapist on the basis of a perception of social role. Even a sophisticated patient must place herself in a vulnerable, less powerful position through a therapist who has more knowledge, training and experience in the therapeutic process. It is the duty of the therapist as fiduciary to attend only to the needs of the patient and to do no harm. Sexual contact is counter-therapeutic behavior that will harm patients (10).

Therapist-patient sexual contact undermines the fiduciary relationship. The patient is vulnerable and she seeks help. The therapist preys on this vulnerability by promising to help, but instead seeks personal sexual gratification. The therapist thereby violates his professional commitment to act in his patient's best interests. To maintain trust, the physician must avoid initiating or responding to any forms of sexual advances. Sexualizing the relationship is a clear breach of trust. The outcome is destructive for both, but the patient suffers the greater damage as the dependent partner in the dyad (16).

Direct harm to the patient that may result from the breach of trust (and perhaps the most lasting of the potential harms resulting from therapist-patient sexual abuse) is a resulting mistrust of others. Feldman-Summers and Jones (24) interviewed women who had been sexually abused by their therapists, those who had been sexually abused by other health care providers, and those who had had no sexual relationships with their therapists. In comparing the women in therapy who were abused with those who were not abused, they found that the victims of sexual abuse had a greater mistrust of men and male therapists in particular, and experienced a greater number of psychological and psychosomatic symptoms after the cessation of treatment. This mistrust may cause the patient to terminate therapy before the underlying problem for which she originally sought help might have been treated successfully. In addition, other psychological problems resulting from the abuse may remain untreated.

HARM ASSOCIATED WITH DISCLOSURE ABOUT SEXUAL ABUSE

In addition to the physical and psychological harm caused by therapist-patient sexual abuse, there may be additional harm to the patient who speaks out against the abuse. There is the very real possibility that others will respond with disbelief, choosing to dismiss the allegations of sexual impropriety or abuse on the grounds that these allegations are made by a "disturbed woman." The victim who calls attention to the problem is likely to be blamed and to experience shame and guilt over her participation. If she chooses to stand up to her betrayer publicly, she must face the added burden of being labeled as unreliable and emotionally disturbed, especially if she had sought psychiatric treatment (25).

An overwhelming sense of powerlessness is associated with the harm that the woman experiences when her credibility is called into question. Alternatively, even if there is a sympathetic response to the disclosure and the patient is believed, she may be harmed by the disclosure should she attempt to have the therapist disciplined or prosecuted. This is a difficult process uniformly described as "daunting, demeaning and retraumatizing" (9).

Conclusion

Therapist-patient sexual contact is unethical: it is a nonconsensual activity that is inherently harmful. As such, it is appropriate to transpose the conclusion of the *Final Report of the Ontario Task Force on Sexual Abuse of Patients* (7) specifically to therapist-patient sexual contact:

> There are NO circumstances—NONE—in which sexual activity between a [therapist] and a patient is acceptable. Sexual activity between a patient and a [therapist] ALWAYS represents sexual abuse, regardless of what rationalization or belief system the [therapist] chooses to use to excuse it. It is ALWAYS the [therapist]'s responsibility to know what is appropriate and never to cross the line into sexual activity.

Acknowledgments

The author would like to thank Jocelyn Downie, Michael Bolton, and Virginia Frisk for helpful comments on an earlier draft of this paper.

Notes

1. Gartrell N, Herman J, Olarte S, et al. Prevalence of psychiatrist-patient sexual contact. In: Gabbard G, ed. *Sexual exploitation in professional relation ships*. Washington D.C.: American Psychiatric Press, Inc., 1989: 3–13.

2. American Psychiatric Association. *Principles of medical ethics with annotations especially applicable to psychiatry*. Washington, D.C.: The American Psychiatric Association, 1986: Sect. 2, #1.

3. American Psychological Association. Ethical principles of psychologists and code of conduct. In: *The American Psychologist* 1992 47 (12): 1605, Sect. 4.06.

4. Mellor C. The Canadian Medical Association Code of Ethics annotated for psychiatrists. The position of the Canadian Psychiatric Association. *Can J Psychiatry* 1980; 25 (5): 432–38.

5. Canadian Psychological Association. Canadian code of ethics for psychologists. In: Baylis F, Downie J, eds. *Codes of ethics: ethics codes, standards, and guidelines for professionals working in a health care setting*. Toronto, ON: The Hospital for Sick Children, 1992: 93–94.

6. Canadian Association of Social Workers. Code of ethics. In: Baylis F, Downie J, eds. *Codes of ethics: ethics codes, standards, and guidelines for professionals working in a health care setting in Canada*. Toronto, ON: The Hospital for Sick Children, 1992: 121.

7. R. v. *Tyhurst* (June 25, 1991), Doc. No. Vancouver CC 901266 (B.C. S.C.).

8. Brickman J, Briere J. Incidence of rape and sexual assault in an urban Canadian population. *International Journal of Women's Studies* 1985: 7.

9. *An independent task force commissioned by the College of Physicians and Surgeons of Ontario. The final report of the task force on sexual abuse of patients.* Toronto, ON: The College of Physicians and Surgeons of Ontario, 1991.

10. Strasburger LH, Jorgenson L, Randles R. Criminalization of psychotherapist-patient sex. *Am J Psychiatry* 1991; 148: 859–63.

11. Gartrell N, Herman J, Olarte S, et al. Psychiatrist-patient sexual contact: results of a national survey, I: prevalence. *Am J Psychiatry* 1986; 143: 1126–31.

12. Pope K, Bouhoutsos J. *Sexual intimacy between therapists and patients.* New York: Praeger, 1986.

13. Faden R, Beauchamp T. *A history and theory of informed consent.* New York: Oxford University Press, 1986: 274–97.

14. Appelbaum PA, Jorgenson L. Psychotherapist-patient sexual contact after termination of treatment: an analysis and a proposal. *Am J Psychiatry* 1991; 148: 1466–73.

15. Dolphin R. Borderline case. *Saturday Night* 1992: February: 59.

16. Sreenivasan U. Sexual exploitation of patients: the position of the Canadian Psychiatric Association. *Can J Psychiatry* 1989; 34 (3): 234–35.

17. Thompson A. *Guide to ethical practice in psychotherapy.* New York: John Wiley and Sons, 1990: 56.

18. Council on Ethical and Judicial Affairs, American Medical Association. Sexual misconduct in the practice of medicine. *JAMA* 1991; 266: 2742.

19. Schoener G, Milgrom JH, Gonsiorek JC. Sexual exploitation of clients by therapists. *Women and Therapy* 1984; 3: 63–69.

20. DeKeseredy W, Hinch R. *Woman abuse.* Toronto, ON: Thompson Educational Publishing, 1991: 15.

21. Committee on Sexual Offenses Against Children and Youths. *Report of the Committee on Sexual Offenses against Children and Youths. The Badgley report. Volumes I and II and summary.* Ottawa, ON: Supply and Services Canada, 1984: 175.

22. MacLeod L. *Battered but not beaten.* Ottawa, ON: Canadian Advisory Council on the Status of Women, 1987.

23. Bouhoutsos J, Holroyd J, Lerman H, et al. Sexual intimacy between psychotherapists and patients. *Professional Psychology: Research and Practice* 1983; 14: 185–96.

24. Feldman-Summers S, Jones G. Psychological impacts of sexual contact between therapist or other health care practitioners and their clients. *J Consult Clin Psychol* 1984; 52: 1054–61.

25. Nadelson C. Afterword. In: Gabbard G. ed. *Sexual exploitation in professional relationships.* Washington D.C.: American Psychiatric Press, Inc., 1989: 230.

Reconsidering the American Psychological Association's Policy on Sex with Former Patients: Is It Justifiable?

Glen O. Gabbard

The new ethics code (American Psychological Association [APA], 1992), although prohibiting sexual intimacies between therapists and patients for at least 2 years after termination, declined to impose a complete ban on posttermination sexual relationships. Therapists might, according to the code, demonstrate that no exploitation occurred because of unusual circumstances. Allowing sex with at least some former patients represented a relatively late alteration of the content in the new code: The first 15 drafts had banned all posttermination sex with patients.

Within 2 months of adoption of the new APA code, the Assembly of the American Psychiatric Association voted to send to their board of directors a recommended policy change that would not recognize any "unusual circumstances" that might legitimize sexual involvement with a former patient. Since that time, an absolute ban on sex with former patients has become an official part of the American Psychiatric Association ethics code. An article by Appelbaum and Jorgenson (1991) served as a major impetus to this change. The article, endorsing a ban on sexual involvement with patients for 1 year after termination, prompted many clinicians to write letters to the editor. John Nemiah (1992), then editor of the *American Journal of Psychiatry,* termed the outpouring of letters "by far the most vigorous and extensive the *Journal* has seen in many years" (p. 979). He also invited Jeremy Lazarus, then chair of the American Psychiatric Association Ethics Committee, to write a special

From *Professional Psychology: Research and Practice* 25, no. 4 (1994): 329–35. Copyright © 1994, American Psychological Association. Reprinted by permission.

editorial that raised questions about the Appelbaum and Jorgensen article for the same issue that contained a sampling of the letters to the editor. Nemiah clarified that he was the "doorman, not the turnkey of the *Journal's* gates" (p. 979) and reemphasized the *Journal's* autonomy from the dictates of American Psychiatric Association policy.

In this article, I invite a reconsideration of the APA's decision to allow sexual involvement with former patients under some conditions. In identifying concerns, arguments, and obstacles, I will not presume to provide a comprehensive and detailed examination of each of the issues, which would be beyond the scope of a journal article. Instead, I will identify issues that need additional discussion among members of the profession and that are crucial to ensure a relevant policy that is in the best interests of patients, society at large, and the profession.

Concerns About Posttermination Sex with Patients

At least five major concerns about the detrimental effects of posttermination relationships do not seem to have been adequately addressed by those supporting such involvements. These concerns were previously discussed in more detail by Brodsky (1985), Brown (1988), Gabbard and Pope (1989), Shopland and VandeCreek (1991), and Vasquez (1991), and I refer the reader seeking additional references to those works.

TRANSFERENCE

Although not universally recognized by all therapists, the concept of transference has been widely accepted, and the mishandling of transference phenomena has been accepted by some courts as a basis for judgments against therapists or counselors in cases involving sexual misconduct (e.g., *Simmons* v. *U.S.*, 1986; *Zipkin* v. *Freeman*, 1968). Transference is usually defined as the displacement of feelings associated with past figures, such as parents, onto the therapist, rendering a sexual relationship with the therapist symbolically incestuous. Research strongly suggests that the transference, even in successfully concluded and carefully terminated cases, tends to persist after the formal sessions cease (Norman, Blacker, Oremland, & Barret, 1976; Oremland, Blacker, & Norman, 1975; Pfeffer, 1963).

Actual sexual involvement with patients after termination as well as a policy that allows patients who are currently in therapy or who have completed therapy to anticipate that they may engage in sex with their therapist at some time in the future may represent a mishandling of posttermination developmental processes relevant to transference. Buckley,

Karasu, and Charles (1981), for example, studied the posttermination experiences of 97 therapists who had themselves completed some form of therapy or analysis. They found that these therapists tended to be working through unresolved transference effects long after the termination of formal treatment.

> Analysis of the data also revealed that thoughts about the therapist reach a peak during the 5- to 10-year period following treatment. . . . All of the respondents in the 5- to 10-year period following therapy reported experiencing thoughts of returning to analysis or therapy. This would seem to be a critical time in the post-therapeutic development. (Buckley et al., 1981, p. 304)

Such research raises serious concerns about posttermination sexual involvement with patients. If transference makes therapist-patient sex symbolically incestuous during treatment, why would its persisting influence not make sex equally incestuous after treatment? Some psychologists argue that their treatment does not make use of transference, and therefore arguments based on transference are irrelevant. Does the profession, for example, have an adequate empirical basis for claiming with reasonable certainty that some patients do not experience transference, or that the transference no longer exists within a particular time period following termination, or that the transference is irrelevant (i.e., that sexual involvement with a former patient would not represent exploiting or mishandling the enduring transference)? If there are such patients, is there adequate evidence that a psychologist can make a formal assessment that a specific former patient falls into this category? If the answer to the last two questions is "yes," the therapist pondering whether to enter a sexual relationship with a former patient would need to rely on another professional to assess whether the transference is nonexistent or irrelevant for a particular patient.

Finally, with what reliability can psychologists determine that active or latent transference of the type that might be exploited or mishandled by a former therapist does not exist for a specific former patient? Unless clinicians are infallible in such assessments, the former patient could be harmed. A reasonable policy regarding posttermination relationships and a former patient's informed choice about assuming any risks in such relationships must rest on knowledge of how often clinicians are correct or incorrect in making determinations about transference issues. Are those assessments always accurate, are they accurate 90% of the time, or are they no more accurate in predicting the patient's clinical status in this regard than the flip of a coin?

INTERNALIZED THERAPIST

Transference, by definition, involves at least some distortion. Patients may form and internalize reasonably accurate representations of their therapists, however, and those representations may be crucial not only during therapy itself but also after termination, to maintain and expand the positive effects of therapy. Geller, Cooley, and Hartley (1981–1982), for example, conducted research with former patients and found that this phenomenon of generally accurate (i.e., nontransferential) representation of the therapist seemed to be an important component of enduring therapeutic effects: "The vividness of the representation and the use of the representation for the purpose of continuing the therapeutic dialogue [in the absence of the therapist] are significantly correlated with self-perceived improvement" (p. 123: see also Orlinsky & Geller, 1993). These findings are consistent with Edelson's (1963) formulation that the challenge of termination is not stopping the therapeutic process, but rather,

> facilitating achievement by the patient of the ability to "hang on" to the therapist (or the experience of the relationship with the therapist) *in his physical absence* in the form of a realistic intrapsychic representation (memories, identification—associated with altered functioning) which is conserved rather than . . . abandoned following separation, thus making mastery of this experience possible. (p. 14)

CONTINUING PROFESSIONAL RESPONSIBILITIES

The notion of a therapist entering into a sexual relationship with a former patient with and toward whom the therapist no longer has any professional relationship or responsibilities is intriguing but perhaps misleading. Aspects of the professional relationship and responsibilities may persist long after termination of even the most brief, superficial, or successful therapy. For example, therapists may be required—by statute, administrative regulation, or professional standard—to maintain records of the treatment for a number of years after termination. In some instances, the therapist may have to relinquish these records to a third party in response to a subpoena and may have to testify as a fact witness regarding the former patient's clinical status in certain forms of litigation. As another example, the patient's rights to appropriate privacy, confidentiality, and privilege endure in perpetuity. Without the patient's informed waiver or other legal basis for exception, the therapist continues to bear a duty to claim privilege on behalf of the former patient should the therapist be asked to disclose information gained in confidence during the course of therapy. The clinical relationship itself is another form of continuing professional responsibility deserving consideration. As many as two thirds of patients who successfully terminate treatment recontact their therapist for a consultation or two during the first 3 years after therapy has ended (Hartlaub, Martin, & Rhine, 1986).

UNEQUAL POWER

Yet another concern, the inherent power imbalance, may not have been adequately addressed in a policy that views some sexual relationships with former patients as ethical. Therapists may have access during the course of therapy to their patients' deepest secrets, hopes, fears, and fantasies. The potential for therapists to exploit this knowledge for purposes not originally intended needs to be recognized. As Brodsky (1985), a coauthor of the first national survey of psychologist-client sexual contact, wrote,

> no matter how the therapy contracts ends, the imbalance of power of the initial interactions can never be erased. Thus, therapists need to agree that once they accept a patient into therapy, that patient becomes off limits to any other relationship. The patient needs to know that the relationship is safe. (p. 59)

Moreover, former patients who come to believe that their trust was exploited and who wish to file a complaint face an implicit threat of blackmail. To file a complaint with the civil courts, a licensing board, or an ethics committee, patients must usually waive their rights to privilege and confidentiality. When they file a complaint, they explicitly (e.g., by signing a waiver for an ethics committee) or implicity (e.g., by placing their mental or emotional state at issue before the courts) allow the former therapist to disclose to third parties the contents of their supposedly confidential communications to the therapist, as well as the therapist's professional opinions about their condition. Thus, in malpractice suits, a patient's deepest secrets may become a matter of public record and literally become front-page news. The notion that therapist and former patient enter a sexual relationship on roughly equal footing may be more apparent than actual.

HARM TO PATIENTS AND THE THERAPEUTIC PROCESS

Allowing posttermination sexual relationships may significantly change the nature of therapy. Rather than viewing their attraction to a therapist as a normal event that may safely emerge in a context with no possibility of ever being consummated, patients may come to recognize that, at least eventually, sexual union with the person serving as their therapist is a real possibility, recognized and condoned by the ethics code. Patients wishing to satisfy this attraction may attempt to hide from the therapist any facets of themselves that may be unattractive, any deeper emotional problems that would make the therapist unwilling to enter a subsequent sexual relationship, and any complications that might prolong the therapy. For patients who feel a powerful attraction to the therapist, therapy may remain a superficial endeavor, a quasicourtship to be completed as quickly as possible so that the legal clock may begin running.

With the knowledge that sexual activity with a patient to whom therapists find themselves strongly attracted is actually possible (at least provided that they can wait the allotted time), therapists might turn a practice into something resembling a dating service. The therapist would be able to screen potential sexual partners or spouses and, by virtue of the role of therapist, to inquire into private areas of the patients' lives and psyches that might be relevant to the therapist's criteria for a potential spouse or sexual partner. Patients who may have wanted or needed a relationship free from sexual possibilities (e.g., those who seek therapy because they have been victims of rape or incest) may find themselves evaluated by therapists as potential future sex partners. In the words of Gordon Bermant, a fellow of the Hastings Center and a former member of the APA Ethics Committee,

> the profession should be able to state its position unequivocally, and mean it, and the public should be able to have complete confidence in the integrity of practitioners to forgo fulfilment of personal gratification based on a relationship that began on a fee for service basis.
>
> Psychotherapists occupy a unique and privileged position vis-à-vis their clients. They are paid to hear and respond to secrets, to advise, counsel, and cure. They are not paid to create future possibilities for themselves, to widen their social spheres of influence or gratification. Nor should they presume to benefit from a free ride on an accident of personal chemistry. (personal communication quoted by Vasquez, 1991, p. 57)

To preserve and support the structure, meaning, and workings of the family, society imposes legal restrictions on sexual activity between parents and their offspring. Consensual sexual activity between a parent and an adult child, for instance, is not permitted, even long after the child has terminated the relationship with the nuclear family, is financially and otherwise independent, is living elsewhere, and there is no longer any possibility of pregnancy. The notion of similarly prohibiting posttermination sex between therapists and patients to preserve and support the structure, meaning, and workings of therapy deserves careful consideration.

Arguments Supporting Policy That Allows Posttermination Sex

Arguments supporting the explicit approval of at least some posttermination sexual relationships, like concerns about such a policy, may not have received sufficient examination. The following subsections present nine arguments frequently set forth as favoring a policy permitting posttermination sexual involvements along with a few brief comments suggesting that such arguments deserve more extensive scrutiny.

CONSTITUTIONAL ARGUMENTS

Some proponents of posttermination relationships assert that any attempt by the professions to prohibit such involvements are inherently unconstitutional. The argument is that people have the right to assemble, the right to pursue happiness, and a right to be free from the regulation of private sexual behavior. According to this view, therapists have a constitutional right to engage in sex with former patients that a professional association cannot abridge.

A careful exploration of this assertion might include, but not be limited to, the following two issues: First, the analogy between the professional's behavior as defined by ethical standards and the citizen's more general constitutional rights may be somewhat misleading. For example, citizens have a constitutional right to free speech. However, professionals submit themselves to both the legally mandated restrictions of privilege (regarding confidential communications from their patients) and the professional associations' mandated restrictions (expressed explicitly through professional ethics codes) regarding confidentiality.

Those acquiring professional status assume additional responsibilities that put limits on what acceptable behavior is. Thus, therapists do not have the right to exercise free speech about information given to them in confidence by those who come to them for help. Moreover, although the restrictions may be legally mandated (e.g., privilege), legitimate ethical codes may impose even more stringent limitations on acceptable behavior than what the law requires. If the statement "what I did was not illegal" were equivalent to "what I did was not unethical," there would be no need for a separate code of professional ethics that might call for a higher standard of responsibility than that required by legislation.

Second, if the argument that the constitution bans a professional organization from prohibiting sexual behavior between two competent adults is accepted, there would be no constitutional basis for prohibiting an adult therapist and adult patient from choosing to engage in private sexual behavior during the course of treatment as well as after termination.

PASSAGE OF TIME

The argument that sexual involvements with patients are safe and ethical when a particular span of time (e.g., 1 or 2 years) has elapsed after termination is questionable on two grounds. First, the concerns raised in the beginning of this article are relevant to this argument and have not been adequately addressed. Concomitants of the original therapeutic relationship such as transference, the internal representations of the therapist, the therapist's continuing professional duties (e.g., privilege), and an imbalance of power may last far beyond a 1- or 2-year period (as both research and theory suggest). Some may continue for as long as the patient lives. Until these concerns are carefully and adequately addressed, it seems unwise to assume that sexual involvements with patients are inherently safe and ethical after a 1- or 2-year wait beyond termination.

Second, research suggests that harm is likely to occur with posttermination sexual involvements. In one study involving 954 cases of therapist-patient sex, clinical assessments indicated that harm occurred in 80% of those cases in which the sexual intimacies were initiated only after termination (Pope & Vetter, 1991). Studies of actions by psychology licensing boards and ethics committees have found that sanctions have been imposed for psychologists who have engaged in sex with patients after termination. One case involved intimacies that occurred 4 years after termination (Gottlieb, Sell, & Schoenfeld, 1988; Sell, Gottlieb, & Schoenfeld, 1986).

LACK OF CONCLUSIVE PROOF OF HARM

Despite studies showing the harm that can happen after sexual involvements with current or former patients, it is possible to argue that there is a lack of conclusive proof that such intimacies cause harm. Those arguments focus on the methodology of the studies in this area. Because the studies examining harm have sometimes used large samples, individual case studies, control groups, and psychometrically sound assessment instruments, critiques have tended to focus on the fact that all studies involve, to some degree, self-selected samples. (For examples of studies using varied approaches, see Bates & Brodsky 1989; Bouhoutsos, Holroyd, Lerman, Forer, & Greenberg, 1983; Feldman-Summers & Jones, 1984, Pope & Vetter, 1991.) Thus, Riskin (1979) argued that the issue of whether sex with patients caused harm could only be definitively decided by research in which patients were randomly assigned to "sex" and "no sex" therapy groups.

From this perspective, however, we have no definitive data (only correlational data) showing that smoking in humans causes harm. The smoking studies to date in which random assignment was used involved only nonhumans (i.e., animal populations, the findings for which cannot be generalized with certainty to humans) and human subjects who were self-selected (i.e., individuals were not randomly assigned to smoking and nonsmoking groups). Although the accumulated research findings on therapist-patient sex in which diverse methodological approaches were used are by no means perfect, at the very least they raise concerns about possible harm to current and former patients that have not been adequately addressed by proponents of sexual relationships with former patients.

From another perspective, it would seem reasonable to ask proponents to present their evidence for the harmlessness of pre- or posttermination sexual involvements with patients using the same epistemological premises. If sex with a current or former patient were a product (e.g., psychotropic medication) or other physical intervention (e.g., electroconvulsive therapy), it would likely not be permissible until its relative safety had been established through systematic study and until it had met whatever criteria its proponents as well as those involved in policy decisions found acceptable. Are there any empirical data suggesting that posttermination sex is reasonably safe?

Indeed, the new code clearly states that the therapist bears the burden of demonstrating that no exploitation has occurred. Is it conceivable that any case could be "justified" as unequivocally nonexploitative? No data exist to suggest that sex with former patients is definitely safe. Although the Pope and Vetter (1991) study might be construed as suggesting that 20% of patients were not harmed, in fact it offers no conclusive proof that posttermination sex is safe. The absence of evidence is not the same thing as evidence of absence.

INSTANCE OF APPARENT HARMLESSNESS

Even in the absence of systematic studies published in peer-reviewed scientific and professional journals suggesting that posttermination sexual involvement with patients is reasonably safe, proponents of such involvements may point to an actual or hypothetical example in which no apparent harm befell the patient. Arguments based on the individual example of harmlessness deserve careful scrutiny. Ethical standards do not depend on the demonstration that an act always causes harm. For example, if a therapist and patient were to collaborate on a business venture, it might be financially profitable for both, but it would still violate professional standards. Similarly, surveys based on anonymous self-reports suggest that most therapists have, at least once, unintentionally breached confidentiality (Pope, Tabachnick, & Keith-Spiegel, 1987). However, the likelihood that not many patients were harmed in no way invalidates the ethical mandate to preserve confidentiality.

Moreover, even when an act is unlikely to cause harm, a legitimate policy may prohibit the act if the nature or extent of the possible harm is considered sufficient. For example, even though most instances of driving while under the influence of alcohol do not result in significant damage to people or property, the policy prohibiting drunk driving is viewed as legitimate and desirable.

ATYPICAL POSSIBILITY

Proponents may argue that an absolute prohibition casts too wide a net by envisioning a remote and highly atypical example. Consider, then, a therapist who sees a patient for one session, then has no contact whatsoever until a chance encounter 20 year later.

Should admittedly atypical instances be used to determine policy when other patients may be put at risk for substantial harm? Should drunk driving laws, for example, be amended to take into account that rare drinker who can hold his or her liquor? Should incest laws be revised to take into account the atypical examples in which a parent and child were separated immediately after the birth of the child and had no contact until a chance encounter 20 or 30 years later?

FAMOUS THERAPISTS HAVE (SUPPOSEDLY) ENGAGED IN SEX WITH PATIENTS

Appealing to an authoritative model is a fallacious argument that is often raised. Prominent therapists have engaged in acts that are currently unacceptable, yet this in no way justifies such acts (Gutheil & Gabbard, 1993). That Freud provided cocaine to his patients, for example, would not justify repealing the laws or professional standards barring therapists from providing cocaine to their patients. Similarly, just because respected public officials and other prominent people have broken the law does not mean that lawless behavior should be legitimized for others.

THERAPISTS CANNOT HELP WHOM THEY FALL IN LOVE WITH

The aura and mysterious power of love may be used to support the notion that therapists should be allowed to engage in sex with their current or former patients. However forceful or attractive this argument seems at first glance, deeper examination is required. Declarations of love do not exonerate an otherwise unethical or illegal act. Parents engaging in incest with their children may experience what they would describe as deep, authentic, and overwhelming feelings of love for the object of their abusive behavior.

Moreover, therapists should be especially aware of the difference between feelings (such as love) and behavior. It may be true that therapists are unable to choose whom they fall in love with, but if they are genuinely able to function as therapists, they can certainly control whom they fall into bed with. Similarly, some therapists may occasionally feel a powerful and overwhelming hate for a patient; this experience, however, in no way justifies acting on the feeling in a way that places the patient at risk for harm.

Finally, in considering this issue, the concept of love often has been invoked in an attempt to rationalize sex with current patients as well as with patients after termination. For example, the notion of "true love" has been classified as one of the 10 most common scenarios of therapist-patient sexual involvement (Pope & Bouhoutsos, 1986, pp. 4, 15–16). Similarly, Gutheil and Gabbard (1992) have noted that many therapists

> profess that their relationship with the patient was "true love" that in no way varied from love relationships outside the therapeutic setting. Obviously, regardless of whatever the subjective feelings of the patient or therapist, misconduct is exploitative in the ethical and legal sense of the term. And from a clinical standpoint, it can never be justified. (pp. 521–522; see also Twemlow & Gabbard, 1989)

MARRIAGE AS JUSTIFICATION

Proponents of posttermination sexual involvements with patients may point to therapists who have married their former patients. This rationale has been used also in attempts to justify some instances of sex with current patients (i.e., instances in which a therapist engaged in sex with a current patient and they later married). Like "true love," the concept of marriage may seem, at first glance, to sanctify or justify a policy permitting posttermination involvements. Also like "true love," this rationale warrants closer scrutiny. The fact of marriage per se is neither helpful nor determinative. The existence of such marriages neither reveals whether or not the former patient was harmed nor clarifies what the policy implications would be of allowing involvements because these marriages do exist.

Certainly abuse occurs in numerous marriages, and marriage as an institution does not—or at least should not—legitimize that abuse. For many years, marriage has been used as a rationalization to protect husbands from the legal consequences of rape and battering. Few laws have been passed to prohibit abuse that occurs in the context of marital relationships. In many instances, for example, state laws prohibiting rape provide specific exemptions for spouses (i.e., they exempt a husband's rape of his wife).

SEX WITH FORMER PATIENTS CAN NEVER BE COMPLETELY ELIMINATED

It may be argued that because a policy of prohibition cannot completely eliminate sexual involvements with patients, some form of involvement should be permitted so as not to encourage disrespect for professional policy more generally. In other words, why implement a policy that cannot easily be enforced? Yet professional policy does not always result in complete compliance (e.g., unintentional breaches of confidentiality mentioned previously). It is unlikely, for example, that a time will come when all therapists without exception refrain from sexual involvements with a current patient. This stubborn reality, however, is not a sufficient reason to allow and tacitly condone questionable behavior. The fact that robberies occur with considerable frequency is not a reason to eliminate or weaken the laws against robbery. It would not make sense, either, to designate a certain quantity of money in every bank as "robbery money" because of the inevitability of robbery.

This rationale is, in some sense, the mirror image of one of the previous justifications: Individual therapists cannot choose whom they fall in love with and therefore should not be held accountable for their behavior. Psychologists may not be able to eliminate sexually exploitative behavior through their ethics code and enforcement procedures. That fact alone, however, should not deter a professional association from establishing an ethics code and a system of accountability that attempts to ensure the protection of the consumer from harm.

Difficulties of Imposing a Permanent Prohibition

Even if the arguments presented here were uniformly accepted, several factors may make a policy prohibiting all instances of sex with those who have become patients difficult to consider and adopt.

1. Gender issues may pose difficulties. The research almost uniformly suggests that sexual involvement with patients, both before and after termination, is a phenomenon in which therapist-participants are overwhelmingly (though not exclusively)

men and patient-participants are overwhelmingly (though not exclusively) women. This significant difference holds, even once the relative proportions of male and female therapists and of male and female patients are adjusted. History suggests that the public generally and the professions more specifically may have considerable difficulty acknowledging the scope of abuse and addressing all its forms (e.g., rape, incest, and spouse battering) in which the modal abuser is a man and the modal victim is a woman (Pope, 1990).

2. As with many forms of victimization, there may be a tendency to blame the victim (Ryan, 1971). For example, this may be manifested in the conceptualization of therapist-patient sex as a phenomenon in which therapists are unable to control their own actions and are helpless when confronted with a seductive patient, whether before or after termination of therapy. Indeed, many victims of therapist-patient sex view themselves as responsible for their therapist's behavior. Management of countertransference is always the therapist's responsibility (Gabbard & Wilkinson, 1994).

3. Therapists may have a tendency to think almost exclusively in terms of ways to allow sexual gratification with at least some individuals who have come to them for help, to the relative exclusion of such notions as the welfare and safety of the consumer. Thus, professionals may bend over backward to find ways to justify sexual involvements rather than starting with a "first, do no harm" principle and ensuring that any involvements are fully consistent with that and other ethical principles.

4. Financial implications may exert disproportionate influence in policy considerations. Sexual misconduct has been a major cause of increased malpractice insurance premiums for psychologists. Imposing more rigorous standards may lead to more violations. In addition, a policy condoning some forms of sexual involvement with patients may tend to make other forms seem less serious—innocence by association—so that sexual involvements with patients are viewed as a shaded continuum that runs from the ethical to the unethical rather than representing a category of clearly unethical behavior.

5. To adopt a prohibition on all sexual involvements with former patients means that psychologists must confront, through their formal policy, their colleagues who have engaged in such involvements. Many of these colleagues may be respected leaders, teachers, and role models. Remnants of the historic conspiracy of silence may persist.

6. Research suggests that most therapists experience, at least occasionally, sexual attraction to those who come to them for professional help and that simply being attracted without acting on it tends to evoke guilt, anxiety, and confusion (Pope, Keith-Spiegel, & Tabachnick, 1986). The topic of sexual involvement with current or former patients may evoke discomfort for many and may make careful consideration of the relevant issues difficult.

Conclusion

The decision of the APA to declare certain forms of posttermination sex as ethical appears to be premature. In the absence of data that would persuasively demonstrate such relationships to be harmless, the prudent course of action would be to proscribe posttermination relationships under the same rationale used to prohibit sex with current patients. When one considers that there are 5 billion people on the planet, the choice of a former patient as a sexual partner must raise serious questions about the judgment and ethics of the psychotherapist.

References

American Psychological Association. (1992). Ethical principles of psychologists and code of conduct. *American Psychologist, 47*, 1597–1611.

Appelbaum, P. S., & Jorgensen, L. (1991). Psychotherapist-patient sexual contact after termination of treatment: An analysis and a proposal. *American Journal of Psychiatry, 148*, 1466–1473.

Bates, C. M., & Brodsky, A. M. (1989). *Sex in the therapy hour: A case of professional incest*. New York: Guilford Press.

Bouhoutsos, J. C., Holroyd, J., Lerman, H., Forer, B., Greenberg, M. (1983). Sexual intimacy between psychotherapists and patients. *Professional Psychology: Research and Practice, 14*, 185–196.

Brodsky, A. M. (1985). Sex between therapists and patients: Ethical grey areas. *Psychotherapy in Private Practice, 14*, 57–62.

Brown, L. S. (1988). Harmful effects of posttermination sexual and romantic relationships between therapists and their former clients. *Psychotherapy, 25*, 249–255.

Buckley, P., Karasu, T. B., & Charles, E. (1981). Psychotherapists view their personal therapy. *Psychotherapy: Theory, Research and Practice, 18*, 299–305.

Edelson, M. (1963). *The termination of intensive psychotherapy*. Springfield, IL: Charles C. Thomas.

Feldman-Summers, S., & Jones, G. (1984). Psychological impacts of sexual contact between therapists or other health care professionals and their clients. *Journal of Consulting and Clinical Psychology, 52*, 1054–1061.

Gabbard, G. O., & Pope, K. (1989). Sexual intimacies after termination: Clinical, ethical, and legal aspects. In G. O. Gabbard (Ed.), *Sexual exploitation in professional relationships* (pp. 115–127).Washington, DC: American Psychiatric Press.

Gabbard, G. O., & Wilkinson, S. (1994). *Management of countertransference with borderline patients*. Washington, DC: American Psychiatric Press.

Geller, J. D., Cooley, R. S., & Hartley, D. (1981–1982). Images of the psychotherapist. *Imagination, Cognition, and Personality*, 1, 123–146.

Gottlieb, M. C., Sell, J. M., & Schoenfeld, L. S. (1988). Social/romantic relationships with present and former clients: State licensing board actions. *Professional Psychology: Research and Practice*, 19, 459–462.

Gutheil, T. G., & Gabbard, G. O. (1992). Obstacles to the dynamic understanding of therapist-patient sexual relations. *American Journal of Psychotherapy*, 46, 515–525.

———. (1993). The concept of boundaries in clinical practice: Theoretical and risk-management dimensions. *American Journal of Psychiatry*, 150, 188–196.

Hartlaub, G. H., Martin, G. C., & Rhine, M. W. (1986). Recontact with the analyst following termination: A survey of 71 cases. *Journal of the American Psychoanalytic Association*, 34, 895–910.

Nemiah, J. C. (1992). Editor's note. *American Journal of Psychiatry*, 149, 979.

Norman, H., Blacker, K., Oremland, J., & Barret, W (1976). The fate of the transference neurosis after termination of a satisfactory analysis. *Journal of the American Psychoanalytic Association*, 24, 471–498.

Oremland, J., Blacker, K., & Norman, H. (1975). Incompleteness in "successful" psychoanalyses: A follow-up case study. *Journal of the American Psychoanalytic Association*, 23, 829–844.

Orlinsky, D. E., & Geller, J. D. (1993). Psychotherapy's internal theater of operation: Patients' representations of their therapists and therapy as a new focus of research. In N. E. Miller, J. Docherty, L Luborsky, & J. Barber (Eds.). *Psychodynamic treatment research*. New York: Basic Books.

Pfeffer, A. (1963). The meaning of the analyst after analysis. *Journal of the American Psychoanalytic Association*, 11, 229–244.

Pope, K. S. (1990). Therapist-patient sex as sex abuse: Six scientific, professional, and practical dilemmas in addressing victimization and rehabilitation. *Professional Psychology: Research and Practice*, 21, 227–239.

Pope, K. S., & Bouhoutsos, J. C. (1986). *Sexual intimacy between therapists and patients*. New York: Praeger.

Pope, K. S., Keith-Spiegel, P. C., & Tabachnick, B. G. (1986). Sexual attraction to patients: The human therapist and the (sometimes) inhuman training system. *American Psychologist*, 41, 147–158.

Pope, K. S., Tabachnick, B. G., & Keith-Spiegel, P. (1987) Ethics of practice: The beliefs and behaviors of psychologists as therapists. *American Psychologist*, 42, 993–1006.

Pope, K. S. & Vetter, V. A. Prior therapist-patient sexual involvement among patients seen by psychologists. *Psychotherapy*, 28, 429–438.

Riskin, L. (1979). Sexual relations between psychotherapists and their patients: Toward research or restraint? *California Law Review*, 67, 1000–1027.

Ryan, W. (1971). *Blaming the victim*. New York: Pantheon Books.

Sell, J. M., Gottlieb, M. C., & Schoenfeld, L. (1986). Ethical considerations of social romantic relationships with present and former clients. *Professional Psychology: Research and Practice, 17*, 504–508.

Shopland, S. N., & VandeCreek, L. (1991). Sex with ex-clients: Theoretical rationales for prohibition. *Ethics and Behavior, 1*, 35–45.

Simmons V. U.S. 805 F.2d 1363, 1365 (9th Cir. 1986).

Twemlow, S. W., & Gabbard, G. O. (1989). The lovesick therapist. In G. O. Gabbard (Ed.), *Sexual exploitation in professional relationships* (pp. 71–87). Washington, DC: American Psychiatric Press.

Vasquez, M. J. T. (1991). Sexual intimacies with clients after termination: Should a prohibition be explicit? *Ethics and Behavior, 1*, 45–61.

Zipkin v. *Freeman*, 436 S. W. 2d 753.761 (Mo. 1968).

Suggestions for Further Reading

Moral and Legal Rights

Berger, Morton, "Ethics and the Therapeutic Relationship: Patient Rights and Therapist Responsibilities." In Rosenbaum, Max, ed. *Ethics and Values in Psychotherapy: A Guidebook.* New York: The Free Press, 1982, ch. 3.

Brakel, Samuel J., John Parry, and Barbara A. Weiner, *The Mentally Disabled and the Law.* Chicago: American Bar Foundation, 1985, chs. 5, 6, 8, 9, 11.

Ennis, Bruce J., and Richard D. Emery, *The Rights of Mental Patients.* New York: Avon Books, 1978.

Friedman, Paul R., *The Rights of Mentally Retarded Persons.* New York: Avon Books, 1976.

Hospital and Community Psychiatry Service, *Rights of the Mentally Disabled.* Washington, D.C.: American Psychiatric Association, 1982.

Kindred, Michael, et al., *The Mentally Retarded Citizen and the Law.* New York: The Free Press, 1976.

Rinas, Joan, and Sheila Clyne-Jackson, "Client's Rights" in *Professional Conduct and Legal Concerns in Mental Health Practice.* Norwalk, Conn.: Appleton & Lange, 1988, ch. 3.

Smith, S. J., and A. J. Davis, "Ethical Dilemmas: Conflicts Among Rights, Duties and Obligations." *American Journal of Nursing* 80, no. 8 (1980): 1463–66.

Suchotliff, Leonard C., et al., "The Struggle for Patients' Rights in a State Hospital." *Mental Hygene* 54 (April 1977): 230–40.

Task Panel on Legal and Ethical Issues, "Mental Health and Human Rights." *Arizona Law Review* 20 (1978): 49–174.

U.S. Department of Health and Human Services, *Implementing Standards to Assure the Rights of Mental Patients,* Rockville, Md.: National Institute of Mental Health, 1977.

Ethics, Values, and Goal Setting in Psychotherapy

American Psychiatric Association, *Principles of Medical Ethics: With Annotations Especially Applicable to Psychiatry*. Washington, D.C.: American Psychiatric Association, 1993.

Brace, Kerry, and Leon VandeCreek, "The Justification of Paternalistic Actions in Psychotherapy." *Ethics and Behavior* 1, no. 2 (1991): 87–103.

Kelly, Tim A., "The Role of Values in Psychotherapy: A Critical Review of Process and Outcome Effects." *Clinical Psychology Review* 10 (1990): 171–86.

Kilburg, Richard R., "Psychologists and Physical Intervention: Ethics, Standards, and Legal Implications." *Psychotherapy* 24, no. 4 (Winter 1988): 516–31.

Michels, Robert, and John M. Oldham, "Value Judgments in Psychoanalytic Theory and Practice." *Psychoanalytic Inquiry* 3, no. 4 (1983): 599–608.

Papanek, Helene, "Ethical Values in Psychotherapy." *Individual Psychology* 43 (March 1991): 86–92.

Vasquez, Melba J. T., "Implications of the 1992 Ethics Code for the Practice of Individual Psychotherapy." *Professional Psychology: Research and Practice* 25, no. 4 (1994): 321–28.

Informed Voluntary Consent in Psychotherapy

Becker, D., and Z. Kahana, "Informed Consent in Demented Patients: A Question of Hours." *Medicine and Law* 12 (1993): 271–76.

Breggin, Peter, *Psychiatric Drugs: Hazards to the Brain*. New York: Springer, 1983, ch. 11.

Dyer, Allen R., *Ethics and Psychiatry: Toward Professional Definition*. Washington, D.C.: American Psychiatric Press, 1988, ch. 6.

Faden, Ruth R., and Thomas L. Beauchamp, *A History and Theory of Informed Consent*. New York: Oxford University Press, 1986.

Greenberg, W. M., and S. Attia, "Multiple Personality Disorder and Informed Consent." *American Journal of Psychiatry* 150, no. 7 (1993): 1126–27.

Hulting, Richard J., "The Informed Consent Doctrine in Mental Health: Legal and Ethical Traditions." *Psychotherapy in Private Practice* 9 (1991): 135–44.

Lidz, Charles W., et al., *Informed Consent: A Study of Decisionmaking in Psychiatry*. New York: The Guilford Press, 1984.

Shapiro, David L., "Informed Consent in Forensic Evaluations." *Psychotherapy in Private Practice* 9 (1991): 145–54.

Assessing Competency

Appelbaum, Paul S., and Loren H. Roth, "Assessing Patients' Capacities to Consent to Treatment." *New England Journal of Medicine* 319, no. 25 (1988): 1635–38.

Buchanan, Allen E., and Dan W. Brock, *Deciding for Others: The Ethics of Surrogate Decision Making.* Cambridge: Cambridge University Press, 1989, ch. 1.

Bursztajn, H. J., et al., "Beyond Cognition: The Role of Disordered Affective States in Impairing Competence to Consent to Treatment." *Bulletin of the American Academy of Psychiatry and Law* 19 (1991): 383–88.

Cutter, Mary Ann G., and Earl E. Shelp, *Competency: A Study of Informal Competency Determinations in Primary Care.* Dordrecht, Netherlands: Kluwer, 1991.

Grisso, Thomas, *Evaluating Competencies: Forensic Assessments and Instruments.* New York: Plenum Press, 1986, ch. 6.

Grisso, Thomas, and Paul S. Appelbaum, "Comparison of Standards for Assessing Patients' Capacities to Make Treatment Decisions." *American Journal of Psychiatry* 151, no. 7 (July 1995): 1033–37.

Janofsky, J. S., R. J. McCarthy, and M. F. Folstein, "The Hopkins Competency Assessment Test: A Brief Method for Evaluating Patients' Capacity to Give Informed Consent." *Hospital and Community Psychiatry* 43, no. 2 (1992): 132–36.

Sternberg, R. J., and J. Kolligian, Jr., eds., *Incompetence: A Conceptual Reconsideration.* New Haven, Conn.: Yale University Press, 1990.

Communicating Truthfully with Patients

Appleton, William S., "The Importance of Psychiatrists' Telling Patients the Truth." *American Journal of Psychiatry* 129 (December 1972): 742–45.

Bok, Sissela, "Shading the Truth in Seeking Informed Consent for Research Purposes." *Kennedy Institute of Ethics Journal* 5, no. 1 (1995): 1–17.

Farber, Leslie H., "Lying on the Couch." *Review of Existential Psychology and Psychiatry* 23, no. 2 (1974): 125–35.

Solovey, A. D., and B. L. Duncan, "Ethics and Strategic Therapy: A Proposed Ethical Direction." *Journal of Marital Family Therapy* 18 (1992): 53–61.

Choosing, Refusing, and Abusing Psychotropic Drugs

Appelbaum, Paul S., *Almost a Revolution: Mental Health Law and The Limits of Change.* New York: Oxford University Press, 1994, ch. 4.

Appelbaum, Paul S., and Thomas G. Gutheil, " 'Rotting with Their Rights On': Constitutional Theory and Clinical Reality in Drug Refusal by Psychiatric Patients." *Bulletin of the American Academy of Psychiatry and Law* 7, no. 3 (1979): 306–15.

Isaac, Rael Jean, and Virginia C. Armat, *Madness in the Streets: How Psychiatry and the Law Abandoned the Mentally Ill.* New York: The Free Press, 1990, ch. 7.

Kapp, Marshall B., "Treatment and Refusal Rights in Mental Health." *American Journal of Orthopsychiatry* 64 (April 1964): 223–34.

Roth, Loren, "The Right to Refuse Psychiatric Treatment: Law and Medicine at the Interface." *Emory Law Journal* 35 (1986): 139–61.

Winick, Bruce J., "The Right to Refuse Mental Health Treatment." *International Journal of Law and Psychiatry* 17, no. 1 (1994): 99–117.

Confidentiality, Warning, and Reporting

American Psychiataric Association, "Model Law on Confidentiality of Health and Social Service Records." *American Journal of Psychiatry* 136 (1979): 137–48.

Appelbaum, Paul S., et al., "Confidentiality: An Empirical Test of the Utilitarian Perspective." *Bulletin of the American Academy of Psychiatric Law* 12, no. 2 (1984): 109–16.

Committee on Confidentiality, American Psychiatric Association, "Guidelines on Confidentiality." *American Journal of Psychiatry* 144 (Nov. 1987): 1522–26.

Dyer, Allen R., *Ethics and Psychiatry: Toward Professional Definition.* Washington, D.C.: American Psychiatric Press, 1988, ch. 4.

Joseph, David, and Joseph Onek, "Confidentiality in Psychiatry." In Sidney Bloch and Paul Chodoff, eds. *Psychiatric Ethics,* 2d ed. New York: Oxford University Press, 1991, ch. 15.

Meyers, Charles J., "Where the Protective Privilege Ends: California Changes the Rules for Dangerous Psychotherapy Patients." *The Journal of Psychiatry and Law* 19 (Summer 1991): 5–31.

Perlin, Michael L., *Law and Psychology Review* 16 (Spring 1962): 56–69.

Slovenko, R., *Psychotherapy, Confidentiality, and Privileged Communication.* Springfield, Ill.: Charles C. Thomas, 1966, ch. 6.

Stone, Alan A., *Law, Psychiatry, and Morality.* Washington, D.C.: American Psychiatric Press, 1984, ch. 7.

Truscott, Derek, "The Psychotherapist's Duty to Protect: An Annotated Bibliography." *The Journal of Psychiatry and Law* 21 (Summer 1993): 221–44.

Weiner, Barbara A., "Provider-Patient Relations: Confidentiality and Liability." In Samuel J. Brakel, John Parry, and Barbara A. Weiner, *The Mentally Disabled and the Law.* Chicago: American Bar Foundation, 1985, ch. 10.

Sex with Patients, Present and Former

Appelbaum, Paul S., and Linda Jorgenson, "Psychotherapist-Patient Sexual Contact After Termination of Treatment: An Analysis and a Proposal." *American Journal of Psychiatry* 148, no. 11 (1991): 1466–73.

Coleman, Phyllis, "Sex in Power Dependency Relationships: Taking Unfair Advantage of the 'Fair' Sex." *Albany Law Review* 53 (1988): 95–141.

Committee on Women in Psychology, "If Sex Enters Into the Psychotherapy Relationship." *Professional Psychology: Research and Practice* 20, no. 2 (1989): 112–15.

Delozier, Pauline P., "Therapist Sexual Misconduct." *Women & Therapy: A Feminist Quarterly* 15 (1994): 55–67.

Gabbard, Glen O., ed. *Sexual Exploitation in Professional Relationships.* Washington D.C.: American Psychiatric Press, 1989.

Gabbard, Glen O., ed. "Psychotherapists Who Transgress Sexual Boundaries with Patients." *Bulletin of the Menninger Clinic* 58, no. 1 (1994): 124–35.

Gabbard, Glen O., Sarah D. Atkinson, and Linda M. Jorgenson, "Can Patients Sexually Harass Their Physicians?" *Archives of Family Medicine* 4 (March 1995): 261–65.

Gartrell, Nanette K., and Barbara E. Sanderson, "Sexual Abuse of Women by Women in Psychotherapy." *Women & Therapy: A Feminist Quarterly* 15 (1994): 39–53.

Keitner, Gabor, and Paul Grof, "Sexual and Emotional Intimacy Between Psychiatric Patients: Formulating a Policy." *Hospital and Community Psychiatry* 32 (March 1981): 188–93.

Lerman, H., *Sexual Intimacies Between Psychotherapists and Patients: An Annotated Bibliography of Mental Health, Legal, and Public Media Literature and Relevant Legal Cases*, 2nd ed. Phoenix, Ariz.: Division of Psychotherapy of the American Psychological Association.

Pope, Gerald G., "Abuse of Psychotherapy: Psychotherapist-Patient Intimacy." *Psychotherapy Psychosomatics* 53 (1990): 191–98.

Pope, Kenneth S., and Jacqueline C. Bouhoutsos, *Sexual Intimacies Between Therapists and Patients*. New York: Praeger, 1986.

Sanderson, B. E., ed., *It's Never OK: A Handbook for Professionals on Sexual Exploitation by Counselors and Therapists*. St. Paul, Minn.: Minnesota Department of Corrections, 1989.

Schoener, Gary R., et al., *Psychotherapists' Sexual Involvement with Clients: Intervention and Prevention*. Minneapolis, Minn.: Walk-in Counseling Center, 1989.

Sederer, Lloyd I., and Mayree Libby, "False Allegations of Sexual Misconduct: Clinical and Institutional Considerations." *Psychiatric Services*, 46, no. 2 (1995): 160–63.

Solursh, Diane S., Lionel P. Solursh, and Nancy R. Williams, "Patient-therapist Sex: 'Just Say No' Isn't Enough." *Medical Law* 12 (1993): 431–38.

Stone, Alan A., *Law, Psychiatry, and Morality*. Washington, D.C.: American Psychiatric Press, 1984, ch. 8.

4.

CONTROVERSIAL BEHAVIOR CONTROL THERAPIES

INTRODUCTION

Perry London wrote in 1977, "Behavior control is the ability to get someone to do one's bidding"; the "someone" could be either oneself or another. Whether we realize and admit it or not, we are all in the business of controlling (that is, influencing) behavior, either that of ourselves or that of other people. What forms of behavior control are most acceptable morally? From the point of view of an ethics that highly values rational autonomy, the most satisfactory method for controlling behavior is the sort of *direct* self-control involved in properly informed volition, willpower, free will, choice, or whatever we wish to call it. Most of us, on reflection, also accept some *indirect* techniques for modifying our own behavior, techniques that help produce desirable changes as a result of performing some previous act. We can modify our own behaviors and mental states indirectly by voluntarily ingesting drugs like coffee, tea, cola drinks, tobacco, alcohol, controlled substances, physician-prescribed psychotropic medications, and by voluntarily submitting to rational persuasion, psychotherapy, psychosurgery, or electroshock. We need criteria to distinguish between acceptable and unacceptable forms of the many indirect techniques of self-modification currently available.

Therapeutic techniques of behavior modification can also be used on others both inside and outside mental hospitals. Many indirect nonmedical forms of behavior modification are also used on others, including parental discipline, public opinion, advertising, religious training, emotional revivals, economic restraints and incentives, education, moral teaching, indoctrination, governmental regulations, laws, courts, prisons, and jails. What forms of indirect control or influence over the behavior of others are morally acceptable? By what criteria can we distinguish between morally acceptable and unacceptable ways of influencing other people's behavior?

Psychotherapy employs many methods of behavior modification, and the readings that follow explore some of the most controversial—psychopharmacology, electroshock, psychosurgery, behavior modification, and sex therapies.

Criteria

Though the list is not exhaustive, the following criteria may be used to distinguish between acceptable and unacceptable forms of indirect behavior modification, whether applied to ourselves or to others. A technique for influencing behavior may be judged to be acceptable to the degree that:

1. It is used with voluntary informed consent on competent adults.
2. Its use does not infringe on basic legal and/or moral rights.
3. There is a high probability of a favorable cost/benefit ratio, using some ideal of intrinsic good and evil.
4. It enhances, or at least does not diminish, a person's capacity for rational autonomy.
5. It involves no physical intrusion into a person's body.
6. It does not have irreversible bad effects. (Irreversible good effects are acceptable if we are confident that we can identify them.)
7. No less objectionable or less restrictive forms of behavior control are readily available.
8. Its effectiveness is proven rather than experimental.
9. Its monetary costs are not prohibitive.

To the degree that these criteria are not satisfied, psychotherapies tend to be unacceptable valuationally and ethically. Using these criteria, try to assess techniques of behavior control commonly used on mental patients, as represented in the following readings. Some introductory comments might be helpful.

Physical Interventions

Along with other catalysts, like budgetary constraints and an enhanced sensitivity to human rights, psychoactive drugs helped to revolutionize the quality of care and of life available to patients in mental hospitals.

Beginning in the 1950s, drugs played a major role in enabling hundreds of thousands of former mental patients to be released from and maintained outside mental hospitals. In their "Introduction to Pharmacotherapy and Mental Disorders," John R. Hughes and Robert A. Pierattini review the major types of psychotropic medication currently used in mental hospitals and outpatient clinics and explore their strengths and limitations.

As for their limitations, most psychoactive medications are not addictive, but some are. They offer only chemical maintenance and do not cure; but the same must be said for insulin shots for diabetes, kidney machines for renal failure, and pacemakers for coronary irregularities. For some mental disabilities, no effective chemotherapies yet exist. Drugs have often been used improperly as "chemical straitjackets" instead of being used therapeutically to restore desirable functioning, including enhanced rational autonomy. Some critics maintain that psychoactive drugs work only by disabling the brain. Inadequate testing has left the safety and effectiveness of many psychotropic drugs in doubt.

Antipsychotic drugs may have highly undesirable long-term side effects like the iatrogenic disease tardive dyskinesia. This usually develops only when high doses of antipsychotic medication are administered for several years, but it may develop more quickly with very high doses. This iatrogenic disease involves irreversible and incurable brain damage that produces rhythmic involuntary movements and loss of muscular control. These typically begin with facial muscles and spread to limbs and trunk; muscles that control breathing, swallowing, and speaking may be affected. Up to forty percent or more of chronic institutionalized patients have this disease. Of course, almost all medications involve trade-offs; and, on reflection, many persons willingly accept the liabilities of drug therapy in exchange for many years of high functioning not available otherwise. Measures like prescribing only minimal effective doses and giving regular "drug holidays" are now used to prevent or delay tardive dyskinesia.

Despite their drawbacks, on the whole, if properly and skillfully used, many psychotropic drugs may measure up well enough by our criteria of acceptability. Hughes and Pierattini explain the benefits as well as the undesirable side effects of psychopharmacotherapy. Their "Introduction to Pharmacotherapy and Mental Disorders," introduces the major mental illnesses, the psychoactive drugs used to treat them, and their favorable effects and unwanted side effects. These authors give a few of the general classes and/or generic names of the drugs used to treat psychic disorders. Here is further information on psychoactive drugs, their generic names, and their trade names.

Chemical Designation	*Generic Name*	*Trade Name*

1. Antipsychotics

Phenothiazines	chlorpromazine	Thorazine
	fluphenazine	Permitil, Prolixin
	molindone	Moban
	perphenazine	Trilafon
	thioridazine	Mellaril
	trifluoperazine	Stelazine
Butyrophenones	haloperidol	Haldol
	droperidol	Inapsine
	pimozide	Orap
Thioxanthenes	chlorprothixene	Taractan
	thiothixene	Navane
Dibenzodiazepine	clozapine	Clozaril

These drugs, often called "Major Tranquilizers," are used to treat symptoms like disorganized thinking, impaired concentration, delusions and hallucinations, and agitation. Common side effects are constipation, blurred vision, dry mouth, muscle stiffness, dizziness, fast heartbeat, sleepiness, shakiness, and restlessness. Less common side effects are difficult urination, eye problems, fainting, muscle spasms, sweating, yellow eyes and skin, excitement, jerky movements of the tongue, head, face, mouth, menstrual changes, shuffling walk, skin rashes, sore throat and fever, sexual impotence, and increased sensitivity to light.

2. Antimanics

Lithium	lithium carbonate	Eskalith, Lithane, Lithotabs, Lithobid, Lithonate
	lithium citrate	Cibalith-S
	carbamazepine	Tegretol
	valproate	Depakene, Depakote
	clonazepam	Klonopin

These drugs are used to treat mood disorders, especially manic episodes that involve excessive talkativeness, elation, increased physical activity, insomnia, hostility, poor judgment, and aggressiveness. Since their effective dose is very close to the lethal dose, regular blood checks are imperative. Common side effects are nausea, decreased sexual ability, dry mouth, increased urination, shakiness, dizziness, and thirstiness. Less common side effects are blurred vision, jerking of arms and legs, weakness, swelling of hands and feet, drowsiness, mental confusion, stomach pains, and slurred speech.

3. Antidepressants

Tricyclics	amitriptyline	Elavil, Endep
	desipramine	Norpramin, Pertofrane
	doxepin	Sinequan, Adapin
	imipramine	Tofranil, Janimine
	nortriptyline	Aventyl, Pamelor
Polycyclics	amoxapine	Asendin
	maprotiline	Ludiomil
MAO inhibitors	isocarboxazid	Marplan
	phenelzine	Nardil
	selegiline	Eldepryl
	tranylcypromine	Parnate
Serotonin-specific	bupropion	Wellbutrin
reuptake inhibitors	fluoxetine	Prozac
	paroxetine	Paxil
	sertraline	Zoloft
	trazodone	Desyrel

These drugs relieve depression, and some of them may alleviate anxiety. They may not take effect for several days or weeks. Common side effects are dry mouth, dry skin, light-headedness, blurred vision, difficulty urinating, numbness, tingling in hands and feet, weight gain or loss, constipation, headaches, rapid pulse, and drowsiness. Less common effects are confusion, disturbed concentration, abdominal swelling, sore throat and fever, disorientation, seizures, and irregular heartbeat. Prozac, Paxil, and Zoloft seem to have fewer immediate undesirable side effects; but because they are so new, their long-term effects are unknown. They are also used to treat conditions other than depression.

4. Antianxiety agents

Benzodiazepine	alprazolam	Xanax
	chlordiazepoxide	Librium, Libritabs, Lipoxide
	diazepam	Valium, Valrelease, Vazepam, Zetran
	lorazepam	Ativan
	oxazepam	Serax
	prazepam	Centrax

These addictive drugs are sometimes called "minor tranquilizers," but this is inappropriate. As Gerald Klerman observed in 1974, "The major tranquilizer–minor tranquilizer distinction is inadequate and inaccurate. It implies that the [antianxiety agents are] basically similar to the phenothiazine group, but contain weaker pharmacologic compounds. This is not accurate and it is far better to see these two classes of compounds as qualitatively different." Antianxiety agents are used to relieve tension and anxiety, panic, agitation, acute muscle spasms, and acute alcoholism. Common side effects are blurred vision, drowsiness, headache, weakness, constipation, diarrhea, nausea, vomiting, stomach pain, difficulty urinating, clumsiness, unsteadiness, dizziness, and slurred speech. Less common are ulcers or sores in the mouth or throat, sore throat and fever, skin rash or itching, mental confusion, hallucinations, unusual excitement, nervousness, irritability, and insomnia.

5. Antiparkinsonian (anticholinergic) agents

benztropine	Cogentin
diphenhydramine	Benadryl
levodopa	Dopar, Larodopa
trihexyphenidyl	Aphen, Artane, Tremin, Trihexane

These drugs are used to relieve the side effects of other psychoactive drugs like muscle stiffness, rigidity, slurred speech, and uncontrollable movements. They have their own side effects such as skin rash, confusion, dizziness, drowsiness, weakness, tachycardia, dry mouth, nausea, vomiting, constipation, blurred vision, urinary retention, elevated temperature, flushing, numbness of fingers, and decreased sweating.

Electroshock

In addition to psychoactive drugs, physically intrusive therapies like electroshock and psychosurgery are available to the psychotherapist. Critics suggest that the ill effects of electroshock can be as intrusive, devastating, and permanent as those of psychosurgery. Severe and enduring memory loss is a serious but low-probability risk. Though rarely used today, this procedure still seems beneficial, though risky, as Louisa Brownell explains, for extreme depression where all else has failed. No one really knows how and why it works when it does. The strategy is to go in, stir up the brain, and hope that things are better afterwards.

Psychosurgery

The modification or destruction of brain tissue for the purpose of altering mental functions like thinking, feeling, willing, and action is called psychosurgery. Although defended in its modern form by Rael Jean Isaac and Virginia C. Armat, it is probably the most objectionable of all the therapies used on mental patients; readers should take seriously the difficulties with electroshock to which they try to reply. Stephen Chorover wrote in 1974, "Psychotherapists have failed to provide balanced accounts of their cases," meaning that psychosurgeons tend to ignore the irreversible ill effects of their work. This has likely changed very little since he wrote.

Peter Breggin identified many value problems connected with psychosurgery in 1982. Worldwide, most of it was, and may still be, performed without the informed consent of patients; and more often than not it was and is performed on women, children, the aged, the institutionalized, and disadvantaged minorities. The notorious obscurity of the concept of "mental illness" is well illustrated by the fact that psychosurgery has been performed to correct neurotic anxieties, hyperactivity, restlessness, warmheartedness, conscientiousness, perfectionism, thoughtfulness, homosexuality, frigidity, promiscuity, strong emotions, gambling, alcoholism, drug addiction, depression, violence, and childhood misbehavior, among others.

What counts as "cure" or therapeutic "success" in psychosurgery? The primary criteria of success for older lobotomies were passivity or manageability, with or without terminating the aforementioned "deviancies," and usually at the price of terminating or drastically reducing practically all distinctively human psychological functions and activities. Lobotomies performed between 1935 and 1952 caused very serious quality-of-life problems; they eliminated many very desirable human capacities along with undesirable behavior. Irreversible ill effects were: a severe blunting of thought, memory, motivation, emotion, spontaneity, creativity, moral sensitivity, love, empathy, enjoyment, self-knowledge, self-control, and so on. The resulting emptiness of consciousness was something that only a Zen Buddhist would envy! Newer psychosurgical techniques, defended in the following article by Isaac and Armat, attempt to avoid these unwanted side effects; but the degree of success is very uncertain.

Psychosurgery presupposes the questionable theory that undesirable behaviors are permanently located in small, definite, independent, and identifiable portions of the brain whose functions do not vary with environmental circumstances, and that undesirable behaviors can be eliminated if these brain areas are destroyed. Unfortunately, the locus of undesirable behaviors in the brain is not easily identifiable, not permanent, not contained in discrete areas that affect nothing else, and not independent of what is happening in the immediate environment. Writing of earlier psychosurgeons' attempts to eliminate aggressiveness, Eliot Valenstein noted in 1978:

> Aggression does not live in the caudate nucleus or in any other single brain area. When we speak of behavior as complex as aggression, it is clear that a large amount of brain is involved. Moreover, any single area

plays a role in many different kinds of behavior—some desirable, some undesirable, depending on circumstances and our own attitudes, at any given moment about what is desirable. The belief that we can stimulate or destroy a given region of the brain and change one and only one type of behavior is sheer fantasy.

Behavior Modification

Almost everything that happens to patients in mental hospitals is called "therapy," including just being in the new environment of the psychiatric ward (milieu therapy), watching television for hours each day (TV therapy), and solitary confinement (time-out therapy). All this therapy is directed supposedly at solving the patient's "real problem," but different schools of psychology have radically divergent accounts of what a patient's problem really is. Some posit deep psychic distortions called functional "mental illnesses" as causes of crazy behavior. Others contend that deviant behaviors are caused by environmental stresses, particularly in the patient's family situation, and that these are the real problem. Some insist that the real problem is organic, a matter of abnormal brain structure and chemistry. Still others repudiate all of the above and claim that the real problem is just the aberrant behaviors themselves, nothing more. Behaviorists holding this view developed behavior modification therapy. They maintain that mental illnesses are merely learned maladaptive behaviors that can be unlearned, especially with a little help.

Behavior modification professes to get at the patient's "real problem" directly, quickly, and economically, without positing mysterious mental causes or nonexistent organic abnormalities and without employing objectionable bodily interventions or years of expensive and ineffective talk therapy. In commenting on the relative ethical merits of what he called "talk therapy" or "insight therapy" versus "action therapy," Perry London wrote in 1977 that insight therapy assumes "that the only proper locus of behavior control is self-control," that this "results from expanding consciousness," and that this can be accomplished "by verbal means." By contrast, action or behavior modification therapy assumes that "the proper locus of behavior control belongs with the therapist," that "his job is to give the patient not self-control but symptom relief," and that "whatever works without damaging the patient is acceptable." Behavior modification strategies use refinements of Pavlovian conditioning—rewarding or positively reinforcing desirable behaviors, and/or negatively reinforcing undesirable ones.

In his essay, Teodoro Ayllon explores the therapeutic and ethical merits and demerits of behavior modification techniques like desensitization, token economies, aversive conditioning, and others. Though not always observed, behavior modification techniques ought never dehumanize patients by violating their basic legal and moral rights, Ayllon affirms. Because patients have rights to the basic necessities of a dignified human existence, behavior therapists should not employ powerful human motivators like depriving patients of food, drink, shelter, safety, privacy, and the like. Unless these fundamentals are assured, the likelihood of abuse is overwhelming. Ingenious behavior therapists still have enormous room for therapeutic maneuvering once essential patient rights are assured.

Finally, many sexual malfunctions classified as mental disorders in *DSM-IV* are treated by psychotherapists and physicians, as L. P. Kok explains. Physical treatments may be used, especially where malfunctions are thought to have organic causes. Sex therapies may be evaluated by cost/benefit analysis, assuming that ethical conditions like informed consent and confidentiality have been met. Some social and behavioral therapies may be ethically problematic, such as using surrogate partners and encouraging masturbation to shift the focus of patients' sexual desires from unacceptable objects (such as children, animals) to more acceptable ones (but mere objects all the same). How do we decide if these treatments are morally appropriate? Consider the answer provided in 1989 by Benedict Ashlep and Kevin O'Rourke, two Roman Catholic moral thinkers. In addition to commending confidentiality and not having sex with patients, they suggest that "persons involved should not be asked to perform actions that are immoral or contrary to their conscience. Thus use of surrogate partners as well as activities otherwise deviant must be rejected" (page 357). Could we accept their general principle, even if we cannot accept all of their examples of unnatural deviancies such as using surrogate partners (regarded even by Thomas Szasz as prostitutes [1980]), reorienting masturbation, and contraception? Consider this question as you read Kok. What else should be considered?

An Introduction to Pharmacotherapy for Mental Disorders

John R. Hughes and Robert A. Pierattini

Both psychotherapy and pharmacotherapy are well-accepted treatments for several mental disorders (American Psychiatric Association, 1989). With some disorders, psychotherapy but not pharmacotherapy is the major therapy (e.g., sexual disorders). Other disorders require pharmacotherapy but not psychotherapy as the major therapy (e.g., bipolar disorders). Finally, in some disorders, both treatments are effective (e.g., major depression) and clinicians and patients can choose either therapy or can combine the two treatments.

Psychologists need to be familiar with pharmacotherapies for several reasons. First, some of their patients will already be on medications when first seen. In one survey, 79% of psychologists reported having patients who receive psychoactive medications (Beitman, 1991). Psychoactive medications can influence the assessment and psychotherapeutic treatment of patients. For example, the side effects of certain medications can change the symptomatic presentation (e.g., tremulousness induced by some antidepressants can resemble anxiety and akinesia induced by some antipsychotics can look like depression). Cessation of such medications can induce new symptoms (e.g., anxiety). Second, psychologists must be familiar with the conditions for which psychoactive medications may be important primary or adjunctive treatments. For example, psychoactive medication for patients with mania or acute psychosis is viewed by many as essential, and referral for medication evaluation would be indicated.

Third, familiarity with pharmacotherapy permits psychologists to recognize inappropriate drug therapy. For example, some patients use tricyclic antidepressants on an ad lib basis and some primary physicians still use antipsychotics to treat anxiety disorders. Finally, psychologists are sometimes asked by patients, families, or social systems to render an opinion about pharmacotherapy for psychological and behavioral symptoms.

There are many existing books on the use of psychoactive medications (American Psychiatric Association, 1989; Baldessarini, 1985; Bassuk, Schoonover, & Gelenberg, 1990; Beitman & Klerman, 1991; Ellison, 1989; Fisher & Greenberg, 1989; Gitlin, 1990; Goldenberg, 1990; Gorman, 1990; Guttmacher, 1988; Hersen, 1986; Julien, 1988; Klein, Gittelman, Quitkin, & Rifkin, 1980; Lader & Herrington, 1990; Lawson & Cooperrider, 1988; Preston & Johnson, 1990; Shader, 1975). A condensation of these books into one chapter can provide only limited coverage of the various disorders, symptoms and medications.

The purpose of the present chapter is to provide a brief overview of the therapeutic use of psychoactive medications. Indications for pharmacotherapy, effects of pharmacotherapy, and appropriateness of medication administration will be considered. This chapter provides several general guidelines. These should not be viewed as standards or rules of expected behavior. As with psychotherapy, the complexity of patient histories and current conditions are such that blind following of a priori rules can be detrimental to the patient. Consideration will be given first to the major disorders and which psychoactive medications might be indicated, how such medications are typically used, and what the major side effects are. Then, the general principles used in prescribing psychoactive medications (e.g., how medications are chosen, monitored, combined with psychotherapy, etc.) will be presented.

Indications for the Use of Psychoactive Medications

Psychoactive medication use is usually based on either diagnostic or symptom-relief indications. A diagnostic indication occurs when a specific disorder is diagnosed and this leads to the selection of a specific pharmacological class of medications. The importance of diagnostics to the choice of psychoactive medications is often overlooked. Its importance resides in the fact that the efficacy of many medications is limited to specific disorders. For example, antidepressants improve the mood of patients with major depressive disorders but do not improve the mood of patients whose depressions are due to recent environmental events (i.e., an adjustment disorder). In fact, such diagnosis/medication specificity has been used to argue the validity of certain psychiatric disorders.

There are several disorders in which medications can be indicated

Table 1
Commonly Used Medications For The Major Psychiatric Disorders

Disorder	Medication
Disorders first evident in infancy, childhood, or adolescence	
Attention-deficit hyperactivity disorder	Stimulants
Tic disorder	Antipsychotics
Organic Mental Disorders (OMD)	
Dementia	
with delirium	Antipsychotics
with delusions	Antipsychotics
with depression	Antidepressants
Psychoactive Substance-induced OMD	
Alcohol withdrawal	Benzodiazepines
Nicotine withdrawal	Nicotine agonists
Opioid withdrawal	Opioid agonists
Sedative/Hypnotic/Anxiolytic withdrawal	Benzodiazepines
OMD Associated with Physical Disorders	
with delirium	Antipsychotics
with delusions	Antipsychotics
with depression	Antidepressants
Psychoactive Substance Use Disorder	
Alcohol dependence	Disulfiram
Nicotine dependence	Nicotine replacement
Opioid dependence	Opioid agonists
Schizophrenia	Antipsychotics
Major depression	Antidepressants
Bipolar disorder	Lithium
with mania	Antipsychotics, Benzodiazepines
with depression	Antidepressants
Generalized anxiety disorder	Benzodiazepines
Panic disorders/agoraphobia	Antidepressants
Obsessive-compulsive disorder	Clomipramine

(Table 1). The three most important classes of disorders are psychotic, mood and anxiety disorders.

PSYCHOPHARMACOLOGICAL TREATMENT OF THE PSYCHOSES

The major psychotic disorder in the *Diagnostic and Statistical Manual of Mental Disorders* (*DSM-III-R*; American Psychiatric Association, 1987) is schizophrenia. The acute phase of this disorder is dominated by "positive" symptoms of illogical thought processes, delusions and hallucinations. Between acute phases, the "negative symptoms" of social isolation, markedly eccentric behavior, blunted or inappropriate affect, odd or magical thinking, perceptual disturbances (illusions, etc.), impaired hygiene, and lack of interests and initiative predominate. Often some negative symptoms occur during the acute period and some positive symptoms remain between acute episodes.

Psychoactive medications used to combat psychotic disorders have been referred to as antipsychotics, major tranquilizers, neuroleptics, or analeptics. The first class of antipsychotics were the phenothiazines which were followed by other effective medications, notably haloperidol. The mechanism of action of traditional antipsychotics is blockage of the D_2 dopamine receptor in the mesolimbic system. Antipsychotics are quite effective in treating an acute episode of positive symptoms. Larger doses are used initially to calm patients suffering from schizophrenia and then decreased. Although antipsychotics usually calm patients within 1–3 days, there is often a 2–8-week lag before these medications significantly improve delusions, hallucinations, and illogical thinking. Traditional antipsychotics are either not effective or, if so, minimally effective for negative symptoms of schizophrenia. Antipsychotics vary little in efficacy but do vary in side effects. High potency medications (e.g., haloperidol) have high potential for extrapyramidal side effects and little for anticholinergic and autonomic side effects. Low potency medications (e.g., chlorpromazine) have less extrapyramidal and more anticholinergic effects. Extrapyramidal symptoms are due to dopamine blockade in the nigrostriatal pathways and include dystonias (involuntary contractions of the tongue, neck muscles, etc.), akathisias (motor restlessness) and parkinsonian-like symptoms (akinesia [slow and difficult movement of large muscle groups], rigidity and slow tremors). Anticholinergic side effects include constipation, dry mouth, difficulty urinating, blurred vision, and sexual dysfunction. Autonomic effects include postural hypotension (an exaggerated fall in blood pressure upon standing resulting in dizziness and the possibility of fainting or falling) and cardiac arrhythmias. Antipsychotics also cause sedation and weight gain. Abrupt cessation of antipsychotics can cause a withdrawal syndrome of insomnia, gastrointestinal problems, sweating, and extrapyramidal side effects.

The class of side effects that has most influenced the use of antipsychotic medications is tardive dyskinesia (Cummings & Wirshing, 1989). Tardive dyskinesia is involuntary muscle movements of the face and tongue that can occur with chronic use of antipsychotics. The risk of tardive dyskinesia increases with age, the dose and duration of use of antipsychotics and concomitant organic brain syndrome. Unfortunately, tardive dyskinesia is often irreversible and untreatable. Thus, many psychiatrists will not use antipsychotics unless it is clear they are essential and other medications cannot substitute.

The exception among antipsychotics is the newly released medication clozapine. Clozapine is an effective antipsychotic that does not appear to work via dopamine blockade, produces little or no extrapyramidal side effects, may affect negative as well as positive symptoms and, importantly, improves 30%-50% of schizophrenics who have not responded to traditional antipsychotics. One problem with clozapine is that in approximately 2% of the patients, white blood cell production is inhibited and this can be fatal. Due to this complication, weekly blood work is necessary to detect this problem early on. The second problem is that clozapine is expensive.

Most of the side effects of antipsychotics are dose related; thus, one usually tries to find the lowest effective dose. However, blood levels of the drug do not appear to be helpful, and it is often difficult to dose-titrate patients.

Schizophrenia is typically a relapsing disorder. Patients who have had two or more episodes are usually placed on a lower dose of the antipsychotic for at least 6 months to decrease relapses. Such therapy decreases the chance of relapse in the first year from 60% to 30%. The duration of maintenance therapy of antipsychotics usually increases with the number of prior episodes and the severity of those episodes.

PSYCHOPHARMACOLOGICAL TREATMENT OF MOOD DISORDERS

Major depression refers to a prolonged depressed mood that has associated symptoms of diminished interest in or pleasure in activities, fatigue, guilt or worthlessness, difficulty thinking and deciding, and thoughts of death. More importantly, several "neurovegetative" signs or symptoms occur as well: weight loss, insomnia or hypersomnia, and psychomotor agitation or retardation. It is the presence of these latter symptoms, a definite onset and course to the depression, and the all-day, everyday mood disturbance that predict a positive response to medication therapy. Because 60% of major depressions reoccur, many patients are placed on 6–12 months of preventive therapy.

Antidepressants are the psychoactive medications of choice for this disorder. Tricyclic (three-ring) antidepressants have traditionally been the mainstay of treatment. Their mechanism of action is thought to be the blockade of reuptake of catecholamines (norepinephrine and serotonin) thereby increasing the amount of catecholamines in the synaptic cleft. Tricyclic antidepressants often take 2-6 weeks to work but are effective in 60%–80% of cases. They can be classified as more serotonergic (e.g., amitriptyline) or more adrenergic (desipramine). The more serotonergic tricyclic antidepressants have more anticholinergic side effects and are more sedating. Other side effects of tricyclic antidepressants include autonomic side effects, weight gain and, when taken in overdoses, especially with alcohol, death. Abrupt cessation of tricyclic antidepressants can produce withdrawal symptoms of rebound insomnia, gastrointestinal problems, nausea, and vomiting. Blood levels are available for several tricyclic antidepressants and these are somewhat related to outcome.

In addition to tricyclic antidepressants, several polycyclic (many-ringed) and noncyclic antidepressants have been marketed in the last 15 years. They appear to be equally efficacious; however, some appear to have fewer side effects (e.g., fluoxetine has less weight gain and anticholinergic effects than tricyclic antidepressants).

Sometimes major depressions include psychotic features (e.g., delusions of having caused some disaster). Antidepressants alone are less effective in these depressions and one must consider the addition of antipsychotic medications. Major depressions that do not respond to tricyclic antidepressants are often treated by adding a second medication such as lithium, thyroid, or amphetamine or by switching to electroconvulsive therapy.

The other class of psychoactive medications effective in major depression is monoamine oxidase (MAO) inhibitors. MAO is an enzyme that breaks down catecholamines in the synaptic cleft; thus, by inhibiting this enzyme, MAO inhibitors increase catecholamines in the cleft. MAO inhibitors require patients to follow a special diet as ingesting tyramine can provoke a hypertensive crisis. This requirement led MAO inhibitors to fall out of favor when tricyclic antidepressants became available. Other common side effects of MAO inhibitors include anticholinergic effects, stimulation, sexual problems, dizziness, insomnia, and agitation. Whether the efficacy of MAO inhibitors for major depression is equivalent to that of tricyclic antidepressants is debatable; thus, MAO inhibitors are often used as a second-line drug. On the other hand, recent evidence suggests MAO inhibitors may be especially effective for "atypical" depressions; that is, those with hypersomnia, hyperphagia, mood swings, rejection sensitivity, and hypochondriasis.

The other major mood disorder is bipolar disorder (manic-depression) which consists of manic states with or without depressive episodes. Manic states are characterized by an elevated or irritable mood plus grandiosity; less need for sleep; loquacity; flight of ideas or tangential speech; distractibility; increased activity; and monetary, sexual, or other indiscretions.

Lithium is the treatment of choice and is effective in 70%–80% of cases. Its mechanism of action is not well understood. Patients typically have blood levels taken daily until lithium blood levels of 0.6–1.2 mEq/l are consistently reached. Often lithium is not completely adequate at first and a sedating medication, which can usually be stopped after 1–2 weeks, is added. The major side effects of lithium are tremors, polyuria, muscle weakness, anorexia, and gastrointestinal problems. Lithium can also induce hypothyroid disorders, conduction defects in the heart, and renal problems but these are rare. Lithium is not a trailquilizer and does not cause sedation. Dehydration with exercise, heat, or other medications, can cause lithium intoxication. Lithium overdoses can be fatal.

Bipolar disorder patients also have depressive episodes that are symptomatically similar to major depression. Although lithium can be used to treat this as well, usually an antidepressant is needed. Lithium is also used as a preventive; thus patients are usually maintained on lithium after their acute episode.

Whether other mood disorders (e.g., dysthymia [chronic depressed mood with fewer vegetative signs]) and organic affective disorders (e.g., from neurological disorders) are responsive to medication therapy is not well documented. Thus, in these disorders it must be decided whether the benefits of a medication trial outweigh its possible costs.

PSYCHOPHARMACOLOGICAL TREATMENT OF ANXIETY DISORDERS

Generalized anxiety disorder is characterized in *DSM-III-R* as unrealistic or excessive anxiety or worry accompanied by symptoms of motor tension (e.g., trembling, restlessness, or fatigue); autonomic hyperactivity (e.g., shortness of breath, dizziness, tachycardia, palpitations, tremor and sweating); and hypervigilance (e.g., easily startled, insomnia, difficulty concentrating). Benzodiazepines are quite effective in reducing this type of anxiety. Their mechanism of action appears to be due to interactions at the benzodiazepine/gamma-aminobutyric acid (GABA)/chlorine (Cl) channel receptor. Prior to the benzodiazepines, barbiturates and other drugs (e.g., meprobamate) were used. Benzodiazepines are far superior to these drugs because benzodiazepines have less abuse potential and are unlikely to result in death in an overdose (unless combined with alcohol and other sedatives).

Benzodiazepines differ in their rate of absorption and elimination. Medications with rapid onset of effects (e.g., diazepam) are useful for quickly sedating patients; however, they are thought to have more abuse liability. Those with a rapid offset and shorter half-lives (e.g., alprazolam) are less likely to accumulate over time but are thought to have more potential to produce withdrawal when stopped. Those with longer half-lives (e.g., prazepam) are able to be used on a daily basis but have more potential for accumulation in the elderly and others unless the dose is appropriately adjusted. Typically, elderly patients require lower doses than do younger patients.

Sedation is the major acute side effect of benzodiazepine. Dizziness, ataxia (balance problems), amnesia, nausea, hypotension and changes in liver function are less common. Another side effect is physical dependence—tolerance and withdrawal. Although significant tolerance occurs in some patients, in most this is not a problem. Benzodiazepine withdrawal may include anxiety, insomnia, tremors, weakness, tachycardia, sweating, hypotension, perceptual disturbances, and, rarely, seizures or delirium. About 30%–50% of patients on benzodiazepine chronically will have significant withdrawal. Since withdrawal symptoms are similar to those of anxiety, it may be difficult to distinguish withdrawal from a return of the anxiety disorder being treated. In addition, a minority of patients cannot stop benzodiazepines despite several attempts, due in part to this withdrawal syndrome. Abuse (i.e., use of benzodiazepine for recreational purposes) is rare among patients unless they have a past history of alcohol or drug abuse.

Whether benzodiazepine should be prescribed chronically for generalized anxiety disorder is controversial. Most physicians try to stop benzodiazepine every so often to verify they are still necessary; however, due to withdrawal symptoms, this is often not accomplished.

Due to the side effects associated with long-term use, many clinicians will try psychological therapies for generalized anxiety disorder before considering benzodiazepines. Others believe the side effects of benzodiazepines are uncommon and cite compliance problems with psychotherapies and use benzodiazepine as a first-line therapy.

Several nonbenzodiazepine medications that have essentially no physical dependence or abuse potential have been tried. Beta-blockers (e.g., propranolol), tricyclic antidepressants, and clonidine are sometimes effective. A new drug, buspirone, may be a significant advance in this area as it appears to be an anxiolytic barren of the side effects mentioned in the previous paragraph. However, many clinicians believe buspirone is less effective than benzodiazepines.

Panic disorder consists of repeated episodes of unprovoked intense anxiety accompanied by autonomic symptoms (see generalized anxiety disorder in the previous paragraph) plus chest pain, fear of dying, et cetera. Tricyclic antidepressants are the mainstay of treatment for panic disorders. Alprazolam and MAO inhibitors have also been recommended but due to their side effect profiles, tricyclic antidepressants are often preferred. The mechanism of action for the tricyclic antidepressants and monoamine oxidase inhibitors in panic disorders is unclear.

Agoraphobia is a fear of being in situations in which it would be difficult to escape from or get help if one suddenly developed embarrassing or incapacitating symptoms. This fear results in a restriction of travel away from home. Panic attacks are often accompanied by agoraphobia but agoraphobia can occur in the absence of panic attacks. Tricyclic antidepressants are also first-line medications in this disorder; however, behavioral and other psychological therapies are often effective.

In obsessive-compulsive disorders, obsessions are defined as recurrent, intrusive and senseless thoughts (which are often fears) and compulsions as repetitive behaviors in response to the obsessions (often rituals to neutralize a feared event). Tricyclic antidepressants are also effective in treating obsessive-compulsive disorders; however, unlike other disorders, a single tricyclic antidepressant, clomipramine, appears to be more effective than others. The mechanism of action for clomipramine is unclear.

Pharmacotherapies for other anxiety disorders (e.g., post-traumatic stress disorder and social phobias) have been tested with varying degrees of success. . . .

Epistemology of Clinicians' and Patients' Beliefs about Psychoactive Medications

Several nonscientific factors may play a role in decisions on whether to use medications or psychotherapy. One possible factor is that both patients and clinicians have biases for or against psychological or pharmacological treatments based on training, clinical experiences or general philosophical grounds. Sometimes a prior experience of the patient or his or her relative or friend (e.g., a failure to respond to a medication) will be the major basis for this belief. It is important to elicit patient beliefs and deal with them early on in the decision to use or not to use psychoactive medication (Bassuk et al., 1990; Beitman & Klerman, 1991; Gorman, 1990; Hersen, 1986; Lawson & Cooperrider, 1988).

Biases that might encourage patients to use medication and avoid psychological treatments include ease of treatment, desire for immediate symptom relief, avoidance of making tough or emotionally taxing decisions, avoiding responsibility for one's problems, and fear of loss of control of emotions in psychotherapy. Biases that might encourage avoiding medications and using psychological treatment include a history of medication sensitivity, fear of side effects, fear of delegating emotional control to medications, reluctance to attribute the problem to biological factors and avoidance of labeling the problem as a psychiatric disorder. . . .

Principles in the Rational Use of Psychoactive Medications

CHOICE OF MEDICATIONS

Usually medications are chosen by pharmacological class. As described previously, despite the advertisements of pharmaceutical companies, medications within a pharmacological class usually have similar efficacy. The history of most psychoactive medications has been one of claims of therapeutic superiority, followed by a reactionary scapegoating of the medication, followed finally by a more reasonable evaluation of the appropriate indications and realistic benefits and liabilities of the new medication as compared to existing medications. Prescribing practices often follow a similar trajectory. For example, benzodiazpines were first enthusiastically prescribed, then avoided as extremely dangerous, and are now used judiciously.

Since efficacy is typically similar within a class, specific medications are usually chosen for other reasons. First and foremost, medications within a class can vary in side effect profiles. For example, some antidepressants are sedating and others stimulating. When taken at night, the former might be helpful to depressed patients with insomnia, whereas when taken during the day, the latter might be more helpful to those who are apathetic or retarded.

Second, psychoactive medications vary by how quickly they are taken up by the blood system and how long effective blood levels are maintained. For example, a benzodiazepine with a long half-life may be preferred so that a patient will have to take the medication only once a day, whereas a benzodiazepine with a short half-life may be preferred in an elderly person who might accumulate the drug over time.

Third, sometimes psychoactive medications are chosen because the patient has responded to the medication before or even because a close family member with a similar disorder has responded to the medication.

Fourth, psychoactive medications vary in route of administration. Liquid medication is used sometimes in noncompliant or elderly patients to insure the medication is delivered. Long-acting injectable medication (i.e., one injection every 2–4 weeks) is sometimes used in patients with schizophrenia as they are often noncompliant to oral medication regimens.

Fifth, generic medications are often prescribed. Psychoactive medications have a generic name (the name of the chemical) and a trade (i.e., brand) name. When a pharmaceutical company develops a medication, through patent laws it has sole rights to market the medication for up to 17 years since its discovery. Once this patent expires other pharmaceutical companies can market the chemical equivalent of the drug (i.e., a generic). Although the substitutability of generics is controversial and may vary across types of medications (Strom, 1987), our opinion is that for the large majority of psychoactive medications, generic substitutes are acceptable.

Sixth, combination products (i.e., two medications in one tablet) are typically not chosen as this limits flexibility in dosing and confuses decisions as to which medication to attribute improvement.

CHOICE OF DOSE AND SCHEDULE

The effects of medications vary by dose, preparation, and other factors. Choosing the right psychoactive medicine but the wrong dose can be equivalent to choosing the wrong medication. In fact, it may be worse, in that an effective medicine is falsely deemed ineffective. This is not unlike stating that the effect of psychological interventions vary by their intensity and duration and that poorly administered psychotherapies can be falsely deemed ineffective.

The effective dose differs greatly across patients. Dose-response relationships often show an inverted U-shaped pattern—at doses below a certain level little effect is seen, at moderate levels efficacy is seen, and at high levels side effects interfere with efficacy. Unfortunately, both the relationship between dose and blood levels and between blood levels and response varies widely across individuals. Blood levels from a given dose of medication often vary 10-fold across individuals (Glassman et al., 1985). These differences can be due to differences in the rate of absorption, distribution among body compartments (e.g., fat vs muscle vs organs), protein binding in the blood, metabolism by the liver, and elimination by the kidney. Thus, the existence of certain medical disorders (e.g., liver or kidney disease) can have a profound effect on absorption and elimination. Use of other substances (e.g., cigarette smoking, caffeine) and other medications (e.g., barbiturates) can increase the elimination of several medications such that a patient using these substances will require higher doses. Response to a given dose of a drug is especially idiosyncratic in several populations, including the elderly, the mentally retarded, those with neurological disease, alcohol/drug abusers, and children.

Doses cited in texts should not be taken as rigid standards. These are the doses the "average" patient will require; thus, many patients will require larger or smaller doses than listed. Effective doses of the same medication vary 20-fold across patients. Because many patients and non-physicians rely on the *PDR*, the *PDR* usually lists conservative dose recommendations and ranges. Effective doses also vary 50-fold across medications within a class. For example, among antipsychotics, 2 mg of haloperidol is similar in effect to 100 mg of chlorpromazine. Patients often think the medication with the higher numerical dose is more toxic and should be avoided. In reality, the relative potency of medications often has little correlation with efficacy or toxicity.

For several medications (e.g., antidepressants and antipsychotics), small doses are prescribed initially and then slowly raised until therapeutic effects or side effects are seen. Sometimes doses are given multiple times per day early on and then switched to single daily dosing. The final dose may be as much as 10 times greater than the initial dose. This dose-titration procedure can be prolonged since the effects of a given dose may not be evident for 2–4 weeks after each dose change.

In contrast, some psychiatric medications (e.g., lithium) are given on a fixed time schedule (e.g., twice a day) and others (e.g., benzodiazepines) are sometimes given ad libitum (for example, when the patient needs some relief). Interestingly, although ad libitum dosing is effective with acute dosing, chronic dosing of benzodiazepines and narcotic analgesics may be more effective with fixed-time dosing than with ad libitum dosing and may be less likely to lead to prescription misuse.

The utility of blood levels of medications varies widely across medications. For example, lithium levels are necessary for its use, whereas the benefits of antidepressant blood levels are more limited (Glassman et al., 1985). At the very least, blood levels can often help determine whether toxic doses are being given and if the patient is taking at least some of the medication.

A common mistake is to use too small a dose for too short a time. For example, many psychiatrists would consider anything short of 4 weeks of an antidepressant at the maximal tolerable dose an inadequate trial. Unfortunately, inadequate treatment is often cited as evidence that a patient will not benefit from a class of medications; thus, falsely denying the patient a possible treatment. A second common mistake is to change doses too quickly. Although some symptoms respond quickly to medication (e.g., acute anxiety), other symptoms have a 2-4 week delay before efficacy is clearly seen (e.g., psychotic and depressive symptoms). A third mistake is to change more than one parameter at a time; for example, lowering the dose of medication and discharging the patient from the hospital the next day.

Whenever possible, medications should be given once daily to improve compliance (Haynes, Taylor, & Sackett, 1979). Medications that are sedating are usually given at night, whereas those with stimulant effects are given early in the day. Usually only enough medication to last until the next visit is given in hopes of reinforcing returning for the next visit or preventing prolonged use without appropriate monitoring. Small amounts of medication (e.g., 1 week supply) are usually given to patients with suicidal ideation or alcohol/drug abuse problems in case the patient attempts to overdose.

Medications are sometimes stopped to determine if the medication is effective or because the period of high risk of relapse has passed. When stopping the use of a medication, it is usually tapered by decreasing the dose over several weeks. This is done for three reasons. First, relapses may occur soon after cessation; thus with a gradual taper, the onset of early symptoms can be detected and medication reinstituted prior to a full-blown relapse. Second, many patients are fearful of stopping medication. A taper is, in effect, a fading procedure for these patients. Third, abrupt cessation can cause withdrawal symptoms.

Withdrawal has traditionally been thought to occur only with dependence-producing drugs; however, as described above, abrupt cessation of several psychiatric drugs that are not abused (e.g., antipsychotics and antidepressants) can lead to a withdrawal syndrome (Dilsaver, 1990). This is probably due to receptor changes responsive to chronic exposure to medication. . . . Medications are essentially removed after five half-lives. A common misperception is that the absence of blood levels of a substance means the absence of any drug effects. However, changes in CNS receptor activity may take longer.

Patients ultimately determine the dose and duration of treatment. Compliance with nonpsychiatric medications is poor (Haynes et al., 1979). Compliance with psychoactive medications is especially problematic due in part to significant side effects from the medication. In addition, some psychiatric patients exhibit disorganized thinking, chaotic lifestyles, denial of having a disorder, denial that medication is needed, social reinforcement of illness behavior, anger at physician or others, and so on. Thus, when treatment fails, noncompliance is one of the first issues to investigate. Techniques to improve compliance have been outlined elsewhere (Haynes et al., 1979). Techniques that are sometimes helpful with psychiatric patients include long-acting injections of medications, home visits, and use of day hospitals or half-way houses.

MONITORING MEDICATION EFFECTS

In most of medicine, the effects of a medication are readily quantifiable (e.g., physical or laboratory changes). With psychoactive medications, the effects of medications can be harder to quantify. In addition, psychoactive medications often take 2–4 weeks to produce their main effects; thus, poor memory can induce clinicians to under- or overestimate the severity of the disorder initially and thus over- or underestimate the efficacy of the psychoactive medication. Thus, it is best to clearly define target symptoms to be helped by the medications and to quantify these either through standardized rating scales or, when possible, operational definitions (Hughes, O'Hara, & Rehm, 1982). Many times significant others can provide such simple ratings. Also, therapists can complete structured interview ratings at the outset of sessions.

SIDE EFFECTS

Side effects occur because few medications are so specific that they do not affect several biological systems. Alternatively, even site-specific medications have diverse effects because specific neurochemical systems influence many forms of behavior.

The use of psychoactive medications is a benefit/risk decision that should include consideration of not only the probability, magnitude, and fidelity of benefit but also the probability, seriousness, and reversibility of side effects. Sometimes psychoactive medications with significant side effects are chosen because alternate treatments are not available and the effect of not treating is likely to be quite detrimental. Informing patients of common or significant potential side effects is critical, and a reasoned discussion of these may ameliorate anxiety about the medications and improve compliance.

The side effects of many psychoactive medications often precede therapeutic effects. Most of the side effects common among psychoactive medications have been described in a previous section. Sedation is an especially common side effect that is potentiated by pre-existing insomnia, alcohol use, and the use of other psychoactive prescription, over-the-counter, or illicit drugs. Prescribers typically warn patients to take care while driving and operating machinery and to abstain from or moderate use of alcohol.

Regulatory agencies require a listing of all side effects in package inserts and the *PDR*. Such lists are quite long because the criteria for calling a symptom a side effect are minimal (i.e., a physician notices a symptom after starting the medication). In fact, none of the standard criteria for assessing causality are necessary: for example, the symptom reoccurs upon rechallenge, the side effect fits with the pharmacological profile of the medication, and so on. In summary, the laundry lists of side effects in the package insert and *PDR* are more useful as a list of possible side effects.

Sometimes side effects can be confused with symptoms of the disorder. For example, the restlessness caused by antipsychotics can be confused with the agitation associated with a worsening of schizophrenia. Side effects can also result from medication interactions (e.g., the use of a diuretic can increase lithium levels and cause lithium intoxication symptoms). A common cause of side effects is intermittent compliance.

Patients who stop a medication for 2–3 days or more may reexperience side effects upon restarting the medication. In fact, astute clinicians use recurrent side effects as an index of suspicion of noncompliance.

There are four approaches to treating initial side effects. First, most side effects abate with time due to tolerance; thus, a common response is to simply wait and see if the side effects abate. Second, side effect profiles differ within a class of medications; thus, one could switch to a different medication. Third, because side effects are usually dose related, one can decrease the dose; however, this also may delay or prevent efficacy. A fourth option is to prescribe a medication to treat the side effects (e.g., antiparkinson medications for extrapyramidal symptoms from antipsychotics). Although this latter option leads to polypharmacy, sometimes the need for treatment is great enough and the options limited such that the addition of an extra medication is justified.

Side effects differ from allergic and toxic effects. Side effects usually occur early in therapy, are dose related, and decrease over time. Allergic effects (e.g., rashes) usually occur at very low doses, are not dose related, and tolerance does not occur. Toxic effects usually occur when medication accumulates over time, when too large a dose is given, or with patient-induced overdoses.

Dependence on or abuse of medication is a side effect about which much confusion exists. Definitions of the terms *abuse* and *dependence* have varied, however, there is some growing consensus (American Psychiatric Association, 1987; Edwards, Arif, & Hodgsen, 1981).

Abuse, which may exist independent of dependence, is usually defined as continuing drug use despite having social or psychological problems from drug use. Dependence can be defined in two ways. The more common way focuses on loss of control of drug use; that is, the drug is used more than was intended, the client is unable to stop using the drug, et cetera. For our purposes we will call this *behavioral dependence*. A second definition focuses on the onset of withdrawal symptoms upon cessation. Tolerance is usually associated with withdrawal and refers to a diminished effect of the drug with repeated dosing. For our purposes, we will call this *physical dependence*.

The probability of abuse and dependence varies greatly across medications. For a given medication, psychiatric patients appear to have a greater probability of abuse and behavioral dependence than general medical patients (Regier et al., 1990; Schneier & Siris, 1987). However, the major factor in predicting abuse and behavioral dependence of prescribed psychoactive medication is a present or past history of alcohol/drug abuse (Portenoy, 1990). In fact, abuse or behavioral dependence on prescribed medication in the absence of such a history is extremely rare.

As discussed in the prior paragraphs, abrupt cessation of several psychoactive medications can induce withdrawal (Dilsaver, 1990). Withdrawal is not the only discontinuation syndrome, and it must be distinguished from rebound symptoms and symptoms indicating a return of the disorder being treated (Pecknold, Swinson, Koch, & Lewis, 1988). Clinically these distinctions can be quite difficult. For example, consider insomnia after cessation of benzodiazepines. Whether this represents withdrawal, rebound, or reemergence of an anxiety disorder is often unclear. Often only abstaining from benzodiazepines for 4 - 6 weeks can clarify the picture. Unfortunately, this is uncomfortable, difficult and unachievable in many patients. In considering withdrawal, it is important to distinguish the withdrawal from medications that may prompt patients to restart medication (e.g., benzodiazepines) from the withdrawal from other medications that rarely cause patients to restart medication (e.g., antipsychotics).

Although abuse, behavioral dependence, and physical dependence often co-exist with illicit drugs, this is often not the case with prescribed psychoactive medications. To illustrate the possible combinations of abuse and dependence, consider the following scenarios. First, a patient with a past history of drug abuse uses benzodiazepines intermittently, often gets into trouble while intoxicated, but can start and stop such use easily and without withdrawal. This is abuse without behavioral or physical dependence. Second, a patient has been using benzodiazepines for 5 years without any problems, has tried to stop in the past and had no significant withdrawal, but cannot seem to stop benzodiazepine use. This is behavioral dependence without abuse or physical dependence. Third, a patient has been using an antidepressant without problems, is asked by the physician to stop it, has withdrawal but successfully stops. This is physical dependence without abuse or behavioral dependence.

USE OF MEDICATION IN SPECIAL POPULATIONS

The diagnosis and treatment of behavioral disorders among children is difficult given (a) the scientific database is small, and (b) there is little data on whether the classic symptom clusters of psychiatric disorders match those of adults (Campbell & Spencer, 1988). However, despite these problems, there is good scientific evidence for the utility of certain psychoactive medications in certain disorders (e.g., stimulants in attention deficit disorder; Kavale, 1982; Rapport, 1984).

One concern with medications in children is that the medication may impede growth, learning, or social development during critical developmental times and, thus, cause what may be irreversible effects. The actual data on this issue are quite mixed (Rapport, 1984). In addition, the very real possibility that the disorder itself is impeding learning and social development is often not considered. Another concern is use of medication leading to illicit drug abuse. Interestingly, this is very rare.

Psychoactive medication is usually used in children when behavioral or psychotherapeutic programs fail. Noncompliance with psychological treatments by children or parents or a lack of resources to implement such treatments often occur. Thus, it is often difficult to decide when to stop trying psychological treatments and add medications.

In children, dosing is often based on body weight. Even so, children vary widely in neurological and intellectual development; thus, idiosyncratic responses are common. In addition, doses for behavioral control and cognitive improvement of children may diverge. For example, low doses of amphetamine improve intellectual performance but not hyperactivity while higher doses of amphetamine improve hyperactivity but worsen intellectual performance (Sprague & Sleator, 1977). Thus, identification of the optimal dose for combined effects is especially important. Finally, "medication holidays" are often used in children to determine if continued medication use is necessary.

Many of the same issues apply to the use of psychoactive medications in the mentally retarded; for example, a poor database, symptom manifestations that may differ from nonretarded adults, noncompliance, and lack of resources for psychological treatments (Aman & Singh, 1988). On the one hand, the mentally retarded often have severe and difficult-to-treat problems, such as self-injurious behavior and physical aggression and failures to respond to behavioral programs do occur. On the other hand, the mentally retarded are at greater risk of developing tardive dyskinesia and other complications (Cummings & Wirshing, 1989). As a result many states have regulations about the indications for and monitoring of medication in the mentally retarded (Rinck, Guidry, & Calkins, 1989).

Mental disorders among the elderly are more difficult to treat with psychoactive medications for several reasons (Jenike, 1989). Physiological changes with aging influence the absorption, binding, distribution, metabolism, and elimination of medications. Many elderly are on several medications, thus increasing the probability of drug interactions. Finally, some elderly have mild symptoms of dementia thereby increasing the probability of noncompliance. All of these can not only impair efficacy but also increase the possibility of side effects. Dosing is usually done cautiously, beginning with very low doses as the elderly often need only half the dose of middle-aged adults.

Women on psychoactive medication may become pregnant (Cohen, Heller, & Rosenbaum, 1989). A clinician should keep this possibility in mind. Almost all psychoactive medications cross the placenta to expose the fetus and are also present in breast milk. Psychoactive medications may cause malformations and perinatal complications (e.g., early delivery). Less well recognized is the possibility that such medications may produce learning and other behavioral deficits in offspring. Thus, when possible, psychoactive medications are discontinued during pregnancy. If continued, the doses of psychoactive medications may be decreased to decrease fetal risk and any resultant increased symptomatology accepted. Two issues arise in stopping or decreasing psychoactive medications during pregnancy. The first is that some patients cannot provide adequate prenatal and self-care without medication and will need to continue medication. The second is that withdrawal effects from too rapid a reduction of medication might harm the fetus.

LEGAL ISSUES

Many states have laws regulating the right to refuse psychoactive medication. Much of the confusion around this issue is whether commitment to a facility implies the right to force medications. Usually danger to self or others are the criteria for both commitment and forcing medication (Appelbaum, 1988; Rinck et al., 1989). There is no legal precedent or tradition to determine when written informed consent should be obtained prior to prescribing a psychotropic drug. Two situations in which informed consent has been recommended include the use of a medication for a disorder not formally approved by the FDA, and the long-term use of antipsychotics (due to the risk of tardive dyskinesia). This latter situation is complicated by the fact that many persons who begin antipsychotics are not able to give true informed consent. However, consent can be sought when delusions and other symptoms have cleared enough to indicate informed consent can be given.

The Drug Enforcement Agency (DEA) regulates medications determined to have significant abuse liability and physicians must have a license from the DEA to prescribe such medications. Several states have introduced triplicate prescription pads for some of these medications. With these pads, a copy of all prescriptions are sent to the state agency responsible for drug abuse litigation. Triplicate prescription systems are intended to make physicians give serious review and consideration before writing prescriptions for these medications. Triplicate plans do decrease prescriptions (Sigier et al., 1984). The debate is whether this is a decrease in inappropriate use of these medications or a decrease in appropriate use of these medications with the result of patients being denied adequate pain relief or other symptom alleviation (Street, 1991).

Pharmacological and Psychological Therapies

Whether psychoactive medication and psychotherapy are combined varies widely across disorders (Hollon & Beck, 1987; Hughes, 1991; Klerman, 1989; Rounsaville, Klerman, & Weissman, 1981). Combined treatment improves outcome beyond either treatment alone in several disorders (i.e., anxiety disorders, depression, nicotine dependence, and schizophrenia). In some disorders, such as schizophrenia and severe depression, pharmacotherapy appears to be essential. For other disorders, psychological treatment appears to be essential (e.g., alcohol dependence).

RELATIVE UTILITY OF PHARMACOLOGICAL VERSUS PSYCHOLOGICAL THERAPIES

Several articles have compared the efficacy of psychoactive medication to psychological treatments for anxiety, depression, and other disorders (Hollon & Beck, 1987). However, efficacy is but one criterion to compare treatments. Other important factors are target outcome, acceptability, availability, safety, universality, and cost-effectiveness (Hollon & Beck, 1987). The utility of a treatment is often determined not by efficacy but by its acceptability and availability. An effective treatment that is not acceptable to many patients (e.g., a medication that has a strong negative impact on sexual desires) or a therapy that is not readily available (e.g., psychotherapists in rural areas) is not very useful.

In terms of target outcome, pharmacological therapy often uses symptom relief as a criterion of success, whereas psychological treatments often use functional criteria (e.g., return to work, etc.). Pharmacotherapy often assumes that symptom relief removes a barrier to functional improvement. Whether this assumption is true probably varies across disorders and patients with the same disorder. There are no sound data on this issue.

COLLABORATION WITH PHYSICIANS

Recent surveys indicate that many psychotherapy patients are being simultaneously treated by a physician and a psychologist (Beitman, 1991). Psychologists should ask about the psychoactive medication their patients are receiving. Some basic information that a psychologist should have about a patient's medication is listed below.

1. What medication (brand name and generic name) is being used.
2. Which DSM disorder or target symptom is being treated.

3. Whether the medication is being used for a diagnosis, for symptom relief, or for prevention.
4. What the expected dose and duration of treatment is.
5. When the medication should begin to work.
6. When and how the patient is to take the medication.
7. How long the patient is to take the medication.
8. What the patient is to do if a dose of medicine is missed.
9. What are the possible side effects of the medication and what should the patient do about them.
10. What are the medication's possible effects on the patient's driving, work, and other activities and what precautions are to be taken.
11. How the medication interacts with alcohol and other drugs.
12. What are the alternative plans if this medication trial fails.

Although patients should know this information, many times physicians fail to make this information clear. Also, existing biases in patients may result in misinterpretation of such information. . . .

Coordinating treatments between physicians and psychologists requires attention and vigilance (Beitman, 1991; Beitman & Klerman, 1991; Ellison, 1989; Gitlin, 1990; Goldenberg, 1990; Guttmacher, 1988; Lader & Herrington, 1990; Lawson & Cooperrider, 1988). Several procedural details need to be explicitly agreed upon: who does the patient call when symptoms worsen or suicidal thoughts occur, how are joint decisions made, and so forth. Finally, some patients are keen to attribute their problem to either a biological cause or a behavior over which they have no control. If physicians and psychologists are not concordant on their view of the problem, the patient can affiliate with the therapist most sympathetic to his or her cause, use one therapist against the other, and not comply with the alternate therapy. . . .

References

Aman, M. G., & Singh, N. N. (1988). *Psychopharmacology of the developmental disabilities.* New York: Springer-Verlag.

American Medical Association Drug Evaluations. (1991). Littleton, MA: Sciences Group.

American Psychiatric Association. (1987). *Diagnostic and statistical manual of mental disorders* (rev. 3rd ed.). Washington, DC: Author.

———. (1989). *Treatment of psychiatric disorders: A task force report of the American Psychiatric Association.* Washington, DC: Author.

Appelbaum, P. S. (1988). The right to refuse treatment with antipsychotic medications: Retrospect and prospect. *American Journal of Psychiatry* 145, 413–19.

Baldessarini, R. (1985). *Chemotherapy in psychiatry.* Cambridge, MA: Harvard University Press.

Barnhart, E. R. (1991). *Physicians' Desk Reference.* Oradell, NJ: Medical Economics Data.

Bassuk, E. L., Schoonover, S. C., & Gelenberg, A. J. (1990). *The practitioner's guide to psychoactive drugs.* New York: Plenum Publishing Corporation.

Beitman, B. D. (1991). Medications during psychotherapy: Case studies of the reciprocal relationship between psychotherapy process and medication use. In B. D. Beitman & G. L. Klerman (Eds.), *Integrating pharmacotherapy and psychotherapy* (pp. 21–44). Washington, DC: American Psychiatric Press.

Beitman, B. D., & Klerman, G. L. (1991). *Integrating pharmacotherapy and psychotherapy.* Washington, DC: American Psychiatric Press.

Campbell, M., & Spencer, E. K. (1988). Psychopharmacology in child and adolescent psychiatry: A review of the past five years. *Journal of the American Academy of Child and Adolescent Psychiatry 27,* 269–79.

Cohen, L. S., Heller, V. L., & Rosenbaum, J. F. (1989). Treatment guidelines for psychotropic drug use in pregnancy. *Psychosomatics 30,* 25–33.

Cummings, J. L., & Wirshing, W. C. (1989). Recognition and differential diagnosis of tardive dyskinesia. *International Journal of Psychiatry in Medicine 19,* 133–44.

Dilsaver, S. T. (1990). Heterocyclic antidepressant, monoamine oxidase inhibitor, and neuroleptic withdrawal phenomena. *Progress in Neuro-Psychopharmacology & Biological Psychiatry 14,* 137–61.

Edwards, G., Arif, A., & Hodgsen, R. (1981). Nomenclature and classification of drug and alcohol-related problems: A WHO memorandum. *Bulletin of the World Health Organization 59,* 225–42.

Ellison, J. M. (1989). *The psychotherapist's guide to pharmacotherapy.* Chicago: Year Book Medical Publishers.

Fisher, S., & Greenberg, R. P. (1989). *The limits of biological treatments for psychological distress: Comparisons with psychotherapy and placebos.* Hillsdale, NJ: Erlbaum.

Gitlin, M. J. (1990). *The psychotherapist's guide to psychopharmacology.* New York: Maxwell Macmillan International.

Glassman, A. H., Schildkraut, J. J., Orsulak, P. J., et al. (1985). Tricyclic antidepressants—Blood level measurements and clinical outcome: An APA Task Force report. *American Journal of Psychiatry 142,* 155–62.

Goldenberg, M. M. (1990). *Pharmacology for the psychotherapist.* Muncie, IN: Accelerated Development.

Gorman, J. M. (1990). *The essential guide to psychiatric drugs.* New York: St. Martin's Press.

Guttmacher, L.B.(1988). *Concise guide to somatic therapies in psychiatry.* Washington, DC: American Psychiatric Press.

Haynes, R. B., Taylor, D. W., & Sackett, D. L. (1979). *Compliance in health care.* Baltimore: Johns Hopkins University Press.

Hersen, M. (1986). *Pharmacological and behavioral treatment: An integrative approach.* New York: Wiley.

Hollon, S. D., & Beck, A. T. (1987). Psychotherapy and drug therapy: Comparisons and combinations. In S. L. Garfield & A. E. Bergin (Eds.), *Handbook of psychotherapy and behavior change* (pp. 437–90). New York: Wiley.

Hughes, J. R. (1991). Combining psychological and pharmacological treatment for smoking. *Journal of Substance Abuse* 3, 337–50.

Hughes, J. R., O'Hara, M. W., & Rehm, L. P. (1982). Measurement of depression in clinical trials: A critical overview. *Journal of Clinical Psychiatry* 43, 85–88.

Jenike, M. A. (1989). *Geriatric psychiatry and psychopharmacology.* Chicago: Yearbook Medical Publisher.

Julien, R. M. (1988). *A primer of drug action* (5th ed.). San Francisco: Freeman.

Kavale, K. (1982). The efficacy of stimulant drug treatment for hyperactivity: A meta-analysis. *Journal of Learning Disabilities* 15, 280–89.

Klein, D. F., Gittelman, R., Quitkin, F., & Rifkin, A. (1980). *Diagnosis and drug treatment of psychiatric disorders: Adults and children.* Baltimore: Williams & Wilkins.

Klerman, G. L. (1989). Drugs and psychotherapy. In S. L. Garfield & A. E. Bergin (Eds.), *Handbook of psychotherapy and behavior change: An empirical analysis* (pp. 777–818). New York: Wiley.

———. (1990). The psychiatric patient's right to effective treatment: Implications of *Osheroff* v. *Chestnut Lodge. American Journal of Psychiatry* 147, 409–18.

Lader, M., & Herrington, R. (1990). *Biological treatments in psychiatry.* New York: Oxford University Press.

Lawson, G. W., & Coopernder, C. A. (1988). *Clinical psychopharmacology: A practical reference for nonmedical psychotherapists.* Rockville, MD: Aspen Publishers, Inc.

Pecknold, J. C., Swinson, R. P., Kuch, K., & Lewis, C. P. (1988). Alprazolam in panic disorder and agoraphobia: Results from a multicenter trial. *Archives of General Psychiatry* 45, 429–36.

Portenoy, R. K. (1990). Chronic opioid therapy in nonmalignant pain. *Journal of Pain and Symptom Management* 5, S46–S62.

Preston, J., & Johnson, J. (1990). *Clinical psychopharmacology made ridiculously simple.* Miami, FL: MedMaster.

Rapport, M. D. (1984). Hyperactivity and stimulant treatment: Abusus non tollit usum. *The Behavior Therapist* 7, 133–34.

Regier, D. A., Fanner, M. E., Rae, D. S., Locke, B. Z., Keith, S. J., Judd, L. L., & Goodwin, F. K. (1990). Comorbidity of mental disorders with alcohol and other drug abuse. *Journal of the American Medical Association* 264, 2511–18.

Rinck, C., Guidry, J., & Catkins, C. F. (1989). Review of states' practices on the use of psychotropic medication. *American Journal on Mental Retardation* 93, 657–68.

Rounsaville, B. J., Klerman, G. L., & Weissman, M. W. (1981). Do psychotherapy and pharmacotherapy for depression conflict? *Archives of General Psychiatry* 38, 24–29.

Schneier, F. R., & Siris, S. G. (1987). A review of psychoactive substance use and abuse in schizophrenia: Patterns of drug choice. *The Journal of Nervous and Mental Disease* 175, 641–52.

Shader, R. I. (1975). *Manual of psychiatric therapeutics.* Boston: Little, Brown.

Sigler, K. A., Guernsey, B. G., Ingrim, N. B., et al. (1984). Effect of a triplicate prescription law on prescribing of Schedule II drugs. *American Journal of Hospital Pharmacy* 41, 108–11.

Sprague, R. L., & Sleator, E. K. (1977). Methylphenidate in hyperkinetic children: Differences in dose effects on learning and social behavior. *Science* 198, 1274–76.

Stone, A. A. (1990). Law, science, and psychiatric malpractice: A response to Klerman's indictment of psychoanalytic psychiatry. *American Journal of Psychiatry* 147, 419–27.

Street, J. P. (1991). Multiple prescription forms don't stop diversion. *American Druggist.*

Strom, B. L. (1987) Generic drug substitution revisited. *New England Journal of Medicine* 316, 1456–62.

Electroconvulsive Therapy— Still Around, Still Controversial

Louisa Brownell

Electroconvulsive therapy, or ECT, is a subject that continues to pro-voke controversy within and among various segments of the mental health community. Nearly 50 years after the techniques were first introduced by Cerletti and Bini in 1938, psychiatrists, other health professionals, patients, and observers continue to disagree about the safety, appropriate uses, administration, effectiveness, and even the purpose of ECT.

The procedures have evolved considerably over the decades. Nowadays, patients are first given a complete physical examination, usually including an EKG and an EEG. Premedication is used to sedate the patient, relax the muscles, and induce sleep. Sometimes oxygen is administered. The patient remains unconscious for about five minutes after the shock is induced then slowly wakes up during the next five to ten minutes.[1] He has no memory of a shock. The combined voltage and time settings constitute the dose. In 1977, it appeared common practice to administer applications ranging in voltage from 70 to 130 and continuing from 0.1 to 0.5 second. Kolb suggested that one usually starts with 80 volts for 0.2 second and if that fails to produce a convulsion, one can increase the voltage to 90 or 100 volts and increase the period of application until a general seizure is induced.[2] Some people believe that it is the seizure itself that is the source of efficacy. Treatments are usually given two or three times a week and number from about five to 30, sometimes followed by maintenance doses.

It appears that both the voltage and length of time of shock may

---

From *Occupational Therapy Forum* 2, no. 20 (1987).

have increased over the last ten years. A study reported in 1986, of sine-wave ECT, had researchers using 130–170 volts for 0.3 to 1.0 second.[3] Another study, referred to in the same article, found researchers using 140 volts for 0.6 second. A third study reported in 1986 cites use of 160 volts for 0.75 second.[4]

The shock may be administered bilaterally, which appears most common, or unilaterally, and it may be administered in a single sine-wave or as a series of brief, lower-voltage pulses. Either way, a generalized seizure is induced.

Physiologically, a number of things happen. According to autopsy reports it appears that a portion of the brain is permanently damaged. The medical literature tends not to dwell on this, saying merely that it is not known exactly how the procedure works. *Journal* articles generally extol the procedure as "safe," apparently meaning that there are few deaths and few fractures as a result of ECT.

Electroshock has been known to produce brain hemorrhage, cerebral edema, and toxic effects resulting from the brain's being exposed to chemicals in the blood that it was ordinarily protected from by the blood-brain barrier. The resulting death of brain cells, which, in turn, result in memory loss, may cause impairment of a severe and long-term nature,[5] although the extent of memory loss has been widely debated. One rationale for the procedure is that by eliminating certain possibly aberrant and dysfunctional neuronal pathways, the brain is forced to develop new and healthier pathways.

Specifically, ECT causes changes in the brain chemicals used to synthesize protein and RNA. The sleep pattern is modified, leading to an increase in total sleep time with diminution of REM sleep. It appears to produce a sustained increase in synthesis and utilization of *norepinephrine* and possibly *dopamine* and *serotonin*.[6] Cerebral dysrhythmia, a slowing of the EEG waves, also occurs; it is long-lasting and possibly permanent. A central vagal discharge leads to a period of brachycardia, with a brief drop in blood pressure followed by tachycardia and a rise in blood pressure. A rise in cerebro-spinal fluid pressure parallels the rise in blood pressure. Apnea always occurs and may, on rare occasions, be prolonged. Prolonged apnea or malignant hyperthermia may also, on rare occasions, occur as a reaction to *succinylcholine,* the muscle relaxant. The occurrence of organic psychosis is a matter of some debate as to frequency; rarely have epilepsy and cardiac arrest followed the shock. When fractures do occur, they are likely to be compression fractures in the neck, or fractures in the femur, acetabulum, or humerus. Dislocation of the jaw has also been reported. Back pain may persist for a few days or weeks.[7] All patients experience confusion in the postictal period and many are disturbed by memory losses and headaches. Less frequently, patients complain of nausea and muscle pain.[8]

What Is the Present Attitude on ECT and Who Is Receiving It?

Phil Brown asserts that a more biomedical and asocial view of mental illness is coming to the forefront in our society. He suggests that renewed biologism, with its emphasis on drugs and medical procedures, stems from psychiatry's attempt to protect its public image and reputation within the medical community. There is, Brown contends, a loss of optimism concerning social treatments and a corresponding paradigm shift. Procedures such as psychosurgery, electroshock, and aversive conditioning may not be increasing, and they may take place in fewer settings, but in absolute numbers of treatments they do not appear to be declining.[9]

A review of literature is complicated by several factors, including differences in research methodologies, the tendency for studies with negative results not to be reported, and lack of clear definitions. "Successful" appears to mean different things, ranging from complete remission of depressive symptoms, through some degree of improved functioning or behavior, to patient behavior which is "more manageable" or indicative of "social" recovery, suggesting residual cognitive impairment. One encounters conclusions such as "it doesn't seem to have as many adverse effects as might be intuitively expected," and "ECT caused no adverse effects in a patient recovering from head injury with prolonged unconsciousness," and "There were benign neurological courses," and "no untoward effects."[10] The same researcher cites studies claiming that ECT has ameliorated the underlying medical illnesses of Parkinson's disease, multiple sclerosis, diabetes mellitus, and other disease. However, if there is any general agreement on who is most benefitted by ECT, it is that severely depressed patients who are at risk of suicide or psychotic exhaustion, who have not responded in a "timely" fashion to other interventions, and those for whom something immediate is needed, can be helped. It would seem that such patients, perhaps, have "little to lose" and much to gain.

Women receive ECT about twice as frequently as men; in Miller's study, 30 of 45 subjects were women.[11] An examination of the use of ECT in California from 1977 to 1983 found 69 percent of the patients to be female.[12] This is surprisingly close to the 70 percent rate of females among psychotherapy patients.[13] It also appears that older people are at more risk for ECT than younger people, although the reasons are not clear.

By diagnosis, various forms of major depression account for the largest share of patients receiving ECT. ECT is not unusual, however, in treating schizophrenics, manic depressive illness sufferers, and occasionally mixed-diagnosis patients, such as depressed borderline patients. To a lesser extent, patients with a surprisingly large variety of illnesses have received ECT. It suggests that a considerable amount of medical curiosity and experimentation has been involved with rather few controls and standardized procedures as regards to dosage and diagnosis. One might question the ethics of administering ECT to epileptics, hydrocephalics (with shunt), pregnant women, people under age 21, and other patients for whom ECT would seem to be risky. Occasionally, disastrous results are reported, such as have occurred using ECT with patients suffering from CNS syphilis, cerebrovascular disease, subdural hematoma, and carbon monoxide poisoning.[14]

A number of psychiatrists, including Kramer and Dubovsky, believe that ECT is greatly underused, implying that there is a vast untapped "market" for ECT, despite the more restrictive regulatory climate in some states. There are laws requiring "informed consent" and also procedures for circumventing that in certain cases.

Memory loss is the best-known and best-documented complication connected with ECT. Current research methodologies make it difficult to compare studies, though not impossible. It should be noted that there appears to be a tendency on the part of some psychiatrists to discount evidence of memory loss as being merely post-ECT depressive symptoms, while others suggest that there are differences in the type of memory loss.

In the 1950s, Irvin Janis conducted a series of studies with ECT patients and matched patients treated with psychotherapy. Follow-up was several months, and memory was tested before and after in terms of basic life history including schooling, job history, family relations, and childhood experiences. Pre-treatment ECT patients often gave long complex answers to single questions, whereas their post-treatment responses to the same material were brief and required many further questions. This phenomenon was not observed in non-ECT patients.[15] Kolb observes that memory loss at first appears to cover a long period prior to treatment and then memory returns somewhat to the period just prior to treatment. It is still impaired to some degree for several weeks or a few months following following the termination of treatment. Kolb states that full return of memory finally occurs and that there is no intellectual impairment; in fact, he claims that with the impairment of retention in memory functioning there is simultaneously an improved capacity for learning.[16] Crowe says something similar: that depressed patients have poor registration and normal retention but after ECT they have normal registration and poor retention.

A follow-up study reported by Crowe states that 55 percent of patients who received bilateral ECT reported memory loss three years later. He says that reports of memory loss are more frequent after bilateral than after unilateral ECT. In another study cited by Crowe, conducted seven months after a course of bilateral ECT, subjects evidenced impaired memory of events immediately before and during the course of treatment. Memory of events up to two years before ECT showed minimal impairment, and more remote memory returned to normal. Anterograde memory tested six months after ECT showed no impairment.

Another study in Crowe's compilation assessed patients before and after ECT, then after four months and seven months. Nineteen cognitive tests were used. The ECT group scored significantly below the control groups, consisting of a group of normal people and depressed patients who did not receive ECT, on nine of the nineteen tests before treatment; no test score deteriorated with treatment, and after four months, performance on only one test separated the ECT recipients from the non-ECT depressed patients. By seven months, the ECT group outperformed the patient-controls on medication on one test, but both patient groups performed at a level somewhat below that of the normal controls on several tests. Similarly, the Northwick Park trial found that by six months later, groups that received ECT or sham therapy did not differ on cognitive testing.[17]

There is some belief that unilateral nondominant hemisphere placement of electrodes during ECT results in less memory loss. That this is so cannot be stated with certainty. Squire reports on a study which showed that one hour after ECT, patients receiving unilateral ECT performed better on a memory recognition test than bilateral patients. By nine hours later, the 25 subjects who had had unilateral ECT performed no better on memory tests than patients who had received bilateral ECT.[18] In addition, brief-pulse ECT resulted in less memory loss than sine-wave ECT during the first hour after treatment, but later there were no differences observed.

There is a view held by some psychiatrists that unilateral electrode placement is not as therapeutically effective as bilateral placement. Electrode placement, however, seems to vary in both forms of ECT, and it has been suggested that unilateral ECT has much the same effect as bilateral ECT when there is a relatively large interelectrode distance.[19]

Miller's study of 45 depressed patients evidently regards the occurrence of treatment delays among 25 patients as a bigger source of concern than their cognitive dysfunction resulting from ECT. He says "we considered the occurrence of cognitive dysfunction or postponement of at least one ECT treatment."[20] The problem, it seems, was that this group of mostly older women (median age, 69) was staying in the hospital, on average, ten days too long. It is not clear what "timely response" to ECT in an acute care setting is, but evidently response was not timely in more than half of the group. Miller states that cognitive disturbances increase with bilateral electrode placement, sine-wave ECT, and high-dosage treatment.

What is the future of electroconvulsive therapy? It seems safe to say that psychiatry will continue to fight for the right to use this, one of their only "medical" treatments, as they wish, and with as little regulation and standardization as possible. Advocates such as Kolb extol the "simplicity of its application, its fewer hazards, and the need for a smaller group of specially trained personnel."[21]

It is more difficult to predict the direction of public opinion and legislation, but certainly they can be influenced by organized medicine.

Reimbursement practices will continue to play a major role. It is interesting that the California survey found little ECT being performed in government hospitals, possibly because they are not reimbursed for the procedure. This is more surprising when one considers that government hospitals are places of last resort and often contain the sickest patients. At present, private voluntary and for-profit hospitals perform most of the ECT done in this country. With impending psychiatric DRGs, and the whole third party reimbursement system pushing for cost containment, ECT may experience an expansion of use. Shorter hospital stays, the desire for rapid-acting interventions, and the profit to be made by using technology instead of labor certainly do not point away from increased ECT use.

It appears that therapists who provide "nonmedical" psychiatric treatments, especially in acute care settings, may find themselves under increasing pressure to generate revenues, justify their positions, and show fast results, at least until the next turn of the wheel toward more holistic approaches to mental health.

Notes

1. Kolb, Lawrence C. *Modern Clinical Psychiatry,* Philadelphia, W.B. Saunders Company, 1977, p. 858.

2. Ibid., p. 857.

3. Squire, Larry P., and Zouzounaris, Joyce A. "ECT and Memory: Brief Pulse Versus Sine-wave," *American Journal of Psychiatry* 143, no. 5 (May 1986): 597.

4. Miller, Michael E., Siris, Samuel G., and Gabriel, Arthur. "Treatment Delays in the Course of Electroconvulsive Therapy," *Hospital & Community Psychiatry* 37, no. 8 (August 1986): 826.

5. Brown, Phil. *The Transfer of Care,* Boston, Routledge & Kegan Paul, 1985, p. 161.

6. Dubovsky, Steven L. "Using Electroconvulsive Therapy for Patients with Neurological Disease," *Hospital & Community Psychiatry* 37, no. 8: 819.

7. Kolb, p. 860.

8. Crowe, Raymond R. "Current Concepts: Electroconvulsive Therapy— A Current Perspective," *New England Journal of Medicine* 311, no. 3 (July 19, 1984): 165.

9. Brown, p. 149.

10. Dubovsky, p. 819.

11. Miller, p. 825.

12. Kramer, Barry Alan. "Use of ECT in California, 1977–1983," *American Journal of Psychiatry* 142, no. 10 (October 1985): 1190.

13. Brown, p. 164.

14. Dubovsky, p. 819.

15. Brown, p. 161.

16. Kolb, p. 860.

17. Crowe, p. 165.

18. Squire, p. 597.

19. Weiner, R. D., Rogers, H. J., Qelch, C. A., et al. "ECT Stimulus Parameters and Electrode Placement: Relevance to Therapeutic and Adverse Effects," in *ECT: Basic Mechanisms*. London, John Libby, 1984. Cited in Squire, p. 597.

20. Miller, p. 826.

21. Kolb, p. 434

Psychosurgery

Rael Jean Isaac and Virginia C. Armat

Psychosurgery was the first and easiest target of those opposed to all psychiatric treatments. The crude early operations had a significant mortality rate and often had a severe negative impact, sometimes so severe as to produce a "vegetable personality"—people who were left without awareness or initiative, and would vegetate on the back wards of hospitals for the rest of their lives. Today, the term "lobotomy" arouses almost universal revulsion.

But Peter Breggin's campaign against psychosurgery, launched in the 1970s, attacked an old treatment at the very time when vastly refined techniques had eliminated its defects and improved understanding had narrowed its use to small subgroups of patients most likely to benefit. Breggin's attacks have made such surgery almost impossible to obtain in the United States. Psychiatrists failed to come to the defense of the new psychosurgery, many of them identifying it with the old lobotomies, which they viewed as barbaric and outmoded. They did not perceive that psychosurgery was merely the first target in what was from the outset a war against all somatic treatments for major mental illness.

The birth of psychosurgery can be traced to an international neurological conference in London in 1935 at which neurophysiologist John Fulton presented the results of experiments he and his colleague at Yale, Carlyle Jacobsen, had conducted with two chimpanzees, Becky and Lucy. The two chimps had been trained to solve elaborate problems in order to obtain food and became upset when they were frustrated in

---

From Rael Jean Isaac and Virginia C. Armat, *Madness in the Streets: How Psychiatry and the Law Abandoned the Mentally Ill* (New York: The Free Press, 1990). Reprinted by permission.

their efforts, shaking and kicking their box, pulling their hair, even throwing their excreta at the scientists. But after Fulton and Jacobsen removed their frontal lobes, the animals became immune to frustration. While their skill in handling the tests had diminished somewhat, they were no longer upset by their failures.

In the audience were two figures who would become the giants of psychosurgery: Egas Moniz and Walter Freeman. Moniz was a distinguished Portuguese scientist, already celebrated for developing cerebral angiography. Fulton reports that after he had read his paper, "Dr. Moniz arose and asked, would it not be feasible to relieve anxiety states in man by surgical means?"[1] Freeman, a young American neurologist, would later modify and disseminate widely the technique that Moniz developed.

Only two months after the London conference, Moniz guided the first surgery on human beings. (The actual operation was performed in Lisbon by a young neurosurgeon, Almeida Lima.) Instead of removing the frontal lobes, as Fulton and Jacobsen had done, Moniz cut fibers connecting the frontal lobes to other areas of the brain. He called the operation "leucotomy" (after the Greek words "leucos" meaning white and "tomos" meaning cutting) and developed a special surgical tool, the leucotome. The leucotome's shaft (cannula) would be inserted into the brain and when it reached the desired plane of section, the surgeon would depress a plunger; a wire looped out and was rotated, cutting a core of brain tissue.

Psychosurgery Comes to the United States

In the United States Freeman, with the aid of neurosurgeon James Watts, pioneered the operation and renamed it "lobotomy," because nerve fibers of a lobe of the brain were cut. As Freeman explained to a group of skeptical psychiatrists: "The [delusional] idea is still there, but it has no emotional drive. . . . I think we have drawn the sting, as it were, of the psychosis or neurosis."[2]

In his own way a community psychiatrist, Freeman felt his life mission was to empty the back wards of state mental hospitals. He recognized that the existing operation could never achieve that end, because it was expensive, requiring the skills of a neurosurgeon, and not likely to be available to patients in the great custodial warehouses maintained by the state. So by the end of 1945 Freeman was looking for a new kind of operation, one, moreover, that would do less extensive damage to personality. Freeman perfected an operation devised by the Italian surgeon A. M. Fiamberti,[3] which reached the frontal lobes from a different direction, avoiding the need for boring holes through the skull. Freeman called the operation, which did not even require an operating room, transorbital lobotomy. His initial operating instrument was in fact an icepick taken from his kitchen drawer.

Freeman, using electroshock in lieu of anesthetic, drew the upper eyelid away from the eyeball to expose the tear duct and then tapped the pick with a hammer to drive through the orbital plate. He would oscillate the instrument to sever fibers at the base of the frontal lobe. The patient would wake up with black eyes but could return immediately to his home or hospital ward "with no restrictions" on his activities, as Freeman would tell the family. Watts, who performed traditional lobotomies, was outraged by the new technique, which he felt diminished the dignity of neurosurgery.[4]

Transorbital lobotomies—or icepick lobotomies as they were dubbed by critics—could be easily performed in state hospitals. It is estimated that by 1955 over 40,000 had been performed in the United States, most of them between 1945 and 1949. Freeman *alone* performed or supervised over 3,500 of the operations in nineteen states and ten foreign countries.[5] Ordinary doctors at backwater state hospitals could master the simple technique. In 1957, science popularizer Paul DeKruif wrote an enthusiastic book about Jack Ferguson, a country doctor (not a psychiatrist) working at Traverse City State Hospital in Michigan, where he was trying the then brand-new, anti-psychotic medications. A few years earlier Ferguson had worked at the state hospital in Logansport, Indiana, where he had pored over Freeman's writings, and then modified the procedure so that it could be completed in three minutes! Ferguson performed hundreds of these operations and told DeKruif that while perhaps two-thirds of the patients behaved better after the operation, "the couldn't plan ahead."[6]

The public image of these procedures did not gain much from Freeman's habit of calling the patients upon whom he had operated "trophies," or terming his mammoth journeys to follow up on what had happened to them "head-hunting expeditions." Yet this effort, which Freeman's one-time partner James Watts, called his "magnificent obsession"[7] was a laudable one. Even in his old age, Freeman would drive 26,000 miles on a single journey,[8] combing the country in search of his former patients, and keeping meticulous records of their progress. (These records, which to this day have not been studied, are kept at the Himmelfarb Health Sciences Library at George Washington University in Washington, D.C., where Freeman taught for many years).[9]

The discovery of anti-psychotic drugs ended the era of lobotomies and by 1960 hospitals no longer permitted even Freeman to operate. Many have condemned the psychiatric profession for permitting such operations, but as Desmond Kelly, an English psychiatrist and expert in modern psychosurgery, points out, the context in which the operations were performed needs to be kept in mind.

It is very easy to look back and to say it was an evil thing, but when you're there it's different. Although there were major personality changes, it enabled an awful lot of schizophrenics to leave psychiatric hospitals . . . but at a price. The difficulty was all the successes were in the community and they didn't tell anyone they had the operation and all the failures were in the hospitals as tombstones of the negative effects of surgery.[10]

The Development of Limbic System Surgery

Lobotomies in their heyday enjoyed widespread public acceptance. It was after they had been discarded, and far superior neurosurgical procedures developed in their place, that modern psychosurgery came under vigorous assault. The *new* operations, emerging in the mid-1960s, were attacked on the basis of the failures of the *old* techniques. As psychiatrist Stewart Shevitz has pointed out, it's as if we were to reject current surgical approaches to coronary heart disease because of the difficulties encountered with the first human heart transplants.[11]

The foundation for modern limbic system surgery was laid in the late 1940s as a result of progress on a number of fronts: in surgical techniques, in identifying the anatomical basis of emotion, and in narrowing the criteria for selecting patients. In 1947 Ernest Spiegel and Henry Wycis at Temple University in Philadelphia pioneered stereotactic surgery. Using three-dimensional brain maps as a guide, they applied a fixating apparatus to the head, which allowed greater precision and far smaller lesions than in the old, blind, freehand operations.[12] At the same time John Fulton, whose chimpanzee experiments had triggered Moniz's first surgery, published the results of his study—based on post mortems of lobotomized individuals—on how the site of the lesion related to the effects of the operation. He concluded that lesions should be confined to one quadrant of the frontal lobe.[13] With stereotactic techniques, it was possible to make the lesion exactly in the area pinpointed by Fulton.

In the late 1940s, Paul MacLean confirmed the existence of the "Papez circuit," named for James W. Papez, a neuroanatomist at Cornell whose 1937 paper "A Proposed Mechanism of Emotion" postulated—with very little evidence at the time—that the anatomical basis for emotion lay in an ensemble of structures deep within the brain: the so-called limbic system. (Limbic means "forming a border around" and these structures border the brain stem.) From now on, neurosurgeons would move in two directions: in one, selected fiber tracts connecting the frontal lobes and specific limbic structures were cut; in the other, lesions were made in the limbic structures themselves, such as the cingulum, midline thalamic areas, and the amygdala. How precisely the surgery worked was not known: brain chemistry might be affected, or interrupted abnormal nerve pathways replaced by normally functioning ones.

The means for making lesions ranged from electrodes to radioactive rods to ultrasound. The new operations had far less risk of complications than the old and did not have their damaging effect on personality or intelligence. By the late 1960s, in the view of California neurosurgeon M. Hunter Brown, limbic system surgery had the "highest benefit to risk ratio of any procedure in neurological surgery."[14]

Spurring development of limbic system surgery in the mid-1960s was the growing recognition that the medications that at first had made psychosurgery seem obsolete did not help everyone. By now psychiatrists and neurosurgeons also had a better understanding of the kinds of patients most likely to be helped by surgery: those, as Robert Arnot pointed out as early as 1940, suffering from a "fixed state of tortured self-concern."[15] Psychosurgery had been used extensively in schizophrenia because of the severity of the illness, but drugs were far more successful in treating psychosis. Severe chronic anxiety, agitated depression, and obsessive compulsive behavior, on the other hand, responded well to surgery.[16]

By 1970 there was enough progress for a Second International Congress on Psychosurgery (the first had been in 1948) to be held in Copenhagen.

Breggin Mounts His Campaign

It was at this promising juncture that Peter Breggin began his fanatical crusade against the principle somatic treatments for the mentally ill. According to Breggin:

> I was sitting in my office in 1970 when I opened up *Psychiatric News* and saw a headline, which read—it was very close to this—"Psychosurgery Said to Be Effective in Certain Neuroses," or something like that. . . . And it was about an international meeting of psychosurgeons in Copenhagen and how psychosurgery was coming back, a second wave. And I was appalled. . . . And I said to myself, someone has to do something about this.[17]

Breggin explains that he wrote to all those mentioned in the article, said he was writing a review of psychosurgery "and would love to include them." In this way he obtained information to be used in his campaign against the treatment, a campaign that would take him to Congress and the media, to law courts, state legislatures, and endless conferences.

Breggin adds: "And it's never stopped since then. Because it became obvious that psychosurgery was nothing more than the ultimate expression of biological psychiatry. That all the treatments damaged the brain; all the treatments worked by destroying function."[18]

Breggin's "research" paper on psychosurgery which was entered into the *Congressional Record* in February 1972 and his testimony in congressional hearings (chaired by Senator Edward Kennedy) early in 1973 relied far more on hysteria than on science. Breggin proclaimed: We are in danger of creating a society in which everyone who deviates from the norm will be in danger of surgical mutilation." Psychosurgery, Breggin warned, was a new form of "totalitarianism," and if America ever became a police state, it would be armed with "lobotomy and psychosurgery."[19] (This was too much for another witness at the Kennedy hearings, Dr. Willard Gaylin, president of the Hastings Institute, who said dryly: "It seems unlikely, if there were some plot to take over the country . . . that psychosurgery would be the method of choice. I doubt that they would find the most efficient technique for mass control would be planting electrodes on a population of 200 million, or psychosurgery, when they have access to a limited national television, and to schools with compulsory education, to psychological inputs and to drugs. . . .[20])

Breggin described psychosurgery as no more than senseless mutilation of the brain, whose effect, *by definition,* had to be harmful, for "improvement in function cannot follow mutilation of the functioning brain."[21] But as British psychiatrist Dr. Desmond Kelly points out:

> Peter Breggin's contention is that you are destroying normal brain tissue and my contention is that these are some of the sickest people I've ever seen in psychiatry and they are so grateful when they come through because although it [the brain tissue] may appear normal under the microscope, it certainly isn't functioning normally. Obsessives are crucified by their illnesses; they may spend sixteen, eighteen hours a day washing, cleaning, their various rituals. They can't work, they can't do anything except ritualize until they finally fall asleep from sheer fatigue, and if that is viewed as the functioning of a normal brain that certainly isn't my definition.[22]

Paul Bridges, consultant psychiatrist at the psychosurgical unit at Brook General Hospital in London, told us that he had invited Breggin, when he was in England, to come and see his patients for himself: "He didn't have time or something like that."[23]

Breggin was no more to be tied down by clinical realities than by scientific evidence; like his mentor Thomas Szasz, he offered rhetorical arguments and denunciation by analogy. From then on, Breggin's attacks on other forms of treatment would consist primarily of equating them with the long-discarded lobotomy. All limbic system surgery was lobotomy. ECT was another type of lobotomy and treatment with neuroleptic drugs "chemical lobotomy."

In his effort to obtain a congressional ban against limbic system surgery, Breggin's initial strategy was to focus on black congressmen. Neurosurgeons Vernon Mark and William Sweet and psychiatrist Frank Ervin, all associated with Harvard Medical School, had sent a foolish joint letter to the *Journal of the American Medical Association* in 1967, at the time of the riots in black ghettoes around the country, citing "medical evidence" that violence was due to biological, not environmental factors, and suggesting psychosurgery as a remedy for the violent behavior of some rioters.

In 1970 Ervin and Mark published *Violence and the Brain,* in which they again suggested that criminal violence could be sharply reduced by psychosurgery. Later one of the authors would agree with the consensus in his field that psychosurgery was appropriate for treatment of aggression only in the presence of a specific brain disorder.[24] But the damage was done: Breggin could plausibly argue that nothing less than "political psychosurgery" was being advocated, and line up black congressmen on the grounds that psychosurgery might be used to control blacks in the ghetto.

While Breggin did not achieve his goal of a legislative ban on psychosurgery, he was successful in obtaining what was then viewed as a prelude toward that end, establishment by Congress in 1974 of a commission to investigate under what circumstances "if any" the continued use of psychosurgery might be appropriate. Breggin boasts of his role in creating the commission, "I created the psychosurgery commission. I lobbied; I sat down in my living room and created that with chief assistant to Senator Glenn Beall from Maryland."[25]

But this particular move backfired. The commission contracted for two studies, conducted by separate teams of scientists and clinicians from MIT and Boston University. The MIT study evaluated eighty-five patients who had received cingulotomies (surgery performed by Dr. H. Thomas Ballantine of Massachusetts General Hospital that makes a lesion in the cingulum, one of the structures in the limbic system), while the Boston University study examined fifty-two patients, who had been ill an average of twenty years, some of whom were evaluated both before and after surgery. Each patient received one of four different limbic system surgical procedures. Both studies, using interviews and objective tests, came to the same conclusions: more than half the patients improved significantly following psychosurgery and *none* of the patients suffered significant neurological or psychological impairment.[26] The results were particularly impressive because only those who were severely disabled and failed to respond to all other treatments had been accepted for surgery.

Although most of the commission's eleven members had approached their task biased against psychosurgery, their report, as critics noted angrily, fell only slightly short of an endorsement. The chairman of the commission explained: "We looked at the data and saw they did not support our prejudices. I, for one, did not expect to come out in favor of psychosurgery. But we saw that some very sick people had been helped by it, and that it did not destroy their intelligence or rob them of feelings. . . . The operation shouldn't be banned."[27]

The report was the more remarkable in that the commission undertook its work in a climate poisoned by near hysteria. The media, uncritically enthusiastic about lobotomies in their heyday, had become extremely hostile now that the risk-benefit ratio had radically shifted in favor of surgery. *Ebony* magazine published a quote from Dr. Alvin Poussaint, a black psychiatrist at Harvard, that whites believed blacks so "animal and savage that whites have to carve on their brains to make them human beings. . . ."[28] Surgeons who performed the operations were intimidated. Breggin boasts: "There were people picketing these guys' [neurosurgeons] houses, picketing the hospitals, women reporters calling them on the phone."[29]

When the commission held public hearings in San Francisco on the commission's recommendation that institutional review boards monitor the surgery, demonstrators stood outside the meeting hall chanting "it didn't end with the Second World War/Eichmann's alive on the fifteenth floor." An article in *Madness Network News* bragged that the commissioners were forced to flee and would probably never return.[30] The Church of Scientology, through its Citizens Commission on Human Rights, also threw itself into the anti-psychosurgery crusade with demonstrations, and pickets. Breggin notes that the Church of Scientology has always been an outright enemy of psychiatry, seeing it as competition for its *own* theory of "psychosis" and treatments.[31] (Scientologists teach that individuals can free themselves of abnormal thought processes through "auditing," a process of tracing past lives, and through the use of an "E-meter"—a battery-powered galvanometer that uses a needle dial wired to two tin cans—can reach a "Clear" status.[32])

Despite the furor, the Commission recommended that psychosurgery continue to be available, and although it opposed such surgery for prisoners, it urged that the operations not be limited to patients able to give informed consent, since this would deprive some seriously ill individuals of a valuable treatment. Indeed the only disappointing finding, from the standpoint of neurosurgeons who performed the operations, was that the commission continued to define psychosurgery as

"experimental" rather than as a well-established procedure. Dr. Ballantine complained: "If I've done the same operation for seventeen years
and 70–80 percent show useful improvement, I don't see how it could
be called innovative."[33]

But if the Commission withstood pressure fairly well (its final report
in 1977 was more qualified in its support than its initial 1976 report,
presumably in response to the outcry evoked by the latter), Department
of Health, Education and Welfare Secretary Joseph Califano wanted
nothing to do with such a political hot potato. Limbic system surgery
could not be banned in the wake of the report, but Califano did not recommend that the operations be available to those too ill to give
informed consent; nor did he follow through on the recommendation
that review boards be established to monitor the surgery and that comprehensive scientific studies of its effectiveness be undertaken. Both
would have given limbic system surgery more legitimacy.

The Kaimowitz Case

Although Breggin's hoped-for congressional ban did not materialize, the
courts dealt psychosurgery a heavy blow. In 1973 Gabe Kaimowitz, an
attorney with Legal Services in Michigan, brought suit to prevent performance of an amygdalotomy on "John Doe," who had been in an
institution for the criminally insane for seventeen years. (Doe's real
name, Louis Smith, became known during the trial.) While in a mental
hospital for psychiatric evaluation, Smith had murdered a student nurse
and raped her dead body.

There were many problems with the proposal to perform surgery on
Smith. The only clear criterion for surgery in cases of aggression is evidence of temporal lobe epilepsy, which was not present in his case. Moreover, while the original intent was to study twenty-four criminal sexual
psychopaths in the state mental health system, comparing the effects of
surgery (an amygdalotomy) with the effects of a drug (cyproterone
acetate) in providing relief from aggression, it was found that Smith was
the only appropriate candidate in the system for surgery.[34] The value of
the experiment in the absence of any other subjects was dubious.

Although technically speaking he had no client (both Smith and his
parents had consented to the operation), Kaimowitz brought suit on the
ground that the coercive atmosphere of a prison made it impossible for
an incarcerated individual to give informed consent to psychosurgery.
The case continued despite the fact that the issue, at least in so far as it
concerned Louis Smith, had dissolved. The three-judge panel in Wayne
County hearing the case set him free on the ground that the "criminal
sexual psychopath" statute under which he had been incarcerated was

unconstitutional. Once free, Smith decided he did not want psychosurgery. Local newspapers reported he was "looking for an apartment and planning to attend community college."[35] (Within a few months he was back in prison, arrested for stealing women's clothes from a store; he was wearing nineteen pairs of women's underpants and ten slips.[36])

The judges ruled that it was impossible for a prisoner to give informed consent to psychosurgery because the risks surrounding it were so great as to make "knowledgeable consent to psychosurgery literally impossible." Breggin was delighted with the outcome. "The judges wrote their opinion and it practically looks like my testimony. They cite the Nuremberg code; they said psychosurgery was destructive of the creative process and described the lobotomy syndrome."[37]

On the other hand, the losing attorney, S. I. Shuman, observes that because the judges in the Kaimowitz case were in effect serving as a medical review committee for a whole field of medicine, they were dependent on the quality of the expert witnesses who testified. Says Shuman: "The medical scientist who gains access as an expert to the institutionalized judicial decision-making process has a professional and political obligation to perform as a scientist and not as a political huckster." Yet, Shuman points out, "the effectiveness of Dr. Breggin's advocacy is in large part due to the fact that it is not scientific."[38]

While members of the mental health bar were delighted that the court had ruled against psychosurgery, the decision's implications made them uneasy. Informed consent, said the judges in Kaimowitz, required not only knowledge, but also voluntariness and competence to make a decision, and these were also absent in the inherently coercive environment of a state mental hospital. (Breggin had told them state mental hospitals were like concentration camps and "that if you're in this oppressive, humiliating, debilitating situation and somebody says he'll volunteer for a freezing experiment, it's only because you're afraid you'll go to the ovens."[39]) Did that mean the involuntary patient could not consent to *any* treatment? What would happen to the "right to treatment" under those circumstances?[40]

Even more serious was the court's ruling that the very fact of institutionalization, by depriving the individual of his sense of self-worth, diminished his competence. The suits brought by the mental health bar depended heavily upon the presumed *competence* of mental patients. Were the judges resurrecting by a back door the old rules that treated mental patients as legally incompetent?

These fears proved unwarranted because other courts never followed up on these elements of the decision. The case only served as precedent for further decisions favorable to the patient liberation bar. For example, the Kaimowitz court decided that psychosurgery violated the First Amendment's guarantee of freedom of speech: by limiting the ability to produce new ideas, it undercut the basis of free expression.[41] This notion would soon be employed by the mental health bar in right to refuse anti-psychotic medication cases. It would be alleged that psychoactive drugs, by interfering with psychotic thought processes, deprived individuals of their constitutional right to freedom of thought and speech.

The Kaimowitz decision had a major impact in discouraging psychosurgery. Breggin boasts that the case brought to an end operations in state mental hospitals. "Up to that point, for example, they were operating in Missouri and I'd go to Missouri and talk on radio and television. Then they would stop it in Missouri and I'd hear about it in California. This really put a blanket on it."[42] Oregon in 1973 and California in 1977 established mandatory psychosurgery review boards whose practical effect was to eliminate the treatment.[43] (Two of the best known neurosurgeons in the field, M. Hunter Brown and Peter Lindstrom—Ingrid Bergman's first husband—were in California.) Neurosurgeons everywhere were reluctant to perform surgery that a court had ruled "clearly experimental," fearing that malpractice suits might be more easily brought—and won—in the wake of the decision. . . .

While all limbic system surgery addresses . . . tortured self-concern, different operations seem to be especially effective in particular disorders. English psychiatrist Desmond Kelly feels limbic leucotomy, the operation he helped to develop in the 1970s, is the best operation for obsessive compulsive disorder. But, he says, "If I had depression I would go to Brook General [hospital] for their operation [stereotactic subcaudate tractotomy]."[44] Dr. Ballantine finds his cingulotomy procedure more effective in depression than in obsessive compulsive behavior, for which he feels Dr. Kelly's operation may be more effective.[45]

Limbic system surgeons are eager for double blind studies that could scientifically establish the value of these operations. In the past the obstacles to such studies have been overwhelming, because subjecting individuals to surgery, which always carries risks, without actually performing the therapeutic procedure is not considered ethical. But now a technique has been developed in Sweden by neurosurgeon Lars Lecksell that requires no incision; the "gamma knife" focuses three beams of gamma rays emitted from a radioactive cobalt source. Each of the rays is too weak to harm tissue by itself: only as they focus together at the desired spot in the brain is tissue destroyed. The technique, which is also used to destroy brain tumors, epilepsy-causing lesions, and deadly arteriovenous masses, makes a double blind study feasible. What stands in the way is the political obstructionism that has so far made all rational consideration of limbic system surgery impossible.

Limbic System Surgery Driven Underground

The commission established by Congress to investigate psychosurgery estimated that in 1971 and 1972 approximately 140 neurosurgeons performed between 400 and 500 operations a year. (Even then, at a time of resurgence of interest in limbic system surgery in the United States, the operations were being performed at only half the rate they were in England and a third the rate they were in Australia.[46]) By 1988, when Thomas Ballantine retired, the number of neurosurgeons performing them was so small that those we spoke to—including Dr. Ballantine—could not even make an estimate of their number. Dr. Charles Fager . . . said he did no more than one a year, and believed only a handful of operations were being done in the United States. Asked if there was any group of doctors who kept each other informed, Dr. Ballantine said: "No. There was in the early 1970s. It's almost a sub rosa procedure."[47]

There is no training whatsoever in medical schools. Dr. Fager says: "The current generation of psychiatrists wouldn't even consider it. The acceptance level has fallen to practically zero."[48] Paul Bridges came from England to give a paper on limbic system surgery at a Philadelphia conference on resistant depression. "They were interested but I had the distinct feeling they were not going to take it on board because of the hassle in America."[49] Dr. Ballantine says: "When you think of the number of patients completely disabled by their affective illnesses, there is an important role for this type of surgery. If it were not for the negative image, a lot more of the surgery would be done."[50]

Breggin's Luddite boast to us was clearly not an idle one. With Dr. Ballantine's retirement, said Breggin: "I think there is no really active psychosurgeon in the United States. I'm sure there are some people doing it but they won't publish because they don't want me to see their publications. They don't want Peter Breggin finding out they're doing it."[51] And indeed one neurosurgeon refused to discuss the operations he had performed with us on the grounds that "it is not professionally safe."

Notes

1. Thomas Ballantine, "A Critical Assessment of Psychiatric Surgery: Past, Present and Future," in Silvano Arieti and Keith Brodie, eds., *American Handbook of Psychiatry*, vol. 7 (New York: Basic Books, 1981), p. 1031.

2. David Shutts, *Lobotomy: Resort to the Knife* (New York: Van Nostrand Reinhold, 1982), p. 70.

3. Paul DeKruif, *A Man Against Insanity* (New York: Harcourt Brace, 1957), p. 100. The new procedure could be performed in minutes rather than the hours required for the earlier operation.

4. David Shutts, op. cit., p. 146.

5. *Appendix: Psychosurgery,* The National Commission for the Protection of Human Subjects of Biomedical and Behavioral Research, U.S. Department of Health, Education and Welfare, Publ. No. Os 77-0003 (Washington, D.C.: U.S. Government Printing Office, 1977), p. I-6.

6. Paul De Kruif, op. cit., p. 103.

7. David Shutts, op. cit., p. 60.

8. Ibid., p. 245. Indomitable to the end, Freeman visited Mexico shortly before his death. Seventy-six years old, suffering from advanced cancer, he traveled 500 miles to Yucatán with two former students, Zigmond Lebensohn and Manuel Suárez, then governor of the Mexican state of Chiapas, and climbed the sheer and difficult steps of a Mayan temple. In Lebensohn's words: "A triumph of will over infirmity, this was a fitting gesture to close the life of a remarkable man whose like we shall never see again" (ibid., p. 249).

9. Ibid., p. 259.

10. Interview, Dr. Desmond Kelly, October 5, 1988. The most famous "tombstone" of the negative effects of surgery was President John Kennedy's sister Rosemary. Mildly retarded, she became mentally ill when she was twenty-one. She suffered from wild moods and tantrums, wandered the streets at night, and became physically abusive. Dr. Freeman had begun performing lobotomies several years earlier, and in 1941 the Kennedys decided to give Rosemary the operation. The result in her case was disastrous. One member of the family claimed the operation "made her go from being mildly retarded to very retarded." Since 1941 Rosemary has been confined to a nursing convent in Wisconsin. See E. Fuller Torrey, *Nowhere to Go* (New York: Harper & Row, 1988), pp. 104–106.

On the other hand, Dr. Paul Bridges, also an English psychiatrist who is an expert on psychosurgery, points out that the Department of Health, in an English study of 10,000 crude operations carried out from 1940 to 1945, "showed that 20%, one fifth of the patients, could be discharged from the hospital after the operation. That's really astonishingly good." Interview, Dr. Bridges, October 13, 1988. Similarly, a series of studies in the United States, including the California-Greystone projects and studies at Boston Psychopathic Hospital, found that lobotomy performed on patients who had failed to respond to other available treatments permitted hospital discharge at a rate substantially exceeding what could otherwise be expected, especially since the patients selected for surgery were often chronic institutionalized schizophrenics. Moreover, the studies found that despite the occurrence of major untoward effects on personality in some cases, there was little or no evidence of intellectual deterioration following surgery. See Herbert G. Vaughan, Jr., "Psychosurgery and Brain Stimulation in Historical Perspective," in Willard M. Gaylin, Josel Meister, and Robert Neville, eds., *Operating on the Mind: The Psychosurgery Conflict* (New York: Basic Books, 1975), p. 41.

11. Stewart A. Shevitz, "Psychosurgery: Some Current Observations," *American Journal of Psychiatry* (March 1976): 267.

12. Thomas Ballantine, "A Critical Assessment," op. cit., p. 1037. The device was a modification of one invented at the turn of the century for use in animal neurophysiology research.

13. Desmond Kelly, *Anxiety and Emotions* (Springfield, Ill.: Charles C. Thomas, 1980), p. 210.

14. *Report and Recommendations: Psychosurgery*. National Commission for the Protection of Human Subjects of Biomedical and Behavioral Research, U.S. Dept. of Health, Education and Welfare Publ. No. OS 77-0001. (Washington, D.C.: U.S. Government Printing Office, 1977), p. 53.

15. Jesse Yap, "Psychosurgery: Its Definition," *American Journal of Forensic Psychiatry* (July 1979): 93.

16. Testimony, neurosurgeon Dr. Charles Fager, to National Commission for the Protection of Human Subjects of Biomedical and Behavioral Research, July 19, 1976. Although psychosurgery was originally used extensively in schizophrenia, as early as 1936 it was apparent to Egas Moniz that agitated depression responded best, while cases of chronic schizophrenia showed little improvement. See Paul Bridges and John Bartlett, "Psychosurgery Yesterday and Today," *British Journal of Psychiatry* 131 (1977): 249.

17. Interview, Dr. Peter Breggin, May 6, 1988.

18. Ibid. One of Breggin's methods of eliciting information has been described by neurosurgeon Thomas Ballantine. Dr. Ballantine writes: "On April 14, 1971, I received a short letter dated April 12, 1971. It said: 'Dear Dr. Ballantine: I read with great interest about the international psychosurgery conference. I would appreciate any reprints you may have concerning your work in this area as well as any other material which you feel might be of interest to a psychiatrist in general practice. Thanks very much. Sincerely, Peter R. Breggin, M.D.' "

Ballantine reports receiving two more letters from Breggin, in which he said he was completing "a review of the literature and a historical study," and requesting Dr. Ballantine's "impressions on the field," the number of cases he had treated with psychosurgery since 1965, his estimate of how many other surgeons were involved in psychosurgery and the techniques used and illustrative material, photograph or diagram, illustrating his technique. The correspondence was cut short when Dr. Ballantine saw a copy of an article by Nicholas von Hoffman in the *Washington Post* of July 16, 1971, entitled "Brain Maim" quoting Breggin as saying that women had "their brains smooshed twice as often as men" by husbands and doctors who wanted to "put an end to their nagging, whining helplessness." He reports sending Breggin a last note: "Is this the article which caused you to request information and reprints from me? Or, have you published an article in a scientific journal on the subject—or, have you prepared such an article for publication?"

Ballantine originally included a detailed account of the correspondence in a chapter on psychosurgery he prepared for *The American Handbook of Psychiatry*, but, in his words, "succumbed to their agonized entreaties and agreed to have all references to Breggin deleted from the published chapter." Unpublished section of manuscript and letter from Dr. Thomas Ballantine to Rael Jean Isaac, November 30, 1989.

19. *Quality of Health Care—Human Experimentation*, 1973 Hearings Before the Subcommittee on Health of the Committee on Labor and Public Welfare, U.S. Senate, 93 Congress, 1st Session, Feb. 23 and March 6, 1973 (Washington, D.C.: U.S. Government Printing Office, 1973), p. 358.

20. Ibid., p. 374.

21. Peter Breggin, "The Return of Lobotomy and Psychosurgery," *Congressional Record*, February 24, 1972, p. 5575.

22. Interview, Dr. Desmond Kelly, October 5, 1988.

23. Interview, Dr. Paul Bridges, October 13, 1988.

24. Vernon H. Mark, "A Psychosurgeon's Case for Psychosurgery," *Psychology Today*, July 1974, p. 28. Mark and Robert Neville are also quoted to this effect in Elliot S. Valenstein, ed., *The Psychosurgery Debate: Scientific, Legal and Ethical Perspectives* (San Francisco: W. H. Freeman, 1980), p. 94,

25. Interview, Dr. Peter Breggin, May 6, 1988.

26. Stephan L. Chorover, "The Psychosurgery Evaluation Studies and Their Impact on the Commission's Report," in Elliot S. Valenstein, ed., op. cit., p. 247.

27. Ibid., p. 248.

28. Samuel I. Shuman, "The Emotional, Medical and Legal Reasons for the Special Concern about Psychosurgery" in Frank Ayd, Jr., ed., *Medical, Moral and Legal Issues in Mental Health Care* (Baltimore: Williams and Wilkins, 1974), p. 72. An exception to this pattern of herd rejection of the treatment was Eugene Methvin's article "Should we Halt the Brain-Probers?" in *Reader's Digest*, February 1979.

29. Interview Dr. Peter Breggin, May 6, 1988.

30. *Madness Network News*, Center Section, Summer 1977, p. 8. See also ibid., Fall 1977, p. 2.

31. Interview, Dr. Peter Breggin, May 6, 1988.

32. Accounts of the Church of Scientology's beliefs and activities can be found in *Newsweek*, Dec. 6, 1982; *Time*, April 5, 1976; *Reader's Digest*, May 1980 and September 1981 (both by Eugene Methvin); *Clinical Psychiatry News*, March, 1981; and *Cult Awareness Network News*, November 1988. Its tactics are illustrated by the letter its Citizens Commission on Human Rights sent to psychiatrists in 1975 offering "amnesty to any psychiatrist or technician who will come forward to confess his or her crimes against humanity." See *News*, Southern California Psychiatric Society, June 1975, p. 10. In 1986 the same gimmick was being used by the Citizens Commission on Human Rights, now formally independent of Scientology, which again produced a flyer offering "Amnesty" to "all psychiatrists, psychologists and psychiatric technicians who truthfully and fully confess their crimes against humanity."

33. Barry Stavro, "Psychosurgery Resurgent," *Politics Today*, January/February 1980, p. 49.

34. Gabe Kaimowitz, "The Case Against Psychosurgery," in Elliot Valenstein, ed., op. cit., pp. 514–15. Kaimowitz was already engaged in a pioneering right-to-refuse antipsychotic medication case when he brought his case against psychosurgery.

35. Jonas Robitscher, "Psychosurgery and Other Somatic Means of Altering Behavior," *Bulletin of the American Academy on Psychiatry and the Law*, 1974, p. 23.

36. Jonas Robitscher, *The Powers of Psychiatry*, (Boston: Houghton Mifflin, 1980), p. 289.

37. Interview, Dr. Peter Breggin, May 6, 1988.

38. S. I. Shuman, "The Emotional, Medical and Legal Reasons," op. cit., pp. 65–66. Shuman (p. 67) notes the problem is exacerbated by the fact that scientists unwilling to be politicians about their science almost universally will not come forward to participate even as scientists in the decisional process. As a result the decision-maker suffers from a double blindness. He receives relevant scientific material filtered through a political screen and is left ignorant of material which is not so filtered.

39. Interview, Dr. Peter Breggin, May 6, 1988.

40. David Wexler, "Mental Health Law and the Movement Toward Voluntary Treatment," *California Law Review* 62 (1974): 681.

41. Jonas Robitscher, *The Powers of Psychiatry*, op. cit., p. 289.

42. Interview, Dr. Peter Breggin, May 6, 1988.

43. Francis C. Pizzuli, "Psychosurgery Legislation and Case Law," in Elliot Valenstein, ed., op. cit., pp. 374–75. Also Stephen Morse, "Regulation of Psychosurgery," in ibid., p. 435.

44. Interview, Dr. Desmond Kelly, October 5, 1988.

45. H. Thomas Ballantine, Jr. "A Critical Assessment of Psychiatric Surgery," op. cit., p. 1043. Ballantine writes that his team has been reluctant to perform limbic leucotomies because of the slight but definite risk of undesirable alterations of personality. Ballantine notes: "In Great Britain this risk is apparently acceptable in view of the potential benefit. In the United States it might not be tolerated at this time." As far as the risks from his own operation are concerned, Dr. Ballantine reports that as of November 1989, 752 cingulotomies had been performed at Massachusetts General Hospital, and there have been only two serious complications: strokes resulting from laceration of a blood vessel during passage of the needle electrodes to the cingulum bundle that is the target of surgery. (Letter to Rael Jean Isaac, November 30, 1989.)

In terms of benefits, Dr. Kelly, studying the postoperative status of 148 patients who underwent stereotactic limbic leucotomy, has found that results have been best in those with obsessional neurosis (84% improved), while good results were obtained with only 60% of patients with a primary diagnosis of anxiety and/or depression. Kelly also found surprisingly good results with the relatively small number (19) of schizophrenic patients in the group, 63% of whom improved. These were selected patients with very distressing psychotic symptoms or high levels of anxiety, depression or obsessions accompanying their illness.

Ballantine's 1975 study of the postoperative status of 154 patients who had undergone cingulotomy for severe affective disorders found 17% to be "well" and an additional 58% "significantly improved." For a discussion of the risk-benefit equation on these operations see Ballantine, "A Critical Assessment of Psychiatric Surgery," op. cit., pp. 1041–42; and John Bartlett, Paul Bridges and Desmond Kelly, "Contemporary Indications for Psychosurgery," *British Journal of Psychiatry* 138 (1981): 507–11. Bartlett, Bridges, and Kelly sum up: "As present day stereotactic operations produce so few side-effects they can be regarded as acceptable forms of treatment for certain intractable psychiatric illnesses, especially when the associated mental anguish, the possibility of death by suicide and the personality deterioration that accompanies these chronic incapacitating conditions is taken into account."

46. *Appendix: Psychosurgery.* National Commission for the Protection of Human Subjects, op. cit., p. I-35.

47. Interview, Dr. H. Thomas Ballantine, Jr., January 12, 1989.

48. Interview, Dr. Charles Fager, January 26, 1989.

49. Interview, Dr. Paul Bridges, October 13, 1988.

50. Interview, Dr. H. Thomas Ballantine, Jr., January 12, 1989.

51. Interview, Dr. Peter Breggin, May 6, 1988.

Behavior Modification in Institutional Settings

Teodoro Ayllon

The major premise underlying behavior modification techniques is that behavior is governed largely by environmental events.[1] A major avenue, therefore, for acquiring new behavior patterns is through either structured or unstructured learning in response to such events. Using established procedures in the area of social learning to set the conditions under which this new learning, and hence new behavior, will be acquired, the behavior therapist can attempt to structure behavior.

This approach has three distinguishing characteristics. First, instead of attempting to explain a psychological problem or emotional conflict in abstract terms, the behavioral therapist examines the individual's unique behavior in relation to his immediate social environment. Second, treatment is then tailored to the individual, and evaluation of treatment effectiveness is accomplished using predetermined criteria based on the individual's unique characteristics. Finally, if evaluation shows that the procedures are ineffective, the treatment is restructured. Thus, the procedures are self-correcting. The approach of behavior modification is, therefore, more pragmatic and empirical than other, largely theoretical, psychological approaches.

Treatment of a child who does not want to go to school may serve to exemplify the behavioralist's approach. Instead of defining the child's psychic conflict as "school phobia," the problem would be behaviorally defined as low or zero school attendance.[2] The advantage of such a tactic is real; it is not a mere exercise in semantics. Evaluation of treatment

From *Arizona Law Review* 17 (1975): 3–19. Copyright © 1975 by the Arizona Board of Regents. Reprinted by permission.

effectiveness is well advanced when the problem can be set in a readily observable and quantifiable domain, as opposed to a reified, mentally-based domain. Thus, 90 or 100 percent school attendance becomes the performance criterion of treatment effectiveness against which the child's progress is measured. Opening the problem and evaluation criteria to quantification and direct observation allows the behavioral therapist to determine whether or not particular techniques change the behavior problem.

Major Techniques of Behavior Modification

SYSTEMATIC DESENSITIZATION

Among the most often used techniques in behavior modification are token economies, aversive conditioning, and systematic desensitization. The last technique is particularly useful in inducing behavioral change in an individual whose unadaptive or neurotic behavior was acquired in an anxiety generating situation.[3] Systematic desensitization therapy amounts to systematic elimination of the anxiety response associated with a given stimulus.[4] For example, phobias in general, such as acrophobia, the fear of crowds, and other psychological problems associated with emotional inhibition,[5] have been treated through systematic desensitization.[6]

The therapy has several distinguishing characteristics. The patient is first put into a state of deep relaxation. While in this state he identifies the different situations that might give rise to his neurotic reaction, and then, if there are more than one, he ranks them in order of the probability that they might trigger the neurotic reaction.[7] The result is a graduated hierarchy of situations that produce anxiety in the patient. By exposing the patient to the least offensive situation and then gradually working up the hierarchy, the therapist can desensitize the subject.[8]

THE TOKEN ECONOMY

Another major technique in behavior modification therapy is the token economy.[9] A quasi-economic system is established within the institution, and desired behavior is rewarded with tokens. Specifically, this set of complementary procedures is characterized by three features. First, as in other behavior modification techniques, the behavior that is the major focus of the treatment is defined in performance rather than psychic terms.[10] Second, a contractual arrangement is established between the patient and the hospital administration setting forth the rewards and penalties associated with certain conduct. For ease of operation, a currency system using tokens is instituted.[11] Third, as motivation to induce the target behaviors, a wide range of backup rewards, privileges, and items are made available to the patient in exchange for tokens. By reducing the time lag between payments of tokens and the purchase of rewards, the currency system can maintain an optimal level of motivation.

The token economy technique has been used in a variety of situations. In mental hospitals the technique has had a series of successful applications. This in large measure is due to the fact that the token economy has been used to eliminate symptoms. For example, auditory hallucinations, hypochondriasis, and chronic refusal to eat have been eliminated using token economies.[12]

The token economy system has been used in schools for both retarded and normal children. In the case of retarded children, treatment objectives have included teaching academic skills such as reading, writing, and arithmetic, as well as social skills such as speech fluency and good eating habits.[13] Schools for normal children have used the system for eliminating discipline problems, raising attention and concentration levels,[14] and enhancing academic performance.[15] The token economy system has recently been applied to the field of criminal corrections. These efforts have involved institutionalized delinquents,[16] youthful offenders,[17] and adult offenders.[18] Treatment objectives have included improving educational and vocational performance, controlling discipline problems, and the rationalized management of detained delinquents.[19] In addition, the token economy has been used to prevent delinquent behavior through placement of predelinquent boys in residential, home-style living arrangements.[20] Treatment objectives in this residential placement program have included modification of undesirable social behavior, development of new behavior in the community, development of self-control, and instillment of responsibility for one's behavior.

AVERSIVE CONDITIONING

Another method of behavior modification is aversive conditioning.[21] It has been defined as "an attempt to associate an undesirable behavior pattern with unpleasant stimulation or to make the unpleasant stimulation a consequence of the undesirable behavior."[22] Aversive conditioning decreases inappropriate or maladaptive behavior by using negative stimuli. For inappropriate behavior, such as when an autistic[23] child bangs his head, a negative stimulus, such as electric shock to the thigh, would be the consequence. For maladaptive behavior, such as homosexuality, the negative stimulus is paired to a stimulus that produces the maladaptive response. For example, the homosexual would be shocked whenever he is sexually aroused by a photo of a nude male. These negative stimuli should decrease head-banging by the autistic child and sexual arousal by the homosexual. The problem, however, is that while these behaviors have been broken, no new adaptive behaviors have been established in their place.[24] Thus, in order to be used effectively, aversive conditioning should be used in conjunction with therapy that will provide positive reinforcement and thereby build appropriate and functional behavior.

Aversive conditioning is typically reserved for behavior problems which will not decrease through any positive conditioning or where the client involved has agreed to this method of treatment. For the most part, aversive conditioning has been used with the most difficult of populations to work with, autistic children. Here, aversive stimuli, such as shock, have been used to save a child's life.[25] This method also has been used with homosexuals, transvestites, and people with fetishes who have agreed to undergo such therapy in a laboratory or a clinic.[26] Aversive conditioning, in the form of shock or chemicals which produce a bad taste, has also been used with alcoholics, drug addicts, and "excessive smokers."[27] In general, these techniques are used only with behaviors which are highly resistant to change by any other type of procedure.

One of the major criticisms of aversive conditioning is that it produces bad side effects such as avoidance, escape, fear, and various other emotional responses. In treatments performed by very competent therapists, however, these negative side effects were not produced in autistic children.[28] Parents, teachers, and some professionals who do not have such competency have clearly produced inappropriate behavior, including anxiety, truancy, stealing, lying, and various nervous habits. Aversive conditioning, therefore, should be used only as a last resort, after all positive programs to change behavior have failed. Even then, it should be carried out only with the greatest of care and only if the persons administering the treatment are accountable for their actions.

Further, the use of aversive conditioning should always be well monitored.[29] The technique of defining behavior in measurable terms, as previously mentioned, is helpful once again, for the degree of success of the aversive therapy can be carefully observed. In this manner, the therapy can be precisely administered, avoiding application of aversive stimuli in unnecessary amounts, and thereby minimizing the collateral production of inappropriate behavior.

ALTERNATIVES TO AVERSIVE CONDITIONING

Because of the problems[30] associated with the use of aversive stimuli, other less objectionable techniques have been developed. Some procedures try to minimize reinforcement of inappropriate behavior. Total withholding of reinforcement is termed extinction.[31] For example, when the class clown starts to disrupt his classroom to get attention, the teacher and other students, using extinction therapy, would totally ignore his antics, thereby refusing the reinforcement he seeks. Withholding reinforcement for brief periods is termed time-out therapy.[32] For example, in one study an autistic child seeking social reinforcement of his tantrums and self-destructive behavior was placed alone in his room for 10 minutes whenever he exhibited such behavior.[33] Similarly, to the prison inmate who views group association as rewarding, placement in solitary confinement also may be considered a form of time-out therapy.[34]

Another alternative to aversion therapy is the response-cost technique. Certain bad behavior will entail a "cost" to the patient; something of value to him is removed from his environment in response to inappropriate behavior.[35] Thus, a cartoon show is turned off when a child sucks his thumb,[36] or a patient in a token economy must return tokens if he engages in inappropriate behavior. In most large settings, such as mental institutions or schools, response-cost and time-out have been used. Response-cost is a particularly useful procedure in settings with a large number of individuals since it can be carried out within the framework of a token economy system.

Although response-cost, time-out, and extinction therapies usually produce less severe side effects than standard aversive therapy, these procedures have certain limitations. They are usually slow in decreasing the target behavior, and, as with aversive conditioning, some undesirable emotional responses may be produced. Therefore, as with other aversion therapy, these techniques should be used in conjunction with a program which builds positive behavior through the use of rewards.

Suggested Guidelines for the Practice of Behavior Modification in Institutions

To ensure a proper respect for the ethical problems inherent in behavior modification[37] and to ensure that the inmate receives those legal rights to which he is entitled,[38] it is imperative that rehabilitation therapy be done with the patient's informed consent and be subject to scrutiny throughout the treatment.[39] In this way the patient participates in and is responsible for his own retraining; he is doing, not being done to. The patient, the therapist, and society gain when the manner of rehabilitation is agreeable, satisfying, and growth producing. Consistent with this view, this article recommends eight guidelines for the behavior therapist in administering treatment.

1. The patient should be informed of the possible outcome of the treatment.[40] The therapist should try to impart as clear an understanding of the anticipated behavior changes as is possible under the circum-

stances. One method for accomplishing this objective would be through the use of some form of written agreement.[41] If the skills that are expected to be acquired are spelled out in an agreement, there would be evidence of compliance with the goal of full disclosure. By using these "contracts," the mutual expectations on the part of both the subject and the therapist would be greatly clarified. A comprehensive therapy contract is now in use[42] which sets forth the expected behavior objectives of the treatment, the nature, methods, and duration of the treatment, and the specific criteria and social values that will be used to evaluate and measure the success of the treatment.[43]

2. The patient should be informed of the procedures that will be used in the treatment.[44] While the outcome may be desirable, the means used to achieve this result may be so personally distasteful as to make the individual's voluntary participation unlikely. For example, given the choice between a treatment using a reward system or one using drug-induced vomiting,[45] it is unlikely that a patient would choose the latter method.

3. The patient should be made to feel that he is free to choose whether or not to participate in a program.[46] This issue is of special concern with prison inmates or with involuntarily-committed mental patients who may feel that participation is necessary to achieve parole or release. Every effort should be made by the therapist to remove such implicitly coercive influences and to dispel any individual fear of retribution. Indeed, coercion could have adverse long range consequences since coercion may lead to extreme resentment on the part of the unwilling participant and intensify a desire for vindication against society upon his release.[47]

Freedom of choice does require that the patient be mature enough to make the choice and cognizant of what he is doing. The latter qualification, however, must not be extended too far. The patient should not be so protected by the requirement of informed consent that even when he knows what procedures will be used and accepts them, he is not allowed to participate in a rehabilitative program. The case of *Kaimowitz* v. *Michigan Department of Mental Health*[48] is an example of such overprotection. Because of the experimental nature of the treatment, the court refused to allow involuntarily-detained mental patients to consent to certain neurosurgical procedures. This is carrying the doctrine of parens patriae to a ridiculous extreme. Essentially, *Kaimowitz* assumed that the patient was not sufficiently mature or aware to know what he wanted for himself. In particular, the criminal patient, such as in *Kaimowitz*, may wish to jeopardize his health in the interest of science, perhaps as a way of repaying a debt to society, as Leopold did with malaria research.[49] The decision should be his.

4. The patient should be able at any time to discontinue his partic-

ipation in a program without incurring prejudice or penalty. What was acceptable to the patient on paper may in fact turn out to be quite unacceptable in practice. Here again, the therapist must safeguard this right. Neither the therapist's rigor nor administrative convenience should be allowed to contravene the individual's wishes.

5. As an adjunct to the right to discontinue treatment, information necessary to make such a decision should be given the patient. He should be informed of his individual progress as often as he desires and in terms that he can readily understand.[50] False hopes of progress may induce continued participation in a program beyond the point at which the patient might otherwise wish to withdraw. Merely evaluating progress before and after treatment is insufficient, and withholding information for the sake of experimental rigor is unacceptable.

6. The patient is entitled to the treatment, rehabilitation, or education which is suited to his individual needs.[51] Requiring conformity to a single type of treatment or the intentional withholding of treatment through placement in an experimental control group is unacceptable. The need to foster individuality and to facilitate growth toward wholeness and self-actualization must be emphasized. The goal of a penal system, for example, if it is to be truly rehabilitative, should be to assist the development of self-esteem through the active encouragement of unique talents. Decisions should not be made for the patient regarding what he will learn while in the institution.

7. The patient should be given the opportunity to express his feelings, views, and attitudes toward a program. While formal assessment before and after the program is acceptable here, the individual must be given the opportunity to express his opinions at any time during his participation. Often, the counseling group is ostensibly used for this purpose, but it is more honored in breach than in practice.[52] For example, there is often great reluctance on the part of prison inmates to go beyond a superficial level of discussion because of the fear that expression of negative feelings might compromise "good behavior."[53] This is unfortunate since group catharsis may serve a valuable function as a tension releasing mechanism, thereby keeping resentment at a minimum and avoiding future Atticas. Thus, if the inmate is to verbalize openly the feelings he is having in a given program, there must be an acceptance of these views by the staff and an absence of fear of retaliation in the inmate. In short, the patient's full participation in a program should be encouraged. His "good boy" docility should not be the primary concern.

8. Only behavioral techniques that enrich the patient's environment beyond a base guarantee of certain social and personal rights should be employed. An individual choosing not to engage in the rewarded activity should simply experience the absence of reward as opposed to coer-

cion to conform to a given behavior. In general, neither sensory nor social deprivation should be considered as standard procedures to influence the individual's conduct. For example, in the START program[54] which took place in Springfield, Missouri, involuntary prison participants were prohibited from possessing reading material or otherwise using any educational, religious, or political material. They were denied the opportunity to view television or listen to a radio, and their actions were under continual surveillance.[55] In other words, the START program totally altered the confinement conditions of the prisoners and forced them to earn back what had rightfully been theirs upon admission into the institution. These kinds of sensory and social deprivations are not standard practices in behavior modification.[56] Further, such heroic means for changing behavior have typically failed to show that alternative techniques were inadequate.

Recommendations for the Use of Behavior Modification in Institutions

Compliance with the guidelines outlined above should provide assurance of effective treatment and awareness of situations of grave ethical concern. In addition to the guidelines, however, certain recommendations regarding methodology in general and the application of specific techniques can be made.

ON THE TOKEN ECONOMY AND COMMUNITY MENTAL HEALTH

The most promising avenue for assuring full protection of the patient's rights may be found in the method of community mental health, which strives to maintain, as extensively as possible, the patient's exposure to his natural environment to ensure that the individual's expectations of himself and society are continued. The token economy system is just such a method since it attempts to maintain the continuity of social expectations and responsibilities that characterize the "natural" contingencies of the outside world.

Nothing will maintain the patient's freedom and responsibility for his own behavior as much as a system that functions as does a token economy—as an extension of the society from which the patient comes. Such an extension guarantees the patient's learning to cope with the demands and responsibilities expected of individuals outside the institution, thereby preventing disculturation. Further, normalization of social interaction is greatly dependent upon a system that enables individuals to exchange goods for services, favors, and other goods. An exchange system[57] helps the parties involved to assess precisely each other's expectations and the rewards or consequences for meeting or failing to meet these expectations.

Careful attention must be given the method and operation of a token economy. A token economy program is characterized by its empirical definition of target behaviors and the results associated with their achievement. Typically, the "rules" of behavior are explicitly and publicly stated, as are the rewards for observing those rules and the benefits which may be obtained in exchange for tokens. This procedure ensures that all individuals have the basis for exercising an informed choice.[58]

The aspect of choice in the token economy is of crucial importance. Choice, to be meaningful, must allow the person to achieve the consequences attendant upon choosing one thing over another. Once the individual discovers that, irrespective of his desires, he will be made to conform to institutional routine, his responsibility for his own actions is terminated. On the other hand, when the individual discovers that his desires will be respected, he will learn that he must bear the consequences of his own choice, and he will, in turn, learn responsibility for his own actions.

Thus, after the consequences of alternative choices have been outlined to the individual it is crucial that his choice be respected, since only in this manner can demeaning and eroding the individual's self-respect and dignity be avoided and responsibility for his own actions assumed. Acceptance of the consequences of one's own choices, however, will require at least a minimum of exposure to the consequences of other choices. Otherwise, the individual will not have an informed basis for choice.

A corollary of the need for individuals to exercise the free choice that is normally associated with community practices such as a token economy is the necessity for patients to have the right to voluntarily assume their own management. This action might include the patient seeking supervised work opportunities in positions which are both useful to the institution and therapeutic to the patient in terms of increased self-confidence and individual responsibility. It must be borne in mind that when patients are treated in mental institutions as if they were in medical hospitals, the objectives of social reeducation often are confused with those of physical restoration. Behavioral reeducation requires that the social environment in which the patient is living resemble closely that of the environment to which he will return. Therefore, if no expectations or demands are made of the patient in the institution, his reentry to a normal environment will only eventuate in failure because of his unpreparedness for such an experience.

To be sure, behavioral techniques enable the patient, upon commitment, to be shielded from all the demands and social pressures that led to his hospitalization. But gradually and systematically, as the patient improves, he is exposed to greater demands so that he learns to cope with most of the situations that he will encounter in the community. While it is appropriate to protect the patient from labor exploitation,[59] it also must be remembered that such protection must be balanced with efforts to keep the patient optimally motivated so as to improve his condition, to allow him to assume responsibility for his own actions, and eventually to permit his return to society.

ON REWARDS AND INCENTIVES

The major aspect of behavior modification is incentives and their use. While the notion of incentives dates from time immemorial, the sophisticated technology associated with their use is recent. Essentially, it is now known that incentives work under certain, and now well-researched, conditions and fail to work when these conditions have not been met. Current technology eliminates the uncertainty in the use of incentives. The naive notion that incentives ought to work has been rejected through research indicating that under certain conditions incentives may have the opposite effect from that expected.

Incentives intended to encourage certain behavior should only be employed after the display of that behavior. For example, if it is desired to encourage participation in a rehabilitative program, incentives should be used only when the individual has demonstrated some participation. Further, incentives must be meaningful to each individual. Since "one man's meat is another man's poison," it is basic to a behavioral approach to discover and develop meaningful incentives. Refusal to do so indicates failure.

What needs to be emphasized is that there are endless permutations and combinations of ways in which the patient may enjoy the rights given to him. For example, one patient may never make a phone call, even if he has the right to make one weekly, but another patient may wish to make a call daily. It is far too easy to standardize the rights of the individual in the institution. What is more difficult is to minimize regimentation, dependence, and eventually apathy. In an effort to enhance individual choice, variability, and differences, in contrast to conformity and regimentation, highly varied opportunities for self-motivation should be used as incentives to help the patients in their own rehabilitation and to reinforce their right to be different.[60]

While standardization of the rights and privileges used as incentives should be avoided, providing certain basic rights and privileges for all patients, such as food, lodging, ground privileges, and privacy, is legally required.[61] These rights and privileges constitute a floor below which guarantees may not drop.[62] Thus, contingent rewards should be made available in addition to those comforts and pleasures already guaranteed to the individual.[63] For example, if all individuals have been assigned a given room and bed, the reward could be the freedom to select the type of room or bed from among a wide range of choices. This effort would be consistent with developing responsibility for making choices. Additionally, withdrawal and return of personal property and privileges already permitted, though not required as basic, should not be the source of rewards. Regaining the possession of one's personal articles or privileges does not meet the contingent-rewards guideline since it is not an additional incentive. By insisting that rewards be additional to those rights and privileges already guaranteed or granted in an institution, deprivation of rewards will be avoided and enrichment of incentives ensured. As a general rule, it would be both effective and legally defensible to use rewards on a contingent basis so long as these rewards go beyond the minimum rights and privileges enjoyed by the patient. In so doing, the result will be an enriched environment that is not limited to the rights and privileges granted the patients.

ON SECLUSION

The solitary confinement of a patient in an empty room is still a treatment commonly used in institutions.[64] To justify the use of this procedure it is necessary that such use be constantly evaluated in terms of its effectiveness and that an additional program based on positive rewards be used concurrently with seclusion. By so doing, the cooling off or confinement period will result in a reduction of disturbed or aggressive behavior as the patient experiences the gross difference between seclusion and his interaction with the rewarding environment.

ON USE OF AVERSIVE OR NOXIOUS STIMULI

Only when the patient's actions present a clear and imminent danger to his own or others' physical integrity may aversive or noxious stimuli be justified.[65] As was the case with seclusion, the patient must be concurrently exposed to a treatment based primarily on positive rewards. In addition, continuous checks must be made on the effectiveness of aversive procedures. Perhaps the best model for such procedures was pioneered in the use of aversive techniques to develop language and social skills in speech-free and self-abusive autistic children.[66] Unquestionably, the objective was desirable. In addition, the relative effects of a mild electric shock delivered to the child upon his displaying self-mutilation were evaluated. When the child ran to the arms of the investigator, the shock was terminated. The fact that this procedure generated an interest in people was considered a notable achievement since autistic children are characterized by their total social detachment. Finally, a socioeducational program based on positive rewards to ensure that the social gains would in time be self-sustaining was administered.

This work demonstrates the proper technical rationale for the use of aversive procedures. Whenever a shock was delivered to the child, care was taken to provide the child with an opportunity to extricate himself from the situation or to terminate the shock by engaging in a learned behavior. This procedure differs from the use of punishment in that the period of punishment is predetermined; it cannot be terminated by the subject. In using aversive stimuli, the individual subjected to it learns how to terminate it and how to avoid it in the future. This gives the subject control over both the onset and the termination of the stimuli. From a therapeutic viewpoint, generating interest in self-protection may well be the lowest level of motivation upon which the therapist can build complex adaptive behavior.

Conclusion

A new technology of behavior modification is rapidly emerging in the areas of therapy and prison rehabilitation. Conclusions may now be drawn as to the effectiveness of specific procedures. Rewards are most effective when they enrich rather than reduce the individual's range of incentives in an institution. Further, aversive procedures are most effective when they are used concurrently with a system of rewards. Because of ethical problems and limited effectiveness, however, aversive procedures, such as electric shock, should be used only in those cases where the individual is physically endangering himself or others. Indeed, heroic procedures such as electric shock are not standard and are of limited value since they teach an individual only what not to do, rather than what to do.

Research shows that it is possible to foster in patients and inmates new behaviors and to develop self-control and responsibility through a motivational system known as the token economy. This system restores to the individual the rights and social obligations found outside the institution. In so doing, the token economy preserves a modicum of social contact between the individual and society at large. Thus, behavior modification, by systematically exposing the individual to rewarding experiences, attempts to teach new and effective ways of meeting the demands of a socially complex world.

Notes

1. Indeed, environmental events shape our character throughout life. The only difference between behavior modification and other approaches to changing behavior is one of degree. Aversive conditioning is common in experience; for example, the child who learns to fear fire after being burned. By systematic application, however, behavior modification succeeds where other approaches fail. See Roos, *Human Rights and Behavior Modification,* 12 MENTAL RETARDATION, June 1974, at 4.

2. Ayllon, Smith & Rogers, *Behavioral Management of School Phobia,* 1 J. BEHAVIOR THERAPY & EXPERIMENTAL PSYCHIATRY 125, 126 (1970).

3. *See generally* Paul, *Outcome of Systematic Desensitization,* in BEHAVIOR THERAPY: APPRAISAL AND STATUS 63 (C. Franks ed. 1969); Russell, *The Power of Behavior Control: A Critique of Behavior Modification Methods,* 30 J. CLINICAL PSYCHOLOGY 111, 117–18 (1974).

4. *See generally,* J. WOLPE, PSYCHOTHERAPY BY RECIPROCAL INHIBITION (1958). Joseph Wolpe pioneered the technique. The historical origin and development is traced in Paul, *supra* note 3, at 64–66.

5. Some examples would be insomnia, shyness, homosexuality, and frigidity.

6. Systematic desensitization has been applied in mental health settings such as clinics and hospitals and in general practice.

7. The procedure is described in detail in Paul, *supra* note 3, at 68–70. The necessity for relaxation is in dispute.

8. For an exhaustive listing of medical articles on systematic desensitization, see W. MORROW, BEHAVIOR THERAPY BIBLIOGRAPHY 1950–1969, 156–57 (1971).

9. The token economy was developed in a ward of chronically psychotic female patients at the Anna State Hospital in Illinois. T. AYLLON & N. AZRIN, THE TOKEN ECONOMY: A MOTIVATION SYSTEM FOR THERAPY AND REHABILITATION at v, 16 (1968) [hereinafter cited as THE TOKEN ECONOMY]. The literature on token economics is now extensive. See Davidson, *Appraisal of Behavior Modification Techniques with Adults in Institutional Settings,* in BEHAVIOR THERAPY: APPRAISAL AND STATUS 220, 229–35 (C. Franks ed. 1969); Kazdin & Bootzin, *The Token Economy: An Evaluation Review,* 5 J. APPLIED BEHAVIOR ANALYSIS 343 (1972). The legal problems have been exposed in Wexler, *Of Rights and Reinforcers,* 11 SAN DIEGO L. REV. 957 (1974) [hereinafter cited as Wexler, *Of Rights and Reinforcers*]; Wexler, *Token and Taboo: Behavior Modification, Token Economies, and the Law,* 61 CALIF. L. REV. 81 (1973).

10. While the performance objectives are often assumed to be clear-cut, the fact is that they are typically couched in terms that are abstract, mental, or largely unobservable. Therefore, for such objectives to be amenable to evaluation, further refinement towards objective definition is necessary.

11. Specially designed tangible items such as points, green stamps, credit cards, and similar symbols have been used as tokens.

12. Ayllon & Azrin, *The Measurement and Reinforcement of Behavior of Psychotics,* 8 J. EXPERIMENTAL ANALYSIS OF BEHAVIOR 357 (1968); Ayllon & Haughton, *Control of the Behavior of Schizophrenic Patients by Food,* 5 J. EXPER-

IMENTAL ANALYSIS OF BEHAVIOR 343 (1962); see Atthowe & Krasner, *Preliminary Report on the Application of Contingent Reinforcement Procedures (Token Economy) on a "Chronic" Psychiatric Ward*, 73 J. ABNORMAL PSYCHOLOGY 37 (1968); Lloyd & Abel, *Performance on a Token Economy Psychiatric Ward: A Two-Year Summary*, 8 BEHAVIOR RESEARCH & THERAPY 1 (1970). *See generally* THE TOKEN ECONOMY, *supra* note 9; Kazdin & Bootzin, *supra* note 9.

13. *Cf.* Birnbrauer, Wolf, Kidder & Tague, *Classroom Behavior of Retarded Pupils with Token Reinforcement*, 2 J. EXPERIMENTAL CHILD PSYCHOLOGY 219 (1965).

14. O'Leary, Becker, Evans & Saudargas, *A Token Reinforcement Program in a Public School: A Replication and Systematic Analysis*, 2 J. APPLIED BEHAVIOR ANALYSIS 3, 8–11 (1969).

15. Ayllon & Roberts, *Eliminating Discipline Problems by Strengthening Academic Performance*, 7 J. APPLIED BEHAVIOR ANALYSIS 71, 74–75 (1974); Lovitt & Curtiss, *Academic Response Rate as a Function of Teacher—And Self-Imposed Contingencies*, 2 J. APPLIED BEHAVIOR ANALYSIS 49, 52 (1969). In one study with disturbed adolescents, however, a token economy designed to increase productivity in classwork resulted in an increase in quantity but a decrease in quality. Cotler, Applegate, King & Kristal, *Establishing a Token Economy Program in a State Hospital Classroom: A Lesson in Training Student and Teacher*, 3 BEHAVIOR THERAPY, 209, 214–17 (1972).

16. Burchard & Tyler, *The Modification of Delinquent Behavior Through Operant Conditioning*, 2 BEHAVIOR RESEARCH & THERAPY 245 (1965).

17. H. COHEN, J. FILIPCZAK & J. BIS, AN INITIAL STUDY OF CONTINGENCIES APPLICABLE TO SPECIAL EDUCATION (1967).

18. Milan & McKee, *Behavior Modification: Principles and Applications in Corrections*, in HANDBOOK OF CRIMINOLOGY (D. Glaser ed. 1974); Boren & Colman, *Some Experiments on Reinforcement Principles Within Psychiatric Ward for Delinquent Soldiers*, 3 J. APPLIED BEHAVIOR ANALYSIS 29 (1970).

19. Again, one of the major problems in the application of behavioral technology to prisons is definition of the inmates' problems and the objectives of the prison. While the inmates' problems have often been conceptualized in a psychological manner involving pathological aggression toward society, this approach limits evaluation of a treatment's effectiveness. A behavioral redefinition of the inmates' problems involves pinpointing the areas of social interaction that require specific skills. A step in that direction is reflected in the selection of behaviors to be taught to the inmates while in prison. In selecting vocational, educational, and social objectives for therapy or treatment, the prison becomes associated with rehabilitative and educational efforts rather than with custodial goals.

20. This program included boys who were in trouble with their school or community or who were largely uncontrollable. Phillips, *Achievement Place: Token Reinforcement Procedures in a Home-Style Rehabilitation Setting for "Pre-Delinquent" Boys*, 1 J. APPLIED BEHAVIOR ANALYSIS 213, 213–14 (1968). Phillips, Phillips, Fixsen & Wolf, *Achievement Place: Modification of the Behaviors of Pre-Delinquent Boys Within a Token Economy*, 4 J. APPLIED BEHAVIOR ANALYSIS 45, 45–46 (1971).

21. *See generally* S. RACHEMAN & J. TEASDALE, AVERSION THERAPY AND

BEHAVIOR DISORDERS: AN ANALYSIS (1969); Rachman & Teasdale, *Aversion Therapy: An Appraisal,* in BEHAVIOR THERAPY APPRAISAL AND STATUS 279–320 (C. Franks ed. 1969). *See also* W. MORROW, *supra* note 8, at 154–55 (collecting sources).

22. S. RACHMAN & J. TEASDALE, *supra* note 21, at xii.

23. Autism is a form of childhood schizophrenia characterized by acting out and withdrawal. The autistic child is apt to perform acts of self-mutilation and head banging. Developmental language disorders and a marked inability to adjust socially are also characteristic. DORLAND'S ILLUSTRATED MEDICAL DICTIONARY 168 (25th ed. 1974).

24. Neither homosexuality nor heterosexuality fills the vacuum created when the other is extinguished. *Money, Strategy, Ethics, Behavior Modification, and Homosexuality,* 2 ARCHIVES OF SEXUAL BEHAVIOR 79 (1972) (editorial). It has been suggested that the proper way to extinguish homosexuality is to reward the subject with a homosexual experience after he achieves a heterosexual experience. Gradually, the number of heterosexual experiences needed to achieve a homosexual experience is increased until the frequency of homosexual activity is minimized or extinguished. Id. at 79–80.

The necessity of shock therapy to reduce homosexuality has been questioned. It has been observed that a male homosexual must be "strongly motivated toward change . . . to subject himself to a series of such shocks after visit. . . . [I]f other forms of psychotherapy were limited only to such a select group of exceptionally motivated homosexuals the results also would be better than average." Marmor, *Dynamic Psychotherapy and Behavior Therapy,* 24 ARCHIVES OF GENERAL PSYCHIATRY 22, 25 (1971).

25. In a laboratory setting, electric shock has been delivered to children who climb to dangerous heights. Risley, *The Effects and Side Effects of Punishing the Autistic Behavior of a Deviant Child,* 1 J. APPLIED BEHAVIOR ANALYSIS 25–30 (1968). Shock also has been delivered to autistic children who engage in severe head banging and self-mutilation. Lovaas & Simmons, *Manipulation of Self-Destruction in Three Retarded Children,* 2 J. APPLIED BEHAVIOR ANALYSIS 143 (1969).

26. See Marks & Gelder, *Transvestism and Fetishism: Clinical and Psychological Changes During Faradic Aversion,* 113 BRITISH J. PSYCHIATRY 711 (1967).

27. *See generally,* A. BANDURA, PRINCIPLES OF BEHAVIOR MODIFICATION 501–54 (1969).

28. *See* Lovaas, Schaeffer & Simmons, *Building Social Behavior in Autistic Children by Use of Electric Shock,* 1 J. EXPERIMENTAL RESEARCH IN PERSONALITY 99, 106–108 (1965); Risley, *supra* note 25, at 21, 32–34.

29. *Accord,* Roos, *supra* note 1, at 5.

30. See text & note 37, *infra.*

31. Ayllon & Michael, *The Psychiatric Nurse as a Behavioral Engineer,* 2 J. EXPERIMENTAL ANALYSIS OF BEHAVIOR 323 (1959). *See generally* Sherman & Baer, *Appraisal of Operant Therapy Techniques with Children and Adults,* in BEHAVIOR THERAPY: APPRAISAL AND STATUS 192, 215–16 (C. Franks ed. 1969).

32. *See generally* Sherman & Baer, *supra* note 31, at 212–13.

33. Wolf, Risley & Mees, *Application of Operant Conditioning Procedures to the Behavior Problems of an Autistic Child,* 1 BEHAVIOR RESEARCH & THERAPY

305, 311 (1964). In another study, children who broke rules applicable to playing pool with other children were isolated for brief periods. Tyler & Brown, *The Use of Swift, Brief Isolation as a Group Control Device for Institutionalized Delinquents*, 5 BEHAVIOR RESEARCH & THERAPY 1, 2 (1967).

34. A recent United States Supreme Court case has held, however, that prisoners may not be placed in solitary confinement without procedural due process guarantees. Wolff v. McDonnell, 418 U.S. 539, 563–67 (1974).

35. Legal strictures require, however, that certain basic rights, food, and privacy not be removed. Wyatt v. Stickney, 344 F. Supp. 373 (D. Ala. 1972), *aff'd sub nom.*, Wyatt v. Aderholt, 503 F.2d 1305 (5th Cir. 1974), *noted in* 51 B.U.L. REV. 530 (1971), 86 HARV. L. REV. 1282 (1973), *and* 25 U. FLA. L. REV. 614 (1973).

36. Baer, *Laboratory Control of Thumbsucking by Withdrawal and Representation of Reinforcement*, 5 J. EXPERIMENTAL ANALYSIS OF BEHAVIOR 525 (1962). See Sherman & Baer, *supra* note 31, at 212.

37. The ethical issues involved in behavior modification have been widely discussed. *See, e.g.*, B. SKINNER, BEYOND FREEDOM AND DIGNITY (1972); Bengelman, *Ethical Issues in Behavioral Control*, 156 J. NERVOUS & MENTAL DISEASE 412 (1973); Cooke & Cooke, *Behavioral Modification: Answers to Some Ethical Issues*, 11 PSYCHOLOGY IN THE SCHOOLS 5 (1974); Halleck, *Legal and Ethical Aspects of Behavior Control*, 131 AM. J. PSYCHIATRY 381 (1974); Roos, *supra* note 1. Behavior modification has been attacked as repressive, dehumanizing, and perhaps even part of a conspiracy to control those citizens who deviate from social norms. Halleck, *supra* at 381. Not all practitioners agree. One psychiatrist remarked that "[o]nly in rare and extreme situations are many people excessively concerned about the minutiae of patients' rights. . . ." Cole, 131 AM. J. PSYCHIATRY 927 (1974) (letter to the editor). In response, it has been charged that such statements are "dangerously naive." Halleck, 131 AM. J. PSYCHIATRY 928 (1974) (letter to the editor).

After arguing that behavior modification techniques contain no new power over mankind, one practitioner interestingly concludes that since there can be no meaningful debate about the ethics of methods that do not work, a discussion of the ethics involved in psychological control is now rather academic. Russell, *supra* note 3, at 132. Even so, this argument is premised upon a misconception—that behavioral techniques are due to a Hawthorne or placebo effect. In other words, whatever behavioral change might follow therapy is not due to the therapy, but to preexisting forces. Those who would advance this point argue that behavioral experiments use no controls and that it is therefore a logical fallacy to assume that the cause of the modified behavior was necessarily the therapy. *See* Opton, *Institutional Behavior Modification as a Fraud and Sham*, 17 ARIZ. L. REV. 20, 22 (1975). In behavioral experiments, however, each person is his own control. The effects of behavior modification can be evaluated by terminating the behavioral procedure and observing whether there is reversion to the sort of behavior that the procedures had attempted to change. This on-off experimental design, called ABA design, is used in all behavioral experiments. *See, e.g.*, Tyler & Brown, *supra* note 33. Indeed, from an ethical standpoint, it is far better to use an ABA design for control than to let a group of patients sit idle, without treatment, merely to constitute a scientifically pure control group.

One more point should be made about the efficacy of behavioral techniques. Opponents argue that it is widely recognized that patients in a token economy eventually will decline to do jobs that are not paid and will request assignment to jobs that do pay. "Crazy they may have been, but not that crazy." Opton, *supra* at 25 n. 17. This both misses and makes the point. Indeed, such behavior is not crazy. The people involved in these programs, however, have never exhibited such behavior before. In the example given, the token economy has taught the principle of economic utility to persons who never before acted in such a manner. This normal behavior was learned.

Certain ethical problems may be irresolvable. For instance, it is difficult to say what one does with a claustrophobic patient who pleads to be released from confinement, assuming he has previously agreed to treatment precisely outlined. Begelman, *supra* at 417. Of course, the patient should be released. The therapy, however, never gets a chance to work. Perhaps the solution lies in more innovative techniques and more gradual treatment.

38. These include all constitutional rights in general and, in particular, the rights to a residence unit with a screen, a comfortable bed, a locker, a chair, a table, nutritional meals, and social interaction, and the rights to have visitors, attend religious services, wear one's own clothes, have clothes laundered, and exercise outdoors. In general, there is a right to the least restrictive conditions necessary to achieve the purposes of commitment. Wyatt v. Stickney, 344 F. Supp. 373, 379–86 (M. D. Ala. 1972), *aff'd sub nom.*, Wyatt v. Aderholt, 503 F. 2d 1305 (5th Cir. 1974).

39. Legally, however, consent is not required in all circumstances. See Friedman, *Legal Regulation of Applied Behavior Analysis in Mental Institutions and Prisons,* 17 ARIZ. L. REV. 39, 68–69 (1975).

40. See Wyatt v. Stickney, 344 F. Supp. 373, 380 (M.D. Ala. 1972), *aff'd sub nom.*, Wyatt v. Aderholt, 503 F.2d 1305 (5th Cir. 1974); Halleck, *supra* note 37, at 384; Roos, *supra* note 1, at 5.

41. These agreements appear to be contracts in the legal sense. There is mutuality of consideration—the therapist develops a treatment plan and the patient agrees to a fee. Failure of performance by the therapist, that is, failure of treatment, results in a reduced fee. Legal problems, however, remain. Should the patient fail to use his best effort to comply or if he terminates the treatment, it is not clear whether the therapist has a claim for his full fee. Neither is it clear whether the therapist, by contracting, has guaranteed certain results.

42. An example of such a contract is reproduced in Ayllon & Skuban, *Accountability in Psychotherapy: A Test Case,* 4 J. BEHAVIOR THERAPY & EXPERIMENTAL PSYCHIATRY 19, 22–23 (1973).

43. While this contract is, of course, intended for therapy rather than penal rehabilitation, it also could be used in a prison, thus paving the way for accountability in our prisons.

44. Wyatt v. Stickney, 344 F. Supp. 373, 380 (M.D. Ala. 1972), *aff'd sub nom.*, Wyatt v. Aderholt, 503 F-2d 1305 (5th Cir. 1974); cf. Halleck, *supra* note 37, at 384.

45. In the case of Knecht v. Gillman, 488 F.2d 1136 (8th Cir. 1973), a vomiting inducing drug called apomorphine was injected whenever certain behavioral requirements were not met, such as getting up on time and working. Although the objectives may be desirable, the extremely negative method of achieving them cannot be justified behaviorally since such behaviors can more easily be developed through positive means such as rewards.

46. See Wyatt v. Stickney, 344 F. Supp. 373, 380 (M.D. Ala. 1972), aff'd sub nom., Wyatt v. Aderholt, 503 F.2d 1305 (5th Cir. 1974).

47. For example, in Springfield, Missouri, in October 1972, a rehabilitative program called START (Special Treatment and Rehabilitative Training) began. This program involved inmates who were arbitrarily denied regular prison conditions without a hearing. For discussions of START, see Friedman, supra note 39, at 92–94; Wexler, Of Rights and Reinforcers, supra note 9, at 963–64.

48. 42 U.S.L.W. 2063 (C.A. 73–19434–AW, Cir. Ct. Wayne County, Mich., July 10, 1973) (partial report).

49. N. LEOPOLD, LIFE PLUS 99 YEARS 305–38 (1958).

50. Any evaluation index, such as a grade or performance rating, must be made known to the patient or inmate so that he can take part in the decision-making body regarding his terminating or continuing a given program.

51. See Wyatt v. Stickney, 344 F. Supp. 373, 384–86 (M.D. Ala. 1972), aff'd sub nom., Wyatt v. Aderholt, 503 F.2d 1305 (5th Cir. 1974).

52. E. WRIGHT, THE POLITICS OF PUNISHMENT: A CRITICAL ANALYSIS OF PRISONS IN AMERICA 61 (1973).

53. Indeed, there is little to indicate that group counseling has made any significant difference to most inmates. Id.

54. See discussion note 47 supra.

55. The right to be free from unreasonable search and seizure, the right to privacy, the right against cruel and unusual punishment, and the freedoms of religion, speech, and association were alleged to be abridged. See Clonce v. Richardson, 379 F. Supp. 338, 352 (W.D. Mo. 1974).

56. Halleck, supra note 37, at 384.

57. Any arbitrary unit of exchange, such as gold, silver, blankets, shells, or cigarettes, could be used.

58. Since an individual choosing not to engage in the rewarded activity would simply experience the absence of reward as opposed to coercion to conform to a given behavior, the requirements of the eighth guideline in the previous section are satisfied. See text accompanying notes 54–56 supra.

59. This could be accomplished with a job rotation rule requiring that a patient not be allowed to hold the same job without interruption for more than a week at a time. See THE TOKEN ECONOMY, supra note 9, at 200–203.

60. Cf. N. KITTRIE, THE RIGHT TO BE DIFFERENT (1971). The methodology to achieve such objectives is available in the token economy. See text & notes 9–20 supra.

61. See discussion note 38 supra. Since many chronically ill patients may forego such rights, there is need for procedures which ensure that patients enjoy them. In this way, the danger of being deprived of items that are self-reinforcing would be avoided. See THE TOKEN ECONOMY, supra note 9, at 88–103.

62. Such free access to privileges and incentives is consistent with the priming rule described in THE TOKEN ECONOMY, *supra* 9, at 91–93.

63. Wexler, *Of Rights and Reinforcers, supra* note 9, at 968–69. Idiosyncratic pleasures, such as feeding kittens, are the most effective reinforcers. Atthowe & Krasner, *supra* note 12, at 38.

64. Roos, *supra* note 1, at 5 (suggesting that a distinction should be drawn between time-out, which is therapeutic, and seclusion, which is long term and merely for the convenience of the staff).

65. For example, head banging, self-mutilation, and violent assaults on others would justify such therapy. Further, punishment and the use of noxious stimuli require the technical supervision of a trained professional since these techniques are easily subject to misuse and abuse.

66. *See* Lovaas, Schaeffer & Simmons, *supra* note 28; Lovaas & Simmons, *supra* note 25.

Management of Sexual Disorders

L. P. Kok

Sexual disorders comprise (a) disorders of function in which sexual functioning is disturbed leading to problems during sexual intercourse, (b) disorders of orientation whereby a nonheterosexual partner or object is sought, and (c) other disorders involving aberrant psychosexual behavior. In managing such problems a thorough psychosexual assessment is required in order to ascertain the exact nature of the problem and what the precipitating, predisposing and prolonging factors are. In disorders of orientation and disorders involving aberrant sexual behaviors, the developmental history and early childhood relationships must be looked into carefully. Laboratory investigations are usually indicated in erectile dysfunction as up to 80% would have an organic aetiology—vascular, neurological and endocrine disorders have to be ruled out. Treatment of the various conditions involves general sexual counselling, behavior therapy including stress management, psychotherapy, marital therapy and drug therapy as indicated. However, in erectile dysfunction, drug treatment(including intracavernosal injections), mechanical aids, or surgery may be indicated; and in transsexualism—for those who are unable to revert to accepting their natural status—a sex reassignment operation is the treatment of choice.

Sexual disorders may be divided into:

a) Disorders of functioning
b) Disorders of orientation
c) Disorders involving a certain behavioral pattern.[1]

From *Singapore Medical Journal* 34: 553–56. Reprinted by permission.

The above 3 categories are however, not mutually exclusive. Table I shows the different types of sexual disorders.

Table I—Disorders of Function*

| | Syndrome | |
Pathology	Male	Female
1) Disorder of interest or libido	Inhibited sexual desire Low sexual interest	Inhibited sexual desire Low sexual interest
2) Disorder of excitement or arousal	Erectile dysfunction (impotence)	General sexual dysfunction (frigidity) Sexual anaesthesia
3) Disorder of orgasm	Anorgasmia Premature ejaculation Delayed ejaculation	Anorgasmia
4) Pain related disorder	Ejaculatory pain	Dyspareunia vaginismus
5) Fear/anxiety related disorder	Erectile dysfunction (performance anxiety) Sexual phobia	Sexual phobia

*Modified from Hawton K. Sex therapy: A practical guide. 1985: 32.

Principles of Management of Sexual Disorders

1) PSYCHOSEXUAL ASSESSMENT

a) *Disorders of sexual functioning*

Although not mandatory, it is helpful if the patient could be seen with his spouse or partner.

During the initial interview a detailed history should be taken to find out the exact nature of the problem, whether the onset was gradual or sudden, whether any precipitating events were present, whether it was situation specific (e.g., with the spouse), whether there were any prolonging factors, what the resulting pattern of behavior and cognition was, and what the reaction of the spouse was.

In addition the sexual development, libido, masturbation and dating history, premarital and marital sexual history, the methods of contraception, family attitudes to sex, and religious upbringing should be looked into. A good medical and drug history has also to be taken, and psychiatric problems ascertained. Possible sources of stress—like work difficulties and relationship problems must also be assessed.

b) *Disorders of sexual orientation*

In disorders of sexual orientation, greater emphasis is placed on the developmental history, relationship with each parent, early childhood experience, initial sexual experience, religious beliefs and problems with the law regarding the sexual activity.

2) PHYSICAL EXAMINATION

After the psychiatric history, a physical examination should be carried out to exclude any general physical problems. In males, the genitalia should be checked for abnormalities of size and shape, for swellings and induration. The sensation of the whole perineal region should also be checked as well as the penile and peripheral pulses. In women complaining of pain on intercourse, inflammatory conditions, atrophic changes, painful scars have to be excluded.

Investigations

Extensive investigations are unnecessary except in erectile dysfunction and retarded ejaculation, and may include:

1) blood tests—GTT for diabetes, sex hormone levels, liver, renal and thyroid function tests.[2,3]
2) assessment of neurological functioning, e.g., sensation in the genitalia and perineal region sacral evoked response (bulbocavernosus reflex time); cystometrography and video cystometry, radiographic examination of the spine may be required.[4]
3) vascular functioning—vasodilator injection[5] to assess the ability of the penile arteries to dilate and whether the venous system is intact and the tumescence is maintained. More sophisticated techniques include duplex ultrasonography of the penis before and after an injection of a vasodilator substance, arteriography and cavernosography. The latter are usually done when invasive treatment is considered.[6]
4) nocturnal penile tumescence[7,8]—this test of whether erection occurs during sleep can often differentiate between organic and psychogenic causes of erection.

PRINCIPLES OF TREATMENT

1) *Discussion of the problem*

As in any other illness the nature of the problem, the diagnosis, causes and options of treatment should be discussed with the patient and partner (if applicable).

2) *Education*

Often an explanation of the anatomy and physiology of sexual organs, the sexual response cycle, psychological reactions to sexual dysfunction in the subject and the partner helps in clarifying the problem and treatment issues.

3) *Helping the couple to communicate*

Couples are often unable to talk about their feelings and problems and the doctor may have to help them discuss their problems in a nonjudgmental, nonemotional way.

4) *Sensate focus (Masters and Johnson's therapy)[9]*

This therapy devised by Masters and Johnson relieves the couple of the pressure to perform thus allowing them to relax, and touch, kiss, hug and massage each other all over in a nondemanding manner. The couple is instructed on what to do and given homework assignments to practice at home. There is an understanding that during the first stage (nongenital sensate focus) the couple does not touch each other's genitalia and breasts. The couple takes turns to do the touching and massaging. Each is responsible for his own pleasure and should communicate to the other if the touching is unpleasant or uncomfortable and how he wants it changed, and also what he finds pleasant about it. During this session the couple learns to trust each other (e.g., a patient with vaginismus will learn to accept that she can be physically close with her spouse without the session ending in sexual intercourse).

During the next phase the couple proceeds to genital touching, without intercourse. Again the aim is for the couple to enjoy the session without monitoring their own performance, or that of their spouse. When the couple is comfortable with this they proceed to a low-keyed intercourse, i.e., vaginal containment, using the woman on top or the lateral (side by side) position. After penetration the couple lies still and focuses on any pleasant sensations they feel. The duration of containment is up to the couple and they can do it two to three times per session, with pleasuring in between.

At the last stage the couple has intercourse with movement, initially slowly and then faster till they are having normal intercourse.

5) *Sexual fantasies and play acting*

Fantasies can be used to increase arousal and improve enjoyment. Often patients or couples find it awkward discussing their fantasies. In this case the doctor can suggest one or two common fantasies. If the couple is willing, they can act out a script which should be pleasurable, fun and erotic. The physician has to use his discretion, as some patients are averse to such suggestions, finding them offensive.

6) *Relaxation therapy*

If anxiety levels are high, e.g., performance anxiety (in erectile dysfunction, premature ejaculation, sexual phobias, vaginismus and dyspareunia) relaxation therapy is useful. In those who are good hypnotic subjects, hypnosis may achieve faster results.

7) *Marital therapy*

If the underlying problem is that of a marital conflict, marital therapy is indicated, and it is after there is some resolution of the conflict and the couple feels more loving towards each other that sex therapy can be initiated—as otherwise sabotage by one or both may occur.

8) *Drug treatment*

Drug treatment may be indicated in conditions like erectile dysfunction or premature ejaculation, in those with high levels of anxiety, or who are depressed. It may also be used in the disorders of sexual orientation (see under specific conditions).

9) *Behavior therapy*

Methods like desensitization, aversive therapy and shaping can be used for disorders of orientation.

10) *Surgery*

This may be indicated in the more severe cases of disorders of function like erectile dysfunction, and vaginismus, and in the disorder of orientation like transsexualism.

11) *Other treatment*

If the sexual problem is part of a wider psychological disturbance, other types of treatment may be indicated, e.g., psychotherapy, cognitive therapy.

SURROGATE PARTNERS

In the Singapore context, surrogate partners are not used. Some male patients may seek commercial partners on their own to test out their sexual functioning, or they practice with their own partners.

Management of Specific Problems

1) IMPOTENCE

Over the past decade there has been a marked change in the treatment of erectile dysfunction, as it became more evident that organic disorders were more predominant in the causation.

The newer methods of treatment[6] include:

a) *Pharmacological treatment*

i) Intracavernosal injection of vasoactive drugs like papaverine,[10] and phentolamine[10, 11] or prostaglandin E_1.[12] Common side effects are pain, haematoma and bruising and priapism. A later side effect is fibrosis or nodule formation. In those with mild to moderate narrowing of the penile vessels, repeated injections may result in marked improvement.

ii) Nitroglycerine paste: There is some evidence that transdermal nitroglycerine pastes used for angina could prove useful.[13]

iii) Oral drugs—These include: x_2 adrenoceptor antagonists, e.g., yohimbine;[14] opiate antagonists, e.g., naltrexone, naloxone;[15] dopamine agonists, e.g., apomorphine and bromocriptine;[16] and appear to be effective in a few patients but no large scale studies have been done.

b) *Suction devices*[17]

These devices consist of a plastic tube placed over the penis. A vacuum is created by a pump and when the organ is erect, a constriction ring is placed over it to maintain erection. Erections have been found to occur in 90% of patients.

c) *Surgery*

i) Penile prosthetic implants—malleable, inflatable (self-contained) and multipart.[18-20]

ii) Vascular surgery of either the arterial or venous system.[21,22]

2) PREMATURE EJACULATION

Premature ejaculation is a condition that is difficult to define, but comprises dissatisfaction by a couple because of rapid ejaculation by the male partner.

The two techniques used for treatment of premature ejaculation are:

a) *Semans stop-start technique*[23]

This involves stroking and masturbation by the subject, or his partner. The important thing is for the subject to be able to ascertain the point of inevitability of ejaculation and to stop the masturbation before this point is reached. After a pause of 1–2 minutes, the stroking can start again. This should be repeated a few times and then the male partner is allowed to ejaculate. With success this procedure is repeated using K-Y jelly.

b) *Squeeze technique*[24]

When about to ejaculate the subject or his partner should hold the head of the penis between the thumb and fore and middle fingers and squeeze firmly till the ejaculatory reflex wears off. Reassurance should be given that this may be accompanied by softening of erection. The procedure is then repeated again after 1–2 minutes for a few times before ejaculation is allowed.

Using these two techniques, control over ejaculation will be established. Once the subject can control himself for about 15 minutes, penetration and vaginal containment can be attempted adopting the female superior position, as this gives the man a greater control over ejaculation. When he feels a high arousal, his partner should lift herself off him and the squeeze method can be used. With success they proceed to normal sexual activity.[25]

Creams

An anaesthetic cream, e.g., lignocaine gel 2% applied to the glans penis is sometimes very helpful in those who are particularly sensitive. This may be used with the above techniques.

Medication

Clomipramine, an antidepressant used in the treatment of depressive illness and obsessive compulsive disorders has as a side effect the property of delaying ejaculation and has been used for premature ejaculation at a dose of 25–75 mg. Prostaglandin E_1[26] has also been used for treatment of this condition, and acts to prevent the rapid detumescence of the penis after ejaculation.

3) RETARDED EJACULATION

Some men with retarded ejaculation may respond well to the sensate focus exercises. Others, especially those who have never ejaculated while awake, require masturbation exercises. Some have a great need of control and are unable to let go. Others tend to spectator a lot. During the masturbation exercises, the focus should be on the pleasurable sensations that he feels.[27] Use of K-Y jelly may help his arousal, as may a vibrator device.[28] Fantasies may be introduced, but often this type of patient finds difficulty fantasizing. Use of magazines, pictures or videotapes (if available) can help him.

4) WOMEN

Orgasmic dysfunction

A woman with orgasmic dysfunction may have strong negative attitudes about sexuality and negative feelings regarding her body, and be unwilling to touch her own genitalia.

Treatment involves reassurance, explanation and programs to desensitize her to the touch of her body like:

a) a genital examination using a mirror to help her identify parts of her body.
b) masturbation exercises to identify the erotic areas of her body, e.g., clitoris or the Graefenberg spot. During the exercises she should be asked to focus on her pleasurable feelings.
c) Kegel's exercises[29]—these exercises strengthen the pubococcygeus muscles and are said to increase the ability to achieve an orgasm in women. These exercises involve contracting and relaxing the vaginal muscles.
d) Sensate focus, masturbation exercises, and eventually intercourse with the partner.

5) VAGINISMUS

This is often associated with sexual phobias—like a fear of being torn apart, of rape, of being damaged. Relaxation exercises and desensitization using graded imagery of sexual contact (from touching to penetration) are taught as well as Kegel's exercises and finger insertion into the vagina using initially her own fingers and later the partner's. Subsequent steps include penetration, vaginal containment and then intercourse.

Surgical methods like using dilators and vaginal molds[30] to stretch the vaginal opening have also been successful.

6) DYSPAREUNIA

When there is a complaint of pain on intercourse a careful vaginal examination should be carried out to exclude organic causes of pain which can be treated accordingly. Dyspareunia of psychogenic origin is usually associated with sexual phobia and vaginismus and is treated according to the principles enumerated above.

Table II—Other sexual disorders

Object	Disorder/condition
A. *Disorder of orientation*	
1) Human sexual partner	Homosexuality*
	Transsexualism
	Pedophilia
2) Dead partner	Necrophilia
3) Nonhuman sexual partner	Zoophilia
4) Object	Fetishism
	Transvestism
B. *Other psychosexual disorders*	
1) Involving pain	Sadomasochism
2) Involving a certain act	Exhibitionism
3) Involving peeping	Voyeurism
4) Involving phoning	Obscene calling

*Homosexuality is a controversial entity and in many countries is not accepted as a disorder or dysfunction, although in Singapore, it is generally still considered as such.

7) DISORDERS OF ORIENTATION

a) *Homosexuality*

If a person (male or female) seeks therapy to change his orientation, the treatment may involve the following:

  i) behavior therapy[31])—shaping his inclination from a homosexual to a heterosexual one, by using graded fantasies with heterosexual components together with masturbation. Gradually he learns to be aroused to heterosexual fantasies. Sometimes a homosexual fantasy can be used and a switch is made to a heterosexual one just before orgasm is reached. In certain subjects a form of aversive therapy can be introduced, e.g., imagining the most feared consequence—i.e., being found out or arrested while practicing a homosexual activity.
  If phobia of women exists, a desensitization program can be started; similarly social skills training can be taught if this is lacking.
  ii) Psychotherapy: This is indicated for those with more deep-seated problems.

b) *Transsexualism*

Transsexuals who come for treatment invariably wish to have the sex reassignment operation. They require a psychiatric assessment to determine their suitability, and then undergo operative procedures to remove their existing gonads and reproductive organs and reconstruct new ones. Regret about the operation and a wish to reverse it is very rare if selection is properly done.[32]

c) *Other orientation disorders*

For these conditions (e.g., pedophilia, exhibitionism and conditions listed in Table II) treatment programs involve essentially shaping of fantasies with masturbation, aversive fantasies and sometimes psychotherapy. In cases where there is a great urgency to control such behavior, drug therapy with an antiandrogen, e.g., cyproterone acetate may be given on a temporary basis till the subject has learned better self-control with psychological means.

Notes

1. Hawton K. *Sex therapy: a practical guide.* Oxford: Oxford University Press, 1985: 123–99.

2. Wagner G, Green R. General medical disorders and erectile failure. In: Wagner G, Green R, eds. *Impotence physiological, psychological, surgical diagnosis and treatment.* New York: Plenum Press, 1981: 37–50.

3. Wagner G, Halstead J, Jensen SB. Diabetes mellitus erectile failure. In: Wagner G, Green R, eds., *Impotence physiological, psychological, surgical diagnosis and treatment.* New York: Plenum Press, 1981: 51–62.

4. Wagner G. Methods for differential diagnosis of psychogenic and organic erectile failure. In: Wagner G, Green R, eds. *Impotence physiological, psychological, surgical diagnosis and treatment.* New York: Plenum Press, 1981: 89–130.

5. Kiely EA, Ignotus P, Williams G. Penile function following intracavernosal injection of vasoactive agents or saline. *Br J Urol* 1987; 59: 473–6.

6. Gregoire A. New treatments for erectile impotence. *Br J. Psychiatry* 1992; 160: 315–26.

7. Fisher C, Gross J, Zuch J. Cycle of penile erection synchronous with dreaming (REM) sleep. *Arch Gen Psychiatry* 1965; 12: 27–45.

8. Fisher C, Shiavi R, Lear H, Edwards A, Davis DM, Welken AP. The assessment of nocturnal REM erection in the differential diagnosis of sexual impotence. *J Sex Marital Ther* 1975; 1: 277–89.

9. Masters WH, Johnson VE. Principles of the new sex therapy. *Am J Psychiatry* 1976; 133: 548–54.

10. Virag R. Intracavernous injection of papaverine for erectile failure. *Lancet* 1982; ii: 928.

11. Kiely EA, Ignotus P, Goldie L. Assessment of the immediate and long term effects of pharmacologically induced penile erections in the treatment of psychogenic and organic impotence. *Br J Urol* 1987; 59: 164–9.

12. Stackl W, Hasum R, Marberger M. Intracavernous injection of prostaglandin E in impotent men. *J Urol* 1988; 140: 66–7.

13. Talley ID, Crawley IS. Transdermal nitrate, penile erection and spousal headache. *Ann Intern Med* 1985; 103: 804.

14. Reid K, Morales A, Harris C, Surridge DHC, Condra M, Owen J, et al. Double blind trial of yohimbine in treatment of psychogenic impotence. *Lancet* 1987; ii: 421–3.

15. Fabri A, Jannine EA, Guessi L, Moretti C, Ulisse S, Francese A, et al. Endorphins in male impotence: evidence of naltrexone stimulation of erectile activity in patient therapy. *Psychoneuroendocrinology* 1989; 14: 103–11.

16. Lal S, Labyea E, Thavundayil JX, Nair NP, Negrete J, Ackman D, et al. Apomorphine induced penile tumescence in impotent patients—preliminary findings. *Prog Neuropsychopharmacol Biol Psychiatry* 1984; 11(2–3): 235–42.

17. Wiles PG. Successful noninvasive management of erectile impotence in diabetic men. *Br Med J* 1988; 296: 161–2.

18. Wagner G. Surgical treatment of erectile failure. In: Wagner G, Green R, eds. *Impotence physiological, psychological, surgical diagnosis and treatment.* New York: Plenum Press, 1981: 155–66.

19. Montague DK. Semi rigid penile prostheses. In: Rajfer J. ed. *Common problems in infertility and impotence.* Chicago: Year Book Med Pub Inc., 1990: 311–16.

20. Bhalchandra GP, Barrett DM. Inflatable penile prostheses. In: Rajfer J. ed. *Common problems in infertility and impotence.* Chicago: Year Book Med Pub Inc., 1990: 332–36.

21. Lue TF. Surgery for venous occlusion. In: Rajfer J, ed. *Common problems in infertility and impotence.* Chicago: Year Book Med Pub Inc., 1990: 311–16.

22. Sharlip ID. Arterial reconstruction in the impotent patient. In: Rajfer J, ed. *Common problems in infertility and impotence.* Chicago: Year Book Med Pub Inc., 1990: 317–23.

23. Semans JM. Premature ejaculation: a new approach. *South Med J* 1956; 49: 353–57.

24. Masters WH, Johnson VE. *Human sexual inadequacy.* London: Churchill, London, 1970: 60–63.

25. Kaplan H. PE: *How to overcome premature ejaculation.* New York: Brunner Mazel, 1989: 43–116.

26. Adikan PG. Physiopharmacology of ejaculation and common ejaculation dysfunction. *Workshop on Male and Female Sexual Dysfunction.* 20–21 February 1993, NUH, Singapore.

27. Kaplan H. *The new sex therapy.* London: Bailliere Tindall, 1976: 316–36.

28. Bancroft J. *Human sexuality and its problems.* Edinburgh: Churchill Livingston, 1989: 523.

29. Kegel AH. Sexual function of the pubococcygeus muscles. *West J Surg Obs and Gynae* 1952; 60: 521–24.

30. Ratnam SS. *Management of dyspareunia and vaginismus. Workshop on Male and Female Sexual Dysfunction.* 20–21 February 1993, NUH, Singapore.

31. Bancroft J, *Human sexuality and its problems.* Edinburgh: Churchill Livingstone, 1989: 509–13.

32. Tsoi WF. A personal communication 1993.

Suggestions for Further Reading

General Discussions

American Psychiatric Association, "Practice Guidelines for Psychiatric Evaluation of Adults." *American Journal of Psychiatry* 152 (Nov. 1995 Supplement), 67–80.

Kilburg, Richard R., "Psychologists and Physical Interventions: Ethics, Standards, and Legal Implications." *Psychotherapy* 25 (Winter 1988): 516–31.

Macklin, Ruth, *Man, Mind, and Morality: The Ethics of Behavior Control.* Englewood Cliffs, N.J.: Prentice-Hall, 1982.

Weiner, Barbara A., "Treatment Rights." In Samuel J. Brakel, John Parry, and Barbara A. Weiner, *The Mentally Disabled and the Law.* Chicago: American Bar Foundation, 1985, ch. 6.

Psychosurgery

Breggin, Peter R., "The Return of Lobotomy and Psychosurgery." In Rem B. Edwards, *Psychiatry and Ethics: Insanity, Rational Autonomy, and Mental Health Care.* Amherst, N.Y.: Prometheus Books, 1982, pp. 350–88.

Chavkin, Samuel, *The Mind Stealers: Psychosurgery and Mind Control.* Boston: Houghton Mifflin, 1978.

Chorover, Stephen L., "Psychosurgery: A Neuropsychological Perspective." *Boston University Law Review* 54 (March 1974): 231, 239–48.

Mark, Vernon, "A Psychosurgeon's Case *for* Psychosurgery." *Psychology Today* 8 (July 1974): 28, 30, 33, 84, 86.

Valenstein, Elliot S., *Great and Desperate Cures: The Rise and Decline of Psychosurgery and Other Radical Treatments for Mental Illness.* New York: Basic Books, 1986.

Valenstein, Elliot S., "Science Fiction Fantasy and the Brain." *Psychology Today* 12 (July 1978): 29–31, 37–39.
———, ed., *The Psychosurgery Debate: Scientific, Legal, and Ethical Perspectives.* San Francisco: W. H. Freeman, 1980.

Electroshock

Abrams, Richard, *Electroconvulsive Therapy*, 2d ed. New York: Oxford University Press, 1992.
American Psychiatric Association, *The Practice of Electroconvulsive Therapy: Recommendations for Treatment, Training, and Privileging.* Washington, D.C.: American Psychiatric Association, 1990.
Breggin, Peter R., *Electroshock: Its Brain-Disabling Effects.* New York: Springer, 1979.
———, "Neuropathology and Cognitive Dysfunction from ECT." *Psychopharmacology Bulletin* 22 (1986): 476–79.
Frank, Leonard Roy, "Electroshock: Death, Brain Damage, Memory Loss, and Brainwashing." *The Journal of Mind and Behavior* 11 (Summer and Autumn 1990): 489–512.
Isaac, Rael Jean, and Virginia C. Armat, *Madness in the Streets: How Psychiatry and the Law Abandoned the Mentally Ill.* New York: The Free Press, 1990, ch. 10.
Lerer, Bernard, et al., *ECT: Basic Mechanisms.* Washington, D.C.: American Psychiatric Association, 1984.
Morgan, Robert, ed., *Electroshock: The Case Against.* Toronto: IPI Publishing, 1991.
Palmer, Robert L., *Electroconvulsive Therapy: An Appraisal.* New York: Oxford University Press, 1981.
Sackeim, Harold E., "The Case for ECT." *Psychology Today* (June 1985): 37–40.

Drug Therapy

American Psychiatric Association, *Treatments of Psychiatric Disorders*, 4 vols. Washington, D.C.: American Psychiatric Association, 1989.
Andreasden, Nancy C., and Donald W. Black, *Textbook of Psychiatry.* Washington, D.C.: American Psychiatric Press, 1995, ch. 26.
Bernstein, Jerrold G., *Clinical Psychopharmacology.* Boston: John Wright, 1984.
Breggin, Peter, *Psychiatric Drugs: Hazards to the Brain.* New York: Springer, 1983.
———, *Toxic Psychiatry.* New York: St. Martin's Press, 1991.
Breggin, Peter R., and Ginger Ross Breggin, *Talking Back to Prozac: What Doctors Aren't Telling You about Today's Most Controversial Drug.* New York: St. Martin's Press, 1995.
Brown, Paul, "Ethical Aspects of Drug Treatment." In Sidney Bloch and Paul Chodoff, eds., *Psychiatric Ethics*, 2d ed. New York: Oxford University Press, 1991, ch. 9.
Gelman, Sheldon, "Mental Hospital Drugs, Professionalism, and the Constitution." *Georgetown Law Review* 72 (1984): 1725–84.

Goodman, Alfred, et al., *Goodman and Gilman's The Pharmacological Basis of Therapeutics*. New York: Macmillan, 1985.

Isaac, Rael Jean, and Virginia C. Armat, *Madness in the Streets: How Psychiatry and the Law Abandoned the Mentally Ill*. New York: The Free Press, 1990, ch. 11.

Kramer, Peter O., *Listening to Prozac*. New York: Viking Press, 1993, especially Ch. 9.

Martorano, Joseph T., "Ethics and Psychopharmacology: Revolution or War?" In Max Rosenbaum, ed., *Ethics and Values in Psychotherapy: A Guidebook*. New York: The Free Press, 1982, ch. 15.

Skull, Andrew T., *Decarceration: Community Treatment and the Deviant—A Radical View*, 2d ed. New Brunswick, N.J.: Rutgers University Press, 1984, ch. 5.

Behavior Modification

American Psychological Association Commission, *Ethical Issues in Behavior Modification*. San Francisco: Jossey-Bass, 1978.

Begelman, D. A., "Ethical Issues in Behavior Control." *The Journal of Nervous and Mental Disease* 156 (1973): 412–19.

———, "Ethical and Legal Issues of Behavior Modification." In: M. Hersen, et al., eds., *Progress in Behavior Modification*, vol. 1. New York: Academic Press, 1975, pp. 159–89.

Erwin, E., *Behavior Therapy: Scientific, Philosophical and Moral Foundations*. Cambridge: Cambridge University Press, 1978, ch. 5.

Flanagan, Stephen, and Robert Paul Liberman, "Ethical Issues in the Practice of Behavior Therapy." In Max Rosenbaum, ed., *Ethics and Values in Psychotherapy: A Guidebook*. New York: The Free Press, 1982, ch. 9.

Kitchner, Richard F., "The Ethical Foundations of Behavior Therapy." *Ethics and Behavior* 1, no. 4, 1991, pp. 221–38.

Krasner, L., "Behavior Modification: Ethical Issues and Future Trends." In H. Leitenbert, ed., *Handbook of Behavior Modification*. New York: Appleton-Century-Crofts, 1976, pp. 627–49.

London, Perry, *Behavior Control*, 2d ed., New York: New American Library, 1977.

Wilson, G. Terence, and Ian M. Evans, "The Therapist-Client Relationship in Behavior Therapy." In Alas S. Gurman and Andrew M. Razin, eds., *Effective Psychotherapy: A Handbook of Research*. New York: Pergamum Press, 1977, ch. 20.

Sex Therapy

Andreasen, Nancy C., and Donald Black, *Introductory Textbook of Psychiatry*, 2d ed. Washington, D.C.: American Psychiatric Press, 1995, ch. 17.

Ashley, Benedict M., and Kevin D. O'Rourke, *Healthcare Ethics: A Theological Analysis*, 3d ed. St. Louis, Mo.: The Catholic Health Care Association of the United States, 1989, ch. 10.

Bancroft, John, "Ethical Aspects of Sexuality and Sex Therapy." In Sidney Bloch and Paul Chodoff, eds., *Psychiatric Ethics,* 2d ed. New York: Oxford University Press, 1991, ch. 11.

Lief, Harold I., "Ethical Problems in Sex Therapy." In Max Rosenbaum, ed., *Ethics and Values in Psychotherapy: A Guidebook.* New York: The Free Press, 1982, ch. 12.

Masters, William H., Virginia E. Johnson, and Robert C. Kolodny, eds., *Ethical Issues in Sex Therapy and Research,* 2 vols. Boston: Little, Brown, 1977.

Schnarch, David, "Joy with Your Underwear Down." *Psychology Today* 27 (July/August 1994): 38–43, 70, 74, 76, 78.

Szasz, Thomas, *Sex by Prescription.* New York: Penguin Books, 1980.

5.

ETHICAL AND CONCEPTUAL ISSUES IN CIVIL COMMITMENT

INTRODUCTION

Admissions to mental hospitals are basically of two types—voluntary and involuntary. In theory, voluntary patients come of their own accord, whereas involuntary patients are coerced into hospitalization. In the first selection of this section, Peter R. Breggin scrutinizes this contrast and highlights the many coercive factors that typically influence voluntary hospitalization. Most such commitments are voluntary only in the sense that they are not ordered by a judge; but intense coercion is usually present in voluntary commitments. Involuntary hospitalization, whether on an emergency, short-term basis or on a regular, long-term basis, is overtly coercive. Over their protests, patients committed through civil and criminal procedures are hospitalized as a consequence of decisions made by others.

Coercion

According to Breggin, "coercion" is the attempt to get someone else to do what you want them to do by using force, the threat of harm, actual harm, or by offering exceptionally enticing positive inducements. When positive incentives are offered to deprived institutionalized persons as persuaders, they are likely to be abnormally potent. Pejorative words like "enticement," "seduction," "undue incentive," or "manipulation," seem fitting because they denote morally questionable activities that tend to subvert rational autonomy. Breggin proposes that "coercion"

417

should be defined in terms of the perceptions of the coerce as well as the intentions of the coercer.

Of course, a coercive act is often morally objectionable, but not always. Threatening would-be lawbreakers with legal penalties is coercive, but legal sanctions as such are not morally wrong, and neither is the coercive punishment of children who misbehave or of criminals who have done wrong. How can we distinguish between justifiable and unjustifiable coercion? Does something about mental patients justify their coercive institutionalization? Articles to follow will address these issues.

Involuntary commitment to mental hospitals can be civil or criminal, depending on whether patients have been charged with a crime; also, some commitments are emergency or temporary, others extended, depending on the duration of the commitment. Many states now authorize involuntary commitment to outpatient treatment. Criminal or forensic commitments will be examined in section 6. Historically, civilly committed patients were coerced into hospitalization for an incredible variety of reasons, such as for treatment, care or custody, for being socially offensive or a social nuisance, for being an economic burden to others, for incapacity to care for themselves or to meet their basic physical needs, or for dangerousness to self or others. Before the 1970s, most states required only "need for care or treatment," but not mental incompetency; mental hospitals were inundated with unwilling persons who were unwanted by society. Civil commitment was so grossly abused that many critics like Thomas Szasz, who calls it a "crime against humanity," advocated that it be abolished totally.

Mental Illness Plus Dangerousness

After the U.S. Supreme Court's 1975 decision in *O'Connor* v. *Donaldson*, all the states tightened up, but did not eliminate, civil commitment laws by restricting coercive, noncriminal psychiatric hospitalization to persons who are both mentally ill *and* dangerous to others or to self, the latter either overtly or through personal neglect. Most states require that the dangerousness be caused by the mental illness, and that involuntary hospitalization be the "least restrictive alternative" available for care, custody, or treatment.

Dangerousness without mental illness does not justify preventive detention. Former felons, drunk drivers, and members of motorcycle gangs are much more dangerous than mentally ill persons; but they cannot be arrested for dangerousness alone. Both dangerousness *and* mental illness are now required for involuntary civil commitment; but what concepts of "dangerousness" and "mental illness" are operative? Thomas

Szasz and the antipsychiatrists believe that the "mental illness" criterion can never be fulfilled, for there is no such thing. Certainly there is no agreed-upon definition of this key concept in the psychiatric or psychological professions, and statutory definitions tend to be incredibly vague, circular, or to rely upon psychiatry for specification. Where dangerous behavior is regarded as sufficient evidence of mental illness (No one would do that without being crazy!), the requirement of both mental illness and dangerousness becomes a vacuous tautology.

"Dangerous acts" has been construed to mean almost anything— hurting someone's feelings, writing bad checks, criticizing an authority, threatening homicide, attempting suicide, or mutilating self or others. As Thomas Szasz explains in his article in this section, people have been judged dangerous just for being prostitutes, vagrants, or married women who disagree with their husbands. In most contemporary commitment laws, however, dangerous acts are narrowly defined as those having a *high probability of imminent and serious physical harm to self or others*, as evidenced by actual threats or overtly aggressive acts. A serious defect of such narrow commitment laws is that they allow innumerable incompetent but harmless people who could be helped to suffer and live homeless in the streets, and to "die with their rights on," as Darold Treffert first put it in 1973.

At the point of overt aggression, the distinction between civil and criminal commitment tends to collapse. Hard evidence for dangerousness to others or self often consists of criminal behaviors such as battery, assault, homicide, or attempted suicide, though the latter is no longer a crime in most states. Szasz's claim that involuntary civil commitment forces people into hospitalization who have not committed any crimes is often untrue. Admittedly, they are not being prosecuted for lawbreaking, and they have not been tried and convicted for it. If insane at the time of the crime, they have not committed a crime, even if they have broken the law, because they lack criminal intent, *mens re*, and are entitled to an insanity defense. They differ most conspicuously from offenders processed through the criminal justice system in that somewhere along the way, an authority decided not to take out a warrant or press charges against them, perhaps for humanitarian reasons, perhaps because they or their families are socially prominent, perhaps because they are truly deemed severely mentally ill.

Many involuntarily committed patients have only threatened harm but have not actually harmed anyone. Predicting dangerousness on the basis of *threats* of harm to others rather than actual harm is very problematic. All incarcerations for dangerousness border on unconstitutional preventive detention; but this is especially obvious where no overtly aggressive acts have been performed.

Other difficulties with the criterion of dangerousness are raised by Thomas Grisso and Paul S. Appelbaum in their following article. If dangerousness, defined as risk of future violent acts, cannot be predicted accurately for the distant future, can it be predicted nevertheless for the immediate future on the basis of clinical knowledge of signs of acute or imminent harmfulness? After these signs have passed, should dangerousness be predicted on the basis of clinical knowledge of individual persons, or on the basis of their belonging to a general class of persons with similar diagnoses, and/or other attributes like youthfulness, masculinity, past violence and arrests for it, current family satisfaction, propensity to take medication, joblessness, and so on? All of these correlate statistically with and are better indicators of future violence than mental illness.

To protect themselves against malpractice suits, mental health professionals greatly overpredict dangerousness far beyond what can be empirically verified. Most predictions of dangerousness are horrendously inaccurate, so society has placed a heavy responsibility upon mental health professionals which they, like everyone else, are ill-equipped to perform. Studies made during the 1960s and 1970s of mental health professionals' abilities to predict dangerousness showed that they were wrong at least 85 percent of the time. An 85 percent inaccuracy rate in predicting dangerousness is very impressive! More recent studies show some improvement, but predictors are still wrong 65 to 75 percent of the time. Why should we preventively detain mental patients for dangerousness when we do not do so for much more dangerous persons such as ex-prison inmates, members of street gangs, or drunken drivers? How can equal protection under the law and due process be assured in civil commitment procedures for persons accused of dangerousness?

Recent research on predicting violence indicates that risk of future harmful acts is not merely a function of probability of harm. The kind, the seriousness, and the probability of harm are integral parts of the notion of risk. A person with a 50 percent risk of committing murder is much more dangerous than one with a 50 percent risk of committing theft. Suppose that we could assign a 70 percent probability to the possibility that five people are likely to do you harm; one is likely to pick your pocket, another to slap your face, another to mug and rob you, another to break your leg, and another to shoot you through the heart. Would you regard them all as equally dangerous, or are some much more dangerous than others despite equal probabilities? Clinical assessments of risk of violent behavior are immensely complex since they take probability, kind, and seriousness of anticipated harms into account. Although there is a calculus for probability, no calculus takes all of these judgmental elements into account. If this is true, can psychiatric predictions of dangerousness be shown to be faulty simply because the behaviors portended are low in probability?

If predicting dangerousness is as problematic as indicated, is it not morally wrong for mental health professionals to engage in it and to lend their authority to horrendous abuse? Grisso and Appelbaum argue that the most serious difficulties with predicting harm can be overcome (which may not be true), and that it is not unethical for mental health professionals to serve the courts as expert witnesses who can reliably predict future violence (as long as standards of predictability are low). Many recent articles (for example, those summarized in Litwack et al. in 1993) contend that earlier studies purporting to show the impossibility of accurately predicting violent future acts were seriously flawed methodologically and conceptually. Grisso and Appelbaum claim that the ability of mental health professionals to predict the probability of violence has improved, though their success is still only 25 to 35 percent at best.

The problem remains: are we content to deprive people of their liberty on the basis of predictions that we know to be wrong more than half of the time? Joseph M. Livermore and his coauthors pointed out in 1968 that "in the criminal law, it is better that ten guilty men go free than that one innocent man suffer." Why should things be so radically different in the domain of involuntary civil commitment?

Incompetency and Need for Treatment

Because mental illness and dangerousness seem so flawed as criteria for depriving people of liberty, many critics have proposed that the states should adopt entirely different standards for involuntary civil commitment. Without repudiating the dangerousness requirement, earlier reformers like Loren Roth (1979) and Joan Callahan (1984) proposed that the mental illness condition be replaced by an incompetency requirement. Callahan called almost every element of contemporary civil commitment laws into account. She argued that "mental illness" is too broad a notion [as extensive as *DSM-IV*] to justify deprivation of liberty, and that it should be replaced by mental incompetence as the primary condition for commitability. Callahan also argued that if genuinely incompetent, the harm to self required for civil commitment need not be physical but might be merely financial or psychological. Callahan maintained that the probability of harm to others need not be high if it is catastrophic, and claimed that the act that will cause the harm, not the harm itself, is the thing that must be imminent. If a patient is truly incompetent, she proposed, the harm to self need not be serious, extreme, or irreversible to justify paternalistic intervention; but she offered no realistic resolution to the quandary of grossly inaccurate predictions of dangerousness.

As Donald Hermann indicates in his article, many states now require not merely mental illness, but severe, substantial, significant or gross impairment, that is, "grave disability," as essential for involuntary civil commitment. These states have, in effect, if not in actual words, adopted the incompetency standard. The wording of commitment statutes may range from "incompetency" to "grave disability," to "lacking sufficient insight or capacity to make a responsible decision concerning treatment."

Hermann accepts the incompetency standard, then takes the next logical step beyond Roth and Callahan to propose that the dangerousness criterion be abandoned, for many good reasons, and that it be replaced by "need for treatment" and "availability of treatment" standards. Also, the "least restrictive alternative" criterion must be replaced by a "most effective treatment" standard. With these criteria, psychiatric professionals would be liberated from the impossible task of predicting dangerousness and could do what they are best prepared to do. Also, only people who are too sick to enjoy liberty would be deprived of it by involuntary hospitalization.

Suicide Prevention

Can involuntary commitment on the basis of dangerousness to oneself be justified when the issue is suicide prevention? Should we allow suicidal persons to "die with their rights on" without paternalistic intervention? We know that an overwhelming majority of them will, if they survive, greatly appreciate and shortly express retrospective gratitude for the intervention. Most people who attempt suicide do not really want to die; they are merely desperate to change something else in their life situation. If they can be nursed through their initial crisis, only about 1 percent will actually kill themselves within a year, but between 5 and 15 percent will kill themselves within fifteen years. There are rational reasons for committing suicide, but the most relevant rule for dealing with suicidal patients when first brought in for emergency hospitalization is still: "When in doubt, treat." After initial evaluation, however, should not the primary consideration be incompetence rather than dangerousness?

Rational suicides can find another chance, assuming that they are not incarcerated forever. Should definite time limits be set for confining suicidal patients, or should the primary condition for release be a return to competency, no matter how short or long a time this takes? Typical suicidal patients are severely depressed and are not paradigms of rational autonomy; their incompetency provides a moral rationale for paternalistic intervention. It often takes three weeks or more for antidepressant drugs or other psychotropic medications to become effective. Treating suicidal patients does not always have a happy ending. Some patients are chronically suicidal and unresponsive to treatment. What then should therapists do?

Coercion of Voluntary Patients in an Open Hospital

Peter R. Breggin

Author's Note (1982)

"Coercion of Voluntary Patients in an Open Hospital" was written twenty [now over thirty] years ago when I was training as an intern in a small psychiatric hospital. The article was a first in the literature—an analysis of the oppression and control of psychiatric patients in an allegedly open, humanistically oriented psychiatric hospital. Unhappily, the article remains a first. I know of no other similar analysis in the official psychiatric literature over the subsequent twenty years.

Psychiatry remains as reluctant as ever to recognize the devastating impact of its treatments upon the minds and brains of its patients. The personal, subjective response of the patient is almost wholly ignored in the psychiatric literature. Meanwhile, in private practice, as well as in clinics and hospitals, the psychiatric patient is subjected to a variety of threats and controls, from the simple authority of the physician to the more concrete menace of *involuntary* drugging, electroshock, and incarceration. Despite many legal attempts to increase the civil liberties of mental patients, it remains true today that even the ostensibly *voluntary* mental patient has almost no protection against assault with the psychiatric armamentorium.

For those psychiatric patients who experience the relatively benign and sometimes helpful experience of psychotherapy in private practice, the threat of psychiatric oppression may seem remote. But should this

From *Archives of General Psychiatry* 10 (1964): 173–81. Copyright © 1964, the American Medical Association. Reprinted by permission.

same patient become "irrational," "self-destructive," "dangerous," "mentally ill," or even "in need of hospital treatment" in the opinion of his well-meaning psychiatrist, his civil liberties can be abrogated, and he can be committed to a mental hospital.

Over the years, I have broadened my criticism of institutional psychiatry as a form of political totalitarianism—the use of state power to control the individual.[1-8] Seldom will the liberty and the integrity of an individual be subjected to a greater threat than when he comes under the scrutiny of psychiatric authorities. In the Western world today, psychiatry remains the greatest threat to the civil liberties and the mental integrity of individual citizens. Few people realize the potential danger to which they expose themselves when they ask for help from a psychiatrist or when they voluntarily enter a mental hospital. But at this moment of great need and vulnerability, the mental patient may find himself in a no-win contest with the overwhelming power and authority of psychiatry.

Introduction

The long history of the open hospital, with its goal to limit the coercion of patients, has recently been reviewed.[6-7] The open hospital may also be a field of study for more subtle forms of coercion that might go unnoticed in other hospitals. The absence of outright locked doors tends to draw attention to these more indirect forms of control over the patient. In an environment dedicated to the elimination of coercion, the staff and the patients will then be exquisitely sensitive to any which continues to manifest itself. In addition, the absence of the locked ward means that any coercion must be directed by an individual doctor against an individual patient, making it more painfully obvious to everyone in the hospital.

This ironic situation provides fertile ground for studying coercion. It might also be used by some as evidence for the inadequacy of open hospitals and by others as evidence for the insidiousness of coercion even within ideal circumstances. The topic is so charged with dramatic ethical, legal, and therapeutic considerations that I might best explain my own bias at the start. I am ethically committed to the principle that coercion should be limited as much as possible but believe that the actual extent of this limitation cannot be decided until we know considerably more about the effects of coercion upon the patient.

Definition of Coercion

By coercion is meant any action, or threat of action, which compels the patient to behave in a manner inconsistent with his own wishes. The compelling aspect can be direct physical or chemical restraint, or it can be indirect threatened recriminations or indirect "force of authority" which convinces the patient that no other legal or medical alternative is available to him.

Coercive behavior falls into the general category of manipulative behavior, in which one person feels that his actions are determined by someone else, despite his own wishes. Coercion may be considered the experience of an unusually constraining or intimidating alternative, so that the individual feels his freedom of choice is preempted.

This is a practical definition in which the reference point is the patient's feeling of being compelled. It is meant to define a common element in the patient's response to such diverse experiences as enforced confinement to a locked ward; self-imposed restriction to an unlocked ward for fear of certification to another hospital; self-imposed restriction to an unlocked ward after receiving the impression that one has no legal right to leave the ward; or self-imposed restriction because one believes that no other medical alternative is available. The focus must be upon the patient's feeling or response, otherwise the patient is subjected to another imposition whereby he loses even his right to decide what is coercive. Defining coercion from the patient's point of view also takes into account individual variations: some patients may not feel coerced by any of these alternatives, either because they do not fear them or because they do not wish to leave the ward, while other patients will be particularly sensitive to the alternatives either because they strongly wish to leave the ward or greatly fear the threats presented to them.

Definition from the patient's point of view is not without ambiguities. For example, it will often be difficult to distinguish between different levels of response in the patient. The patient may say that he feels coerced, while he behaves as if he is not, or the patient may deny feeling coerced while he acts as if he is. Equally difficult, the patient may perceive coercion in a situation where few others would. These problems cannot be avoided, since coercion is relative to the individual, and to the situation. Life itself exists along a continuum of coercion in which the individual often feels that his behavior is in part determined by direct constraints or threats. The definition cannot do away with the ambiguities and relativity inherent in the situation, but it can draw attention to the patient's response to various constraints, pressures, or threats within the hospital environment. . . .

The Physician's Use of Coercion

There are many reasons why the resident therapist may at times feel the need to act against the patient's will, even in the open hospital.

First, he may believe he has an ethical, professional, or religious responsibility to help the patient, even if the patient does not want help. The physician may believe that the patient, like a child, is unable to make the best decision for himself, and therefore must have someone else "take over" for him. The physician knows that patients often resist the initial efforts of their therapists, only to thank them later. He knows that many patients, and society in general, *expect* him to take this responsibility. He may perceive at times that the patient often *wants* him to be coercive. In addition, his medical training has conditioned him to trust his own judgment in determining what will be of benefit to the patient.[9]

Second, the therapist may be motivated to coerce the patient by a sense of responsibility toward the patient's family and toward the society. The therapist may wish to mitigate the patient's hostility, or to restrain the patient from physically or psychologically harming others. He may also wish to rehabilitate the patient into a socially and economically productive human being. He may believe these goals at times transcend the patient's immediate, and perhaps irresponsible, wishes.

Third, the therapist may be concerned about placing himself in legal jeopardy if he does not accept responsibility for his patient and society. For example, he may fear being sued by the family of a patient who harms or kills himself. He may also place his residency appointment in jeopardy if he does not at times coerce his patient. In any contemporary hospital, no matter how "open" its attitude, his superiors will at times hold him responsible for his patient's welfare and the society's welfare. Thus, legal and professional survival add impetus to any other motives which might influence him to coerce his patient.

Fourth, the therapist may be motivated to protect or enhance his own self-image and prestige through the actions of his patient. Thus, he may wish to coerce his patients into avoiding or performing certain acts. A patient who kills someone else, or who kills himself, can deal a severe blow to the resident therapist's self-image and prestige. To a lesser extent, a patient who does not respond in an appropriate fashion to psychotherapy is bound to reflect upon the therapist. An example of this is found in a recent paper which encourages psychiatrists to use the relative number of patients who sign out Against Medical Advice as a reflection of the resident's ineptitude.[4] Such an attitude on the part of supervisors is bound to encourage trainees to coerce their patients into more acceptable forms of behavior. At S.P.H. [Syracuse Psychiatric Hospital] any such arbitrary "grading system" would be frowned upon. Nonetheless, the residents sometimes feel that the proportion of their patients certified reflects upon them. While few residents, if any, would rationally accept so gross a standard of therapeutic success or failure, most would admit to embarrassment and a sense of failure when one of their patients is certified to a larger state hospital. When it appears that a patient is "in danger of getting certified," a strong impulse then arises to modify the patient's behavior by restricting his liberty, by threat of certification, by electroconvulsive treatment, or by heavy tranquilization.

Fifth, the therapist might coerce the patient for motives entirely inappropriate for the situation. To give an example with infinite variations, one resident became aware that he refused his patient weekend passes in part because he resented her wish to visit home rather than to attend the Saturday therapy session. Many motives to coerce might result from counter-transference of various intensities, many of which the therapist-in-training might not recognize. There is little reason to presume that first or second year residents, or really anyone, would be immune to these motives. Supervision by more highly trained psychiatrists might mitigate some of these motives, if the supervision and the supervisor were oriented in this way. On the other hand, the supervisor usually has his own coercive powers over the trainee, setting an example for one individual to coerce another. In addition, since the supervisor's use of coercion will depend in part upon his evaluation of the trainee's patient, the resident may feel the need to coerce his patient into behavior consistent with the supervisor's expectations.

Finally, the therapist may feel that the existence of the larger state hospitals creates a situation in which, in order to avoid even greater coercion, he must himself act coercively upon the patient. For example, he may anticipate that certain acting out by his patient will eventually lead to certification by the staff. He might then compromise his own antipathy to coercion by using a little "prophylactic coercion," hoping a few restrictions on the patient's liberty, or electroconvulsive therapy, will discourage further acting out. Similarly, if he has a very low opinion of the larger state hospital, he may feel that the "danger of being sent away" is greater than the danger of temporarily coercing his patient. He may feel that separation from the psychotherapy would harm the patient at a crucial time when the patient is acting out. However, even if the therapist has no desire at all to coerce the patient, he may indirectly increase the threat of coercion by communicating his own anxiety about the threat to the patient. For example, the therapist may tell the patient, "I would not want to see you committed, but I feel you should know that your present behavior will lead the hospital administration to advise your commitment."

If the physician decides to use coercion, three basic methods are available to him: restriction of liberty, certification to a larger hospital, or treatment with electroconvulsive therapy and large doses of medication. Each of these can be coercive when used as threats, as direct constraints, or as punishments. In each case, the patient feels compelled to act against his will.

Despite the absence of locked doors, control over the patient's physical liberty remains the most frequent means of coercion. The physician may limit the patient's freedom to move around the hospital, he may refuse weekend passes, or he may insist that the patient remain in the hospital for the full 25 days stipulated in the voluntary admission form. In many instances, nearly every therapeutic hour with a hospitalized patient will revolve around direct or indirect bargaining for increased liberties with improved behavior. For example, the patient may request a pass to leave the ward, and the physician may respond that the patient's behavior still lacks sufficient self-control. No matter what the therapist's attitude, the coerciveness of the implication cannot be avoided—if the patient does not change his behavior, he will not be given more freedom.

From the physician's point of view, coercion through real or threatened physical restriction is often very taxing and very disagreeable. Although most patients will not defy his legal authority, he must on occasion further implement his restrictions to the ward. This is very difficult in an open hospital and places a great deal of strain upon the ward personnel who are directly responsible for watching the patient's movements, and for restraining him, somehow, without the locked door. The use of restrictions on liberty is also frankly contrary to the "open door" attitude, and often extremely repugnant to the physician.

The second means of coercion, threatened or actual certification to a larger state hospital, is so pervasive that it hardly needs to be mentioned by the therapist. This threat is so obvious and overwhelming to many patients, that the physician has little power to increase or ameliorate it. Nearly everyone on the staff is very reluctant to certify anyone, but more than one patient is still certified every month. The effect of this on the remainder of patients will be discussed in the next section.

The third means of coercion is threatened or actual treatment with drugs or electroconvulsive therapy. Many patients will bargain to diminish their drug doses, much as they will bargain to decrease their physical restrictions. Many dislike the associated side effects of phenothiazines, including the dryness of the mouth, chapped lips, blurred vision, stuffy nose, and gastrointestinal symptoms, as well as the more disturbing changes in motor control and affect which almost invariably accompany larger doses. The use of drugs is entirely the prerogative of the physician and is most often a clear method of restraint when the patient is suicidal or homicidal. From the physician's point of view, the drugs have many disadvantages in restraining doses. First, the side-effects often interfere with psychotherapy. Second, it is sometimes difficult to make the patient take the drug. Third, the use of the drug for coercion prejudices the patient against any further use of the drugs.

Electroconvulsive therapy is a more potent means of coercion. In my own experience, most patients have terror of the treatment. Those few who have requested the treatment, still expressed a great fear of it. At S.P.H., the patient and the therapist usually both dislike the use of electroconvulsive therapy. Most patients refuse to sign permission, and the hospital then asks the patients' nearest relatives to sign. The legal implication of the family's consent has never been tested in New York State and is not clearly stated in any law. The device is nonetheless a strong inducement to the patients, who believe it legally binding. This is an example of coercion by implying to the patient that he has no other legal alternative.

In summary, the resident therapist may have many motives to coerce his patient. Some may be characteristic of all human relationships. Some are basic to current legal and social attitudes toward the mentally ill. A number are characteristic of an open hospital which must operate in a fundamentally closed society, represented by the larger state hospitals. If the physician decides to use coercion, he has three basic means: (1) control over the patient's liberty and length of stay in the hospital; (2) certification to a larger state hospital; (3) treatment with drugs or electroconvulsive therapy. Each of these may be used coercively as threats, punishments, or a means of restraint.

The Patient's Response to Coercion

Most patients sign a voluntary admission to the hospital. However, many of these admissions occur as a result of direct or indirect coercion by the patient's family. The patient may be brought to the hospital in a chaotic fashion by his family in the midst of a disintegrating social situation. Usually one or more other members of the family have decided that the patient's admission is the only feasible and immediate solution to the situation.

Often the patient will balk at the last minute when he is told that admission means he can be held for 25 days against his will. At this time, the family may pressure the patient by threats to certify him, or by threats to withdraw support. More rarely, the patient will be accompanied by the police or parole officer who may exert more direct coercion.

On occasion, the resident admitting officer for the day will admit the patient involuntarily at the request of the family and the family physician. More often, the resident is caught up as a passive observer in the family conflict. If he has interviewed the patient through the formal preadmissions clinic, or if he can ascertain quickly that the patient is grossly psychotic, he may also urge the patient to accept a voluntary admission. He may ameliorate the patient's fear of being held 25 days by emphasizing the open doors, and by implying that the patient could not really be held against his will, even though the law permits it.

Very likely more patients would balk at signing the voluntary admission if aware that they could be committed from S.P.H. to a larger state hospital, or that they might feel intimidated to stay considerably longer than the 25 days, or that they might be given electroconvulsive treatment against their will. For this reason, the admitting officer seldom mentions these eventualities at the time of admission. However, soon after admission the patient learns about these possibilities from direct observation of other patients, from discussions with other patients, or through his own experience. This is one of the reasons why the patient often begins to clamor for discharge within ten days or two weeks of hospitalization. He is afraid that the longer he stays the more danger there is that one or more threats will materialize. His fears usually culminate at the time of the official staff meeting which takes place about two weeks after each patient's admission.

Of all the fears, fear of commitment to the large state hospital is by far the most pervasive and intense. From his own prior knowledge and from hospital scuttlebutt, the patient learns that the larger state hospital (1) carries a greater social stigma; (2) has much tighter controls on personal freedom, including locked doors; (3) is more isolated from friends and family, with more limited visiting hours; (4) places more emphasis on chemical and electroconvulsive therapy; and (5) tends to hold patients for longer periods.

Beyond these specific fears about the larger hospital, there is an indefinable awe. In part, it stems from the not-too-distant past when most large state hospitals were "snakepits." In part, it stems from a fear of being mentally ill. Commitment to the larger hospital implies a degree of mental illness far greater than implied in the original voluntary admission to S.P.H. Similarly, the patient may feel that commitment implies incurability. On top of all this, the patient often looks upon commitment as an outright rejection by his physicians and family.

Fear of commitment to the larger state hospital can be reinforced by some commitments of other patients which he is likely to witness in the small hospital. Often the other patients will display overwhelming anxiety concerning their commitment. They may be given large doses of drugs, or transferred to the third floor for closer observation just prior to commitment. Then they are whisked off to the other hospital, leaving behind a wake of spreading fear throughout the hospital.

For many patients, the fear of commitment to the larger state hospital becomes a major motive during the hospital stay. Thus the smaller hospital, despite its open doors, becomes in some ways an annex or way station to the other hospital. For some patients, the threat becomes as real as if the smaller hospital were no more than a ward attached to the larger hospital.

The patient who lives under the threat of commitment, as well as the threat of a prolonged hospitalization, greater restrictions, or electroconvulsive therapy, soon develops ideas about what kind of behavior is likely to cause these threats to materialize. These ideas are often thrashed out in patient bull sessions in preparation for staff meetings. They include the following: (1) failure to respond satisfactorily to therapy, or failure to show an interest in therapy; (2) unmanageable or destructive behavior; (3) suicidal attempts or repeated suicidal threats; (4) immoral acts; (5) behavior disturbing to other patients; (6) repeated attempts to run away from the hospital; (7) any behavior which antagonizes hospital doctors, nurses or personnel; and (8) any behavior which antagonizes the patient's family.

The fear that running away will lead to eventual commitment to the larger hospital is especially important, for it most directly modifies the hospital's "open door policy." It effectively "locks the door." The patient may realize that he would rarely be forcibly returned to the hospital after running away, but he may feel that the hospital would thereafter deny him readmission. This would limit his future alternatives to the larger hospitals. Indirectly, then, the fear of the larger hospital might compel him to stay on in the ward.

In summary, the patient learns, soon after admission, that his voluntary status leaves him vulnerable to certain eventualities, the most disturbing being involuntary electroconvulsive therapy and certification to a larger state hospital. He also tries to find out what kind of behavior will cause these threats to materialize, so that he can modify his behavior accordingly.

Illustration of Cases

The following cases are illustrations of how coercion may affect different patients and their physicians.

The first patient is a 20-year-old girl who became suicidal, stuporous, and mute during her first few months at college. She was diagnosed schizophrenic and was voluntarily hospitalized three times in rapid succession during the next several months. She felt that each hospitalization brought her closer to being "sent away," yet she herself recognized the need for each hospitalization, and may have unconsciously wished for commitment and more prolonged treatment at the larger hospital. Prior to her third voluntary admission, her out-patient therapist had to reassure her that she would again be discharged if she showed some improvement. After a few weeks, her new hospital therapist felt she was making progress, but the hospital administration felt it was time to commit her for long-term treatment. Her new therapist told the patient he himself was against her commitment. The patient confided she imagined the larger hospital as a kind of Hell, and she threatened to run away. However, when the commitment papers were finally signed, she did a turnabout, and tearfully thanked everyone for committing her. She asked for tranquilizers to make her transition to the new hospital easier.

The second patient is a 26-year-old man who had developed paranoid schizophrenia during his first year of college. At that time he had been admitted voluntarily and then given electroconvulsive therapy against his wishes. He bitterly remembered these treatments and partly for this reason refused voluntary admission a second time. He was brought in involuntarily. After several weeks of psychotherapy his paranoid ideation ceased to function overtly in the patient-physician relationship. When his period of involuntary hospitalization drew to a close, he reluctantly agreed to sign a voluntary admission for continued hospitalization. In retrospect, he probably did this out of fear that he would otherwise be committed. When the therapist subsequently had to leave the hospital prior to the completion of therapy, the therapist decided to commit the patient for further treatment at a larger hospital. The patient again became acutely paranoid. At first he denounced his therapist but then tried to mollify him. He was finally placed on large doses of chlorpromazine to prevent his fleeing the hospital prior to commitment.

The first patient was always reluctant to be admitted voluntarily, for fear of eventual certification, and when certification did occur, she threatened to run away. Eventually, her basically passive-dependent orientation led her to "accept what's best." In the second case, the patient resisted admission at the start, but accepted voluntary status later on during his hospitalization. Very possibly, he thought that he would be certified if he refused voluntary status, as he would have been. When he was eventually certified, his basically paranoid orientation led him to reincorporate the therapist into his paranoid system. However, when he realized that the display of paranoid ideation and hostility would only further insure his certification, he attempted to mollify his therapist.

Often, the threat of commitment is itself potent enough to obviate the need for commitment. The third case, an addict to meperidine (Demerol), was admitted involuntarily at night when the doors are locked. In the morning, after several hours of unmanageable behavior, he fled past the attendant. The police were called to pick up the patient, who was thought dangerous to his wife. They were instructed to return him to jail in preparation for more speedy commitment to the larger state hospital. However, the policeman turned out to be an old high school chum of the patient. He warned the patient about the danger of commitment and returned him to the hospital. Despite the apprehension of the doctors, the patient was docile after this.

The vast majority of patients would not yield such clear-cut illustrations of coercion. One example, from an unusual follow-up opportunity, demonstrates that responses to coercion may be concealed from the therapist. The patient is a 35-year-old mother of four children who came in voluntarily after several months of bitter struggle between herself and her husband. In the last days before admission the patient had become agitated, threatened suicide, and finally became mute and stuporous. Rapport seemed to develop quickly between the patient and the therapist, and the patient made a remarkable symptomatic improvement after ventilating her rage and receiving support for her self-esteem. She appeared as the victim of an extremely sadomasochistic relationship. After the patient's discharge in two weeks, she somewhat reluctantly entered into a weekly family therapy project with the same therapist. During the first session, one daughter told how the patient's husband had threatened her with commitment to a larger state hospital just prior to her voluntary admission. During the second session, another daughter made a slip of the tongue which uncovered that the patient had always included the therapist among those hostile male figures whom she had to resist passively. She had put up a front of rapport during her hospitalization to insure her speedy discharge and to guard against the threat of commitment to the larger state hospital. To what extent some kernel of rapport did exist could not be ascertained against the background of motivation to deceive.

Comment

The proportion of patients actually affected by direct and threatened coercion, and the degree to which these patients accordingly modify their behavior, require some quantification. Many psychiatrists have already stated the opinion that so long as the threat of coercion exists, most or all patients will respond to it.[1,3,5,8,10,11] I have the impression that nearly every patient is affected by the threat of coercion but that only the more intact patients are able to modify their behavior in response. Thus the case illustrations present two schizophrenic patients who were unable to disguise their symptoms despite the threat of coercion, and a drug addict and a neurotic patient who were able to modify their behavior and, in the latter case, to disguise the response to the coercion. Beyond this kind of impression, it is not at present possible to quantify the degree of response, since every patient, voluntary or involuntary, is subjected to the same threats. Under these conditions, there are no control groups upon which to base a study of the effect of coercion.

Because the effects of coercion are not fully understood, it is not easy to decide if we should, or could, do away with all coercion in mental hospitals. However, there are some cogent reasons to do away with the pretense about coercion and to recognize, as some have already done,[1] that the voluntary mental hospital experience is thoroughly permeated with coercion. If we gloss over the implications of coercion, we put the patient into a dangerous double bind. On the one hand, we tell him he is voluntary and encourage him to establish a relationship of mutual confidence. On the other hand, we use actual restraint, certification, and undesired treatments to control or intimidate him. On top of this, we then close our eyes to the problem and thus indirectly warn against too much concern about the realistic ambiguities of the situation. As one patient confided, "Is it true, Doctor, that you get committed if you look too eager to go home?" Naturally, openness and frankness about the pervasiveness of coercion is likely to help the physician as well as the voluntary patient, for it encourages a feeling of greater self-respect on the part of the physician and removes a taboo from important areas of the patient-physician relationship.

A concrete step can be taken to increase frankness and honesty in this regard. A requirement could be made that the patient be informed prior to admission about the possibilities of involuntary treatment, restrictions on liberty, and certification. In New York State this would be little more time-consuming or difficult than the current requirement that the patient be told prior to admission that he can be held for 15 days against his will at the discretion of the staff, and that he may then be required to give ten days' notice before leaving.

After being given this information, some patients might choose not to sign a voluntary admission. This occasionally happens now, when the patient is told that he can be held against his will. In keeping with the spirit of the voluntary admission, this should be the patient's prerogative. If the patient eventually does need involuntary hospitalization, the community then has means for obtaining this more directly through the various forms of mental hospital commitment. In New York State, for example, there is no lack of these forms and therefore little reason for physicians to fear for the future of patients who might refuse voluntary admission.

Frank recognition of the implications of voluntary admission would seem justified on ethical grounds, as well as on therapeutic grounds. Hopefully, frank recognition might also lead to codification of more real legal distinctions between voluntary and involuntary admissions in our state laws pertaining to the mentally ill. This would further the goal of a more frank and unambiguous patient-physician relationship. It would also make possible comparative studies of the effects of voluntary and involuntary hospitalization, studies now hampered by the absence of truly voluntary admissions.

Summary

An open hospital environment provides the opportunity for observing the more covert and indirect means of coercion found in most mental hospitals. Coercion is viewed from the patient's point of view as any action, or threat of action, which makes the patient feel compelled to behave in a manner contrary to his own wishes. Special attention is given to restriction of liberty around the hospital, certification to a larger and more remote state hospital, and involuntary treatment with drugs or electroconvulsions. Each of these can function coercively as a direct means of constraint, as a threat, or as a punishment. Case illustrations are given. The therapist's wish to coerce the patient is also presented.

A suggestion is made to inform voluntary patients prior to admission about the eventualities of coercion in the hospital. This would establish a more frank patient-physician relationship at the start and encourage future definitive legal distinctions between voluntary and involuntary patients.

References to Author's Note

1. Breggin, Peter R.: "Psychotherapy as Applied Ethics," *Psychiatry* 34: 59–75, 1971.

2. Breggin, Peter R.: *The Crazy from the Sane* (a novel), Lyle Stuart Publisher, New York, 1971.

3. Breggin, Peter R.: *After the Good War* (a novel), Stein and Day Publisher, New York, 1972.

4. Breggin, Peter R.: "Therapy as Applied Utopian Politics," *Mental Health and Society* 1: 129–46, 1974.

5. Breggin, Peter R.: "Psychiatry and Psychotherapy as Political Processes," *American Journal of Psychotherapy* 29:369–82, 1975.

6. Breggin, Peter R.: "Needed: Voluntaristic Psychiatry," *Reason,* September, 1975.

7. Breggin, Peter R.: *The Psychology of Freedom,* Prometheus Books, Amherst, 1980.

8. Breggin, Peter R.: "A Libertarian Critique of Psychiatry and Psychology," *Psychiatric Quarterly,* in press.

References

1. Bickford, J. A. F.: "Shadow and Substance: Some Changes in the Mental Hospital," *Lancet* 1: 423-424, 1958.

2. Cameron, D. E.: "An Open Psychiatric Hospital," *Mod. Hosp.* 74: 84–88, 1950.

3. "Freedom in Mental Hospitals: The End and the Means," *Lancet* 2: 964–66, 1954.

4. Greenwald, A. F., and Bartemeier, L. H.: "Psychiatric Discharges Against Medical Advice," *Arch. Gen. Psychiat.* 8: 117–19, 1963.

5. Hunt, R. C.: "Ingredients of a Rehabilitation Program," in *An Approach to the Prevention of Disability from Chronic Psychoses: The Open Mental Hospital Within the Community,* New York, Milbank Memorial Fund, 1958, pp. 9–28, cited in Rubin and Goldberg.[7]

6. Knoff, W. F.: "Modern Treatment of the 'Insane': An Historical View of Nonrestraint," *NY J. Med.* 60: 2236–43, 1960.

7. Rubin, B., and Goldberg, A.: "An Investigation of Openness in the Psychiatric Hospital," *Arch. Gen. Psychiat.* 8: 269–76, 1963.

8. Szasz, T.: Discussions at the State University of New York, Upstate Medical Center, Department of Psychiatry.

9. Szasz, T., and Hollender, M. H.: "A Contribution to the Philosophy of Medicine: The Basic Modes of the Doctor-Patient Relationship," *AMA Arch. Intern. Med.* 97: 585, 1956.

10. "The Unlocked Door," *Lancet* 2: 953–54, 1954.

11. Winston, F.: "Beyond the Open Door," *Ment. Hyg.* 46: 11–19, 1962.

Involuntary Civil Commitment: A Crime Against Humanity

Thomas S. Szasz

I

For some time now I have maintained that commitment—that is, the detention of persons in mental institutions against their will—is a form of imprisonment;[1] that such deprivation of liberty is contrary to the moral principles embodied in the Declaration of Independence and the Constitution of the United States;[2] and that it is a crass violation of contemporary concepts of fundamental human rights.[3] The practice of "sane" men incarcerating their "insane" fellow men in "mental hospitals" can be compared to that of white men enslaving black men. In short, I consider commitment a crime against humanity.

Existing social institutions and practices, especially if honored by prolonged usage, are generally experienced and accepted as good and valuable. For thousands of years slavery was considered a "natural" social arrangement for the securing of human labor; it was sanctioned by public opinion, religious dogma, church, and state;[4] it was abolished a mere one hundred years ago in the United States; and it is still a prevalent social practice in some parts of the world, notably in Africa.[5] Since its origin approximately three centuries ago, commitment of the insane has enjoyed equally widespread support; physicians, lawyers, and the laity have asserted, as if with a single voice, the therapeutic desirability and social necessity of institutional psychiatry. My claim that commitment is a crime against humanity may thus be countered—as indeed it has been—by maintaining, first, that the practice is beneficial for the mentally ill, and second, that it is necessary for the protection of the mentally healthy members of society.

Illustrative of the first argument is Slovenko's assertion that "Reliance solely on voluntary hospital admission procedures ignores the fact that some persons may desire care and custody but cannot communicate their desire directly."[6] Imprisonment in mental hospitals is here portrayed—by a professor of law!—as a service provided to persons by the state because they "desire" it but do not know how to ask for it. Felix defends involuntary mental hospitalization by asserting simply, "We *do* [his italics] deal with illnesses of the mind."[7]

Illustrative of the second argument is Guttmacher's characterization of my book *Law, Liberty, and Psychiatry* as ". . . a pernicious book . . . certain to produce intolerable and unwarranted anxiety in the families of psychiatric patients."[8] This is an admission of the fact that the families of "psychiatric patients" frequently resort to the use of force in order to control their "loved ones," and that when attention is directed to this practice it creates embarrassment and guilt. On the other hand, Felix simply defines the psychiatrist's duty as the protection of society: "Tomorrow's psychiatrist will be, as is his counterpart today, one of the gatekeepers of his community."[9]

These conventional explanations of the nature and uses of commitment are, however, but culturally accepted justifications for certain quasi-medical forms of social control, exercised especially against individuals and groups whose behavior does not violate criminal laws but threatens established social values.

II

What is the evidence that commitment does not serve the purpose of helping or treating people whose behavior deviates from or threatens prevailing social norms or moral standards; and who, because they inconvenience their families, neighbors, or superiors, may be incriminated as "mentally ill"?

1. THE MEDICAL EVIDENCE

Mental illness is a metaphor. If by "disease" we mean a disorder of the physicochemical machinery of the human body, then we can assert that what we call functional mental diseases are not diseases at all.[10] Persons said to be suffering from such disorders are socially deviant or inept, or in conflict with individuals, groups, or institutions. Since they do not suffer from disease, it is impossible to "treat" them for any sickness.

Although the term "mentally ill" is usually applied to persons who do not suffer from bodily disease, it is sometimes applied also to persons who do (for example, to individuals intoxicated with alcohol or other drugs, or to elderly people suffering from degenerative disease of the brain). However, when patients with demonstrable diseases of the brain are involuntarily hospitalized, the primary purpose is to exercise social control over their behavior;[11] treatment of the disease is, at best, a secondary consideration. Frequently, therapy is nonexistent, and custodial care is dubbed "treatment."

In short, the commitment of persons suffering from functional psychoses" serves moral and social, rather than medical and therapeutic, purposes. Hence, even if, as a result of future research, certain conditions now believed to be "functional" mental illnesses were to be shown to be "organic," my argument against involuntary mental hospitalization would remain unaffected.

2. THE MORAL EVIDENCE

In free societies, the relationship between physician and patient is predicated on the legal presumption that the individual "owns" his body and his personality.[12] The physician can examine and treat a patient only with his consent; the latter is free to reject treatment (for example, an operation for cancer).[13] After death, "ownership" of the person's body is transferred to his heirs; the physician must obtain permission from the patient's relatives for a post-mortem examination. John Stuart Mill explicitly affirmed that ". . . each person is the proper guardian of his own health, whether bodily, or mental and spiritual."[14] Commitment is incompatible with this moral principle.

3. THE HISTORICAL EVIDENCE

Commitment practices flourished long before there were any mental or psychiatric "treatments" of "mental diseases." Indeed, madness or mental illness was not always a necessary condition for commitment. For example, in the seventeenth century, "children of artisans and other poor inhabitants of Paris up to the age of 25, . . . girls who were debauched or in evident danger of being debauched, . . . and other "misérables" of the community, such as epileptics, people with venereal diseases, and poor people with chronic diseases of all sorts, were all considered fit subjects for confinement in the Hôpital Général.[15] And, in 1860, when Mrs. Packard was incarcerated for disagreeing with her minister-husband,[16] the commitment laws of the State of Illinois explicitly proclaimed that ". . . married women . . . may be entered or detained in the hospital at the request of the husband of the woman or the guardian . . . , without the evidence of insanity required in other cases."[17] It is surely no coincidence that this piece of legislation was enacted and enforced at about the same time that Mill published his essay *The Subjection of Women*.[18]

4. THE LITERARY EVIDENCE

Involuntary mental hospitalization plays a significant part in numerous short stories and novels from many countries. In none that I have encountered is commitment portrayed as helpful to the hospitalized person; instead, it is always depicted as an arrangement serving interests antagonistic to those of the so-called patient.[19]

III

The claim that commitment of the "mentally ill" is necessary for the protection of the "mentally healthy" is more difficult to refute, not because it is valid, but because the danger that "mental patients" supposedly pose is of such an extremely vague nature.

1. THE MEDICAL EVIDENCE

The same reasoning applies as earlier: if "mental illness" is not a disease, there is no medical justification for protection from disease. Hence, the analogy between mental illness and contagious disease falls to the ground: The justification for isolating or otherwise constraining patients with tuberculosis or typhoid fever cannot be extended to patients with "mental illness."

Moreover, because the accepted contemporary psychiatric view of mental illness fails to distinguish between illness as a biological condition and as a social role,[20] it is not only false, but also dangerously misleading, especially if used to justify social action. In this view, regardless of its "causes"—anatomical, genetic, chemical, psychological, or social—mental illness has "objective existence." A person either has or has not a mental illness; he is either mentally sick or mentally healthy. Even if a person is cast in the role of mental patient against his will, his "mental illness" exists "objectively"; and even if, as in the case of the Very Important Person, he is never treated as a mental patient, his "mental illness" still exists "objectively"—apart from the activities of the psychiatrist.[21]

The upshot is that the term "mental illness" is perfectly suited for mystification: It disregards the crucial question of whether the individual assumes the role of mental patient voluntarily, and hence wishes to engage in some sort of interaction with a psychiatrist; or whether he is cast in that role against his will, and hence is opposed to such a relationship. This obscurity is then usually employed strategically, either by the subject himself to advance *his* interests, or by the subject's adversaries to advance *their* interests.

In contrast to this view, I maintain, first, that the involuntarily hospitalized mental patient is, by definition, the occupant of an ascribed role; and, second, that the "mental disease" of such a person—unless the use of this term is restricted to demonstrable lesions or malfunctions of the brain—is always the product of interaction between psychiatrist and patient.

2. THE MORAL EVIDENCE

The crucial ingredient in involuntary mental hospitalization is coercion. Since coercion is the exercise of power, it is always a moral and political act. Accordingly, regardless of its medical justification, commitment is primarily a moral and political phenomenon—just as, regardless of its anthropological and economic justifications, slavery was primarily a moral and political phenomenon.

Although psychiatric methods of coercion are indisputably useful for those who employ them, they are clearly not indispensable for dealing with the problems that so-called mental patients pose for those about them. If an individual threatens others by virtue of his beliefs or actions, he could be dealt with by methods other than "medical": if his conduct is ethically offensive, moral sanctions against him might be appropriate; if forbidden by law, legal sanctions might be appropriate. In my opinion, both informal, moral sanctions, such as social ostracism or divorce, and formal, judicial sanctions, such as fine and imprisonment, are more dignified and less injurious to the human spirit than the quasi-medical psychiatric sanction of involuntary mental hospitalization.[22]

3. THE HISTORICAL EVIDENCE

To be sure, confinement of so-called mentally ill persons does protect the community from certain problems. If it didn't, the arrangement would not have come into being and would not have persisted. However, the question we ought to ask is not *whether* commitment protects the community from "dangerous mental patients," but rather from precisely *what danger* it protects and by *what means?* In what way were prostitutes or vagrants dangerous in seventeenth century Paris? Or married women in nineteenth-century Illinois?

It is significant, moreover, that there is hardly a prominent person who, during the past fifty years or so, has not been diagnosed by a psychiatrist as suffering from some type of "mental illness." Barry Goldwater was called "paranoid schizophrenic";[23] Whittaker Chambers, a "psychopathic personality";[24] Woodrow Wilson, a "neurotic" frequently "very close to psychosis";[25] and Jesus, "a born degenerate" with a "fixed delusional system," and a "paranoid" with a "clinical picture [so typical] that it is hardly conceivable that people can even question the accuracy of the diagnosis."[26] The list is endless.

Sometimes, psychiatrists declare the same person sane *and* insane, depending on the political dictates of their superiors and the social demand of the moment. Before his trial and execution, Adolph Eichmann was examined by several psychiatrists, all of whom declared him to be normal; after he was put to death, "medical evidence" of his insanity was released and widely circulated.

According to Hannah Arendt, "Half a dozen psychiatrists had certified him [Eichmann] as 'normal.' " One psychiatrist asserted, ". . . his whole psychological outlook, his attitude toward his wife and children, mother and father, sisters and friends, was 'not only normal but most desirable.' . . . And the minister who regularly visited him in prison declared that Eichmann was 'a man with very positive ideas.' "[27] After Eichmann was executed, Gideon Hausner, the Attorney General of Israel, who had prosecuted him, disclosed in an article in the *Saturday Evening Post* that psychiatrists diagnosed Eichmann as " 'a man obsessed with a dangerous and insatiable urge to kill,' 'a perverted, sadistic personality.' "[28]

Whether or not men like those mentioned above are considered "dangerous" depends on the observer's religious beliefs, political convictions, and social situation. Furthermore, the "dangerousness" of such persons—whatever we may think of them—is not analogous to that of a person with tuberculosis or typhoid fever; nor would rendering such a person "non-dangerous" be comparable to rendering a patient with a contagious disease non-infectious.

In short, I hold—and I submit that the historical evidence bears me out—that people are committed to mental hospitals neither because they are "dangerous," nor because they are "mentally ill," but rather because they are society's scapegoats, whose persecution is justified by psychiatric propaganda and rhetoric.[29]

4. THE LITERARY EVIDENCE

No one contests that involuntary mental hospitalization of the so-called dangerously insane "protects" the community. Disagreement centers on the nature of the threat facing society, and on the methods and legitimacy of the protection it employs. In this connection, we may recall that slavery, too, "protected" the community: it freed the slaveowners from manual labor. Commitment likewise shields the non-hospitalized members of society: first, from having to accommodate themselves to the annoying or idiosyncratic demands of certain members of the community who have not violated any criminal statutes; and, second, from having to prosecute, try, convict, and punish members of the community who have broken the law but who either might not be convicted in court, or, if they would be, might not be restrained as effectively or as long in prison as in a mental hospital. The literary evidence cited earlier fully supports this interpretation of the function of involuntary mental hospitalization.

IV

I have suggested that commitment constitutes a social arrangement whereby one part of society secures certain advantages for itself at the expense of another part. To do so, the oppressors must possess an ideology to justify their aims and actions; and they must be able to enlist the police power of the state to impose their will on the oppressed members. What makes such an arrangement a "crime against humanity"? It may be argued that the use of state power is legitimate when law-abiding citizens punish lawbreakers. What is the difference between this use of state power and its use in commitment?

In the first place, the difference between committing the "insane" and imprisoning the "criminal" is the same as that between the rule of man and the rule of law:[30] whereas the "insane" are subjected to the coercive controls of the state because persons more powerful than they have labeled them as "psychotic," "criminals" are subjected to such controls because they have violated legal rules applicable equally to all.

The second difference between these two proceedings lies in their professed aims. The principal purpose of imprisoning criminals is to protect the liberties of the law-abiding members of society.[31] Since the individual subject to commitment is not considered a threat to liberty in the same way as the accused criminal is (if he were, he would be prosecuted), his removal from society cannot be justified on the same grounds. Justification for commitment must thus rest on its therapeutic promise and potential: it will help restore the "patient" to "mental health." But if this can be accomplished only at the cost of robbing the individual of liberty, "involuntary mental hospitalization" becomes only a verbal camouflage for what is, in effect, punishment. This "therapeutic" punishment differs, however, from traditional judicial punishment, in that the accused criminal enjoys a rich panoply of constitutional protections against false accusation and oppressive prosecution, whereas the accused mental patient is deprived of these protections.[32] . . .

Notes

1. Szasz, T. S.: "Commitment of the mentally ill: Treatment or social restraint?" *J. Nerv. & Ment. Dis.* 125: 293–307 (Apr.–June), 1957.

2. Szasz, T. S.: *Law, Liberty, and Psychiatry: An Inquiry into the Social Uses of Mental Health Practices* (New York: Macmillan, 1963), pp. 149–90.

3. Ibid., pp. 223–55.

4. Davis, D. B.: *The Problem of Slavery in Western Culture* (Ithaca, N.Y.: Cornell University Press, 1966).

5. See Cohen, R.: "Slavery in Africa." *Trans-Action* 4: 44–56 (Jan.–Feb.), 1967; Tobin, R. L.: "Slavery still plagues the earth." *Saturday Review,* May 6, 1967, pp. 24–25.

6. Slovenko, R.: "The psychiatric patient, liberty, and the law." *Amer. J. Psychiatry* 121: 534–39 (Dec.), 1964, p. 536.

7. Felix, R. H.: "The image of the psychiatrist: Past, present, and future." *Amer.J. Psychiatry* 121: 318–22 (Oct.), 1964, p. 320.

8. Guttmacher, M. S.: "Critique of views of Thomas Szasz on legal psychiatry." *AMA Arch. Gen. Psychiatry* 10: 238–45 (March), 1964, p. 244.

9. Felix, op. cit., p. 231.

10. See Szasz, T. S.: "The myth of mental illness." This volume, ch. 1; *The Myth of Mental Illness: Foundations of a Theory of Personal Conduct* (New York: Hoeber-Harper, 1961); "Mental illness is a myth." *The New York Times Magazine,* June 12, 1966, pp. 30 and 90–92.

11. See, for example, Noyes, A. P.: *Modern Clinical Psychiatry,* 4th ed. (Philadelphia: Saunders, 1956), p. 278.

12. Szasz, T. S.: "The ethics of birth control; or, who owns your body?" *The Humanist* 20: 332–36 (Nov.–Dec.) 1960.

13. Hirsch, B. D.: "Informed consent to treatment," in Averbach, A. and Belli, M. M., eds., *Tort and Medical Yearbook* (Indianapolis: Bobbs-Merrill, 1961), Vol. 1, pp. 631–38.

14. Mill, J. S.: *On Liberty* [1859] (Chicago: Regnery, 1955), p. 18.

15. Rosen, G.: "Social attitudes to irrationality and madness in 17th and 18th century Europe." *J. Hist. Med. & Allied Sciences* 18: 220–40 (1963), p. 223.

16. Packard, E. P.: *Modern Persecution, or Insane Asylums Unveiled,* 2 Vols. (Hartford: Case, Lockwood, and Brainard, 1873).

17. Illinois Statute Book, Sessions Laws 15, Section 10, 1851. Quoted in Packard, E. P.: *The Prisoner's Hidden Life* (Chicago: published by the author, 1868), p. 37.

18. Mill, J. S.: *The Subjection of Women* [1869] (London: Dent, 1965).

19. See, for example, Chekhov, A. P.: *Ward No. 6* [1892], in *Seven Short Novels by Chekhov* (New York: Bantam Books, 1963), pp. 106–57; De Assis, M.: *The Psychiatrist* [1881–82], in De Assis, M., *The Psychiatrist and Other Stories* (Berkeley and Los Angeles: University of California Press, 1963), pp. 1–45; London, J.: *The Iron Heel* [1907] (New York: Sagamore Press, 1957); Porter, K. A.: *Noon Wine* [1937], in Porter, K. A., *Pale Horse, Pale Rider: Three Short*

Novels (New York: Signet, 1965), pp. 62–112; Kesey, K.: *One Flew Over the Cuckoo's Nest* (New York: Viking, 1962); Tarsis, V.: *Ward 7: An Autobiographical Novel* (London and Glasgow: Collins and Harvill, 1965).

20. See Szasz, T. S.: "Alcoholism: A socio-ethical perspective." *Western Medicine* 7: 15–21 (Dec.), 1966.

21. See, for example, Rogow, A. A.: *James Forrestal: A Study of Personality, Politics, and Policy* (New York: Macmillan, 1964); for a detailed criticism of this view, see Szasz, T. S.: "Psychiatric classification as a strategy of personal constraint." *Ideology and Insanity,* pp. 190–217.

22. Szasz, T. S.: *Psychiatric Justice* (New York: Macmillan, 1965).

23. "The Unconscious of a Conservative: A Special Issue on the Mind of Barry Goldwater." *Fact,* Sept.–Oct. 1964.

24. Zeligs, M. A.: *Friendship and Fratricide: An Analysis of Whittaker Chambers and Alger Hiss* (New York: Viking, 1967).

25. Freud, S. and Bullitt, W. C.: *Thomas Woodrow Wilson: A Psychological Study* (Boston: Houghton Mifflin, 1967).

26. Quoted in Schweitzer, A.: *The Psychiatric Study of Jesus* [1913], transl. by Charles R. Joy (Boston: Beacon Press, 1956), pp. 37, 40–41.

27. Arendt, H.: *Eichmann in Jerusalem: A Report on the Banality of Evil* (New York: Viking, 1963), p. 22.

28. Ibid., pp. 22–23.

29. For a full articulation and documentation of this thesis, see Szasz, T. S.: *The Manufacture of Madness: A Comparative Study of the Inquisition and the Mental Health Movement* (New York: Harper & Row, 1970).

30. Hayek, F. A.: *The Constitution of Liberty* (Chicago: University of Chicago Press, 1960), especially pp. 162–92.

31. Mabbott, J. D.: "Punishment" [1939], in Olafson, F. A., ed., *Justice and Social Policy: A Collection of Essays* (Englewood Cliffs, N.J.: Prentice-Hall, 1961), pp. 39–54.

32. For documentation, see Szasz, T. S.: *Law, Liberty, and Psychiatry: An Inquiry into the Social Uses of Mental Health Practices* (New York: Macmillan, 1963); *Psychiatric Justice* (New York: Macmillan, 1965).

Is It Unethical to Offer Predictions of Future Violence?

Thomas Grisso and Paul S. Appelbaum

For many years, scholars have been warning mental health professionals that the results of our research on predictors of future violence set serious limits for experts who testify about future dangerous behavior (e.g., Cocozza & Steadman, 1976; Ennis & Litwack, 1974; Monahan, 1981). Megargee's (1981) conclusion is representative: "The identification of the potentially violent individual with sufficient accuracy to warrant preventative detention . . . is an impossible quest" (p. 181).

Recognition of these predictive limits often has given rise to recommendations that clinicians should not render opinions about "dangerousness" or future violence in legal forums. For example, the American Psychiatric Association (1974) long ago suggested that "clinicians should avoid 'conclusory' judgments" (p. 33) about such matters in expert testimony. This recommendation seems to have been reached most often with regard to testimony in criminal cases (Brody, 1990), although Stone's (1975) review of the empirical evidence led him to recommend that violence prediction should be placed outside the clinician's role in civil commitment as well.

More recently, some analysts of the state of the art in violence prediction have stated outright that which earlier writers may only have implied: It is unethical to do what our research says we cannot do reliably. Melton, Petrila, Poythress, and Slobogin (1987), after concluding that "there is no specialized clinical knowledge that permits categorical, or even relative, conclusions about dangerousness" (p. 204), observed

From *Law and Human Behavior* 16, no. 6 (1992): 621–33. Copyright © 1992, Plenum Publishing Corp. Reprinted by permission.

that "in view of this research, clinicians may decide that they cannot ethically offer prediction testimony" (p. 205). Ethicist Philippa Foot (1990) stated the point more forcefully in the context of capital sentencing, admonishing clinicians to refuse to offer predictive testimony that they know is unreliable: "Such a refusal," she observed, "seems right in the center of the area of professional ethics" (p. 213).

Ewing's (1983, 1985, 1991) statements of this position have been the most sweeping: "[There] is good reason to conclude that psychologists and psychiatrists act unethically when they render predictions of dangerousness that provide a legal basis for restricting another person's interest in life and liberty" (Ewing, 1991, p. 162). The foundation for this assertion is that "such predictions cannot be said to be founded on a scientific basis. . . . The psychiatrist or psychologist who makes a prediction of dangerousness violates his or her ethical obligation to register judgments that rest on a scientific basis" (Ewing, 1983, pp. 417–18).

Ewing's conclusions were reached after his review of research on clinical judgment, expert testimony, and legal considerations in delinquency and criminal cases involving questions of detention and sentencing. But the broad reference to violence predictions affecting restrictions of liberty suggests, as have others (e.g., Stone, 1975), that predictions in matters concerning juvenile and adult offenders are not the only ones that are being condemned. Emergency and involuntary admissions to mental hospitals, as well as decisions about discharge, also involve violence predictions and potential restrictions of liberty. So do the decisions of psychotherapists who fulfill legal obligations to protect children or other persons when they become aware of potential violence by their clients. Therefore, it would appear that a broad-based conclusion that predictions of future violence are unethical indicts most mental health professionals in general clinical or forensic work of unethical behavior at least some time in their careers, and a substantial proportion of them on a daily basis.

We believe that a more differentiated analysis of predictive testimony about future violence, which we offer in this article, does not support an assertion that experts' judgments about violent behavior are necessarily or always unethical, even in legal cases involving potential loss of liberty.[1] We submit that there may be several ethically significant dimensions along which predictions of future violence can be differentiated, which are not taken into account by a blanket condemnation of predictive testimony. These dimensions include, but may not be limited to, (a) the nature of the predictive testimony, (b) the foundation for the predictive testimony, and (c) the legal consequences of the prediction.[2]

The Nature of the Predictive Testimony

Let us presume that when critics have spoken against "predictions of dangerousness," they have been referring to "predictions of future violent behavior."[3] Expert testimony about future violence can take several forms, all of which might be considered predictions as the term is used broadly in the behavioral and social sciences. We can cite no authority for the forms of testimony that such predictions take, but the following are examples from our experience:

a. *Dichotomous*: Statement that a particular behavior (or type of behavior) will or will not occur in the future. ("In my opinion, he will engage in serious violent behavior in the future.")

b. *Dichotomous with Qualified Confidence*: Dichotomous statement, with additional testimony concerning expert's confidence in his or her opinion. ("In my opinion, he will engage in a serious violent behavior in the future, and I believe that it is more likely than not [or 'reasonably certain' or 'very certain'] that my judgment would prove accurate.")

c. *Risk, Individual-Based*: Statement of the degree of likelihood that this individual will engage in a particular behavior (or type of behavior) in the future. ("In my opinion, there is a 40% probability that he will engage in serious violent behavior in the future.")

d. *Risk, Class-Based*: Statement of likelihood or probability, but offered in reference to a class of persons of which the individual is alleged to be a member. ("In my opinion, about 25% of people with this individual's characteristics engage in violent behavior after release from a mental hospital.") May be combined with individual-based. (". . . but I believe that he presents somewhat greater/less risk than that group" [e.g., based on future environmental circumstances].)

All of these forms of testimony may be construed as predictions.[4] They attempt to inform the listener about the clinician's professional opinion concerning behaviors that may occur in the future. Statements of risk are no less predictions than statements in dichotomous form; they simply provide additional information concerning the likelihood that others will be right or wrong in drawing their own dichotomous conclusion.

Broad arguments for a ban on predictions of violent behavior appear not to have been limited to dichotomous statements of prediction, but would prohibit all types of predictive testimony involving questions of future violence and restriction of liberty. The scope of the applicable definition of *prediction* may be significant in evaluating arguments such as Ewing's (1991). If one intends to condemn all forms of predictive testimony as unethical, and if the basis for this conclusion is inadequate scientific support for predictions, then the conclusion is wrong if there is reasonable scientific support for any of the above forms of predictive testimony. It would seem that there is.

Let us consider first the evidence as it relates to dichotomous predictive testimony, our types *a* and *b*. Research demonstrating the lack of scientific support for the validity of predictions of future violence is derived primarily from publications in the 1970s, which have been reviewed extensively (e.g., Monahan, 1981; Webster & Menzies, 1987). Collectively, those studies demonstrated that even for groups with characteristics that often are associated with violent behavior, no more than 20%–40% of individuals, at best, were identified later (e.g., on parole) as engaging in violent acts resulting in recidivism. Reviews of the literature concluded that clinicians have no ability, or no special ability, to predict whether or not a person will engage in a violent act in the future and that they would be right in at best about one in three cases in which they made such predictions (e.g., Cocozza & Steadman, 1976, 1978; Ennis & Emery, 1978; Ennis & Litwack, 1974).[5]

In a thoughtful, critical review of this literature, Litwack and Schlesinger (1987) have argued that "none of these statements has been established by the relevant research findings and, in all probability, they are simply wrong" (p. 206). Their primary argument was that the design of the studies simply did not allow such sweeping conclusions. Given that some studies demonstrated a high number of false-positive predictions in certain circumstances with certain populations, it still did not follow that there were no circumstances in which clinicians might make more accurate predictions or might have something more to offer than laypersons.

An example of Litwack and Schlesinger's (1987) reasoning is provided by their analysis of the court's majority and dissenting opinions in *Schall* v. *Martin* (1984). Both opinions interpreted past research as indicating that accurate predictions of juveniles' future violence (for purposes of justifying pretrial preventive detention) could not be made. Yet Litwack and Schlesinger observed (as did Monahan, 1981) that there is no research contradicting the notion that predictions of violence might be more accurate in certain cases, especially those in which there is a known history of recent, repeated violence. In other words, research has yet to show "that there is no identifiable subclass of juvenile arrestees about whom predictions can reasonably be made" (Litwack & Schlesinger, 1987, p. 232).

In one sense, Litwack and Schlesinger's observations appear to challenge the conclusion that all dichotomous predictions are unethical. Research on the invalidity of such predictions has focused only on certain populations and circumstances; one might argue, therefore, that the impropriety of dichotomous predictions in those types of cases need not extend to other types of cases for which validity has not yet been challenged. This reasoning is less persuasive, however, if it is also unethical (as some critics have claimed: Dix, 1980) to make dichotomous predictions when we *do not know* their validity for the type of case at hand because of the *absence* of relevant research. Dichotomous predictions of future violence, therefore, remain vulnerable to arguments that they violate ethical propriety.

Turning now to predictive testimony of types *c* and *d,* some of the same studies of the 1970s that challenged the validity of dichotomous predictions provided the earliest scientific support for offering predictive testimony in the form of probabilistic or comparative risk statements. For example, the State of Michigan's (1978) Parole Risk Study identified a small class of parolees with a 40% rate of violent recidivism. Accurate classification of a parole candidate in that group, therefore, would allow scientifically supported predictive testimony that the risk of violent recidivism was much greater for this person than for most parolees (for whom the baserate was shown to be about 10%).

Much more sophisticated research during the 1980s significantly augmented the scientific support for identification of groups with relatively high baserates of future violence (e.g., Binder & McNiel, 1988; Klassen & O'Connor, 1988, 1990; Link, Cullen, & Andrews, 1990; Swanson, Holzer, Ganju, & Jono, 1990). For example, studies identified hospitalized groups, based on a combination of background and demographic characteristics, for which the risk of subsequent violent behavior in the community was over 50% (Klassen & O'Connor, 1988), as well as groups identified merely by a reliable diagnosis (alcohol or drug abuse/dependence) for which prior-year baserates of violence in the community were 25%–35%, or 12–17 times greater than for persons with no DSM-III diagnosis (Swanson et al., 1990).

These newer studies, of course, do not provide scientific evidence with which to claim validity for predictive testimony in dichotomous form (predictive testimony of types a and b in our characterization above).[6] They merely provide research support, in some cases, for predictive testimony that offers courts a sense of the relative risk of violence associated with individuals in question (predictive testimony of types c and d). Yet this is enough to contradict the generalized assertion that *all* predictive testimony regarding future violence is unethical for lack of a scientific basis.

One might argue, however, that the very nature of this scientific basis for the ethical propriety of some predictive testimony actually negates the value of the testimony for legal decision makers. The risk probabilities found in research for the highest risk groups are rarely above 50% (and often less than 30%). As such, ethically supportable risk-related statements will almost always constitute an acknowledgment, by inference, that it is more likely than not that violence will *not* occur. This argument would conclude that courts may have no need for predictive testimony, if there are rarely any cases in which it could support scientifically the proposition that certain individuals will, "more likely than not," be violent.

The argument presumes, however, that *legal* decisions identifying a person as "dangerous" (for purposes of authorizing restriction of liberty) require a finding of relative certainty (or at least likelihood of greater than 0.5) that the individual will be violent. Yet few statutes make this requirement. Using various terminology, they simply require "a likelihood" or a significant probability.[7] For example, New York state's statutes authorizing the pretrial (preventive) detention of juveniles reviewed in *Schall* v. *Martin* (1984) (a U.S. Supreme Court decision strongly criticized by Ewing [1985] as misinterpreting the value of expert testimony on future violence) required merely that "there is a serious risk" that the juvenile will commit a criminal act if not detained. For civil commitment and many other legal purposes, Massachusetts requires a "likelihood of serious harm," further defined as a "substantial risk of physical harm" (Massachusetts General Laws, Ch. 123, Sec. 1).

Statutes like these do not require a finding that the person *will* commit a future violent act, but that a *sufficient risk* exists to warrant restriction of liberty (Monahan & Wexler, 1978). Given accurate and scientifically supportable predictive testimony about degree of risk, it is up to society (usually its representative on the bench) to determine whether 40%, 30%, or even 20% risk of future violence might reach a threshold justifying a particular legal intervention (Morse, 1978).[8]

How society's legal decision makers perform this judgment has been suggested by other writers, who have described other factors that decision makers are likely to take into account in interaction with the degree of risk in a particular case. Brooks (1974), for example, noted that *dangerousness* could be defined not simply as a function of the probability of future harm, but as an interaction between probability and other factors: the expected magnitude of harm, its expected frequency, and its imminence. Similarly, Gottfredson and Gottfredson (1988) offered empirical evidence that dangerousness judgments fit a model based on an interaction of "risk" (probability of future harm) and " stakes" (the nature of the harm expected). Their evidence supported the notion that society's decisions to restrict liberty require a higher threshold of risk when the type of harm expected is not serious and allow a lower threshold of risk to justify liberty restrictions when the type of harm expected is more violent. Risk assessments also interact with society's moral judgments in determining justifiable restrictions of liberty. For example, in the context of sentencing in criminal cases, Monahan (1982) described a "modified desert model" in which society determines the upper and lower limits for prison sentences on the basis of moral perceptions of classes of offenses, while the degree of risk that the person might offend again may be used for judgments about the actual length of sentence within those limits.

Massachusetts' definition of "likelihood of serious harm," for purposes of criminal and civil legal decisions, offers one of the most straightforward acknowledgments of a risk-oriented perspective when it defines *dangerousness* as "evidence that others are placed in *reasonable fear* of violent behavior" (M.G.L., Ch. 123. Sec. 1; emphasis added). From a legal perspective, future violence need not be "more likely than not" before society is justified in being afraid.[9]

In summary, not all predictive statements about future violence are unethical owing to lack of scientific support because predictive testimony stated as a risk estimate sometimes is scientifically supported. Moreover, the fact that the scientific evidence manifests significant false-positive rates does not detract from the potential value of risk estimates for courts' legal decisions about restrictions of liberty.

This conclusion, of course, does not resolve all questions concerning the ethical propriety of predictive testimony. Both individual professionals and professional organizations must go beyond the nature of the predictive testimony itself to consider at least two other factors when weighing the ethical propriety of predictive testimony. The remainder of our discussion explores these additional factors.

The Foundation of the Predictive Testimony

As the preceding discussion makes clear, the scientific basis for predictions of future violence is derived from studies identifying particular characteristics of research subjects who subsequently engaged in violent behavior. This suggests three important limitations on the appropriateness even of predictive risk statements, consistent with a general standard of competence in clinicians' performance of evaluations (Section 1: American Psychiatric Association, 1989; Principle 1: American Psychological Association, 1981).

First, the person about whom the estimate of risk is being made must be similar to the research subjects in the studies from which the predictive model is derived. Second, the estimate of risk must be based on types of data comparable to those available in the studies that are being relied upon. Third, the expert's evaluation process and methods by which data are gathered must be sufficiently reliable to assure accurate identification of the relevant characteristics of the individual in question.

Many of the arguments against the use of predictions by mental health professionals have focused on a single type of situation in which none of these limiting conditions has been respected: the prediction of a defendant's future violent behavior at the sentencing phase of a capital trial (Ewing, 1983). In that situation, mental health professionals have testified routinely about the likelihood of future violence when there were no data about comparable groups of subjects (Dix, 1980), or when such data began to be available (Marquart, Ekland-Olsen, & Sorenson, 1989; Marquart & Sorenson, 1989), often in disregard of them. Moreover, such testimony often has been based on evaluation procedures or methods that manifest little regard for a reliable description of the defendant's characteristics. Such is the case when predictions are offered on the basis of information provided in a hypothetical question posed by the prosecutor, typically without the expert having had an opportunity to examine the defendant or to become acquainted with documentary evidence relevant to the defendant's history (Appelbaum, 1984).

The ethics of predictions of future violence in such a context indeed are questionable. But it is not clear that one can generalize from these troublesome practices to all other predictive testimony. For example, predictive testimony may be ethically appropriate when a mental health professional who has examined a potential patient offers testimony at a commitment hearing about an increased risk of future violence, based on (a) data suggesting that certain diagnostic groups, or persons manifesting certain symptoms, are at increased risk for violent behavior, and (b) data indicating that the prospective patient reliably can be associated with those groups. The closer the match between the characteristics of the subject of the prediction and the data available about those characteristics in the studies on which the predictive statement is based, the less problematic such testimony will be.

In summary, predictive testimony sometimes has met the foundational criteria described here and sometimes has not. But the frequent failure of experts to have satisfied these conditions in a particular situation (sentencing in capital trials) does not warrant the conclusion that *all* violence predictions are unethical.

The Legal Consequences of the Prediction

Thus far we have provided reasoning for two assertions. *First,* not all predictive testimony about future violence can be challenged as unethical on

empirical grounds because predictive testimony in the form of probabilistic or comparative risk statements in some cases can rest upon an
empirical foundation based on reliable research findings. *Second,* though
experts sometimes have failed to abide by accepted principles for applying this empirical base in individual assessments, this certainly is not
always (or even usually) the case. The unethical or incompetent behavior of some clinicians does not render all violence predictions unethical.
One further dimension requires consideration, however, when weighing
the ethical status of predictions about future violence. It pertains to the
legal consequences of our predictions.

We sometimes have the necessary research support and assessment
data to state a probability of violence in a given case. That probability
usually will be less than 0.5. As noted in our first discussion, this probability may be sufficient to lead the fact-finder to conclude that the identified level of risk satisfies a sociolegal definition of dangerousness for
purposes of restricting liberties. When decision makers are satisfied that
a level of risk below 0.5 warrants the restriction of liberty, however,
across cases the majority of persons about whom the decision is being
made will be the "victims" of a high false-positive rate.

Society may believe that it is justified in "mistakenly" restricting the
liberties of a majority in order to achieve the proper objectives in relation to the minority who are "correctly" restricted. Yet that which society can justify for itself may not always satisfy the ethical obligations of
clinicians, as interpreted individually or by their professional organizations. For example, psychologists are urged by their profession's ethical
standards to be alert to, and to refuse to engage in or condone, unjustifiable decisions by others as a consequence of their own actions, and to
make known their concern about conflicts of these types that they
encounter in their work (American Psychological Association, 1981:
Principle 1[f], 2[b] and [d]). Psychiatrists are urged to respect the rights
of patients and to seek changes in laws when they are contrary to the best
interests of patients (American Psychiatric Association, 1989: Section 3
and 4). Therefore independent of that which is accepted by society or
the law, professionals have an obligation to consider the potential effects
of their testimony about risk statements with high false-positive rates and
to question whether the law's use of their testimony violates their professional ethical standards.

When we participate in legal proceedings in which our predictive testimony results in decisions with high false-positive rates and their consequences, do we practice unethically? There are at least three ways that
one might address the question.

First, one can argue that *any* restriction of liberty based on predictive testimony about risk involving large false-positive rates constitutes a

misuse of psychological or psychiatric information by the legal system. This position would be based on either of two views: (1) that it is wrong for society to restrict liberties on the basis of less than 0.5 probability of future violence, and that to do so demeans the rights of the individual, is "unjustifiable," and does not "promote human welfare" (e.g., American Psychological Association, 1981: Preamble, and Principle 3[b]), or (2) that even with an expert's attempts to inform the court about the limits of testimony based on probabilities with high false-positive rates, there is an unacceptable potential for misunderstanding or misuse of the information in the legal forum. Experts who testify about risk probabilities with high false-positive rates, therefore, would be perceived as participating unethically in the process.

A second approach would leave questions of justification to the courts and society to determine, not the mental health professional. Statutes and procedures of law define the conditions under which society "justly" restricts the liberties of its citizens. The expert who provides reliable risk probability information (and clearly explains its limitations) to courts within that legal framework engages in ethical practice, according to this view, even if the legal outcome deprives the individual of liberty "mistakenly." The duties of the forensic expert are different in this regard from those of the clinician in a doctor-patient relationship, wherein the obligation to maximize the welfare of the patient is paramount. Therefore, the consequences of a court's restrictions of liberty present no ethical burden for the expert beyond that of presenting reliable testimony and clearly explaining its limitations.

A third position is intermediate in relation to the other two. It would not leave questions of justification only to the courts. On the other hand, it would observe that not all types of liberty restrictions are of equal consequence, especially given variability across circumstances (e.g., civil commitment vs. capital sentencing) in potential, counterbalancing benefits to the person whose liberty is restricted. This position might also recognize variability in the quality of legal justice across jurisdictions (e.g., known patterns of racial bias in sentencing in certain jurisdictions). This perspective would see predictive testimony about risk probabilities with high false-positive rates as neither ethical nor unethical per se. Instead, it would encourage professional debate regarding the circumstances (e.g., degree and type of liberty restrictions associated with the legal question, types of benefits that may accrue) in which the various magnitudes of false-positive error resulting from risk probability testimony would be ethically acceptable or unacceptable in relation to the balance of consequences for the individual and society.

Our purpose here is not to evaluate, endorse, or refine any of these approaches. We merely observe that they reach different answers to the question of ethical propriety in predictive testimony about risk probabilities. The second approach would not consider such predictive testimony unethical, and the third might consider it unethical for certain types of legal proceedings, but not for all.

The first approach would, indeed, see all such testimony as unethical. If it is to be used as a basis for arguing that risk-related predictive testimony should be banned because it contributes to unjust legal decisions, then its proponents should make explicit the assumptions and unanswered questions underlying the position so that it can be debated on its merits. For example, on what basis are our professional associations to determine that society's justifications for restrictions of liberty (based partly on our testimony) are wrong? What is the foundation for the argument that our testimony, if carefully presented, will be misunderstood or misused by legal fact-finders? Do the gains in "human welfare" associated with a prohibition on risk-related testimony outweigh the potential negative effects on "human welfare"?[10]

Absent a clearer view of that position, a consideration of the three perspectives does not support a summary judgment that predictive testimony based on risk probabilities with high false-positive rates is per se unethical, especially if offered with an eye to clinicians' obligations to make clear the limits of their predictive statements.

Conclusion

A careful analysis of predictions of future violence demonstrates that there are several types of predictive testimony, varying along at least three ethically relevant dimensions: the nature, foundation, and consequences of the prediction. We suspect that further reflection will discern others. Proponents of a ban on all predictive testimony by mental health professionals have often reasoned from a single paradigm: testimony at sentencing hearings in capital cases, and sometimes other criminal contexts, where the characteristics of the predictions are not necessarily similar to those made elsewhere. Proponents of that position may indeed have identified circumstances in which predictive statements cannot be considered ethical; but by our reasoning, this conclusion cannot blithely be generalized to all other contexts. Therefore, we would not advise psychology, psychiatry, or the courts to conclude that all predictions of dangerousness are unethical.

Notes

1. For the purposes of this paper, we do not challenge the implied standard for ethical expert testimony reflected in the critiques cited above: that

expert testimony lacking a scientific foundation (i.e., empirical data supportive of the expert's conclusions) is always ethically problematic. We argue below that even if this conclusion is accepted, predictions related to future violence are not necessarily unethical. Nevertheless, we do not mean to imply that expert testimony not supported by empirical research data is always unethical, particularly in circumstances in which such data are not available, and the expert does not imply that the opinion offered rests on a scientific basis (e.g., the expert bases an opinion on his or her own experience or the anecdotal experience of others).

2. One could base an argument about the ethical impropriety of predictive testimony on two broad approaches: (1) that violence predictions violate ethical principles in theory (that is, predictive testimony *cannot* be offered ethically), or (2) although it could be offered ethically, in actual practice experts so frequently misuse such predictions that the practice in general should be construed as violating ethical obligations. The arguments in this article discuss ethical propriety primarily in theory, not in actual practice. It is common knowledge that some mental health professionals offer predictive testimony in unethical ways; but little is known about "average" practice among mental health professionals nationally when they testify regarding predictions of violence. One should note, however, that professional organizations could potentially use either theoretical or state-of-the-practice arguments, if made successfully, to prohibit a particular type of professional service.

3. Future discourse in this area might be facilitated by ridding ourselves of the phrase *predictions of dangerousness*. It has no logical meaning in the context of the behavioral and social sciences. To "predict" is to make a statement about the likelihood of a future event or behavior. *Dangerousness* seems to refer not to an event or behavior, but to a condition that exists as a function of the presence of someone or something perceived as "dangerous." Other definitions are possible, but whatever dangerousness means, it is not a behavior or an event offering a logical criterion for predictive efforts in research or clinical practice.

4. Melton et al. (1987) have described another type of testimony about future violence in which the clinician goes no further than identifying for the court any factors relevant to the case that augment or mitigate the prospect of future violence (e.g., "His record of past violence increases the likelihood of future acts of similar type, although his advancing age suggests decreasing risk."). Undoubtedly this is the appropriate level of testimony in some cases; we do not include it in our list of testimonial types merely because, when it is offered without more, this testimony stops short of a predictive statement.

5. We note in passing, however, that this research notwithstanding, there may be cases in which empirical evidence would support a conclusion that a particular person would almost certainly be violent in the future. Ewing's (1987) review of the lives of 100 battered women provides some excellent examples. Weekly physical abuse of a wife over a period of years would seem to be sufficient evidence to justify a prediction—barring some intervention, unlikely change in living arrangements, or the wife's death—that it will happen again. To offer such a prediction as expert testimony would not seem unethical for lack of a scientific basis. The point is not particularly interesting, however, because in most cases of this type, an expert's opinion would be superfluous.

6. We note, however, that they do offer a logical contradiction to the assertion that dichotomous predictions never have scientific support. Many of the studies identify classes of individuals for which the baserate of violent behavior approaches zero. These results could offer scientific support for testifying that it is virtually certain that an individual in question would *not* engage in a violent act.

7. Several analysts of predictive testimony on future violence (e.g.. Brody, 1990; Stone, 1975: Cocozza & Steadman, 1976) have used the legal standard of proof (e.g., beyond a reasonable doubt, characterized as "95% certain") to identify the required level of the expert's or fact-finder's certainty that future violence will occur. We do not agree with this interpretation. Legal standards of proof refer to the certainty of the fact-finder that the person in question has been accurately identified as presenting a risk of violence meeting an abstract criterion (e.g., "significant," "substantial," "serious"), whatever actual probability that might be. To the extent that this burden applies to the clinician, the standard of proof may express the degree of certainty with which the clinician must be able to form an opinion that the probability of future violence, whether it is 0.1, 0.2, or 0.5, has been obtained and applied accurately to the person in question. Monahan and Wexler (1978) provided a more detailed discussion of this distinction.

8. When experts use terms such as *substantial* or *significant* to refer to these levels of risk, they should be prepared to explain the difference between a relatively "significant risk" (which may nevertheless involve a high false-positive rate) and an absolute "high probability."

9. This notion has been acknowledged in other jurisdictions as well. For example, the First Circuit Court of Appeals in *Rogers* v. *Okin* (1980) recognized that in certain life-threatening circumstances, "It would be patently unreasonable to require that [clinicians] determine that the probability of the feared violence occurring is greater than fifty percent before they can act" (p. 656). Moreover, some research suggests that ordinary citizens in fact do conclude that coercion should be applied in some circumstances in which the levels of risk of endangering behavior are well below 50% (Slovic, 1991).

10. Two examples of potential negative consequences of the first position may be offered. *First,* a blanket prohibition of risk probability testimony involving high false-positive rates would disallow not only predictions of violence, but also predictions of nonviolence. According to past research, our predictions that individuals will *not* engage in future violence are quite likely to be accurate (low false-negatives). Therefore, testimony about nonviolence is immune to consequentialist arguments that focus on unjust restrictions of liberty as a result of the effects of testimony on legal dispositions. Prohibiting risk-related predictive testimony could deprive individuals of testimony that might reduce the likelihood of liberty restrictions due to alleged violence potential. *Second,* additional questions are raised by the apparent limitation of the argument (that testimony on future violence is unethical) to situations in which "liberty" is at stake (e.g., Ewing, 1991). If cases involving restrictions on liberty are construed narrowly as only referring to decisions about detention or release, we arrive at the para-

doxical argument that the same testimony about a child abuser's future violence that could not be offered at a parole hearing could be tendered at a custody proceeding. On the other hand, if liberty is construed broadly, such that, for example, denial of access to one's child consequent to a custody determination infringes liberty, then testimony on future violence would never be permissible. We question whether proponents of the view that predictions of future violence are unethical truly desire to exclude testimony from child custody hearings (presuming the testimony meets scientific standards) that a parent has a 40% likelihood of harming his or her child.

References

American Psychiatric Association (1974). *Clinical aspects of the violent individual.* Washington, D.C.: American Psychiatric Association.

——— (1989). *Principles of medical ethics with annotations especially applicable to psychiatry.* Washington, D.C.: American Psychiatric Association.

American Psychological Association (1981). *Ethical principles of psychologists.* Washington, D.C.: American Psychological Association.

Appelbaum, P. (1984). Hypotheticals, psychiatric testimony, and the death sentence. *Bulletin of the American Academy of Psychiatry and the Law* 12, 169–77.

Binder, R., & McNiel, D. (1988). Effects of diagnosis and context on dangerousness. *American Journal of Psychiatry* 145, 728–32.

Brody, B. (1990). Prediction of dangerousness in different contexts. In R. Rosner & R. Weinstock (Eds.), *Ethical practice in psychiatry and the law* (pp. 185–96). New York: Plenum.

Brooks, A. (1974). *Law, psychiatry and the mental health system.* Boston: Little, Brown.

Cocozza, J., & Steadman, H. (1976). The failure of psychiatric predictions of dangerousness: Clear and convincing evidence. *Rutgers Law Review* 29, 1084–1101.

——— (1978). Prediction in psychiatry: An example of misplaced confidence in experts. *Social Problems* 25, 265–76.

Dix, G. (1980). Clinical evaluation of the "dangerousness" of "normal" criminal defendants. *Virginia Law Review* 66, 523–81.

Ennis, B., & Emery, R. (1978). *The rights of mental patients.* New York: Avon.

Ennis, B., & Litwack, T. (1974). Psychiatry and the presumption of expertise: Flipping coins in the courtroom. *California Law Review* 62, 693–752.

Ewing, C. (1983). "Dr. Death" and the case for an ethical ban on psychiatric and psychological predictions of dangerousness in capital sentencing proceedings. *American Journal of Law and Medicine* 8, 407–28.

——— (1985). *Schall* v. *Martin:* Preventive detention and dangerousness through the looking glass. *Buffalo Law Review* 34, 173–226.

——— (1987). *Battered women who kill.* Lexington, MA: Heath.

——— (1991). Preventive detention and execution: The constitutionality of punishing future crimes. *Law and Human Behavior* 15, 139–63.

Foot, P. (1990). Ethics and the death penalty: Participation of forensic psychiatrists in capital trials. In R. Rosner and R. Weinstock (Eds.). *Ethical practice in psychiatry and the law* (pp. 207–17). New York: Plenum.

Gottfredson, D., & Gottfredson, S. (1988). Stakes and risks in the prediction of violent criminal behavior. *Violence and Victims* 3, 247–62.

Klassen, D., & O'Connor, W. (1988). A prospective study of predictors of violence in adult male mental health admissions. *Law and Human Behavior* 12, 143–58.

———— (1990). Assessing the risk of violence in released mental patients: A cross-validational study. *Psychological Assessment* 1, 75–81.

Link, B., Cullen, F., & Andrews, H. (1990, August). *Violent and illegal behavior of current and former mental patients compared to community controls.* Paper presented at the meeting of the Society for the Study of Social Problems.

Litwack, T., & Schlesinger, L. (1987). Assessing and predicting violence: Research, law, and application. In I. Weiner & A. Hess (Eds.), *Handbook of forensic psychology* (pp. 205–57). New York: Wiley.

Marquart, J., Ekland-Olsen, S., & Sorenson, J. (1989). Gazing into the crystal ball: Can jurors accurately predict dangerousness in capital cases? *Law and Society Review* 23, 449–68.

Marquart, J., & Sorensen, J. (1989). A national study of the *Furman*-committed inmates: Assessing the threat to society from capital offenders. *Loyola of Los Angeles Law Review* 23, 5–28.

Megargee, E. (1981). Methodological problems in the prediction of violence. In J. Hays, T. Roberts, & K. Solway (Eds.), *Violence and the violent individual* (pp. 179–91). New York: Spectrum.

Melton, G., Petrila, J., Poythress, N., & Slobogin, C. (1987). *Psychological evaluations for the courts.* New York: Guilford.

Monahan, J. (1981). *The clinical prediction of violent behavior.* Rockville, MD: National Institute of Mental Health.

Monahan, J. (1982). The case for prediction in the modified desert model of criminal sentencing. *International Journal of Law and Psychiatry* 5, 103–13.

Monahan, J., & Wexler, D. (1978). A definite maybe: Proof and probability in civil commitment. *Law and Human Behavior* 2, 37–42.

Morse, S. (1978). Crazy behavior, morals, and science: An analysis of mental health law. *Southern California Law Review* 51, 527–654.

Rogers v. *Okin*, 634 F.2d 650 (1st Cir., 1980).

Schall v. *Martin*, 467 U.S. 253 (1984).

Slovic, P. (1991, January). *Studies of perceived risk and perceived dangerousness of mentally ill persons.* Paper presented at the meeting of the MacArthur Foundation Research Network on Mental Health and the Law, Key West, FL.

State of Michigan, Department of Connections (June 29, 1978). *The parole risk study.* Unpublished manuscript.

Stone, A. (1975). *Mental health and law: A system in transition.* Rockville, MD: National Institute of Mental Health.

Swanson, J., Holzer, C., Ganju, V., & Jono, R. (1990). Violence and psychiatric disorder in the community: Evidence from the Epidemiologic Catchment Area Surveys. *Hospital and Community Psychiatry* 41, 761–70.

Webster, C., & Menzies, R. (1987). The clinical prediction of dangerousness. In D. Weisstub (Ed.), *Law and mental health: International perspectives,* Vol. 3 (pp. 158–208). New York: Pergamon.

A Critique of Revisions in Procedural, Substantive, and Dispositional Criteria in Involuntary Civil Commitment

Donald H. J. Hermann

Anyone spending time in a major urban center in the United States must be shocked by the significant number of mentally ill persons living on the streets—the "bag people" who sleep in doorways, on steam grates, on subway stairs.[1] These people represent a new lifestyle made possible in part by a policy of deinstitutionalization of the mentally ill, which has been motivated largely by economic considerations and rationalized as a matter of mental health law reform.[2] Another major factor contributing to the increasing denial of treatment to the mentally ill has been a revision of the mental health statutes. A number of jurisdictions now require, as a prerequisite to involuntary commitment, both a finding of dangerousness to self or others and that treatment be done in the least restrictive institutional setting.[3] The policy of deinstitutionalization and these reforms of commitment law ignore the reality of mental illness—many mentally ill persons lack the ability to make rational decisions about their treatment needs.[4]

This essay examines the efficacy of the procedural and substantive reforms in civil commitment law that courts and legislatures have made in the last decade and a half. In light of this examination, the Essay suggests some doctrinal revisions that are necessary to assure adequate treatment for mentally ill persons who lack the rational capacity to understand their own needs or how to meet those needs.

The current law of civil commitment reflects the extensive reform of the last two decades.[5] Historically, the process of involuntary civil com-

From *Vanderbilt Law Review* 39, no. 1 (January 1986): 83–106. Copyright © 1986, *Vanderbilt Law Review*. Reprinted by permission.

mitment limited an individual's civil rights in favor of achieving social control by compelling treatment in conformity with the police power and a *parens patriae* policy.[6] During the last two decades, however, this process has been challenged in the courts and subjected to legislative revision.[7] This reassessment has produced three principal reforms: the imposition of procedural rights for those subjected to commitment proceedings,[8] the constriction of substantive commitment criteria,[9] and the adoption of the least restrictive alternative disposition requirement.[10] While the development of procedural rights raises obstacles to the imposition of effective treatment, this development, on the whole, has been desirable. On the other hand, the constriction of commitment criteria and the formulation and requirement of the least restrictive alternative for disposition have been mistaken: these developments raise inappropriate barriers to providing effective treatment to persons who are in need of such treatment.

Procedural Requirements in Involuntary Civil Commitment

Through a series of cases the United States Supreme Court clearly has established that involuntary civil commitment in a state facility constitutes an invasion of an individual's constitutionally protected interests and therefore requires compliance with due process. . . .

. . . The Supreme Court has established that some degree of procedural due process must be provided before the state may forcibly deprive a mentally ill person of his liberty. Although the Court has not definitively determined the type of hearing required for civil commitment under the due process clause, on the basis of the Court's lead, state courts and legislatures have recognized a range of civil rights of persons who are subject to involuntary commitment; these include: prior notice,[11] an opportunity to be heard,[12] the right to counsel,[13] and the right to judicial review of an initial commitment order.[14] . . .

The Supreme Court's decisions evidence a balanced judicial concern with patient rights.[15] The early civil commitment cases emphasized the civil rights of patients by requiring procedural safeguards and demanding that the state establish a proper basis for any restrictions on liberty.[16] Subsequent cases revealed an emerging concern with clinical or treatment rights.[17] Establishing a burden of proof that lies between that used in civil cases and that used in criminal cases demonstrates the Court's sensitivity to the need for balancing the individual's interest in personal liberty against the state's interest in providing that person with needed treatment.[18] The most recent cases reveal an even greater concern with the clinical needs of patients.[19] Deference to the judgment of admitting physicians as a basis for involuntary commitment of juveniles[20] and recognition of professional judgment in decisions on treatment modalities in civil commitment of retarded persons[21] suggest that the Court is concerned with maintaining a proper balance between protecting civil liberties and providing effective treatment.

The judicial reform of commitment law has been limited largely to procedural matters with which the courts properly feel most qualified to deal. Courts have demonstrated a pronounced reluctance to alter the substantive basis for commitment, which has been viewed as essentially involving medical criteria. Instead, state legislatures have been the locus of change in the substantive criteria for commitment.

Substantive Bases for Involuntary Civil Commitment

While commitment criteria vary from state to state, most states have adopted substantive standards for commitment that employ two elements. First, all states require that an individual must be found mentally ill as determined by medical authorities.[22] The second element varies in form and scope from state to state. Most states allow commitment upon a showing that an individual is dangerous to self or others.[23] For instance, in California a person may be certified for a one hundred and eighty day commitment period if "[t]he person had attempted, or inflicted physical harm upon the person of another, that act having resulted in his or her being taken into custody and who presents, as a result of mental disorder or mental defect, a demonstrated danger of inflicting substantial physical harm upon others."[24] Some state legislatures and courts require that dangerousness be established by a recent overt act or threat.[25]

A few states also allow commitment of those who are gravely disabled.[26] Several states do not use the term "gravely disabled" when setting forth substantive commitment criteria but nevertheless set forth descriptions of conditions that may fairly be considered equivalent to a standard of "grave disability."[27] For instance, Florida permits commitment of a person if "[h]e is manifestly incapable of surviving alone or with the help of willing and responsible family or friends, including available alternative services, and, without treatment, he is likely to suffer from neglect or refuse to care for himself, and such neglect or refusal poses a real and present threat of substantial harm to his well-being."[28] Illinois permits commitment of a "person who is mentally ill and who because of his illness is unable to provide for his basic physical needs so as to guard himself from serious harm."[29] Finally, some states, such as New Jersey[30] and New York,[31] merely require a showing that an individual is in need of treatment.

Many of the present civil commitment criteria are the products of a twenty-year reform effort.[32] The statutory reform was prompted by an increase in concern for civil liberties[33] and by empirical studies providing evidence of poor diagnosis and treatment.[34] Legislatures increasingly have restricted their reliance on *parens patriae* as a justification for commitment and have substituted instead a greater reliance on police power.[35] Thus, there has been a general movement away from a concern for a person's treatment needs and toward a concern for a person's dangerousness.[36] By placing stress on the legal concept of dangerousness rather than on the medical concept of need for treatment, legislatures have chosen a legal rather than a medical or psychiatric model of commitment.[37] This narrow legal analytical framework results in a substantial rejection of and insensitivity to psychiatric concerns and ignores the basic needs of the mentally ill.[38] Thus, while procedural safeguards are necessary to prevent abuse of involuntary commitment, medical criteria other than dangerousness are necessary to provide a means for meeting the treatment needs of the mentally ill, particularly those who are incompetent to make treatment decisions.[39]

Civil commitment traditionally has been justified on the grounds that it protects the mentally ill from harming themselves or others and provides them with care, custody, and treatment.[40] The use of state power to prevent harm to others is clearly an exercise of police power,[41] while state-enforced treatment is an exercise of *parens patriae* power.[42] Preventing harm to self involves both police power and *parens patriae* power. The revisions of civil commitment law in the direction of a single standard of dangerousness[43] therefore reflect a determination that *parens patriae* standing alone is an insufficient basis for commitment of the incompetent mentally ill.[44]

The grounds for rejecting the *parens patriae* standards of "grave disability" and "need of mental treatment" include an asserted unreliability of medical diagnosis;[45] a failure of statutes and regulations to define mental illness adequately;[46] judgment that treatment often is not provided or not successful;[47] and a concern with loss of liberty, stigmatization, and invasion of privacy.[48] The United States District Court for the District of Nebraska applied this rationale in *Doremus* v. *Farrell*,[49] decided in 1975. The court reasoned as follows:

> Considering the fundamental rights involved in civil commitment, the *parens patriae* power must require a compelling interest of the state to justify the deprivation of liberty. In the mental health field, where diagnosis and treatment are uncertain, the need for treatment without some degree of imminent harm to the person or dangerousness to society is not a compelling justification. . . . To permit involuntary commitment upon finding of "mental illness" and the need for treatment alone would be tantamount to condoning the State's commitment of persons

deemed socially undesirable for the purpose of indoctrination or con-
forming the individual's beliefs to the beliefs of the State. Due process
and equal protection require that the Standards for commitment must
be (a) that the person is mentally ill and poses a serious threat of substantial harm to himself or to others; and (b) that this threat of harm
has been evidenced by a recent overt act or threat. The threat of harm
to oneself may be through neglect or inability to care for oneself.[50]

At one level this reasoning fails to recognize the reality of mental illness,
which can be debilitating to the person and provide a real source of
social disruption.[51] The view expressed by the *Doremus* court—particularly its labeling of mental health treatment as a process of "indoctrination"—demonstrates a hostility toward and lack of understanding of
mental health treatment. On another level this reasoning is simply inconsistent with the scope of the dangerousness standard. To the extent that
the dangerousness standard includes "threat of harm to oneself," it is
broad enough to permit commitment on exactly the same basis as a
"need of treatment" or "incompetence" standard. Ironically, those
courts and legislatures that have adopted reasoning similar to the *Doremus* court's and explicitly have rejected need of treatment as a grounds
for commitment nevertheless implicitly have recognized incompetence
as a basis for *parens patriae* commitments.[52] They manifest this recognition whenever they permit commitment on a showing that a person is
"unable to provide for his basic personal needs and is not receiving such
care as is necessary for his health or safety,"[53] which on its face should
include an inability to understand one's need for mental health treatment or an inability to obtain such treatment. What is needed is further
statutory reform that will give explicit recognition to incompetence as a
basis for commitment.

Courts and legislatures must recognize that the dangerousness criterion for civil commitment has serious problems. Empirical studies reveal
that psychiatrists and sociologists are notoriously inaccurate at predicting
dangerousness and in fact have a pronounced tendency to overpredict.[54]
The most effective predictive criteria yield a sixty to seventy percent false
positive rate—persons incorrectly predicted as dangerous.[55] Moreover,
psychiatrists rarely claim to be able to treat dangerousness.[56] The assertion that dangerousness results from mental illness and will be eliminated
by treatment is simply unsubstantiated. By making dangerousness the
principal substantive criterion, legislatures have chosen to base civil commitment on the very criterion that the mental health system is least able
to diagnose and treat.[57] At a minimum, courts and legislatures should
supplement the dangerousness standard by requiring a finding that the
person is likely to respond to available treatment. Otherwise, civil com-

mitment becomes merely a form of preventive detention.[58] Furthermore, if nontreatable, dangerous persons are to be civilly committed, the reliability of prediction should be increased by requiring the finding of a recent overt dangerous act,[59] and confinement should be for a limited fixed period under a rubric of crisis intervention.[60] Better yet, the criminal justice system should deal with nontreatable, dangerous persons by explicitly adopting a scheme of preventive detention.[61] Once courts and legislatures recognize the inherent problems of a civil commitment system based on dangerousness criteria, they can begin to develop further the standards for therapeutic commitment.

The elimination of the "need of treatment" standard standing alone may be necessary to avoid imposition of treatment when a person is competent to make treatment decisions.[62] There is a need, however, to create a statutory basis for providing treatment for those who are mentally ill and not capable of evaluating their own condition and making an appropriate treatment decision.[63] This *parens patriae* concern may be met by an additional or alternative standard other than "dangerousness." The commitment criteria should be enlarged to provide that those mentally ill persons who need treatment and who are incapable of exercising a rational choice between seeking treatment or continuing in their present situation can be involuntarily treated.[64] While it makes no sense to presume incompetence from the fact of mental illness alone,[65] it also does not make sense to presume that all mentally ill persons are competent to make a rational treatment decision.[66] Ensuring that its citizens have a minimal opportunity to assert their human autonomy and freedom in a rational fashion should be recognized as a compelling state interest justifying the use of the state's coercive power.[67]

A standard that would satisfy this treatment need might be formulated as follows: Commitment is permitted for a person who is mentally ill and in need of care or treatment in a mental hospital but because of illness lacks sufficient insight or capacity to make a rational decision concerning treatment.[68] This standard would require a mental health professional to ascertain an individual's competency to make a rational treatment choice.[69] Involuntary commitment would not be permitted under this standard unless the professional could demonstrate to the committing authority the specific manner in which a patient lacked relevant insight or capacity for rational choice.

Under the above standard, psychotic individuals who are out of touch with reality usually would qualify since they generally are not aware of their mental illness, usually are not aware of treatment alternatives available to them, and frequently are not able to provide for their basic needs or deal reasonably within the context of their daily lives.[70] Persons not subject to commitment under this standard would include those who are aware of their mental disorder and the effect their illness may have on their daily lives and also are aware of treatment alternatives, including the risks and benefits of those alternatives.[71] Because such persons have sufficient insight into their condition and into ways to change it if they so desire, their autonomy should be respected.

For commitment to be upheld under this standard, the state also should be required to demonstrate that appropriate and effective treatment is available and will be offered.[72] In fact the criteria for treatment under any standard should require the state to make a showing that effective treatment will be made available to any persons whom the state seeks to involuntarily commit.[73] Furthermore, under an incompetence standard, the treatment objective should be limited to restoring the individual's capacity for making rational treatment decisions.[74] This limitation would insure that the nature and duration of the commitment is consistent with the legitimate purposes of *parens patriae* commitment. Thus, commitment under such a standard would have as its objective not the complete restoration to full mental health of the patient but the restoration of the patient's capacity to engage in rational choice. Under this scheme, once competence is restored, a patient would be free to terminate hospitalization or, if he chooses, to continue treatment as a voluntary patient.

Parens patriae commitment on the basis of incompetence is an appropriate and limited state response to the factual reality of a person's condition and disability. Unlike the current standards for commitment, which limit commitment to those found to be dangerous, an incompetence standard is not a state response to a mere prediction of dangerous future conduct. Moreover, under an incompetence standard, psychiatric expertise is used in an appropriate manner by the legal system. Rather than predicting future conduct, the medical authority must determine the extent to which a mental disorder has affected a person's capacity for rational choice. This use of the medical authority is thus in accord with the essential expertise of psychiatrists, which consists of diagnosing and treating mental illness—not of predicting future dangerous behavior.[75] Courts have recognized the legitimacy of professional medical judgments within the procedural context;[76] legislatures similarly should recognize the proper scope of medical judgment in establishing substantive standards for commitment.

Least Restrictive Alternative versus Most Effective Treatment Alternative

One consequence of the adoption of a dangerousness standard for civil commitment has been the imposition of a dispositional requirement that the patient be provided with the least restrictive treatment alternative.[77]

This requirement represents a balancing of the liberty interests of the patient with the requirements of social protection.[78] This balancing reflects the fact that civil commitment under a dangerousness standard is an exercise of police power resulting in a form of preventive detention.[79] A standard for commitment that is based on a finding of lack of competence and need of treatment demands instead that a patient be provided the *most effective* treatment alternative rather than the *least restrictive* alternative. A dangerousness standard leads to concern that the mentally ill will not be unnecessarily deprived of liberty; it thus has little to do with the treatment concerns of the mentally ill. An incompetence standard focuses solely on the need for the treatment. In this sense, the move toward a dangerousness standard for commitment has entailed an abdication of responsibility for treatment and care of those who are incompetent. Adoption of an incompetence standard reflects the view that beneficial treatment, though involuntarily received, ultimately may increase personal welfare, freedom, and autonomy.

It should be pointed out that the least restrictive alternative concept was first developed in cases involving the curtailment of civil liberties. In the 1960 *Sheldon* v. *Tucker*[80] decision, the Supreme Court ruled that a state was constitutionally compelled to achieve its goal of combatting subversion by choosing the means that least interfered with individuals' basic civil rights.[81] The Court observed:

> [T]his Court has held that, even though the government's purpose be legitimate and substantial, that purpose cannot be pursued by means that broadly stifle fundamental personal liberties when the end can be more narrowly achieved. The breadth of legislative abridgement must be viewed in the light of less drastic means for achieving the same purpose.[82]

This concept of the least restrictive alternative was first applied in the mental health area by the United States Court of Appeals for the District of Columbia in 1966 in *Lake* v. *Cameron*.[83] The court held:

> [T]he court may order . . . hospitalization for an indeterminate period, or order any other alternative course of treatment which the court believes will be in the best interests of the person or the public. . . . Deprivations of liberty solely because of dangers to the ill persons themselves should not go beyond what is necessary for their protection.[84]

It is clear from this opinion that the least restrictive alternative is required because of the application of a dangerousness standard for commitment. The least restrictive alternative is applied because of the need to balance the liberty interest of the patient against the danger posed by his behavior.

Lake v. *Cameron* ultimately suggests that the standard of the least restrictive alternative favors community placement over involuntary hospitalization.[85] Observers, however, have suggested that some patients experience more freedom in the setting of a mental hospital than in available community placements.[86] More significantly, some mental health professionals have maintained that the goal of placement should not be the least restrictive alternative but the most optimal setting for the patient.[87]

The adoption of the least restrictive alternative reflects a view that equates the degree of governmental involvement with the degree of restriction. This approach makes sense only as long as intervention is permitted to further the governmental interests of providing protection from dangerous behavior at the cost of individual liberty. If, however, the intervention is aimed at developing mental competence by providing needed treatment, the standard for appropriate dispositional alternatives changes. Instead of the least restrictive alternative, the committing authority should aim at identifying the most effective treatment alternative. Under such a standard, the judgment of medical authorities should determine the most efficacious treatment modality that will satisfy the treatment needs of the patient. Legal support for this view can be found in the Supreme Court's *Youngberg* v. *Romeo*[88] opinion in which the Court observed that "[i]t is not appropriate for courts to specify which of several professionally acceptable choices should have been made."[89] Rather, the proper dispositional alternative should be one that adopts the most effective treatment alternative as determined by medical authorities based on a professional diagnosis and a professional determination of the efficacy and availability of a particular treatment plan.

Conclusion

The Supreme Court in its more recent procedural decisions has revived the *parens patriae* doctrine as a justification for involuntary civil commitment. This development is clear from a reading of *Addington* v. *Texas*,[90] *Parham* v. *J.R.*,[91] and *Youngberg* v. *Romeo*.[92] While the Court has recognized a range of procedural requirements that protect the civil liberty interests of persons subject to civil commitment, it has at the same time increasingly given recognition to treatment and clinical rights of persons involuntarily committed to mental health facilities. On the other hand, many legislatures and courts have focused only on the civil liberty interests of persons subject to involuntary civil commitment. These courts and legislatures thus have limited commitment to cases of mentally ill and dangerous persons and have required a disposition that is the least restrictive alternative. There is, however, a need to provide commitment criteria that will permit the state to meet the treatment needs of the mentally ill who are not capable of making rational decisions about their treatment needs. By adopting a standard that requires a finding of lack of competence, the state is best able to satisfy the needs of citizens afflicted with serious mental illness and who are otherwise condemned to a life of suffering. Statutory revision, therefore, should focus on satisfying the needs of the mentally ill because their needs cannot and are not being met under statutes that limit commitment under a dangerousness standard and require the least restrictive dispositional alternative. To meet these needs, commitment statutes should be revised to require proof of incompetence, a showing of susceptibility to and availability of treatment, and provision of the most effective treatment.

Notes

1. *See* Hermann, *Mental Patient Release Program Leaves Many to Face Harsh Fate*, N.Y. Times, Nov. 18, 1979, at 1, col. 5. This column describes the human misery of a New York City men's shelter:

> The fetid odor of unclean bodies and the gray-blue haze of cigarette smoke hang like smog about the destitute clientele of the Men's Shelter on the Bowery in Manhattan.
>
> Nearly 1,300 men visit the shelter each day. By and large, they come from New York State's psychiatric hospitals, which have released 83,659 adult patients "to the community" over the last four years—nearly 40,000 of them to New York City.
>
> On the first floor, ragged men with vacant eyes sit in the "Big Room' on plastic chairs attached in rows. As many as 250 men will sit all night if there are no beds available in the nearby flophouses.
>
> Some men will wash themselves in the second floor shower, but many refuse. Others must be deloused or they cannot stay.
>
> . . . The people in the Men's Shelter, the "shopping-bag ladies" at Pennsylvania Station, the disheveled characters outside the single-room-occupancy hotels on the west side—all have no contact with community mental-health centers or hospital outpatient clinics. If they were told about them, they do not know or have forgotten how to get there. Many do not realize they will need care or are unwilling to go.

2. *See* C. WARREN, THE COURT OF LAST RESORT: MENTAL ILLNESS AND THE LAW 21–24 (1982). Warren maintains that the primary factor motivating political and legal authorities to adopt a policy of deinstitutionalization was fiscal. In Warren's view, the adoption of statutes such as that in California, which mandates the least restrictive alternative treatment, was motivated in large part by a desire to reduce the funding for mental health treatment. While the reformers urged the adoption of the least restrictive form of confinement consistent with patient needs on therapeutic and civil libertarian grounds, the legislature largely was moved by fiscal considerations. The state could thus replace costly hospitalization with less expensive alternatives such as nursing homes, day care centers, and community health clinics.

3. *See* Peele, *The Legal System and the Homeless,* in TASK FORCE REPORT OF THE AMERICAN PSYCHIATRIC ASSOCIATION: THE HOMELESS MENTALLY ILL 261 (H. Lamb ed. 1984) [hereinafter cited as Peele]. The author observes:

> Over the past two decades many legislative and judicial actions have directly and adversely affected the homeless mentally ill. . . . [These include] current trends and philosophy in relation to advocacy, the principles of least restrictive alternative, malpractice and civil liability, commitment laws, the right to treatment, and the right to refuse treatment; we believe that many of these trends have contributed to homelessness.

Id.

4. *See* Arce, Tadlock, Vergare & Shapiro, *A Psychiatric Profile of Street People Admitted to an Emergency Shelter,* 34 HOSP. & COMMUNITY PSYCHIATRY 812, 812–17 (1983); Lipton, Sabatini & Katz, *Down and Out in the City: The Homeless Mentally Ill,* 34 HOSP. & COMMUNITY PSYCHIATRY 817, 817–18 (1983). These studies of the homeless in New York and Philadelphia both conclude that the vast majority of the homeless studied were mentally ill and had a history of psychiatric hospitalization. In Philadelphia, of the 193 persons studied, 84% were mentally ill, including 37% who were schizophrenic and 25% who were alcoholics or drug addicts. In New York, of 100 persons studied, almost all were mentally ill, with 72% diagnosed as schizophrenic.

5. *See generally* Hermann, Book Review, 31 BUFFALO L. REV. 611, 611–14 (1983) (reviewing C. WARREN, THE COURT OF LAST RESORT: MENTAL ILLNESS AND THE LAW [1982]).

6. *See* R. Reisner, LAW AND THE MENTAL HEATH SYSTEM 319–20 (1985) (discussing the difference between a state's police power and its *parens patriae* power). Together, the police power and the *parens patriae* power provide the legal foundation for state laws regarding civil commitment of the mentally disabled. When the state seeks to hospitalize a mentally disabled individual because he or she is dangerous *to others,* it is acting under its police power. When the state seeks to hospitalize a mentally disabled individual because he or she is dangerous to himself or herself, it is acting under its *parens patriae* power.

7. *See* S. HERR, S. ARONS & R. WALLACE, LEGAL RIGHTS AND MENTAL-HEALTH CARE 3 (1983). The authors observe:

> Until recently, action to secure the enforceable legal rights of consumers of mental-health care was almost nonexistent. . . . In the wake of the civil-rights movement of the 1960s and the growth of public legal services in the 1970s, these patterns began to change.
>
> . . . Legislative reforms and court decisions accelerated the release of patients from large mental institutions, tightened procedures for admission or commitment, and enunciated patients' rights by setting minimum standards of care and other remedies.

Id. (footnote omitted); *see also* PRESIDENT'S COMM'N ON MENTAL HEALTH, REPORT TO THE PRESIDENT 3–4 (1978).

8. *See, e.g.,* Lessard v. Schmidt, 349 F. Supp. 1078 (E.D. Wis. 1972). *vacated and remanded,* 414 U.S. 473 (1974), *redecided,* 379 F. Supp. 1376 (E.D. Wis. 1974), *vacated and remanded on other grounds,* 421 U.S. 957 (1975), *redecided,* 413 F. Supp. 1318 (E.D. Wis. 1976) (minimal due process

requirements should be met in cases of involuntary commitment, including notice and opportunity to be heard, application of specified standards for commitment, provision of counsel and application of rules of evidence).

9. *See, e.g.,* IDAHO CODE § 66–329(i) (1980) (restricting criteria for extended confinement of the mentally ill in terms of both evidentiary weight and substantive criteria: "If, upon completion of the hearing and consideration of the record, the court finds beyond a reasonable doubt that the proposed patient (1) is mentally ill or mentally retarded, and (2) is, because of his ailment, likely to injure himself or others, it shall order his commitment. . . ."). *But see* N.Y. MENTAL HYG. LAW § 9.01 (McKinney 1978 & Supp. 1985) (providing in part; " 'in need of involuntary care and treatment' means that a person has a mental illness for which care and treatment as a patient in a hospital is essential to such person's welfare and whose judgment is so impaired that he is unable to understand the need for such care and treatment"); *id.* § 9.31 (providing involuntary hospitalization of persons in need of care and treatment without specifying an evidentiary standard to be applied in making such a determination); *cf. In re* Rochman, 104 Misc. 2d 218, 428 N.Y.S.2d 168 (N.Y. Sup. Ct. 1980) (holding that when psychiatric patient applied for a hearing to determine the need for involuntary care and treatment, he did not have the burden of proving by a fair preponderance of evidence that he could be released safely; rather, the state had the burden of establishing by 'clear and convincing proof' that the patient was mentally ill and needed treatment). *But cf. In re* Hurley, 104 Misc. 2d 582, 428 N.Y.S.2d 604 (N.Y. Sup. Ct. 1980) (patient who, after a period of confinement, filed petition for a hearing to determine the need for involuntary care and treatment had the burden of proving by a fair preponderance of the evidence that he could be released safely).

10. *See, e.g.,* Lake v. Cameron, 364 F.2d 657, 661 (D.C. Cir. 1966) (construing the District of Columbia mental health care law to require that the least drastic method of treatment be provided); *see also* ILL. ANN. STAT. ch. 91½, § 3–81 (Smith-Hurd Supp. 1985) (providing in part: "The court shall order the least restrictive alternative for treatment which is appropriate.").

11. *See, e.g.,* ILL. ANN. STAT. ch. 91½, § 3–206 (Smith-Hurd Supp. 1985); *see also* Doremus v. Farrell, 407 F. Supp. 509, 515 (D. Neb. 1975) (discussing the requirements of notice under Nebraska law).

12. *See, e.g.,* ILL. ANN. STAT. ch. 91½, § 3–205 (Smith-Hurd Supp. 1985); *see also* Stamus v. Leonardt, 414 F. Supp. 439, 447 (S.D. Iowa 1976) (holding that the restriction on the plaintiff's right to be present during her civil commitment hearing was an unconstitutional deprivation of her due process rights).

13. *See, e.g.,* ILL. ANN. STAT. ch. 91½, §§ 3–205, 3–805 (Smith-Hurd Supp. 1980); *see also* Lynch v. Baxley, 386 F. Supp. 378, 389 (M.D. Ala. 1974) (noting that the subject of an involuntary civil commitment proceeding has a right to have counsel present during all significant stages of the commitment process), *rev'd on other grounds,* 651 F.2d 387 (5th Cir. 1981).

14. *See, e.g.,* ILL. ANN. STAT. ch. 91½, § 3–816 (Smith-Hurd Supp. 1985).

15. Supreme Court decisions have established a series of due process rights that fall short of those provided to criminal suspects but that nonetheless are directed at guaranteeing the trustworthiness of the determinations needed to

make a civil commitment decision. At the same time the Court has evidenced a concern with providing civilly committed persons with needed treatment; although here too the Court has taken care to avoid judicial control of clinical judgments and setting treatment standards that are not feasible given institutional and financial constraints. *See* generally Monahan, Three Lingering Issues in Patient Rights, in PSYCHIATRIC PATIENT RIGHTS AND PATIENT ADVOCACY: ISSUES AND EVIDENCE 264–65 (B. Bloom & S. Asher eds. 1982) (examining the differences both in nature and success in advocacy of procedural and treatment rights).

16. *See, e.g.,* Lessard v. Schmidt, 349 F. Supp. 1078 (E.D. Wis. 1972), *vacated and remanded,* 414 U.S. 473 (1974), *redecided,* 379 F. Supp. 1376 (E.D. Wis. 1974), *vacated and remanded on other grounds,* 421 U.S. 957 (1975), *redecided,* 413 F. Supp. 1318 (E.D. Wis. 1976) (holding that minimal due process requirements must be met in cases of involuntary hospitalization).

17. *See, e.g.,* O'Connor v. Donaldson, 422 U.S. 563 (1975) (holding that custodial confinement without treatment was constitutionally deficient for non-dangerous individuals capable of living in freedom by themselves or with the help of family and friends).

18. Addington v. Texas, 441 U.S. 418 (1979) (holding that in cases of involuntary civil commitment, the standard of proof required by the fourteenth amendment is clear and convincing evidence that the person is mentally ill).

19. *See, e.g.,* Youngberg v. Romeo, 457 U.S. 307 (1982) (holding that mentally retarded residents of state institutions have constitutional rights to the basic necessities of life, reasonably safe living conditions, freedom from undue restraints, and the minimally adequate training needed to enhance or further their abilities to exercise other constitutional rights).

20. *See* Parham v. J.R., 442 U.S. 584 (1979) (holding that parents have plenary authority, subject to independent medical judgment, to commit their children to a state mental hospital without a formal precommitment hearing).

21. *See* Youngberg v. Romeo, 457 U.S. 307 (1982) (holding that decisions made by mental health professionals are presumptively valid).

22. *See, e.g.,* ALA. CODE § 22–52–10(a)(1) (1984) (requiring a finding "that the person sought to be committed is mentally ill").

23. *See, e.g.,* N.M. STAT. ANN. § 43–1–11(c) (1984) (providing for involuntary commitment upon a finding by clear and convincing evidence that "(1) as a result of mental disorder, the client presents a likelihood of serious harm to himself or others; (2) the client needs and is likely to benefit from the proposed treatment; and (3) the proposed commitment is consistent with the treatment needs of the client and with the least drastic means principle").

24. CAL. WELF. & INST. CODE § 5–300(b) (West 1984).

25. *See, e.g.,* ALA. CODE § 22–52–10(3) (1984) (requiring "that the threat of substantial harm has been evidenced by a recent overt act"); *see also* ARIZ. REV. STAT. ANN. § 36–501(3)(Supp. 1984) (providing that danger to others must be "based upon a history of either: (a) [h]aving seriously threatened, in the recent past by verbal or nonverbal acts or both, to engage in behavior which will likely result in serious physical harm to another person, . . . [or] (b) [h]aving inflicted or having attempted to inflict serious physical harm upon another person within one hundred eighty days preceding the fixing of the petition").

26. *See, e.g.,* CONN. GEN. STAT. ANN. § 17–178(c) (West Supp. 1985) (providing in part: "If, on such hearing, the court finds by clear and convincing evidence that the person complained of is mentally ill and dangerous to himself or herself or others or *gravely disabled,* it shall make an order for his or her commitment, considering whether or not a less restrictive placement is available, to a hospital for mental illness to be claimed in such order, there to be confined for the period of the duration of such mental illness or until he or she is discharged in due course of law") (emphasis added).

27. *See, e.g.,* VT. STAT. ANN. tit. 18, § 7101(17)(B)(ii) (Supp. 1985) (providing that a person may be shown to pose a danger to himself by establishing that "he has behaved in such a manner as to indicate that he is unable, without supervision and the assistance of others, to satisfy his need for nourishment, personal or medical care, shelter, or self-protection and safety, so that it is probable that death, substantial physical bodily injury, serious mental deterioration or serious physical debilitation or disease will ensue unless adequate treatment is afforded").

28. FLA. STAT. ANN. § 394.467(l)(b)(1)(b)(1) (Supp. 1985).

29. ILL. ANN. STAT. ch. 9½, § 1–119(2) (Smith-Hurd Supp. 1985).

30. N.J. STAT. ANN. §§ 30:4–44, 30:4–45 (West 1977) (providing that the court shall determine whether the respondent is suffering from mental illness). The Code provides: " 'Mental illness' shall mean mental disease to such an extent that a person so afflicted requires care and treatment for his own welfare, or the welfare of others, or of the community." *Id.* § 30:4–23.

31. N.Y. MENTAL HYG. LAW § 9.32 (McKinney 1978 & Supp. 1985) (providing for a "hearing on the question of need for involuntary care and treatment"). The Code provides: " 'in need of care and treatment' means that a person has a mental illness for which inpatient care and treatment in a hospital is appropriate." *Id.* § 9.01.

32. *See* generally Peele, *supra* note 3, at 285. The report states:

> Because of renewed concern about the civil rights of the mentally ill, the pendulum swung again in the early 1960s to more extensive procedures and narrow admission criteria. Standards emphasizing that for commitment a patient must be dangerous as well as mentally ill, limitations on the loss of rights of patient, mandatory times of judicial review, and an increase in procedural safeguards became prominent in the standards legislated in the 1960s and 1970s. While some states still consider the need for psychiatric treatment an adequate criterion for involuntary treatment, by and large state legislation requires that the individual be not only mentally ill but also likely to harm others, likely to harm himself, or likely to be harmed if not hospitalized.

Id.

33. *See, e.g.,* Livermore, Malmquist & Meehl, *On the Justifications for Civil Commitment,* 117 U. PA. L. REV. 75 (1968); see also Ennis, *Civil Liberties and Mental Illness,* 7 CRIM. L. BULL. 101 (1971).

34. *See, e.g.,* Dix, *Acute Psychiatric Hospitalization of the Mentally Ill in the Metropolis: An Empirical Study,* 1968 WASH. U.L.Q. 485, 503–21 (1968); *see also* Wexler & Scoville, *The Administration of Psychiatric Justice: Theory and Practice in Arizona,* 13 ARIZ. L. REV. 1 (1971).

35. *See supra* notes 47–49 and accompanying text.

36. States limiting involuntary commitment to those mentally ill persons who are dangerous to themselves or others include: ALA. CODE § 22–52–37 (a)(7) (1984) (adopted in 1975); D.C. CODE ANN. § 21–545(b) (1981) (adopted in 1965); HAWAII REV. STAT. § 334–602 (Supp. 1984) (adopted in 1984); KY. REV. STAT. ANN. § 202A.026 (Baldwin 1982) (adopted in 1982); ME. REV. STAT. ANN. § 34–B, § 3864(5)(E) (Supp. 1985) (adopted in 1983); MD. HEALTH-GENERAL CODE ANN. § 10–617(a)(Supp. 1985) (adopted in 1982); N.H. REV. STAT. ANN. § 135–B:26 (1977) (adopted in 1973); N.M. STAT. ANN. § 43–1–11(c) (1984) (adopted in 1977); N.C. GEN. STAT. § 122–58.7(i) (Supp. 1983) (adopted in 1973); PA. CONS. STAT. § 4405 (1969 & Supp. 1985) (adopted in 1966); TENN. CODE ANN. §§ 33–6–103, –104 (Supp. 1985) (adopted in 1965); W. VA. CODE § 27–5–4(d) (Supp. 1985) (adopted in 1955).

37. *See* Dershowitz, *Psychiatry in the Legal Process: A Knife That Cuts Both Ways,* in THE PATH OF THE LAW FROM 1967, 82–83 (A. Sutherland ed. 1968). The author urges the adoption of a legal rather than a medical model for development of the civil commitment law; Professor Dershowitz argues that "no legal rule should ever be phrased in medical terms; that no legal decision should ever be turned over to the psychiatrist; that there is no such thing as a legal problem which cannot—and should not—be phrased in terms familiar to lawyers. And civil commitment of the mentally ill is a legal problem; whenever compulsion is used or freedom denied—whether by the state, the church, the union, the university, or the psychiatrist—the issue becomes a legal one; and lawyers must be quick to immerse themselves in it." *Id. But see* Stone, *Comment,* 132 AM. J. PSYCHIATRY 829–31 (1975) (maintaining that the purpose of civil commitment is not for legal control but for treatment; for example, hospitalization in the case of suicidal or homicidal behavior is not for the purpose of preventing that behavior but for the purpose of treating the underlying disorder).

38. *See* Chodoff, *The Case for Involuntary Hospitalization of the Mentally Ill,* 133 AM. J. PSYCHIATRY 496, 498 (1976). The author argues: "Despite the revisionist efforts of the anti-psychiatrist, mental illness *does* exist. . . . [I]t does encompass those few desperately sick people for whom involuntary commitment must be considered." *Id.* (emphasis added). According to Chodoff, the criteria for involuntary treatment should include: (1) the presence of a mental illness, (2) a serious disruption of functioning together with an impairment of judgment of such a degree that the individual is incapable of considering his condition and making decisions about it in his own interest, and (3) the need for case and treatment. *Id.* at 498–99; see *also* Stone, *supra* note 61, at 830. Stone maintains that psychiatry involves the identification of the presence of clinical states and of the appropriate interventions or treatment to remedy those conditions.

39. *See* Klein, *Legal Doctrine at the Crossroads, Mental Health Law Project Summary of Activities* 7, 8 (Mar. 1976). The author provides examples of the type of nondangerous persons who need treatment but who are not likely to be voluntary patients:

For example, some depressed people believe they are unworthy of help. There are also paranoids who reject treatment on such grounds as that the psychiatrist

> "is a CIA agent who will plant a tape recorder in my head." And, perhaps most significantly, there are numerous extremely passive people, including many elderly, who simply will not seek treatment on their own. If they are not treated involuntarily and here I think the concept of "involuntariness" is largely metaphysical—we know by recent experience that many of them will wander aimlessly through our blighted inner cities, subject to a host of dangers.

Id.; *see also* Peele, *supra* note 3, at 270–71 (noting that the legal system needs to reconsider the commitment law reforms of the last two decades, which have contributed to the plight of the homeless mentally ill and have made it too easy for those who need help to refuse treatment).

It should be noted that the Supreme Court in O'Connor v. Donaldson explicitly declined to address the question "whether the [s]tate may compulsorily confine a nondangerous, mentally ill individual for the purpose of treatment" 422 U.S. 563, 573 (1975). So at present, there is no constitutional barrier to involuntarily committing the nondangerous mentally ill.

40. *See, e.g.*, Jones v. United States, 463 U.S. 354, 368 (1983) ("The purpose . . . of civil commitment, is to treat the individual's mental illness and protect him and society from his potential dangerousness.").

41. *See, e.g.*, Rogers v. Okin, 634 F.2d 650, 654 (1st Cir. 1980), *vacated and remanded sub nom.* Mills v. Rogers, 457 U.S. 291 (1982) (noting that under its police power, "the state has a legitimate interest in protecting persons from physical harm at the hands of the mentally ill").

42. *Id.* at 657 (observing that "[t]here is no doubt that '[t]he state has a legitimate interest under its *parens patriae* powers in providing care to its citizens who are unable to care for themselves' ") (quoting Addington v. Texas, 441 U.S. 418, 426 [1979]).

43. *See, e.g.*, State *ex rel.* Hawks v. Lazaro, 202 S.E.2d 109, 123 (W. Va. 1974) (stating that "[s]ociety is entitled to protect itself against predatory acts on the part of the anti-social people, regardless of the cause of their anti-social actions. Therefore, if the state can prove that an individual is likely to injure others if left at liberty, it may hospitalize him. The state is also entitled to prevent a person from injuring himself in the very specific sense of doing physical damage to himself, either actively or passively.").

44. *See, e.g.*, Lessard v. Schmidt, 349 F. Supp. 1078, 1093–94 (E.D. Wis.), *vacated*, 414 U.S. 473 (1974) (holding that a finding of dangerousness was required for a constitutionally valid civil commitment).

45. *See, e.g.*, Ennis & Litwack, *Psychiatry and the Presumption of Expertise: Flipping Coins in the Courtroom*, 62 CALIF. L REV. 693, 707 (1974) (concluding that the empirical data revealed that psychiatrists could not reliably make judgments about the need for hospitalization and treatment, and the effects of hospitalization and treatment).

46. *See, e.g.*, Livermore, Malmquist & Meehl, *On the Justification for Civil Commitment*, 117 U. PA. L. REV. 75, 80 (1968) (concluding that the definition of "mental illness" was dependent on the norms of adjustment applied by the mental health professional, effectively masked the actual norms being applied and was thus expandable to include anyone the case worker chose to so classify.)

47. *See, e.g.,* Greenberg, *Involuntary Psychiatric Commitments to Prevent Suicide,* 49 N.Y.U. L. REV. 227, 256 (1974) (reporting that few controlled studies of the effectiveness of treatment measures had been reported and concluding that these results had been either inconsistent or negative).

48. *See, e.g.,* T. SZASZ, LAW LIBERTY AND PSYCHIATRY 40–41 (1963) (arguing against compulsory hospitalization of mentally ill persons because of the extensive deprivations of civil rights that commitment entails).

49. 407 F. Supp. 509 (D. Neb. 1975).

50. *Id.* at 514–15.

51. *See* Treffert, *Dying with Their Rights* On, 130 AM. J. PSYCHIATRY 1041, 1041 (1973) (reporting that under a law that provided commitment only upon a showing of " 'extreme *likelihood* that if the person is not confined he will do *immediate* harm to himself or others' . . . a 49-year-old anorexic woman starved herself to death; a 70-year-old man died a self-perpetuating, metabolic, toxic death; and a 19-year-old student, while unable to qualify for commitment under the new guidelines, was able to hang herself. Each of these patients needed commitment; none qualified. Each outcome was entirely predictable. Each of these patients went to his or her grave with his rights entirely intact.") (emphasis in original).

52. *See, e.g.,* TEX. REV. CIV. STAT. ANN. art. 5547–50(b) (Vernon Supp. 1984–85). The statute provides:

> Upon the hearing, the judge or the jury, if one has been requested, shall determine that the person requires court-ordered mental health services only if it finds, on a basis of clear and convincing evidence, that: (1) the person is mentally ill; and (2) a a result of that mental illness the person: (i) is likely to cause serious harm to himself; or (ii) is likely to cause serious harm to others; or (iii) will, if not treated, continue to suffer severe and abnormal mental emotional, or physical distress and will continue to experience deterioration of his ability to function independently *and is unable to make a rational and informed decision as to whether or not to submit to treatment.*

Id. (emphasis added); *see also* Colyar v. Third Judicial Dist. Ct., 469 F. Supp. 424 (D. Utah 1979). The *Colyar* court held:

> Given that in order to be involuntarily committed a mentally ill person must be shown to be a danger to himself or others, and that such danger may include the incapacity to provide the basic necessities of life, the court feels constrained to hold that the state must also show that the individual is incapable of making a rational choice regarding the acceptance of care or treatment.
>
> . . . [T]he involuntary commitment of the mentally ill under the *parens patriae* power must reflect the following considerations: The committing authority must find, as a threshold requirement, that the proposed patient is incapable of making a rational treatment decision. The purpose of this requirement is to require the committing court to "distinguish between those persons whose decisions to refuse treatment must be accepted as final from those whose choices may be validly overridden through *parens patriae* commitment."

Id. at 431, 434 (quoting *Developments in the Law—Civil Commitment of the Mentally Ill,* 87 HARV. L REV. 1190, 1216 [1974]).

53. OR. REV. STAT. § 426.005(2) (1983).

54. *See* Cocozza & Steadman, *The Failure of Psychiatric Predictions of Dangerousness: Clear and Convincing Evidence,* 29 RUTGERS L REV. 1084, 1085 (1976).

55. *See* Ennis & Litwack, *supra* note 45, at 714.

56. *See* B. ENNIS & R. EMORY, THE RIGHTS OF MENTAL PATIENTS 46–47 (1978) (reporting that no method of treatment, including behavioral conditioning, has been shown to be successful in reducing dangerous behavior in mentally ill persons).

57. *See* A. STONE, MENTAL HEALTH AND LAW: A SYSTEM IN TRANSITION 36–37 (1975) (suggesting that there is little evidence that mental disorders and the dangerous behaviors that supposedly ensue from them are particularly ameliorable through mental health treatments).

58. *See, e.g.,* People v. Sansone, 18 Ill. App. 3d 315, 323–24, 309 N.E.2d 733, 739, *leave to appeal denied,* 56 Ill. 2d 584 (1974) (holding that a person committed as mentally ill and dangerous to self or others was entitled to treatment to alleviate his condition). *See generally* Dershowitz, *Preventive Confinement.* 51 TEX. L. REV. 1277 (1973).

59. *See generally* Comment, *Overt Dangerous Behavior as a Constitutional Requirement for Involuntary Civil Commitment of the Mentally Ill,* 44 U. CHI. L REV. 562 (1977). Various state statutes now include provisions requiring an overt act to establish dangerousness. *See* ALA. CODE § 22–52–10(a)(3) (1984) (providing "that the threat of substantial harm has been evidenced by a recent overt act"); *see also* MICH. COMP. LAWS ANN. § 330.1401(a) (West 1980) (providing for commitment of "[a] person who is mentally ill, and as a result of that mental illness can reasonably be expected within the near future to intentionally or unintentionally seriously physically injure himself or another person, and who has engaged in an act or made significant threats that are substantially supportive of the expectation").

60. *See generally* Peszke, *Is Dangerousness an Issue for Physicians in Emergency Commitment?* 132 AM. J. PSYCHIATRY 825 (1975).

61. *See* Note, *Mental Illness: A Suspect Classification?* 83 YALE L.J. 1237, 1261–62 (1974) (suggesting that the dangerous mentally ill are no more dangerous than the dangerous nonmentally ill, so that the grounds for involuntary institutionalization creates a grossly underinclusive class). *See generally* Morse, *A Preference for Liberty: The Case Against Involuntary Commitment of the Mentally Disordered,* 70 CALIF. L. Rev. 54, 67 (1982) (arguing for the abolition of involuntary civil commitment but acknowledging the need to confine those people who have demonstrated dangerous behavior).

62. *See* Commonwealth *ex rel.* Finken v. Roop, 234 Pa. Super. 155, 339 A.2d 764 (1975), *cert. denied,* 424 U.S. 960 (1976) (holding that an involuntary commitment requirement that a person be "in need of care at a [mental health] facility" was overbroad and vague); *see also* Colyar v. Third Judicial Dist. Ct., 469 F. Supp. 424 (D. Utah 1979) (invalidating as unconstitutionally vague a statute that authorized civil commitment of a mentally ill individual in need of custodial care and treatment in a mental health facility and lacking insight to make responsible decisions about his need for care and treatment; the statute failed to require the committing authority to determine whether the person's refusal was rational).

63. Recent studies establish that a large percentage of current mental patients lack capacity to make informed decisions concerning treatment. *See* Appelbaum, Murkin & Bateman, *Empirical Assessment of Competency to Consent to Psychiatric Hospitalization,* 138 AM. J. PSYCHIATRY 1170 (1981); Olin & Olin, *Informed Consent in Voluntary Hospital Admissions,* 132 AM. J. PSYCHIATRY 938 (1975); Pryce, *Clinical Research upon Mentally Ill Subjects Who Cannot Give Informed Consent,* 133 BRIT. J. PSYCHIATRY 366 (1978).

64. *See* Stromberg & Stone, *A Model State Law on Civil Commitment of the Mentally Ill,* 20 HARV. J. ON LEGIS. 275, 302 (1983) (reporting that individuals afflicted with severe mental disorders may be unable to pay attention or assimilate information, or disorganized thoughts may preclude them from engaging in anything resembling a rational thinking process).

65. *See* Winters v. Miller, 446 F.2d 65 (2d Cir.), *cert. denied,* 404 U.S. 985 (1971). The court observed that:

> [T]he law is quite clear in New York that a finding of "mental illness" even by a judge or jury, and commitment to a hospital, does not raise even a presumption that the patient is "incompetent" or unable adequately to manage his own affairs. Absent a specific finding of incompetence, the mental patient retains the right to sue or defend in his own name, to sell or dispose of his property, to marry, draft a will, and, in general to manage his own affairs.

Id. at 68.

66. *See* Colyar v. Third Judicial Dist. Ct., 469 F. Supp. 424, 431 (D. Utah 1979) (holding that a finding of mental illness did not create a presumption of lack of capacity to make rational decisions, but noting that the committing authority could find in an appropriate case that a mentally ill patient was incapable of making a rational treatment decision).

67. *See* Jacobson v. Massachusetts, 197 U.S. 11, 20 (1905) (recognizing the authority of the state in its sovereign capacity to enact laws that protect the public's health, safety, morals, and welfare); *see also* Hawaii v. Standard Oil Co., 405 U.S. 251, 257 (1972) (observing that *parens patriae* power was predicated upon the state acting in a protective role to assure the health, welfare, and well-being of individual citizens who could not care for themselves).

68. State statutes currently containing provisions that could be fairly construed to provide for commitment of the mentally disabled who are unable to make rational treatment decisions include: COLO. REV. STAT. §§ 27–10–102, –106 (1982) (providing for commitment of the "gravely disabled," which "means a condition in which a person, as a result of mental illness, is unable to take care of his basic personal needs or is making irrational or grossly irresponsible decisions concerning his person and lacks the capacity to understand this is so"); CONN. GEN. STAT. ANN. §§ 17–176, –177 (West Supp. 1985) (providing in part that " 'gravely disabled' means that a person, as a result of mental or emotional impairment, is in danger of serious harm as a result of an inability or failure to provide for his or her own basic human needs such as essential food, clothing, shelter or safety and that hospital treatment is necessary and available and that such person is mentally incapable of determining whether or not to accept such treatment because his judgment is impaired by his mental illness");

DEL. CODE ANN. tit. 16, §§ 5001, 5010 (1983) (providing in part: " 'Mentally ill person' means a person suffering from a mental disorder or condition which requires such person to be observed and treated at a mental hospital for his own welfare and which . . . renders such person unable to make responsible decisions with respect to his hospitalization"); FLA. STAT. ANN. § 394.467 (West Supp. 1985) (providing for involuntary commitment of person found mentally ill and unable to determine for himself whether treatment is necessary and who without treatment is unable to care for himself; MO. ANN. STAT. §§ 632.005–.335 (Vernon Supp. 1985) (providing for commitment of person who, as a result of mental illness, present likelihood of serious physical harm, which is defined as "a substantial risk that serious physical harm to a person will result because of impairment in his capacity . . . and need for treatment as evidenced by his inability to provide for his own basic necessities of food, clothing, shelter, safety or medical care"); S.C. CODE ANN. § 44–17–580 (LAW. Co-op. 1984) (providing for commitment of a mentally ill person who "lacks sufficient insight or capacity to make responsible decisions with respect to his treatment"); S.D. CODIFIED LAWS §§ 27A–1–1, –9–18 (1984) (providing for commitment of persons mentally ill and in need of treatment and defining "mentally ill" to include persons who lack sufficient understanding or capacity to make responsible decisions concerning his person so as to interfere grossly with his capacity to meet the ordinary demands of life"); UTAH CODE ANN. § 64–7–36(10)(c) (Supp. 1985) (providing for hospitalization of mentally ill person when "[t]he patient lacks the ability to engage in a rational decision-making process regarding the acceptance of mental treatment as demonstrated by evidence of inability to weigh the possible costs and benefits of treatment").

69. See Stomberg & Stone, supra note 64, at 299–300 (suggesting that the treatment team conscientiously try to explain to a patient the nature and effects of proposed hospitalization or treatment before attempting to make a specific assessment of a patient's capacity for making a treatment decision).

70. See, e.g., AMERICAN PSYCHIATRIC ASS'N. TASK FORCE ON NOMENCLATURE AND STATISTICS, DIAGNOSTIC AND STATISTICAL MANUAL OF MENTAL DISORDERS 367–68 (3d ed. 1980) (describing "psychotic" behavior as inaccurately drawing inferences concerning external reality despite evidence to the contrary).

71. See, e.g., Rogers v. Commissioner, 390 Mass. 489, ___, 458 N.E. 2d 308, 313 (1983) ("'[A] finding [of incompetence], apart from evidence as to mental illness, should consist of facts showing a proposed ward's inability to think or act for himself as to matters concerning his personal health, safety, and general welfare.' " [quoting Fazio v. Fazio, 375 Mass. 394, 403, 378 N.E.2d 951, 957 (1978)]).

72. See, e.g., UTAH CODE ANN. § 64–7–36(10)(e) (Supp. 1983) (providing the following requirement for hospitalization of a patient lacking rational decisionmaking ability. "The hospital or mental health facility in which the individual is to be hospitalized pursuant to this act can provide the individual with treatment that is adequate and appropriate to the individual's conditions and needs. In the absence of required findings of the court after the hearing, the court shall forthwith dismiss the proceedings.").

73. See Wyatt v. Stickney, 325 F. Supp. 781, 784, reh'g granted, 334 F.

Supp. 1341, 1342 (M.D. Ala. 1971), *redecided.* 344 F. Supp. 373 (M.D. Ala. 1972), *redecided,* 344 F. Supp. 387 (M.D. Ala. 1972), *aff'd in part and remanded in part sub nom.* Wyatt v. Aderholt, 503 F.2d 1305, 1312 (5th Cir. 1974) (reasoning that absent the opportunity to receive treatment, mentally disabled persons in an institution were not patients but mere residents with indefinite sentences; treatment and not custodial care was found to be the purpose of involuntary commitment).

74. The standard for release in civil commitment logically should be the same as the standard for initial commitment of the mentally ill. *See* Note, *Due Process for All-Constitutional Standards for Involuntary Civil Commitment and Release,* 34 U. CHI. L. REV. 633, 658 (1967); Comment, *The New Mental Health Codes: Safeguards in Compulsory Commitment and Release,* 61 N.W. U.L. REV. 977, 1007–08 (1967).

75. *See* Stone *supra* note 37, at 830 (maintaining that psychiatry has the ability to concern itself with the presence of clinical states and to identify those that require drastic intervention for appropriate treatment rather than predicting future events or dangerous acts).

76. *See* Youngberg v. Romeo, 457 U.S. 307, 323 (1992) (recognizing presumptive validity of decisions of mental health professionals).

77. *See* Lake v. Cameron, 364 F.2d 657, 660 (D.C. Cir. 1966) (finding that "[d]eprivations of liberty solely because of dangerousness to the ill persons themselves should not go beyond what is necessary for their protection"). Several state statutes specifically require committing courts to consider less restrictive alternatives. *See, e.g.,* ALA. CODE § 22–52–10(a)(5) (1984); ARIZ. REV. STAT. ANN. § 36–540 (Supp. 1983); ILL. ANN. STAT. Ch. 91½, § 3–812 (Smith-Hurd Supp. 1985); MICH. COMP. LAWS ANN. § 330.1468(2)(c) (West Supp. 1985); VA. CODE § 37.1–84.1(6) (1984); WASH. REV. CODE ANN. § 71.05–320(1) (West 1986).

78. *See, e.g.,* Lessard v. Smith, 349 F. Supp. 1078 (E.D. Wis. 1972), *vacated,* 414 U.S. 473 (1974). The court reasoned:

> [E]ven if the standard for an adjudication of mental illness and potential dangerousness are satisfied, a court should order full-time involuntary hospitalization only as a last resort. A basic concept in American Justice is the principle that "even though the governmental purpose cannot be legitimate and substantial, that purpose be pursued by means that broadly stifle fundamental personal liberties when the end can be more narrowly achieved. The breadth of legislation abridgment must be viewed in the light of less drastic means for achieving the same basic purpose."

Id. at 1096 (quoting Shelton v. Tucker, 364 US. 479, 488 [1960]).

79. *See generally* Dershowitz, *supra* note 58, at 1286; Hermann, *Preventive Detention, A Scientific View of Man, and State Power,* 1973 U. ILL. L.F. 673, 682.

80. 364 U.S. 479 (1960).

81. *Id.* at 490.

82. *Id.* at 488.

83. 364 F.2d 657 (D.C. Cir. 1966).

84. *Id.* at 659–60 (quoting D.C. CODE ANN. § 21–545[b] [Supp. V 1966]).

85. *Id.* at 661.

86. *See, e.g.*, Bachrach, *Is the Least Restrictive Environment Always the Best? Sociological and Termantic Implications*, 31 HOSP. COMMUNITY PSYCHIATRY 97–103 (1960).

87. *See, e.g.*, Perr, *The Most Beneficial Alternative: A Counterpoint to the Least Restrictive Alternative*, 6 BULL. AM. ACAD. PSYCHIATRY L. iv, iv–vii (1978).

88. 457 US. 307 (1982).

89. *Id.* at 321.

90. 441 US. 418 (1979).

91. 442 U.S. 584 (1979).

92. 457 U.S. 307 (1982).

Suggestions for Further Reading

Coercion in Involuntary Civil Commitment

American Psychiatric Association, "Guidelines for Legislation on the Psychiatric Hospitalization of Adults." In *Issues in Forensic Psychiatry*. Washington, D.C.: American Psychiatric Press, 1984, pp. 27–55.

American Psychiatric Association, "A Model State Law on Civil Commitment of the Mentally Ill." In *Issues in Forensic Psychiatry*. Washington, D.C.: American Psychiatric Press, 1984, pp. 57–180.

Brakel, Samuel J., "Involuntary Institutionalization." In Samuel J. Brakel, John Parry, and Barbara A. Weiner, *The Mentally Disabled and the Law*. Chicago: American Bar Foundation, 1985, ch. 1.

Breggin, Peter, *Psychiatric Drugs: Hazards to the Brain*. New York: Springer, 1983, ch. 12.

Buchanan, Allen E., and Dan W. Brock, *Deciding for Others: The Ethics of Surrogate Decision Making*. Cambridge: Cambridge University Press, 1989, chs. 1 and 7.

Chodoff, Paul, "Involuntary Hospitalization of the Mentally Ill as a Moral Issue." *American Journal of Psychiatry* 141, no. 3 (1984): 384–89.

Dresser, Rebecca S., "Involuntary Confinement: Legal and Psychiatric Perspectives." *Journal of Medicine and Philosophy* 9, no. 3 (August 1984): 295–99.

Isaac, Rael Jean, and Virginia C. Armat, *Madness in the Streets: How Psychiatry and the Law Abandoned the Mentally Ill*. New York: The Free Press, 1990, chs. 5 and 6.

Livermore, Joseph M., Carl P. Malmquist, and Paul E. Meehl, "On the Justifications for Civil Commitment." *University of Pennsylvania Law Review* 117 (1968): 75–96.

Miller, Robert, "The Ethics of Involuntary Commitment to Mental Health Treatment." In Sidney Bloch and Paul Chodoff, *Psychiatraic Ethics,* 2d ed. New York: Oxford University Press, 1991, ch. 13.

Miller, Robert, "Need-for-Treatment Criteria for Involuntary Civil Commitment." *American Journal of Psychiatry* 149 (Oct. 1992): 1380–84.

Parry, John, "Involuntary Civil Commitment in the 90s: A Constitutional Perspective." *Mental and Physical Disability Law Reporter* 18, no. 3 (1994): 320–28.

Reznek, Lawrie, *The Philosophical Defence of Psychiatry*. London: Routledge, 1991, ch. 13.

Steiner, Jerome, "Ethical Issues in the Institutionalization of Patients." In Max Rosenbaum, ed. *Ethics and Values in Psychotherapy: A Guidebook*. New York: The Free Press, 1982, ch. 7.

Treffert, Darold A., "Dying with Their Rights On." *American Journal of Psychiatry* 130 (1973): 1041.

———, "The Obviously Ill Patient in Need of Treatment: A Fourth Standard for Civil Commitment." *Hospital and Community Psychiatry* 36 (March 1985) pp. 259–64.

Turkheimer, Eric, and Charles Parry, "Why the Gap? Practice and Policy in Civil Commitment Hearings." *American Psychologist* 47 (May 1992): 646–55.

Predicting Dangerousness

Hughes, Douglas H., "Can the Clinician Predict Suicide?" *Psychiatric Services* 46, no. 5 (1995): 449–51.

Kozol, H. L., R. J. Boucher, R. F. Garofalo, "The Diagnosis and Treatment of Dangerousness." *Crime and Delinquency* 19 (1972): 371–92.

Lidz, C. W., E. P. Mulvey, and W. P. Gardner, "The Accuracy of Prediction of Violence to Others." *Journal of the American Medical Association* 269 (1993): 1007–11.

Litwack, Thomas R., "Assessments of Dangerousness: Legal, Research, and Clinical Developments." *Administration and Policy in Mental Health* 21 (May 1994): 361–77.

———, "On the Ethics of Dangerousness Assessments." *Law and Human Behavior* 17, no. 4 (1993): 479–85.

Litwack, Thomas R., Stuart M. Kirschner, and Renate C. Wack, "The Assessment of Dangerousness and Predictions of Violence: Recent Research and Future Prospects." *Psychiatric Quarterly* 64 (Fall 1993): 245–73.

Mulvey, Edward P., "Assessing the Evidence of a Link Between Mental Illness and Violence." *Hospital and Community Psychiatry*, 45 (July 1994): 663–68.

Rosen, A., "Detection of Suicidal Patients: An Example of Some Limitations in the Prediction of Infrequent Events." *Journal of Consulting Psychology* 18 (1954): 397–403.

Schaffer, C. Edward, Jr., W. F. Waters, and S. G. Adams, Jr., "Dangerousness: Assessing the Risk of Violent Behavior." *Journal of Consulting and Clinical Psychology* 62, no. 5 (1994): 1064–68.

Schwitzgebel, R. K., "Treatment and Policy Considerations." In McGarry, A. Louis, et al., *Civil Commitment and Social Policy*. Rockville, Md.: U.S. Department of Health and Human Services, 1981, pp. 25–46.

Shah, Saleem A., "Dangerousness and Civil Commitment of the Mentally Ill: Some Public Policy Considerations." *The American Journal of Psychiatary* 132 (1975): 501–505.

Steadman, H. J., and J. Coccoza, "The Prediction of Dangerousness—Baxstrom: A Case Study." In G. Cooke, ed., *The Role of the Forensic Psychologist.* Springfield, Ill.: Charles C. Thomas, 1980, pp. 204–15.

Thornberry, T. P., and J. E. Jacoby, *The Criminally Insane: A Community Follow Up of Mentally Ill Offenders.* Chicago: University of Chicago Press, 1979.

Torrey, E. Fuller, "Violent Behavior by Individuals with Serious Mental Illness." *Hospital and Community Psychiatry,* 45 (July 1994): 653–62.

Suicide Prevention

Andreasen, Nancy C., and Donald W. Black, *Introductory Textbook of Psychology,* 2d ed. Washington, D.C.: American Psychiatric Press, 1995, ch. 20.

Battin, M. Pabst, *Ethical Issues in Suicide.* Englewood Cliffs, N.J.: Prentice-Hall, 1982.

Beauchamp, Tom L., and Robert M. Veatch, *Ethical Issues in Death and Dying.* Upper Saddle River, N. J.: Prentice Hall, 1995, ch. 3.

Brody, Baruch A., ed., *Suicide and Euthanasia: Historical and Contemporary Themes.* Dordrecht, Holland: Kluwer Academic Publishers, 1989.

Coleman, Phyllis, and Ronald A. Shellow, "Suicide: Unpredictable and Unavoidable—Proposed Guidelines Provide Rational Test for Physician's Liability." *Nebraska Law Review* 71 (1992): 643–93.

Greenberg, David F., "Involuntary Psychiatric Commitments to Prevent Suicide." *New York University Law Review* 49 (1974): 227–45.

Heyd, David, and Sidney Bloch, "The Ethics of Suicide." In Sidney Bloch, and Paul Chodoff, eds., *Psychiatric Ethics,* 2d ed. New York: Oxford University Press, 1991, ch. 12.

Maltsberger, John T., "Calculated Risk Taking in the Treatment of Suicidal Patients: Ethical and Legal Problems." *Death Studies* 18 (1994): 439–52.

Matthews, Martha Alys, "Suicidal Competence and the Patient's Right to Refuse Lifesaving Treatment." *California Law Review* 75 (March 1987): 707–58.

Shneidman, Edwin S., "Rational Suicide and Psychiatric Disorders." *New England Journal of Medicine* 326, no. 13 (March 26, 1992): 889–91.

Siegl, Karolynn, "Rational Suicide: Considerations for the Clinician." *Psychiatric Quarterly* 54 (Summer 1982): 77–84.

Slaby, Andrew E., "Psychopharmacotherapy of Suicide." *Death Studies* 18 (1994): 483–95. (Many issues of *Death Studies* contain good articles on suicide.)

Szasz, Thomas, "The Case Against Suicide Prevention." *American Psychologist* 41 (July 1986): 806–12.

6.

ETHICAL ISSUES IN FORENSIC PSYCHIATRY

INTRODUCTION

Responsibility and Rational Autonomy

Previous articles touched on responsibility and its relation to blameworthiness and insanity, but now these concepts must be scrutinized more carefully, as must the relevance, or irrelevance, to responsibility of determinism—the view that necessary and sufficient antecedent causal conditions exist to bring about every detail of every event. Being responsible for x seems to mean being the cause of x; but what kind of causation is required?

Libertarians, who affirm free will, acknowledge that being responsible for our choices and actions involves a rational ability to understand open alternatives, but they think that responsibility is incompatible with making causally predetermined choices. Responsibility presupposes free will, the capacity for making originative or creative choices that transcend given causal conditions. Libertarians interpret rational autonomy indeterministically. Responsibility, libertarians claim, involves originative or creative causality. Without creative volitional autonomy we could not be morally or legally praiseworthy or blameworthy precisely because we would not be responsible for, that is, we did not originate, our choices and the acts that issue from them. We cannot freely choose an alternative unless we understand it, so libertarianism does not deny that responsibility involves rationality as well as free will, or that irrational people are nonresponsible.

Hard determinists, as William James called them, accept the libertarian analysis of responsibility and agree that it presupposes free will, but they conclude that there is no such thing as responsibility in a rigidly deterministic universe (like ours?). They give up responsibility, along with all the other moral concepts and practices with which it has an essential logical connection, and they lament that this is simply the price to be paid for adopting a deterministic metaphysics. Hard determinists are rare.

Soft determinists, by comparison, are compatabilists who contend that we are responsible moral agents even though determinism is true. Soft determinists contend that responsibility presupposes nothing more than (1) rationality, the ability to understand, and/or (2) autonomy, the ability to make choices (even if they are predetermined), and/or (3) freedom of action, the ability to do what we choose to do in the absence of external constraints and restraints. Originative choosing is irrelevant, they insist. Soft determinists conceive of rational autonomy deterministically. Some deny that choice or willpower is relevant to responsibility and exclusively emphasize the capacity to understand; others proclaim that choice and freedom of action are essential; but they all deny that responsible choices need be creative or originative.

Soft determinists deny that determinism is incompatible with responsibility, choice-making, blameworthiness, and the moral and legal practices of praising and rewarding, blaming and punishing. We can and normally do have freedom of action (the ability to *do* what we want and choose without external hindrance) in a deterministic universe devoid of freedom of will (the ability to make originative choices); this is all that responsible agency requires. Since Jonathan Edwards, soft determinists typically maintain that people are free and responsible for their acts if (1) they know or understand what they are doing, (2) they are adequately motivated to do it, and (3) they choose to do it in the absence of immediate and unusually powerful *external* constraints and restraints.

Lawrie Reznek emphasizes (1) and seems to presuppose (2) and (3). While accepting (1), (2), and (3) as necessary for responsible action, the libertarian champion of free will contends that we must add that (4) people make internally uncaused and genuinely originative and creative choices. Free and creative choices are uncaused in the sense that given causal conditions (like understanding, anticipating, and desiring the alternatives) make choices possible; but they are not sufficient for their occurrence. Creative choices are limited by these conditions, but they transcend them and are not fully predictable from them. Free choices are caused in that they presuppose necessary conditions; they are uncaused in that given causal conditions are not sufficient to determine choices.

On both views of responsibility, people are blameworthy and justly subject to blame or punishment if they are responsible for their acts, and the acts are wrong. Both agree that if an agent is nonresponsible for a prohibited act, then a nonresponsibility defense is warranted. But which concept of responsibility, the libertarian's or the soft determinist's, is the most plausible, and why?

Nonresponsibility and the Insanity Defense

Further exploration of the free will vs. determinism debate is beyond the scope of this introduction, but we should note its relevance to whether mentally ill persons are responsible agents who are praiseworthy for their good behavior, or blameworthy and justly punishable for their misdeeds. To the extent that responsibility presupposes understanding, libertarians and soft determinists can agree that insane persons who are irrationally incompetent should not be blamed or punished for their misdeeds because they suffer from an inability to understand. Articles in this section by the American Psychiatric Association and by Lawrie Reznek explain how, in our legal tradition, the old (1843) M'Naghten test grants an insanity defense to wrongdoers who suffer from "a defect of reason." Nonrationality entails nonresponsibility.

However, nonresponsibility may involve more than a defect of reason. Later legal tests like the Durham rule (1954) and that of the American Law Institute (1961) add defects of self-control as exculpatory conditions. But what kind of self-control is required? Does self-control consist of creative effortful choosing, or is volitional effort that is completely determined by antecedent causal conditions sufficient, as long as there is external freedom of action? Does rational autonomy involve creative or uncreative choices?

In one sense, free will is of little practical significance, for without it we could simply adopt a deterministic concept of responsibility (points [1] through [3] above) and go right on about the business of dealing with moral and legal offenders. Interestingly, the law seldom if ever asks if choices are originative or fully determined; the issue is philosophically significant nevertheless. Yes, autonomy can be defined without introjecting free will, as soft determinists insist; but libertarians are convinced that this omits something essential for human worth or dignity—our ability to originate our own decisions. Although the question is seldom raised in the courtroom and in ordinary life, perhaps we simply assume that our decisions originate with us until circumstances like mental incompetence arise that call it into question.

We tend to excuse *psychotics* primarily because they are deficient in rationality; but we tend to excuse *neurotics* (who usually *know* what they are doing but can't help it) mainly because they are deficient in self-control or willpower, because their decisions are compelled by powers in themselves over which they have no conscious volition or control. When neurotics assume responsibility, they do so unrealistically and blame themselves for innumerable evils far beyond their control. Our concept of moral "responsibility" has at least two distinct meanings that should not be confused. It means (1) "causing through choice or self-activity" or (2) "having and assuming duties or obligations." Neurotics exaggerate responsibility in both senses and assume both culpability and obligations far beyond their powers. They are inordinately responsible, but the duties and offenses they assume are misdirected and misconceived.

Forensic Commitments

Instead of being jailed, many persons charged with criminal offenses are hospitalized involuntarily in psychiatric institutions. Some forensic patients await a determination of their competency to stand trial; others are being treated for restoration to such competency; and those who are extremely impaired have little prospect of restoration to either competency or liberty. Some were tried and found "not guilty" because insane at the time of their crimes. Yet they are involuntarily institutionalized even though innocent, and they may spend more time in a psychiatric institution than they would have served in prison had they been found guilty. Many public misconceptions exist about persons found not guilty by reason of insanity, such as that large numbers of criminals plead and succeed with the insanity defense, and that they are then released immediately back into society like all other innocent persons. Actually, only a small number of insanity pleas are made each year, and insanity acquittals, often for nonviolent crimes, are rare indeed. Involuntary institutionalization, often in maximum security mental hospitals, almost inevitably follows upon insanity acquittals.

Though inappropriate, offenders judged "not guilty by reason of insanity" or "guilty but mentally ill" are frequently committed involuntarily to mental hospitals for punishment disguised as rehabilitation. Theoretically, there are significant differences between *punishing* convicted criminals in penal institutions and *treating* those acquitted of crimes committed because of insanity. Convicted criminals are punished for several reasons: to prevent and deter similar offenses, to rehabilitate, and to extract that sweet revenge that we dignify with the epithets of "justice" or "retribution." Mental institutions also aim at prevention, deterrence, and rehabilitation; but they differ in theory from penal institutions in that it is improper to use them to extract societal revenge. In practice, however, there is often little difference between the two in any of these respects. Revenge is not readily combined with rehabilitation.

Competency to *stand trial* may be confused with sanity (competency and responsibility) *at the time of the crime,* but they are absolutely different. Legally, criteria for determining competency to stand trial and guilt for criminality are quite distinct. Criminal guilt presupposes that offenders were capable of knowing and/or controlling their behavior at the time of their crime. To stand trial, the accused must be able, well after the crime, to understand the nature and circumstances of the offense and to cooperate with legal counsel in developing and presenting a defense.

In his article Louis McGarry explains the testing of competency to stand trial. Competency to stand trial is a very specific type of competency, quite distinct from competency to conduct business, make wills or contracts, marry, vote, or choose and refuse treatment. Our laws and courts do not allow mental patients to be declared generally incompetent for everything. The presumption of competency in all respects remains fully intact until it is successfully challenged. Formal competency hearings occur during the final stages of such challenges. Each competency hearing must be issue- or task-specific. In practice, it may be difficult to distinguish between incompetency due to mental illness and ignorance of the court system that results from cultural deprivation.

Chemical Sanity

Psychoactive drugs are usually prescribed to restore competency to stand trial, but many states now tentatively recognize a right to refuse such medication. Some courts and legal authorities champion a right not to be drugged to stand trial.

Defenders of chemical sanity contend that treatment, especially with psychoactive drugs, can restore an offender's rational or volitional competency, thus facilitating a speedy trial. Drug therapy in conjunction with counseling, not talk therapy alone, is definitely the treatment of choice for schizophrenia and other psychoses. No amount of talking will restore a serious chemical imbalance or structural defect in the dopamine circuit of a schizophrenic's brain. Recently available CT, PET, and MRI scans disclose that during acute psychotic episodes the rational forebrain of schizophrenics hardly functions, while sensory and emotional regions of the brain are hyperactive. Schizophrenics are being overwhelmed with emotions and sensory images, often hallucinatory, while lacking a critical cognitive perspective on what is happening to them. Brain scans also show that psychotropic drugs, used skillfully, can correct many of the functional imbalances suffered by psychotics.

Despite the efficacy of psychoactive drugs, chemical competency to stand trial is vigorously contested. Some opponents find the very idea abhorrent, unmindful perhaps that ordinary competency depends upon normal brain chemistry, and that drug therapy can facilitate a return toward a more normal brain chemistry. If properly used, psychoactive drugs can help restore memory, a sense of personal identity and varying degrees of rational and volitional capacity. This happens often, despite all protests.

Lawyers are concerned that juries may fail to grasp the distinction between competency at the time of the trial and sanity at the time of the crime. It is their job to ensure that this distinction is properly appreciated, but many attorneys and defendants believe (1) that the best way to do this is to allow a jury to see the patient in an unmedicated state, and (2) that the calm reasonableness of chemical sanity defeats this objective. The article by Karl G. Williams explains the 1992 U.S. Supreme Court decision to uphold the right not to be drugged to stand trial in the *Riggins* v. *Nevada* case.

An interesting conundrum results from the right to avoid chemical competency to stand trial. If defendants are extremely confused and out of control *before* the administration of drugs, their competency to accept or refuse therapy is in doubt. Since there cannot be an unjustified infringement of autonomy where no autonomy exists, involuntary treatment would otherwise be quite appropriate here. If, however, defendants refuse further therapy *after* drugs have restored self-control and rational comprehension, they will likely become incompetent thereafter to stand trial (and to choose or refuse drug therapy), so no jury will have a chance see them in an unmedicated state. Being incompetent to stand trial, and having competently refused medication necessary to sustain their competency, they will be incarcerated indefinitely in a mental institution. Respecting their chemical competency results in the annihilation of their chemical competency! So is it, or is it not, in the patient's "best interest" to stand trial? Is it really better to be committed to indeterminate, perhaps lifelong, craziness and incarceration in a mental institution than to serve a sane, fixed, and frequently shorter sentence in a penal institution? Problems about chemical competency become even more acute when the issue is competency to be executed (Byers, 1994) and when dealing with multiple personalities (Appelbaum and Alexander, 1994).

American Psychiatric Association Statement on the Insanity Defense

Insanity Defense Work Group

Long before there was psychiatry, there was the insanity defense. The idea that the insane should not be punished for otherwise criminal acts began to develop in the twelfth century as part of the more general idea that criminal punishment should be imposed only on persons who were morally blameworthy. In the thirteenth century, Bracton, the first medieval jurist to deal with the subject of insanity and crime, stated, "For a crime is not committed unless the will to harm be present." The earliest documented case of a jury acquittal on grounds of unsound mind occurred in 1505.[1]

In his treatise on the *History of the Pleas of the Crown*[2] published posthumously in 1736, England's Lord Mathew Hale explained that the insanity defense was rooted in the fundamental moral assumptions of the criminal law: "Man is naturally endowed with these two great faculties, understanding and liberty of will. . . . The consent of the will is that which renders human actions either commendable or culpable. . . . [I]t follows that, where there is a total defect of the understanding, there is no free act of the will."

Thus it is a longstanding premise of the criminal law that unless a defendant intentionally chooses to commit a crime, he is not morally blameworthy, and he should not be punished. By singling out certain defendants as either lacking free will or, alternatively, lacking sufficient understanding of what they do, the insanity defense becomes the exception that proves the rule. In the law's moral paradigm, other criminal

From the *American Journal of Psychiatry* 140, no. 6 (June 1983): 681–88. Copyright © 1983, the American Psychiatric Association. Reprinted by permission.

defendants, those who do not receive an insanity defense, are thus found blameworthy.

Despite these general premises in the criminal law, many questions have persisted about the insanity defense such as how best to define criminal insanity (what the legal test should be) and what should happen to criminal defendants once they are found "insane." The history of the insanity defense has been one of periodic revisions of standards, public debate, and contention. This has been the case especially when the insanity defense is highlighted by a case involving a defendant who has attempted to harm a well-known person.

The modern formulation of the insanity defense derives from the "rules" stated by the House of Lords in Daniel M'Naghten's case in 1843. M'Naghten was indicted for having shot Edward Drummond, secretary to Robert Peel, the Prime Minister of England. The thrust of the medical testimony was that M'Naghten was suffering from what today would be described as delusions of persecution symptomatic of paranoid schizophrenia. The jury returned a verdict of not guilty by reason of insanity. This verdict became the subject of considerable popular alarm and was regarded with particular concern by Queen Victoria. As a result, the House of Lords asked the judges of that body to give an advisory opinion regarding the answers to five questions "on the law governing such cases." The combined answers to two of these questions have come to be known as M'Naghten's Rules.

> [T]o establish a defense on the ground of insanity, it must be clearly proved that, at the time of the committing of the act, the party accused was labouring under such a defect of reason, from disease of the mind, as not to know the nature and quality of the act he was doing; or if he did know it, that he did not know he was doing what was wrong.

M'Naghten quickly became the prevailing approach to the insanity defense in England and in the United States, even though this formulation was criticized often because of its emphasis on the defendant's lack of intellectual or cognitive understanding of what he was doing as the sole justification for legal insanity. M'Naghten's case was followed by a public response not unlike that of the public's response to the John Hinckley case.

> Ye people of England exult and be glad
> For ye're now at the will of the merciless mad . . .
> For crime is no crime—when the mind is unsettled.[3]

Over the last 150 years, legal formulations for insanity other than M'Naghten have, from time to time, been adopted in certain jurisdictions, e.g., the "irresistible impulse" formulation.[4,5] Judge David Bazelon was midwife to the "product of mental illness" test for insanity employed in the District of Columbia from 1954 through 1972.[6] However, the "product of mental illness" test was originally formulated in New Hampshire in 1869.[7,8]

The alternative formulation for the insanity defense best known besides M'Naghten is that proposed by the drafters of the Model Penal Code during the 1950s, the so-called ALI (American Law Institute) test. Section 4.01 of the Model Penal Code provides: "A person is not responsible for criminal conduct if at the time of such conduct as a result of mental disease or defect he lacks substantial capacity either to appreciate the criminality (wrongfulness) of his conduct or to conform his conduct to the requirements of law." This was the test employed in the Hinckley case.

The ALI (Model Penal Code) approach to insanity differs from M'Naghten in three respects. First, ALI substitutes the concept of "appreciation" for that of cognitive understanding in the definition of insanity, thus apparently introducing an affective, more emotional, more personalized approach for evaluating the nature of a defendant's knowledge or understanding. Second, the ALI definition for insanity does not insist upon a defendant's total lack of appreciation (knowledge) of the nature of his conduct but instead that he only "lacks substantial capacity." Finally, ALI, like the "irresistible impulse" test, incorporates a so-called volitional approach to insanity, thus adding as an independent criterion for insanity the defendant's ability (or inability) to control his actions.

Through court rulings, the ALI approach to criminal insanity has been adopted in all federal jurisdictions. It has been adopted by legislation or judicial ruling in about half the states. Some variation of M'Naghten is the exclusive test of insanity in about one-third of the states. A handful of states (six) supplement M'Naghten with some variation of the "irresistible impulse" test. Only New Hampshire continues to use the "product of mental illness" test. Montana and Idaho have abolished the insanity defense in recent years or at least that form of the defense that requires the defendant to meet one of the above-mentioned special legal tests or formulations for insanity.

Interestingly, the United States Supreme Court has never ruled whether the availability for defendants of an insanity defense is constitutionally compelled. Nor has the legislature of the United States (the Congress) yet adopted one or another of the traditional insanity defense formulations for use in the federal courts. Earlier in the twentieth century, three state courts (Washington, Mississippi, and Louisiana) ruled that recognition of the insanity defense was constitutionally required.

Despite the attention given to the insanity defense by legal scholars and the continuing debates about the role that psychiatry should play in the administration of defense, it should be noted that successful invocation of the defense is rare (probably involving a fraction of 1 percent of all felony cases).[9,10] While philosophically important for the criminal law, the insanity defense is empirically unimportant. Making changes in the insanity defense will hardly be the panacea for reducing crime.

Historically, defendants who were found insane also did not usually regain their freedom. Instead, they often spent many years, if not their whole lifetimes, locked away in institutions for the criminally insane. Information also suggests that despite the prominence given the insanity defense through well-publicized trials, the majority of such successful defenses, rather than being awarded by juries after criminal trials, occur instead by concurrence between the prosecution and defense. Thus, in many instances, the insanity defense functions in a noncontroversial manner to divert mentally ill offenders from the criminal justice system to the mental health system.

As has . . . been summarized by persons testifying before Congress in the wake of the John Hinckley verdict, there is also a great deal that is unknown and not very well studied about the insanity defense. For example, contrary to popular belief, what little evidence there is suggests that the insanity defense is not solely or exclusively a defense of the rich.[11] Nor is it a defense that is confined to defendants who are accused only of violent crimes.

During the last ten years, interest in abolishing or modifying the insanity defense has been renewed because of several factors. Public officials, speaking for a growing conservative consensus and a public understandably disturbed by the failures of the entire criminal justice system, have championed the cause that the insanity defense is one more indication that the country is "soft on crime." Thus, in 1973 President Nixon called for the abolition of the insanity defense, noting that this proposal was "the most significant feature of the Administration's proposed criminal code."

A 1981 Attorney General's Task Force on Violent Crime proposed federal legislation to create a verdict of "guilty but mentally ill," similar to legislation that had been passed in a few states such as Illinois and Michigan.

The hardening of American attitudes about crime has not been, however, the only cause of concern about the insanity defense. Over the last decade, as a consequence of some civil libertarian-type court rulings that insanity acquittees may not be subjected to procedures for confinement that are more restrictive than those used for civil patients who have not committed criminal acts, the insanity defense became a more attractive alternative for defendants to plead. As noted by Stone, over the last decade [the 1970s] and for the first time in history, a successful plea of insanity had "real bite."[12] Modern psychiatric treatment, particularly the use of antipsychotic drugs, permits the seeming restoration of sanity for many defendants, even if it cannot be known with certainty whether such acquittees still remain dangerous.

The consequence of the aforementioned trends has been the rapid release from hospitals for a segment of insanity acquittees in some states. In Michigan, following the McQuillan[13] decision, 55.6 percent of "not guilty by reason of insanity" patients were discharged following a 60-day diagnostic commitment.[14] In contrast, over 90 percent of insanity acquittees are hospitalized in Illinois after the 30-day diagnostic hearing, with their average length of hospitalization being 39 months. Once their release is approved by the court, it is almost always under the condition of participation in a mandatory, court-ordered outpatient program. The exodus of insanity acquittees in some states has alarmed both the public and the psychiatric profession, which traditionally has been expected to play some continuing role in the social control of persons found not guilty by reason of insanity. The public's perception that a successful plea of insanity is a good way to "beat the rap" contributes to a belief that the criminal insanity defense is not only fundamentally unfair ("for after all, he did do it") but also that insanity is a dangerous doctrine.

The Hinckley Verdict

The ruling of the District of Columbia jury in the John Hinckley case catalyzed many of the above and related issues concerning the insanity defense and its administration. Following the Hinckley verdict, some twenty bills were under discussion or were introduced in the Congress that would codify, for the first time, a federal approach toward insanity and also restrict the defense. The debate has focused on the wording of the insanity defense, its potential abolition, and on post-trial mechanisms for containing the insane. The Reagan administration . . . proposed, in effect, to abolish the traditional insanity defense and to substitute instead a "mens rea" approach. A person would be found not guilty by reason of insanity only if the person lacked "mens rea," the required mental state that is part of the definition of a crime. Another approach proposes a limited M'Naghten-type criterion to define insanity.

Other debates have focused upon procedural issues in the law of insanity. In Mr. Hinckley's case, as is presently the case in about half the states, the government had the burden of persuasion to prove the defendant's sanity beyond a reasonable doubt. The other states include insanity among the so-called affirmative defenses, placing the burden of proving insanity upon the defendant rather than making the government prove sanity. One proposed change of the insanity defense is to shift the burden of proof to the defendant, rather than to the state.

Another focus of discussion, both prior to and following Mr. Hinckley's case, has been on the nature and quality of psychiatric testimony in insanity trials. In particular, there has been criticism of psychiatric testimony about whether defendants meet (or fail to meet) the relevant legal test for insanity in a given jurisdiction. To some extent the public appears confused by the so-called battle of the experts. Unfortunately, public criticism about the "battle of the experts" fails to recognize or acknowledge advances in psychiatric nosology and diagnosis that indicate a high degree of diagnostic reliability for psychiatry—80 percent or so—so long, that is, as psychiatric testimony is restricted to medical and scientific, and not legal or moral, issues (see, for example, reference 15). Sanity is, of course, a legal issue, not a medical one. The "battle of the experts" is also to a certain extent foreordained by the structure of the adversary system. Experts often disagree in many types of criminal and civil trials. For example, other medical experts may disagree on the interpretation of X-rays, engineers on structural issues, and economists on market concentration issues. American jurisprudence requires that each side (defense and prosecution) make the best case it can in the search for the just outcome.

The APA Position

SHOULD THE INSANITY DEFENSE BE ABOLISHED?

The American Psychiatric Association, speaking as citizens as well as psychiatrists, believes that the insanity defense should be retained in some form. The insanity defense rests upon one of the fundamental premises of the criminal law, that punishment for wrongful deeds should be predicated upon moral culpability. However, within the framework of English and American law, defendants who lack the ability (the capacity) to rationally control their behavior do not possess free will. They cannot be said to have "chosen to do wrong." Therefore, they should not be punished or handled similarly to all other criminal defendants. Retention of the insanity defense is essential to the moral integrity of the criminal law.

The aforementioned points do not, of course, mean that the insanity defense is necessarily "good for psychiatry," "good for all criminals" who invoke the plea, or even always "good for the public." In fact, the opposite may be the case. Psychiatrists, indeed even some psychiatric patients, might be less stigmatized, less susceptible to criticism by the media and the public were the insanity defense to be abolished. Thus the Association's view that the insanity defense should not now be abolished is not one that it takes out of self-interest. Only a minority of psychiatrists testify in criminal trials. Members of the American Psychiatric Association, however, recognize the importance of the insanity defense for the criminal law, as well as its importance for genuinely mentally ill defendants who on moral and medical grounds require psychiatric treatment (in addition to restraint), rather than receiving solely custody and punishment.

To the extent that changes need to be made in the insanity defense, the Association, therefore, recommends consideration of some of the ideas discussed below concerning the legal definition of insanity, the burden of proof, the role that psychiatrists can or should play within the insanity defense, and the post-verdict disposition of persons found insane.

SHOULD A "GUILTY BUT MENTALLY ILL" VERDICT BE ADOPTED IN THE LAW TO EITHER SUPPLEMENT OR TAKE THE PLACE OF THE TRADITIONAL INSANITY DEFENSE?

While some psychiatrists believe that the "guilty but mentally ill" verdict has merit for dealing with problems posed by the insanity defense, the American Psychiatric Association is extremely skeptical of this approach. Currently nine states are experimenting with a "guilty but mentally ill" verdict or its equivalent. They permit a "guilty but mentally ill" verdict as an alternative choice for jurors to the traditional insanity defense. Were, however, "guilty but mentally ill" to be the *only* verdict possible (besides guilt or innocence), this would be the abolitionist position in disguise. The idea of moral blameworthiness would be diminished within the law. This does not seem right.

There are also problems with "guilty but mentally ill" as an alternative choice to the traditional insanity defense. "Guilty but mentally ill" offers a compromise for the jury. Persons who might otherwise have qualified for an insanity verdict may instead be siphoned into a category of "guilty but mentally ill." Thus some defendants who might otherwise be found not guilty through an insanity defense will be found "guilty but mentally ill" instead.

The "guilty but mentally ill" approach may become the easy way out. Juries may avoid grappling with the difficult moral issues inherent in adjudicating guilt or innocence, jurors instead settling conveniently on "guilty but mentally ill." The deliberations of jurors in deciding cases are, however, vital to set societal standards and to give meaning to societal ideas about responsibility and nonresponsibility. An important symbolic function of the criminal law is lost through the "guilty but mentally ill" approach.

There are other problems with "guilty but mentally ill." Providing mental health treatment for persons in jails and prisons has, over the years, proved a refractory problem.[16] Yet the "guilty but mentally ill" approach makes sense only if meaningful mental health treatment is given defendants following such a verdict. In times of financial stress, the likelihood that meaningful treatment for persons "guilty but mentally ill" will be mandated and paid for by state legislatures is, however, slight. This has been the outcome in Michigan, the state that first embarked upon the "guilty but mentally ill" approach) where even though they have been found "guilty but mentally ill," felons have received no more treatment than they would have prior to the new law.

Alternatively, whatever limited funds are available for the treatment of mentally ill inmates may be devoted to "guilty but mentally ill defendants," ignoring the treatment needs of other mentally ill but conventionally sentenced prisoners who require mental health treatment in prison.

The "guilty but mentally ill" plea may cause important moral, legal, psychiatric, and pragmatic problems to receive a whitewash without fundamental progress being made. We note that under conventional sentencing procedures already in place, judges may presently order mental health treatment for offenders in need of it. Furthermore, a jury verdict is an awkward device for making dispositional decisions concerning a person's need for mental health treatment.

SHOULD THE LEGAL STANDARDS NOW IN USE CONCERNING THE INSANITY DEFENSE BE MODIFIED?

While the American Psychiatric Association is not opposed to state legislatures (or the U.S. Congress) making statutory changes in the language of insanity, we also note that the exact wording of the insanity defense has never, through scientific studies or the case approach, been shown to be the major determinant of whether a defendant is acquitted by reason of insanity.[9] Substantive standards for insanity provide instructions for the jury (or other legal decisionmakers) concerning the legal standard for insanity which a defendant must meet. There is no perfect correlation, however, between legal insanity standards and psychiatric or mental states that defendants exhibit and which psychiatrists describe. For example, while some legal scholars and practitioners believe that using the word "appreciate" (rather than "knowing" or "understanding"') expands the insanity dialogue to include a broader and more comprehensive view of human behavior and thinking, this may not necessarily be so. Of much greater practical significance is whether the standard employed is interpreted by individual trial judges to permit or not permit psychiatric testimony concerning the broad range of mental functioning of possible relevance for a jury's deliberation. But this matter is not easily legislated.

The above commentary does not mean that given the present state of psychiatric knowledge psychiatrists cannot present meaningful testimony relevant to determining a defendant's understanding or appreciation of his act. Many psychiatrists, however, believe that psychiatric information relevant to determining whether a defendant understood the nature of his act, and whether he appreciated its wrongfulness, is more reliable and has a stronger scientific basis than, for example, does psychiatric information relevant to whether a defendant was able to control his behavior. The line between an irresistible impulse and an impulse not resisted is probably no sharper than that between twilight and dusk. Psychiatry is a deterministic discipline that views all human behavior as, to a large extent, "caused." The concept of volition is the subject of some disagreement among psychiatrists. Many psychiatrists therefore believe that psychiatric testimony (particularly that of a conclusory nature) about volition is more likely to produce confusion for jurors than is psychiatric testimony relevant to a defendant's appreciation or understanding.

Another major consideration in articulating standards for the insanity defense is the definition of mental disease or defect. Definitions of mental disease or defect sometimes, but not always, accompany insanity defense standards. Under Durham,[6] the "product of mental illness" approach, a series of legal cases in the District of Columbia suggested that (for purposes of criminal insanity) "sociopathy" or other personality disorders could be "productive" of insanity. It was assumed by the law that such disorders could impair behavior control. But this is generally not the experience of psychiatry. Allowing insanity acquittals in cases involving persons who manifest primarily "personality disorders" such as antisocial personality disorder (sociopathy) does not accord with modern psychiatric knowledge or psychiatric beliefs concerning the extent to which such persons do have control over their behavior. Persons with antisocial personality disorders should, at least for heuristic reasons, be held accountable for their behavior. The American Psychiatric Association, therefore, suggests that any revision of the insanity defense standards should indicate that mental disorders potentially leading to exculpation must be *serious*. Such disorders should usually be of the severity (if not always of the quality) of conditions that psychiatrists diagnose as psychoses.

The following standard, recently proposed by Bonnie,[17] is one which the American Psychiatric Association believes does permit relevant psychiatric testimony to be brought to bear on the great majority of cases where criminal responsibility is at issue:

> A person charged with a criminal offense should be found not guilty by
> reason of insanity if it is shown that as a result of mental disease or men-
> tal retardation he was unable to appreciate the wrongfulness of his con-
> duct at the time of the offense.
>
> As used in this standard, the terms mental disease or mental retar-
> dation include only those severely abnormal mental conditions that
> grossly and demonstrably impair a person's perception or understand-
> ing of reality, and that are not attributable primarily to the voluntary
> ingestion of alcohol or other psychoactive substances.

In practice there is considerable overlap between a psychotic person's defective understanding or appreciation and his ability to control
his behavior. Most psychotic persons who fail a volitional test for insanity will also fall a cognitive-type test when such a test is applied to their
behavior, thus rendering the volitional test superfluous in judging them.

SHOULD THE BURDEN OF PROOF IN INSANITY CASES ALWAYS REST WITH THE PROSECUTION?

The case of John Hinckley brought renewed attention to who has the
burden of proof in insanity cases. In the Hinckley case, the state had the
burden to prove Mr. Hinckley's sanity beyond a reasonable doubt. This
was a considerable burden for the state to overcome. Legal scholars
believe that who bears the burden of proof in a legal case is a matter of
considerable import. This is especially so when what is to be proven is
inherently uncertain. And if anything can be agreed upon about criminal insanity, it is that insanity is a matter of some uncertainty.

At present about half of the states and all the Federal Courts require
that once a defendant introduces into the proceeding any evidence of
insanity, the state then bears the burden to prove the defendant was
instead sane. An equal number of states and the District of Columbia,
however, assign the burden of proof to the defendant, who must then
prove his insanity by "a preponderance of the evidence" or by an even
higher standard of proof.

The American Psychiatric Association is exceedingly reluctant to
take a position about assigning the burden of proof in insanity cases.
This matter is clearly one for legislative judgment. For public policy, the
issue is, in part, whether the rights of the individual or the rights of the
state are to be given more or less weight in criminal insanity trials or, as
is sometimes stated, which types of errors do we deem more or less tolerable in insanity trials. Given the inherent uncertainties involved in psychiatric testimony regarding the defense and the ever-present problems
relating abstract legal principles to controversies of such emotion, who

bears the burden of proof in insanity trials may be quite important. This is particularly so when what must be proved must also be proved "beyond a reasonable doubt." As suggested by the United States Supreme Court in the *Addington* case,[18] psychiatric evidence is usually not sufficiently clear-cut to prove or disprove many legal facts "beyond a reasonable doubt."

It is commonly believed that the likely effect of assigning the burden of proof (burden of persuasion) to defendants rather than to the state in insanity trials will be to decrease the number of such successful defenses. This matter clearly requires further empirical study.

SHOULD PSYCHIATRIC TESTIMONY BE LIMITED TO STATEMENTS OF MENTAL CONDITION?

This area for potential reform of the insanity defense is one of the most controversial. Some proposals would limit psychiatric testimony in insanity defense trials to statements of mental condition, i.e., to statements of conventional psychiatric diagnoses, to provision of accounts of how and why the defendant acted as he did at the time of the commission of the act, to explanations in medical and psychological terms about how the act was affected or influenced by the person's mental illness. However, under this approach, psychiatrists would not be permitted to testify about so-called ultimate issues such as whether or not the defendant was, in their judgment, "sane" or "insane," "responsible" or not, etc. A further limitation upon psychiatric "ultimate issue" testimony would be to restrict the psychiatrist from testifying about whether a defendant did or did not meet the particular legal test for insanity at issue. Thus the law could prevent psychiatrists from testifying in a conclusory fashion whether the defendant "lacked substantial capacity to conform his behavior to the requirements of law," "lacked substantial capacity to appreciate the criminality of his act," was not able to distinguish "right from wrong" at the time of the act, and so forth.

The American Psychiatric Association is not opposed to legislatures restricting psychiatric testimony about the aforementioned ultimate legal issues concerning the insanity defense. We adopt this position because it is clear that psychiatrists are experts in medicine, not the law. As such, the psychiatrist's first obligation and expertise in the courtroom is to "do psychiatry," i.e., to present medical information and opinion about the defendant's mental state and motivation and to explain in detail the reason for his medical-psychiatric conclusions. When, however, "ultimate issue" questions are formulated by the law and put to the expert witness who must then say "yea" or "nay," then the expert witness is required to make a leap in logic. He no longer addresses himself to medical concepts but instead must infer or intuit what is in fact unspeakable, namely, the *probable relationship* between medical concepts and legal or moral constructs such as free will. These impermissible leaps in logic made by expert witnesses confuse the jury.[19] Juries thus find themselves listening to conclusory and seemingly contradictory psychiatric testimony that defendants are either "sane" or "insane" or that they do or do not meet the relevant legal test for insanity. This state of affairs does considerable injustice to psychiatry and, we believe, possibly to criminal defendants. These psychiatric disagreements about technical, legal, and/or moral matters cause less than fully understanding juries or the public to conclude that psychiatrists cannot agree. In fact, in many criminal insanity trials both prosecution and defense psychiatrists do agree about the nature and even the extent of mental disorder exhibited by the defendant at the time of the act.

Psychiatrists, of course, must be permitted to testify fully about the defendant's psychiatric diagnosis, mental state, and motivation (in clinical and commonsense terms) at the time of the alleged act so as to permit the jury or judge to reach the ultimate conclusion about which they, and only they, are expert. Determining whether a criminal defendant was legally insane is a matter for legal fact-finders, not for experts.

WHAT SHOULD BE DONE WITH DEFENDANTS FOLLOWING "NOT GUILTY BY REASON OF INSANITY" VERDICTS?

This is the area for reform where the American Psychiatric Association believes that the most significant changes can and should be made in the present administration of the insanity defense. We believe that neither the law, the public, psychiatry, nor the victims of violence have been well served by the general approach and reform of the last ten years [the 1970s], which has obscured the quasi-criminal nature of the insanity defense and of the status of insanity acquittees.

The American Psychiatric Association is concerned particularly about insanity acquittals of persons charged with violent crime. In our view, it is a mistake to analogize such insanity acquittees as fully equivalent to civil committees who, when all has been said and done, have not usually already demonstrated their clear-cut potential for dangerous behavior because they have not yet committed a highly dangerous act. Because mental illness frequently affects the patient's ability to seek or accept treatment, we believe that civil commitment, as a system of detention and treatment, should be predicated on the severity of the patient's illness and/or in some instances on the mental patient's potential for perpetrating future violence against others. The usual civil committee has not, however, committed nor will he commit in the future a major crime. Most mentally ill persons are not violent.[20] By contrast, the "dangerousness" of insanity acquittees who have perpetrated violence has already been demonstrated. Their future dangerousness need not be inferred; it may be assumed at least for a reasonable period of time. The American Psychiatric Association is therefore quite skeptical about procedures now implemented in many states requiring periodic decision-making by mental health professionals (or by others) concerning a requirement that insanity acquittees who have committed previous violent offenses be repetitively adjudicated as "dangerous," thereupon provoking their release once future dangerousness cannot be clearly demonstrated in accord with the standard of proof required.

While there are no easy solutions to these problems, the following are some potential alternatives for the future.

First, the law should recognize that the nature of in-hospital psychiatric intervention has changed over the last decade. Greater emphasis is now placed upon psychopharmacological management of the hospitalized person. Such treatment, while clearly helpful in reducing the overt signs and symptoms of mental illness, does not necessarily mean, however, that "cure" has been achieved—nor that a patient's "nondangerousness" is assured. Continuing, even compelled, psychiatric treatment is often required for this population once the patient is released from the hospital.

Although some insanity acquittees will recover in such facilities, there can be no public guarantee. Therefore, the presumption should be that after initial hospitalization a long period of conditional release with careful supervision and outpatient treatment will be necessary to protect the public and to complete the appropriate treatment programs. Unfortunately, however, many jurisdictions have neither the trained personnel nor appropriate outpatient facilities and resources to provide for such close management of previously violent persons who are conditionally released. Where statutes provide for conditional release and judges allow it without these necessary resources, the public is subjected to great risk and the insanity acquittee is deprived of an opportunity for a necessary phase of treatment.

At any hearing that might order the conditional release of an insanity acquittee, the following questions must be answered affirmatively. Has a coherent and well-structured plan of supervision, management, and treatment been put into place? Is this plan highly likely to guarantee public safety while maximizing the chances for rehabilitation of the insanity acquittee? Are the necessary staff and resources available to implement the plan? Is there in place a procedure to reconfine the insanity acquittee who fails to meet the expectations of the plan?

For some acquittees contingent release is not possible because of the risk to society, the lack of resources, or other relevant legal considerations. Yet because psychiatry has no more to offer the acquittee, continued confinement cannot be justified on therapeutic or psychiatric grounds. When there exists no realistic therapeutic justification for confinement, the psychiatric facility becomes a prison. The American Psychiatric Association believes this hypocrisy must be confronted and remedied. One appropriate alternative is to transfer the locus of responsibility and confinement for such acquittees to a nontreatment facility that can provide the necessary security.

The American Psychiatric Association believes that the decision to release an insanity acquittee should not be made *solely* by psychiatrists or *solely* on the basis of psychiatric testimony about the patient's mental condition or predictions of future dangerousness. While this may not be the only model, such decisions should be made instead by a group similar in composition to a parole board. In this respect, the American Psychiatric Association is impressed with a model program presently in operation in the State of Oregon under the aegis of a Psychiatric Security Review Board.[21, 22] In Oregon a multidisciplinary board is given jurisdiction over insanity acquittees. The board retains control of the insanity acquittee for a period of time as long as the criminal sentence that might have been awarded were the person to have been found guilty of the act. Confinement and release decisions for acquittees are made by an experienced body that is not naive about the nature of violent behavior committed by mental patients and that allows a quasi-criminal approach for managing such persons. Psychiatrists participate in the work of the Oregon board, but they do not have primary responsibility. The Association believes that this is as it should be since the decision to confine and release persons who have done violence to society involves more than psychiatric considerations. The interest of society, the interest of the criminal justice system, and the interest of those who have been or might be victimized by violence must also be addressed in confinement and release decisions.

In line with the above views, the American Psychiatric Association suggests the following guidelines for legislation dealing with the disposition of violent insanity acquittees.

1. Special legislation should be designed for those persons charged with violent offenses who have been found "not guilty by reason of insanity."
2. Confinement and release decisions should be made by a board constituted to include psychiatrists and other professionals representing the criminal justice system—akin to a parole board.
3. Release should be conditional upon having a treatment supervi-

sion plan in place with the necessary resources available to implement it.

4. The board having jurisdiction over released insanity acquittees should have clear authority to reconfine.

5. When psychiatric treatment within a hospital setting has obtained the maximal treatment benefit possible but the board believes that for other reasons confinement is still necessary, the insanity acquittee should be transferred to the most appropriate nonhospital facility.

In general, the American Psychiatric Association favors legislation to identify insanity acquittees who have committed violent acts as a special group of persons who, because of the important societal interests involved, should not be handled similarly to other civil committees.

Although efforts to treat mentally disordered offenders have met with limited success, we should also increase our commitment to developing and implementing new treatment approaches for those adjudicated insane. There are practical as well as humanistic reasons for making this recommendation. A certain number of those who plead insanity will, whatever their disposition, eventually be released to society. To whatever extent their sanity is restored or their capacity to adhere to proper conduct is enhanced, the public will receive that much more protection from crime.

Notes

1. Robitscher J, Haynes AK: In defense of the insanity defense. *Emory Law Journal* 31:9–60. 1982.

2. Low T, Jeffries J, Bonnie R: *Criminal Law: Cases and Materials.* Mineola, NY, Foundation Press, 1982, p. 653.

3. *The Times,* 1843: Cited in Sutcliffe and after (edtl.). *Lancet* 1: 1241–42, l981.

4. Weiner BA: Not guilty by reason of insanity: a sane approach. *Chicago-Kent Law Review* 56: 1057–85, 1980.

5. *Smith* v. *United States,* 36 F 2d 548, 549 DC Cir (1929).

6. *Durham* v. *United States,* 214 F 2d 862 DC Cir (1954).

7. *State* v. *Pike,* 49 NH 399 (1869).

8. *State* v. *Jones,* 50 NH 369 (1871).

9. Pasewark RA: Insanity plea: a review of the research literature. *Journal of Psychiatry & Law* 9: 357–401, 1981.

10. Steadman HJ: Testimony before Subcommittee on Criminal Justice, Committee on the Judiciary, House of Representatives, July 22, 1982.

11. Steadman HJ, Keitner L, Braff J, et al: Factors associated with a successful insanity plea. *Am J Psychiatry* 140: 401–405, 1983.

12. Stone AA: The insanity defense on trial. *Hosp Community Psychiatry* 33: 636–40, 1982.

13. *People* v. *McQuillan.* 392 Mich 511, 221 NW 2d 569 (1974).

14. Criss ML, Racine DR: Impact of change in legal standard for those adjudicated not guilty by reason of insanity 1975–1979. *Bull Am Acad Psychiatry Law* 8: 261–71, 1980.

15. Spitzer RL, Forman JBW, Nee J: *DSM-III* field trials, 1: initial interrater diagnostic reliability. *Am J Psychiatry* 136: 815–17, 1979.

16. Roth LH: *Correctional psychiatry, in Modern Legal Medicine, Psychiatry and Forensic Science.* Edited by Carran W, McGarry AL, Petty C. Philadelphia, FA Davis Co., 1980.

17. Bonnie RJ: The moral basis of the insanity defense. *American Bar Association Journal* 69: 194–97, 1983.

18. *Addington* v. *Texas,* 99 S Ct 1804, 1811 (1979).

19. Shah SA: Some interactions of law and mental health in the handling of social deviance. *Catholic University Law Review* 23: 674–719, 1974.

20. Rabkin JG: Criminal behavior of discharged mental patients: a critical appraisal of the research. *Psychol Bull* 86: 1–27, 1979.

21. Rogers JL: 1981 Oregon legislation relating to the insanity defense and the Psychiatric Security Review Board. *Willamette Law Review* 18: 23–48, 1982.

22. Bloom JL, Bloom JD: Disposition of insanity defense cases in Oregon. *Bull Am Acad Psychiatry Law* 9: 93–99, 1981.

Psychiatry and Responsibility

Lawrie Reznek

[Does] having a mental illness excuse a patient from being responsible for his actions?

MENTAL ILLNESS AND RESPONSIBILITY

When a psychotically depressed mother kills her children because she is convinced they are better off dead, we judge she is not responsible for her actions and excuse her from blame. Similarly for a schizophrenic who kills innocent people because he believes they are hostile Russian agents, for a kleptomaniac who steals a range of objects for which he has no conceivable use, and for an epileptic who strangles someone during a seizure. Can we justify these intuitions? Szasz argues not:

> If "mental illness" is a bona fide illness, then it follows, logically and linguistically, that it must be treated like any other illness. Hence, mental hygiene laws must be repealed. There are no special laws for patients with peptic ulcer or pneumonia; why then should there be special laws for patients with depression or schizophrenia? (Szasz, 1974 p. xii)

Since bodily diseases like pneumonia do not provide excuses for criminal actions like murder, Szasz argues that neither should mental illnesses. Having a disease per se seems unable to excuse someone from responsibility. Jennifer Radden argues that this is the major flaw in the medical paradigm:

From: Lawrie Reznek, *The Philosophical Defence of Psychiatry* (New York: Routledge, 1991).

509

> The failure of the medical model to accommodate our moral intuition that insanity excuses wrong-doing is a neglected aspect of the standard critiques of that model. It is, moreover, the fundamental failing of a disease model. . . . We want to excuse the insane criminal or wrong-doer. Yet if we adopt a medical model we must explain why diseases constitute excuses—and they do not appear to do so. (Radden, 1985, p. 42)

However, I will argue that the medical paradigm is not flawed in this way and that the responsibility thesis is defensible.

In considering whether someone is responsible for his actions, we are guided by the intuition that it is only just to punish those who are responsible for their actions. If our intuitions strongly suggest that we ought not to punish someone, this suggests we do not judge him responsible for his action. It is because we feel it would be unjust to punish the mentally ill offenders described above that we do not consider them responsible for their actions. What we need to do now is to explain why they are not responsible.

Our intuitions suggest that a person is only responsible for his voluntary actions. A voluntary action is an action performed intentionally, and a person is responsible for his actions if he "could have done otherwise." This latter idea is embodied in the policeman test—if a man would have done otherwise had there been a policeman at his elbow, he is responsible for his action. Conversely, a man is not responsible for involuntary actions—i.e., what happens to him. If he has a vaso-vagal attack at the wheel of his car and kills a pedestrian, we do not regard him as responsible because fainting is not a voluntary action. The law recognizes that we are only responsible for voluntary actions (Williams, 1983). If a person kills someone while sleep-walking, he is excused from responsibility because he is judged not to have formed any intent and thereby not to have acted voluntarily.

Our intuitions also suggest that ignorance and compulsion excuse a person from responsibility for his actions (Aristotle, 1955). If a man gives his wife her medicine, and unwittingly administers poison and kills her, he is not responsible for her death. And if a man acts under the threat of death to his family—i.e., under compulsion—then he is not fully responsible for his actions. We cannot expect a reasonable man to act otherwise.

On this basis, it can be shown that mental illnesses excuse. The idea that mental illness excuses because it causes ignorance is reflected in the McNaughton Rules. In 1843, Daniel McNaughton shot and killed Edward Drummond, the private secretary to the prime minister, Sir Robert Peel, mistaking him for the prime minister. He was suffering from the delusion that Peel and others were persecuting him. At his trial,

the defense of insanity was successfully used. The House of Lords justified this decision to Queen Victoria (whose would-be assassin had also
recently been excused on such grounds) with the McNaughton Rules:

> To establish a defence it must on the grounds of insanity, it must be
> conclusively proved that, at the time of the committing of the act, the
> party accused was labouring under such a defect of reason, from the
> disease of the mind, as not to know the nature and quality of the act he
> was doing; or if he did know it, that he did not know what he was
> doing was wrong. (*Regina* v. *McNaughton*, 1843)

To be excused, the person must suffer from a disease of the mind which
causes factual or moral ignorance.

In addition, a mental illness can excuse if it causes "internal compulsion." The law, at least in England and Scotland, admits that a person
can have diminished responsibility:

> Where a person kills or is party to the killing of another, he shall not be
> convicted of murder if he was suffering from such abnormality of mind
> . . . as substantially impaired his mental responsibility for his acts and omis-
> sions in doing so or being a party to the killing. (Homicide Act, 1957)

If a person is compelled to do something because of some mental condition, then he is excused from full responsibility.

On this view, if a person acts because of ignorance or compulsion,
and if mental illness is causally sufficient for this, then the agent is not
responsible for his actions. Or if a person does something while failing
to form an intent, he is not responsible. When a schizophrenic kills
because of a delusion (ignorance), he is not responsible because he is
ignorant of what he does. When a kleptomaniac steals because of some
compulsion, he is not responsible because he would have stolen with
security guards "at his elbow"—he could not have done otherwise.
When an epileptic kills because of a seizure, we excuse him because this
was not a voluntary action.

There are a number of problems with this explanation. First, an
epileptic may know he behaves violently in a psychomotor seizure, and
may voluntarily induce a seizure by flicking his hand back and forth in
front of his eyes in order to be violent. While it is true that, immediately
before the violent act, he is unable to form an intent, he is nevertheless
responsible for his violent action because he *did* form an intent to be violent in this way. Similarly, a schizophrenic may omit his medication
knowing he will come to believe people are merely irritating insects to
be killed. If he kills while laboring under this delusion, he is nevertheless
still responsible because he is responsible for this ignorance.

Second, while the schizophrenic and depressive are ignorant—the former thinks that innocent people are Russian agents and the latter that life for his family will be an endless torment—and while they are not responsible for their illnesses, this ignorance is not sufficient to excuse. To count as an excuse, those actions must be justified if performed *without* ignorance. But if Russian agents had indeed infiltrated society intent on undermining it, killing them would not be justified—he ought to go to the police instead. Similarly, if life was going to be an endless torment for the depressive's family, killing them is not justified—she ought to discuss the matter with them and leave them the choice. Therefore, ignorance cannot provide an excuse here. But we still feel the schizophrenic and the depressive are not responsible.

Third, there are other cases where mental illness excuses but where no ignorance and compulsion can be found. In 1966 a sniper in the University of Texas killed several people. There was little evidence that he was suffering from ignorance or some irresistible impulse, but a brain tumor was found which presumably caused his actions. Jennifer Radden argues that the sniper was either ignorant of the source of his desire to kill, or he was not. If he was ignorant, this ignorance excuses and he was not responsible. If he was not ignorant, then assuming him to be of normal moral constitution, he would have refrained from acting unless the desire was irresistible (Radden, 1985, p. 36).

But this is wrong. First, the ignorance it supposedly causes cannot excuse. While it is true that the sniper does not know that the tumor caused his desire to kill, I am certainly unaware of the physical causes of my desires. But this does not make me ignorant in such a way that I am not responsible for my actions! On this criterion, we will *all* fail to be responsible for our actions. And second, the tumor may still excuse while not causing ignorance or an irresistible impulse. It may have caused personality changes making him have little respect for the lives of others. But Radden feels personality change cannot excuse:

> There is a good reason why we should be reluctant to excuse the criminal action of a person suffering long-term personality change. It is because the element of knowledge would appear to enter critically into this case. . . . Because with knowledge comes foresight and predictive and preventive powers, persons able to understand the disease's role in their motivation and action would be culpable in the same way as the alcoholic and drug addict. They could predict and thus would be held responsible for preventing the illegal actions by avoiding the occasion and means of criminality, or by actively seeking treatment and alleviation for that symptom of their condition. (Radden, 1985, p. 39)

But this is also wrong. A person who has undergone a personality change may not be ignorant of his new character—he may predict that he will kill. But as a result of the personality change, he may not care enough about others any more to be interested in preventing this. We do not regard the sniper as responsible because we feel that it was not *he* who committed these acts.

Another explanation why mental illness excuses argues it does so by causing a pervasive disturbance of rationality:

> Rationality is the fundamental premise by virtue of which we under-stand ourselves as human beings; that is, as creatures capable of adjust-ing their actions as reasonably efficient means to intelligible ends. Being mentally ill means being incapacitated from acting rationally in this fun-damental sense. . . . Why does severely diminished rationality excuse? It is because our notions of who is eligible to be held morally responsible depend on our ability to make out rather regularly practical syllogisms for actions. One is a moral agent only if one is a rational agent. (Moore, 1980, p. 60)

This view has a prima facie plausibility because it can explain why ratio-nal agents are responsible for their actions. A person is rational if he is able to let good reasons determine his beliefs and his actions. The crude policeman test presupposes that if a person is given a sufficiently good reason, embodied in the presence of a policeman at his elbow, not to do something, he will behave otherwise—i.e. the test presupposes rational-ity. Let us see if this irrationality criterion can do better than the tradi-tional view and show how mental illness excuses.

The criterion appears to do better than the reference to ignorance and compulsion. The schizophrenic with the delusion that Russian agents have infiltrated society ought not to have killed them even if his belief was true. Therefore, the ignorance criterion does not work. How-ever, schizophrenia also serves to undermine the agent's reasoning pow-ers such that he may well not have understood that there was any option. Therefore, we ought to excuse him. Similarly, we judge that the depres-sive ought not to have killed her family even if her belief in a bleak future was true. However, we ought to excuse her because severe depression distorts the agent's powers of reasoning such that she might well not have figured there was any alternative. If mental illness so undermines a person's rational faculty that he/she is unable to work out what he/she has most reason to do, then he/she is not responsible for those actions. We judge that the kleptomaniac is not responsible because rationality is undermined by the disorder—he recognizes that he has most reason not to steal, but finds he is unable to be rational. It is because the mental illness undermines his rationality so that he is no longer able to do what he has most reason to do, that we consider the mental illness to be an excuse. Someone is only responsible if he is rational, because only if he is rational is it the case that he could have done otherwise. So all in all, the criterion of irrationality appears to do quite well.

However, it comes into difficulties when it encounters the case of the personality change discussed above. The man undergoing the personality change should be excused from his crimes. However, this was not because the resultant personality was in any way irrational—he simply had radically different desires and concerns. We do not regard the sniper as responsible because he was not responsible for acquiring the tumor which gave him radically different desires and attitudes. While this different personality acted rationally (on the basis of these new desires and attitudes), we think the original person is innocent—it would be a travesty of justice if we were to excise the tumor and then convict him of murder. Therefore this explanation of how mental illness excuses also falters.

Any justification of the excusing property of mental illness must take account of the fact that not all mental illnesses excuse the sufferer from blame. Someone with hypochondriasis is not excused from defrauding an insurance company, and exhibitionism does not provide an excuse for armed robbery. It seems reasonable to conclude that if a mental illness is to excuse, it must be causally related to the behavior it is excusing. This suggests the following argument: from the conceptual premise that if an agent is not responsible for his disease, he is not responsible for the effects of that disease, and the factual premise that an agent is not responsible for his diseases, we can conclude that he is not responsible for any behavior that is the effect of the disease. Is this argument sound?

The factual premise seems true. We are only responsible for voluntary actions and not for what happens to us. But diseases are by definition involuntary processes—i.e., not actions. If disabilities and symptoms were forms of action, being reproducible at will, they would not be symptoms of disease. But since they are not forms of action, we cannot be responsible for them. And hence it appears to follow that we cannot be held responsible for the diseases that we have.

However, the premise is false. There are cases where we *are* responsible for diseases we have. A man who knowingly goes to bed with a woman with gonorrhea *is* responsible for getting the disease. The law recognizes this in its judgement on crimes committed under the influence of alcohol or drugs. Even though it may be the case that one is not responsible for one's actions while under the influence of alcohol or drugs, because one is responsible for putting oneself under the influence of alcohol or drugs, one is responsible for the crimes committed (Williams, 1983). Were this not the case, then a person wishing to commit violence could take a drug like PCP known to cause violent outbursts. But if we amend the factual premise to the assumption that an agent is not responsible for the diseases he has not knowingly caused or failed to treat, then it is true.

The conceptual premise is also false. A man might not be responsible for acquiring diabetes mellitus, but whether he becomes symptomatic depends on whether he takes insulin. Knowing that his symptoms depend on his taking insulin, if he refuses to take his insulin, becoming comatose at the wheel of his car and killing a cyclist, he *is* responsible.

It is only where diseases are not knowingly caused, and where the causal relationship between the disease and the effects is one of causal sufficiency, that the premise seems true. If the disease is causally sufficient for the behavior, then the agent is not responsible for it. This is because there is no room for the agent to intervene to prevent the occurrence of this behavior. In the diabetes case, there *is* room for this intervention—the diabetes is only necessary for a coma—and hence the agent remains responsible. Thus we have a justification why mental illness excuses—if a mental illness was not knowingly caused, and is causally sufficient for some behavior, then the agent is not responsible for that behavior.

But this requirement is too strong. The relationship between mental illness and the "resulting" behavior is not one of causal sufficiency. Rather, the disease in most cases is only necessary for the behavior. For example, schizophrenia may be sufficient for abnormal beliefs, but is not sufficient for the resulting action—e.g., it may be sufficient for the belief that Russian agents have infiltrated society, but is not sufficient for the action—this depends on other factors like the desire to rid society of such agents. Because the mental illness is only a necessary condition for the behavior, we cannot explain why it excuses with this argument. There may be mental illnesses, like temporal lobe epilepsy, where the disorder is sufficient for the automatic behavior during a seizure, and where such a justification applies. But there are many more where this justification will fail to apply.

We need an explanation why the schizophrenic is responsible while the diabetic is not when in both cases the disease is necessary for the behavior. We need an explanation why a disease that causes a new desire (to kill) in the sniper undermines his responsibility, but the disease of TB that causes anger towards the state for not improving living standards (responsible for the disease) and subsequent terrorist activity does not undermine responsibility. We also need an explanation why the man who induces a psychomotor seizure is responsible. Finally, we need an explanation why the kleptomaniac who acts irrationally is not responsible, while someone who chooses irrationally to fulfill a dare to steal is responsible.

The explanation lies with the notion of autonomy. Someone is responsible only if he is autonomous—if his actions are *fully* voluntary—and diseases can undermine autonomy. Someone is autonomous if he determines his own life without interference. To expand, we must understand what it is for *him* to determine his life. For the self to determine his life, he must act rationally in accordance with his own desires. If a man acts because of a post-hypnotic suggestion, we do not think that he acts autonomously— it is not *he* who acts. Generalizing, we regard alien desires—i.e., desires acquired in abnormal ways, like hypnosis or disease—as undermining autonomy. If a man acts in a drugged state with his rational faculty undermined, we do not take him to be autonomous. In addition, factors that undermine the agent's rationality, such as impulse disorders or addictions, also undermine autonomy. Finally, outside pressures such as coercion undermine autonomy. Any notion that hopes to explain why an agent is responsible must explain why we should only praise or blame him. And the notion of autonomy does just this. If an agent acts because of alien desires, or because his rationality is undermined, or because he is being coerced, it is not *he* who is acting. Only when the self determines his actions do we consider it fair to praise or blame him.

Thus we can hypothesize that it is only where disease undermines autonomy that it can excuse the person from responsibility. In the TB case, the formation of the new desire (for justice) occurs in the normal way—the agent perceives that someone has caused his TB and desires retribution. Although the disease causes the desire, it does so *in a normal way*—the new desire is not alien and therefore autonomy is not undermined. But in the case of the sniper, the new desire (to kill others) is *not* caused in a normal sort of way—the disease directly causes the desire without the agent accurately perceiving he has a new need—his new desire is alien. For this reason his autonomy is undermined. In fact, the change most calculated to undermine autonomy is personality change—if an alien process produces a new set of desires and attitudes, then it is no longer the (original) self who determines his future. In the case of the schizophrenic, the new belief is caused in an abnormal way— it is not acquired on the basis of the available evidence because the disease has undermined rationality. Hence autonomy has been undermined. While in the diabetes case, the desire (to acquire symptoms) *is* formed in a normal way, and hence he is responsible for the death. Similarly for the epileptic who induces his seizure. The kleptomaniac has his rationality undermined by his illness in that he is unable to stop himself doing what he recognizes he has most reason not to do—his action is not determined by normal rational deliberation and autonomy is undermined. While the person acting on the dare, though irrational, is acting after rational deliberation (to take the risk). To illustrate:

Epilepsy Case:
Disease—A→Action

Not autonomous
Not responsible

Self-induced Epilepsy Case:
Desire + Belief—N→Disease—A→Action

Autonomous
Responsible

Sniper Case:
Disease—A→Desire, + Belief—N→Action

Not autonomous
Not responsible

TB Case:
Disease—N→Desire, + Belief—N→Action

Autonomous
Responsible

Schizophrenia Case:
Disease—A→Belief, + Desire—N→Action

Not autonomous
Not responsible

Kleptomania Case:
Desire + Belief + Disease—A→Action

Not autonomous
Not responsible

Dare Case:
Desire + Belief—N→Action

Autonomous
Responsible

| —N→ | = | causes in normal way |
| —A→ | = | causes in abnormal way |

While this is probably an oversimplification, it illustrates that only if behavior is determined in a certain way (by rational deliberation on desires and beliefs normally formed) will the agent be responsible.

It might be considered odd that one sort of cause undermines responsibility while another does not. But this is the only reasonable position to take. Being responsible is not a matter of actions being uncaused—if they had no causes, we would have no control over them. We would find ourselves stealing when we had no good reason, and this would hardly be a state of affairs where we would be responsible. Being responsible is a matter of one's actions being caused *in a certain way*—by reasons caused in the right sort of way. Only if our actions are under the control of reasons normally formed are we responsible. This entails that if our actions fall under the control of other sorts of processes, we cease to be responsible. And this is precisely the position we have arrived at.

Thus the responsibility thesis is defensible. And there *is* a logical connection between mental illness and responsibility. Diseases can undermine autonomy, and autonomy is required for responsibility. Hence we can explain why diseases excuse a person from responsibility. QED.

References

Aristotle (1955), *Ethics,* Harmondsworth, Penguin.

Moore, M. (1980), "Legal conceptions of mental illness," in B. Brody and T. Engelhardt (eds.), *Mental Illness: Law and Public Policy,* Dordrecht, Reidel, pp. 25–69.

Radden, J. (1985), *Madness and Reason,* London, George Allen & Unwin.

Regina v. *McNaughton* (1843), *English Reports,* 718: 722–23.

Szasz, T. (1974), *Law, Liberty, and Psychiatry,* London, Routledge.

Williams, G. (1983), *Textbook of Criminal Law,* London, Stevens & Son.

The Nature of Competency to Stand Trial

A. Louis McGarry

To be fit for trial, it is assumed that a person must have minimal effective and cognitive resources available to him to assume the role of a defendant in court. Lacking these resources, the individual would be deprived of his due process right to testify in his own defense, to confront witnesses against him, and to maintain an effective *psychological presence* in court beyond his mere physical presence there. The issue of competency is thus an essentially legal issue, not a psychiatric issue. The criteria for competency to stand trial are concerned with the protection of the individual in the criminal system in order that he may be assured of a fair trial. No other area of the person's physical or emotional health is an issue. Whether or not the person has physical or psychological defects is irrelevant except to the extent that they substantially interfere with fitness for trial.

The common law criteria for competency are defined as (1) an ability to cooperate with one's attorney in one's own defense, (2) an awareness and understanding of the nature and object of the proceedings, (3) an understanding of the consequences of the proceedings. Within the framework of these criteria, a judgment must be made as to whether an accused person should stand trial without undue delay or whether the trial should be deferred until such time as the accused shall meet a minimal standard based on these criteria.

The determination of competency in the broadest sense must be

From *Competency to Stand Trial and Mental Illness,* Department of Health, Education, and Welfare publication no. (HSM) 73–9105, 1973. Copyright © 1973 by A. Louis McGarry. Reprinted by permission of the author.

based on some evaluation of these criteria. It must be a prediction because the judgment of the actual performance of the defendant in the role of defendant has not occurred. An assessment of the defendant's ability to perform adequately at his trial must be made by individuals considered most expert to evaluate fitness for trial.

It is important that the assessment or evaluation of the defendant be made with a clear understanding of the requirements of the legal system. Psychological evaluation must be directed toward determining how well the individual will be able to meet the minimum requirements of the three common law criteria for competency. Issues such as legal responsibility for the offense or possibility of rehabilitation are not relevant considerations. Also, mental illness or pathology per se are not equivalent to incapacity to stand trial, although such matters may be involved in a determination of competency.

The test which follows has been developed for the purpose of quickly screening defendants in order to make recommendations regarding their competency to stand trial.

COMPETENCY TO STAND TRIAL ASSESSMENT INSTRUMENT

	Total	Severe	Moderate	Mild	None	Unratable
			Degree of Incapacity			
1. Appraisal of available legal defenses	1	2	3	4	5	6
2. Unmanageable behavior	1	2	3	4	5	6
3. Quality of relating to attorney	1	2	3	4	5	6
4. Planning of legal strategy, including guilty plea to lesser charges where pertinent	1	2	3	4	5	6
5. Appraisal of role of:						
a. Defense counsel	1	2	3	4	5	6
b. Prosecuting attorney	1	2	3	4	5	6
c. Judge	1	2	3	4	5	6
d. Jury	1	2	3	4	5	6
e. Defendant	1	2	3	4	5	6
f. Witnesses	1	2	3	4	5	6
6. Understanding of court procedure	1	2	3	4	5	6
7. Appreciation of charges	1	2	3	4	5	6
8. Appreciation of range and nature of possible penalties	1	2	3	4	5	6
9. Appraisal of likely outcome	1	2	3	4	5	6
10. Capacity to disclose to attorney available pertinent facts surrounding the offense including the defendant's movements, timing, mental state, actions at the time of the offense	1	2	3	4	5	6

COMPETENCY TO STAND TRIAL ASSESSMENT INSTRUMENT (CONTINUED)

11. Capacity to realistically challenge prosecution witness	1	2	3	4	5	6
12. Capacity to testify relevantly	1	2	3	4	5	6
13. Self-defeating v. self-serving motivation (legal sense)	1	2	3	4	5	6

Examinee _____ Examiner _____

Date _____

The instrument which this code book describes was designed to improve communication between the behavioral science disciplines (particularly psychiatry) and the law in an area of mutual responsibility—the determination of competency to stand trial. Prior attempts at such communication have suffered from the understandable tendency of each of these disciplines to adhere to the language and concepts of their own discipline. Thus the findings of the clinician have not been delivered in a form and language which are appropriate to the needs of the court. Insofar as clinical opinion has been delivered to the courts in this area, it has tended to be global, conclusional, and not substantiated by relevant clinical data.

We sought, therefore, to develop an instrument which delivered clinical opinion to the court in language, form, and substance sufficiently common to the disciplines involved to provide a basis for adequate and relevant communication. The purpose of the instrument is to standardize, objectify, and quantify the relevant criteria for competency to stand trial.

The instrument may be described as a series of thirteen functions related to an accused's ability to cope with the trial process in an adequately self-protective fashion. These functions or items were culled from appellate cases, the legal literature, and our clinical and courtroom experience. The total series is intended to cover all possible grounds for a finding of incompetency. The weight which the court may be expected to assign to one or another of the items will not be equal, nor is it intended to be. Neither will the weight assigned to a given item by the court in reaching a finding on competency for a particular defendant necessarily apply to the next defendant. For example, in the court's view, it may be far more critical to the defense of a particular defendant that he be able to "testify relevantly" than for another defendant whose attorney does not intend to put him on the stand. Consideration of the weight to be assigned a given item in the case of the particular defendant goes beyond the scope of what should be expected of the examining clinician. The task for the clinician is the providing of objective data, the import of which is the responsibility of the court.

This instrument is designed to reflect the competency status of a defendant at the time of examination. It is not a predictive instrument. Our experience indicates that with the passage of time and variations in clinical status, even from day to day, a given defendant will vary in the scores attained. This is particularly true of patient-defendants recovering from an acute psychosis.

It is important to note at the onset that the inability to function indicated by low scores on this instrument must arise from mental illness and/or mental retardation and not, for example, from ideological motivation. When there is doubt as to its connection with abnormal and mental processes, the item should not be scored and it should be indicated that the opinion does not reach reasonable clinical certainty on the particular item.

At the very least, individual items which are scored at one or two (out of a scale of five) should be substantiated by diagnostic and clinical data of adequate richness to establish a serious degree of mental illness or retardation and the manner in which such disability relates to the low degree of functioning in the particular item.

It should be noted that defendants with mental disability of a serious degree, including psychosis and moderate mental retardation, frequently are quite competent and may achieve high scores on any or all of the items. Mental disability is relevant to a competency determination only insofar as it is manifested by malfunctioning in one or more of the specific items of the instrument.

In the scoring of this instrument a basic assumption is that the accused will be adequately aided by counsel. A second basic assumption is that the professional who is using this instrument has at least a basic understanding of and experience in the realities of the criminal justice system.

Each item in the instrument is scaled from 1 to 5 ranging from "total incapacity" at one to "no incapacity" at five. If the instrument is used for outpatient or in-court screening purposes, a majority or a substantial accumulation of scores of three or lower in the thirteen items could be regarded as grounds for a period of inpatient observation and more intensive workup.

In our experience with patient-defendants who are in good contact, the examination and scoring, using this instrument, usually does not require more than one hour. Grossly psychotic or passive, concrete and under-responsive defendants obviously may require more extended examination. Care should be taken not to resort to leading questions.

The device of offering two or three alternative choices to such defendants has been found to be useful. . . .

A score of *one* on the instrument indicates that for the item scored a close to or total lack of capacity to function exists of the order of a mute or incoherent person or a severe retardate.

A score of *two* indicates that for the item scored there is severely impaired functioning and a substantial question of adequacy for the particular function.

A score of *three* indicates that there is moderately impaired functioning and a question of adequacy for the particular function.

A score of *four* indicates that for the item scored there is mildly impaired functioning and little question of adequacy for the particular function. An individual can be mildly impaired on the basis of lack of experience in the legal process or sociocultural deprivation with or without attendant psychic pathology.

A score of *five* indicates that for the item scored there is no impairment and no question that the defendant can function adequately for the particular function.

A score of *six* indicates that the available data do not permit a rating which is within reasonable clinical certainty. . . .

Right of a Defendant to Refuse Antipsychotic Medication during a Criminal Trial

Karl G. Williams

A criminal defendant has the right to refuse or be free from antipsychotic medication during the trial process unless the prosecution can prove an "overriding justification" for its use. The United States Supreme Court in *Riggins* v. *Nevada* (112 S.Ct. 1810 [1992]) requires state courts to make a detailed showing that antipsychotic medication is medically appropriate and essential for the defendant's safety or the safety of others and that the state (prosecution) has exhausted the alternatives that are less intrusive than compelled medication.

Background

David Riggins was arrested shortly after the November 1987 stabbing death of Paul Wade. Following his arrest, Riggins complained to a prison psychiatrist about hearing "voices." The psychiatrist, after learning of Riggins's prior successful treatment with thioridazine, prescribed therapy with thioridazine 100 mg per day. The problem persisted and the daily dose was gradually increased to a peak of 800 mg in divided doses.

In January 1988, Riggins was receiving thioridazine 450 mg per day. During a hearing to determine Riggins's competence to stand trial, psychiatrists presented conflicting testimony about Riggins's ability to understand the processes of his criminal trial and to work effectively with counsel in his defense. In a brief order that provided little insight into the reasoning involved, the judge found Riggins legally sane and competent to stand trial.

From *American Journal of Hospital Pharm.* 50 (1993): 1937–38. Copyright © 1993, American Society of Health-System Pharmacists, Inc. All rights reserved. Reprinted by permission.

Riggins was charged by the state prosecutor with murder and robbery with the use of a deadly weapon. He pleaded not guilty by reason of insanity. Conviction for any crime requires that the defendant not only commit the act but also have the intent to commit the act. The defense reasoned that because Riggins was insane at the time of the crime, he was unable to form the mental intent required for conviction.

Because thioridazine therapy affected Riggins's mental state, appearance, and demeanor, his attorneys made a motion to have it discontinued. In theory, the medication could hinder the defendant's ability to assert the insanity defense by making him look and act relaxed (or even somnolent) rather than psychotic. Because of its depressant effect, thioridazine was argued to interfere with Riggins's ability to communicate with his attorneys, understand and react to testimony presented, and understand the procedural events of the trial. Together, these alterations amounted to the deprivation of his right under the Sixth Amendment to the U.S. Constitution to a full and fair trial. Forced medication would also deprive Riggins of a significant "liberty" interest under the due process clause of the Fourteenth Amendment—the right to make personal medical decisions.

The trial court held a hearing on the motion to discontinue the thioridazine therapy. Four psychiatrists were asked whether Riggins would be unable to function competently in the trial process without medication. Two of the experts were uncertain, one stated Riggins's competence would not be affected, and one thought Riggins would become incompetent to stand trial. The judge, again with little explanation, denied the motion to discontinue therapy.

Riggins was tried and found guilty of murder and robbery with the use of a deadly weapon. The jury imposed the death penalty. The defense appealed on the grounds that denying the motion to discontinue thioridazine had deprived the defendant of due process and unfairly prejudiced him at trial. The Supreme Court of Nevada denied the appeal, upholding Riggins's conviction and sentence. Because the appellate arguments were based in part on rights under the Constitution, the defendant sought review by the U.S. Supreme Court. The court decided to hear the case because of the novel question posed: What are the dimensions of the inquiry required of a state court in assessing a criminal defendant's right to refuse antipsychotic medication?

Court case

The U.S. Supreme Court decided that the approach of the Nevada courts was inadequate to protect Riggins's constitutional rights and reversed his conviction by a majority of seven to two. Justice Sandra Day

O'Connor wrote the majority opinion. Her review focused on the nature of the trial court's inquiry and ruling on the motion to discontinue thioridazine therapy. She addressed the question of how a trial court should weigh the criminal defendant's constitutional interest in being free from antipsychotic medication against the state's interest in bringing accused criminals to trial. O'Connor cited a recent case, *Washington v. Harper* (494 U.S. 210 [1990]), as a framework for analyzing the facts presented in *Riggins*.

The question raised in *Harper* regarded the circumstances under which the administrators of a prison could override an inmate's (Harper's) right to refuse antipsychotic medication. In *Harper* the court held that because of the high frequency and often alarming nature of adverse effects from phenothiazine-like agents, the prisoner's Fourteenth Amendment liberty interest required an "overriding justification and determination of medical appropriateness" before antipsychotic medication could be compelled. In the *Riggins* opinion, O'Connor concluded that "the Fourteenth Amendment affords at least as much protection to persons the state detains for trial." Therefore the trial court in *Riggins* had to require the prosecution to prove that the thioridazine was medically appropriate and essential for the safety of the defendant or others. Since the trial court had not done this, the "substantial probability of trial prejudice" required reversal of Riggins's conviction and retrial.

O'Connor refused to decide the most controversial question raised by this case: Would a criminal defendant be allowed to refuse antipsychotic medication if that would make him or her legally incompetent to stand trial? The issue had not been addressed fully by the lower courts, and the defense had failed to argue the position that the constitutional right to be free of antipsychotic medication overrides the state's fundamental interest in bringing an accused criminal to trial. Because of the incomplete record, the issue of whether "synthetic competence" (a phrase used in the concurring opinion by Justice Anthony Kennedy that means behavior modified by pharmaceuticals to the extent that a court could be persuaded that there exists competence to stand trial) could be compelled by the prosecution was not properly presented and could not be decided.

Although he concurred with the majority, Kennedy, who wrote the *Harper* opinion (in which the prison inmate's right to refuse was allowed to be overridden), presented his view of the propriety of using involuntary medication to restore or maintain competence to stand trial. He agreed with O'Connor that the trial court record did not allow complete review of this issue but thought that it was unlikely that a state could satisfy the evidentiary burden required "given our present understanding of the properties of these drugs." The burden a state prosecutor must overcome is much more substantial than that of the prison officials in *Harper* because the "functional competence" the prison officials sought to restore in inmate Harper was much less than the competence required to stand trial. Because of the poorly understood adverse effects of phenothiazines and related drugs, Kennedy doubted that it could be shown that the defendant could work effectively with counsel or escape the unfair prejudice resulting from alterations in behavior and demeanor.

Justice Clarence Thomas, joined in part by Justice Antonin Scalia, wrote a dissenting opinion that upheld the Nevada courts. He argued that the defendant did not prove that he was actually prejudiced by the trial court's action. (O'Connor addressed this position in the majority opinion, saying that trying to prove prejudice would be "futile" and "guesswork.") In a section of the dissenting opinion that Scalia refused to join, Thomas also suggested that treatment was not forced on Riggins simply because the trial court denied the motion to discontinue it. Finally, Thomas took issue with the remedy of reversing Riggins's conviction; assuming there was a violation of the defendant's constitutional rights, separate civil remedies were available and Riggins should be satisfied with those, Thomas reasoned.

Comment

A federal constitutional right to refuse antipsychotic medication with phenothiazine derivatives was first elucidated in the late 1970s (*Rennie v. Klein*, 462 F. Supp. 1131 [D.N.J. 19 78] and *Rogers v. Okin*, 478 F. Supp. 1342 [D. Mass. 1979]). This right was based on a fundamental privacy interest firmly established in the common-law regulation of medicine—self-determination in medical care. (If a patient was given a medical treatment to which he or she did not consent, the patient could sue the physician for battery. Today the tort of negligent nondisclosure is the more likely basis of action for failure to obtain informed consent.) As early cases dealing with the right to refuse progressed from the trial courts through the appeals process, the dimensions of the right to refuse under federal law became attenuated, less sweeping, and poorly defined.

With *Riggins* and *Harper,* the proposition that there is a right to refuse under the U.S. Constitution has been be firmly established. It arises from the due process clause of the Fourteenth Amendment, which says, "no person shall be deprived of life, liberty or property without due process of law." Because this language is not self-defining, however, the dimensions of the liberty interest as it relates to the right to refuse antipsychotic medication are unclear.

One way to understand the outcomes of *Riggins* and *Harper* is to consider the status of the defendant. Harper was a convicted prison inmate and Riggins was an accused criminal. Harper's liberty interest was less compelling than the state's interest in the efficient operation of the prison. The court ruled that Harper's due process rights were satisfied by the prison's internal review. Riggins was entitled to review by a court because of society's need to protect the trial process. Neither decision was deduced from the liberty interest of the defendant, although the court seems to have said that the right to refuse antipsychotic medication is something different from the right to refuse "ordinary" medication.

In her *Riggins* opinion, O'Connor interpreted *Harper* as requiring an "overriding justification and a determination of medical appropriateness" before a hospital prison inmate could be compelled to take antipsychotic medication. This analysis of the inmate's liberty interest is an advance in interpretation from the *Harper* opinion itself, which offered very little guidance. In an effort to further define the issues, Kennedy wrote an unusual and enlightening concurring opinion in *Riggins* that addressed a question not before the Court. The question was about the state's power to use antipsychotic medication to restore or maintain a defendant's competency to stand trial.

Article III, Section 2 of the U.S. Constitution provides that "judicial power shall extend" to various "cases" and "controversies." Over the years this has been construed to mean that the federal courts (including the Supreme Court) are powerless to find an act of government, such as a criminal conviction, unconstitutional outside the context of a properly presented question. An issue is said to lack "ripeness" if it is not presented and argued in the context of a fully litigated case or controversy. The question of the synthetic competence of Riggins to stand trial could not be decided because it was not ripe for review.

Kennedy's opinion on synthetic competence, which he wrote despite the issue's lack of ripeness, showed an understanding of pharmacology and toxicology of phenothiazines, an appreciation for the lack of sufficient medical knowledge about these agents, and an awareness of their contribution to society. He doubted that it was possible that a state prosecutor could show, with the medical certainty required to protect the institution of trial, that a defendant being treated with antipsychotic medication would be able to work with counsel or participate in the defense. In other words, a criminal defendant who is found incompetent to stand trial without medication would probably be incompetent with medication.

An accused murderer who becomes functionally competent will probably not be released because of the magnitude of the crime, but neither will he or she be allowed to waive the high standard of competence articulated by Kennedy (112 S.Ct. 1810, 1817) to stand trial. This hypothetical situation creates a "limbo" for the accused. Kennedy believes that this limbo, which requires keeping incompetent defendants in mental health facilities, "is a burden that must be borne by society to protect the integrity of the trial process." The accused patient bears a substantial burden as well.

The *Riggins* decision did not establish principles about the right to refuse antipsychotic medication. While drug policymakers wait for another case involving involuntary treatment with antipsychotic medication to come along and wind its way through hearings, trial, and the appellate process, the Court has signaled, through Kennedy, that it is educated about this class of medication and takes a very jaundiced view of its involuntary use.

Suggestions for Further Reading

General Discussions

Appelbaum, Paul S., "Forensic Psychiatry: The Need for Self-Regulation." *Bulletin of the American Academy of Psychiatry and Law* 20, no. 2 (1992): 153–62.

Bursztajn, Harold J., Albert E. Scherr, and Archie Brodsky, "The Rebirth of Forensic Psychiatry in Light of Recent Historical Trends in Criminal Responsibility." *Psychiatric Clinics of North America* 17 (Sept. 1994): 611–35.

Committee on Ethical Guidelines for Forensic Psychologists, "Specialty Guidelines for Forensic Psychologists." *Law and Human Behavior* 15 (1991): 655–65.

Rappeport, Jonas, "Ethics and Forensic Psychiatry." In Sidney Bloch and Paul Chodoff, *Psychiatraic Ethics,* 2d ed. New York: Oxford University Press, 1991, ch. 18.

Responsibility and the Insanity Defense

Appelbaum, Paul S., *Almost a Revolution: Mental Health and the Limits of Change.* New York: Oxford University Press, 1994, ch. 5.

Appelbaum, Paul S., and Alexander Greer, "Who's On Trial? Multiple Personalities and the Insanity Defense." *Hospital and Community Psychiatry* 45, no. 10 (1994): 965–66.

Bayer, Ronald, "The Insanity Defense in Retreat." *Hastings Center Report* (December 1983): 13–16.

Bumby, Kurt M., "Reviewing the Guilty but Mentally Ill Alternative: A Case of the Blind 'Pleading' the Blind." *The Journal of Psychiatry and Law* 21 (Summer 1993): 191–217.

Elliot, Carl, "Moral Responsibility, Psychiatric Disorders and Duress." *Journal of Applied Philosophy* 7, no. 2 (1990): 203–13.

Fields, L., "Blameworthiness, Insanity and Diminished Responsibility." *International Journal of Moral and Social Studies* 7, no. 2 (1992): 139–52.

Fingarette, Herbert, and Hasse, Ann Fingarette, *Mental Disabilities and Criminal Responsibility*. Berkeley, Calif.: University of California Press, 1979.

Gaylin, Willard, *The Killing of Bonnie Garland: A Question of Justice*. New York: Simon & Schuster, 1982.

Grisso, T., *Evaluating Competencies: Forensic Assessments and Instruments*. New York: Plenum Books, 1986.

Halpern, Abraham L., "Misuse of Post-Acquittal Hospitalization for Punitive Purposes." *Psychiatric Annals* 22 (November 1992): 561–65.

Moore, Michael S., *Law and Psychiatry: Rethinking the Relationship*. New York: Cambridge University Press, 1984.

Morse, S., "Failed Explanations and Criminal Responsibility." *Virginia Law Review* 68 (1982): 971–1084.

Roberts, Caton F., and Stephen L. Golding, "The Social Construction of Criminal Responsibility and Insanity." *Law and Human Behavior* 15, no. 4 (1991): 349–76.

Reznek, Lawrie, *The Philosophical Defence of Psychiatry*. London: Routledge, 1991, ch. 12.

Rylchlak, Joseph F., and Ronald J. Rylchlak, "The Insanity Defense and the Question of Human Agency." *New Ideas in Psychology* 8, no. 1 (1990): 3–24.

Stone, Alan A., "The Insanity Defense on Trial." *Hospital and Community Psychiatry* 33 (August 1982): 636–40.

Weiner, Barbara A., "Mental Disability and the Criminal Law." In Samuel J. Brakel, John Parry, and Barbara A. Weiner, *The Mentally Disabled and the Law*. Chicago: American Bar Foundation, 1985, ch. 12, part 3.

Competence to Stand Trial, Chemical Sanity

Byers, Keith A., "Incompetency, Execution, and the Use of Antipsychotic Drugs." *Arkansas Law Review* 47, no. 2 (1994): 361–91.

Dixon, Jennifer L., "The Right of the Mentally Ill to Refuse Antipsychotic Drugs During Trial." *New England Journal on Criminal and Civil Confinement* 19 (Winter 1993): 373–95.

Domb, Brian, "A New Twist in the War on Drugs: The Constitutional Right of a Mentally Ill Criminal Defendant To Refuse Antipsychotic Medication That Would Make Him Competent To Stand Trial." *Medical Trial Technique Quarterly* 40, no. 1 (1993): 57–101.

Grisso, T., *Competency to Stand Trial Evaluations: A Manual for Practice*. Sarasota, Fl.: Professional Resource Exchange, 1988.

Yandell, Christi, "The Case Against Forced Administration of Antipsychotic Drugs to Induce Competency to Stand Trial." *American Journal of Criminal Law* 21 (1994): 311–19.

Weiner, Barbara A., "Mental Disability and the Criminal Law." In Samuel J. Brakel, John Parry, and Barbara A. Weiner, *The Mentally Disabled and the Law*. Chicago: American Bar Foundation, 1985, ch. 12, part 2.

Expert Witnesses

Appelbaum, Paul S., "The Parable of the Forensic Psychiatrist: Ethics and the Problem of Doing Harm." *International Journal of Law and Psychiatry* 13 (1990): 249–59.

Faust, D., and J. Ziskin, "The Expert Witness in Psychology and Psychiatry." *Science* 241 (1988): 31–35.

Hambacher, William O., "Expert Witnessing: Guidelines and Practical Suggestions." *American Journal of Forensic Psychology* 12, no. 2 (1994): 17–35.

Healy, Francis B., "Is Psychological Evidence 'Expert'?" *Forensic Psychology* 5 (1993): 17–34.

7.

ETHICAL ISSUES IN CUSTODIAL CARE AND DEINSTITUTIONALIZATION

INTRODUCTION

What quality of life and of medical care are available to mental hospital patients, and how do these compare to resources available to them outside the mental hospital? The meaningless routines and non-therapeutic environment of understaffed and underfinanced custodial care institutions as they existed in the third quarter of the twentieth century are well understood, and they represent a low mark against which more modern and progressive psychiatric institutions can measure their progress. Unfortunately, despite all efforts at reform, institutions or wards providing little more than minimal custodial care are still to be found. Mental illness is not a high-status, high-priority illness like cancer or heart disease, and our society is unwilling to spend the money necessary for adequate mental health treatment and research.

Institutionalization of persons alleged to be mentally deficient or disturbed reached its peak in the United States during the late 1950s and early 1960s. By 1980 patient populations in mental hospitals had been reduced by more than two-thirds as a result of a nationwide emphasis on returning mental patients to "the community," which turned out in practice to be any place (including other kinds of institutions) outside mental hospitals.

Accounting for Deinstitutionalization

What really lies behind the emphasis on deinstitutionalization? Many considerations explain it. Beginning with the discovery of thorazine in

533

1952, the introduction of new, powerful, and effective drugs in the mid-fifties helped to revolutionize the care and maintenance of psychiatric patients both inside and outside mental institutions. The antipsychiatric crusaders who so persistently called attention to the often horrible living conditions and flagrant violations of the moral and civil rights of mental hospital patients also had a significant consciousness-raising effect. The public came to realize more and more that mental hospitals were being used and abused as warehouses or dumping grounds for unwanted people who had no business being in mental hospitals in the first place.

Economics was probably the most effective impetus behind deinstitutionalization. As we saw earlier, judicial decisions mandating that involuntary patients be treated or released resulted more often than not in release; even minimal treatment was deemed too expensive. Although incredibly cheap compared to other hospitals, public mental hospitals are costly to taxpayers. Saving money for taxpayers, or at least making taxpayers think they are saving money, largely explains deinstitutionalization.

Statistics on reductions in patient populations are deceptive. It is not true that hundreds of thousands of persons released from mental hospitals since the 1960s lived independently afterwards and actively enjoyed all the freedoms of democracy and the amenities of middle class existence. Most deinstitutionalization was reinstitutionalization in nursing homes, smaller community mental health centers and hospitals, group homes, foster homes, cheap welfare hotels, missions, flophouses, jails, prisons, and reformatories. The deinstitutionalization process coincided with a national effort to separate the mentally ill from the mentally retarded, and thousands released from mental hospitals were promptly reinstitutionalized in newly built facilities for the mentally retarded. When institutionalization reached its peak in the late fifties and early sixties, 1 percent of our population was institutionalized. After deinstitutionalization ran its course, the figure was still 1 percent.

The economic statistics of deinstitutionalization are also extremely misleading. The new institutions into which former mental hospital patients were shifted also cost money, but the federal government pays the bills through Medicare and Medicaid in nursing homes, psychiatric units of general hospitals, and for an initial period in regional mental health centers. For the most part, city, county, and state governments pay for public mental hospitals. The real game of deinstitutionalization was to transfer mental patients into programs that federal funds would finance. This permitted mayors, state governors, and legislators to boast of enormous savings in local and state tax dollars—while hoping that voters were too obtuse to comprehend that taxpayers still pay the bills after the burden has been shifted to the federal level.

Perhaps deinstitutionalization resulted in some savings to taxpayers where patients returned to live with families, friends, or on the streets. Even here the federal government pays much of the costs through Medicaid if they get sick and through Supplemental Security Income checks for the disabled. Many patients try to exist "independently" on $458 or so per month (a 1995 figure that increases slightly each year) from such checks by living in rundown welfare hotels or foster homes. In return for this sum, these residences provide the basic necessities (food, lodging, and fuel) and still attempt to make a reasonable profit. Obviously, the quality of service bought by these limited funds is low indeed; and it is no small wonder that many patients prefer mental hospitals to the diminished quality of life and of medical care that deinstitutionalization offers. Jonathan Borus noted in 1981, "The state hospital took responsibility not only for mental-health care but also for the patient's housing, food, finances, medical care, medications, work activities, and social relations. The deinstitutionalized patient's limited abilities to cope are often overwhelmed when he or she is forced to seek these types of care from multiple, uncoordinated community agencies."

This section's article by Paul S. Appelbaum explores and deplores deinstitutionalization and indicates that neither the ethical ideal of promoting the rational autonomy of mental patients nor the economic goal of saving government money has been well served by deinstitutionalization.

Many mental hospital patients have good reasons for wanting to remain where they are, or to return to hospitalization after a short and frustrating taste of freedom. Some lawyers and most antipsychiatrists find the thought unthinkable, but thousands of mental patients, "crazy but not stupid," review their realistic options and choose hospitalization. In fact, many homeless or otherwise miserable, involuntarily deinstitutionalized patients "act out" deliberately with violent behavior so that they can meet readmission requirements; thus, the dangerousness requirement actually encourages dangerousness!

The intense coercion to which involuntary mental patients are subjected when hospitalized has received much scrutiny, but the era of deinstitutionalization also brought intense and problematic coercion to bear upon the discharge process. If it is a morally objectionable violation of rational autonomy to institutionalize persons against their will, why is it not equally objectionable to deinstitutionalize them against their will? Should they be coerced to assume responsibility for managing their own lives when they do not wish to be autonomous? If the state has spent years creating institutional dependence, has it incurred an obligation to support what it has created when institutional life is preferred to freedom? How much pressure should be exerted to persuade individuals to go who do not wish to leave, especially those with passive, dependent personalities who find institutionalization so appealing? Have taxpayers any rights against "freeloaders" on the safety net system who are capable of functioning outside public hospitals but who repeatedly "act out" to forestall dismissal or regain admission? What quality of life and of medical care are such persons entitled to receive at public expense? Mental health professionals must answer such difficult questions every working day; society has provided them with no clear ethical guidelines for doing so.

Crazy in the Streets

Paul S. Appelbaum

I

They are an inescapable presence in urban America. In New York City they live in subway tunnels and on steam grates, and die in cardboard boxes on windswept street corners. The Los Angeles City Council has opened its chambers to them, allowing them to seek refuge from the Southern California winter on its hard marble floors. Pioneer Square in Seattle, Lafayette Park in Washington, the old downtown in Atlanta have all become places of refuge for these pitiable figures, so hard to tell apart: clothes tattered, skins stained by the streets, backs bent in a perpetual search for something edible, smokable, or tradable that may have found its way to the pavement below.

Riddled by psychotic illnesses, abandoned by the systems that once pledged to care for them as long as they needed care, they are the deinstitutionalized mentally ill, the detritus of the latest fashion in mental-health policy. The lucky ones live in board-and-care homes where they can be assured of their next meal; perhaps they have a place to go a few hours a week for support, coffee, even an effort at restoring their productive capacity. Those less fortunate live in our public places, existing on the beneficence of their fellow men and God. It is extraordinary how quickly we have become immune to their presence. Where we might once have felt compassion, revulsion, or fear, now we feel almost nothing at all.

From: *Commentary* 83, no. 5 (May 1987): 34–39. All rights reserved. Reprinted by permission.

There are times, of course, when the reality of the deinstitutionalized breaks through our defenses. Three days after the Statue of Liberty extravaganza in New York harbor last July [1986], in the shadow of the icon of huddled masses, a psychotic man ran amok on the Staten Island ferry, slashing at enemies in a war entirely of his own imagining. Two victims died. Investigations ensued. For a moment we became aware of the world of shelters and emergency rooms, a world where even those willing to accept help and clearly in need of it are turned away because the state has deliberately dismantled the system where they might once have received care. Briefly, the curious wondered, how did this come to be?

Like its victims, the policy of deinstitutionalization has been taken for granted. It is difficult to recall that mentally ill persons ever were treated differently. Yet the process that came to be called deinstitutionalization (no one knows when the term was coined) only began in the mid-1950s, and did not move into high gear until a decade later. Although the term itself suggests a unitary policy, deinstitutionalization has had complex roots, and at different times has sought diverse goals. Its failure, however, was all but preordained by several of the forces that gave it birth. Any attempt to correct the debacle that has attended the contraction—some might say implosion—of our public mental-health systems will require an understanding of those forces.

II

The idea that the states bear some responsibility for the care of the mentally ill was not immediately obvious to the founders of this country. Through the colonial and federalist periods, care of psychotic and other dependent persons was the responsibility of local communities. They responded then as many of them do today. Almshouses and jails were overrun with the mentally ill, who, though thrown together with the criminal, tubercular, and mendicant, were often treated with a cruelty visited on none of the others.

Change came in the second quarter of the 19th century. New interest was stimulated among a small number of physicians in a system of treatment of the mentally ill begun in a Quaker hospital in England and called "moral" care. The name—with its ironic allusion to the immorality that had governed most other efforts to deal with the mentally ill—denoted a therapeutic system based on the radical idea that the mentally ill were more like us than unlike. If they were treated with kindness, encouraged to establish order in their lives, given the opportunity to work at productive trades, and provided with models of behavior, their mental illnesses might dissipate.

The belief that the mentally ill could be treated, and thus need not be relegated to the cellars of local jails, was championed by Dorothea Dix, a spinster Sunday-school teacher from Massachusetts, who traversed the country, cataloguing the barbarities inflicted on mentally ill persons and petitioning legislatures to establish facilities where moral treatment might be applied. Her efforts and those of others resulted in the creation of a network of state-operated hospitals. As the states assumed ever wider responsibility for the mentally ill, the hospitals grew in size, absorbing the denizens of the jails and poorhouses.

In the wake of the Civil War, as the burdens created by waves of immigration stood unrelieved by increases in funding, the public hospitals surrendered the goal of active treatment. They continued to expand, but changed into enormous holding units, to which the mentally ill were sent and from which many never emerged. Once again sliding to the bottom of the list of social priorities, the mentally ill were often treated with brutality. At best, they suffered from benign indifference to anything more than their needs for shelter and food.

Such had been the condition of public mental hospitals for nearly eighty years as World War II came to a close. Periodic efforts at reform had left them largely untouched. Over one-half million patients languished in their wards, accounting for half of all the occupants of hospital beds in the country. The state hospitals had swelled to bloated proportions. Pilgrim State Hospital on Long Island, New York's largest, held nearly 20,000 patients. St. Elizabeths in Washington, D.C., the only mental hospital operated directly by the federal government, had its own railroad and post office. Most facilities, located away from major population centers, used patients to work large farms on their grounds, thus defraying a good part of the costs of running the institution.

A new generation of psychiatrists, returning from the war, began to express their disquiet with the system as it was. They had seen how rapid-treatment models in hospitals close to the front and the introduction of group therapy had drastically cut the morbidity of psychiatric conditions evident earlier in World War I. With the belief that patients need not spend their lives sitting idly in smoky, locked wards, they determined to tackle a situation which Albert Deutsch had described as the "shame of the states."

These psychiatrists and their disciples, emphasizing the desirability of preparing patients for return to the community, began to introduce reforms into the state systems. Wards that had been locked for nearly a century were opened; male and female patients were allowed to mix. Active treatment programs were begun, and many patients, particularly elderly ones, were screened prior to admission, with efforts made to divert them where possible to more appropriate settings. The effects soon became evident. More than a century of inexorable growth in state-hospital populations began to reverse itself in 1955, when the number of residents peaked at just over 558,000. The first phase of deinstitutionalization was under way.

A second factor was introduced at this point. In 1952, French scientists searching for a better antihistamine discovered chlorpromazine, the first medication with the power to mute and even reverse the symptoms of psychosis. Introduced in this country in 1954 under the trade name Thorazine (elsewhere the medication was called Largactil, a name that better conveys the enormous hope that accompanied its debut), the drug rapidly and permanently altered the treatment of severe mental illness. The ineffective treatments of the past, from bleedings and purgings, cold baths and whirling chairs, to barbiturates and lobotomies, were supplanted by a genuinely effective medication. Thorazine's limitations and side-effects would become better known in the future; for now the emphasis was on its ability to suppress the most flagrant symptoms of psychosis.

Patients bedeviled by hallucinatory voices and ridden by irrational fears, who previously could have been managed only in inpatient units, now became tractable. They still suffered from schizophrenia, still manifested the blunted emotions, confused thinking, odd postures that the disease inflicts. But the symptoms which had made it impossible for them to live outside the hospital could, in many cases, be controlled.

Psychiatrists still argue over whether the new ideas of hospital and community treatment or the introduction of Thorazine provided the initial push that lowered state-hospital censuses. The truth is that both factors probably played a role, with the medications allowing the new psychiatric enthusiasm for community-based care to be applied to a larger group of patients than might otherwise have been the case. The effects of the first stage of deinstitutionalization can be seen in the figures for patients resident in state psychiatric facilities. By 1965 that number had decreased gradually but steadily to 475,000.

III

Until the mid-1960s, deinstitutionalization had been a pragmatic innovation; its driving force was the conviction that some patients could be treated and maintained in the community. Although large-scale studies supporting this belief were lacking, psychiatrists' everyday experiences confirmed its validity. Further, control of the process of discharging patients was solidly in the hands of mental-health professionals. By the end of the first decade of deinstitutionalization, however, the process was in the midst of being transformed.

What had begun as an empirical venture was now about to become a movement. Deinstitutionalization was captured by the proponents of a variety of ideologies, who sensed its value for their causes. Although their underlying philosophies were often at odds, they agreed on what seemed a simple statement of mission: all patients should be treated in the community or in short-term facilities. The state hospitals should be closed.

Some of the earliest advocates of this position were themselves psychiatrists. Unlike their predecessors, who first let light and air into the back wards, these practitioners were not content to whittle away at the number of patients in state hospitals. They sought systemic changes. The pragmatism of the psychiatrists, persuaded on their return from the war that many patients could be treated without long-term hospitalization, was transmuted into a rigid credo. No patient should be confined in a massive state facility, it was now declared. All treatment should take place in the community.

These advocates, who saw themselves as part of a new subspecialty of community psychiatry, were heavily influenced by the sociologists of institutional life, notably Erving Goffman, the author of *Asylums*. That book, based on a year of observing patients and staff at St. Elizabeths Hospital in Washington, D.C., catalogued the ways, subtle and blatant, in which patients were forced by the demands of a large institution into an unthinking conformity of behavior and thought. The rules that constrained their behavior, Gorman wrote, derived not from a consideration of therapeutic needs, but from the desires of hospital staff members to simplify their own tasks. From Goffman's work a new syndrome was defined—"institutionalism": the progressive loss of functional abilities caused by the denial of opportunities to make choices for oneself, and leading to a state of chronic dependency. Robbed of their ability to function on their own, state-hospital patients had no alternative but to remain in an environment in which their lives were directed by others.

Community psychiatry embellished Goffman's charges. Articles in professional journals began to allege that the chronic disability accompanying psychiatric illnesses, particularly schizophrenia, was not a result of the disease process itself, but an effect of archaic treatment methods in which patients were uprooted from their own communities. With the attachments of a lifetime severed, often irretrievably, patients lost the incentive and then the will to maintain their abilities to relate to others and function in social environments. Thus, state hospitals, in addition to subjecting patients to abominable physical conditions—the stuff of exposés since the 1860s—were exacerbating and embedding the very symptoms they purported to treat. The only way to prevent the development of a new generation of dysfunctional chronic patients was to close the hospitals.

Of course, alternative places of treatment would have to be created. In 1963, the new community psychiatrists persuaded a President already interested in mental-health issues and a receptive Congress that, with a new approach, chronicity could be averted. The consensus that emerged was embodied in the Community Mental Health Center Act of 1963. With seed money from the federal government, the law encouraged the development of outpatient clinics in every area of the country. Ultimately, it was hoped, no citizen would live outside one of the 2,000 designated "catchment areas" in which community-based treatment could be provided.

Psychiatric proponents of closing the state hospitals found unlikely allies in a group of civil-libertarian attorneys who were now turning their attention to the mentally ill. Fresh from victories in the civil-rights movement, and armed with potent new constitutional interpretations that restricted the power of the state to infringe personal liberties, these lawyers sought the dismantling of state hospitals as the first step in eliminating all coercive treatment of the mentally ill. They sought this end not simply because they believed that encouraging autonomy reduced chronicity, as the community psychiatrists claimed, but because in their own hierarchy of values individual autonomy was paramount.

Mentally ill persons seemed particularly appropriate targets for a crusade against governmental power, for the state was depriving them of liberty—with ostensibly benevolent aims, yet in conditions that belied the goal of treatment. It appeared to these critics that ultimately the state was concerned most with maintaining imbalances of power that favored the privileged classes and with suppressing dissent. By confining and discrediting the more obstreperous members of the lower classes, the mental-health system served as a pillar of the ruling elite.

Critiques of this sort were not rare in the late 1960s, when skepticism of established power was, for many, a prerequisite of intellectual discourse. Its application to psychiatry was encouraged, however, by the writings of iconoclastic psychiatrists like Thomas Szasz, who maintained that mental illness was a "myth," perpetuated only as a mechanism for social control, and R. D. Laing, whose books touted the value of the psychotic experience for elevating one's perceptions of the meaning of life. Additional academic support for Szasz's views came from sociologists known as labeling theorists who believed that deviance was a creation of the person with the power so to name it.

Whereas the community psychiatrists initially sought to achieve their ends through a legislative reconstruction of the mental-health system, the civil-libertarian attorneys favored the judicial route. They attacked the major mechanism for entry into the public mental-health system, the statutes governing involuntary commitment. These laws, they charged, were unconstitutionally broad in allowing any mentally ill person in need of treatment to be hospitalized against his will. Surely individual liberty could not legitimately be abridged in the absence of a substantial threat to a person's life or to the life of others. In addition, they alleged that the wording of the statutes, many little changed for one hundred years, was impermissibly vague; particularly problematic for the civil libertarians were the definitions of mental illness and the circumstances that rendered one committable.

In an era of judicial activism, many courts, both federal and state, agreed. Involuntary commitment came to be limited to persons exhibiting danger to themselves or others; strict, criminal-law-style procedures came to be required, including judicial hearings with legal representation. As the trend in the courts became apparent, many legislatures altered their statutes in anticipation of decisions in their own jurisdictions, or in emulation of California, where civil libertarians won legislative approval of a tightened statute even without the threat of court action.

The final common pathway of this complex set of interests led through the state legislatures. Although concerns about better treatment for chronic patients and the enhancement of individual liberty were not foreign here, more mundane concerns made themselves felt as well. The old state mental hospitals took up a significant proportion of most state budgets, in some jurisdictions the largest single allocation. Advocates of closing the old facilities were not reticent in claiming enormous cost savings if patients were transferred to community-based care. And even if real costs remained constant, the availability of new federal entitlement programs such as Supplemental Security Income and Medicaid, to which outpatients but not inpatients would have access, promised a shift in the cost of supporting these people from the states to the federal government.

In many states, this was the final straw. The possibility that patients could be cared for in the community at less expense, perhaps with better results, and certainly with greater liberty, was an irresistible attraction. Deinstitutionalization was too valuable a tool of social policy to remain a discretionary option of state-hospital psychiatrists. It now became an avowed goal of the states. Quotas were set for reductions in state-hospital populations; timetables were drawn up for the closure of facilities. Individual discretion in the release of patients was overridden by legislative and administrative fiat. Patients were to be released at all costs. New admissions were to be discouraged, in some cases prohibited. In the words of Joseph Morrissey, if the first phase of deinstitutionalization reflected an opening of the back wards, the second phase was marked by a closing of the front door.*

Thus did deinstitutionalization assume the form in which we know it today.

---

*A good comprehensive history of deinstitutionalization has yet to be written. The best of the existing, essay-length works is Joseph Morrissey's "Deinstitutionalizing the Mentally Ill: Process, Outcomes, and New Directions," in W. R. Gove, ed., *Deviance and Mental Illness* (Sage Publications, 1982). Morrissey focuses in particular on the experiences in Massachusetts, New York, and California.

IV

If a decrease in patient population is the sole measure for gauging the outcome of deinstitutionalization, the success of the policy is unquestionable. From 1965 to 1975, inpatient populations in state hospitals fell from 475,000 to 193,000. By 1980, the figure was 137,000, and today all indications are that the number is even smaller. Relatively few of the state hospitals closed. The majority shrank from bustling colonies with thousands of patients to enclaves of a few hundred patients, clustered in a few buildings in largely abandoned campuses.

Yet by the mid-1970s professionals in the field and policy analysts had begun to ask whether the underlying goals espoused by the advocates of deinstitutionalization were really being met. Are the majority of the mentally ill, by whatever measure one chooses to apply, better off now than before the depopulation of the state hospitals? The inescapable answer is that they are not.

A large part of the reason for the movement's failure stems from its overly optimistic belief in the ability of many mentally ill persons to function on their own, without the much-maligned structure of state-hospital care. Rather than liberating patients from the constraints of institutional life, the movement to reduce the role of state hospitals merely shifted the locus of their regimented existences. Indeed, *trans*institutionalization may be a better term to describe the process that occurred. It is estimated that 750,000 chronic mentally ill persons now live in nursing homes, a figure nearly 50 percent higher than the state-hospital population at its 1955 apogee. Additional hundreds of thousands live in board-and-care homes or other group residences. Many of these facilities, particularly the nursing homes, have locked wards nearly indistinguishable from the old state hospitals. They are, in psychiatrist H. Richard lamb's evocative phrase, the asylums in the community.

Many of the mentally ill, of course, have drifted away entirely from any form of care. Given the freedom to choose, they have chosen to live on the streets; according to various estimates they comprise between 40 and 60 percent of homeless persons. They filter into overcrowded shelters—as Juan Gonzalez did before becoming the agent of his fantasies on the Staten Island ferry—where they may experience fleeting contact with mental-health personnel. The lack of external structure is reflected in their internal disorganization. Whatever chance they had to wire together their shattered egos has been lost.

What of the hopes of the community psychiatrists that liberating patients from state hospitals would prevent the development of the chronic dependency which stigmatizes the mentally ill and inhibits their reintegration into the community? They learned a sad lesson suspected by many of their colleagues all along. The withdrawal, apathy, bizarre thinking, and oddities of behavior which Goffman and his students attributed to "institutionalism" appear even in populations maintained outside of institutions. They are the effects of the underlying psychiatric illnesses, usually schizophrenia, not of the efforts to treat those conditions. And contrary to the claims of the labeling theorists, it is the peculiar behavior of severely psychotic persons, not the fact that they were once hospitalized and "labeled" ill, that stigmatizes and isolates them in the community. Studies of discharged patients demonstrate that those who continue to display the signs of their illnesses and disrupt the lives of others are the ones who suffer social discrimination.

To some extent, the community psychiatrists never had a chance to test their theories. The community mental-health centers in which they envisioned care taking place were, for the most part, never built. Fewer than half of the projected 2,000 centers reached operation. Of those that did, many turned from the severely ill to more desirable patients, less disturbed, easier to treat, more gratifying, and above all, as federal subsidies were phased out, able to pay for their own care. A few model programs, working with a selected group of cooperative patients, are all the community psychiatrists have to show for their dreams. But the evidence suggests that even optimal levels of community care cannot enable many mentally ill persons to live on their own.

The goals of the civil libertarians, except in the narrowest sense, have fared little better. If one conceives that liberty is enhanced merely by the release of patients from the hospitals to the streets, then perhaps one might glean some satisfaction from the course of deinstitutionalization to date. But if individual autonomy implies the ability to make reasoned choices in the context of a coherent plan for one's life, then one must conclude that few of the deinstitutionalized have achieved autonomy. One study found fewer than half the residents of a large board-and-care home with a desire to change anything at all about their lives, no matter how unrealistic their objectives might be. If the façade of autonomy has been expanded, the reality has suffered.

Finally, and with fitting irony, not even the hope that deinstitutionalization would save money has been realized. It was originally anticipated that the closing of state hospitals would allow the transfer of their budgetary allocations to community facilities. But state hospitals proved difficult to close. As many hospitals existed in 1980 as in 1955, despite a fourfold reduction in patients. Even with current, broad definitions of who can survive in the community, tens of thousands of patients nationwide continue to require institutional care, often long-term. They are so regressed, self-destructive, violent, or otherwise disruptive that no community can tolerate them in its midst. Moreover, the communities that derive jobs from the facilities have fought hard to preserve them. As censuses have fallen, per-capita costs of care have increased, pushed up even further by pressure to improve the level of care for those who remain. Many costs for the treatment of outpatients have been redistributed, with the federal and local governments bearing heavier burdens; but no one has ever demonstrated overall savings. Even as the quality of life for many mentally ill persons has fallen, state mental-health budgets have continued to expand.

V

Both the failure of deinstitutionalization and our seeming paralysis in correcting it stem from the same source: the transformation of deinstitutionalization from a pragmatic enterprise to an ideological crusade. The goal of the first phase of the process—to treat in the community all mentally ill persons who did not require full-time supervision and might do equally well or better in alternate settings—was hardly objectionable. Had state-hospital populations been reduced in a deliberate manner, with patients released no faster than treatment, housing, and rehabilitative facilities became available in the community, the visions of psychiatry's Young Turks of the 1950s might well have been realized.

Once the release of state-hospital patients became a matter of faith, however, this individualized approach was thrown to the winds. In the Manichean view that soon predominated, confinement in state hospitals came to be seen as invariably bad. Freedom was always to be preferred, both for its own sake and because it had a desirable, albeit mysterious therapeutic value. Further, we came to doubt our own benevolent impulses, yielding to those who claimed that any effort to act for the welfare of others was illegitimate and doomed to end with their oppression. Thus, although we may now recognize the failure of deinstitutionalization, we as a society have been unable to reverse course; these same ideologies continue to dominate our policies not by the power of logic but by the force of habit.

It is time to rethink these presuppositions. That freedom per se will not cure mental illness is evident from the abject condition of so many of the deinstitutionalized. More difficult to deal with is the belief that, even if the lives of hundreds of thousands of mentally ill persons have been made objectively more miserable by the emptying of our state hospitals, we have no right to deprive people of liberty, even for their own benefit. In the currently fashionable jargon of bioethics, the value of autonomy always trumps the value of beneficence.

Interestingly, this position is now being challenged by a number of our leading public philosophers, who have called attention to its neglected costs. Robert Burt of the Yale Law School and Daniel Callahan of the Hastings Center, for example, have taken aim at the belief that the freedom to do as we please should be our primary societal value. This emphasis on individual autonomy, they point out, has come to mean that in making our choices, as long as we do not actively infringe on the prerogatives of others, we face no obligation to consider them and their needs. The result has been the creation of an atomistic community in which, relieved of the duty to care for others, we pursue our goals in disregard of the suffering that surrounds us. This lack of an obligation to care for others has been transmuted in some cases into an actual duty to ignore their suffering, lest we act in such a way as to limit their autonomy.

Although Burt and Callahan have not addressed themselves to mental-health policy per se, there is no better illustration of their thesis. The right to liberty has become an excuse for failing to address, even failing to recognize, the needs of the thousands of abandoned men and women we sweep by in our streets, in our parks, and in the train and bus stations where they gather for warmth. We have persuaded ourselves that it is better to ignore them—that we have an obligation to ignore them—because their autonomy would be endangered by our concern.

But the impulse to act for the benefit of others is the adhesive substance that binds human communities together. A value system that looses those bonds by glorifying individual autonomy threatens the cohesion of the polity. Nobody wants to live in a society characterized by unrestrained intervention (even with benevolent intent), but that does not mean we must reject altogether the notion that doing good for others, despite their reluctance, is morally appropriate under some conditions.

Meaningful autonomy does not consist merely in the ability to make choices for oneself. Witness the psychotic ex-patients on the streets, who withdraw into rarely used doorways, rigidly still for hours at a time, hoping, like chameleons on the forest floor, that immobility will help them fade into the grimy urban background, bringing safety and temporary peace from a world which they envision as a terrifying series of threats. Can the choices they make, limited as they are to the selection of a doorway for the day, be called a significant embodiment of human autonomy? Or is their behavior rather to be understood on the level of a simple reflex—autonomous only in a strictly formal sense?

Far from impinging on their autonomy, treatment of such psychotics, even coercive treatment, would not only hold out some hope of mitigating their condition but might simultaneously increase their capacity for more sophisticated autonomous choices. To adopt the typological scheme of the philosopher Bruce Miller, patients might thereby be enabled to move from mere freedom of action to choices that reflect congruence with personal values, effective rational deliberation, and moral reflection. Our intervention, though depriving them of the right to autonomy in the short term, may enhance that quality in the long run. In such circumstances, benevolence and autonomy are no longer antagonistic principles.

VI

Deinstitutionalization is a remnant of a different era in our political life, one in which we sought broadly-framed solutions to human problems that have defied man's creativity for millennia. In the 1960s and '70s we declared war on poverty, and we determined to wipe out injustice and bigotry; government, we believed, had the tools and resources to accomplish these ends; all that was needed was the will.

This set of beliefs, applied to the mentally ill, allowed us to ignore the failure of a century-and-a-half of mental-health reform in this country, in the conviction that this time we had the answer. The problem, as it was defined, was the system of large state hospitals. Like a cancer, it could be easily excised. And the will was there.

Unfortunately, the analysis was wrong. The problems of severe mental illness have proved resistant to unitary solutions. For some patients, discharge from the state hospitals was a blessing. For all too many others, it was the ultimate curse. Far from a panacea, the policy created as many problems as it solved, perhaps more. To be sure, it is never easy to admit that massive social initiatives have been misconceived. The time has come, however, to lay deinstitutionalization to rest.

It would not be difficult to outline a reasonable program to restore some sense to the care of the mentally ill: moderate expansion of beds in state facilities, especially for the most severely ill patients; good community-based services for those patients—and their number is not small—who could prosper outside of an institution with proper supports; and greater authority for the state to detain and treat the severely mentally ill for their own benefit, even if they pose no immediate threat to their lives or those of others.

Deinstitutionalization has been a tragedy, but it need not be an irreversible one.

Suggestions for Further Reading

Custodial Care

Carter, Michele A., "Ethical Framework for Care of the Chronically Ill." *Holistic Nursing Practice* 8 (1993): 67–77.

Fowlkes, Martha R., "Business as Usual—At the State Mental Hospital." *Psychiatry* 38 (1975): 55–64.

Lidz, Charles W., and Robert M. Arnold, "Institutional Constraints on Autonomy." *Generations* (1990): 65–68.

Simon, Walter B., "On Reluctance to Leave the Public Mental Hospital." *Psychiatry* 28 (1965): 145–56.

Vail, D. G., *Dehumanization and the Institutional Career*. Springfield, Ill.: Charles C. Thomas, 1966.

Wieglus, K., "Custodial and Therapeutic Patient Relationships." *Ethics in Science and Medicine* 3 (July 1976): 71–94.

Deinstitutionalization

Borus, Jonathan, F., "Deinstitutionalization of the Chronically Mentally Ill." *New England Journal of Medicine* 305 (1981): 339–42.

Brown, P., *The Transfer of Care*. Boston: Routledge and Kegan Paul, 1985.

Gralnick, Alexander, "Deinstitutionalization: Origins and Signs of Failure." *The American Journal of Social Psychiatry* 3 (Fall 1983): 8–12.

Isaac, Rael Jean, and Virginia C. Armat, *Madness in the Streets: How Psychiatry and the Law Abandoned the Mentally Ill*. New York: The Free Press, 1990.

Lamb, H. Richard, "Lessons Learned from Deinstitutionalization in the U.S." *British Journal of Psychiatry* 162 (May 1993): 587–92.

———, ed., *The Homeless Mentally Ill*. Washington, D.C.: American Psychiatric Association, 1984.

Mollica, Richard F., "From Asylum to Community: The Threatened Disintegration of Public Psychiatry." *The New England Journal of Medicine* 308 (Febuary 17, 1983): 367–73.

Mosher, L., and L. Burti, *Community Mental Health.* New York: W. W. Norton, 1989.

Peele, Roger, "The Ethics of Deinstitutionalization." In Sidney Bloch and Paul Chodoff, eds. *Psychiatraic Ethics,* 2d ed. New York: Oxford University Press, 1991, ch. 14.

Scull, Andrew T., *Decarceration,* 2d ed. Cambridge: Oxford Polity Press, 1984.

Torrey, E. Fuller, *Nowhere to Go: The Tragic Odessey of the Homeless Mentally Ill.* New York: Harper & Row, 1988.

Warren, C., "New Forms of Social Control: The Myth of Deinstitutionalization." *American Behavioral Scientist* 24 (1981): 724–40.

Contributors

The American Psychiatric Association Insanity Defense Work Group was composed of Loren Roth, M.D., Shervert H. Frazier, M.D., Allan Beigel, M.D., Robert L. Spitzer, M.D., and ex-officio Alan A. Stone, M.D., and Joel Klein, Esq.

Paul S. Appelbaum is the A. F. Zeleznik Professor of Psychiatry and director of the Law and Psychiatry Program at the University of Massachusetts Medical School.

Virginia C. Armat writes on contemporary social issues and is on the administrative faculty of George Mason University.

Teodoro Ayllon, Ph.D., is professor of psychology and special education at Georgia State University, Atlanta.

Françoise Baylis, Ph.D., was associate professor pf philosophy in the medical ethics program at the University of Tennessee, Knoxville, and is now with Bioethics Education and Research at Dalhousie University, Halifax, Nova Scotia, Canada.

Kerry Brace is with the Counseling and Psychological Services Center, West Virginia University, Morgantown, West Virginia.

Peter R. Breggin, M.D., P.A., is a psychiatrist in Bethesda, Maryland, and a prolific critic of physicalistic approaches to psychotherapy.

Louisa Brownell, M.S. in Occupational Therapy, was completing a master's degree in Management of Human Services at Brandeis University when she wrote her article on electroconvulsive therapy.

Paula J. Caplan, Ph.D., is professor of applied psychology at Ontario Institute for Studies in Education, Toronta, Canada, and assistant professor of psychiatry at the University of Toronto.

Jennifer I. Downey, M.D., is with the Department of Psychiatry, Columbia University College of Physicians and Surgeons, New York, New York.

James F. Drane, Ph.D., is professor of philosophy at Edinboro University of Pennsylvania.

Rem B. Edwards, Ph.D., is Lindsay Young Professor of Philosophy at the University of Tennessee, Knoxville, and a senior member of the medical ethics faculty.

Richard C. Friedman, M.D., is with the Department of Psychiatry, Columbia University College of Physicians and Surgeons, and the Department of Psychology, Adelphi University, New York, New York.

Glen O. Gabbard is Bessie Walker Callaway Distinguished Professor of Psychoanalysis and Education in the Karl Menninger School of Psychiatry and Mental Health Sciences, and clinical professor of psychiatry at the University of Kansas School of Medicine, Kansas City, Kansas.

Thomas Grisso is with the Department of Psychiatry, University of Massachusetts Medical Center, Worchester, Massachusetts.

Donald H. J. Hermann, J.D., Ph.D., is professor of law and philosophy at DePaul University.

John R. Hughes, Ph.D., is professor of psychiatry, psychology, and family practice at the University of Vermont and is medical director of the University of Vermont Substance Abuse Treatment Center.

Rael Jean Isaac, Ph.D., writes on political issues for several national periodicals.

L. P. Kok, M.D., is an associate professor in the Department of Psychological Medicine, National University Hospital, Singapore.

A. Louis McGarry, M.D., was medical director of the Division of Forensic Services and professor of psychiatry at the State University of New York, Stony Brook.

Michael S. Moore, J.D., is the Robert Kingsley Professor of Law at the University of Southern California, Los Angeles.

Michael Norko, M.D., is unit chief at the Whiting Forensic Institute, Middletown, Connecticut.

Robert A. Pierattini, Ph.D., is clinical assistant professor of psychology at the University of Vermont and the director of the University of Vermont's Psychopharmacology Consultation Service.

Lawrie Reznek, M.D., Ph.D., is with the Department of Psychiatry, the Toronto Hospital, Toronto, Canada. Formerly he was senior registrar at the Royal Edinburgh Hospital.

Heather Sones, R.N., graduated from the University of Saskatchewan.

David Stier was a medical student at Yale University, New Haven, Connecticut.

Thomas S. Szasz, M.D., is professor of psychiatry emeritus at the Health Science College, State University of New York, and Upstate Medical Center, Syracuse.

Robert M. Veatch, Ph.D., is currently a professor at the Kennedy Institute of Ethics, Georgetown University, Washington, D.C.

Jerome C. Wakefield is with the Columbia University School of Social Work and the Institute for Health, Health Care Policy, and Aging Research, Rutgers University.

Robert M. Wettstein, M.D., is with the Department of Psychiatry, University of Pittsburgh School of Medicine, and Western Psychiatric Institute and Clinic.

Karl G. Williams, M.S., J.D., is assistant professor of pharmacy law and administration, University of Wyoming School of Pharmacy, Laramie.

Bruce J. Winick is professor of law at the University of Miami School of Law, Coral Gables, Florida.

Robert Wright is the editor of New Republic Books.

Howard Zonana is director, Law and Psychiatry Division, Yale University School of Medicine, Department of Psychiatry, New Haven, Connecticut.